Beginning
ASP.NET 2.0 and Databases

Beginning ASP.NET 2.0 and Databases

John Kauffman and Bradley Millington

Wiley Publishing, Inc.

Beginning ASP.NET 2.0 and Databases

Published by
Wiley Publishing, Inc.
10475 Crosspoint Boulevard
Indianapolis, IN 46256
www.wiley.com

Copyright © 2006 by Wiley Publishing, Inc., Indianapolis, Indiana

Published simultaneously in Canada

ISBN-13: 978-0-471-78134-9
ISBN-10: 0-471-78134-7

Manufactured in the United States of America

10 9 8 7 6 5 4 3 2 1

1MA/RX/QX/QW/IN

Library of Congress Control Number: 2006015830

No part of this publication may be reproduced, stored in a retrieval system or transmitted in any form or by any means, electronic, mechanical, photocopying, recording, scanning or otherwise, except as permitted under Sections 107 or 108 of the 1976 United States Copyright Act, without either the prior written permission of the Publisher, or authorization through payment of the appropriate per-copy fee to the Copyright Clearance Center, 222 Rosewood Drive, Danvers, MA 01923, (978) 750-8400, fax (978) 646-8600. Requests to the Publisher for permission should be addressed to the Legal Department, Wiley Publishing, Inc., 10475 Crosspoint Blvd., Indianapolis, IN 46256, (317) 572-3447, fax (317) 572-4355, or online at http://www.wiley.com/go/permissions.

LIMIT OF LIABILITY/DISCLAIMER OF WARRANTY: THE PUBLISHER AND THE AUTHOR MAKE NO REPRESENTATIONS OR WARRANTIES WITH RESPECT TO THE ACCURACY OR COMPLETENESS OF THE CONTENTS OF THIS WORK AND SPECIFICALLY DISCLAIM ALL WARRANTIES, INCLUDING WITHOUT LIMITATION WARRANTIES OF FITNESS FOR A PARTICULAR PURPOSE. NO WARRANTY MAY BE CREATED OR EXTENDED BY SALES OR PROMOTIONAL MATERIALS. THE ADVICE AND STRATEGIES CONTAINED HEREIN MAY NOT BE SUITABLE FOR EVERY SITUATION. THIS WORK IS SOLD WITH THE UNDERSTANDING THAT THE PUBLISHER IS NOT ENGAGED IN RENDERING LEGAL, ACCOUNTING, OR OTHER PROFESSIONAL SERVICES. IF PROFESSIONAL ASSISTANCE IS REQUIRED, THE SERVICES OF A COMPETENT PROFESSIONAL PERSON SHOULD BE SOUGHT. NEITHER THE PUBLISHER NOR THE AUTHOR SHALL BE LIABLE FOR DAMAGES ARISING HEREFROM. THE FACT THAT AN ORGANIZATION OR WEBSITE IS REFERRED TO IN THIS WORK AS A CITATION AND/OR A POTENTIAL SOURCE OF FURTHER INFORMATION DOES NOT MEAN THAT THE AUTHOR OR THE PUBLISHER ENDORSES THE INFORMATION THE ORGANIZATION OR WEBSITE MAY PROVIDE OR RECOMMENDATIONS IT MAY MAKE. FURTHER, READERS SHOULD BE AWARE THAT INTERNET WEBSITES LISTED IN THIS WORK MAY HAVE CHANGED OR DISAPPEARED BETWEEN WHEN THIS WORK WAS WRITTEN AND WHEN IT IS READ.

For general information on our other products and services please contact our Customer Care Department within the United States at (800) 762-2974, outside the United States at (317) 572-3993 or fax (317) 572-4002.

Trademarks: Wiley, the Wiley logo, Wrox, the Wrox logo, Programmer to Programmer, and related trade dress are trademarks or registered trademarks of John Wiley & Sons, Inc. and/or its affiliates, in the United States and other countries, and may not be used without written permission. Microsoft is a registered trademark of Microsoft Corporation. All other trademarks are the property of their respective owners. Wiley Publishing, Inc., is not associated with any product or vendor mentioned in this book.

Wiley also publishes its books in a variety of electronic formats. Some content that appears in print may not be available in electronic books.

About the Authors

John Kauffman has written numerous books about ASP and the incorporation of data into ASP pages. Born in Philadelphia and educated at Penn State, he has lived, taught, and programmed on three continents as he follows his wife's diplomatic assignments.

When not writing, he spends his time sailing, teaching electronics to high school groups, and chauffeuring his kids to hockey and music practices.

Bradley Millington is a Microsoft Program Manager for the Web Platform and Tools Team with primary responsibility for the database controls in ASP.NET. He is a well-known frequent speaker at Microsoft technical conferences including TechEd and PDC.

Credits

Senior Acquisitions Editor
Jim Minatel

Development Editor
Jennifer Eberhardt

Technical Editors
Eilon Lipton
Polita Paulus

Production Editor
Pamela Hanley

Copy Editor
Foxxe Editorial

Editorial Manager
Mary Beth Wakefield

Production Manager
Tim Tate

Vice President and Executive Group Publisher
Richard Swadley

Vice President and Executive Publisher
Joseph B. Wikert

Project Coordinator
Ryan Steffen

Quality Control Technicians
John Greenough
Brian Walls

Graphics and Layout
Jennifer Click
Carrie A. Foster
Lauren Goddard
Barbara Moore
Lynsey Osborn
Alicia B. South

Proofreading and Indexing
Techbooks

This book is dedicated to my wife's extended family in appreciation for all they have done for me over the last twenty years. Aunt Ethel has been a gracious and generous hostess on so many occasions. Glenn has provided hours of intellectual stimulation in his quest to understand the grandest questions of the universe. Angela provided an open heart and wonderful meals on many extended stays at her home. Stephanie, Diego, Linda, and Dae Gwon have been wonderful hosts during visits to Pittsburgh, Venice, and Sunnyvale, especially when they tolerated our jet-lagged children running around their homes at two in the morning. My thanks to Leigh for his encouragement to our children and patient explanations of his research in the function of the human brain. Tam has generously provided her organizational skills on numerous occasions with travel plans and accommodations, while her daughters have given us another look at the world through children's eyes. And Dave has been so much fun for all of us and is now an inspiration and role model for my son. My thanks to all of you for your generosity, love, and acceptance over the last two decades.

John Kauffman

Contents

Introduction

The ASP.NET 2.0 team has done a tremendous job with the 2.0 version on two fronts. First, it is far easier to use data with ASP now than with any version in the past. Second, site designers can perform more complex tasks with data than at any time in the past. Faster development and expanded capability are two achievements that have made this book a joy to write. I feel privileged to be the bearer of such good news to the ASP community.

This book is a major update of its predecessor, *Beginning ASP.NET 2.0 Databases Beta Edition*. Because we were lucky enough to have the beta edition published in 2005 as a starting point for this new final release edition, we were able to add significant new coverage in this final release book. Even after Microsoft released ASP.NET 2.0 and the related toolset in the fall of 2005, Microsoft's Web Platform and Tools team continued to release additional tools for ASP.NET developers and we have been able to include coverage of many of those additional tools in this book. We also had the time to have all of the code retested by a second set of technical editors, further improving this book for you.

Audience

The target audience for this book remains the same as prior versions. Each chapter and exercise is completely explained, provided the reader has a basic understanding of using ASP without data. The normal prerequisite for this book is an understanding of *Beginning ASP.NET 2.0* (with VB code examples ISBN: 0-7645-8850-8 or with C# examples ISBN: 0-470-04258-3) by an author team including John Kauffman. Alternatively, the reader should be comfortable with ASP.NET version 1.x or ASP version 3.0.

Readers should also have some familiarity with databases. This book does not delve into the details of designing or administering a database.

How to Use This Book

This book is presented as a progression from simple to complex topics. In general, I recommend that you start at the beginning and work your way through to the end, doing every exercise. There are several exceptions.

Chapters 2 through 4 describe connections to Access (Chapter 2), SQL Server (Chapter 3), and other data sources (Chapter 4). If you know you will only be using one of the Microsoft SQL Server versions (7.0, 2000, 2005, SQL Server 2005 Express Edition, or MSDE), the concepts of Chapter 3 provide your technique and you can skip Chapter 2. As chapter 2 explains, while Access is suitable for learning the ASP.NET 2.0 and database techniques, it isn't recommended for a production web server setting. So even if you are using Access now, it would be appropriate to learn ASP.NET 2.0 and databases with SQL Server too reading chapter 3, using the free SQL Server 2005 Express Edition. Chapter 4 on working with ASP.NET 2.0 and other data sources you can read on an "as needed" basis.

Conventions

To help you get the most from the text and keep track of what's happening, a number of conventions are used throughout the book.

Try It Out

The *Try It Out* is an exercise you should work through, following the text in the book.

1. They usually consist of a set of steps.
2. Each step has a number.
3. Follow the steps in order.

How It Works

After most *Try It Outs*, the code you've typed is explained in detail.

Boxes like this one hold important, not-to-be-forgotten information that is directly relevant to the surrounding text.

Tips, hints, tricks, and asides to the current discussion are offset and placed in italics like this.

As for styles in the text:

- Important words are *highlighted* when introduced.
- Keyboard strokes are shown like this: Ctrl+A.
- File names, URLs, and code within the text appear like so: `persistence.properties`.
- Code is presented in two different ways:

```
In code examples, new and important code is highlighted with a gray background.
```

```
The gray highlighting is not used for code that's less important in the present
context, or has been shown before.
```

Source Code

As you work through the examples in this book, you may choose either to type in all the code manually or to use the source code files that accompany the book. All of the source code used in this book is available for download at `http://www.wrox.com`. Once at the site, simply locate the book's title (either by using the Search box or by using one of the title lists) and click the Download Code link on the book's detail page to obtain all the source code for the book.

Because many books have similar titles, you may find it easiest to search by ISBN; for this book, the ISBN is 0-471-78134-7.

Once you download the code, just decompress it with your favorite compression tool. Alternatively, you can go to the main Wrox code download page at `http://www.wrox.com/dynamic/books/download.aspx` to see the code available for this book and all other Wrox books.

Errata

We make every effort to ensure that there are no errors in the text or code. However, no one is perfect, and mistakes do occur. If you find an error in one of our books, like a spelling mistake or faulty piece of code, we would be grateful for your feedback. By sending in errata you may save another reader hours of frustration and you will be helping us provide even higher quality information.

To find the errata page for this book, go to `http://www.wrox.com` and locate the title using the Search box or one of the title lists. Then, on the book details page, click the Book Errata link. On this page, you can view all errata that has been posted for this book. A complete book list, including links to each book's errata, is also available at `www.wrox.com/misc-pages/booklist.shtml`.

If you don't spot "your" error on the Book Errata page, go to `www.wrox.com/contact/techsupport.shtml` and complete the form there to send us the error you have found. We'll check the information and, if appropriate, post a message to the book's errata page and fix the problem in subsequent editions of the book.

p2p.wrox.com

For author and peer discussion, join the P2P forums at `p2p.wrox.com`. The forums are a Web-based system for you to post messages relating to Wrox books and related technologies and interact with other readers and technology users. The forums offer a subscription feature to e-mail you topics of interest of your choosing when new posts are made to the forums. Wrox authors, editors, other industry experts, and your fellow readers are present on these forums.

At `http://p2p.wrox.com`, you will find a number of forums that help you not only as you read this book, but also as you develop your own applications. To join the forums, just follow these steps:

1. Go to `p2p.wrox.com`, click the Register link, read the terms of use, and click Agree.
2. Complete the required information to join, as well as any optional information you wish to provide, and then click Submit.
3. You will receive an e-mail with information describing how to verify your account and complete the joining process.

You can read messages in the forums without joining P2P but to post your own messages, you must join.

Once you join, you can post new messages and respond to messages other users post. You can read messages at any time on the Web. If you would like to have new messages from a particular forum e-mailed to you, click the Subscribe to this Forum icon by the forum name in the forum listing.

For more information on how to use the Wrox P2P, be sure to read the P2P FAQs for answers to questions about how the forum software works and many common questions specific to P2P and Wrox books. To read the FAQs, click the FAQ link on any P2P page.

Introduction to ASP.NET 2.0 and ADO.NET

The speed and power that ASP.NET 2.0 and the .NET Framework 2.0 bring to the beginning programmer make it a joy to write this edition. We believe you will find many moments when you just won't believe the quality of results you can achieve with so little effort. We think you will often say, as other programmers did at the first demos, "Wow, this is the way it should be." Your managers and clients will be equally impressed by the speed and accuracy with which you produce Web sites.

This chapter presents an introduction to the topic of using data in an ASP.NET 2.0 Web page, an explanation of how to set up a machine to use ASP.NET 2.0 with software and data for this book, and a set of initial demonstrations of the powerful features you will learn to use. Some of the material reviews knowledge covered in the prerequisites for a basic knowledge of ASP.NET and familiarity with basic database tasks). The sections are organized as follows:

- Overview of the technologies, including the .NET 2.0 Framework, ASP.NET 2.0, and ADO.NET; a short review of how the older versions (1.*x*) worked with data; and a review of some key terminology
- Discussion of the components needed to use data on ASP.NET 2.0 pages
- Setup for this book
- Demonstration of several ASP.NET 2.0 pages that utilize data

As in previous editions, we include a list of common mistakes, a thorough summary, and some questions for you to check your knowledge.

Overview of the .NET Technologies

About a million developers have been creating Web sites using the .NET Framework in its first version. So in the summer of 2003, many ears perked up when rumors came out of Microsoft that a new version was available, a version that promised to decrease the number of lines of code required to create ASP.NET pages by 70 percent. Such a significant increase in productivity does not come often in the world of programming.

When samples of ASP.NET 2.0 code were demonstrated in the fall of 2003 at the Microsoft Professional Developer's Conference, the result exceeded the expectation. A Web page that warranted a budget of several hours of programmer time in the first version of ASP.NET could easily be built in a few minutes using ASP.NET 2.0. Simply stated, any programmer that continues to create ASP.NET pages in version 1 after the final release of the .NET Framework 2.0 is spending a lot of extra time to accomplish the same results.

Perhaps more than in any other area, ASP.NET 2.0 offers advances in the ease of incorporating data into a page. Programmers no longer need to have detailed knowledge of connection, command, data reader, and data adapter objects to implement common data scenarios. ASP.NET 2.0 makes basic data use simple and brings more complex use of data within the grasp of beginners.

Introduction to the .NET Framework

Microsoft developed .NET as a philosophy and set of technologies for computers to work together in the world of the Internet. The overall objective was to provide a smooth flow of information and processes across a wide range of systems and devices. .NET is not a language or a specific product. Rather, it is a set of standards and guidelines that are incorporated into almost all Microsoft products released since about 2002.

.NET embraces a standardized format for the exchange of information using the open-standards XML format. Extensible Markup Language (XML) eliminates the need for a requestor to have any specialized knowledge about how the data store holds information — the data can always come out in the self-describing XML format. Likewise, almost all data stores now have the capability to serve up their information in XML, making them appealing to all .NET data consumers. .NET supports other standards for information exchange (e.g. t-SQL, cryptographically strong streams, and non–XML-compliant HTML). But in the beginning, you will most frequently need to connect to XML.

.NET supports the Web Services standard for software to request the running of code in remote software using the open-platform standard Simple Object Access Protocol (SOAP) and the language XML. A .NET Web site can find out from another Web site what services it offers and then consume those services. This makes it possible for a Web site to obtain HTML, calculated results, or sets of data from other Web sites.

As part of its .NET initiative, Microsoft released a runtime, a set of programming tools, and a set of application program interfaces (APIs), called the .NET Framework, to enable the development community to build client-server applications, .NET client and server applications, and XML Web Services.

The .NET Framework is composed of the Common Language Runtime (CLR) and a unified set of class libraries. The CLR provides a fully managed execution environment for running applications, providing several services such as assembly loading and unloading, process and memory management, security enforcement, and just-in-time compilation. What gives the Common Language Runtime its name is the capability to author applications in a wide variety of languages, and compile source code to an intermediate language that the CLR understands and can run regardless of the original source language. This "language independence" is a key feature of the CLR (and also of ASP.NET), and it allows developers to work in their preferred language, such as C#, VB.NET, or Cobol while leveraging all features in the .NET Framework.

The .NET Framework also includes a set of *class libraries*, which are large sets of code that can be used by programmers. They provide common functionality that applications may need. These class libraries can be accessed from any language supported by the .NET Framework. The services (and corresponding namespaces) offered by these class libraries include the following:

- **System Types** ***(System)*:** Includes definitions for most simple data types, conversion functions between types, some mathematical functions, arrays, and ways to handle exceptions.
- **Input/Output** ***(System.IO)*:** Includes classes to read and write to data streams (for example, output to an external device such as a Pocket PC) and to files on drives.
- **Data Access** ***(System.Data)*:** Includes classes to interact with external data, typically a database. This namespace includes most of ADO.NET, which is used by the ASP.NET 2.0 data controls, and thus is of particular interest to this book.
- **Security** ***(System.Security)*:** Includes the classes to implement the foundations of security, particularly the system of permissions.
- **Data Structures** ***(System.Collections)*:** Includes classes to organize and maintain sets of data within .NET including lists, dictionaries, and hash tables. (Note that the System.Data namespace is for communicating with sets of external data.)
- **Configuration** ***(System.Configuration)*:** Includes classes to establish configuration settings and to handle errors using the settings.
- **Networking** ***(System.Net)*:** Includes classes to work with networking protocols such as IP and Sockets.
- **Reflection** ***(System.Reflection)*:** Includes classes that allow a program to look at itself to identify its own characteristics, such as specialty data types and the organization of the code.
- **Globalization** ***(System.Globalization)*:** Includes classes that hold culture-specific settings such as syntax of dates and currency.
- **Painting and Drawing** ***(System.Drawing)*:** Includes classes that can interface with the graphical user interface. This namespace includes many classes for specific types of renderings, including Pen, Brush, and Imaging.
- **Tracing and Diagnostics** ***(System.Diagnostics)*:** Includes classes to analyze problems, including the dissection of system processes, process counters, and event logs.
- **Windows (Client) Application Model** ***(System.Windows.Forms)*:** Includes classes that allow implementation of the Windows user interface.
- **Web Application Model** ***(System.Web)*:** Includes classes that provide a programming model for producing Web pages. The Web page code runs on the server and renders HTML to the client's browser. This class includes over a dozen subclasses that focus on various types of browsers and server services. These are of great interest in this text because System.Web is, essentially, ASP.NET.

Note that the .NET Framework contains two application programming models, one for client applications (System.Windows.Forms) and one for Web-based applications (System.Web). This book is concerned with the latter model. The System.Web namespace in the .NET Framework is the portion of the .NET Framework that provides ASP.NET functionality. Looking at the above list, we can see that ASP.NET is just one part of the overall .NET Framework for building applications.

Introduction to ASP.NET

ASP.NET is a programming model for building Web-based applications. It is essentially a runtime and set of .NET Framework class libraries that can be used to build dynamic Web pages. ASP.NET runs within the context of a Web server, such as Microsoft Internet Information Server (IIS), and processes programming instructions on the server to service browser requests. Unlike static HTML files, which are served directly from the Web server, ASP.NET pages are built on the server to produce dynamic results. The final rendering of a page might be constructed from a variety of different instructions or data sources.

ASP.NET pages are created by a programmer as a combination of text, markup (such as HTML), and ASP.NET server-specific tags and script, which are then stored with the `.aspx` extension on the Web server. You can think of a stored ASP.NET page as a set of instructions for how to build an HTML page. When the page is requested, the server-side logic is processed to create a page in HTML that the client browser can display. Because the rendered output is HTML markup (no proprietary code), any browser can read it. All the dynamic processing happens on the Web server. ASP.NET server-specific tags are very powerful; they include the capability to react to user actions, connect to data stores, and automatically build very complex HTML structures.

As previously mentioned, ASP.NET represents one part of the .NET Framework and, consequently, ASP.NET pages can take advantage of all of the services offered by that framework, including networking, data access, security, and much more. The fact that all of these framework services are available to ASP.NET enables you to build rich Web applications more easily than ever before. You can spend less time reinventing the basic building blocks that all applications need and instead spend more time focusing on the specific logic that is unique to your application.

ASP.NET also introduces Web programming innovations that greatly improve the development model over classic Active Server Pages (ASP):

- **Language-independence:** Because ASP.NET is part of the .NET Framework, ASP.NET applications can be constructed in the language of your choice, for example Visual C#, Visual Basic .NET, or J#. Classic ASP (versions 1, 2, and 3), on the other hand, was generally used only with JScript or VBScript pages.
- **Compiled instead of interpreted:** Unlike classic ASP, which interprets programming instructions every time the page is requested, ASP.NET dynamically compiles pages on the server into native programming instructions that can be run much, much faster. Frequently, an ASP.NET page will run an order of magnitude faster than the same page written in Classic ASP.
- **Event-driven programming model:** In classic ASP, pages are always executed in a top-down linear fashion, and HTML markup is often mixed in with the programming instructions. Anyone with experience in Classic ASP knows that this can make your pages difficult to read, and even more difficult to maintain. ASP.NET introduces an event-driven model that allows you to separate code from markup content and to factor code into meaningful units for handling specific tasks, such as responding to a button click from the client. This VB-like eventing model greatly improves the readability and maintainability of your pages.
- **Server controls:** Classic ASP requires you to dynamically construct a page rendering by piecing together HTML fragments in code, which often results in writing the same code over and over again across your applications. (How many times have you constructed a table of data from a database query?) One of the great advancements that ASP.NET brings to Web programming is Microsoft's encapsulation of code to perform common behavior into server controls that can be

easily reused within an application. A *server control* is created declaratively, just like an HTML tag, but represents a programmable object on the server that can interact with your code and output a custom dynamic HTML rendering. ASP.NET includes over 80 server controls that encapsulate behavior that ranges from standard form elements to complex controls such as grids and menus.

- **Design time improvements to controls (when used with Visual Web Developer):** Developers can decrease the time it takes to develop a complex page by using design time interfaces such as the Smart Tasks panels, tag-level navigation bars, and wizards that can set control properties.

If you have worked in Classic ASP, you will be amazed at the increase in your productivity with ASP.NET 2.0. If you have never worked in Classic ASP, you can buy a beer for someone who did and listen to the war stories.

Introduction to ASP.NET 2.0

The first ASP.NET versions (1.0 and 1.1) rapidly spread throughout the developer community from a pre-release in 2001 to 2005. Programmers quickly appreciated that they could spend a lot less time programming using the power and flexibility of the .NET Framework, and CIOs saw that they could devote more resources to high-level improvements to their IT structure when programmers were spending less time troubleshooting custom code. ASP.NET was truly a monumental release that simplified the lives of Web developers.

However, even prior to the release of version 1.0, the ASP.NET team was already working on ASP.NET 2.0. The team set the following ambitious design goals:

- Remove 70 percent of the lines of code needed to build a typical Web application.
- Provide a set of extensible application services that provide the building blocks for common application scenarios such as membership, roles, personalization, and navigation.
- Create a rich set of scenario-based server controls that are able to leverage the aforementioned services to deliver complete and customizable user interfaces that expose those services with a minimum of code.
- Improve page-processing performance to increase the overall Web server throughput.
- Provide administration features that enhance the deployment, management, and operations of ASP.NET.
- Improve the tools for hosting companies to support multiple sites and to migrate developers' projects to public deployment.
- Enable nearly all features of ASP.NET to be easily extended or replaced with custom implementations for advanced scenarios.

Let's pause to reflect on that first goal: the removal of 70 percent of the code needed today to write a dynamic Web application. How is this possible? The ASP.NET team looked closely at the variety of common scenarios being implemented in custom code today, and specifically looked for ways to encapsulate those scenarios into building blocks (server controls or classes that provide services) that could accomplish those tasks automatically. For example, most Web applications need security, navigation, or personalization services to provide custom experiences for users. In ASP.NET 2.0, these scenarios are exposed as a set of configurable application services and server controls that talk to those application services. By providing these class libraries, Microsoft greatly reduced the amount of code that must be written by programmers to implement common scenarios.

Among all the common scenarios, however, one stood apart as absolutely essential to every application. Data access is the common thread that drives most dynamic Web applications, and so it is no surprise that the ASP.NET team defined some very aggressive goals toward reducing the amount of code and concepts necessary to perform data access in ASP.NET 2.0 applications. The goals that were specific to data include the following:

- Enable a declarative (no-code) way to define a source of data in ASP.NET.
- Enable a declarative (no-code) way to display data in controls, without having to explicitly data-bind at the right time in the page execution life cycle.
- Enable a declarative (no-code) way to perform common data scenarios such as sorting, paging, filtering, updating, inserting, and deleting data.
- Enable a rich set of UI controls for displaying data, including flexible grid/details controls with the capability to both display and manipulate data.
- Enable an extensible model for building custom data sources to support new types of data.
- Enable an extensible model for building custom controls for displaying data in new ways.

The result of the preceding objectives is a set of server controls that programmers can use to add data interactions to a page. The data-specific controls are divided into two groups: data source controls and data-bound controls. *Data source controls* create the connection to stores of data (databases or other repositories). The *data-bound controls* take the information from the data source controls and create a rendering on the page. This simple two-control pattern is available in many combinations.

A number of data source controls are available for many types of databases and even nonrelational data sources. Although additional controls are already in development by third parties, the following five data source controls ship with ASP.NET 2.0:

- **SqlDataSource control:** To connect to the Microsoft SQL Server and other T-SQL databases that have a managed provider
- **AccessDataSource control:** To connect to Microsoft Access files (extension of `.MDB`)
- **ObjectDataSource:** To connect to middle-tier business objects
- **XmlDataSource:** To connect XML content
- **SiteMapDataSource:** To connect XML files in the format of the ASP.NET 2.0 site map (or site data through a custom provider)

Data-bound controls include many that are familiar from ASP.NET 1.*x*, as well as some that are completely new for ASP.NET 2.0:

- **GridView and DataGrid:** For tabular data. `GridView` is new for version 2, whereas the legacy `DataGrid` remains largely unchanged for ASP.NET 1.*x*.
- **DetailsView and FormView:** Display data for one record at a time.

- **DataList and Repeater:** Display multiple data records in flexible layouts defined by the page programmer.
- **ListBox, DropDownList, BulletedList, CheckBoxList, and RadioButtonList:** Display a group of options with the expectation that the user will make a selection.
- **AdRotator:** Display an advertisement from a store of advertisements. This control was offered in ASP.NET version 1.*x* but has been updated to be compatible with data source controls.
- **TreeView and MenuView:** Display hierarchical data.

Taken together, the data source controls and data-bound controls represent the majority of effort in this book.

Introduction to ADO.NET

Working behind the scenes in all versions of ASP is ADO, the ActiveX Data Objects. *ADO.NET* is a set of class libraries in the .NET Framework that makes it easier to use data in your applications. Microsoft has gathered the best practices in data connections from the past several decades and written the code to implement those practices. The code is wrapped up into several objects that can be easily used by other software, including ASP. In this section we will take a short look at ADO.NET so you have some feel for the technology. Keep in mind that for most scenarios in ASP.NET 2.0, you do not need to work directly with ADO.NET.

The classes within ADO.NET handle much of the plumbing and database-specific intricacies so that when ASP.NET page designers want to read or write data, they can write fewer lines of code. ADO.NET, like ASP.NET, is not a language; rather, it is a collection of classes that provide common functionality. You can use those classes from a programming language such as Visual Basic or C#.

You can think of ADO.NET as a very smart translation layer between a data store (like SQL Server) and a data consumer (like an ASP.NET page). ADO.NET classes can generate commands that are appropriate to carry out tasks in the data store. But, as you will see, ASP.NET 2.0 offers server-side data controls that make it even easier to work with ADO.NET, sometimes eliminating the need to use ADO.NET objects directly.

Review of ASP.NET 1.x and ADO.NET for Data Access

This section is one of the few places where we discuss ASP.NET 1.*x*, meaning version 1.0 or 1.1. We do so for purposes of comparison. Pay close attention in each sentence to its application for ASP.NET 1.*x* (last version) versus ASP.NET 2.0 (the topic of this book).

Many readers will already have experience with earlier versions of ASP.NET. This short section recalls that model for the purposes of demonstrating how, in version 1.*x*, you worked directly with the ADO.NET objects to bring data into a Web page. For those readers who never used earlier versions, view the code that follows as a curiosity of history, akin to a study of surgery techniques prior to the discovery of ether. In the past, a typical simple ASP.NET version 1.*x* page required the following code. Note that although the following is presented only in Visual Basic, the rest of the techniques in this book are covered in VB.NET and C#.

```
<script runat="server">
  Sub Page_Load(ByVal sender As Object, ByVal e As System.EventArgs)
    BulletedList1.DataSource = GetAuthorsByState("CA")
    BulletedList1.DataBind()
  End Sub

  Shared Function GetAuthorsByState(ByVal state As String) As System.Data.DataSet\
         Dim connectionString As String =
                 "server=(local);database=pubs;trusted_connection=true"
         Dim dbConnection As System.Data.IDbConnection = New
                 System.Data.SqlClient.SqlConnection(connectionString)

    Dim queryString As String =
         "SELECT [authors].[au_lname] FROM [authors] WHERE ([authors].[state] =
@state)"
    Dim dbCommand As System.Data.IDbCommand = New System.Data.SqlClient.SqlCommand
    dbCommand.CommandText = queryString
    dbCommand.Connection = dbConnection

    Dim dbParam_state As System.Data.IDataParameter = New
         System.Data.SqlClient.SqlParameter
    dbParam_state.ParameterName = "@state"
    dbParam_state.Value = state
    dbParam_state.DbType = System.Data.DbType.StringFixedLength
    dbCommand.Parameters.Add(dbParam_state)

    Dim dataAdapter As System.Data.IDbDataAdapter = New
         System.Data.SqlClient.SqlDataAdapter
    dataAdapter.SelectCommand = dbCommand
    Dim dataSet As System.Data.DataSet = New System.Data.DataSet
    dataAdapter.Fill(dataSet)

    Return dataSet
  End Function
</script>
<html><head runat="server"><title>Untitled Page</title></head>
<body>
    <form id="form1" runat="server"><div>
      <asp:BulletedList ID="BulletedList1"
         DataTextField="au_lname" Runat="server" />
    </div></form>
</body></html>
```

The preceding example executes a `SQL SELECT` statement that reads the information about some authors from a database and then binds the result to a bulleted list control. The page has a method named `GetAuthorsByState` that creates several ADO.NET objects to accomplish this task:

- A `SqlConnection` object represents the connection to the database server.
- A `SqlCommand` object represents the `SQL SELECT` command to execute.
- A `SqlParameter` object represents a value to be substituted for a marker in the command.
- A `SqlDataAdapter` represents the capability to fill a `DataSet` object from a command.
- A `DataSet` represents the command result, which may be bound to the `BulletedList`.

In the Page_Load event, the GetAuthorsByState method is called to retrieve the DataSet result and assign it to the BulletedList's DataSource property. We then call DataBind() to force the BulletedList to create itself from the data result. The fact that we need to call DataBind() at the appropriate time in the page execution life cycle is a key step that ASP.NET 2.0 seeks to eliminate in the most common cases. In fact, in most cases, ASP.NET 2.0 completely eliminates the need to interact with ADO.NET. However, it is useful to understand the relationship between the aforementioned ADO.NET objects to discuss how ASP.NET 2.0 improves upon that model.

ASP.NET 2.0 and Data Access

Having endured a long winter of discontent with ASP.NET 1.*x*, we can now turn to the pearl of ASP.NET 2.0. Version 2.0 gives us an improved set of tools for data access that eliminates much, if not all, of the code that was required to perform data-binding in ASP.NET 1.*x*. First, you no longer have to programmatically instantiate, set properties of, and call methods of ADO.NET objects as in the preceding listing. Instead, you can add simple server-side data controls to your page and set their attributes declaratively. When the page is rendered, ASP.NET 2.0 will automatically perform all of the object instantiation and method calls to set up and display your data. Compare the following listing in ASP.NET 2.0 to the previous listing.

```
<html>
<head runat="server"><title>Demo</title></head>
<body>
    <form id="form1" runat="server">
        <asp:SqlDataSource ID="SqlDataSource1" Runat="server"
            SelectCommand="SELECT au_lname FROM authors WHERE (state = @state)"
            ConnectionString='<%$ ConnectionStrings:Pubs %>' >
            <SelectParameters>
                <asp:Parameter Type="String" DefaultValue="CA" Name="state" />
            </SelectParameters>
        </asp:SqlDataSource>

         <asp:BulletedList ID="BulletedList1" Runat="server"
             DataSourceID="SqlDataSource1"
             DataTextField="Au_lname">
        </asp:BulletedList>
    </form>
</body></html>
```

Note in the preceding ASP.NET 2.0 code that two server-side controls are used. The first is a data source control, in this case the SqlDataSource control. Behind the scenes the control sets up all of the ADO.NET connection objects needed for the display of data, including the Connection, Command, and DataReader or Dataset objects. Then, a data-bound control named BulletedList is used to take the data of the data source control and actually render it to the page.

The second improvement occurs because the server-side controls are sensitive to events in the page life cycle. Appropriate actions are taken by the ASP.NET 2.0 server-side controls during the page life cycle. Notice that there is no reference in the ASP.NET 2.0 page to any event in the page life cycle. Students of earlier versions of ASP.NET were typically confused by the intricacies of when in a page life to perform various tasks, such as data-binding. Thus, many ASP.NET 1.*x* pages suffered from code that either called DataBind in the wrong event or called DataBind duplicate times in multiple events. These timings are now automatic with the ASP.NET 2.0 server-side data controls.

Review of Terminology

To round out the introductory material, this section provides a review of some of the terminology used throughout the book.

- **Access:** An RDMS that is based on the MDB (Access) file format, the JET engine, and a series of tools for building and using databases. Access is inexpensive, easy to learn, widely understood, and currently deployed on many machines. However, it does not support more than a few concurrent users.
- **ADO.NET:** A collection of classes that acts as an intermediary between data stores (such as Access or an XML file) and a data consumer (such as an ASP.NET page).
- **ASP.NET:** A set of class libraries in the .NET Framework for building and running dynamic Web applications.
- **Command:** An ADO.NET object that represents a SQL statement that can be passed to a database.
- **Common Language Runtime (CLR):** The .NET runtime environment. It enables programmers to write in one of many languages, and then compile the code to a single, uniform language for deployment.
- **Connection:** An ADO.NET object that represents a unique path between a data consumer and data provider.
- **Data Engine (MSDE):** Similar to SSE, but based on an earlier version of the SQL Server engine. MSDE will work for the exercises in this book.
- **Data store:** A place where data is kept and usually managed. All RDMS are data stores, but some data stores are not RDMS because they are not relational.
- **Database or Relational Database Management System (RDMS):** The software that enables reading and manipulation of data. Most systems include tools to design and test databases as well as tools to optimize sets of procedures. An RDMS must store data in compliance with some form of normalization (a relational format). These databases include SQL Server, Oracle, Access, and the other main database products.
- **Database schema (or database metadata):** The structure of the database, including the design of the tables and relationships. Schema does not include the actual data values.
- **Data-bound control:** A server-side control that takes data from a data source control and renders it on the page. Data-bound controls abstract from the programmer the HTML tags such as `<table>`. Data-bound controls are available to render tables, lists, trees, and other structures.
- **Data source control:** A server-side control that creates a connection to a database. It provides an abstraction of the data store and makes programming ASP.NET 2.0 pages faster and easier to build. Data source controls are available for Microsoft SQL Server, Microsoft Access, XML, and other sources of data.
- **DataSet:** An ADO.NET object representing a group of data organized into rows and columns.
- **Dynamic Web pages:** Files stored on the Web server as code and then converted to HTML at the moment they are requested. When they are converted, they can take into account the real-time situation of the user and the owners of the Web site, and thus take different forms for different requests.

- **Extensible Markup Language (XML):** A markup language commonly used for data in which each value is stored and described. XML is not particularly efficient (the space required for the descriptions generally exceeds the size of the data), but it is easily read by many different data management systems.
- **Integrated Development Environment (IDE):** A set of tools that assists programmers in developing code.
- **Internet Information Server (IIS):** A built-in Web server in Windows that serves Web pages to requestors via TCP/IP. IIS operating on Windows 2000, 2003, or Windows XP Professional has the capability to use the .NET 2.0 Framework classes to serve ASP.NET 2.0 Web pages.
- **JET:** A database engine that runs in the background and uses MDB (Access) files. JET accepts commands directly from other software (such as .NET or Access) to read or modify MDB files.
- **.NET Framework:** A group of classes written by Microsoft that make applications easier and faster to develop and more suitable for operation over the Internet.
- **Parameter:** An ADO.NET object that represents a variable piece of data that can be sent to the SQL Server with the `Command Object` (SQL statement) and inserted by the SQL Server prior to execution of the statement
- **Server control:** An object that derives from `System.Web.UI.Control` that performs its tasks on the server to contribute to an HTML page that is sent to the browser. Server-side controls can maintain a state through `ViewState`.
- **SQL Server:** An enterprise-strength RDMS designed to support large amounts of data and many concurrent users.
- **SQL Server Express (SSE):** A database engine (currently free) based on the Microsoft SQL Server database engine. Unlike SQL Server, SSE is limited in the number of simultaneous data connections it can serve and has only a few utilities. This book uses SSE in most examples.
- **Structured Query Language (SQL):** A language used by data consumers to request a read or write from a data provider. For over a decade, SQL has been the standard for communication with an RDMS.
- **ViewState control:** A string (frequently very long) that describes the current state of the page and is posted back to the server when the page is refreshed. The server uses the `ViewState` string to then take the next appropriate action for the user.
- **Visual Studio (VS):** A very powerful IDE that is optimized for .NET development. Visual Studio includes an editor to design pages, an Explorer-like file manager, and many tools increase developer productivity.
- **Visual Web Developer Express (VWD):** Another IDE from Microsoft that is similar in look and feel to VS but with a reduced set of features. Currently VWD Express is free, so we use it in this book.
- **Web Page Editor:** Software that allows pages to be opened and changed. One of the most basic editors is Notepad. Visual Studio, Visual Web Developer, and ASP.NET Web Matrix include an editor with other tools to improve productivity.

With these past few sections, we have defined ASP.NET 2.0 and its importance. Now, we will describe the prerequisites and then we can move on to creating our first few pages.

Requirements for Using ASP.NET 2.0

This section describes and discusses the options for the components you need to add data to your ASP.NET 2.0 pages. The next section steps you through the actual installations of the four prerequisites needed for using databases with ASP.NET 2.0:

- A Web server
- The .NET Framework version 2.0
- An editor to create ASPX pages
- Database management system

A Web Server

Web pages must be processed by a Web server to be available to a browser. Two options work with the .NET Framework, one for deployment and one for development. IIS handles the load of a public Web site, but may also be used for development purposes. If you have already turned on IIS on your development machine, you will find that the .NET Framework automatically registers itself with IIS and is available for you to create ASP.NET pages.

If IIS is not turned on, you can easily enable it in Windows:

1. Check that you have updated your installation of Windows with the latest service packs and security patches. (This is a good habit to get into.)
2. Click through Start➪Control Panel➪Add & Remove Programs.
3. Select Add/Remove Windows Components, add a check mark to IIS, and click OK to install.

Microsoft also provides a lightweight alternative to IIS named the ASP.NET Development Server (code-named Cassini) that is better suited to developers and students than IIS. The ASP.NET Development Server comes with Visual Studio and Visual Web Developer and installs automatically. When a page is run from the Visual Web Developer, ASP.NET Development Server will automatically start its Web service on a random port and invoke your browser with a request for your page sent to `http://localhost:xxxx/MySiteName/MyPageName.aspx`. The `xxxx` represents a random number of the port that is opened for the Web server (the number is randomized to prevent people from searching the Internet for developers who happen to have a specific port open at that moment). Instead of IIS, ASP.NET Development Server will serve the page, including processing ASP.NET code and server controls. Evidence of the server activity appears as an icon system tray.

> **ASP.NET Development Server is designed for developers and does not support requests from remote computers. For this book either Web server will work. Both servers use the same ASPX pages, so there is no need for any changes in syntax or commands.**

The .NET Framework Version 2.0

The .NET 2.0 Framework includes the classes that enable ASP.NET 2.0, including its data connection capabilities. The framework is available for download in three ways:

- The first is the version named .NET Framework 2.0 Redist, which is about 20MB.
- The second version includes the Software Development Kit (SDK), which includes the .NET Framework documentation, samples, and several SDK tools. However, the SDK download is significantly larger than the Redist, and this book does not rely on features in the SDK. If you are not in a rush, you can download the .NET 2.0 Framework and order the SDK on CD, as described on the download page.
- The third alternative is to use the version that is automatically downloaded and installed with Visual Studio or Visual Web Developer (VWD) Express. That route is easiest and is adequate for this book. A description of the install of VWD Express follows.

If you have the .NET Framework version 1.0 or 1.1 installed, you can also install the .NET Framework 2.0 on the same machine. If you have already installed version 1.0 or 1.1 of the .NET Framework and either of those versions is already registered in IIS, the .NET Framework 2.0 setup will not *automatically* register 2.0 with IIS because this would potentially upgrade applications to the new version without the user's consent.

In order to register .NET 2.0 Framework if version 1.*x* is installed, run in a command prompt window `aspnet_regiis -i` from the .NET 2.0 Framework installation directory; for example, `\WINDOWS\Microsoft .NET\Framework\<version>`. This command line utility will upgrade the server and all apps on it to use 2.0.

> **Although it is possible to run both 1.*x* applications and 2.0 applications side by side on the same machine, the steps for doing so are more involved and outside the scope of this book.**

An Editor to Create Web Pages

ASP.NET pages must be written using some type of editor. Most readers will select one of the following three options, depending on their budget and interest in learning to use new software. This book uses Microsoft VWD Express.

Visual Studio

Visual Studio (VS) provides very powerful tools to design complex Web pages that employ multiple resources from throughout the enterprise. Objectives that require 10 or 20 lines of typing in Notepad are performed in VS with a single drag and drop or by clicking through a wizard. After the drag and drop, VS types all of the tags, attributes, and code to produce the feature. VS also provides intelligent assistance to typing so that you generally have to type only a character or two and VS will complete the syntax (called "IntelliSense" technology). Debugging features, including trace and immediate windows (called stacks), are built into the product. For readers of this book, a key VS feature is the capability to read and display database information at design time, so you do not need to have Access or a SQL tool open to see the structure and data of your database. Visual Studio includes many tools for multiple programming languages and tools for collaboration of multiple developers at a price starting at around US $500. This book does not discuss the installation of Visual Studio.

Visual Web Developer Express

Visual Web Developer (VWD) Express is a new product from Microsoft and includes most features of Visual Studio needed for Web site development, but at a much lower price (not known at time of writing). All of the exercises in this text can be performed using VWD, as it includes ASP.NET Development Server, the visual design interface, all of the controls we discuss, and the debugging features. VWD does not include some of the large-scale deployment features of the Visual Studio used by teams of developers, but for the purposes of this book you will not need them.

Notepad and Other Editors

Notepad is free with Windows and can be used as a no-frills text editor to create ASP.NET 2.0 pages. Remember that ASPX files are saved as text files, as are HTML files. Therefore, every exercise in this book can be typed into a text file using Notepad, saved with an *.aspx* extension (not `.txt`), and run. On the other hand, Notepad does not offer much assistance other than cut, copy, and paste. If you use Notepad, be prepared to do a lot of typing, look up a lot of syntax, and perform a lot of troubleshooting.

Additional editor options are likely to appear. Microsoft may add ASP.NET 2.0 capabilities to FrontPage, its Web designer–oriented site development tool. Also, editors may be forthcoming from third parties. However, as long as VWD Express is a free download, its advantages far outstrip the other options. This book uses VWD Express for all exercises and demonstration figures. The resulting code is then generally presented so you can see the source and so typists can enter the page into Notepad or another editor.

A Database Management System

A Web site needs a way to manage the data. ASP.NET 2.0 files will not, by themselves, hold or manage data. Several choices are listed here; we use SQL Server Express (SSE) in this book.

- **Microsoft Access:** Familiar and already widely deployed but not recommended for use in a production Web site. Access works for learning and development purposes, however (more details follow).
- **Microsoft SQL Server:** A powerful choice for public deployment but expensive and more difficult to set up and manage, particularly on a desktop development machine.
- **SQL Server Express (SSE):** A lightweight and free database engine based on the SQL Server engine. SSE is used to support this book's examples in most cases.
- **Other relational databases:** Examples that can be used include Oracle or MySql. This book discusses using their data but not how to install or manage them.
- **Nonrelational stores of data:** Examples include text files, XML files, or Excel spreadsheets, in some cases.

Let's look at some details for each of these five options.

Microsoft Access

Microsoft Access is sold as part of Microsoft Office Professional or as a separate purchase. When you install Access, you automatically get a sample database named `Northwind.mdb` and the JET database engine. You can also download the `Northwind.mdb` file from the following location (or search Microsoft.com for "Northwind.mdb download"):

```
http://www.Microsoft.com/downloads/details.aspx?FamilyID=c6661372-8dbe-422b-8676-
c632d66c529c&DisplayLang=en
```

When using Access as a source of data for Web sites, even in development environments, you should be aware of two major problems:

- Access was not designed to scale to large numbers of users. When loads begin to increase, Access uses large amounts of server resources. Therefore, it is unsuitable for deployment in scenarios with more than five or ten users.
- The second problem concerns the syntax of passing information to Access when modifying data. Access relies on a model where the order of the data passed to a parameterized command determines the fields where the data is stored. This creates a number of problems for the page designer, as you will see in later chapters. Microsoft SQL Server, MSDE, and SQL Server Express use a different model where the parameter values are named; thus, order is unimportant.

For the reasons just described, this book recommends that you *not* use Access for working with data in ASP.NET; instead, download the SQL Server Express (SSE) database engine described shortly.

Microsoft SQL Server

Microsoft SQL Server is an enterprise-level database management system designed to scale and perform for the needs of entire organizations. It makes an ideal RDMS for public Web sites with high volumes and the need for integration with other Microsoft products.

Microsoft, to this point, has offered time-limited trial versions of the product at `www.Microsoft.com/sql`. SQL is generally installed by a database administrator, and the steps are outside the scope of this book. If you are installing it yourself, we suggest you select the mixed authentication security model and be sure to install the sample databases. If you are using an existing SQL server installation at your workplace, you may have to ask your administrator to reinstall the Northwind and Pubs sample databases. You will also need to know the name of the server, instance, user ID, and password.

SQL Server Express

The SQL Server Express (SSE) edition provides an engine that holds a database and responds to T-SQL statement commands. SSE is built from Microsoft SQL Server and, thus, responds exactly like the full-scale SQL Server. SSE is the next generation to Microsoft Data Engine (MSDE), and the upgrade path to SQL Server is seamless. As of this writing, SSE does not include graphical tools for managing the database, changing the schema, or modifying data, although you will be able to use Visual Studio or Visual Web Developer to perform some of these tasks. Keep your eyes open for Microsoft to add a basic GUI interface. If your machine has SQL Enterprise Tools on it (part of the SQL Server software), then you can use it to manage SSE instances. There are several advantages to SSE over other sources of data for readers of this book:

- SSE is free and installs automatically with VWD.
- Developers spend little time acclimating to SSE — it operates as a background service without a visual interface to learn.
- The data format and organization is the same as Microsoft SQL Server, so when you are ready to deploy there are very easy and well-documented solutions. Many Web-hosting companies have extensive experience importing SSE databases to SQL Server.

The biggest disadvantage is that as of this writing, there is no GUI interface for installing or importing a new database. We will talk you through the steps of installing your sample databases for this book using VWD Express.

Other Relational Databases

ASP.NET 2.0 can use other sources of data, including MySql, Oracle, and any other database for which a provider exists. Those connections are covered in Chapter 4. In theory, you could build `Northwind.mbd` in one of those systems for the purpose of writing the exercises in this text. This book does not cover installation or maintenance of these other sources.

Nonrelational Stores of Data

Another option is data stored in files or streams. For example, XML has emerged as an important format for storing and transferring data. Other data formats, such as Excel, can also be used in special cases. These file-based data stores exist independently of any database management system. They can be used directly by ASP.NET 2.0. In the rare cases that these are the only sources of data, there is no need to install a database management system.

Now that we've covered the components needed at a theoretical level, it is time to get out the keyboard and actually set up your machine for the exercises in this book.

Setup for This Book

We've discussed the software needed for running, creating, and testing data-driven ASPX pages, and it is now time to walk you through the setup. We will also perform some steps that are specific for this book, not for ASP.NET 2.0 in general.

Install Visual Web Developer Express, SSE, and the ASP.NET Development Server

Visual Web Developer is a one-stop package for most of what is needed in this book. Its install wizard installs all of the Microsoft-provided components discussed in the previous section: the .NET Framework 2.0, the ASPX development environment including the page editor (VWD Express), the ASP.NET Development Server, and SQL Server Express.

1. Shut down any open applications.
2. Visit the Developer Express page at `http://lab.msdn.microsoft.com/express` and follow the instructions for downloading and installing Visual Web Developer Express. While on that page, check for any notices regarding best practices, security, and changes to the install procedure.

3. Select the Visual Web Developer Express download and run it.
4. When and if prompted, you need to install VWD, SSE, and the .NET Framework. The help library is recommended; the SDK is optional (it provides sample code and FAQs).
5. VWD will give you the option to install SSE. Agree, and (if asked about features) select SQL Server Database Services, SQL Command Line Tools, Connectivity Components, and the Management Tools. The SSE installation may proceed in the background. The default authentication mode will be Windows Authentication. If the install pauses and prompts you to specify the authentication, then select Windows Authentication.
6. Finish the install and reboot.

> **After finishing the setup of this chapter, you may also want to download the set of Quick Start sample applications. They have simple install instructions and give you a useful, applied reference.**

After this step, you can perform two confirmations. Your Start➪Programs will now contain Visual Web Developer 2005 Express Edition. Your Start➪Control Panel➪Administrative Tools➪Services will display SQL Server running. Note that your SSE instance will be named `(local)\SQLExpress`. Another syntax for the name is `.\SQLExpress` (note the leading period). This instance name will come up many times in this book and can be a source of error if not typed correctly. You can now use SSE as your database management system, but keep in mind that the engine does not yet hold a database.

Download This Book's Files

The materials needed for the exercises in this book are available from the publisher:

1. Create a folder to hold the downloads for this book. We suggest you use `C:\TempBegAspNet2DB`. Note that although we park the download files here, the site will be created in the normal folder for IIS's Web applications, `C:\Websites`.
2. Go to `www.wrox.com`, get the download files for this book, and store them in `C:\TempBegAspNet2DB`. Extract the files to the same folder.

The download will contain notes on the install, the sample database setup files, demonstration pages used in the text, and all of the exercises. Read the install notes.

Create the Practice Web Site

Before doing any other steps, we will create the Web site used in this book. The site will be stored in the `C:\Websites` folder (created automatically by IIS) within which we will create a `BegAspNet2DB` folder.

1. Start VWD. You will see a Start Page in the center of the screen that is similar to Figure 1-1 (but with an empty list of recent projects). This is useful in the future, but close it for now.
2. Select File➪NewWebSite to see the New Web Site dialog box, as shown in Figure 1-2. Select the template type ASP.NET Web Site and locate the site in `C:\Websites\BegAspNet2Db`. Accept the defaults for File System and language of Visual Basic.

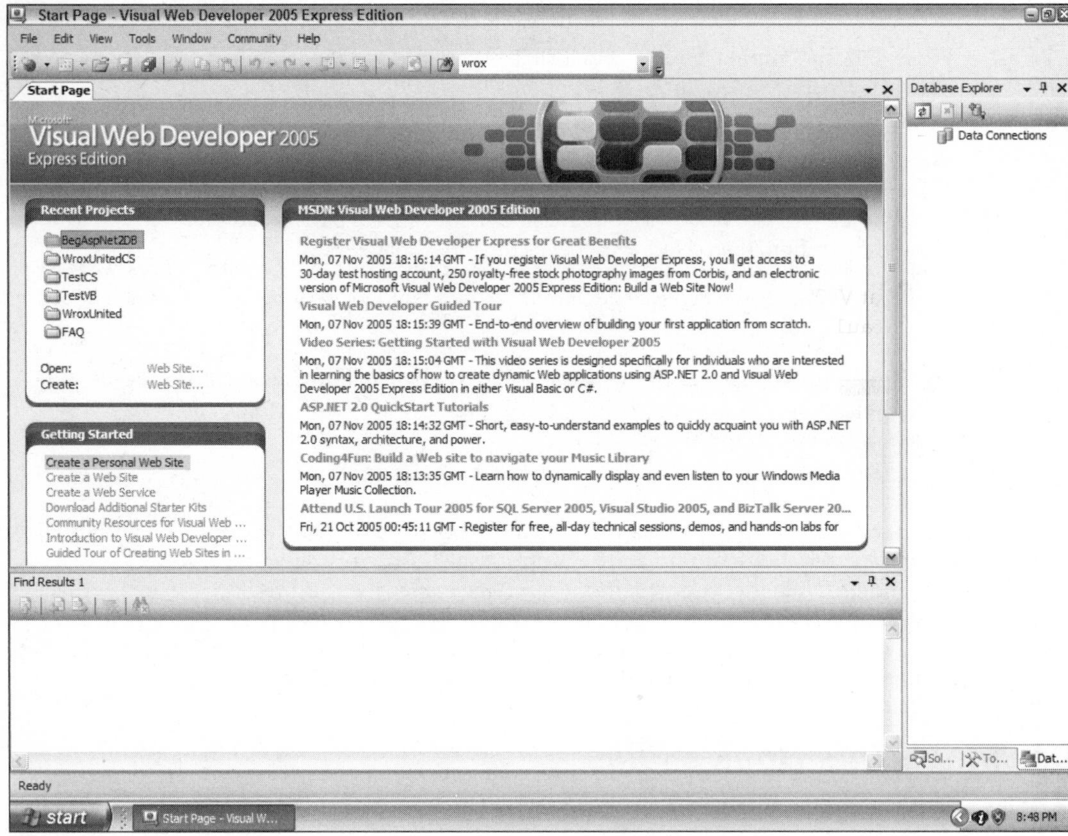

Figure 1-1

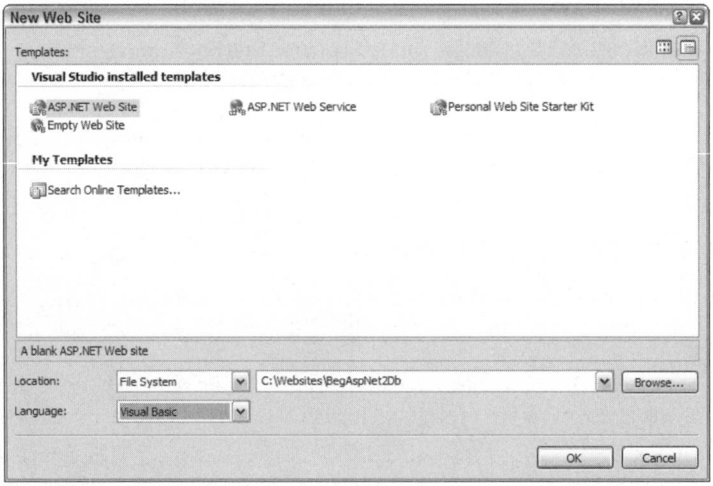

Figure 1-2

3. VWD will automatically build the framework of a site and present to you a default page as in Figure 1-2. In the lower-left corner, click the Design view (WYSIWYG—What You See Is What You Get) that is currently empty or a Source view of the same page (see tabs in Figure 1-3).

Figure 1-3

4. Take a look in the Solution Explorer by selecting View⇨Solution Explorer or press Ctr+Alt+L. Note that VWD has created the root and `App_Data` folders. Within the root are the `web.config` and `Default.aspx` pages and a folder for `App_Data` (see Figure 1-4).

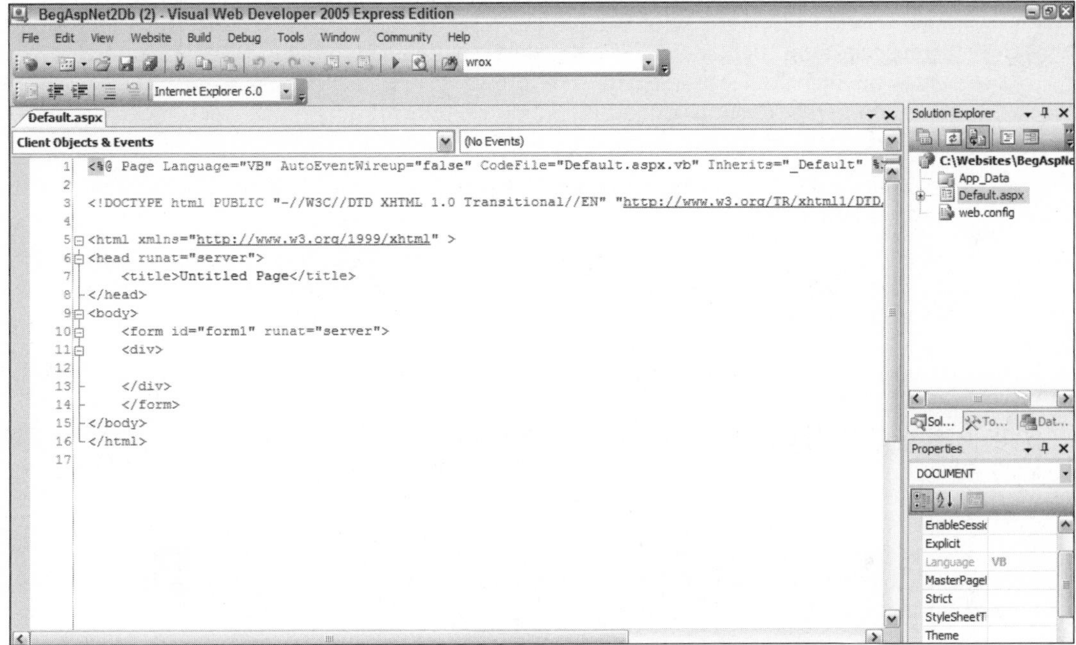

Figure 1-4

Later in the chapter, we will begin adding pages into folders we create named `ch01`, `ch02`, and so on.

Install the Sample Databases

In the download files, we provide two files of data used for data transfer—`Northwind.mdf` and `Pubs.mdf`—the same databases we have all come to know and love through many versions of Access and SQL Server. We also include `Northwind` in Access format for some demonstrations (`.mdb` file). These download files can be added to your site (and explored) in the following steps. First we physically copy the files into our site. Then we establish logical connections to them as sources of data.

1. In VWD's Solution Explorer, right-click on `App_Data` and select add Existing Item. Browse to your download for this book, select `App_Data\Northwind.mdf`, and click OK. Repeat for `Pubs.mdf` and `Northwind.mdb`.
2. Switch to the Database Explorer by clicking the tab that sits, by default, on the right side of the screen, as shown in Figure 1-5. If the tab is not visible, click through the menu: View➪Database Explorer.

Figure 1-5

3. Click on the Connect to Database icon and select Add Connection. In the Add Connection dialog box, select a Data source of Microsoft SQL Server Database file. This is a little confusing because the term "data source" refers to the type of source — that is, SQL format, Access format, and so on. In the Database file name box, browse to `App_Data\Northwind.mdf` and click Open. Accept the default logon using Windows Authentication, click Test Connection, and then click OK.
4. Repeat for the `Pubs.mdf` file both the Add Existing Item in the Solution Explorer and the Add new connection in the Database Explorer.
5. Finally, repeat for the `Northwind.mdb` (Access format) file. In Solution Explorer select Add Existing Item the same as we did for the `.mdf` files. However, in Database Explorer, in the Add Connection dialog box use as a data source "Microsoft Access Database File."

Note that your Data Explorer (Server Explorer) now has connection entries for `Northwind` (two connections) and `Pubs`, which will remain available when you open this site in the future. You can expand the entry to see the tables, and when you right-click on a table you will be offered an option to Show Table Data. You can demonstrate the power of this view by changing some small value, such as the spelling of a person's name. After a database in `.mdf` (or `.mdb`) format is copied into your `App_Data` directory, you can use VWD as a front end to examine and change the data of a database.

That finishes the setup steps. We will finish the chapter with a few quick demonstrations of the ease and power of using ASP.NET 2.0 to access data on Web site pages.

Demonstrations

To finish off the first chapter, we will create several pages that demonstrate using ASP.NET 2.0 pages with data. We will talk you through creating the pages using the VWD tools. In addition, each of these pages is available in this book's download at `www.wrox.com`. Also, check at that location for the latest updates and warnings for these exercises. To create these pages, you must have completed all of the install steps earlier in this chapter.

Try It Out — Creating a GridView Table from SQL with Paging and Sorting

In this exercise we quickly build a page that uses a `GridView` control to produce a table of author names that supports sorting and paging. Then we add a clickable filtering process to show authors living in just one state. We finish with a link to a second page that shows more details about one of the authors.

1. Continue using VWD with your BegAspNet2DB site open. If a Default page is open, you can close it.
2. In the Solution Explorer (if not visible on the right, press Ctrl+Alt+L to turn on), right-click on the name of the site, and click New Folder. Name it `ch01`.
3. Right-click on the new `ch01` folder, and add a new item using the template Web Form. Name it `TIO-0101-GridViewSQL`. Set the language to Visual Basic and leave the other settings at their defaults (Select master page = off and Place code in separate file = off), as shown in Figure 1-6. Once the new page appears on the VWD screen you will see, at the bottom left, tabs for Design and Source views. Switch to Design view.

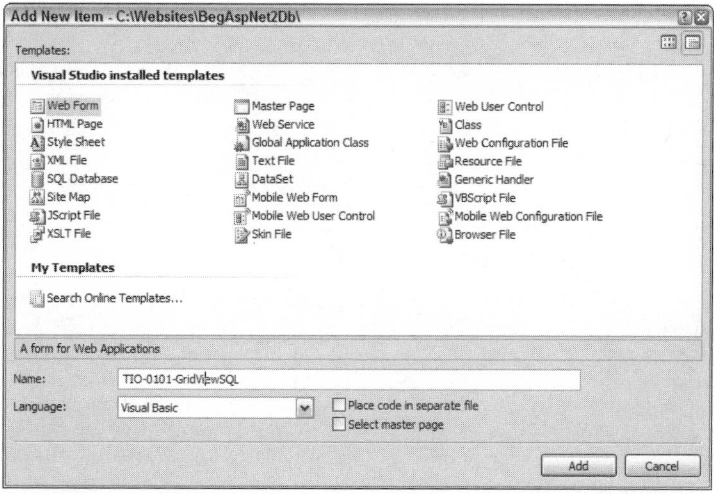

Figure 1-6

4. Select Menu: View⇨Database Explorer (Server Explorer) to display the explorer of data connections.
5. Expand the Pubs connection, Tables folder, and the Authors table as shown in Figure 1-7. Using Control+click, select the four fields `au_id`, `au_lname`, `au_fname`, and `state`. Drag them onto the blank page. VWD will automatically create a `GridView` and a `SqlData Source` control.

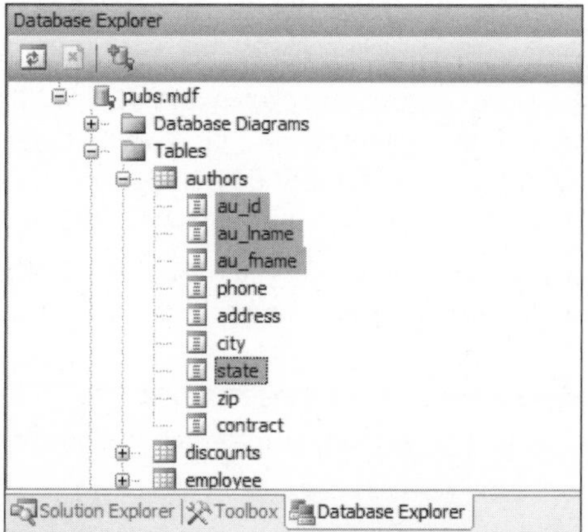

Figure 1-7

6. The Tasks menu automatically opens next to the new control, as in Figure 1-8. (Alternatively, open it by selecting the `GridView` and clicking on the small arrow at the top right of the control.) Enable paging and sorting, and then click AutoFormat and select one that you like (we use Professional). Click Apply and click OK.

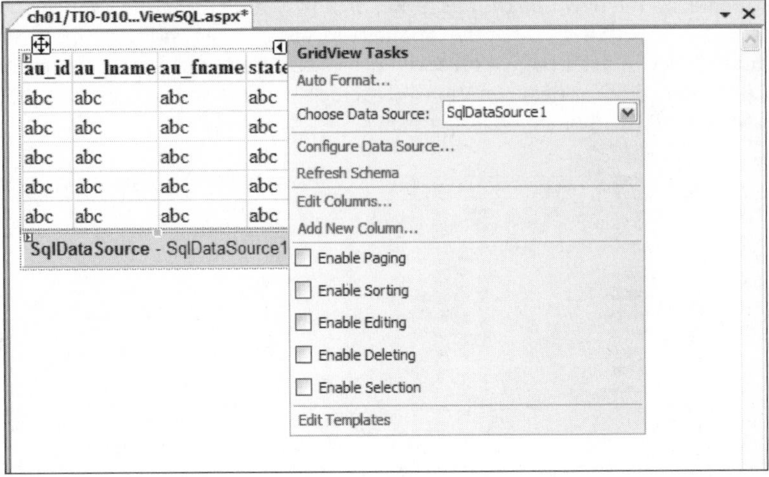

Figure 1-8

7. Save the page with Ctrl+S and press F5 to run it. When warned about debugging being disabled, select to modify the `web.config` file to enable debugging and click OK. In ASP.NET 2.0, the first viewing of a page is delayed as the framework compiles and optimizes the code. Subsequent requests are much faster.

> **Depending on your security settings, you may get a firewall blocked warning; if so, unblock the firewall for just the `WebDeveloper.WebExpress.exe`.**

8. In your browser, play with the sorting (click header of each column) and paging (numbers at bottom of table). Note that we have used drag-and-drop, but no code, to create a sophisticated display of data on the page. Close the browser so that the page is unlocked for improvements in VWD.

9. An alternative way to show data uses two steps. First, create the data source control. Then create the data-bound control. Although slower than the drag-and-drop, it provides more control over the process. In prelude, we will create a little working room above the `GridView` by pressing Ctrl+Home, pressing Enter twice, and then pressing Ctrl+Home again. In the next steps, we will first add a data source control and then add the data-bound control

10. Display the toolbar by clicking on Menu:View➪Toolbox. If the sections of the Toolbox are collapsed (you see only the dark gray headings of Standard, Data, Validation . . .), expand the Standard and Data sections. Drag a `SqlDataSource` control to the top of the page, as shown in Figure 1-9.

Figure 1-9

11. The Smart Tasks panel will automatically open, as shown in Figure 1-10; click Configure Data Source. Drop down the list of connections, select `pubsConnectionString1`, and click Next. Select the table named `Authors`, and click just one column from the check boxes: State. Turn on Return only unique rows, and click Next. Test the query and then click Finish. You now have a `SqlDataSource` control named `SqlDataSource2`, the first step in this two-step method to add data to the page.

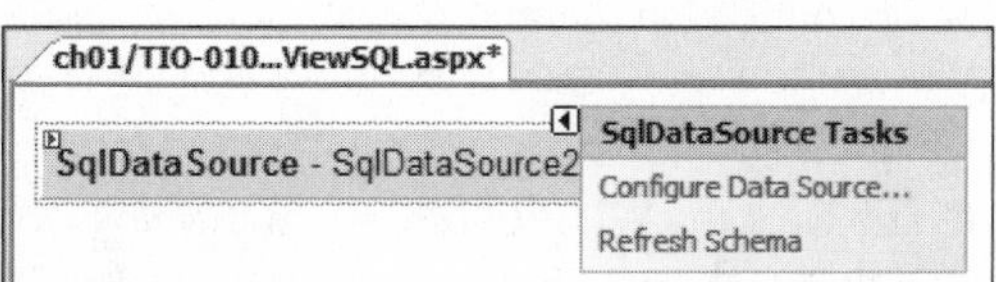

Figure 1-10

12. Display the list of distinct states by dragging a list box from the Standard section of the Toolbox to the top of the page. In the list box's Smart Tasks panel, click Choose Data Source and select `SqlDataSource2` (the distinct states list). The display and value fields can both remain "state," as shown in Figure 1-11. Click OK. Back on the Smart Tasks panel, click Enable AutoPostBack and close the task menu, save, and press Ctrl+F5 to view in your browser. You now have a list control on the page along with an invisible `SqlDataSource` control. Close the browser before returning to VWD.

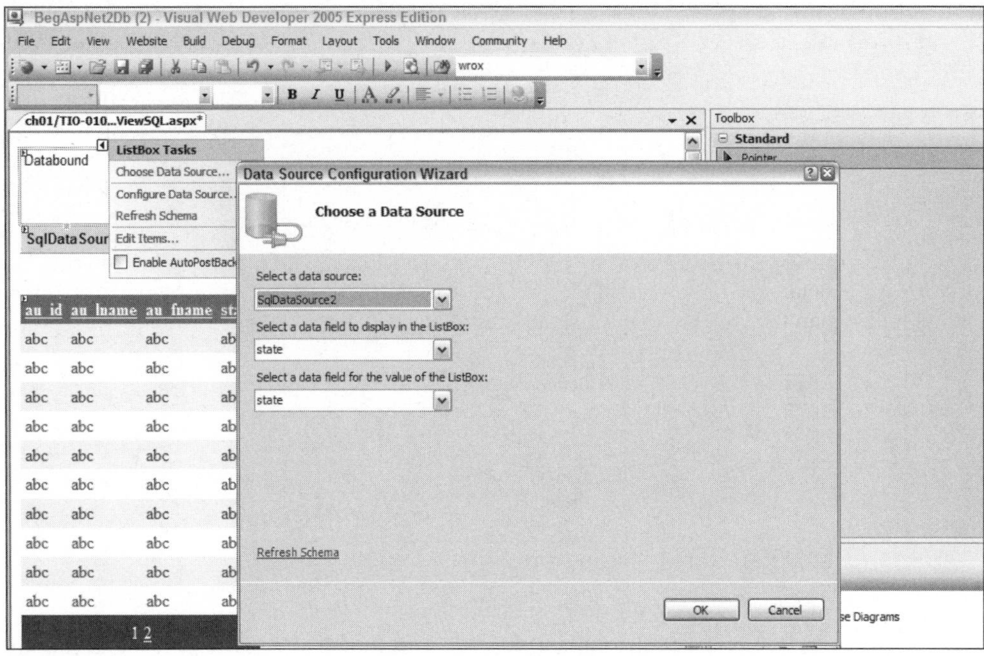

Figure 1-11

13. This step links the list box to the `GridView`, so only authors from the selected state appear. Stay in Design view, and select the `SqlDataSource1` control (below the `GridView`—be careful you don't use the `SqlDataSource2` control) and open its Smart Tasks panel. Click Configure Data Source, keep the same connection (named `pubsConnectionString1`), and click Next. You should see the option button set to specify columns and check-offs for the four fields (`id`, `firstname`, `lastname`, and `state`).

    Stay in the wizard, and click the WHERE button. In this box, you specify which authors to show. You want only those whose `state` value equals the selection in the States list box. Under the Column list, select State. The operator can stay as equals, and the source should be set to Control. Note the new options to pick a Control ID; you want `ListBox1`. Set the default value by typing in the string **CA** to start with a view of just authors in California. Click the Add button to append that `WHERE` clause to your SQL statement. Click OK and click Next.

    In the next page of the wizard, test the query using the default value of CA. Click Finish and then close the Common Tasks menu. If you are asked to refresh the control, click Yes.

14. Save and then run the file. Select various states and note the change in the table. Close the browser when you are done.

15. Now, you will create a second page to display details about one author from our `GridView`. In VWD, click your Solution Explorer tab so it is on top (or press Ctrl+Alt+L). Right-click on `ch01` and add a new item of template type Web Form and name it `TIO0101-DetailsViewSql.aspx`. Accept the other defaults and click `Add`. At the bottom left of the screen, select the Design view. Drag and drop a `DetailsView` control from the toolbar (Data section).

The Smart Tasks panel opens. Choose a New data source and select the type of database (which, by default, means a Microsoft SQL Server database), and click OK. Choose the connection named `pubsConnectionString1` and click Next. Check on the Specify columns from a table, select the name of `authors`, and click the asterisk (all columns). Click the WHERE button and set the `au_id` column equal to a source of `querystring` using the QueryString field `au_id` that you type in. Set a default value of `213-46-8915`, as shown in Figure 1-12. Click Add and double-check that the SQL expression shows `[au-id]=@au_id`. Click OK, click Next, test the query (click OK to accept default values in test and click Finish.

Close the `DetailsView` control's Smart Tasks panel menu, save, and press F5 to run. You will see the details on only one author, and you will see them presented in a `DetailsView` control rather than the GridView of the first part of the exercise. Close your browser.

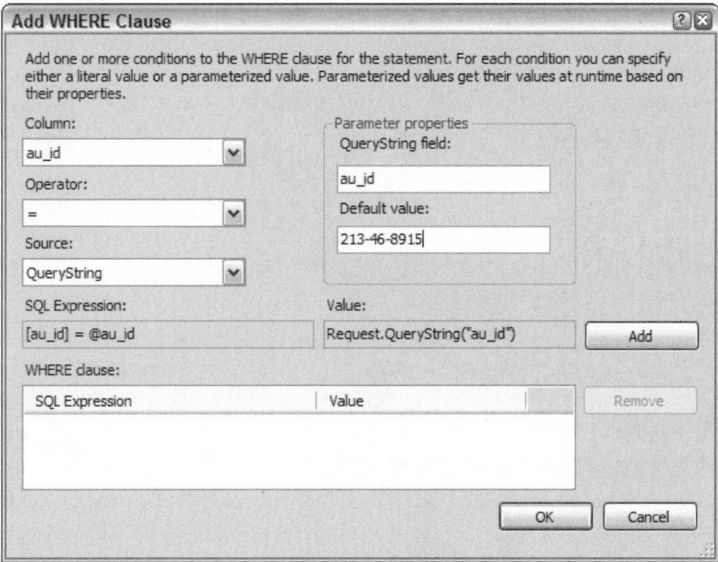

Figure 1-12

16. Now that you have a page to show details about an author, you can finish by giving the user a way to click the GridView of our first page to jump to the details page. In VWD, open `TIO-1-GridViewSql.aspx` in Design view. Select the GridView and expand the small top-right arrow to see the Smart Tasks panel. Select Edit columns to see the Fields dialog box. Select Hyperlink in the Available Fields and click Add. Keep your hyperlink field selected in the lower left, and go to the properties on the right to set the following:

```
Text =  View Details...
DataNavigateUrlFields =  au_id
DataNavigateUrlFormatString = TIO0101-DetailsViewSql.aspx?au_id={0}
```

Click OK and close the Smart Tasks panel.

17. Save the file and then run it. Observe the behavior in the browser.

How It Works

This exercise covered a lot of small steps. When finished, you have two pages of medium complexity (similar to the type that will be discussed in detail in the middle chapters of this book). For now, there are five general concepts you should observe:

- All of the steps were performed in the VWD designer interface. You did not write any Visual Basic or C# code, nor did you directly write any HTML tags or set tag attributes.
- Take a look at the code that VWD generated for you by clicking the Source view of the file `TIO-1-GridViewSQL` (or looking at the preceding code listing). Note that there is nothing in the initial `<script>` tags. All of the characters on the page are in HTML-like syntax with opening and closing tags, hierarchical tags, and attributes within tags. (We say *HTML-like* because in some cases ASP.NET tags are not 100 percent HTML-compliant.)
- Look at the general pattern of the pages. There are pairs of controls: data source controls (`SqlDataSource`) and data-bound controls (`GridView`, `DetailsView`, and `Listbox`). The first gives you a connection to a database. The second displays data. For example, at the top of the GridView page, you have an `<asp:SqlDataSource>` and then an `<asp:ListBox>` that uses the `SqlDataSource` as its `DataSourceID`. You will study this pattern in detail throughout the book.
- Notice how a data source control can have its data controlled by another control on the page. The `SqlDataSource` for the `GridView` has a `WHERE` clause that is modified by the value the user selects in the list box. The information is passed in the form of `@state` in a tag called `<SelectParameters>`.
- You can pass a parameter from one page to the next in the querystring, and that parameter can be used to modify the data source on the new page. For example, in the `HyperlinkField` tag of the `GridView`, you specified to pass the `au_id` field. The `DataNavigateUrlFormatString` added the target page's text to the `au_id` value. Then on the Details page, you set your `SqlDataSource SelectCommand` to use the querystring value.
- ASP.NET offers an `AutoPostback` feature that causes the `ViewState` to be sent back to the server and induces the server to process a new page (generally using some change in the page, such as the user's list selection) and send the new page to the browser.

Overall, even on a first try, in less than 15 minutes you can produce pages with functionality that would have taken many hours in earlier versions of ASP.

Try It Out Creating a DataList from Access

In this exercise we use a `DataList` control to display data with flexibility to arrange our fields within a template space. For variety, we will use an Access data source.

1. Continue using VWD with the BegAspNet2DB Web site open.
2. Right-click the site's `ch01` folder and Add a New Item using the Web Form template with the name `TIO-0102-DataListAccess.aspx`.
3. In Design view, drag a DataList control from the Data section of the Toolbox to the page. From the Smart Tasks panel, select New Data Source from the data source list. Select the data source type of Access database, accept the default name of `AccessDataSource1`, and click OK.

Choose a database file by browsing to `C:\websites\BegAspNet2Db\App_Data\Northwind.mdb and clicking OK`. Click Next and, for the Name (which means the name of a table or query), select Categories and check the ID, Name, and Description fields. Click Next and run the test query. Then click Finish.

4. You now have a `DataList` control that uses an `AccessDataSource` control that returns the Categories table of Northwind. Test it in your browser and then close the browser before continuing.

5. Back in VWD, select the `DataList`, open its Smart Tasks panel (small arrow at top right) and click the property builder to set some overall properties for the `DataList`. Change the columns to 3 in the `Repeat layout - Columns` property and the direction to horizontal. Click Apply and OK.

6. Now you configure the display of each record's data. Continuing with the `DataList` selected, in its Smart Tasks panel, click Edit Templates. You can now add and format controls within the `ItemTemplate` space.

   First, select and delete the six controls in the template. Check that your insertion bar is in the editable space, and then type the word **Item**. Now click through Menu:Layout⇨Insert Table. Set the table to be 2 rows by 2 columns with a border of 2, and set the Cell Properties Background Color to a light shade of yellow. Click OK to finish all of the dialog boxes and create the table in the `DataList`'s template.

7. Now we will get some data-bound controls into the template. In the top-left cell, we will place the Northwind logo. Prepare by creating an `Images` folder in the root of the site (select the root of the site, right-click, and select New Folder).

   Right-click the new `Images` folder and choose Add Existing Item. Browse to the downloads for this book and select the file named `NorthwindLogo.bmp`. (You can use any other `.bmp` or `.gif` if you don't have the download.) Open the toolbar, find the Standard section, and then drag into the top-left cell of the table an image control (not Image Map or Image Button). Do not use the Image Smart Tasks panel in this case (because we want all records to show the Northwinds logo). Select the image control and, in the Properties window, set the `ImageUrl` to `~\Images\NorthWindLogo.bmp`, as shown in Figure 1-13.

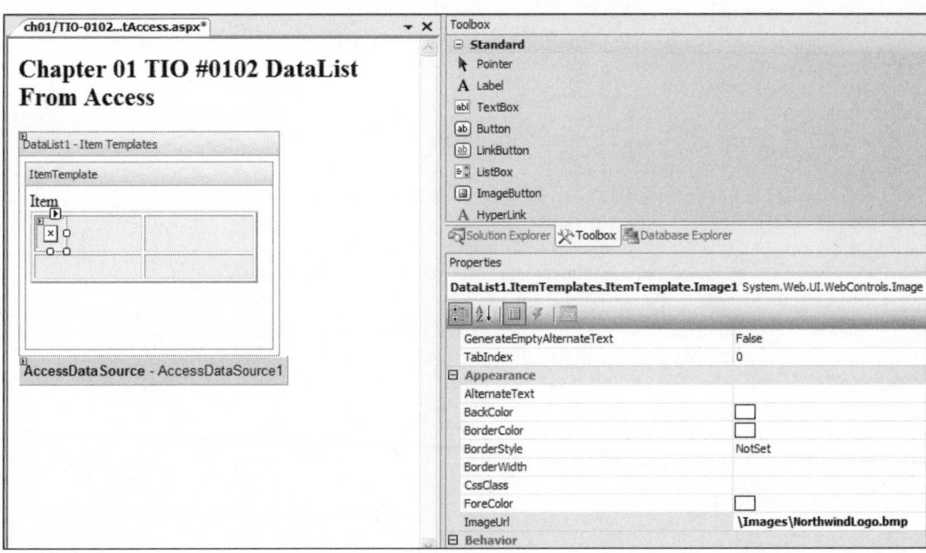

Figure 1-13

8. Into the top-right cell, drag a label from the Toolbox and click Edit Data Bindings in the Smart Tasks panel. Bind its text property to the `category ID` field, as shown in Figure 1-14, and click OK. Into the bottom-left cell, drag a label and bind its text to the description field. Into the bottom-right cell, add a label and bind its text to the category name field.

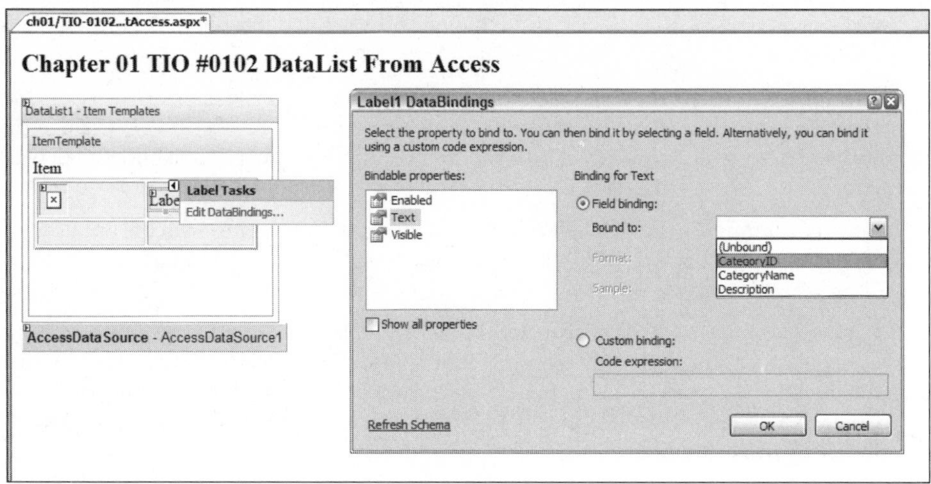

Figure 1-14

9. Now that the cells are filled, select the right column by clicking on the arrow that appears when you position the mouse cursor right at the top of the column. Once selected, in the Properties window, set align to center. Select the left column, and set its width in the Properties window to 600. Finish by opening the `DataList`'s Smart Tasks panel (arrow at top right of entire `DataList` control) and clicking on End Template Editing.

10. Save the document and press Ctrl+F5 to run it. Your page should resemble the following code and display the results in your browser, as shown in Figure 1-15.

```
<%@ Page Language="VB" %>
<!DOCTYPE html PUBLIC "-//W3C//DTD XHTML 1.0 Transitional//EN"
"http://www.w3.org/TR/xhtml1/DTD/xhtml1-transitional.dtd">
<script runat="server">
</script>
<html xmlns="http://www.w3.org/1999/xhtml" >
<head id="Head1" runat="server">
    <title>TIO-0102-DataListAccess.aspx</title>
</head>
<body>
        <h2>Chapter 01 TIO #0102 DataList From Access </h2>
    <form id="form1" runat="server">
    <div>
        <asp:DataList ID="DataList1" runat="server" DataKeyField="CategoryID"
DataSourceID="AccessDataSource1"
            RepeatColumns="3" RepeatDirection="Horizontal">
            <ItemTemplate>
                Item<table border="2">
                    <tr>
                        <td style="background-color: lightgoldenrodyellow"
width="600">
```

```
                              <asp:Image ID="Image1" runat="server"
ImageUrl="~/Images/NorthWindLogo.bmp" /></td>
                            <td align="center" style="width: 100px; background-color:
lightgoldenrodyellow">
                              <asp:Label ID="Label1" runat="server" Text='<%#
Eval("CategoryID") %>'></asp:Label></td>
                        </tr>
                        <tr>
                            <td style="background-color: lightgoldenrodyellow"
width="600">
                              <asp:Label ID="Label2" runat="server" Text='<%#
Eval("Description") %>'></asp:Label></td>
                            <td align="center" style="width: 100px; background-color:
lightgoldenrodyellow">
                              <asp:Label ID="Label3" runat="server" Text='<%#
Eval("CategoryName") %>'></asp:Label></td>
                        </tr>
                    </table>
                    <br />
                    <br />
                </ItemTemplate>
            </asp:DataList><asp:AccessDataSource ID="AccessDataSource1" runat="server"
DataFile="~/App_Data/Northwind.mdb"
                SelectCommand="SELECT [CategoryID], [CategoryName], [Description] FROM
[Categories]">
            </asp:AccessDataSource>

        </div>
        </form>
</body>
</html>
```

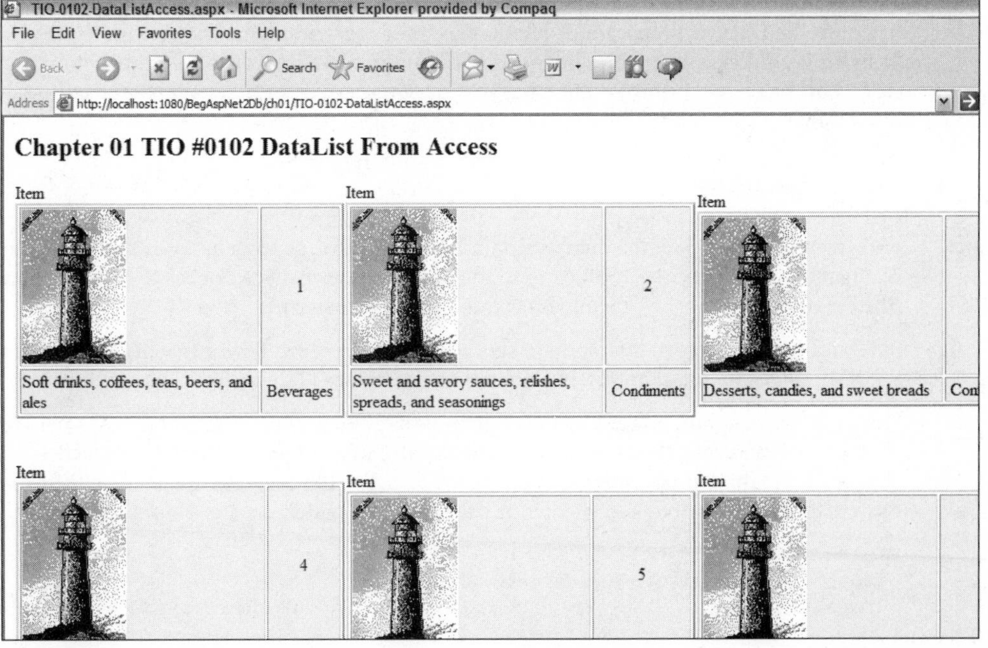

Figure 1-15

How It Works

You can see the same patterns here as in the first exercise. Instead of writing code, you use VWD drag-and-drop to put ASP.NET 2.0 data controls onto the page. You can build a page in just a few minutes. As before, you added a data-bound control (`DataList`) and it automatically walked you through setting up its data source control (`AccessDataSource`).

The `DataList` control starts the same way as the `GridView`, by specifying its `DataSource` control. Then we revised the rendering through the control's item template. In this template, we added and formatted controls and bound them to fields in the underlying data source control. The template controls will then display the appropriate value for their record in the `DataList`. In this case, you started with a table to organize the space in the template and filled the cells with three labels. When the `DataList` is rendered, you see a more flexible layout than you had with a `GridView`. All of the topics discussed in this demonstration will be fodder for deeper analysis in later chapters of the book.

Try It Out Using a TreeView Based on XML Data

Your sources of data are not limited to relational databases, and your data displays do not have to be in rectangular grids. In this exercise, you will read data from an XML file and display it in hierarchical fashion in a `TreeView` control. You will also see how to handle an event on a `TreeView` control when a selection is made, one of the few cases where you have to write code.

1. Select your site's `App_Data` folder (created by VWD), right-click, and select Add Existing Item. Browse to the downloads for this book and select the file named `Bookstore.XML` from the downloads into your `App_Data` folder. Repeat the process to get `closedbook.gif`, `notepad.gif`, and `folder.gif` into your `Images` folder (feel free to import all the images of the download, we will use them throughout the book). In your `ch01` folder, create a new Web Form page named `TIO-0103-TreeViewXML.aspx`.

2. Start by adding a data source control as follows. In Design view, drag an `XmlDataSource` control from the Data section of the Toolbox onto the page, and then click Configure Data Source from the common tasks menu. You need to fill in only two items (double-check your syntax and case). For the Data File, browse to `\App_Data\Bookstore.xml`. For the `XPath` expression, type the following with careful attention to case.

```
Data File:                    ~/Data/Bookstore.xml
XPath expression:             Bookstore/genre[@name='Fiction']/book
```

3. Now we need to display the data in a data-bound control, so drag a `TreeView` control from the Navigation section for the Toolbox onto the page and set its Data Source to `XmlDataSource1` (the default name for the control you created in the last step).

4. Save and run the page at this point to see, as shown in Figure 1-16, a tree of the generic names of the XML nodes (book, chapter), but not the actual values (Tale of Two Cities, Introduction).

5. Exit your browser and go back to the page in Design view. Open the Smart Tasks panel menu for the `TreeView` and click `EditTreeNode DataBinding`. In the available list, click `Book` and click Add. Set three properties for book, as follows. For the `ImageUrl`, use the ellipses icon to browse to the `closedbook.gif` in your site's `Images` folder.

```
DataMember:      Book
TextField:       Title
ImageUrl (careful - NOT ImageUrlField):       ~/Images/closedbook.gif
```

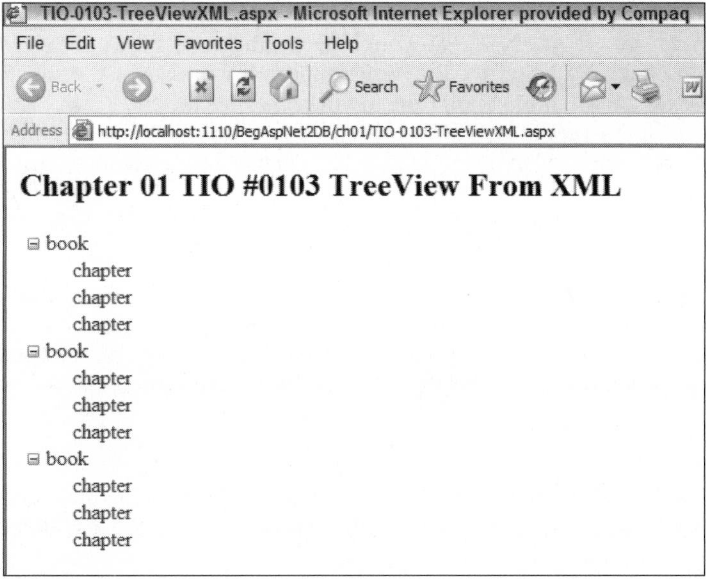

Figure 1-16

6. Staying in the DataBindings dialog box, select the chapter node in the "Available data bindings" and click Add. Then set its `DataMember` to chapter, `TextField` to name, and `ImageUrl` to `notepad.gif`. Click Apply and OK to close.

7. Save the page and view it in your browser, as shown in Figure 1-17.

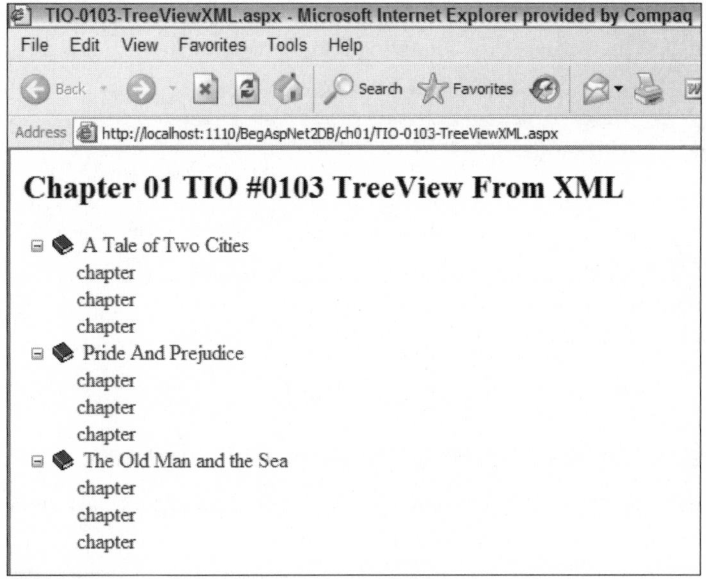

Figure 1-17

8. You will add one last feature to demonstrate that you can handle events in a similar fashion to older versions of ASP.NET. Exit your browser and go to VWD. In Design view, select the `TreeView` control. Display the Properties window by pressing F4. At the top of the Properties window, click the lightning bolt icon and then double-click the `SelectedNodeChanged` event. VWD will automatically switch to source view and type the first and last lines of an event handler. You can now type in the highlighted line below. Don't test the code in the browser until after the next step, wherein we add a short bit of code. The first option uses Visual Basic, and we demonstrate C# following that.

VB

```
<%@ Page Language="VB" %>
<script runat="server">
  Sub TreeView_Select(ByVal sender As Object, ByVal e As EventArgs)
    Response.Write("You selected: " & TreeView1.SelectedNode.Value)
  End Sub
</script>
```

The second option employs C#, as follows, if you chose to use C# when you created the page. Note both a change in the code and in the initial `Page Language` setting.

C#

```
<%@ Page Language="c#" >
<script runat="server">
    void TreeView_Select(Object sender, EventArgs e)
    {
        Response.Write("You selected: " + TreeView1.SelectedNode.Value);
    }
</script>
```

9. Take a look at the line added automatically by VWD that instructs the `TreeView` control to use your new event handler when any value of the tree is clicked. Staying in Source view, scroll down to and then observe the following highlighted line in the `<asp:TreeView>` control:

```
<asp:TreeView ID="TreeView1" Runat="server"
       OnSelectedNodeChanged="TreeView_Select"
      DataSourceID="XmlDataSource1">
```

10. Save the file and run it. When you click on any item in the tree, the event is triggered and the page displays a small note repeating the value of the text under the click. The finished file looks like the following:

C#

```
<%@ Page Language="c#" AutoEventWireup="false" ClassName="TIO_3_TreeViewXML_aspx"
%>

<script runat="server">
    void TreeView_Select(Object sender, EventArgs e)
    {
        Response.Write("You selected: " + TreeView1.SelectedNode.Value);
    }
</script>
...
```

VB

```
<%@ Page Language="VB" AutoEventWireup="false" ClassName="TIO_3_TreeViewXML_aspx"
%>
<script runat="server">
    Sub TreeView_Select(ByVal sender As Object, ByVal e As EventArgs)
        Response.Write("You selected: " & TreeView1.SelectedNode.Value)
    End Sub
</script>

<!DOCTYPE html PUBLIC "-//W3C//DTD XHTML 1//EN"
"http://www.w3.org/TR/xhtml1/DTD/xhtml1.dtd">

<html xmlns="http://www.w3.org/1999/xhtml" >
<head runat="server">
    <title>Chapter 1 TIO #3 TreeView from XML</title>
</head>
<body>
    <h2>
Chapter 1 TIO #3 TreeView from XML
    </h2>
    <form id="form1" runat="server">
    <div>
        <asp:XmlDataSource ID="XmlDataSource1" Runat="server"
            DataFile="~/Data/Bookstore.xml"
            XPath="Bookstore/genre[@name='Fiction']/book" />

        <asp:TreeView ID="TreeView1" Runat="server"
            DataSourceID="XmlDataSource1"
            OnSelectedNodeChanged="TreeView_Select" >
            <DataBindings>
                <asp:TreeNodeBinding ImageUrl="~/Images/closedbook.gif"
TextField="Title" DataMember="book" />
                <asp:TreeNodeBinding ImageUrl="~/Images/notepad.gif"
TextField="name" DataMember="chapter" />
            </DataBindings>
        </asp:TreeView>

    </div>
    </form>
</body>
</html>
```

How It Works

The same themes emerge in this third example. You create a data source control (`XmlDataSource`) and a data-bound control (`TreeView`). By default, the tree shows the names of the nodes rather than their values. But even at this level, you have achieved an expanding and collapsing tree with just a few clicks. Then, in the Edit TreeNode Bindings dialog box, you determined what actual values and images to display at each level.

Note two items that you will cover in more depth later. In specifying the XML file, you started the path with a tilde (~). This represents the root of the Web site. If the site is deployed to another physical location on a drive, the link will continue to work. Also, note how the `XPath` string is used to limit the number of books displayed. There are five titles in the XML file. If you change the central part of the `XPath` to `[@name='NonFiction']`, you can see the other two books.

The last exercise ended with a little coding. ASP.NET supports many languages, but the most common are Visual Basic and C#. We cover both in this book. The language is set in a directive at the top of the page, which VWD automatically creates based on your selection when creating the page. As in earlier versions of ASP.NET, you can set an event to call an event handler with custom code. In this case, the `TreeView` has an `OnSelectedNode` event that will send the value of the node that was selected to the event handler. You can display that with a simple `Response.Write`.

Common Mistakes

Near the end of each chapter, we provide a list of some common mistakes that beginning programmers make with the material covered in that chapter. Of course there are lots of ways to go wrong, but these are the ones that come up most often when we teach, observe code, or answer questions. If you are having difficulty getting a page to work, we suggest you run through this list of mistakes to help guide your troubleshooting. In addition, reading through these scenarios will serve as a review of the chapter's concepts.

- Modifying the wrong data source control when more than one data source control is on a page
- Attempting to use an Access MDB file that has password protection (see Chapter 4 for information on using secured MDB files)

Summary

This chapter reviewed some basic ASP.NET 2.0 topics, covered setting up your machine for the book, and walked you through three exercises that displayed data.

Recall from your study of ASP.NET 2.0 that pages are stored as a combination of text, HTML tags, scripts, and ASP.NET 2.0 server-side controls. When a page is requested, IIS directs the request to ASP.NET 2.0, which processes the page using the ASP.NET 2.0 controls and code to build a pure HTML page. Therefore, you achieve two objectives. First, you can build each page to suit the individual requestor and the current needs of the business (the pages are dynamic). Second, any browser can read the page because it is delivered as pure HTML.

The .NET Framework is a collection of classes written by Microsoft that enable programmers to quickly and easily create solutions for their organization. ASP.NET, a set of classes in the namespace `System.Web`, provides very powerful controls for building dynamic Web pages. ASP.NET 2.0 greatly reduces the amount of coding for common data scenarios, compared to earlier versions of ASP. In most cases, the decisions about ADO.NET object parameters and the timing of bindings are handled automatically. The page architecture follows a pattern of having two controls to show data. The first is a data source control that establishes a connection to a database. The second is a data-bound control that displays the data.

This chapter discussed various software options to implement data on ASP.NET 2.0 pages. The .NET Framework 2.0 must be installed. You have two Web server options: Public deployment requires IIS, whereas development can use the lighter-weight ASP.NET Development Server that comes with Visual Web Developer. To create pages, we use Visual Web Developer Express because it offers many tools in its IDE and is available for free. Several alternatives for a database management system were discussed also. This book uses SQL Server Express (SSE) because it is free, overcomes the problems of using

Access, and easily scales to Microsoft SQL Server at the time of deployment. Last, you copied to your site two databases (`Northwind.mdf` and `Pubs.mdf`) that you will use for examples in this book.

The exercises in this chapter revealed that it takes just a few ASP.NET tags with a half-dozen attributes each to display and modify data. You used data source controls (`SqlDataSource`, `AccessDataSource`, and `XmlDataSource`) to create a conduit to the data. Then you used data-bound controls (GridView, `DataList`, and `TreeView`) to display the data. You did not have to use any `<script>` code to perform the data-binding tasks, although you did demonstrate that you could write an event handler as in earlier versions.

One control can have its parameters set by another control, for example in the first Try It Out when the data source for the `GridView` was changed by the selection in the `ListBox`. Those parameters were passed easily across pages as when you sent a record ID to the details page. Overall, understand that none of these pages would take more than ten minutes to type and troubleshoot using the drag-and-drop tools of Visual Web Developer.

The next few chapters examine data source controls. Topics include Access, SQL data source control, and connecting to other databases. Following that, several chapters discuss displaying data using various data-bound controls.

Exercises

1. What is the basic pattern for showing data on an ASP.NET 2.0 page?
2. Name several types of data source controls that ship with ASP.NET 2.0.
3. Name several ways that ASP.NET 2.0 can display data.
4. What is the difference between the .NET Framework 2.0 and ASP.NET 2.0?
5. Compare SQL Server, MSDE, and SSE, and make some observations.

Connecting to an Access Database

The first chapter provided an overview of ASP.NET 2.0 and databases. This chapter discusses how to create and modify data source controls that connect to a Microsoft Access database. The next few chapters discuss connecting to different types of databases and cover the same concepts for Microsoft SQL Server and other data sources.

This chapter covers the following topics:

- Introduction to Microsoft Access and the JET Database Engine
- Pros and cons of using Access as a data source
- Connecting to a Microsoft Access Database in Visual Studio or Visual Web Developer (VWD)
- Introduction to the `AccessDataSource` control
- Variations in SQL statements for selecting data
- Variations in MDB file location
- Managing MDB file permissions
- Handling connection failures

Introduction to Microsoft Access and the JET Database Engine

Microsoft Access is one of the most common database management systems in use today. Part of the Microsoft Office family of products, Access is readily available to information workers at both work and home. If you are reading this book, chances are good that you have had some experience with Access at one time or another. To understand what is happening in this chapter, you must be able to differentiate between Microsoft Access, MDB files, and the JET database engine.

Microsoft Access provides basic tools. Some are concerned with the back end (the machine-level organizing and storing of data), whereas others are for the front end (the human interface for reading, writing, and managing the data). These aids can be categorized as follows:

- **Tables:** Structures to hold data
- **The JET engine:** Code to instruct the machine to read and write to that data
- **Design view of forms and reports:** An environment for developers to create a front end for the data
- **Data view of forms and reports:** Tools that can run the front end

In Access, you have a complete package for both the front and back ends of data management. But when working with ASP.NET pages, you don't need all of the tools for the front end (designing and running forms and reports). All you need are the back-end tools: the ability to hold data and to instruct the machine to read and write data. The ASP.NET page itself will serve as the front-end form to allow the user to interact with the data.

Microsoft makes it easy to use just the back-end functions of Access in a tool called the *JET engine*. You can think of JET as Access without forms or reports. Instead, JET gets its instructions to read or write data as commands from code (in our case ASP.NET 2.0). JET can read and write to tables and execute queries, while ignoring the form and report objects in the MDB.

JET is installed on any machine on which you have set up Access or Visual Basic (and some other software). You do not have to do anything to turn on JET; it is a service, not an application that must be started like Access. For this book, you can use Access to examine or create MDB files, but ASP.NET data sources will use JET directly to work with Access (MDB) files on an ASP.NET page.

Pros and Cons of Using Access in Web Applications

Access works very well as a desktop database, and the interface is familiar to many readers. Many small offices have resources already stored in Access MDB files. You'll find it easy to open up the database and examine it using the Access tools. However, Access does not scale to support more than a few users simultaneously.

The problem with Access is that it was never designed to handle execution in a fast-paced, multi-threaded environment such as a Web server. Access was designed and intended as a single- or few-user desktop database. When used in a Web server environment, Access simply does not provide enough performance to run a public Web site effectively and may actually produce unpredictable results under these conditions. For this reason, you will have difficulty finding a host that is willing to run JET to support a Web site on its hosting machines.

Access also creates development challenges when using parameterized SQL statements, particularly when values must be provided in order to be written to the database. When using parameters, Access correlates the values to fields based on the order in which the values are presented. This is sometimes difficult to manage if the order of fields in your form does not match the order of fields in your SQL statement. Named parameters (instead of ordered parameters) are available in other database systems and are much easier to use and less prone to errors.

Although Microsoft Access is a reasonable database for learning ASP.NET and performing initial development, it is almost never the right solution for running a production Web site. If you are considering using Access, we suggest that you read the next chapter and switch your focus to using SQL Server, SQL Server Express or another database system designed for multiple users.

Connecting to a Microsoft Access Database in Visual Web Developer

Although you can use the Microsoft Access design tools to create and explore the contents of an Access database, Microsoft has also made it easy to use Visual Web Developer (VWD) to explore the contents of an Access database. Once Visual Studio has established a connection to your database, you can browse the database schema (the form of the tables and columns, but not the data contained in them) or change the data content directly from within VWD. Note that in order to *create* an Access database or *alter* the database schema, you must use Microsoft Access.

As previously mentioned, the MDB file format is the container that stores data for a Microsoft Access database. When you save a database in Access, this file is created on your hard disk. To use an Access database in an ASP.NET application, you will need to know the path to this file, for example:

```
C:\Documents and Settings\Owner\Desktop\MyDatabase.mdb
```

Databases generally require a username and password for initial entry. Although it is possible to protect the contents of an Access database by requiring these credentials, Access databases do not require this information by default. For the sake of the examples in this chapter, the sample database will not require a username or password.

We will save our discussion of how to connect to a password-protected database for Chapter 4 for reasons that will be made apparent in that chapter.

It is important to understand the structure (schema) of a database before you begin to use it. At a minimum, you must know the names of tables or queries that you want to use as well as the names of their columns (fields). If you intend to write or change data, you should also have an understanding of the relationships so that data dependencies are not broken. This section will demonstrate how to use VWD to connect to an Access MDB file on your disk. From there you can browse the database contents and familiarize yourself with the schema, including the names of tables and the names and data types of columns (fields).

At this point it is a good idea to run a few tests of any SQL statements you plan to use to see if you get the expected results. Remember to close any Design view windows before using the MDB as a source of data in an ASP.NET page because Access objects that are open in Design view are locked from reads and writes.

Because VWD provides powerful tools to see the schema of a database without leaving the IDE, let's walk through some of these tools in the first Try It Out.

Try It Out Exploring an Access MDB File in Visual Web Developer

In this exercise, you copy a database into your Web site and then look at its structure using tools in VWD. You put data on a Web page in the next Try It Out.

You must be using Visual Studio (VS) or VWD to perform this exercise. VWD uses the term Database Explorer *while VS uses* Server Explorer *(it includes additional features for connecting to more than just databases). However, both provide the same functionality for connecting to databases.*

If you are writing your pages in Notepad or another text editor, do only the first two steps (make folders and copy the database), and then explore the Northwind database directly in Access. Close the database prior to using it as a source of data in your ASP.NET pages. Of course, you must have completed the Chapter 1 setup of ASP.NET 2.0 and the .NET Framework to run the sample pages in this text.

1. If you haven't done so already in Chapter 1, perform the tasks in this step.

   Set up your software as described in the first chapter by installing the VWD Express (which includes the .NET Framework 2.0, VWD, and SSE). Then check that you have Access or the JET engine by looking at Start⇨Control Panel⇨Add Programs and searching for Microsoft Office/ Access or Microsoft Visual Studio.

   If you didn't create a Web site for this book in Chapter 1, do it now as follows:

   Open VWD and choose New Web Site from the File menu. Then type the path **C:\Websites\BegAspNet2Db** and click OK. Notice that this directory is opened and an `App_Data` subdirectory is automatically created for you. Check that you have a copy of `Northwind.mdb`, which you should have downloaded from `www.Wrox.com` or the Microsoft site, as described in Chapter 1. In Solution Explorer, right-click the `App_Data` directory and Add Existing Item. Browse to the `Northwind.mdb` file, and click Add.

2. Within VWD, the Solution Explorer should be visible. If not, use View⇨Solution Explorer to display.

3. Right-click the `C:\Websites\BegAspNet2Db` directory in VWD, and choose Add New Folder to add another subdirectory named `Ch02`.

4. Click View⇨Database Explorer and note how the Database Explorer (called the Server Explorer in the VS) now shares a space with (that is, it is overlaid upon) the Solution Explorer. You may want to make the panel holding the Database and Solution Explorer about half the screen width for this exercise.

5. Note that at the bottom of the panel you have tabs to switch between a view of the Web files (Solution Explorer), a view of the sources of data (Database Explorer), and the Toolbox, as shown in Figure 2-1. Also note that you cannot expand and look into an MDB from the Solution Explorer window (although you can see that the file exists in the `App_Data` folder, and can double-click an MDB file to open it in Access). You must switch to Database Explorer view to delve into the MDB's schema.

6. Note that VWD automatically displays in the Data Explorer the data files that are physically located in the `App_Data` folder. Not only are they displayed, but beneath the covers they have been automatically *attached*, meaning that they are available to data source controls.

7. In the Database Explorer, expand the level of Data Connections and then expand your connection to `Northwind.mdb`. You can now view the objects in the MDB. Expand `Tables` and then expand `Employees` and `Products`.

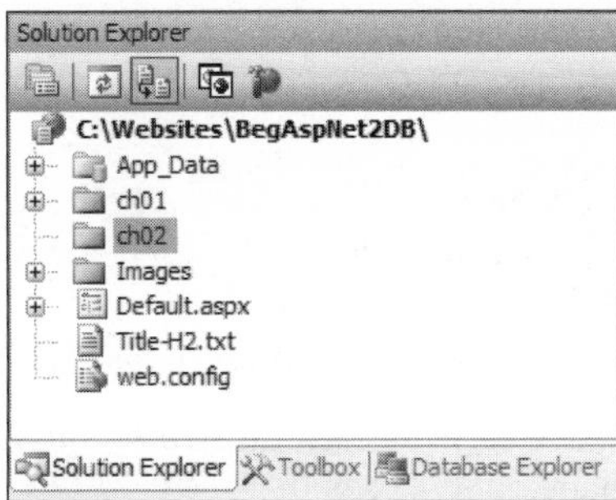

Figure 2-1

At this point, you can see each column name in these tables. For MDB files, you cannot see the properties of the columns or modify the table structure. However, for MDF (SQL Server) files you have more options.

8. Right-click `Northwind.mdb`, and choose New Query to start the VWD Query Builder.

9. Select the `Products` table, click the Add button, and then close the table dialog box by clicking Close. Inside the Query Builder, select the `ProductID` and `ProductName` fields by clicking the check box next to each column name.

10. Right-click anywhere in the Query Builder and choose Execute SQL to run the command. Notice that the query executes and the results are displayed in the bottom of the dialog box. You can also manually edit the SQL statement to write your own queries, as shown in Figure 2-2.

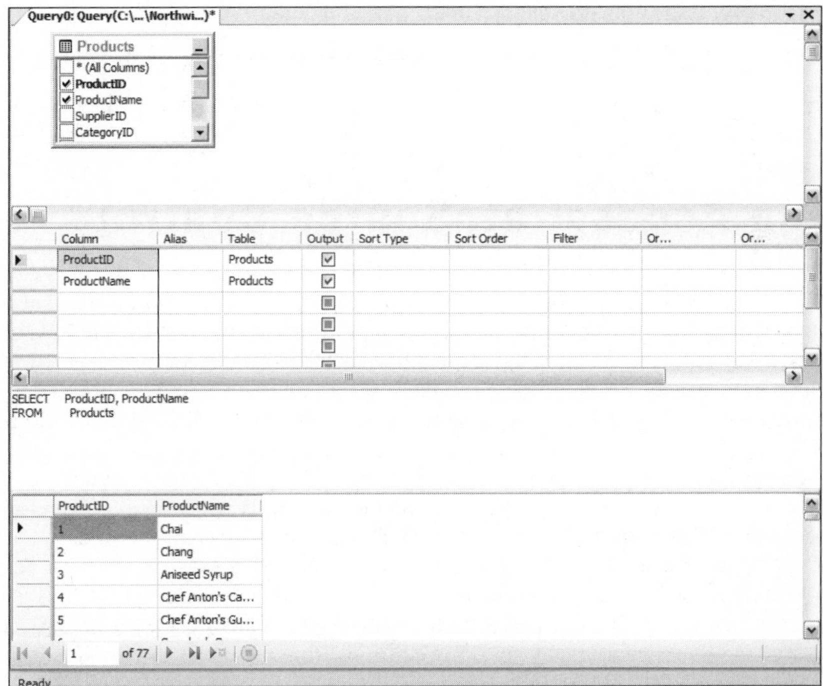

Figure 2-2

11. Close the Query Builder and note that VWD prompts you to save this query as a document you can reopen for future use. (You can click Cancel for now to dismiss the prompt; no need to save it.

12. Right-click the `Products` table node in the Database Explorer and choose Show Table Data. Notice that VWD opens a new document window where you can view and update the data in the `Products` table directly.

13. Close the Show Table Data document window.

14. Double-check that you have closed all windows and collapsed the `Northwind.mdb` so that there is no database in edit mode.

How It Works

When you connect to an Access database using the Database Explorer (or Server Explorer), VWD will open and read the MDB file and display the database schema (tables and columns) in a hierarchical tree. When you click on a node in this tree, you can view the properties of the selected schema object in the Property Grid. You can also right-click to open the Query Builder against this database and execute SQL queries. These queries may be saved and reopened for future use. Using the Database Explorer and Query Builder allows you to easily explore database files from within the Visual Web Developer IDE.

Note that when you open a table or query in Design view, Access locks the object for its own exclusive use. So, if you are modifying the structure of a table in Access and then switch over to use the new table in VWD or your browser, you may be blocked from even reading the table's values. You must close the Design view in Access and then go back to Visual Studio to change your Web page.

Keep in mind also that adding a database to the Server Explorer does not add a data source control to an ASP.NET page. Presence in the Data Connections makes the preview features available only in the IDE.

In the next section, you actually connect a page to an MDB file using a data source control.

Using an AccessDataSource Control

ASP.NET 2.0 includes an `AccessDataSource` control for exposing data from an Access database to an ASP.NET 2.0 (.aspx) page. The control has a simple set of properties. The most important property of `AccessDataSource` is the `DataFile` property, which points to the path of the MDB file on disk. The other property that the `AccessDataSource` must have is the `SelectCommand` property, which assigns a statement that indicates the resultset (table and columns) to return. The `SelectCommand` must be defined using SQL syntax (actually, a subset of SQL named T-SQL). See Appendix Afor more information.

In VWD, you can add the `AccessDataSource` control to your page in one of two ways. If your MDB file is added to your Database Explorer, as demonstrated in `TIO-0201` (the previous exercise), you can drag and drop column names onto the page and VWD will automatically create an `AccessDataSource` control and a `GridView` to display the data for you. If you do not want the `GridView` or you want to customize the controls, you can add just an `AccessDataSource` control from the Toolbox and walk through its configuration wizard to set it up. The wizard prompts you to browse for the data file and then allows you to specify the `SelectCommand` by choosing columns from the tables in your database.

If you are typing your pages outside of VWD, you can match the following code:

```
<asp:AccessDataSource ID="MySourceName" Runat="server"    DataFile="MyMDBName.mdb"
   SelectCommand="SELECT MyField1, MyField2 FROM MyTable">
</asp:AccessDataSource>
```

Again, note the simplicity. All you provide is an `ID`, the name of an MDB file, and a `SelectCommand`.

This chapter is about a data source control, but recall that a data source control does not render anything visible on the page. So to give you a visual way to test your data source controls, the next Try It Out exercise explains the basic steps to display data in a table using the `GridView` control (an evolution from ASP.NET version 1's `DataGrid` control). Note that the focus is not on the configuration or customization of the `GridView` in this chapter; rather, the focus is on the data source control. Chapter 5 explores the `GridView` control in much more detail.

Try It Out — Connecting to an MDB and Displaying with the GridView

In this exercise, you display information about products sold by Northwind on your page.

1. Start VWD and use the Solution Explorer to navigate to `C:\Websites\BegAspNet2Db\ch02\`.
2. Add a page named `TIO-0202-DisplayMdbData` from the template Web Form. Change to Design view using the tabs at the bottom.
3. Before you start to actually work with ASP.NET, go to the top of the page, type a heading such as **Demonstration of Connection to an MDB Source** and put similar text into the title. Although this step is not discussed in every exercise, we suggest that you include a title and HTML text in each of your pages so that you do not lose track of which page you are viewing. See the How It Works section that follows this Try It Out for a fancier alternative.

```
<%@ Page Language="VB" %>
<!DOCTYPE html PUBLIC "-//W3C//DTD XHTML 1.0 Transitional//EN"
"http://www.w3.org/TR/xhtml1/DTD/xhtml1-transitional.dtd">
<script runat="server">
</script>
<html xmlns="http://www.w3.org/1999/xhtml" >
     <head>
         <title>TIO-0202 Display MDB Data</title>
     </head>
     <body>
         <h3>ch02 TIO-0202 Demonstration of Connection to an MDB Source </h3>
     <body>
     </html>
```

4. Choose View⇨Toolbox to display the Toolbox (or use Ctrl+Alt+X) and expand the Toolbox's Data panel.
5. The control's Smart Tasks panel should appear automatically. If not, select the new data source control and then click the small arrow on the top right to open the Smart Tasks panel. Click Configure Data Source.
6. In the Choose a Database step, click the Browse button and select `C:\Websites\BegAspNet2Db\App_Data\Northwind.mdb`. Note that VWD converts the file spec to a relative reference, where the tilde (~) represents the root of the site. Click Next.
7. In the Configure Select Statement box, select the Specify Columns option and then for Name, select the `Products` table. Check the asterisk (*) to select all columns. Click Next, Test Query, and Finish.

The Test Query option runs your query before you finish the wizard and shows you the results. If you see there is a problem in the resultset, you can click the Back button and revise your SQL statement.

8. Select the Data control, right-click, and select Properties (or display the Properties window with F4). Change its ID to `NorthwindProductsAccDataSource`.
9. In the Toolbox, double-click GridView (in the Toolbox's Data section) to add the control to the page and enter its Smart Tasks panel. Click on Choose Data Source, and select from the list `NorthwindProductsAccDataSource`.
10. Select the `GridView` and in the Properties panel change its ID from `GridView1` to `NorthwindProductsGridView`. Your page should now appear in Source view as follows:

```
<%@ Page Language="VB" %>
<!DOCTYPE html PUBLIC "-//W3C//DTD XHTML 1.0 Transitional//EN"
"http://www.w3.org/TR/xhtml1/DTD/xhtml1-transitional.dtd">
<script runat="server">
</script>
<html xmlns="http://www.w3.org/1999/xhtml" >
<head id="Head1" runat="server">
    <title>TIO-0202-DisplayMDBData.aspx</title>
</head>
<body>
        <h2>Chapter 02 TIO #0202 Display MDB Data</h2>
    <form id="form1" runat="server">
    <div>
        <asp:AccessDataSource ID="NorthwindProductsAccDataSource" runat="server"
            DataFile="~/App_Data/Northwind.mdb"
            SelectCommand="SELECT * FROM [Products]"></asp:AccessDataSource>
        <asp:GridView ID="NorthwindProductsGridVIew" runat="server"
            AutoGenerateColumns="False"
            DataKeyNames="ProductID"
            DataSourceID="NorthwindProductsAccDataSource">
            <Columns>
                <asp:BoundField DataField="ProductID" HeaderText="ProductID"
                    InsertVisible="False"
                    ReadOnly="True"
                    SortExpression="ProductID" />
                <asp:BoundField DataField="ProductName" HeaderText="ProductName"
                    SortExpression="ProductName" />
                <asp:BoundField DataField="SupplierID" HeaderText="SupplierID"
                    SortExpression="SupplierID" />
                <asp:BoundField DataField="CategoryID" HeaderText="CategoryID"
                    SortExpression="CategoryID" />
                <asp:BoundField DataField="QuantityPerUnit"
                    HeaderText="QuantityPerUnit"
                    SortExpression="QuantityPerUnit" />
                <asp:BoundField DataField="UnitPrice" HeaderText="UnitPrice"
                    SortExpression="UnitPrice" />
                <asp:BoundField DataField="UnitsInStock" HeaderText="UnitsInStock"
                    SortExpression="UnitsInStock" />
                <asp:BoundField DataField="UnitsOnOrder" HeaderText="UnitsOnOrder"
                    SortExpression="UnitsOnOrder" />
                <asp:BoundField DataField="ReorderLevel" HeaderText="ReorderLevel"
                    SortExpression="ReorderLevel" />
                <asp:CheckBoxField DataField="Discontinued"
HeaderText="Discontinued"
```

```
                    SortExpression="Discontinued" />
            </Columns>
        </asp:GridView>
    </div>
    </form>
</body>
</html>
```

11. Press F5 to run the page and see it in the browser, which should look similar to the page shown in Figure 2-3.

12. Finish by displaying data from an MDB view instead of a table. Close the browser and return to VWD. Save the file with a new name: **ch02_TIO_2_DisplayMDBData-View.aspx**. Select the `AccessDataSource` and open its Common Task Menu by clicking the small arrow at the top right of the control. Click on Configure Data Source and Next to pass by the selection of the MDB file. In the screen to Configure Select Statement, change the Name to **Sales by Category** and check the asterisk to get all fields. This view (called a query in Access) brings together four tables in SQL join statements, limits the number of records used in one table, and does some grouping and aggregation of data to get totals. Click Next, click Test Query, and then click Finish. Accept the refresh of the `GridView` if asked by VWD. Your data source control will now look like the following:

```
<asp:AccessDataSource ID="NorthwindProductsAccDataSource" runat="server"
DataFile="~/App_Data/Northwind.mdb"
SelectCommand="SELECT * FROM [Products]">
</asp:AccessDataSource>
```

13. Open your browser and view the page, which should look like Figure 2-4.

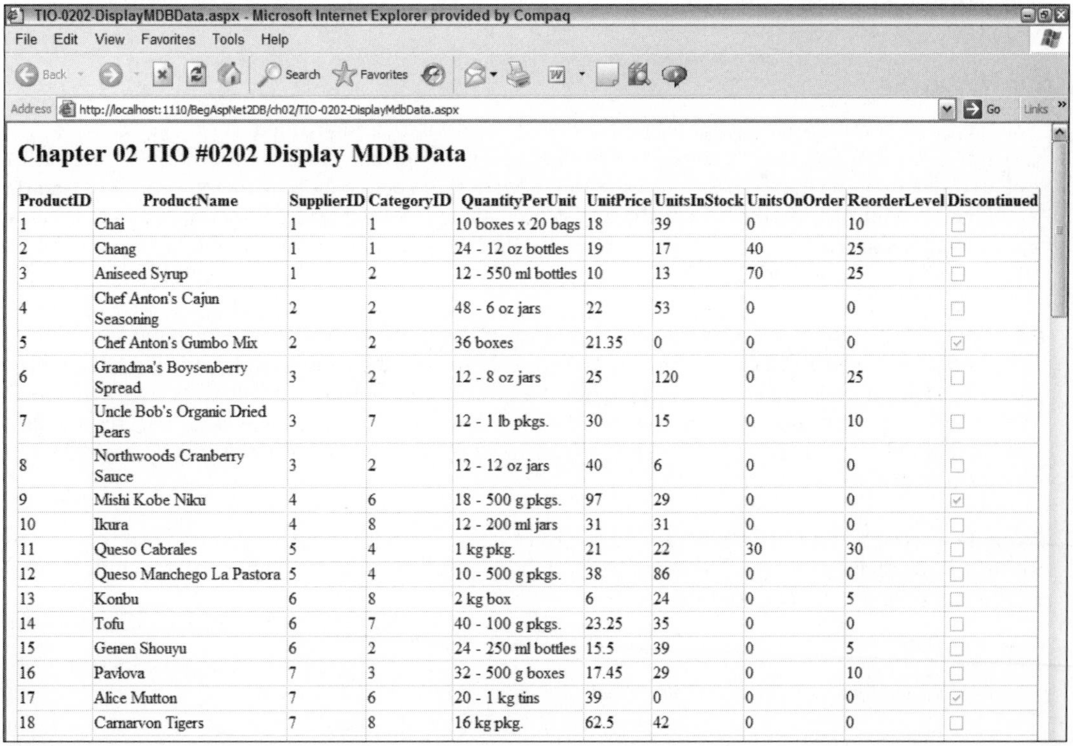

TIO-0202-DisplayMDBData.aspx - Microsoft Internet Explorer provided by Compaq

File Edit View Favorites Tools Help

Address http://localhost:1110/BegAspNet2DB/ch02/TIO-0202-DisplayMdbData.aspx

Chapter 02 TIO #0202 Display MDB Data

ProductID	ProductName	SupplierID	CategoryID	QuantityPerUnit	UnitPrice	UnitsInStock	UnitsOnOrder	ReorderLevel	Discontinued
1	Chai	1	1	10 boxes x 20 bags	18	39	0	10	☐
2	Chang	1	1	24 - 12 oz bottles	19	17	40	25	☐
3	Aniseed Syrup	1	2	12 - 550 ml bottles	10	13	70	25	☐
4	Chef Anton's Cajun Seasoning	2	2	48 - 6 oz jars	22	53	0	0	☐
5	Chef Anton's Gumbo Mix	2	2	36 boxes	21.35	0	0	0	☑
6	Grandma's Boysenberry Spread	3	2	12 - 8 oz jars	25	120	0	25	☐
7	Uncle Bob's Organic Dried Pears	3	7	12 - 1 lb pkgs.	30	15	0	10	☐
8	Northwoods Cranberry Sauce	3	2	12 - 12 oz jars	40	6	0	0	☐
9	Mishi Kobe Niku	4	6	18 - 500 g pkgs.	97	29	0	0	☑
10	Ikura	4	8	12 - 200 ml jars	31	31	0	0	☐
11	Queso Cabrales	5	4	1 kg pkg.	21	22	30	30	☐
12	Queso Manchego La Pastora	5	4	10 - 500 g pkgs.	38	86	0	0	☐
13	Konbu	6	8	2 kg box	6	24	0	5	☐
14	Tofu	6	7	40 - 100 g pkgs.	23.25	35	0	0	☐
15	Genen Shouyu	6	2	24 - 250 ml bottles	15.5	39	0	5	☐
16	Pavlova	7	3	32 - 500 g boxes	17.45	29	0	10	☐
17	Alice Mutton	7	6	20 - 1 kg tins	39	0	0	0	☑
18	Carnarvon Tigers	7	8	16 kg pkg.	62.5	42	0	0	☐

Figure 2-3

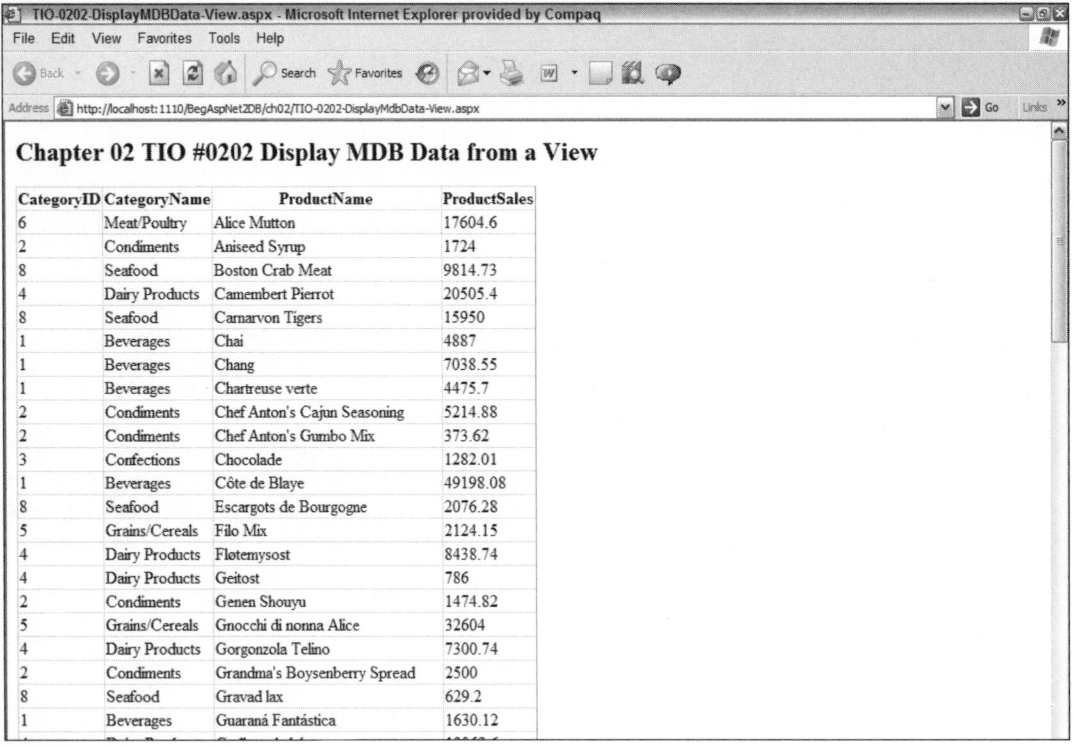

CategoryID	CategoryName	ProductName	ProductSales
6	Meat/Poultry	Alice Mutton	17604.6
2	Condiments	Aniseed Syrup	1724
8	Seafood	Boston Crab Meat	9814.73
4	Dairy Products	Camembert Pierrot	20505.4
8	Seafood	Carnarvon Tigers	15950
1	Beverages	Chai	4887
1	Beverages	Chang	7038.55
1	Beverages	Chartreuse verte	4475.7
2	Condiments	Chef Anton's Cajun Seasoning	5214.88
2	Condiments	Chef Anton's Gumbo Mix	373.62
3	Confections	Chocolade	1282.01
1	Beverages	Côte de Blaye	49198.08
8	Seafood	Escargots de Bourgogne	2076.28
5	Grains/Cereals	Filo Mix	2124.15
4	Dairy Products	Fløtemysost	8438.74
4	Dairy Products	Geitost	786
2	Condiments	Genen Shouyu	1474.82
5	Grains/Cereals	Gnocchi di nonna Alice	32604
4	Dairy Products	Gorgonzola Telino	7300.74
2	Condiments	Grandma's Boysenberry Spread	2500
8	Seafood	Gravad lax	629.2
1	Beverages	Guaraná Fantástica	1630.12

Figure 2-4

How It Works

You have two controls on the page. The first, the `AccessDataSource` named `NorthWindProductsAccDataSource`, does all of the work of connecting to the ADO.NET objects that talk to the JET engine that communicates with the MDB file. The second, the `GridView`, takes that data and formats it into HTML that can be displayed on the page. Note that it is very important to give each control a useful ID (name). Then you must be sure that the data-bound control (the `GridView`) uses its `DataSourceID` property to identify its data source as the `AccessDataSource` control.

Displaying data from Views, Queries, or Stored Procedures is no more difficult; the names of these objects can be used instead of table names in Access. However, there are two caveats. First, if a table or query has spaces in its name, you must enclose the entire name in square brackets. Second, queries that require user input (for example, Northwind's "sales by year" needs to know which year) require techniques that we do not cover in this book for Access, but we will study in depth for SQL Server in Chapters 11 and 12.

With the preceding few steps, you can see on your page a display of data from your `AccessDataSource` control. Later chapters go into great detail about the `GridView`, but this chapter will continue its focus on the `AccessDataSource` control.

If you want to get fancy with the title tag in your pages, you can use a line of code to automatically display the page name. This allows you to use Save As to rename files without updating the title. You need both shaded lines, including the `Import System.IO`.

```
<%@ Page Language="VB" %>
<%@ Import Namespace="System.IO" %>
<!DOCTYPE html PUBLIC "-//W3C//DTD XHTML 1.0 Transitional//EN"
"http://www.w3.org/TR/xhtml1/DTD/xhtml1-transitional.dtd">
<script runat="server">
</script>
<html xmlns="http://www.w3.org/1999/xhtml" >
<head id="Head1" runat="server">
    <title><%Response.Write(New FileInfo(Request.FilePath).Name)%></title>
</head>
<body>
        <h2>Chapter 11 TIO #1103 </h2>
...
```

Variations in Select Statements

When you create a data source in VWD, the wizard asks you to specify columns to display or to create a custom SQL statement. In the preceding Try It Out, you simply checked a few columns. You can specify more complex SQL statements in several ways:

- By using the Advanced, Order By, or Where buttons of the dialog box
- By typing a custom SQL statement in the AccessDataSource Wizard (invoked by the Configure Data Source smart task on the control)
- By typing the statement into the property grid
- By typing the statement directly into the tag in the Source view

For simple queries that return one or more columns from a single table, selecting columns in the AccessDataSource wizard is the preferred technique because it reduces typos and syntax errors. In this wizard, you can select either a table or a query name from the Name drop-down list. You can then select individual columns in the table or query by checking either all of the columns (*) or any set of columns. If you click the Order By button, you can sort by any column in the source. The field selected in Then By will be used if the first column has a tie. As you choose options from this wizard, notice that the actual SQL syntax of the `SelectCommand` is displayed at all times in a read-only textbox located at the bottom of the dialog box.

> **The WHERE button in this wizard allows you to create parameterized SQL statements, which are discussed in Chapter 9. For now, we will overlook this option, but it is important that before deployment you use parameters, as discussed later in the book.**

In a deployed site, avoid ever directly concatenating user input into a SQL statement. Concatenating leaves your site open to SQL injection attacks, a hacking technique that uses spurious characters from user input to negate the intended SQL statement and then substitutes a damaging statement amended to the end of the string. Using the parameters collection sends the user input through the ADO.NET parameters collection, which eliminates the possibility of SQL injection issues.

Although the Configure Data Source Wizard has many options to help you build up a SQL statement quickly, at times you will want to type or modify your SQL statement directly into the tag's `SelectCommand`. The AccessDataSource wizard allows you to do this. On the wizard page where you can choose tables, queries, and columns, you can choose a radio button option to "Specify a custom SQL statement or stored procedure." Selecting this option and clicking the Next button in the wizard takes you to a separate page where you can define a custom statement by typing it directly in a text area. You can also use the Visual Studio Query Builder to visually construct a custom statement here using a tool very similar to the Access Query Builder.

If you don't want to use the wizard, you can optionally type a custom SQL statement in the property grid for the `AccessDataSource` control or just switch to Source view and type the statement on the `SelectCommand` property of the `AccessDataSource` control tag.

There are many texts on SQL (one in the same style as this book is *Beginning SQL Programming,* ISBN 1-861001-80-0), and this book provides a brief introduction in Appendix A. If you want to go beyond the appendix topics, we suggest you start with commands that return only a portion of the records (`TOP` and `DISTINCT`), syntax to alias a field (`AS`), and the techniques to return fields from two related tables (`JOIN`). The following exercise explores a few variations on SQL statements.

Try It Out — Alternating Select Statements for an AccessDataSource

In this exercise, you display only certain columns and certain records from the `Products` table of `Northwind`. You will also create a page to display data from a query. Note that in this exercise the criteria for the selection reside in your source code. At this point in the book, we are not employing user input to make selections but start doing so in Chapter 9.

1. Create a file in `C:\Websites\BegAspNet2Db\ch02\` named `TIO_0203_AlternateSelectCommands-1.aspx`. We use the `-1` because we will build more than one version of the page in this exercise.

2. In Design view, add an `AccessDataSource` control with the ID `Northwind` and set the MDB to your `\App_Data\Northwind.mdb`. As you walk through the dialog boxes, set the `Select` command to retrieve all fields from the `Products` table `("name" = Products)`. After finishing the wizard, take a look in the Source view and observe the statement you created, as follows:

```
SELECT * FROM Products
```

3. Add a `GridView`, give it an ID of `NorthwindGrid`, and set its source to `Northwind`. Save the page. The following shows the entire page as it appears in source view at this point:

```
...     <title>TIO-0203-AlternateSelectCommands-1.aspx</title>
</head>
<body>
        <h2>Chapter 02 TIO #0203 Alternate Select Commands version 1</h2>
    <form id="form1" runat="server">
    <div>
        <asp:AccessDataSource ID="NorthwindAccDataSource" runat="server"
            DataFile="~/App_Data/Northwind.mdb"
            SelectCommand="SELECT * FROM [Products]" >
```

```
    </asp:AccessDataSource>
    <asp:GridView ID="GridView1" runat="server"
        AutoGenerateColumns="False"
        DataKeyNames="ProductID"
        DataSourceID="NorthwindAccDataSource">
        <Columns>
            <asp:BoundField DataField="ProductID" HeaderText="ProductID"
                InsertVisible="False"
                ReadOnly="True"
                SortExpression="ProductID" />
            <asp:BoundField DataField="ProductName" HeaderText="ProductName"
                SortExpression="ProductName" />
            <asp:BoundField DataField="SupplierID" HeaderText="SupplierID"
                 SortExpression="SupplierID" />
            <asp:BoundField DataField="CategoryID" HeaderText="CategoryID"
                SortExpression="CategoryID" />
            <asp:BoundField DataField="QuantityPerUnit"
                HeaderText="QuantityPerUnit"
                SortExpression="QuantityPerUnit" />
            <asp:BoundField DataField="UnitPrice" HeaderText="UnitPrice"
                SortExpression="UnitPrice" />
            <asp:BoundField DataField="UnitsInStock" HeaderText="UnitsInStock"
                SortExpression="UnitsInStock" />
            <asp:BoundField DataField="UnitsOnOrder" HeaderText="UnitsOnOrder"
                SortExpression="UnitsOnOrder" />
            <asp:BoundField DataField="ReorderLevel" HeaderText="ReorderLevel"
                SortExpression="ReorderLevel" />
            <asp:CheckBoxField DataField="Discontinued"
                HeaderText="Discontinued"
                SortExpression="Discontinued" />
        </Columns>
    </asp:GridView>
</div></form></body></html>
```

4. Go back to the Design view and select the AccessDataSource (not the GridView). Open its smart tasks panel and click Configure Data Source. In the Configure Select Statement window, select "Specify a custom SQL statement" and then click Next. Modify the SQL statement in the editor, as follows:

```
SELECT * FROM [Products] WHERE (CategoryID = 3)
```

5. Click Next and test the query. Click OK and finish out the dialog boxes. Take a look at the page in Source view and focus on the following:

```
<asp:accessdatasource id="NorthwindAccDataSource" runat="server"
    selectcommand="
        SELECT *
        FROM [Products]
        WHERE (CategoryID = 3)"
    datafile="~/App_Data/Northwind.mdb">
</asp:accessdatasource>
```

6. Try building some of the following Select commands using the dialog box, typing in the Source view, or using a combination.

```
SELECT * FROM Products WHERE ProductID = 12
SELECT * FROM Products WHERE ProductName = 'Northwoods Cranberry Sauce'
SELECT * FROM Products WHERE ProductID < 11
SELECT * FROM Products WHERE ProductID <11 ORDER BY ProductName ASC
SELECT * FROM Products WHERE SupplierID = 6 OR SupplierID = 8
SELECT * FROM Products WHERE SupplierID = 24 AND UnitPrice > 10
```

7. Save the file and then run it. Observe the behavior in the browser.

Feel free to try other combinations of SQL clauses before closing the page.

How It Works

In the first steps, you set up an `AccessDataSource` control and a `GridView` as before. But then you began experimenting with the `Select` command. Adding and removing columns with the check boxes is intuitive. You can also directly type or edit SQL statements in the editor window. You added `WHERE` clauses that limit which records are returned from the MDB file. If your column names do not have spaces or other special characters, you can omit the `[ ]`. If names include spaces or other special characters, you must use those brackets.

Variations in MDB File Location

Your MDB file may be stored in various physical places on your disk: the same folder as the Web page, a subfolder beneath the Web page, or any other folder on the machine. In Visual Web Developer, you can often just browse for the file in the Designer, and the correct path to the MDB file will be set for you. However, if you are typing your code, you will need to follow the syntax presented in this section.

The `DataFile` property of the `AccessDataSource` control can contain a path that is either fully qualified (starting with the drive letter, for example) or is specified relative to the location of the page that contains the `AccessDataSource`. The path may also be application-relative, which uses URL syntax to refer to the path. This syntax substitutes the tilde (~) character for the application root directory, for example `~/App_Data/Northwind.mdb`. Using application-relative paths enables you to easily move the page from one location to another without breaking the reference to the database, and we recommend that you use them whenever possible.

First, observe the fully qualified path syntax, which contains the entire path to the MDB file starting at the root of the computer drive where the file is located:

```
<asp:accessdatasource ...
datafile="C:\WebSites\MyWebApplication1\App_Data\MyMdb.mdb">
```

Although this syntax works, it has the disadvantage of making your application less portable. If you move this application to another machine, the drive or full path to the file may be different, and you would potentially need to modify the `DataFile` property every time you moved the page.

An improvement on the fully qualified syntax uses relative-path syntax, which specifies only the portion of the path that is different from the full path to the page containing the `AccessDataSource`. Here is the syntax for a database file in the same folder as the page, specified as a relative path. (Note that this is not the recommended location; you learn why in a minute.)

```
<asp:accessdatasource ... datafile="MyMdb.mdb">
```

Because in the preceding example the page and the MDB file are in the same directory, there is no difference between the paths to these files; hence, you need to specify only the filename itself. The following relative-path syntax is very similar to the preceding one if the MDB is in a folder down one or more levels. In this case, you need to specify only the subfolder name, followed by a slash and the MDB filename:

```
<asp:accessdatasource ... datafile="MyDaughterFolder/MyMdb.mdb">
```

If the MDB file were located in the page's parent directory, you could also use the double-period syntax to specify one level up from the current location:

```
<asp:accessdatasource ... datafile="../MyMdb.mdb">
```

Using relative-path syntax, you can easily move the application from location to location without breaking the paths to your MDB file. Because the page and MDB file always travel together (provided the MDB file is part of the application), the relative location between these files always stays the same. However, what happens when you want to move the path around inside of the application, for example, moving the page into a subdirectory? In this case, the relative location between the page and MDB file changes, and the relative-path syntax is then incorrect.

The application-relative syntax alleviates this problem. In this case, the path is always specified relative to the application root directory, instead of relative to the page itself. The root is represented by a tilde (~). There is a clear advantage to always locating your data files in the `App_Data` folder. VWD will look in this one folder (only) to set up automatic attachments when the application is opened.

```
<asp:accessdatasource ... datafile="~/App_Data/MyMdb.mdb">
```

When you get to SQL databases in Chapter 3, another abbreviation uses the syntax `|DataDirectory|\MyFile.mdb`.

Now you can easily move around the application, or move around pages within the application without breaking your reference to the database. For this reason, you should use application-relative paths whenever possible.

The following is MDB that is outside of the Web site folder (such as `C:\MyCustomers\Customers.mdb`):

```
### datafile=" \MyMdb.mdb"
```

The following is MDB on a different machine on a mapped network drive (like P:):

```
### datafile=" \MyMdb.mdb"Another machine on the network to which there is not a
mapped network drive (like
MyServer2://C:\MyCUstomers\Customers.mdb)datafile="\\MyMachine\MyShareName\
MySubFolder\MyMdb.mdb"
```

Managing MDB File Permissions

An MDB database is just another file on your disk, and as such, it is subject to all the same file access permissions issues that would apply to any other file. This means that to read from (and write to, as you will see later in this book) a database file, the identity under which your application runs must be given appropriate permission to read from and write to the file itself in Windows.

In the examples so far, we have not encountered permission problems. This is convenient when you are using the VWD Web Server, a lightweight process that runs under the identity of the user running VWD. That is, the VWD Web Server runs as *you*, and you already have permission to read and write the MDB file to which your page connects.

After deployment, however, your pages will be served by IIS, and the situation becomes a little more complicated. In IIS, ASP.NET pages are run by default under the identity of a special limited-privilege user account on your machine. Under IIS 5.1, this account is named ASPNET. Under IIS 6 or later, this account is named Network Service, which belongs to a Windows group named IIS_WPG ("worker process group"). To use Access databases under IIS, these accounts need permission to read and optionally write to the directory containing the MDB file.

It's fortunate that VWD goes an extra step toward helping you establish these permissions by automatically granting this permission to the ASPNET or Network Service accounts when the database is located under the `App_Data` subdirectory under the application root. This special directory is always granted the correct permissions, provided you are using VWD to develop pages on the local machine.

The `App_Data` directory has additional benefits as well—for example, preventing any files from being served to requesting Web browsers. This means that by placing your MDB files in the application's local `App_Data` directory, you protect those files from inadvertent or deliberate download by your application's clients. For this reason, we highly recommend using the `App_Data` directory for storing your MDB files.

If you must store your MDB files elsewhere, or if you just need to specify the permissions to the database directory manually (for example, if you are working against a remote Web server), you can use Windows to configure permissions for the ASPNET and/or Network Service accounts.

To set permissions manually, follow these steps:

1. Navigate to the folder where the MDB file is located using Windows Explorer.
2. Right-click this directory and choose Properties.
3. Select the Security tab and click the Add button.
4. Add either the local ASPNET account (IIS 5.1) or IIS_WPG group (IIS 6).
5. Click OK; then apply the appropriate permissions to this directory.

For more information, refer to the white paper entitled "Running ASP.NET 1.1 and IIS 6.0" available on the ASP.NET Web site: `www.asp.net/faq/AspNetAndIIS6.aspx`.

Handling Access Connection Failures Gracefully

Errors and failures inevitably happen from time to time in an application. What happens when someone "improves" your server's file system by adding a new level of folders above your MDB? What if the name of your MDB has been changed? What if the MDB has been corrupted? Each of these problems prevents a successful connection to the data and causes a page failure. Good coding practice dictates that you try to make any failure as graceful as possible.

Before discussing the actual commands, understand that the `AccessDataSource` control is derived from the `SqlDataSource` control. In most cases, this is only a background issue. But when handling exceptions, you must use events and methods that actually reside (and are thus named) in the underlying `SqlDataSource` control.

The technique for a soft landing uses an event handler (shown in Step 5 of TIO 02-04) that is called when the `AccessDataSource` control undergoes its `OnSelected` event. That event is raised internally when the data-bound control (`GridView`) requests data from the data source control. The code to handle a connection error checks an exception argument that the data source control passes. The `AccessDataSource` control does not have a derived argument for this event; you have to use the argument type from its parent, `SqlDataSourceStatusEventArgs`. The code checks if the exception argument is null; if so, nothing happens. If the exception argument has a value, the value is checked. If the argument is of an OLE DB Exception type, a warning label on the page can have its text set to a message. Again, note the terminology. It would be clearer if there were an "AccessException" type, but there isn't. You use the more generic object `OleDbException` and finish the script with a command that the exception was handled. That allows the `GridView` to continue rendering, albeit without data, and prevents the general beige-background ASP.NET 2.0 failure page. Because the `GridView` did not get any data, it displays an alternate table: one with a single cell that shows the message in the `EmptyDataText` property.

Don't despair if you have difficulty following these steps; the next exercise will demonstrate. For now, you can just cut and paste the code into your pages to see it work. In Chapter 17, we discuss the details of how to create an alternate rendering of the `GridView` in case of connection failure and provide more details on handling an error event.

Try It Out Handling AccessDataSource Connection Failures

1. In your `ch02` folder, create a file named `TIO-0204-ConnectionFailure-1PreCode.aspx` and set it to use the C# language. In Design view, add to the page an `AccessDataSource` control pointing to `Northwind` that selects all columns from the Products table.
2. Add a `GridView` that displays the information from the data source control. Also, add a label control and name it (set its ID property) `"Message"`.
3. Save and check your page in your browser. You should have no problems seeing the products sold by Northwind. Close the page in the browser.
4. Switch back to VWD and use Design view. Select the `GridView`, and in the Properties pane, change the `AutoGenerateColumns` to `true` and set the `EmptyDataText` to `"No data records were returned"`. Stay in VWD, and switch to Source view. From the `GridView`, remove the entire section of `<columns>`. You should be left with a very simple page, as follows:

```
<html>
<head id="Head1" runat="server">
    <title>TIO-0204ConnectionFailure-1-PreCode</title>
</head>
<body>
<h3>Chapter 2 TIO #4 Connection Failure to Access</h3>
    <form id="form1" runat="server">
        <asp:label ID="Message" runat="server"/><br/><br/>
        <asp:gridview id="GridView1"  runat="server"
            datasourceid="AccessDataSource1"
            AutoGenerateColumns="true"
            EmptyDataText="No data records were returned" />
        <asp:AccessDataSource ID="AccessDataSource1" Runat="server"
            selectcommand="Select * From Products"
            datafile="~/App_Data/Northwind.mdb"/>
    </form></body></html>
```

5. Now you will add code to deal with an exception. Save the page as `TIO-0204-ConnectionFailure-1-CS.aspx`. In Design view, select the `AccessDataSource` control, and in its Properties pane click the lightning icon at the top. Double-click Selected from the list of events. VWD switches to Source view and makes two changes. The first is adding a property to the `AcccessDataSource` control as follows:

```
<asp:AccessDataSource ID="AccessDataSource1" runat="server"
DataFile="~/App_Data/Northwind.mdb"
SelectCommand="SELECT * FROM [Products]"
OnSelected="AccessDataSource1_Selected"   >
</asp:AccessDataSource>
```

Second, at the top of the page VWD creates the framework for an event handler within the `<script>` tags, as shown in the code that follows. Add the shaded lines to the framework. The first example is in C# and the second in VB. Enter only one.

C#

```
<%@ page language="C#" %>
<script runat="server">

    protected void AccessDataSource1_Selected(object sender,
SqlDataSourceStatusEventArgs e)
    {
        if (e.Exception is System.Data.OleDb.OleDbException)
            {
                Message.Text = "There was a problem opening a connection to the
database.  Please contact the system administrator for this site.";
                //Optionally set GridView1.Visible = false;
                e.ExceptionHandled = true;
            }
    }
</script>
<html> ...
```

VB

```
<%@ Page Language="VB" %>
<!DOCTYPE html PUBLIC "-//W3C//DTD XHTML 1.1//EN"
"http://www.w3.org/TR/xhtml11/DTD/xhtml11.dtd">
```

```
<script runat="server">

    Sub AccessDataSource1_Selected(ByVal sender As Object, ByVal e As
SqlDataSourceStatusEventArgs)
        If (Not e.Exception Is Nothing) Then
            If TypeOf e.Exception Is System.Data.OleDb.OleDbException Then
                Message.Text = "There was a problem opening a connection to the
database. Please contact the system administrator for this site."
                ' Optionally set GridView1.Visible = false
                e.ExceptionHandled = True
            End If
        End If
    End Sub

</script>
<html> ...
```

6. Save and run the page. Because the `AccessDataSource` can still connect to the MDB, there should still be no problems. Close the browser.
7. Move the `Northwind.mdb` file out of `App_Data` and into your `C:\Temp` folder so that the connection will fail. Attempt to run the page and observe that the failure is handled gracefully.
8. Move `Northwind.mdb` back to `C:\BegAspNetDb\App_Data`.
9. Change your code to attempt to connect to `Southwind.mdb`. Run the page and observe that your browser shows a more elegant failure message. Close the browser, change your source code back to Northwind, and save the page.

How It Works

First, recall that the `AccessDataSource` control is a derivative of the `SqlDataSource` control and uses the set of exceptions applicable for all OLE DB data sources. Don't be surprised when we refer to objects with SQL or OLE DB names rather than with Access names.

Observe that three modifications were made to the page to handle connection failures:

- You added a property to the `GridView` data source control to display a message if the `GridView` did not get any data from the data source control.
- You added a property to the data source control that invokes the `AccessDataSource1_Selected` event handler when the `OnSelected` event occurs. Note that this event is located on the `SqlDataSource`. Although the user does not directly select data from the `AccessDataSource` control (there isn't even a rendering to the user), the data selection occurs internally in the `AccessDataSource` control when the `GridView` requests data from the data source control.
- You wrote the event handler. The event handler will receive an event argument that contains several properties, one of which will be an exception. There is no type named `AccessDataSourceStatusEventArgs`. Instead, you receive the type from which the `AccessDataSource` is derived: the `SqlDataSource`. If no problems exist, the exception property will be empty. If an exception was created by the `OleDbException` then the code reacts with a friendly notice of problems. Again, note that there is no such type as an `AccessException`. Instead, `AccessDataSource` holds an exception created by ADO.NET in

the more generic object named `OleDbException`. Although there can be many types of exceptions, in this part of the book we focused on exceptions raised by a failure to make a connection to an MDB. The same kind of error handler can be developed for using bad command syntax, attempting to get data from a table or query that doesn't exist, passing parameters of the wrong type, and other faults.

The biggest trick to this code is keeping straight the objects with three different names. You are using an Access file (MDB) for your data source and thus use the `AccessDataSource` control. But you are using the underlying `SqlDataSource` for your event arguments. Last, you are using the generic OLE DB set of exceptions. Most mistakes occur when you try to use ASP.NET 2.0 objects named Access at all of these points in the syntax.

Common Mistakes

The following list provides a record of the most common errors made by students in a lab setting and is a good place to start if you are having problems:

- **Including incorrect name or path for the MDB file:** Recheck the exact name of the MDB and the path. To avoid errors in the pathnames, you can use the Browse button in the Configure Data Source Wizard for `AccessDataSource`.
- **Having incorrect permissions to access the MDB file:** If a `UserID` and `password` are required by the MDB file, you must use the techniques explained in Chapter 4.
- **Trying to use a data-bound control when there is no data source control:** A data-bound control must have a source of data — that is, a data source control — specified by its `DataSourceID` property.
- **Setting the data-bound control to the wrong data source:** If you are using more than one data source control, be extra careful to accurately name each control. Then double-check for each data-bound control that the `DataSourceID` property refers to the correct data source control.
- **Attempting to use an MDB when JET is not installed on the machine:** Although it is rare for JET not to be installed, check that the server has JET available. It is easy to copy the MDB file, but you also must have installed the Access software or the JET engine.
- **Having errors in table or column names:** This mistake usually arises when typing; it is less problematic when using the designer wizards or drag-and-drop in Visual Studio and VWD.
- **Using Incorrect SQL statement syntax:** Make sure you spell the keywords correctly. You must include a comma between each item in a list, such as a group of field names. Literal strings must be in single quotes, but numbers are not. Whenever possible, build your statements using the data source control's Configure Data Source dialog box. You can also test SQL statements directly in the Access Query Design tool or Visual Studio Query Builder.
- **Trying to use an MDB object that is locked:** An MDB table or query that is currently open in Access in design mode (Design view) is locked to all reads and writes. Close the object in Access before attempting to use it in an ASP.NET page, either at design time or at runtime.
- **Attempting to change a locked page:** VWD Design view is unavailable for a page that is still open in a browser. To use Design view, you must first close the browser. (You can edit in Source view, save, and refresh your browser to see changes.)

Summary

This chapter discussed techniques for connecting an ASP.NET 2.0 Web page to a Microsoft Access database. It covered some general ideas and then focused on the theme and variations of using the `AccessDataSource` control to read from an Access MDB file. These techniques make values in the database available for a data-bound control to display. To see the data in this chapter, we used a `GridView` data-bound control with default settings.

Also, we discussed the fact that while Access MDB files and the JET engine are useful tools for students or small offices, a public Web site will overwhelm the ability of JET to handle multiple simultaneous users. Furthermore, JET has a model for changing data that creates additional problems for programmers. For these reasons, you can use Access for learning or development but switch to a full-strength database management system for your production applications.

Successful page designers spend time preparing to use data. It is important to know the file's path and be familiar with the tables, queries, and columns within the MDB file. Ensure that you have a login that has been granted the permissions you will need. You may want to use VWD or Access to open and explore the MDB to understand its structure and constraints before you design the ASPX page.

You can modify the `SelectCommand` to contain any `SELECT` statement allowable by SQL. The Configure Data Source Wizard for `AccessDataSource` contains very effective tools to build a statement by clicking within the designer.

When using an MDB, you must allow permissions for the MDB file for two instances, VWD (mostly design time) and IIS (at deployment). If you create your Web site using VWD Menu, File⇨New⇨ Website, VWD automatically creates a folder named `App_Data` within which there are permissions for files for the developer based on the Windows login. But at the time of deployment, it will not be the developer requesting use of the files. Rather, permission must be granted to the IIS process. Again, if you created the Web site in VWD, these permissions were automatically set up for you. If you created the Web site in folders created outside of VWD, you must create the IIS permissions by hand, as described in the chapter.

Finally, we discussed that connections may occasionally fail, particularly if security or location of the MDB changes. The small amount of code demonstrated in the Try It Out "Handling AccessDataSource Connection Failures" can modify the page so that it handles failure gracefully. The code runs whenever the `GridView` is created or refreshed. The code checks whether there were exceptions from the source of data and renders a failure message to the screen.

Now that you are comfortable reading from an MDB file, the next chapter moves on to the technique of connecting with more robust sources of information: the Microsoft SQL Server and MSDE.

Exercises

1. Describe the difference between the terms Access, JET, and MDB file.
2. What two basic ASP.NET 2.0 server-side controls are required to display data from an MDB file?
3. Explain the advantage of using syntax *a* instead of syntax *b*, which follow:

a. `C:\Websites\MySite\App_Data\MyFile.mdb`

b. `~\App_Data\MyFile.mdb`

4. List disadvantages to using Access as a source of data for Web sites.
5. If you want to write more sophisticated `SelectCommands`, what language should you study?
6. When handling an Access connection failure, you will use objects with three names. Fill in the following table:

Purpose	Object Name
Connection with the MDB file	
Transfer arguments to the event handler	
Hold the exceptions raised by the connection	

Connecting to SQL Server and SQL Server Express

For the past 30 years, most organized data has been stored in some form of relational database such as Microsoft SQL Server. These systems feature the kind of scalability, robustness, and management features that can support even the largest and busiest Web sites. The `SqlDataSource` control is designed to connect these databases to data-bound controls on your page and will be your workhorse for the rest of the book. This chapter focuses on using the `SqlDataSource` control with two Microsoft products: SQL Server and the new SQL Server Express (SSE) database engine.

This chapter is divided into seven sections (plus the usual list of common mistakes to help with troubleshooting, a summary, and some questions for you to review your progress):

- Introduction to SQL Server and connection strings
- Using the `SqlDataSource` control
- Understanding security in SQL Server
- Storing the connection string in the `web.config` file
- Choosing between `DataSet` and `DataReader`
- Discovering the schema (structure) of an unfamiliar database
- Handling connection failures with the `SqlDataSource`

Introduction to SQL Server and Connection Strings

A site that expects to have more than a few simultaneous users will have to employ a more scalable data source than Microsoft Access. This chapter explains how to use data from Microsoft SQL Server, an enterprise-strength relational database management system (RDBMS).

The full version of SQL Server includes three main parts or groups of functions. Note that there are no built-in tools for creating a user interface (front end) to the database. That is left to tools such as Windows Forms or ASP.NET for Web pages. The three main parts of SQL Server include:

1. The SQL Server engine, which actually organizes the data and reads or writes in response to commands in code. This also includes tools such as the Query Analyzer and Data Transformation Services.
2. SQL Management Studio (or Enterprise Manager in older versions), which provides a central point for all database management functions, including the creation of new databases.
3. Tools for administering a database, ranging from backup utilities to replication schemes.

Although the full version of SQL Server has invaluable benefits for large-scale enterprises, many developers don't need the capacity and entire suite of tools (and the price tag that comes with them). Fortunately, Microsoft makes available a free version called SQL Server Express (SSE) that uses the same engine but has a different management interface and fewer tools. SSE is more focused on supporting local databases or development needs and, thus, is limited in its capacity (4GB) and restricted so that only local connections are served. This means that you cannot run SSE on a different machine than the Web server, except in very specialized scenarios. SSE installs automatically when you download and install VWD Express.

In addition to the SQL Server Management Suite Express (SSMSE), you can easily use Visual Studio or Visual Web Developer to develop and manage SSE databases. For developers, SSE allows testing on a local machine against a RDBMS that behaves exactly like the full Microsoft SQL Server product. You may have worked with an older incarnation named MSDE, which was based on SQL Server 2000; SSE is based on the 2005 version of SQL Server. SSE is used throughout this book.

Unless specifically noted otherwise, all of the techniques presented here apply for all three forms of SQL Server (full SQL Server [versions 7.0, 2000, and 2005], SSE, and the older MSDE). Thus, the generic term *SQL Server* encompasses all three.

SSE itself is an engine without development or management tools. You can download the SSMSE to provide an interface. You can also use the Database Explorer tool built into VWD, as will be our primary route in this book. Note that the Database Explorer in Visual Web Developer can change data and schemas in local databases, but in remote databases it can change only the data (not the schema). In the full Visual Studio version, you are able to alter the schema of remote database servers. The Database Explorer in Visual Studio is called the Server Explorer because it includes some additional capabilities for working against nondatabase servers. In this book, we will, once or twice, use tools from SSMSE or even the `osql.exe` command line tool to achieve tasks not available in VWD's Database Explorer. A third alternative for database schema modification is to open Access and link to an external table in your SSE database.

Working with SQL Server requires familiarity with some vocabulary. SQL Server is installed on a machine that becomes a *server* and can be referenced by its machine name. If SQL Server is on the same machine as the requesting software, the machine can be referred to as `(local)` or with the shortcut symbol of a period (full stop). The engine can be installed more than once on a machine, and each installation is called an *instance*. SSE installs as an instance named `SQLExpress`, so you could reference this on the local machine as `(local)\SQLExpress` or `.\SQLExpress`.

Within an instance, you can create *databases*. Databases have *tables* with fields and records. Databases can also have *views*, which are a set of tables, fields, and constraints available to data consumers. *Stored procedures* (*SPROCs*) are collections of T-SQL statements, encapsulated under a single procedure name, that can carry out complex tasks or queries against the data. In order to use SSE, the requestor must be authenticated as a legitimate user.

A database is stored by SQL Server as an `.MDF` file. If your database is primarily for your Web site, then the MDF will most likely be stored in your site's `App_Data` folder. MDF files stored in `App_Data`, as we will see later in this chapter, will automatically have a connection created by VWD in its Database Explorer. Alternatively, the MDF may be stored on another machine that provides data services to the entire enterprise but for which a connection string must be explicitly created.

Preparing to Use a SQL Server Database

Any time you spend up front studying your database will reduce mistakes when you design pages to use the data. Check that you have the following kinds of information in hand before writing a page that uses SQL Server:

- **Server, instance, and database names:** Confirm the exact spelling of the server name, instance, and database name. If there is only one instance of the full SQL Server on a server, it will probably be the default instance, and you do not need to use an instance name. But even if there is only one instance of SSE on the server, you must refer to the server explicitly as (local) `\SQLExpress`. Clarify with the database administrator whether you will be testing against live data or a development copy of the database.
- **Security information:** You will need to know your user ID and password to authenticate and gain access to the database for development. Also, check whether the SSE uses Windows or SQL authentication. (The Chapter 1 install of SSE used Windows authentication.)
- **Database schema:** Understand the schema (structure of tables, columns, constraints, etc.) of the database. Obtain the exact spelling of tables and field names, autogenerated or locked fields, dependencies, and constraints. Carefully note the presence of underscore characters and spaces in object names. Find out from the administrator whether you will be using tables directly or whether you will be using views and SPROCs. The use of SPROCs may require parameters of specific data types. Use Visual Web Developer's Database Explorer to see the components of the database or use SQL queries to check this metadata, as explained near the end of this chapter in the section "Discovering the Schema of an Unfamiliar Database."
- **Test your SQL statements (optional):** You may have doubts about the syntax or logic of your SQL statements. You will find it more efficient to test the statements using a development tool such as the SQL Server Query Analyzer rather than checking them for the first time in an ASPX page.

Once you have done your homework, the next step is to consider the settings of your connection string.

Specifying Connection Strings

The major difference between the syntax of the `AccessDataSource` control (discussed in Chapter 2) and the `SqlDataSource` control lies in the way you specify which database to use. For an MDB, we merely provide the file's name and path. The `SqlDataSource` control uses a *connection string* to hold the name of the server and instance, database, login, and other information. A connection string has a different syntax than we are accustomed to using in Visual Basic or C# and is the source of mistakes for many developers. A typical connection string follows.

```
Data Source =.\SQLExpress;AttachDbFileName=|DataDirectory|\MyDataFileName.
mdf;Integrated Security=True;User Instance=true"
```

When specifying the connection string on the `SqlDataSource` control, you set its `ConnectionString` property, for example:

```
ConnectionString="Data
Source=.\SQLExpress;AttachDbFileName=|DataDirectory|\MyDataFileName.mdf;Integrated
Security=True;User Instance=true"
```

Using alternate formatting on multiple lines improves the readability of the printed page of this text, as in the following. But it is better not to break the lines in your actual site.

```
connectionString="
        Data Source=.\SQLExpress;
        AttachDbFileName=|DataDirectory|\MyDataFileName.mdf;
        Integrated Security=True;
        User Instance=true"
```

First, note the syntax. The entire string resides within double quotation marks in the source code. When specifying the string in the property window of VWD, you do not need the quotes because VWD will add them. Inside the quotes are a series of pairs in the format `Criteria=value`. Semicolons separate these pairs. Note that quotes are not used around the values. Also note that even though some of the criteria include spaces (for example, `Integrated Security`), they are not encased in quotes or brackets. This syntax is not difficult to understand, but because it is different from the syntax of languages such as VB, C#, and SQL, mistakes are common.

Let us take a moment to dissect the component parts of this string. Within a connection string can be many values, only a few of which concern us at this point in the book.

The database identifiers start with a `Data Source` value that is the network name of the machine hosting SQL Server. The machine name `(= Data source)` is available in Windows. For Windows XP, use Start➪My Computer, and then right-click and select Properties➪Computer Name tab➪Full Computer Name. For Windows 2000, right-click My Computer on the desktop and select Properties➪Network Identification. If you know that the database server will be running on the same machine as the Web server where ASP.NET will run, you can also specify the server name with the local identifier of a period (a full stop). The instance can be added with `Instance=MyInstance`. More commonly, the instance is appended to the server name as `MyServer\MyInstance` or `.\MyInstance`. You may also see code that uses the term (local) to represent the local machine, as in `(local)\MyInstance` but there are a few cases where this will not work. When setting the name of the file to attach, you should use the special `|DataDirectory| syntax`, which will point to the `App_Data` folder of your site.

> **SSE, by default, installs with its own instance. Referring to `(local)` alone will fail. You must refer to your SSE as `.\SQLExpress`.**
>
> **ASP.NET also accepts the syntax of `Server=.\SQLExpress` and it will compile the same as `Data Source=.\SQLExpress`.**

Security settings are discussed later in this chapter. For now, understand that for Windows authentication, you should use the attribute `Integrated Security=true` (`trusted_connection=true` also works). When using SQL authentication, you use two values: `UserID=MyUserName; password=MyPassword`, where `MyUserName` and `MyPassword` are replaced with your own credentials. This text uses Windows authentication.

Last, we set the `UserInstance` to true because we want SSE to spawn a new instance of SSE that sets the requestor as Administrator for that instance and thus automatically has rights to the entire database.

If you are familiar with earlier versions of ASP, you may be wondering about the provider. The default provider for the `SqlDataSource` *control is the .NET Framework Data Provider for SQL Server* (`System.Data.SqlClient`)*, so you do not need to specify a provider in the* `SqlDataSource` *in this chapter. However, there is no default provider in a connection string within the* `web.config`*, so you must state the provider there. The next chapter will discuss specifying nondefault providers for other databases.*

Using the SqlDataSource Control

When you use the `SqlDataSource` control to select data, you can start with just three properties plus the authentication information. When using Windows Authentication, you can use `Integrated Security=true`.

```
<asp:SqlDataSource ID="MySourceControlName" Runat="server"
     connectionString="
     Data Source=.\SQLExpress;
     AttachDbFileName=|DataDirectory|\MyDataFileName.mdf;
     Integrated Security=True;
     User Instance=true"
     ProviderName="System.Data.SqlClient"



     SelectCommand="SELECT Field1, [Field With Space] FROM MyTable">
</asp:SqlDataSource>
```

First is the connection string, as previously discussed, and second is the `SelectCommand`, which determines what information is extracted from the SQL Server database. Within the `SelectCommand`, you can use any legitimate SQL `SELECT` statement (including those discussed in the Try It Out "Alternating Select Statements for an AccessDataSource" in Chapter 2 or in Appendix A).

Many SQL Server administrators will not allow users to directly access tables. SQL statements that attempt to access tables will be denied. Instead, the database administrator sets up limited permissions on SPROCs or views. These mechanisms present only parts of tables or tables with restrictions on what data can be modified. The syntax to connect to a view follows:

```
SelectCommand="SELECT * from MyView"
```

If the table, query, SPROC, or view has a space in its name, enclose the entire name in brackets. You must also set the `SelectCommandType`. For example, for a SPROC you must use the following:

```
ConnectionString="..."
            SelectCommandType="StoredProcedure"
            SelectCommand="[My Sproc]"   >
```

You may have noticed the `FilterExpression` *property in the* `SqlDataSource` *and wonder how it compares with using a* `WHERE` *clause in the data source* `SelectCommand`*. Filtering is useful when you want to adjust the visible data after the* `SelectCommand` *query has been executed. This book covers this topic as it is relevant to caching scenarios in Chapter 15.*

ASP.NET 2.0 data source controls support reading from SPROCs, queries from Access or views, as follows:

```
ConnectionString="..."
 SelectCommandType="StoredProcedure"
 SelectCommand="MySproc"
```

With a connection string and a SelectCommand, you can create a page to use data from a SQL Server.

Try It Out Creating a SqlDataSource — Simple Example

In this exercise, you want to display a `GridView` of the products from the SQL version of `Northwind` in a grid (table) format. In this first exercise, you will start with the technique of first adding a data source control and then a data-bound control. To make the first example very simple, we will keep the connection string in the page and not store it in the configuration file (`web.config`).

1. Ensure that you have installed SSE (as explained in Chapter 1), including the sample database `Northwind.mdf`. You must close and open VWD at least once since adding `Northwind.mdf` to your `App_Data` folder. This exercise will not work with data stored outside `App_Data` because a few additional steps are needed to create the connection string. Future examples in the book will explain that technique.

2. Create a folder `ch03` and, within it, a file named `TIO-0301-SqlSimple-1.ASPX`. Display the Toolbox by selecting Menu⇨View⇨Toolbox (Ctrl+Alt+X). Note that the Toolbox has a Data section that can be expanded.

3. In Design view, drag a `SqlDataSource` control from the data section of the toolbar onto the page. In the Smart Tasks panel, click on "configure data source" to open the list of connections. Because `Northwind.mdf` was in the `App_Data` folder when VWD opened, VWD automatically created a connection in its Database Explorer and now offers that connection with the name `Northwind.mdf`. Select the `Northwind.mdf` option, and click Next. For this exercise, do not save the connection string in the application configuration file. Your next step is the dialog to

"Configure the Select Statement." Choose "Specify columns from a table," and then select the table Products. In the Columns list, click on the `ProductID`, `ProductName`, and `UnitPrice`. Click Next and Test Query, and then click Finish. That completes the creation of your `SqlDataSource` control.

4. From the Toolbox Data section, drag a `GridView` data-bound control to the page. In the Smart Tasks panel, drop down the list of data sources, Choose `SqlDataSource1` and close the Smart Tasks panel. That configures the data-bound control. Save and run your page, which appears as follows in Source view:

```
...
<title>TIO-0301-SqlSimple.aspx</title>
</head>
<body>
        <h2>Chapter 3 TIO #0301 SQL Simple</h2>
    <form id="form1" runat="server">
    <div>
        <asp:SqlDataSource ID="SqlDataSource1" runat="server"
ConnectionString="DataSource=.\SQLEXPRESS;
                AttachDbFilename=|DataDirectory|\Northwind.mdf;
                Integrated Security=True;
                User Instance=True"
         ProviderName="System.Data.SqlClient"
         SelectCommand="SELECT [ProductID], [ProductName], [UnitPrice]
                FROM [Products]">
        </asp:SqlDataSource>

        <asp:GridView ID="GridView1" runat="server"
            AutoGenerateColumns="False"
            DataKeyNames="ProductID"
            DataSourceID="SqlDataSource1">
            <Columns>
                <asp:BoundField DataField="ProductID" HeaderText="ProductID"
                    InsertVisible="False"
                    ReadOnly="True"
                    SortExpression="ProductID" />
                <asp:BoundField DataField="ProductName"
                    HeaderText="ProductName"
                    SortExpression="ProductName" />
                <asp:BoundField DataField="UnitPrice"
                    HeaderText="UnitPrice"
                    SortExpression="UnitPrice" />
            </Columns>
        </asp:GridView>
</div></form></body></html>
```

5. Close the browser and compare your page in Source view with the code listing above.

How It Works

Notice that within the `<form>` of the page, there are two controls. The `SqlDataSource` has a `ConnectionString` and `SelectCommand`. The `GridView` has several columns bound to the `SqlDataSource` control's fields. When it comes to syntax, the `SqlDataSource` varies little from the `AccessDataSource` used in Chapter 2. The big difference is the use of a connection string (instead of specifying a data file). This similarity means that your knowledge of one control will help you understand the other data source control.

The connection string passes three values to the `SqlDataSource`. Note that they are all within one pair of double quotes and separated by semicolons.

- Data source that is the server and instance name
- `AttachDbFileName` that is the relative path and name of the MDF file or `InitialCatalog` that points to the database to use within SQL
- The security authentication scheme, where `Integrated` means Windows authentication

When referring to the local server, VWD uses a leading period, which is one of three allowable syntaxes. The other two are the name of the machine or the specific term `(local)`. The name of the machine is followed by the instance. In our case, when VWD installed SQL Express for us automatically, it created an instance of `SQLEXPRESS`.

In the second part of the connection string, VWD uses the syntax of vertical bar characters surrounding the specific term `DataDirectory`. This refers to the `App_Data` folder of the site. It is important to use this syntax rather than a literal path so that when the site is deployed, the connection string still knows where the MDF folder is located. ASP.NET 2.0 will substitute for `|DataDirectory|` the actual path to the `App_Data` folder.

There are two alternates to identify the database to use within the instance of the server. `AttachDbFileName` will dynamically attach the MDF file based on its path. `InitialCatalog` will identify a database within the site and then attach it.

Understanding Security in SQL Server

Any database that has Web exposure must have some type of security scheme. There are many levels of security measures, but they all begin with authentication. *Authentication* is the process whereby software establishes who is using the services. We all authenticate ourselves everyday by providing user IDs and passwords when we use our company computers, visit certain Web sites, or even use ATM machines. Authentication consists of three parts:

1. Somehow, the prospective user must present authentication data, typically a user ID and a password.
2. Somewhere in the site there must be a database of allowed users and their passwords.
3. There must be software that actually does the look-up and reports back whether the prospective user is authenticated or rejected.

In this chapter, we cover authentication options in detail. In Chapters 13 to 16, we also talk about some additional techniques to avoid security breaches. However, security layers such as establishing permissions within a database are covered in texts on database administration.

Be aware that authentication and permissions are not the same. Authentication establishes *who* is trying to use the data. Permissions authorize *which users* can perform *which tasks* with the data. The process of establishing that a given user has permission to access a particular database or object within a database is called *authorization*. A prospective user can be authenticated (established as a known user ID and correct password), but they may not be authorized to actually access the database (or individual objects within the database). Both authentication and authorization must be in place for a functional security system.

Authentication Options in SQL Server

An installation of SQL Server has three options for authentication, and they differ by which software performs the authentication:

- **Windows authentication:** Windows authentication (also called Trusted Authentication or Integrated Security) accepts that the user was authenticated when they logged into Windows and then passes to SQL Server a security token. The data of known users and their passwords is kept in only Windows, and Windows performs the checking algorithms. When Windows authentication is used by ASP.NET, the connection string does not provide a username or password; it only provides an instruction to use Windows authentication. The ASP.NET process runs as a local user named `ASPNET` or on IIS 6.0 as a user named `Network Service`. That "user" logs on to Windows when it starts, and this is the account that needs access granted to the database when Windows authentication is used.
- **SQL authentication:** SQL authentication authenticates users in SQL Server, using data stored in SQL Server and software built into SQL Server (without any reference to a user in the operating system). When SQL authentication is used, the connection string must pass to SQL Server the user ID and password. SQL authentication easily supports multiple Web sites running in the ASP.NET process to connect to each of their databases with unique sets of credentials, providing reasonable isolation between applications. This is the most common authentication scheme used for deployed Web applications, especially in shared hosting scenarios.
- **Mixed Mode:** Mixed Mode is a configuration of SQL Server that allows either Windows authentication or SQL authentication.

There are many ways to define the "user" that is attempting to authenticate with SQL Server. The most typical configuration authenticates the ASP.NET application as a whole, rather than the actual end user sitting at the browser. In this case, the ASP.NET application usually supplies the same set of SQL authentication credentials to the database regardless of the user that is browsing the application. When using Windows authentication, the credentials presented to SQL Server are those of the process containing the application (either ASPNET or Network Service), and so all applications running in the same process are viewed by SQL Server as the same user.

One way to provide independent Windows credentials for each application is to run each application in its own process (i.e., an "application pool" in IIS 6.0), but instructions for configuring this are outside the scope of this book. In rare cases, an end user at the browser will actually be entering an ID and password that get passed to the SQL Server. But most of the time when an end user enters an ID and password into the browser, it is to be authenticated into the ASP.NET 2.0 site itself, not the database. Once the browser user has been authenticated and allowed to access the site, the database connections are just using the credentials of the application itself. As an aside, note that ASP.NET 2.0 offers a set of easy-to-use controls for authenticating visitors to a site and displaying custom content for them (`Login`, `LoginStatus`, `LoginView`, `CreateUserWizard`, `PasswordRecovery`, and others).

When choosing a form of authentication for your application, you should also consider the security implications of each. When using Windows authentication, the user (that is, the Web site) must have a user ID and password for Windows as a whole. Because of the small possibilities that a hacker could gain access to other parts of the operating system through this user account, we typically want to run the application as a very-low-privileged user. Both the default `ASPNET` and `Network Service` accounts fall into this category. On the other hand, SQL authentication only authorizes access to the SQL Server software, and this user has no authority in the Windows operating system itself.

SQL authentication also has security implications. First, a user ID and password for the SQL Server has to be stored in the Web site so that it can be presented to SQL Server at the time of authentication. Storing this information is always a potential point of security failure, because the connection string can be easily discovered by anyone with access to the application files. However, as you will see later in this chapter, ASP.NET provides a safe way to store the connection string (including the SQL authentication user ID and password) in the `web.config` file in an encrypted format that protects the string from exposure in plain text. Another problem with SQL authentication arises from sloppy programming. Older versions of SQL Server, by default, had one user called sa with no password. This sa user is a powerful user that can access any database on the system. Any destructive hacker will attempt to authenticate him- or herself as this user just to check if the database administrator has been careful to change or remove the account. Because of this, SQL Server 2005 and SSE now require you to put a strong password on the `sa` account before the installation will complete.

A major implication for the two types of authentication is the ability of multiple Web sites to coexist on one server. Because all ASP.NET applications run as this same user, in Windows authentication they all present themselves to the SQL Server as the same, so there is the potential for users and programmers of one Web site to access data from another Web site on the same server (host). (Although it is possible to run each application in a unique ASP.NET process, each as a separate user, or to impersonate the Windows user identity of the browser client making the connection request, these topics are outside the scope of this book.) SQL authentication can require each Web site to present different credentials. Those different users/Web sites can be entitled to a different set of permissions, as shown in the following table.

Characteristic	Windows Authentication	SQL Authentication (Used in This Text)
Alternate Name	Trusted Authentication Integrated Security	None, but Mixed Mode Authentication allows Windows or SQL authentication
Typical Environment	Intranet	Internet
Location of List of Users and Authentication Process	Windows	SQL Server
SSE Install	Default	Requires special setup.

Connection String	`Trusted_connection=true`
	
	Or
	
	`Integrated Security=true`
		`user=username;`
		`password=password`

Characteristic	Windows Authentication	SQL Authentication (Used in This Text)
User for ASP.NET Web Apps	ASP.NET process called ASPNET (IIS 5.x) or Network Service (IIS 6).	A SQL User (usually the Web site) with an ID and password different from the OS.
Strength	Generally better security; activity of a user can be traced across both SQL events and Windows events.	Deploys to host without needing an account in the OS. Normal technique for hosted intranet sites. More flexibility for applications to use different credentials to connect to each of their databases.
Weakness	A Windows credential for a Web app is more likely to accidentally give rights to more in the OS than necessary.	Passwords are stored in the Web app (in Windows authentication they are not). Be sure your passwords are stored in the `web.config` file and encrypted. Allows poor practice of a Web app using `sa` credentials. Always create a new credential for the ASP.NET Web app and give it only those rights needed.

Having looked at the two options, we can now discuss the specifics of implementing them with ASP.NET 2.0.

Authentication with SQL Server Express

When you install SQL Server or SSE, you select which mode of authentication to use. In SQL Server, a wizard assists you in the authentication setup. For SSE, you will get Windows authentication by default. SSE does not offer pure SQL authentication, but it does offer the Mixed Mode. To install with Mixed Mode, you must take specific steps. Normally (as we directed earlier in the book), you install VWD Express and let it automatically install SSE. In that case, there is no user interface for the SSE installation; it just happens behind the scenes as directed by the VWD Express Install. All defaults are used, including Windows Authentication.

If you want to use SQL authentication, you must start an explicit SSE installation by using the SSE installation interface that can be downloaded and installed prior to installing VWD Express. The SSE installer with the user interface gives you a wizard in which you can select SQL Authentication. This text uses the default, Windows Authentication.

If your SQL Server or SSE is already installed, you can figure out which authentication scheme was specified by opening RegEdit (back it up, of course), looking in HKey_Local_Machine/Software/Microsoft/Microsoft SQL Server, and searching for LoginMode. A Registry subkey value of 1 means Windows authentication, and a value of 2 means Mixed Authentication mode. However, the values of registry keys can change from release to release of products, so if this is crucial you should check the documentation for your version of SQL Server.

Database Rights with SQL Server Express

Once a user is authenticated (proven to be a given user by presenting valid credentials), there is the matter of rights to using data in SQL Server Express. To understand the granting of rights, it is important to know that SSE is designed for other applications than just Web developers. For example, SSE may be supporting multiple clients using Windows Forms. Therefore, the security model is not optimized for just ASP.NET. Fortunately, we as ASP.NET 2.0 users have some tools available to ensure that our Web sites have a good security model.

SSE, by default, only allows Administrators of the OS to attach a database to an instance of SSE (attachment is a step that must occur before any reading or writing). When you work on a development machine, you normally have administrator rights in the OS, so SSE gives you rights to attach a database. But we would prefer a model in which a different username could have access to databases but without being given Admin rights in the OS.

The solution is to include in the connection string a property called UserInstance=true. When received by SSE, that property will start a new instance of SSE with administrator rights granted to the user that sent the connection string. That is no improvement for us when running a site on the ASP.NET Development Server on our development machine (where we are administrators anyhow). But it is important if the site is running on IIS. In that case the process is running with the name of ASPNET (IIS 5 and earlier) or NetworkService (IIS 6 and later). Then the user instance is started and these "users" have rights to attach a database but do not have to be made administrators on the server.

The take home message is to use the UserInstance=true in your connection strings. You get no benefit on the development server, but it will enable database attachments when your site is deployed and runs under IIS.

Authentication Requirements for the SqlDataSource Control

Now, knowing the way SQL Server employs security, consider how the data consumer (in our case, the data source control) will meet the requirements. First, there is the use of data by VWD at design time and VWD Web Server (testing with ASP.NET Development Server). Second, you will want to access the data from IIS after deployment. These two data consumers have different identities. At design time, VWD and VWD Web Server use the identity of your account that is logged on to Windows. IIS uses the identity of the process, either ASPNET or Network Service by default.

If your SQL Server uses Windows authentication, your `SqlDataSource` control needs to include the following in its connection string: `Integrated Security=true` (or, synonymously, `Trusted_connection=true`). This parameter will instruct SQL Server to authenticate the user based on the user's Windows login. If you were the user logged in when you installed SSE, your credentials were given access rights to SSE. Using VWD and VWD Web Server will work fine because the VWD Web Server is running under your Windows account and, thus, has permission to access SSE. However, even though your application works inside of VWD at design time, it may not work when the site is moved to IIS.

IIS operates under an explicit user account named ASPNET (or Network Services in IIS6/Windows 2003 Server). Therefore, the administrator of the machine that hosts SQL Server must add the ASP.NET process account as a login, make it a user of the database, and give it permissions to access the database. That procedure is beyond the scope of this book but is no different from configuring security for any other Windows user account in SQL Server.

If your SQL Server is using Windows authentication, you can do this book's exercises with VWD and VWD Web Server. Your pages will work on IIS only after granting the ASP.NET process account permission to your database or using SSE with the `UserInstance=True` in the connection string.

If your SQL Server uses SQL Authentication, SQL will do its own authentication. There is no dependence on Windows users. Include in your connection string the two parameters `user=username; password=password`. Now you can use your page from VWD, VWD Web Server, or IIS, because there is no requirement for setting up user accounts in Windows. However, we need to use an account in SQL Server. The only default account is `sa`. Prior to deployment, you should create another account in SQL Server that has only the rights needed to execute your ASPX pages. Failure to create an alternative account to `sa` (and password protect `sa`) will expose your site to one of the most widely known and easily exploited security failures. Any hacker knows to try a login of `userID='sa'` with an empty password.

If you install SSE in the background as a part of the VWD installation (as we do in this book), then it will use the default, Windows Authentication. But if you install SSE using its own installation tools, you will get a dialog box that prompts you to create a password for the default `sa` account. You must use a strong password that, in this case, means that you should use at least seven characters and ensure a mix of letters, numbers, and symbols. In most situations beyond a student exercise, you will want a specific account for each database and application. Avoid giving an application rights to the data of any other application.

Storing the Connection String in the web.config File

Users of older versions of ASP frequently stored the connection string right in the ASP page. Recall that the connection string holds information about the data server name and (in the case of SQL authentication) the user account, sometimes even including the password. Having that information in the code is bad practice for two reasons. First, the information can be seen by every programmer on the design team (however, it cannot be seen on a browser by site visitors). Second, it must be maintained or updated in every place throughout the Web site that has a connection. Updating passwords becomes an onerous job.

ASP.NET 2.0 gives you the option to move the connection string to a `connectionStrings` section of the `web.config` file, give the string a name, and encrypt it. Then ASP.NET 2.0 pages just refer to the connection string by name. The steps required to store a connection string to `web.config` are not difficult. VWD provides both manual and automatic options. We will start with the automatic steps and then describe the manual method from the Designer.

The Designer automatically stores the connection string in `web.config` when you drag a data source control to the page. Alternatively, when you run through the Configure Data Source Wizard, there will be a page with an option (turned on by default) to store the connection in the "application configuration file," meaning `web.config`.

Try It Out Storing the Connection String in web.config

Like the last Try It Out, this exercise displays a `GridView` of the products from the SQL version of `Northwind`. However, this exercise uses the better practice of storing the connection string in the `web.config` file.

1. Open your `web.config` file (located in the list of files in the Solution Explorer). Scroll down to the section named `ConnectionStrings`. There may be an `<add>` tag with a string, depending on the exercises that you did in chapters one and two. Close `web.config`.
2. Create a new file named `TIO-0302-ConnectionStringInWebConfig-1.ASPX`. In VWD Design view, drag a `GridView` onto the page. In its Smart Tasks panel, drop down the Choose Data Source list and select New Data Source. The data will come from a database, and we will keep the default name of `SqlDataSource1`. Click OK. Drop down the list of connections, and select `Northwind.mdf`. This time (different from the previous Try It Out), accept the default option to save the connection string, but give it the name of `MdfNorthwind`, and click Next. Specify the columns for the table named `Products` and select the Product ID, name, and UnitPrice. Click Next, test the query, and then click Finish.
3. Run the page to see that it works. Close your browser and, back in VWD, look at the page in Source view. Whereas in the last exercise you saw a connection string with the server name and filename, you now see only a reference, as follows:

```
...
<h2>Chapter 3 TIO #2 Connection String in web.config</h2>
      <asp:SqlDataSource ID="SqlDataSource1" runat="server"
          ConnectionString="<%$ ConnectionStrings:MdfNorthwind %>"
          SelectCommand="SELECT [ProductID], [ProductName], [UnitPrice]
              FROM [Products]">
      </asp:SqlDataSource>
```

4. Still in VWD, in the root of your Web application, open the file named `web.config`. Search for the tag `<connectionStrings>`, and observe that the connection information is now in the `web.config`.

```
<?xml version="1.0"?> ...
<configuration xmlns="http://schemas.microsoft.com/.NetConfiguration/v2.0">
```

```
<appSettings/>
<connectionStrings>
 ... perhaps some other connection strings ...
 <add name="MdfNorthwind" connectionString="Data Source=.\SQLEXPRESS;
        AttachDbFilename=|DataDirectory|\Northwind.mdf;
        Integrated Security=True;
        User Instance=True"
         providerName="System.Data.SqlClient" />
</connectionStrings>
```

5. Use the same technique as Step 2 to create a `GridView` that shows the authors names from the `Pubs` database. Accept the default option to save the connection string to the application file (`web.config`), and give it the name `MdfPubs`. We will use this connection in later chapters of the book.

> **Examples in this book, starting with the next exercise, keep the connection string in the `web.config` file but with no encryption. Future exercises will assume that you have done this Try It Out.**

How It Works

In this exercise, you created a page with data in the secondmost-automated way—by dragging a `GridView` onto the page and walking through the wizard. (The most automated way, assuming that you want a `GridView`, is to drag fields from the Database Explorer). The wizard routed you into the steps to create a new `SqlDataSource` control and then offered the option to store the connection string in the "application file," meaning `web.config`. When you turned on this option, you stored in the page only a reference to a connection string, not the actual string. Because the connection string can hold a user ID and password, you want to keep it as secure as possible, that is, off the ASPX page.

You then looked in the `web.config` file. Within this file was a section named `<connectionstrings>`, within which VWD created for you two `<add>` tags to hold the names `MdfNorthwind` and `MdfPubs` and their connection strings. These connection strings will be available to all pages within the application.

Manually Adding a Connection String to the web.config File

Creating a connection string in `web.config` merely involves editing the file. You open the `web.config` file located in the root of your site, find the section delimited by `<connectionStrings>` (or add it yourself if it is not there), and type an `<add>` tag, as follows. The tag has three attributes: `name`, `connectionString`, and `providerName`. The `name` attribute is just an ordinary name for the connection string that you will use within your pages. The `connectionString` attribute should be set to the full connection string value for connecting to your database, as described at the start of this chapter. The `providerName` attribute is discussed later in this book; for now, we will just add it as follows. The first example is for Windows authentication (as we use in this book).

```
<configuration>
<connectionStrings>
```

```
  <add
          name="MyConnectionStringName"
          ConnectionString="Data Source=MyServer;
                 Database=MyDatabase;
                 Integrated Security=true;
                 User Instance=true"
          providerName="System.Data.SqlClient" /></connectionStrings>
</configuration>
```

The `web.config` file can contain multiple connection strings, as follows:

```
<configuration>
<connectionStrings>
  <add
          name="MyConnectionStringONE"
          ConnectionString="Data Source=MyServerONE;
          Database=MyDatabaseONE;
        Integrated Security=true;
          User Instance=true"
providerName="System.Data.SqlClient" />
  <add
          name="MyConnectionStringTWO"
          ConnectionString="Data Source=MyServerTWO;
          Database=MyDatabaseTWO;
         Integrated Security=true;
          User Instance=true"
providerName="System.Data.SqlClient" />

  <add
          name="MyConnectionStringTHREE"
          ConnectionString="Data Source=MyServerTHREE;
          Database=MyDatabaseTHREE;
        Integrated Security=true;
          User Instance=true"
providerName="System.Data.SqlClient" />

</connectionStrings>
</configuration>
```

When using SQL authentication, you will also need to present the credentials as follows:

```
<configuration>
<connectionStrings>
  <add
          name="MyConnectionStringName"
          ConnectionString="Data Source=MyServer;
                User ID=MyUserID;
                Password=MyPassword,
                Database=MyDatabase"
providerName="System.Data.SqlClient "/>
</connectionStrings>
</configuration>
```

Each of the preceding listings goes in the web.config file. Then we use the name of that string in our ASPX page with the following syntax. Note how the syntax is written to execute a single statement <%$ %> that returns a string. The <%$ ... %> syntax is called an *expression* in ASP.NET 2.0, and in this case we use a connectionString expression to evaluate a connection string value. There are other expressions available in ASP.NET 2.0 that are outside the scope of this book.

```
<asp:sqldatasource runat="server"
    ID="MySmartDataSource"
    ConnectionString="<%$ connectionsStrings:MyConnectionStringName %>"
    SelectCommand="..."
/>
```

The statement reads the connection string from the set of connection strings in the web.config file. The web.config file is the default location and does not have to be specified.

Encrypting Connection Strings

Although the contents of the web.config would not be visible to a browser, they would be visible to the development team and administrators at the hosting company. To prevent compromising of the system, ASP.NET 2.0 offers an encryption utility to hide the connection string information within the web.config file. The information will be automatically decrypted by ASP.NET when the connection string is requested by an ASPX page.

The encryption should be performed on the server that is actually used for public deployment because the default key used to perform the encryption derives from the machine where the application will be run. So, even if you successfully encrypt the key on your development machine, once you deploy the key to another machine, ASP.NET won't be able to decrypt it (because the deployment machine doesn't have the private key). There are ways around this (deploying the same key to all your machines, for example), but those techniques are outside the scope of this book.

You can perform an encryption from the command line as follows:

1. Close VWD.
2. Click Start⇨Run⇨cmd and change directory to the C:\WINDOWS\Microsoft.net\Framework\v2.0.50727 (the final release version).
3. If C:\Websites\BegAspNet2Db is the root of your site, enter the following line:

```
aspnet_regiis -pef connectionStrings c:\Websites\BegAspNet2Db
```

You will see the messages shown in Figure 3-1.

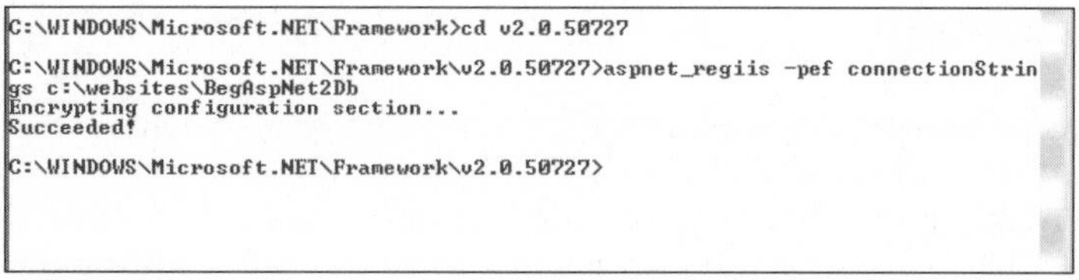

```
C:\WINDOWS\Microsoft.NET\Framework>cd v2.0.50727

C:\WINDOWS\Microsoft.NET\Framework\v2.0.50727>aspnet_regiis -pef connectionStrin
gs c:\websites\BegAspNet2Db
Encrypting configuration section...
Succeeded!

C:\WINDOWS\Microsoft.NET\Framework\v2.0.50727>
```

Figure 3-1

The command line tool for encrypting connection strings can also take a virtual path syntax (the path in IIS metabase) instead of your specifying the fully qualified path to the `web.config` file, as follows:

```
aspnet_regiis -pe connectionStrings -app /BegAspNet2Db
```

Once this encryption has been performed, the `web.config` file can be opened, but the connection strings will be garbled, as follows:

```
<?xml version="1.0"?>
<configuration xmlns="http://schemas.microsoft.com/.NetConfiguration/v2.0">
  <appSettings/>
  <connectionStrings configProtectionProvider="RsaProtectedConfigurationProvider">

<EncryptedData Type="http://www.w3.org/2001/04/xmlenc#Element"
   xmlns="http://www.w3.org/2001/04/xmlenc#">
   <EncryptionMethod Algorithm="http://www.w3.org/2001/04/xmlenc#tripledes-cbc" />

<KeyInfo xmlns="http://www.w3.org/2000/09/xmldsig#">
    <EncryptedKey xmlns="http://www.w3.org/2001/04/xmlenc#">
     <EncryptionMethod Algorithm="http://www.w3.org/2001/04/xmlenc#rsa-1_5" />
<KeyInfo xmlns="http://www.w3.org/2000/09/xmldsig#">
      <KeyName>Rsa Key</KeyName>
     </KeyInfo>
<CipherData>
<CipherValue>z/ltjvphw0Qzgy+CKQjmfjcmtAC5YHik3LDRbxBR6D6Bnr45cr/lwf7DeK8p6tINfpNBUs
tRxt8VzkN/NtWl+qpC8vm8I7OUk4NCRBKdTSgUskoi884OHBzElOM+5TyrQ/mUo1ciza81iAAWW2A48UQan
HJqilPJGR+T0BqI6Oc=</CipherValue>
</CipherData>
</EncryptedKey>
</KeyInfo>

<CipherData>

<CipherValue>RQM6/Y4DU+tiHQ2btu/Y6/jOuqzcRxffB4sIL7KDrKI1kBqNA9cas6+3V5tHwA...
PS0cHHOjo0wrI5GxJ517LNhCrWInJRfXJ7jNvx8jK/66wtaU</CipherValue>
</CipherData>
</EncryptedData>
</connectionStrings>
...
</configuration>
```

The connection data will be decrypted automatically when needed by ASP.NET. However, you can decrypt the connection information manually if you need to make modifications, such as changing the password, by using the following line:

```
aspnet_regiis -pdf connectionStrings c:\Websites\BegAspNet2Db
```

To repeat, the encryption process employs a key that is based on the machine where the encryption algorithm is executed. The process of decryption (either by hand or in the process of serving a page) must occur on the same machine as the encryption. Moving a `web.config` to another machine, for example as part of an XCOPY deployment (simple copy and paste including all subdirectories), will render the `web.config` undecryptable, so it is recommended that you encrypt your connection strings *after* you deploy your Web site to its final destination machine.

Keep in mind that VWD is a tool for development. The VWD testing Web server was never designed to support public sites. So, although you can encrypt a `web.config` when using VWD, it is not the typical case. The typical pattern is to create and test pages in VWD that use an unencrypted connection stored in `web.config`. You then use XCOPY or FTP to deploy the site to your host machine that runs IIS. Prior to going public, you would run the encryption on the hosting machine.

Try It Out — Encrypting Connection Strings in web.config

In this exercise, we will walk through the steps to encrypt the connections strings. After viewing the encryption keys, we will decrypt them.

1. There is no need to create new files for this exercise, but we have included a placeholder page in the download named `TIO-0303-EncrytpionOfConnectionStrings`.
2. Click on the Windows Start menu, and click Run. Type `CMD` and change the directory to `C:\WINDOWS\Microsoft.net\Framework\ v2.0.50727`.
3. Type the following command, and press Enter. Don't worry if there is odd word wrapping.

```
aspnet_regiis -pef connectionStrings c:\Websites\BegAspNet2Db
```

4. In VWD, open your `web.config` and observe the set of `<cipher>` tags that replace your `MdfNorthwind` and `MdfPubs`. The syntax is not important, since you will not do any editing within these tags. Run the page from the last Try It Out to prove that the connection string properly and automatically decrypts.
5. Close VWD and return to your command prompt window. Type the following, and press Enter:

```
aspnet_regiis -pdf connectionStrings c:\Websites\BegAspNet2Db
```

Alternatively, instead of typing, you can retrieve your last command by pressing the up arrow key, and then change from `-pef` *to* `-pdf`.

6. Close the command prompt and reopen VWD. Open `web.config`, and observe that your connection strings are in human language again.

How It Works

The encryption is performed with the utility from Windows' command line. To be safe, close VWD when running these commands. Once you get to the .NET Framework directory, the command can be entered using the `-pef` switch for encryption and`-pdf` for decryption. As you observed in `web.config`, the encrypted state replaces the contents of the `<connectionString>` tags with new subtags that identify the encryption scheme and keys. Although we did not test it in this exercise, keep in mind that the decryption function relies on information specific to the machine on which the encryption occurred. Therefore, encryption should be performed on the deployment machine.

Choosing between DataSet and DataReader

The `SqlDataSource` control will obtain data from the database in one of two ways, according to the value of the `DataSourceMode` property: `DataReader` or `DataSet` (the default). A `DataReader` streams the information, whereas the `DataSet` will hold the values in memory and allow the data-bound control to perform tasks such as sorting and paging. This distinction is of little importance to a Web application, because the end-user code never gets access to the underlying `DataSet` or `DataReader`. The `DataSet` or `DataReader` is discarded at the end of the request, so it does not persist in memory across requests. The sole determination of the ability to write data using a data source control is having `Update-`, `Delete-` or `Insert-Commands` defined, as we will study in Chapters 11 and 12. This works irrespective of whether the data source returns a `DataSet` or `DataReader` from the `SelectMethod`.

The trade-offs are performance, capability in presentation, and cache enabling as summarized in the table below. There are many variables, but in common scenarios, a `DataReader` will be faster and than a `DataSet` and will use less memory on the IIS server. As a general rule, you should use a `DataReader` when your data source control is only populating a list or a data-bound control that does not need caching, paging, and dynamic sorting. You should also use it if your data-bound control will offer sorting or paging of records, in which case you will need to accept the cost of using a `DataSet` (the default when `DataSourceMode` is not explicitly set). For more information about paging and sorting behavior, refer to Chapter 7. Last, caching scenarios, as we cover in Chapter 17, require the use of a `DataSet`.

Value	Advantages	Cautions
`DataReader`	Faster	Doesn't support caching, paging, and dynamic sorting
`DataSet`	Supports caching, sorting and paging	Slower

We can see these differences in the following Try It Out.

Try It Out — Setting the SqlDataSource DataSourceModes of DataSet and DataReader

In a short exercise we will set the data source mode to `DataReader` for a `SqlDataSource` bound to a `DropDownList`. Then we will add a `GridView` and see that paging will fail if its data source control is changed from `DataSet` (default) to `DataReader` mode. Although we have not discussed paging and sorting in depth, you may recall that we did turn it on in Demonstration 1 in of Chapter 1.

1. Create a page named `TIO-0304-DataMode-1.aspx`. In Design view, drag a `DropDownList` control to the page. Choose Data Source, select New, and set it to use your `MdfNorthwind` connection created in the Try It Out "Storing the Connection String in web.config" earlier in this chapter. This time use the `Shippers` table and the `ShipperID` and `CompanyName`. Back in the `DropDownList` wizard, set the field to display to `CompanyName` and the field for value to `ShipperID`.

   Because this information will rarely change, we just want to get it into the page as fast as possible. Select the data source control, and in the Properties window (press F4 if the Properties window is not visible), change the `DataSourceMode` property to `DataReader`. Run the page, although you will not be able to sense that it is faster.

2. Now, we will demonstrate a failure from a mismatch between the `DataSourceMode` property and our intention to use paging in a `GridView` control. Drag and drop a `GridView` control onto the page, and configure the Data Source to a new database, keeping the default name of `SqlDataSource2`. Use your `MdfNorthwind` connection, and select the table named `Products`

and just the ProductID and Name fields. Click Next and Finish. By default, the SqlDataSource control will be in DataSet mode.

With the GridView selected, in the common tasks panel enable paging. Save, run, and observe in your browser that the page loads without problems and that paging in the GridView works correctly.

3. Close the browser and go back to the page in VWD design mode. Select the SqlDataSource2 control and look in the Properties window. Find the DataSourceMode (under the Designer group) and double-click it to change the option to DataReader. Save the page as TIO-0304-DataMode-2, and when you view it in the browser, note the error.

How It Works

The DataReader is faster. However, the SqlDataSource does not support paging or sorting when using the DataReader mode. Because the ability to quickly feed data to a relatively static control is ideal for a DropDownList, in Step 1 we set the list's data source control to a DataReader. You saw in Step 2 that the default data mode is DataSet. When you switched to DataReader, the paging failed. Note that there are many cases when using a DataReader makes sense, such as quickly populating a ListBox or BulletedList.

Discovering the Schema of an Unfamiliar Database

It is important to understand the structure (schema) of a database before you begin to use it. At a minimum, you must know the names of tables or queries that you want to use, as well as the names of their columns (fields). If you intend to write or change data, you should also have an understanding of the relationships so that data dependencies are not broken.

The Database Explorer in VWD provides most of the capability needed to understand (or create) the structure of a database. The database can be expanded and then the table section expanded. Select one table name, and notice that you automatically get a row count in the Properties window. If you expand the table node, you can select any field name within that table and see its properties. Right-clicking on a table and selecting Open Table Definition will reveal properties for all columns at once.

VWD supports a few more tricks. You can see the data of a table by right-clicking on the table and selecting Show Table Data. At the bottom of the grid is a blank row to add a new record. You can edit an existing row by double-clicking in the field of interest. A particularly useful feature is the ability to double-click on a stored procedure to see the SQL that is in the procedure. Or you can select a procedure, right–click, and then click on Execute. If you supply parameters (if needed), the procedure will execute, and the results will appear in an output window.

> **If you own the full edition of SQL Server you can explore database structure with the SQL Server Enterprise Manager.**

If you don't have any of these tools available, or want to dig deeper, you can discover the schema by using SQL commands. Programmers usually do this on some temporary pages; in the end, this is not part of deployment. These statements are a little tricky to start, but they do follow a logical pattern. This topic is covered in depth, including all of the nomenclature, in Chapter 16 of *Beginning SQL Programming* by Kauffman et al., ISBN 1-861001-80-0.

SQL Server contains schema tables that describe the schema of the data they hold. Schema tables can be read like other data once you know their table and column names. The following table lists those most commonly used.

Schema Table Name (all schema names begin with INFORMATION_SCHEMA)	Most Useful Columns
.SCHEMATA	Catalog_Name (database name)
.TABLES	Table_Name Table_Catalog (which database holds the table) Table_Type (base table or a view)
.COLUMNS (shows all columns of all tables)	Column_Name Table_Name (location of the column) Data_Type Column_Default
.VIEWS	Table_Name (the view name) View_Definition
.ROUTINES (stored procedures)	Routine_Name Routine_Definition

The basic syntax to explore a database schema follows.

```
<asp:SqlDataSource ID="SchemaDataSource" Runat="server"
    ConnectionString="  ...   "
    SelectCommand="SELECT Table_Name, Table_Catalog
            FROM INFORMATION_SCHEMA.Tables">
</asp:SqlDataSource>

<asp:GridView ID="SchemaGridView" Runat="server"
DataSourceID="SchemaDataSource"
AutoGenerateColumns="true">
</asp:GridView>
```

Note that if this is the first time you have looked at the schema of a database, you will see more information than you could have imagined. However, it is easy to ignore the extraneous information. Human minds have been separating the wheat from the chaff for tens of thousands of years; they convert well from grain to code. You can refine your search by using a `WHERE` clause in the `SelectCommand`, as explored in the next exercise.

Try It Out Determining a Database Schema

Imagine that Northwind will be hiring people in China and Canada. You are wondering if you can accommodate postal codes with six digits and a mix of numbers and letters. In this Try It Out, your objective will be to learn the data type and size of the postal codes for employees in Northwind stored on your SQL Server. Assume that you have no information about Northwind other than what a vague colleague scribbled on the back of a lotto ticket: server = (local)\SQLExpress and database name = Northwind.

1. In your ch03 folder, create a file named TIO-0305-DatabaseStructure-1.aspx. Start with trying to get the largest level of schema, a list of databases on the server, as follows. In the Toolbox, double-click a GridView to put one on the page. Create a new data source control of the database type, and accept the default name. In the step to configure the Select statement, choose to specify a custom statement and enter the following:

```
Select * from INFORMATION_SCHEMA.Tables
```

2. Open the GridView's Smart Tasks panel, and Click Edit Columns. If necessary, turn on the "Auto-generate fields" option in the lower-left corner. Select each of the selected fields, and click the red X button for delete. Click OK. Save the code, and test it in your browser.

```
...
    <title>Ch03-TIO0305-DatabaseStructure-ver01</title>
</head>
<body>
Chapter 03 TIO #0305 DatabaseStructure ver 1
    <form id="form1" runat="server">
    <div>

        <asp:GridView ID="GridView1" Runat="server"
            DataSourceID="SqlDataSource1"
            AutoGenerateColumns="true">
        </asp:GridView>

        <asp:SqlDataSource ID="SqlDataSource1" Runat="server"
             ConnectionString="<%$ ConnectionStrings:MdfNorthwind %>"
            SelectCommand="Select * from INFORMATION_SCHEMA.Tables">
        </asp:SqlDataSource>
    </div></form></body></html>
```

3. View the results in a browser. Note in the right column that you are seeing a list of views as well as tables. Close the browser, and in VWD source view restrict the records returned as follows (only the value for the SelectCommand is shown). Save this as TIO-0305-DatabaseStructure-2.

```
SELECT * from INFORMATION_SCHEMA.Tables WHERE Table_Type='Base Table'
```

4. Looking at the column TABLE_NAME, you can see "Employees" as an obvious candidate table that holds the Postal Codes column you are seeking. Try showing a list of columns by changing the Select Command to the one below, and save it as: TIO-0305-DatabaseStructure-3.

```
SELECT * from INFORMATION_SCHEMA.Columns
```

5. The information is there, but you see the columns of all the tables. Restrict the result to just columns in the Employees table, as follows. Save it as `TIO-0305-DatabaseStructure-4`.

```
SELECT * from INFORMATION_SCHEMA.Columns WHERE Table_Name='Employees'
```

6. Now, you can easily see that the data type is `nVarChar`. The `Char` means that the data type can hold characters, and the `Var` means a variable number of characters. The `n` means that the characters are encoded using the Unicode scheme (they can even accommodate Asian characters). You can also see that the size has been set to a maximum of 10 characters. You now know that your database can support employee zip codes from China (for example, 1000600) and Canada (for example, J5K S1K).

How It Works

Once you have a guide to the names of objects in the RDMS schema, you can display all of the metadata that you need to work with the database on a developmental ASPX page. Start with a `SELECT` command that shows the databases, for which you do not need to specify a database in the `ConnectionString`. Then use the object names from the table that precedes this Try It Out to obtain records about the database. Keeping the `GridView` property `AutogenerateColumns=true` eliminates the need to know anything about the column schema when you create the ASPX page.

Handling Failures with SqlDataSource

In spite of taking precautions, there will be times when `SqlDataSource` fails. Rather than return a nondescript failed page, you want to present the user with a more graceful and informative failure notice. The strategy is very similar to the discussion late in the last chapter on failed connections when using the `AccessDataSource`.

When the `GridView` is created or refreshed, it requests a set of data from the data source control. The data source control executes the `SELECT` command. After the `SELECT` command has been executed, the data source control raises the `Selected` event and sends data (if it exists) and any exceptions (errors). You write a procedure to be executed on the `Selected` event in which you check for exceptions and then check whether they are from SQL. If they are, then you provide an informative error message to the user. Note that the `Selected` event here means that the data source control has executed the `SELECT` command. This use of the term *select* has nothing to do with the user clicking on (selecting) a control in the browser.

Try It Out Handling Connection Failures

In this exercise, you'll display a `GridView` of shippers used by `Northwind` and add an event handler to gracefully deal with failures. Then you will create an error in our connection string and observe. You can write this page using either C# or VB; samples of both are provided. This exercise is very similar to the one for connection failures with the `AccessDataSource` control.

1. In your `ch03` folder, create a file named `TIO-0306-HandleFailure.aspx`. In Design view, drag a `GridView` to the page, and in the Smart Tasks panel, choose a data source of New. Select Database, name the database `NwShipperDataSource`, and use the `MdfNorthwind` connection. Set it to read all the fields and all the records from `Northwind`'s Shippers table. Name the

`GridView` control `NwShipperGridView`. If you are unsure of the technique, review the first Try It Out exercise of this chapter. Check the page in your browser.

2. Close the page in the browser, and add a label named `FailMessage` with an empty string for the default `Text` value. Select the `GridView` and in the Properties window for `EmptyDataText` give it a value such as "No records to display" (more details on this property when the `GridView` is discussed in Chapter 5).

   Switch to Source view and at the upper-left corner drop down the list of objects and select `NwShipperDataSource`. At the top right, drop the list of events and click on Selected. VWD will add the following highlighted line to the `SqlDataSource` control. You will build that procedure in a minute (more details on handling events in general in Chapter 16).

```
<asp:SqlDataSource ID="NwShipperDataSource" Runat="server"
    ConnectionString="<%$ ConnectionStrings:MdfNorthwind %>"
    SelectCommand="Select * FROM Shippers"
    OnSelected="NwShipperDataSource_Selected"/>
```

3. Now, add the procedure in either C# or Visual Basic:

C#

```
<script runat="server">
    void NwShipperDataSource_Selected(object sender, SqlDataSourceStatusEventArgs
e)
    {
        if (e.Exception is System.Data.SqlClient.SqlException)
        {
            FailMessage.Text = "There was a problem.";
            //Optionally set GridView1.Visible = false;
            e.ExceptionHandled = true;
        }
    }
</script>
```

VB

```
<script runat="server">
    Protected Sub NwShipperDataSource_Selected(ByVal sender As Object, ByVal e As
System.Web.UI.WebControls.SqlDataSourceStatusEventArgs)
        If (Not e.Exception Is Nothing) Then
            If TypeOf e.Exception Is System.Data.SqlClient.SqlException Then
                FailMessage.Text = "There was a problem. Please contact the system
administrator for this site."
                ' Optionally set GridView1.Visible = false
                e.ExceptionHandled = True
            End If
        End If
    End Sub
</script>
```

4. Save and test your page; it should work fine. Now induce a failure. Close the browser, and in VWD source view, find the `SqlDataSource` and change the `SelectCommand` to `"SELECTXXX * FROM [Shippers]"`.

Save and run the page.

How It Works

At the moment the GridView is created or refreshed, it requests data from the SqlDataSource control. The request triggers the SqlDataSource control to execute the SELECT command. Immediately after the SELECT command is executed, an event called Selected occurs. At that point, you will know if there was a failure in running the SELECT command. So, you specify in the SqlDataSource control an event handler named NwShipperDataSource_Selected, as follows:

```
<asp:sqldatasource
 . . .
Onselected="NwShipperDataSource_Selected"/>
```

In the event handler, you will receive several pieces of information, including a set of event arguments passed as the type SqlDataSourceStatusEventArgs in a variable named e.

```
void NwShipperDataSource_OnSelected(object sender, SqlDataSourceStatusEventArgs e)
```

One property of SqlDataSourceStatusEventArgs is named Exceptions. It contains an object that represents a description of any problems that were encountered when the data source's SELECT command was executed. Looking into the script, our code checks for the existence of exceptions by using the is operator, which will be false if the value is NULL, as follows. At the same time, it will determine whether the problem is of the SQL exception type.

```
        if (e.Exception is System.Data.SqlClient.SqlException)
```

If the exception is from SQL Server, you perform two or three tasks. The first is to put an error message into the ConnFailMessage label. Second, you have the option not to display the GridView at all.

```
ConnFailMessage.Text = "There was a problem opening a connection.";
//Optionally set GridView1.Visible = false;
```

Third, you set a variable that states you have handled the exception and the page should finish loading.

```
e.ExceptionHandled = true;
```

If ExceptionHandled was not set to true, the page would throw an unhandled exception and revert to the ASP.NET error page, and you would not have achieved your graceful connection failure.

Note that you could create other types of errors. For example, if you changed the name of the connectionString to Southwind then there would not be a match to any entry in the web.config file. You would get a parser error, and thus any code triggered by the SqlDataSource control would never execute.

We can never anticipate everything that will go wrong. But this framework will catch most kinds of problems with the SqlDataSource control, and you can elaborate upon it, perhaps by presenting a more detailed message based on the value in the System.Data.SqlClient.SqlException.

Common Mistakes

The following list describes mistakes commonly made in trying to accomplish the tasks described in this chapter:

- Mistaking the syntax connection string. Like all string properties on ASP.NET controls, the entire string is placed within double quotation marks. Data is presented in `name=value` pairs, which are separated by semicolons. Quotes are not used around individual values.
- Putting the `ConnectionString` into the wrong `web.config` file. The string must be in the `web.config` file in the root of the Web site that will use the string.
- Attempting to use sorting and paging when `SqlDataSource` is in `DataReader` mode. Change your data source control to `DataSourceMode = DataReader`.
- Forgetting to grant permission to the ASP.NET Windows user when using Windows authentication in the connection string.
- Attempting to use the wrong user ID or password for the RDBMS when using SQL Authentication.
- Attempting to use data from an RDBMS that is not properly configured and running. Check that your login information and select commands work with another interface to the RDBMS, such as SQL Server's Query Analyzer.
- Making syntax errors or typos in `SELECT` commands.
- Forgetting to set `ExceptionHandled = true` in a connection handler event so that the error is considered resolved enough to continue running the page (even though the page will likely now be presenting a custom error message).

Summary

If your Web site will have more than a few visitors or if it will be hosted outside of a simple network, avoid using Access. An alternative with a logical upgrade path is Microsoft SQL Server, an enterprise-strength RDBMS. For development, you can use a free product called SQL Server Express (SSE) that contains just the database engine from SQL Server. Pages written to use SSE are the exact same in syntax as those for SQL Server, so deployment is seamless. In this chapter, all of the techniques discussed and pages written for SQL Server work fine against the full SQL Server or SSE.

The `SqlDataSource` control has one major variation from the `AccessDataSource` control of the last chapter. The SQL version uses a connection string to provide information about the target database and the security information for authentication. Be careful of the syntax because it is different from other languages used in this book. You specify the database in values for the SQL Server, instance, and database. There is no need to specify a provider in the `SqlDataSource` because the default provider is for SQL Server. Prior to deployment, the connection string should be stored in the `web.config` file and encrypted as described. The connection string in `web.config` does not have a default provider, and so it must be specified.

SQL Server installs with one of two security schemes. Windows authentication (Trusted Authentication) lets Windows keep the list of users and perform the task of checking prospective users against the list.

Examples in this book use Windows authentication. For Windows authentication, we use `Integrated Security=true` (or `Trusted_Connection=True`) in the connection string. SQL authentication requires that the connection string include the user ID and password. If there is no authentication information in the connection string, then SSE will use the `sa` account by default, but that account's password should be changed prior to deployment. For SQL authentication, we use `User ID=MyUserID;password=MyPassword`.

The `SqlDataSource` will handle data in one of two modes: `DataReader` or `DataSet`. Use `DataReader` mode when you're only filling a list or a `GridView` that will not use paging, sorting, or caching. For all other cases use the default `DataSet`.

There are several ways to discover the structure (schema) of a database. Normally, you will use one of the GUI tools, including SQL Server Enterprise Manager, the Visual Studio QueryBuilder, and the VWD Database Explorer. But if these are not available, the SQL language offers a way to discover the schema of an unfamiliar database by using SQL statements. These are of the general form `SELECT * FROM Information_Schema.MyObject`, where `MyObject` can be databases, tables, columns, or other structures. Many of these commands return large amounts of information about the minutiae of the database, but commonly needed information, such as the exact spelling of column names, is also in the report.

Although you take care to avoid the possibility of a `SqlDataSource` control failing to connect, it may happen. Instead of the default failure page, you can handle the error. Start by setting the `OnSelected` property of the source control to a procedure. When the data-bound control asks for values, the `SqlDataSource` control will execute the `SELECT` command and then raise the `Selected` event and pass to it any exceptions (errors). In the procedure, we check for the existence of errors, and if they exist, we check to see whether they are of a SQL type. If there was a connection error, we give the user a message and inform the `SqlDataSource` control that we have handled the error so that ASP.NET delivers our error-modified page instead of the default failure page.

The next chapter takes a look at connections to other databases that may be found in the enterprise. Then we move on to several chapters that drill down into the techniques to display data.

Exercises

1. What is the difference between SQL Server, MSDE, and SSE?
2. What is the syntax to refer to an SSE instance on your local machine?
3. What are the benefits of storing the `ConnectionString` in the `web.config` file?
4. What event is of interest when detecting and responding to a connection failure?
5. What arguments are of interest when detecting and responding to a connection failure?

4

Connecting to Other Relational Databases

So far, you have studied an easy scenario in Chapter 2 (connecting to Microsoft Access MDB files with no password security) and a very common scenario in Chapter 3 (connecting to Microsoft SQL Server and SSE). Of course, there are many other sources from which you might want to read data, and this chapter explores how ASP.NET 2.0 enables you to connect to those databases. We will be moving beyond the defaults of the `SqlDataSource` control to implement alternate providers and additional values in the connection string. This chapter also looks at the case of using Access with a security scheme. Note that although we cover many sources of data in this chapter, we do not cover XML sources, which are covered thoroughly in Chapter 14. Our expansion on the `SqlDataSource` control in this chapter includes:

- Understanding the relationship between layers of connectivity software and looking at the supported ADO.NET providers and how to use them in ASP.NET 2.0
- Connecting to an Access MDB file that has a security scheme
- Connecting to Oracle and MySQL
- Connecting to Excel
- Connecting to other databases

And, as always, we include a list of common mistakes, a summary, and some exercises to review what you've studied.

This chapter is not a guide to installing or using databases. It assumes that if you are connecting to Oracle, MySQL, or another database, you already have it installed and are familiar with its specific procedures and terminology. Most readers will not do all of the exercises. We suggest that you do only those exercises that connect to databases you have installed. We do not recommend that readers set up these databases just for the exercises.

Introduction to Connections with Providers

Chapters 1 and 2 discussed two types of connections:

- **Using the** `AccessDataSource` control where there is no requirement for a connection string or provider; only the name and path of an MDB file are needed. However, recall that you cannot use this technique on an MDB with a security scheme installed because there is no way to pass the authentication information.
- **Using the** `SqlDataSource` control to connect to Microsoft SQL Server, SSE or MSDE, where you use a connection string to pass the name of the server, the name of the database, and the user's ID and password. There is no need to designate a provider because the `SqlDataSource` control uses the provider for SQL Server as its default.

In this chapter, we move on to more complex examples that require more exact specifications for how to connect to the database, such as naming a provider.

The terminology in this chapter can be confusing. In particular, the terms *SQL* and *provider* are used by more than one layer of software and not always with the exact same meaning. The SQL language is widely used throughout the database world. Therefore, the term *sql* shows up in many places and names. The definition is not always the same and causes problems for many students. Keep in mind that the *sql* in *SqlDataSource* control is not specific for Microsoft SQL Server. It means that the control is usable with any data source that can understand the SQL language. More specifically, it can connect to any database that is represented by a managed data provider. A data provider is a set of APIs that enable connecting to a specific type of database back end. This chapter demonstrates using the `SqlDataSource` control with Access, Oracle, MySQL, and Excel.

> **The *sql* in *SqlDataSource* control means a SQL-enabled source of data, not necessarily Microsoft SQL Server.**

Understanding the Relationship between Layers of Connectivity Software

Before looking at new kinds of connections, let's consider some theory. It would be wonderful if Microsoft and third parties offered sets of data source controls that automatically connected directly to each kind of database, with no other intermediate software. Unfortunately, we are not there yet for technical, business, and historical reasons. Instead, we have a stack of several layers of software. The commands and data pass through these layers between the data store and the ASP.NET 2.0 page.

The essential point here is to understand the layers of software through which requests or values are passed between your rendered ASPX page and the tables in the database. When reading data, requests will be passed down from the ASPX page to the database, and values will be passed up from the database to the ASPX page. The topmost layer (the ASPX page) is the highest level and most abstract. The lowest layer (lowest in the following list) represents the values in the database.

The following layers of software and code are used to work with data on an ASPX page:

- **ASP.NET (.ASPX) page:** The highest level, this layer is the template used to build the HTML sent to the browser. The page is saved with a `.aspx` extension and contains two types of

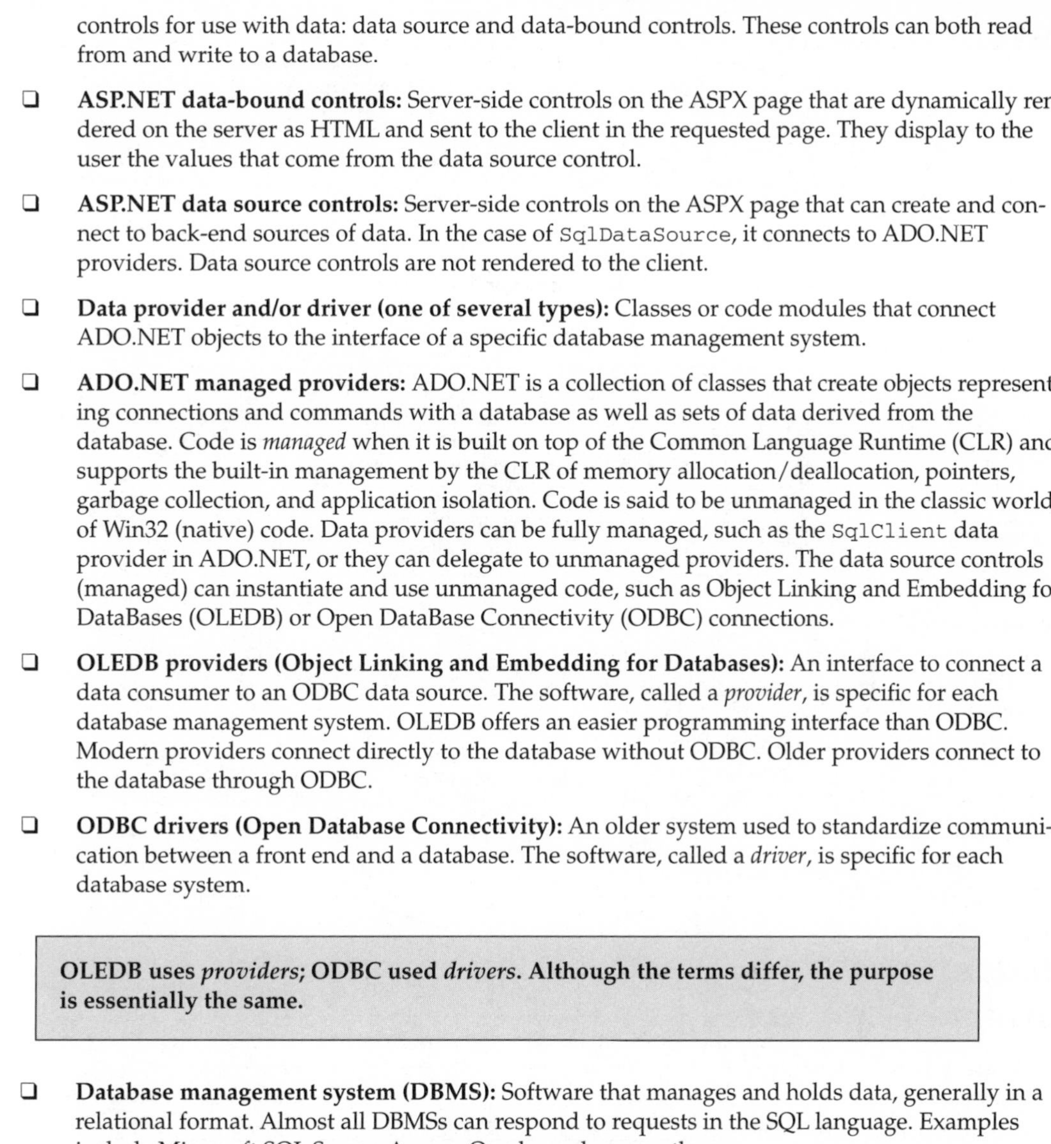

controls for use with data: data source and data-bound controls. These controls can both read from and write to a database.

- **ASP.NET data-bound controls:** Server-side controls on the ASPX page that are dynamically rendered on the server as HTML and sent to the client in the requested page. They display to the user the values that come from the data source control.
- **ASP.NET data source controls:** Server-side controls on the ASPX page that can create and connect to back-end sources of data. In the case of `SqlDataSource`, it connects to ADO.NET providers. Data source controls are not rendered to the client.
- **Data provider and/or driver (one of several types):** Classes or code modules that connect ADO.NET objects to the interface of a specific database management system.
- **ADO.NET managed providers:** ADO.NET is a collection of classes that create objects representing connections and commands with a database as well as sets of data derived from the database. Code is *managed* when it is built on top of the Common Language Runtime (CLR) and supports the built-in management by the CLR of memory allocation/deallocation, pointers, garbage collection, and application isolation. Code is said to be unmanaged in the classic world of Win32 (native) code. Data providers can be fully managed, such as the `SqlClient` data provider in ADO.NET, or they can delegate to unmanaged providers. The data source controls (managed) can instantiate and use unmanaged code, such as Object Linking and Embedding for DataBases (OLEDB) or Open DataBase Connectivity (ODBC) connections.
- **OLEDB providers (Object Linking and Embedding for Databases):** An interface to connect a data consumer to an ODBC data source. The software, called a *provider*, is specific for each database management system. OLEDB offers an easier programming interface than ODBC. Modern providers connect directly to the database without ODBC. Older providers connect to the database through ODBC.
- **ODBC drivers (Open Database Connectivity):** An older system used to standardize communication between a front end and a database. The software, called a *driver*, is specific for each database system.

> **OLEDB uses *providers*; ODBC used *drivers*. Although the terms differ, the purpose is essentially the same.**

- **Database management system (DBMS):** Software that manages and holds data, generally in a relational format. Almost all DBMSs can respond to requests in the SQL language. Examples include Microsoft SQL Server, Access, Oracle, and many others.
- **Database:** A set of information within the DBMS that is related to a single topic. The information is organized into tables containing rows (records) and columns (fields). Tables depend upon each other through a set of relationships.

We can see this graphically in Figure 4-1 for reading data. When an ASPX page requests data, the request flows from the data-bound control through the data source control to a managed data provider and then down to the database management system (possibly going through additional OLEDB and/or ODBC layers). The data is then gathered by the DBMS and passed up through the ODBC and/or OLEDB layers, through the provider layer, and through the data source control. It is then displayed on the page by the data-bound control.

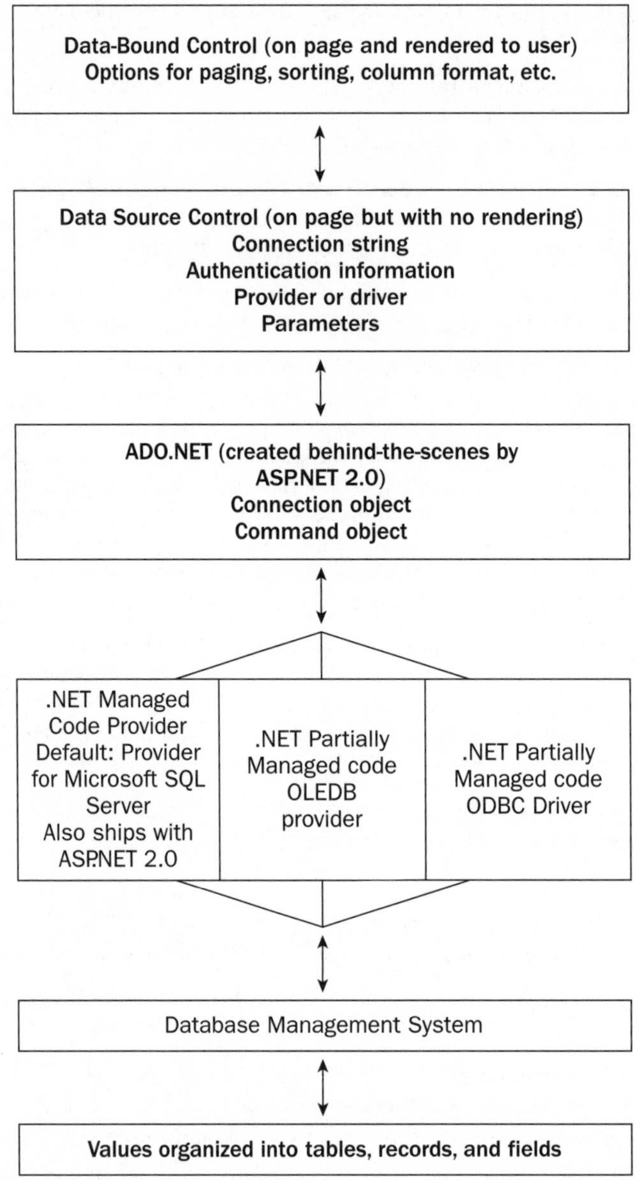

Figure 4-1

Looking at Figure 4-1, we can follow the request for data flows from the data-bound control down through the stack to the data store. Then the data values are passed back up through the stack. Note that there are three options in the ADO.NET layer, depending on the combinations of providers and drivers used. This chapter focuses on the OLEDB provider and ODBC driver layers of the stack. The provider translates between the specific protocol of the DBMS and the general protocol of the ODBC or OLEDB layers.

Understanding Supported ADO.NET Providers

Microsoft wrote four managed ADO.NET providers and included them with the .NET Framework 2.0. Microsoft may support additional providers in the future, as will third parties. These providers can be divided into two groups:

- **Native fully managed providers:** Contain managed code optimized for one data source. They connect directly to the database.
  - **SqlClient provider:** Designed for the Microsoft SQL Server. This is the default provider for `SqlDataSource`, so we did not have to specify it in our examples in Chapter 2.
  - **Oracle provider:** Designed for the Oracle database. Note that other parties may publish their own versions of an Oracle provider in the future.
- **Partially managed providers:** Contain managed code that delegates control to a native (unmanaged) provider or driver to do the actual work of connecting to the database. A partially managed provider can't function on its own; there must also be a native provider or driver installed on the machine. The native provider can come from the vendor of the database (such as `www.MySQL.com` or `www.SAP.com`), from Microsoft, or from a third party.
  - **OLEDB provider:** Delegates to a native OLEDB provider.
  - **ODBC Provider:** Delegates control to an ODBC driver.

Although they have similar names, do not confuse the providers (for example, `SqlClient`*) with the data source controls (for example,* `SqlDataSource`*). Data source controls read from the ADO.NET object at a higher level in the information stack. Alternatively,* `XmlDataSource` *and* `ObjectDataSource` *(discussed later in the book) normally do not use ADO.NET.*

Using ADO.NET Providers in ASP.NET 2.0

All of the code for using providers resides within the `SqlDataSource` control on the ASPX page. The `ProviderName` property of a `SqlDataSource` control specifies an ADO.NET provider that is registered under the `<DbProviderFactories>` config section in `machine.config` (located in `\WINDOWS\Microsoft.NET\ Framework\<version>\CONFIG`). The syntax when using providers is a bit tricky for three reasons:

- The `ProviderName` property for each `SqlDataSource` control has a default, which means that in some cases the properties do not have to be set at all (as in the Chapter 3 examples).
- The syntax of specifying a provider uses terms, such as `SQL`, that are used at different levels with different meanings.
- The syntax within a `ProviderName` varies for different providers.

Keeping in mind these pitfalls, we will organize the syntax in ways that are easy to remember.

When connecting to a data source through a provider, you need to perform three or five steps (the extra two are for the OLEDB and ODBC partially managed providers that require the additional native provider).

1. When using the OLEDB or ODBC providers, install the native provider or driver for the database you are using. The most common providers (including SQLOLEDB and JET) are typically already installed on the system from your installation of SSE or Access.
2. In VWD, add to the page a `SqlDataSource` control.
3. Set the `ProviderName` property of the `SqlDataSource` to one of the four providers previously listed (`System.Data.SqlClient`, `System.Data.OracleClient`, `System.Data.OleDb`, or `System.Data.Odbc`).
4. Create the connection string with values such as `Server`, `Database`, `UserID`, and so on.
5. When using the OLEDB or ODBC provider, add to the connection string the name of the native provider or driver to use. The syntax for each native provider or driver is slightly different and should be described in the documentation for that native provider.

Visual Web Developer makes these steps easier when you configure a data source control using the Provider tab of the Server Explorer Connection Dialog. We will look at the resulting specific syntax momentarily.

As a review from Chapter 3, the syntax for connecting to a Microsoft SQL Server database follows. Note that we are using the `System.Data.SqlClient` provider, which is the default `ProviderName` in the `SqlDataSource` control, so there is no reference to providers.

```
<asp:SqlDataSource ID="NorthwindProductsSqlDataSource"  Runat="server"
 ConnectionString="Data Source=.\SQLEXPRESS;
        AttachDbFilename=|DataDirectory|\Northwind.mdf;
        Integrated Security=True;
        User Instance=True"
SelectCommand="Select * FROM [Employees]"/>

"
```

The preceding code, using a default, is the same as the following code, which is explicit for the same provider.

```
<asp:SqlDataSource ID="NorthwindProductsSqlDataSource"  Runat="server"
ConnectionString=
          "Data Source=.\SQLEXPRESS;
        AttachDbFilename=|DataDirectory|\Northwind.mdf;
        Integrated Security=True;
        User Instance=True"
ProviderName=System.Data.SqlClient
SelectCommand="SELECT * FROM MyTable" />
```

If you want to use the Oracle managed provider supplied with the framework, you have to specify the `ProviderName`, as follows. Note here that the `sql` in `SqlDataSource` refers to connecting to a database that can understand the SQL language. It does not necessarily mean a connection to Microsoft SQL Server (or MSDE or SSE). The following code is broken to several lines to make it easier for you to read. When it is used in your site, you should have the value of the `ConnectionString` property on one line.

```
<asp:SqlDataSource ID="MyOracleSqlDataSource"  Runat="server"
 ProviderName=System.Data.OracleClient
```

```
        ConnectionString=
          "Data Source=MyOracleServer;
          User ID=MyID;
          Password=MyPassword;
          Integrated Security=SSPI"
    SelectCommand=" ... />
```

Note that the preceding two cases used fully managed providers (`SqlClient` and `Oracle`), so providing the name of a native provider in the connection string wasn't necessary.

When using the OLEDB or ODBC providers, you must specify a native provider that will actually do the work, because these providers just delegate the provider tasks to a native provider. For example, if you wanted to use a native provider for Microsoft SQL Server from a third party, say AcmeDev, you would specify your `ProviderName` as the generic OLEDB, and then in the connection string, you would provide the name of the native provider from `AcmeDev`, as follows:

```
<asp:SqlDataSource ID="MyAcmeSqlDataSource"  Runat="server"
  ProviderName=System.Data.OleDb
  ConnectionString=
          "Provider=AcmeDev.MsSqlServerProvider.OLEDB.1.2.3;
          Server=MySqlServer;
          User ID=MyUSer;
          Password=MyPass;"
  SelectCommand="SELECT * FROM MyTable"/>
```

The same two-part syntax is used for an ODBC driver from a third party. Suppose that you have an ODBC driver for Excel from AcmeDev. You specify your `ProviderName` as the generic ODBC, and then in the connection string, you provide the name of the native driver from `AcmeDev`, as follows. Note the peculiarity here in that you use the same `ProviderName` property even though you end up using an ODBC driver.

```
<asp:SqlDataSource ID="MyBonzoExcelDataSource"  Runat="server"
  ProviderName="System.Data.ODBC"
  ConnectionString=
          "Driver=AcmeDev.ExcelDriver.ODBC.4.5.6;
          FieldName=MySheet.xls;"
  SelectCommand="JanuaryRange "/>
```

Overall, keep the following points in mind:

- The `SqlDataSource` can connect to any managed data provider that is registered in `machine.config` under the section `<system.data><DbProviderFactories>`.
- The .NET Framework includes four built-in ADO.NET providers: `SqlClient`, `OLEDB`, `ODBC`, and `Oracle`.
- You can specify which provider the `SqlDataSource` uses by setting the `ProviderName` property to the fully qualified name of the provider, for example, `System.Data.SqlClient` or `System.Data.OleDb`. Note that these names are case-sensitive and must be typed exactly as they appear in `machine.config`.

- The `SqlClient` provider is the default provider used by `SqlDataSource` when the `ProviderName` property is not specified.
- When using the OLEDB or ODBC providers, the connection string must contain an additional specification of the underlying native provider to use for connecting to your specific database system. Additionally, the native provider or driver must be installed on the machine.

Connecting to an Access MDB File When a Password Is Used

We used Access MDB files in many examples in Chapter 2. Recall that we did not have to get involved in connection strings or providers; we just used the `AccessDataSource` control and gave the path and name of the MDB file. But also recall that we left you with the caveat that this would not work with an Access database that had a security scheme.

The problem is simple: When using the `AccessDataSource` control, there is no property (or underlying mechanism) for sending a user ID or password. The reason is that Microsoft wants to encourage storing sensitive data (such as usernames and passwords) in the `web.config` file, where it can be properly secured and encrypted. This option is enabled by using the `SqlDataSource` control (with the OLEDB provider) to connect to secured Access database. The credentials can be specified as part of the connection string, and this connection string can be stored in `web.config`. We discussed placing connections strings in the `web.config` file in Chapter 3.

> **This is not a book on Access. Make sure that you thoroughly understand Access security before installing a security scheme. We suggest that you make a backup of the unsecured MDB until you know that your security protocol is working. Security rules applied in Access can be irreversible and might even require a reinstall of the software.**

It seems odd to work with an Access MDB file using a `SqlDataSource`, but the AccessDataSource is designed for the simplest connection. If we want to pass authentication information, we must move up to the capabilities of the more sophisticated `SqlDataSource` and treat Access as any other SQL-enabled data management system. (As an aside, the `AccessDataSource` object is actually derived from the `SqlDataSource` object. So, in context of how the ASP.NET 2.0 classes were written, using the `SqlDataSource` to talk to an Access MDB, it is not as big a jump as might appear.)

If an Access security scheme has been established for your MDB file, you must use a connection technique that allows relaying login information in the connection string. There are four differences from the technique used in Chapter 2 to connect to an MDB file. You must:

- Use a `SqlDataSource` control (instead of `AccessDataControl` techniques used in Chapter 2).
- Use the partially managed OLEDB provider and the native JET provider (instead of default providers for the `AccessDataSource`).

- ❑ Include the UserID and Password attributes in the connection string (not needed in simpler Ch02 solutions).
- ❑ In some cases, include the name of the workgroup security file (not needed in Chapter 2).

There are two types of security for Access. One is a simple database password that is global for all users and can be specified using Tools⇨Security⇨Set Database Password in Access. For this configuration, simply include the Database Password attribute in the connection string and keep the connection string in the web.config file as follows; the line breaks have been added for clarity in this text. (We will discuss the code on the actual ASPX page in the next section.)

```
<add name="NorthwindConnectionString"
ConnectionString="Provider=Microsoft.Jet.OLEDB.4.0;
Data Source=|DataDirectory|\MyFileWithPassword.mdb;"
Persist Security Info=True;
Database Password=MyPasswordForTheDatabase;
providerName="System.Data.OleDb" />
```

Access also offers user-level security, which allows the definition of users and assigns to them permissions for specific objects in the database. To configure this type of security, run through the User-Level Security Wizard in Access to create a workgroup information file. This file defines the users and permissions that are valid for a given database (or optionally all databases). Once this workgroup file has been created in Access, switch to Visual Web Developer and specify the path to the workgroup file as a Jet OLEDB:System Database attribute in the connection string, along with the specific credentials (User ID and Password) used to connect to the database, as follows (again, this is for the web.config file). Note that both the data MDB file and the associated security file extended with .MDW are defined in the string. As in other connection string listings, this would all be on one line on the actual site.

```
<add name="NorthwindConnectionString"
ConnectionString="Provider=Microsoft.Jet.OLEDB.4.0;
  Data Source=|DataDirectory|\MyFileWithPassword.mdb;
Persist Security Info=True;
User ID=MyUserId;
Password=MyPassword;
Jet OLEDB:System Database='|DataDirectory|\Security.mdw' "
providerName="System.Data.OleDb" />
```

Trick: Although the web.config section is called <connectionStrings>, a given "connection string" can hold more information then just the connection string proper. In our case, it can also hold the name of a provider. This name is inside the <add> tag but outside the connection string proper.

Now that we have a connection string created in the web.config file we can turn our attention to the ASPX page. Instead of the AccessDataSource we used in Chapter 2, we will use a SqlDataSource as covered in Chapter 3, as follows:

```
<asp:SqlDataSource ID="SqlDataSource1" Runat="server"
    ConnectionString="<%$ ConnectionStrings:NorthWindConnectionString %>"
    SelectCommand=" ... ">
</asp:SqlDataSource>
```

> **Again, this is not a text on setting up a security scheme in Access, but if a scheme exists, you can connect to the file as described in the preceding paragraphs.**

One additional trap can crop up with Access. The site must have the security rights to use the Access file. During development this is usually not a problem, since the user of VWD, Access and the development server is the same — the person logged in to Windows. But at deployment the site changes to using IIS and then the "user" becomes an account named ASPNET, and that user may not have rights to the MDB file or its folder. Therefore, using standard Windows user management, the administrator of the deployed site must give read and/or write permissions for the ASPNET process to use the MDB file.

Try It Out Connecting to an Access MDB with a Password

Prior to adding a security scheme to Access, you should understand the database security theory. A security scheme can prevent you from using data in an MDB file or even opening any MDB file from Access. The consequences of a mistake are reduced if you use an installation of Access on a separate machine that is not used for a production MDB.

1. In your `C:\Websites\BegAspNEt2Db\App_Data` folder, create a copy of `Northwind` named `NorthwindPass.mdb`. In Access 2003, open `NorthWindPass` for exclusive use, as follows. Click File⇨Open, and navigate to the `C:\Websites\BegAspNet2Db\App_Data` folder. Single-click on `NorthWindPass`. Observe that in the lower-right corner the Open button now has a drop-down option. Expand the Open button, and click on Open Exclusive. Add a password by clicking Tools⇨Security⇨Set Database Password. We will use `north56wind`. Close the MDB file and reopen it to check that the password is required. Close `NorthWindPass.MDB` and close Access.
2. Add a connection string to the `web.config` file, as follows:

```
<connectionStrings>
     <add name="MdbNorthwindPassword"
                providerName="System.Data.OleDb"
                connectionString="Provider='Microsoft.Jet.OLEDB.4.0';
                Data Source="|DataDirectory|\NorthwindPass.mdb"
                Persist Security Info=True;
                Database Password=north56wind"
     />
</connectionStrings>
```

3. Create a folder named `C:\Websites\BegASpNet2DB\ch04`, and in it a page named `TIO-0401-MdbWithPassword.ASPX`. In Source view, add a `SqlDataSource` control (not an `AccessDataSource`), and connect it to the nascent connection string in the `web.config`. You will be prompted for the MDB password. Set the select command to read the `Customer ID` and Name from the Customers table. You will be prompted again for the password. Add a `GridView` that displays the values.

```
<body>
    <form id="form1" runat="server">
    <div>
        <asp:SqlDataSource ID="SqlDataSource1" Runat="server"
         ConnectionString="<%$ connectionStrings:MdbNorthwindPassword %>"
         SelectCommand="SELECT  CustomerID, Name FROM Customers">
```

```
            </asp:SqlDataSource>

            <asp:GridView ID="GridView1" Runat="server"
            DataSourceID="SqlDataSource1"
            AutoGenerateColumns=true
            >
            </asp:GridView>
        </div>
        </form>
    </body>
```

4. Save the page, which should be similar to the preceding, and view it in your browser.

How It Works

In this example, you have four key changes in the data source control compared with the no-password examples of Chapter 2.

Start with your focus on the `web.config` file. The default provider for `SqlDataSource` is for Microsoft SQL Server, so you must override the default by specifying an alternate provider. In this case, you are using the generic OLEDB provider by setting a parameter within the <add> tag (but outside the actual connection string).

```
providerName="System.Data.OleDb"
```

Second, you are using a generic provider (OLEDB). That means it just delegates the work to a native provider. Therefore, inside the connection string, you must specify which native provider will actually do the work.

```
connectionString="
  Provider=Microsoft.Jet.OLEDB.4.0;
```

Last, you provide the usual values needed for a connection string, including the path and name of the MDB, the user ID, and password.

```
            Data Source=|DataDirectory|\NorthwindPass.mdb
    Persist Security Info=True;
    Database Password=north56wind"
```

You finish in the actual ASPX page. To do this, you need to pass authentication credentials and that requires a connection string. `AccessDataSource` does not support a connection string, so instead we use `SqlDataSource`.

```
<asp:SqlDataSource . . .
```

Other than those four points of syntax, the connection is the same as in Chapters 2 and 3. Note that you are prompted twice or more during use of the data source control setup wizards. These checks arise when VWD is attempting to read information such as the names of its fields, from the database in order to build the wizard pages.

Try It Out — Connecting to an MDB File with Workgroup Security

Now, we will set up an Access MDB file that employs user-level security and connect to it with an ASPX page.

1. Start in Windows Explorer where you make a copy of: `C:\Websites\BegAspNet2Db\App_Data\Northwind.mdb` and name it `NorthwindWorkgroup.mdb`. Open the new file in Access 2003. Click on Tools⇨Security⇨User-Level Security Wizard and go through the steps, as follows:

    a. Create a new workgroup file, click Next, accept the WID, and make the workgroup information file the default workgroup file, and click Next again.

    b. Allow verification of all objects, click Next, add the Full Data Users group to your file, and click Next again.

    c. Do not grant rights to the Users group and click Next. Add a new user named `aspxpage` with the password `north78wind` and be sure to click the "Add this user to list" button, and then click Next.

    d. Drop down the list of "Group or user names" to select `aspxpage`, and then turn on the checkbox next to Full Data Users. Click Next and Finish.

    You can save and print the security setup report, but it is not needed for this exercise.

2. Test your security scheme by closing the MDB and closing Access and then opening `NorthwindWorkgroup` and supplying the `aspxpage` and `north78wind` credentials. Close Access.

3. Switch to VWD, open `web.config` and add a connection string as follows:

```
<add name="MdbNorthwindWorkgroup"
connectionString="Provider='Microsoft.Jet.OLEDB.4.0';
 Data Source='C:\WebSites\BegAspNet2Db\App_Data\NorthwindWorkGroup.mdb';
 Persist Security Info=True;
 User ID=aspxpage;
 Password=north78wind;
 Jet OLEDB:System Database=|DataDirectory|\Security.mdw"
providerName="System.Data.OleDb" />
```

4. Create a file named `TIO-0402-MdbWorkgroup.aspx`. Add a `SqlDataSource` that uses the `AccessNorthwindWorkgroup` connection string from the `web.config` file. Add a `GridView` that displays the information, as follows:

```
<%@ Page Language="VB" %>
<!DOCTYPE html PUBLIC "-//W3C//DTD XHTML 1.1//EN"
"http://www.w3.org/TR/xhtml11/DTD/xhtml11.dtd">
<script runat="server">
</script>
<html xmlns="http://www.w3.org/1999/xhtml" >
<head runat="server">
    <title>Ch04-Tio0402-MdbWithWorkgroup</title>
</head>
<body>
    <h2>Chapter 04 Tio #2 Mdb With Workgroup</h2>
    <form id="form1" runat="server">
    <div>
```

```
      <asp:SqlDataSource ID="SqlDataSource1" runat="server"
             ConnectionString="<%$ ConnectionStrings:AccessNorthwindWorkgroup %>"
             ProviderName="<%$
ConnectionStrings:AccessNorthwindWorkgroup.ProviderName %>"
             SelectCommand=
"SELECT [ProductID], [ProductName] FROM [Alphabetical List of Products]">
      </asp:SqlDataSource>

        <asp:GridView ID="GridView1" Runat="server"
        DataSourceID="SqlDataSource1"
        AutoGenerateColumns=true
        >
        </asp:GridView>
    </div></form></body></html>
```

5. Save the code and test it in your browser.

How It Works

Recall that Access 2003 supports two types of security schemes. This Try It Out demonstrated the simple password. The Try It Out employs the scheme where users and groups are created and then given specific rights. These credentials are stored (encrypted, of course) in a file named `Security.mdw`. After making a working copy of `Northwind` named `NorthWindWorkgroup`, you went through the Security Wizard. This is not a text on Access security, but if you follow the preceding steps, you will end up with a new user named `aspxpage` with the password `north78wind` that is in the group of Full Data Users.

Next, you added a connection string in the `web.config` that was different from the first Try It Out in this chapter in three ways. First, you specified the username. Second, you set the `Password` property to refer to the specific user's password, not the general database password, as in the last exercise. Third, you specified the location of the security file.

Back in the ASPX page, you have little to do. Recall that you use a `SqlDataSource` instead of the `AccessDataSource` so that you can specify the OLEDB provider that can pass credentials. Then you just specify the correct connection string from the `web.config` file.

But, as we have warned, Access has a number of problems for a publicly deployed database. A far better choice is Microsoft SQL Server. Alternatively, you may have to connect to an Oracle database, as we will discuss next.

Connecting to Oracle Database

Oracle Database is one of the most widely used databases in business. If you work in a medium to large organization, you will probably have to obtain at least some of your site's data from Oracle Database.

Oracle Database can understand the SQL language, so you can connect with the `SqlDataSource` control. That control's provider, by default, is for Microsoft SQL Server, so you will have to override the default with one of the three other providers that ship with ASP.NET 2.0. Although you could use the generic OLEDB provider, it is more efficient to use the fully managed native Oracle provider written by Microsoft.

Keep in mind four points when writing up the code or clicking through the VWD designer:

1. Use a `SqlDataSource` control because Oracle understands the SQL language.
2. In the data source control, set the `ProviderName` to `System.Data.OracleClient`.
3. Within the connection string, you do not need to specify a native provider because the Oracle fully managed provider already has the native component.
4. In the connection string, use `Data Source=Oracle8i;Integrated Security=SSPI`.

Then on the ASPX page, a typical data source control for Oracle follows:

```
<asp:SqlDataSource ID="SqlDataSource1"
ProviderName="System.Data.OracleClient"
ConnectionString="
  Data Source=Oracle8i;
  User ID=MyID;
  Password=MyPassword;
  Integrated Security=SSPI"
SelectCommand=" ... "
Runat="server" />
```

Connecting to MySQL

MySQL is a database management system popular with open source Web sites. Implementations are available to run on several operating systems, including Windows. The software is free for most uses from the `www.MySQL.com` site.

There are two ways to connect to a MySQL database.

- **ODBC driver:** This driver is officially supported by MySQL and available at `www.mysql.com/products/connector/odbc`.
- **OLEDB provider:** This provider is available for use with ASP.NET, but is not yet officially supported by ADO.NET. See the latest at `www.mysql.com/products/connector/net`. You can also check for new developments in MySQL connections at `www.dev.mysql.com`, `www.ByteFX.com`, and `www.CrLab.com`.

In this section, we will use the ODBC driver. Both the OLEDB and ODBC options use, on the ASPX page, the ASP.NET 2.0 `SqlDataSource` control.

Syntax for an ODBC Connection to MySQL

The ODBC technique requires the `SqlDataSource` to specify a `ProviderName=System.Data.Odbc` and a connection string, as follows. Notice that because we set the ProviderName to ODBC, we now use a `Driver = . . .` in the connection string (OLEDB uses a `Provider = . . .`).

```
<asp:SqlDataSource ID=...>
ProviderName="System.Data.Odbc"
ConnectionString=
 "Driver={MySQL ODBC 3.51 Driver};
```

```
server=MyServer;
database=MyDatabase;
uid=MyUserName;
password=MyPassword;
option=3"
```

The option setting is a sum value of various aspects of ODBC that are not implemented in this driver. A value of 3 denotes possible errors in the width of a column and the value for number of affected rows.

You can add a MySQL connection to your Database Explorer window to view the names of tables and fields. However, drag-and-drop of fields from a MySQL source in the Database Explorer to the ASPX page is not yet implemented. To add the MySQL connection:

1. Click Add to Database.
2. Click on the Provider icon and select .NET Framework Data Provider for ODBC.
3. While still in the Connection Properties dialog box, click the Connection icon, select Use Connection String, and enter the following:

```
Driver={MySQL ODBC 3.51 Driver}; server=localhost; option=3
```

4. Enter the UserID and Password in the provided textboxes.
5. Where asked to type the initial catalog, type the name of the database to use within the MySQL install.

Alternatively, you can use the VWD to guide you through the setup, albeit with a couple of catches: Drag a GridView to the page and for Choose Data Source select `<new data source>`.

1. Select the SQL Database and give it an ID. At the Choose Connection dialog box, click New.
2. Click the Provider icon and select ODBC.
3. Click the Connection icon, and enter the same connection string as the last paragraph, the user ID, password, and initial catalog (database).
4. Test if desired, and then click OK to see that your connection is now `ODBC.localhost via TCP/IP.mysql`.
5. Click Next and give the connection a name for the `web.config` file. Be prepared for some error messages at this time. The third-party driver for SQL does not support display of tables at this point. You can click on Specify a Custom SQL and click Next to get a textbox to type your SQL statement.
6. In the test query dialog, you may get several error messages from the beta software, but the test results will appear. Click Finish, and the properties of the `GridView` and `SqlDataSource` will be built by VWD.

Try It Out Connecting to a MySQL Database

This exercise is optional and should be done only by readers intending to work with MySQL. We do not recommend installing MySQL if it is only for the purpose of this exercise. We do not lead you through the steps of creating a database in MySQL; we assume that you have a MySQL installation named `localhost` with a user named `root`. You will need to know the root account password.

1. Download MySQL ODBC Driver-MyODBC 3.51 from www.mysql.com/products/connector/odbc. Unzip the download, and execute the MyODBC-<version>.exe file. Accept the license agreement, and click OK to finish.

2. Create a new page in C:\Websites\BegAspNet2Db\ch04 named TIO-0403-Connection-MySql.aspx. Add a SqlDataSource, but do not click on Configure Data Source in the Smart Tasks panel. Switch to Source view, and type the following code. (Be sure to substitute your actual root password.) Note that the Set the SQL SELECT command to SELECT Host, User,Password,Create_priv FROM User that provides some information from the general User table that is in all installations of MySQL.

```
<asp:SqlDataSource ID="SqlDataSource1" Runat="server"
         ProviderName="System.Data.Odbc"
         ConnectionString= "DRIVER={MySQL ODBC 3.51 Driver};
                          SERVER=localhost;
                          DATABASE=mysql;
                          UID=root;
                          PASSWORD=MyRootPassword;
                          OPTION=3"
      SelectCommand="SELECT host, user, create_priv, password FROM user"
>
</asp:SqlDataSource>
```

3. Add a GridView that displays the values (accept the default of AutogenerateFields=true).

```
<%@ Page Language="VB" %>
<!DOCTYPE html PUBLIC "-//W3C//DTD XHTML 1.1//EN"
"http://www.w3.org/TR/xhtml11/DTD/xhtml11.dtd">
<script runat="server">
</script>
<html xmlns="http://www.w3.org/1999/xhtml" >
<head runat="server">
    <title>Ch04-TIO-0403-ConnectionToMySql</title>
</head>
<body>
Chapter 04 TIO #3 Connection to mySql
    <form id="form1" runat="server">
    <div>
        <asp:GridView ID="GridView1" Runat="server"
            DataSourceID="SqlDataSource1">
        </asp:GridView>

        <asp:SqlDataSource ID="SqlDataSource1" Runat="server"
         ProviderName="System.Data.Odbc"
         ConnectionString= "DRIVER={MySQL ODBC 3.51 Driver};
                          SERVER=localhost;
                          DATABASE=mysql;
                          UID=root;
                          PASSWORD=MyRootPassword;
                          OPTION=3"
      SelectCommand="SELECT host, user, create_priv, password FROM user"
      >
        </asp:SqlDataSource>
    </div>
```

```
    </form>
</body>
</html>
```

4. Save the code and view it in the browser. You should see four data items for each user in the MySQL administrative database.

How It Works

This technique starts with installing a special ODBC driver for MySQL. Then, on the page, you can employ the `SqlDataSource` with the specification of a `ProviderName` (the generic ODBC provider) and a connection string. In the connection string, you specify the driver you installed for MySQL. The other connection string values are similar to those used with SSE in Chapter 3. The exception is the `Option=3` setting that warns the programmer of shortcomings in this combination of driver and client.

ASP.NET 2.0's `SqlDataSource` control allows connection to any set of information that supports ODBC or OLEDB. For example, in the following case, we will read data from a spreadsheet instead of a database.

Connecting to Excel

The JET engine that we used for Access is also able to connect to an Excel spreadsheet if we add an `Extended Property`, which identifies that we will be using Excel, version 8.0 or higher. For the examples below we will use the following spreadsheet stored as `Fruits.xls`. The shaded range has been given the `RangeName` of `LowerHalf`.

Name	Qty	Color
apple	11	red
banana	22	yellow
current	33	purple
durian	44	Green

To make a connection, we use the `System.Data.OleDb` provider with the JET provider in the connection string. As always, it is better to keep connection strings all on one line in your actual project, but in the following we have added line breaks to make it easier to read.

```
<asp:SqlDataSource ID="SqlDataSource1" runat="server"
            ConnectionString="Provider=Microsoft.Jet.OLEDB.4.0;
                Data Source=C:\MyPath\MyExcelFile.xls;
                Extended Properties='Excel 8.0' "
            ProviderName="System.Data.OleDb"
            SelectCommand="SELECT * FROM [sheet1$]">
</asp:SqlDataSource>
```

If your XLS file is the App_Data folder of your site, you can refer to it with the following syntax:

```
ConnectionString="... Data Source=|DataDirectory|MyExcelFile.xls; ... "
```

You can specify if row one contains headers instead of actual values, as follows. When this HDR value is set to yes then your row one values will become the field names. If it is set to no, then your field names will be F1, F2, and so on.

```
Extended Properties='Excel 8.0';HDR=Yes"
Extended Properties='Excel 8.0';HDR=No"
```

When selecting for specific columns (as opposed to using * for all columns) because you must refer to the columns as dictated by the HDR value as in the two samples below. However, the lower sample will return the first row of the worksheet as if it were an actual record holding values.

```
<asp:SqlDataSource ID="SqlDataSource1" runat="server"
            ConnectionString="Provider=Microsoft.Jet.OLEDB.4.0;
                Data Source=|DataDirectory|Fruits.xls;
                Extended Properties='Excel 8.0';HDR=yes"
            ProviderName="System.Data.OleDb"
            SelectCommand="SELECT Name, Color FROM [sheet1$]">
</asp:SqlDataSource>

<asp:SqlDataSource ID="SqlDataSource1" runat="server"
            ConnectionString="Provider=Microsoft.Jet.OLEDB.4.0;
                Data Source=|DataDirectory|Fruits.xls;
                Extended Properties='Excel 8.0';HDR=no "
            ProviderName="System.Data.OleDb"
            SelectCommand="SELECT F1,F3 FROM [sheet1$]">
</asp:SqlDataSource>
```

WHERE clauses in the SelectCommand work fine and are no different from other data sources.

You can drill down to less then a sheet in two ways. First, use Excel to create named ranges in your workbook. You can then refer to a range (for example, LowerHalf) as in the first example below. Alternatively, you can provide the address of a range of cells as in the second example below. However, be careful when using addresses with the HDR=yes property because the first row of the range will be considered field names.

```
            SelectCommand="SELECT * FROM LowerHalf">
            SelectCommand="SELECT * FROM [Sheet1$B2:D4]">
```

Last, you can also connect using ODBC like we did to MySQL, as follows:

```
"Driver={Microsoft Excel Driver
(*.xls)};DriverId=790;Dbq=C:\MyExcel.xls;DefaultDir=c:\mypath;"
```

Connecting to Other Databases

Many additional databases can serve as a source of values for ASPX pages. In general, you can connect to them using either ODBC (older and slower) or OLEDB (faster and more robust). Currently, almost every source of data has an ODBC driver that can be used with the `SqlDataSource` control. OLEDB providers will doubtlessly enter the market.

> **Use of XML formatted data is covered in Chapter 14.**

ODBC, the most universal of data access techniques, is strong when a single application needs to use data from different sources. But ODBC involves the most layers and, thus, provides lower performance. OLEDB, a native .NET provider, is much faster than ODBC. The managed code takes care of memory management and security. It is also easier to use syntax specific to your database management system. The disadvantage is that OLEDB is less widely used and may not work for all data sources for your site. You also have to wait until the final version of the .NET Framework 2.0 when third-party managed providers will be supported.

Searching the Web will yield information on new drivers and providers. For example, software developer Carl Prothman maintains many permutations of connection strings and links to drivers and providers at `www.able-consulting.com/ADO_Conn.htm`. I hope he will be expanding his samples to include connections for .NET 2.0.

Exploring Common Mistakes

The following lists include some common mistakes not covered in Chapters 2 and 3 that developers make when trying to connect to other sources of data.

- Confusing the *sql* part of various names. For the SqlDataSource control, the term means that the control works with any database that understands the SQL language.
- Attempting to use the `AccessDataSource` control for an MDB with a security scheme.
- Specifying a fully qualified path to an Access MDB file in the connection string. This prohibits deployment to another machine that may have a different drive or folder path structure. Use this syntax: `=|DataDirectory|\MyFileName.xxx`
- Using a partially managed provider (OLEDB or ODBC) without including a native provider in the connection string.
- Reversing the names of the providers. The partially managed provider (OLEDB or ODBC) goes in the `SqlDataSource` control's `ProviderName` property. The name of the native provider (for example, `Microsoft.Jet.OLEDB.4.0`) goes in the connection string's `Provider` setting.
- Not having the correct native provider installed for an OLEDB or ODBC connection.
- Not typing the name of a provider exactly as it appears in the Framework. Provider names are case-sensitive — for example, `System.Data.OleDb`, *not* `System.Data.OLEDB` or just `OLEDB`.
- Attempting to use a provider that is not registered in `machine.config` under `<system.data><DbProviderFactories>`.
- Using a syntax error when specifying the `Provider` attribute in an OLEDB or ODBC connection string. The syntax for each native provider differs slightly, so consult the provider's documentation to be sure of the required format.

- Using terminology from one DBMS in another, for example, confusing how the term *database* differs between Microsoft SQL Server and Oracle.
- Not using the correct SQL syntax for the particular database system you are using.

Summary

For connection to simple databases (Access with no password, Chapter 2) or the default database (Microsoft SQL Server, Chapter 3), you did not have to worry about providers. But for other connections, you must have a better understanding of the layers of software and know how to use providers. At the highest level of the stack sits the ASPX page that holds the data-bound controls and the data source controls. The data source controls create and use ADO.NET objects, which in turn talk to OLEDB providers and ODBC drivers. Providers and drivers translate from the standard OLEDB or ODBC protocol to the specific internals of the database management system.

Four providers come with the .NET 2.0 Framework. Two are written in managed code and are specific for Microsoft SQL Server DBMS and for Oracle. The other two are partially managed providers that can be used with any data source that has its own (native) provider or driver. These generics merely delegate the tasks to the native providers. For example, we saw how to download a native provider for MySQL that works with the partially managed `System.Data.Odbc` provider.

When you use a provider, you have to declare it in the `ProviderName` of the `SqlDataSource` control. If you are using a partially managed (generic) provider, you must also specify the native provider in the connection string. Be careful to avoid confusing these two provider properties. Below are the possibilities with a short reminder of their syntax.

The `SqlDataSource` control with default provider (Microsoft SQL Server, Access, Oracle):

```
<asp:SqlDataSource ...
ConnectionString= " ... "   />
```

The `SqlDataSource` control with nondefault managed provider (Access with passwords, third-party managed providers):

```
<asp:SqlDataSource
 ProviderName=System.Data.MyManagedProvider
 ConnectionString= " ... "   />
```

The `SqlDataSource` control with nondefault partially managed provider and native provider (OLEDB and ODBC):

```
<asp:SqlDataSource ID="MyAcmeSqlDataSource"  Runat="server"
 ProviderName=System.Data.MyPartiallyManagedProvider
 ConnectionString=
         "Provider=MyNativeProvider ...  "  />
```

When using an Access MDB file with a security scheme, you must understand the Access security model. If there is only a file password, you can simply add that to the connection string. If there is user-level security, you must specify the name and location of the security file as well as a username and password. The `AccessDataSource` cannot pass a connection string with the authentication information, so you must switch to using the `SqlDataSource` control.

We can also use the `SqlDataSource` with an OLEDB provider to connect to Excel. The unmanaged provider (within the connection string) is for JET, the same as for Access. The syntax to determine which cells to read is different from that of other sources. Particularly watch the `HDR` property that determines if the top line of the selection is composed of column headers or values.

Third parties are constantly developing providers, including fully managed providers. Keep alert to the sites for your specific database and when available and certified, use those providers instead of the partially managed solutions.

This brings to an end our first group of chapters. We have been focused on the general architecture of ASP.NET 2.0 and how to connect to three general classes of databases by using data source controls. Next we move to the second section of the book wherein we discuss how to display data to the user.

Exercises

1. Describe the major differences between connecting to an unsecured MDB file and a password-protected MDB file.
2. Name the two files specified in a connection string to an MDB with user-level security.
3. When setting up a MySQL, you are asked for the initial catalog. What does that mean in MySQL terminology?
4. Why didn't we specify a provider in Chapter 3 when connecting to Microsoft SQL Server?
5. Which data source control is used to connect to MySQL and Oracle?
6. In earlier versions of ASP.NET, it was necessary to instantiate ADO.NET classes. Why is this not necessary in ASP.NET 2.0?
7. What additional piece of software must be obtained to connect to a MySQL database?
8. Contrast the `Password` property of the connection string when used with an Access MDB file password security scheme and an Access workgroup security scheme.

Displaying Data in Tables

The last several chapters focused on creating a conduit for information between our page and a source of data. We have not discussed in detail the display of that data, using the same `GridView` of `Northwind` products in almost every example. With this chapter, you now enter a new section of the book (Chapters 5 to 10), wherein the focus is on how to make the display of data as effective as possible for your business goals. The `GridView` control remains the core of interest in this chapter; it is the most powerful of the data-bound controls in ASP.NET 2.0. You'll also look at its sibling, the `DetailsView` control, which presents data from one record at a time.

This chapter covers the following:

- Displaying data in ASP.NET 2.0
- An introduction to the `GridView` control
- Connecting a `GridView` to data
- Customizing the `GridView`'s columns
- The `DetailsView` control
- Common mistakes

Displaying Data in ASP.NET 2.0

To begin our discussion, we will start with a review of the general plan of how to display data in ASP.NET 2.0 and then examine the `GridView` data-bound control.

Review of Data-Bound and Data Source Controls

As previously discussed, the use of data in ASP.NET 2.0 pages relies on two types of controls. Data source controls provide a conduit for data between the page and the store of data, whereas data-bound controls display the data on the page. This entire section (Chapters 5 to 10) covers displaying data.

> **Modifying data (adding, changing, and deleting) is covered in the next block of chapters (Chapters 11 and 12).**

There are many ways to display data to a reader on a printed page. A Web page provides fewer options in layout, but they include tables, charts, lists, trees, and arrays of radio buttons and check boxes. ASP.NET 2.0 has controls for each of these formats as well as the ability for them to work with each other so that selection in a list can change which records are displayed in a table. Some data-bound controls can automatically take advantage of capabilities of the data source controls, including paging, sorting, editing, deleting, and inserting. If you are using Visual Web Developer (VWD) or Visual Studio (VS), most of the formatting and behavior can be set with drag-and-drop or property choices. But even if you are typing in Notepad, the tasks are easy.

Types of Data-Bound Controls

ASP.NET 2.0 offers the following data-bound controls:

- **GridView:** A tabular representation of multiple records and multiple fields that also offers the capacity to page, sort, change, and delete data. The `GridView` as a whole is covered in this chapter. (Formatting the `GridView` is covered in Chapter 6. Chapter 7 explains the techniques of paging and sorting in a `GridView`. Additional material is covered in Chapter 9 on Filtering and Master-Details.)
- **DetailsView:** A tabular representation of multiple fields from only one record at a time. Allows record navigation (paging), editing, deleting, and creating new records. The `DetailsView` control is discussed at the end of this chapter and further in Chapter 9.
- **FormView:** A control that renders a single data item at a time as a custom user-defined template (optionally containing other controls). Like `DetailsView`, `FormView` also allows record navigation (paging), editing, deleting, and creating new records. (`FormViews` are covered in Chapter 10.)
- **DataList and Repeater:** A tabular representation of multiple records and multiple fields from each record, generally with all the fields in a single space, not spread out with one value per cell. The fields are arranged within templates. The DataList will render all the fields of one record within one HTML cell. The `Repeater` does not render to an HTML table. (This topic is covered in Chapter 8.)
- **TreeView and Menu:** Hierarchical presentations of data in an expandable/collapsible tree or menu. (Hierarchical data source and data-bound controls are discussed in Chapter 14.)
- **Selectable List Controls:** Controls for rendering lists of data values, usually displaying one data field and using another field for the underlying value of the list item. These include `DropDownList`, `ListBox`, `BulletedList`, `CheckBoxList`, and `RadioButtonList`. (This topic is covered in Chapter 8.)

It may come as a surprise not to see controls such as `Label` and `TextBox`, as used in earlier versions of ASP.NET. These are still available but are added into the template portions of one of the preceding controls. The concept and practice of templating are discussed in detail in Chapter 10.

Introduction to the GridView Control

The `GridView` control provides the fastest, easiest, and most feature-rich display of tabular data. If you are familiar with ASP.NET 1.*x*, the `GridView` control is the successor to the `DataGrid` control. The object model for `GridView` is essentially the same, but its principle advantage over `DataGrid` is the ability to automatically bind to a data source control and take advantage of sorting, paging, and modifying data through that control. As with other ASP.NET 2.0 controls, these tasks can be achieved with almost zero user code.

Capabilities of the GridView Control

Before delving into the details of using the `GridView`, let's quickly cover its capabilities. Each of these is discussed in detail over the next few chapters.

- **Displaying data:** Performs all tasks necessary to create an HTML table on the page.
- **Formatting data:** Supports formatting at the level of the entire grid, a column or a row. Furthermore, the GridView can display buttons, check boxes, links, or images, depending on the underlying data.
- **Paging data:** Automatically divides the entire set of records into smaller sets called *pages*. A page of records can be displayed along with navigation tools to move from page to page.
- **Sorting data:** Sorts data initially and then re-sorts data, as requested by the user, through a click on a column heading.
- **Updating data:** Supports changing a row of data by entering into an update mode. Changes from the user are sent back to modify the data in the underlying database.
- **Deleting data:** Directly deletes an entire record through a simple user interface.
- **Row selection:** Allows the user to select a row. That selection then becomes a parameter available to define the display of other controls.
- **Row navigation:** Displays links for each row that navigate to a separate page, with the option to pass information in the querystring.

Note that the `GridView` does not directly support the creation of new records (Inserting), but it can be used in conjunction with the `DetailsView` control to add a record to the data source.

When you consider the amount of coding it took to produce a similar set of functions in classic ASP (or even ASP.NET version 1.*x*), you can understand our enthusiasm about the `GridView` in ASP.NET 2.0.

GridView Rendering Elements

A `GridView` renders with eight kinds of rows, as described in the following table. Note that Selected Row, Edit Row, and Alternate Data Row are special designations assigned to one of the data rows.

Row	Description
Header Row	Single row that generally holds the name of each field displayed as a column header.
Data Row	Repeated rows holding field values with the basic formatting.
Alternate Data Row	Every other data row with an alternate formatting.
Selected Row	The one data row that has been selected.
Edit Row	The one data row that is being edited.
Footer Row	Single row that generally holds the name of each field as column footers. Useful in a tall table, where column headers may be scrolled out of view. This column can also be used to render column totals (requires custom code).
Pager Row	Single row that holds page navigation tools. Has no column dividers.
Empty Data Row	A single cell shown instead of the data rows if no records are provided by the data source control.

Connecting a GridView to Data

The key property of a `GridView` (beyond its own `ID` and `runat`) is the DataSourceID property, which determines the data source control that will provide the values. The `GridView` retrieves data from the data source and automatically generates a table on the page to display the values. You've already seen examples of the basic syntax in earlier chapters. The following code sample is available in the download as Ch05/Sample0501 GridView Simple.aspx.

```
<body>
    <form id="form1" runat="server">
    <div>

        <asp:GridView ID="GridView1" runat="server"
            DataSourceID="SqlDataSource1">
        </asp:GridView>

        <asp:SqlDataSource ID="SqlDataSource1" runat="server"
            ConnectionString="<%$ ConnectionStrings:MdfNorthwind %>"
            SelectCommand="SELECT * FROM [Products]">
        </asp:SqlDataSource>

    </div></form></body>
```

In this example, the `GridView` is automatically generating its columns at runtime based on the fields returned from the data source control. The `AutoGenerateColumns` property is set, by default, to `true`.

You can exercise much more control over how the data is displayed by setting additional properties of the GridView.

Drag and Drop Fields from Data Explorer

The VWD designer greatly accelerates the addition of GridView controls to the page. Recall from Chapter 1 that you can add a database to your Data Explorer window (Server Explorer in Visual Studio). You can then expand that database's tables to see the field names. Those field names can be selected and dragged to the page; then VWD will do all of the work to create a data source control and GridView to display the values. Depending on the type of connection, the data source is either a SqlDataSource or an AccessDataSource. Drag-and-drop sets a lot of properties on the GridView and data source to enable column reordering, automatic updates, inserts, and deletes (topics that are covered later). This chapter primarily focuses on displaying data, so in the following sections we'll create a GridView manually by dragging and dropping from the Toolbox and setting only those properties that we discuss.

Drag and Drop Controls from the Toolbox

When you drag a GridView from the Toolbox, the control starts out with only ID and runat properties. You can then customize additional properties of the GridView using the property grid, Source view, or the GridView's Smart Tasks panel in Design view.

Try It Out Basic GridView

In this exercise, you will add a GridView to the page and then use the Smart Tasks panel to create a data source control.

First, here is a reminder about the location of connection strings. Starting with Chapter 3 of this book, we have been using connections named MdfNorthwind and MdfPubs stored in the web.config file in the root of the application. If you did not create those connections, return to Chapter 3 and step through the Try It Out "Storing the Connection String in web.config." Alternatively, there is a sample web.config file in the downloadable files for this text. Your web.config file should already contain the following entries.

```
<connectionStrings>
    <add name="MdfNorthwind"
         connectionString="Server=.\SQLExpress;
         AttachDbFileName=|DataDirectory|\Northwind.mdf;
         Integrated Security=True;
         User Instance=true"
         ProviderName="System.Data.SqlClient" />
    <add name="MdfPubs"
         connectionString="Server=.\SQLExpress;
         AttachDbFileName=|DataDirectory|\Pubs.mdf;
         Integrated Security=True;
         User Instance=true"
         providerName="System.Data.SqlClient" />
</connectionStrings>
```

1. Create a new folder named ch05 and, within it, a new page named `TIO-0501-GridViewBasic_ver01.aspx`.

2. In Design view, drag and drop a `GridView` control from the Toolbox. Note that the Smart Tasks panel automatically opens. From the Choose Data Source drop-down list, select `<New Data Source>`.

3. VWD will walk you through the configuration for a data source control. In this case, you will select the SQL database type of source and choose the data connection named `MdfNorthwind`. Select all columns from the Products table (careful, do not choose "Alphabetical list of products") to display and then click Next, Test Query, and Finish.

4. Save your work and test the page in your browser. Note that you did not have to perform a separate step to create a data source control first; VWD created it behind the scenes as you started to walk through the wizard.

   The source code for your page will resemble the following:

```
<%@ Page Language="VB" %>
<html>
<head>
<title>TIO-0501-GridViewBasic_ver01.aspx</title>
 </head>
<body>
    <form id="form1" runat="server">
      <asp:GridView ID="GridView1"  Runat="server"
        DataSourceID="SqlDataSource1"
        AutoGenerateColumns="False" DataKeyNames="ProductID">
        <Columns>
            <asp:BoundField ReadOnly="True" HeaderText="ProductID"
InsertVisible="False" DataField="ProductID"
                SortExpression="ProductID"></asp:BoundField>
            <asp:BoundField HeaderText="ProductName" DataField="ProductName"
SortExpression="ProductName"></asp:BoundField>
            <asp:BoundField HeaderText="SupplierID" DataField="SupplierID"
SortExpression="SupplierID"></asp:BoundField>
            <asp:BoundField HeaderText="CategoryID" DataField="CategoryID"
SortExpression="CategoryID"></asp:BoundField>
            <asp:BoundField HeaderText="QuantityPerUnit"
DataField="QuantityPerUnit" SortExpression="QuantityPerUnit"></asp:BoundField>
            <asp:BoundField HeaderText="UnitPrice" DataField="UnitPrice"
SortExpression="UnitPrice"></asp:BoundField>
            <asp:BoundField HeaderText="UnitsInStock" DataField="UnitsInStock"
SortExpression="UnitsInStock"></asp:BoundField>
            <asp:BoundField HeaderText="UnitsOnOrder" DataField="UnitsOnOrder"
SortExpression="UnitsOnOrder"></asp:BoundField>
            <asp:BoundField HeaderText="ReorderLevel" DataField="ReorderLevel"
SortExpression="ReorderLevel"></asp:BoundField>
            <asp:CheckBoxField HeaderText="Discontinued"
SortExpression="Discontinued" DataField="Discontinued"></asp:CheckBoxField>
        </Columns>
      </asp:GridView>

      <asp:SqlDataSource ID="SqlDataSource1" Runat="server"
      ConnectionString="<%$ ConnectionStrings:MdfNorthwind %>"
```

```
        SelectCommand="SELECT * FROM [Products]"/>
    </form>
</body>
</html>
```

Try creating the same page in an even easier way.

1. Create a page named TIO-0501-GridViewBasic-ver02.aspx. Switch to Design view, if necessary.
2. View the Database Explorer window. Expand (local)\SQLExpress\Northwind and then Tables.
3. Drag the name of the Products table onto the page. Ignore the open Smart Tasks panel and run the page. VWD automatically created the correct SqlDataSource control with a pointer to the connection string in the web.config file.

Although this latter technique is very fast, it does introduce additional tags that are not covered until later in the text. You can take a look at the ASPX page in Source view, but don't be shocked by the amount of code.

How It Works

The Choose Data Source task of the GridView's Smart Tasks panel creates the data source control on the page and sets the DataSourceID property of the GridView control. The data source in this example has two properties set: ConnectionString and SelectCommand. The GridView creates asp:BoundField objects in its Columns collection, matching the fields selected by the data source. Unlike the first example, where the GridView automatically generated its columns at runtime using the fields from the data source, in this case, the GridView uses the bound fields to determine which of the fields from the data source to display. Notice that the AutoGenerateColumns property is set to False, which means that only fields defined in the Columns collection will be displayed.

In version two we used the absolute simplest step to get a GridView displayed on a page: one drag and drop. How much easier could Microsoft have made it? But if you peruse the source code, you will see that there are quite a few more tags and properties the VWD employs in order to handle various potential scenarios. By the end of this book, you will be very familiar with most of that code.

Although wizards are designed to make your work easier, there can be confusion when working your way through the steps of the wizards. One set of panels sets up the *data source control*. Within that wizard, a panel sets the *connection* for the data source control. If you are not using an existing connection (saved in web.config), then you will be routed through a second wizard that creates a new connection for you. Then you are returned to the remaining panels of the wizard to create the data source control.

Having created a basic GridView, we now want to modify the columns so that they meet more specific objectives.

Customizing the GridView's Columns

The preceding example showed how the `GridView` can explicitly define the fields included in its Columns collection instead of automatically generating columns at runtime. This section demonstrates the variety of column types that the `GridView` can display. The `GridView` displays columns in the order they are defined in the collection within the <Columns> tags. Note that the terms *columns* and *fields* are essentially interchangeable, but columns tends to refer to the final result in the `GridView` rendering, whereas fields tends to refer to the labels used in the data store.

Selecting Columns in the Edit Columns Dialog Box

VWD offers a handy tool for adding, moving, and deleting columns from a `GridView`. On the control's Smart Tasks panel, click Edit Columns. In the lower-left corner, there is a check box to turn the AutoGenerateColumns feature on or off. When defining column fields in this dialog box, the AutoGenerateColumns feature should usually be turned off. At the top left are types of columns. To add a column, simply select a type and click Add. Then, on the right, you can set properties for the selected column. Note the up and down arrows that allow you to change a column's position as well as the X button that allows you to remove a column.

Types of Column Fields

ASP.NET 2.0 supports seven types of columns (fields), as follows:

- **Bound fields:** Show values from a field provided by the `DataSource` as a `Label`, or as a `TextBox` in edit mode
- **CheckBox fields:** Display a Boolean value as a checked or unchecked `CheckBox`
- **Button fields:** Give the user a clickable interface to run code the programmer writes
- **Command fields:** Allow the user to invoke one of three standard methods of the `GridView`: edit, delete, or select records
- **Hyperlink fields:** Allow the user to navigate to another page
- **Image fields:** Display a JPG, GIF, or other image file and (optionally) react to a user click on the image with a hyperlink to another page
- **Template fields:** Contain one or more controls within each cell as designed by the programmer in regards to layout, format, and data binding (see Chapter 10)

Bound Field

Bound fields will show data from a field delivered by the data source control. Which field to display is determined by the `DataField` property. Keep in mind that if an alias was assigned to a field in the data source control's `SelectCommand`, you must use that alias in the `BoundColumn.DataField`.

A tricky but useful attribute you can use is the `DataFormatString`. To format a number, you must enclose your specification within braces. Additional internal quotes are not required. Within the braces, you start with a zero and a colon (*0:*). This represents the first item of data within the field. Because you will show only one item of data per field, there is no need to use any value other than zero. After the colon, place a letter code for the format of the display followed by a number to set the number of decimal places. For example, a number with three decimal places could be formatted as follows:

```
<asp:BoundColumn ... DataFormatString="{0:F3}" ... >
```

The following table lists numeric data format options.

Letter Code	Format	Example	Result If Value Is 3.1416 and Windows Is Set to USA Conventions
C	Currency with currency sign	`{0:C2}`	$3.14 Note rounding
E	Exponential	`{0:E4}`	3.1416E+000
F	Fixed	`{0:F3}` Note rounding	3.142
G	General	`{0:G3}`	3.14 Same as currency but without symbol
P	Percent	`{0:P0}`	%314 (Value must be 0.0314 to get %3.14)

For dates and times, you can use the format codes listed in the following table:

Letter Code	Format Pattern (Picked Up from Windows Regional Options)	Example	Result If Value Is 14:23:45 on 13 January 2006 and Windows Is Set to USA Conventions
d (Lowercase d)	Short date pattern	`{0:d}`	1/13/2006
D (Uppercase D)	Long date pattern	`{0:D}`	Friday, January 13, 2006
t (Lowercase t)	Short time pattern	`{0:t}`	2:23 PM
T (Uppercase T)	Long time pattern and date	`{0:T}`	2:23:45 PM
F (Uppercase F)	Short time pattern and date	`{0:F}`	Friday, January 13, 2006 2:23:45 PM
m or M (Either case)	Month and day pattern	`{0:m}`	January 13
y or Y (Either case)	Year and month pattern	`{0:y}`	January 2006

Other options are available and described when you search in Visual Web Developer Help for "Formatting Overview," "Formatting Types," "Date and Time Format Strings," and "Numeric Format Strings."

Literal text can also be added to the format, as follows. Note that if you are using `DataFormatString`, you must turn off HTML encoding.

```
<asp:BoundColumn ...
         HtmlEncode="false"
         DataFormatString="My prefix {0:x} My suffix"
```

For example, if you wanted to make a note on a page that orders of Northwind will be delivered by the date in the `RequiredDate` field, you could use the following (full page available in download `Sample-0502-FormatWithLiteralText.ASPX`).

```
<asp:GridView ID="GridView1" runat="server"
    AutoGenerateColumns="False"
    DataSourceID="SqlDataSource1">
    <Columns>
    <asp:BoundField DataField="OrderID"
        HeaderText="OrderID" />
    <asp:BoundField DataField="RequiredDate"
         HtmlEncode="false"
         HeaderText="RequiredDate"
         DataFormatString="Delivery set for {0:D} or earlier"/>
    </Columns>
</asp:GridView>
```

CheckBox Field

A `CheckBoxField` binds to Boolean data and then automatically displays the results as the `Checked` value of a `CheckBox`. The most important attribute is the `DataField` that determines the linked field of the `GridView`'s `DataSource`. You must use add a field that is a Boolean or Bit data type. The `CheckBoxField` property can display a short text to the right of the check box. Note the `ReadOnly` property to protect data, which leaves the checkbox unchangeable. We will discuss features associated with writing data in Chapters 11 and 12.

```
<asp:GridView ID="GridView1" Runat="server"
   DataSourceID="SqlDataSource1"
  AutoGenerateColumns="False" >
  <Columns>
   ...
   <asp:CheckBoxField HeaderText="Discontinued"
   DataField="Discontinued" />
   ...
  </Columns>
</asp:GridView>
```

Try It Out — Bound Field and CheckBox Field Columns

In this exercise, you will display some fields from the Northwind Products table.

1. Start with a new page named `TIO-0502-BoundAndCheckBoxColumns-1.aspx`. Add a `SqlDataSource` control and configure to use the existing connection named `MdfNorthwind`. Specify the columns to come from the `Products` table and return all fields.

2. Drag a `GridView` to the page and, on the Smart Tasks panel, set the data source to the nascent `SqlDataSource1` control created in Step 1. Continuing in the Smart Tasks panel, click on Edit Columns. Ensure that Auto-Generate Fields is turned off. Note that, by default, all of the fields have been added to the Selected Fields list (so they will all be shown). Test the page in the browser. Note the third and fourth columns are for the product and supplier IDs.

3. Close the browser, and back in VWD design view, open the `GridView`'s Smart Tasks panel. Click on Edit columns and in the lower-left corner box marked Selected fields, select Category ID and click the Delete icon. Repeat this for Supplier ID. Save as version 2, view in the browser and note the absence of those fields.

4. Close the browser and go back to editing columns in the VWD. Select the bound column for `UnitPrice` and in the `Boundfield` properties panel on the right, set its `DataFormatString` to show currency with three decimal places with the designator `{0:c3}`. Set `HtmlEncode` to `false`. Close the Edit Columns dialog box and the Smart Tasks panel, save as version 3, and view in the browser.

5. This time, back in the edit columns box, select `UnitsInStock` and add the words `on hand` after the number by using a suffix in the `DataFormatString`. Save the code as version 4 and test it in your browser.

6. To finish, go back to VWD design view and observe that our `GridView` has one `CheckBox` field: Discontinued. Switch to VWD source view (or look at the code listing below) and note toward the bottom of the page the list of `<asp:BoundField>` controls and the single `<asp:CheckBoxField>` object. VWD set this up for us automatically. In the end, your page should resemble the following:

```
<title>TIO-0502-BoundAndCheckColumns</title>
</head>
<body>
        <h2>Chapter 05 TIO #0502 Bound and Check Columns</h2>
    <form id="form1" runat="server">
    <div>
        <asp:SqlDataSource ID="SqlDataSource1" runat="server" ConnectionString="<%$
ConnectionStrings:MdfNorthwind %>"
            SelectCommand="SELECT * FROM [Products]"></asp:SqlDataSource>
    <asp:GridView ID="GridView1" runat="server" AutoGenerateColumns="False"
DataKeyNames="ProductID"
        DataSourceID="SqlDataSource1">
        <Columns>
            <asp:BoundField DataField="ProductID" HeaderText="ProductID"
InsertVisible="False" ReadOnly="True" SortExpression="ProductID" />
            <asp:BoundField DataField="ProductName" HeaderText="ProductName"
SortExpression="ProductName" />
            <asp:BoundField DataField="QuantityPerUnit"
HeaderText="QuantityPerUnit" SortExpression="QuantityPerUnit" />
            <asp:BoundField DataField="UnitPrice" HeaderText="UnitPrice"
SortExpression="UnitPrice" DataFormatString="{0:c3}" HtmlEcode="false"/>
            <asp:BoundField DataField="UnitsInStock" HeaderText="UnitsInStock"
SortExpression="UnitsInStock" DataFormatString="{0}on hand" />
            <asp:BoundField DataField="UnitsOnOrder" HeaderText="UnitsOnOrder"
SortExpression="UnitsOnOrder" />
            <asp:BoundField DataField="ReorderLevel" HeaderText="ReorderLevel"
SortExpression="ReorderLevel" />
```

```
            <asp:CheckBoxField DataField="Discontinued" HeaderText="Discontinued"
SortExpression="Discontinued" />
        </Columns>
    </asp:GridView>
</div></form></body></html>
```

How It Works

Bound fields will make up the majority of your `GridView` columns; they display values from the database. You can add or remove them using a handy dialog box that invokes from the Edit Columns task in the `GridView`'s Smart Tasks panel or by clicking the ellipsis in the `Columns` property in the property grid. Data field values can be formatted using the `DataStringFormat` property set to a valid .NET Framework format string (examples given in the preceding text). If your table has a Boolean value, you can display it using the `CheckBoxField`, which is a derivative of the `BoundField`.

HyperLink Field

A hyperlink field allows the grid to render a hyperlink for one of the columns in the grid. It allows you to redirect the user when the link is clicked, with the target of redirection dependent on which record the user clicks. For example, in a `GridView` of employees, each record could have a hyperlink and each could automatically be linked to the home page of that employee.

You set two properties for a hyperlink column that dictate the text and the URL for the link. Each of those properties can be hard-coded to a literal value for all rows, or it can come from a field of your data source. First, you must set the hyperlink's text that will appear in the hyperlink column. The Text property will use the same literal string for all records, as follows:

```
<asp:HyperLinkField ... Text="Click here for this Employee's home page" ...>
```

An alternative is to pick up a value from the database using the DataTextField property, as follows. You can optionally format this field value using the DataTextFormatString property.

```
<asp:HyperLinkField ... DataTextField="EmployeeHomePageName" ...>
```

The second setting is the target URL of the hyperlink. Again, this can be hard-coded with the `NavigateUrl` property, but that would not be very useful, because all records would hyperlink to the same target. More useful is the `DataNavigateUrlFields` property that allows you to target a page whose URL is saved in the database, as follows (note that the syntax for the property ends in an "s," the reason for which is described in the following text):

```
<asp:HyperLinkField ... DataNavigateUrlFields="EmployeeHomePage" ...>
```

Assuming that the `EmployeeHomePage` field in the preceding example contains a simple page name such as `JohnsPage.aspx`, you might want to prepend to this field value a full page to the location where the employee home pages are stored. You can do this using the `DataNavigateUrlFormatString` property, as follows:

```
<asp:HyperLinkField ... DataNavigateFormatString="../EmployeeWebs/{0}"
```

To navigate outside your Web site, you must use a literal `http` designation, as follows:

```
<asp:HyperLinkField ... DataNavigateFormatString="http://{0}"
```

Note that this format string property works the same way as the `DataFormatString` property of `BoundField` previously described. The `{0}` marker in the format string is a placeholder for the actual field value that is substituted when the page runs.

So, why does `DataNavigateUrlFields` end with an "s" (plural), when we are assigning it only a single field name? The answer is, as you might have guessed, this property can contain multiple field names. The reason you might want to do this is to pass field values along the querystring to a single-page URL, instead of requiring a unique target page for each row in the grid. For example, instead of navigating to `JohnsPage.aspx`, you might go to a single page for all employees, passing their first and last names:

```
EmployeeHomePage.aspx?FirstName=John&LastName=Kauffman
```

You would specify the `FirstName` and `LastName` fields in `DataNavigateUrlFields` (separated by a comma) and then use the format string to complete the rest of the URL, as in the following example:

```
    <asp:HyperLinkField DataNavigateUrlFields="FirstName,LastName"
DataNavigateUrlFormatString="EmployeeHomePage.aspx?FirstName={0}&LastName={1}" />
```

A hyperlink can also invoke your email software. Set the `NavigateUrlFormatString="mailto:{0}"` and `NavigateUrlField="MyEMailField"` that contains a complete email address, as in the following example:

```
<asp:HyperLinkField DataNavigateUrlFields="EmailAddress"
DataNavigateUrlFormatString="mailto:{0}" />
```

Many companies have standardized email addresses that may not be saved in a field. For example, an address such as `NancyDevalio@Northwind.com` cannot be saved in a field. Other databases may contain part of the email address, for example `NDevalio3`, and assume that the company domain will be the same for all. Building these types of email addresses is not hard but requires using templates and code for binding as covered in Chapter 10. We will give you the syntax here for the completeness of this section.

```
<ItemTemplate>
<a href='mailto:<%# Eval("FirstName") %><%# Eval("LastName")
%>@Northwind.com'>Click here to send message
</a>
</ItemTemplate>
```

Try It Out — HyperLink Field Columns

We'll start with a simple example that adds a hyperlink column to a list of employees. Then you will activate the hyperlink to go to another page and display how to carry your employee ID to the new page.

1. Create a new page named `TIO-0503-Hyperlink-1.aspx`. Add a `SqlDataSource` control and a `GridView` to show from the Northwind Employees table the `EmployeeID`, `LastName`, `FirstName` and `PhotoPath`. Save the page and take a look at it in the browser. Note that although we see the hyperlink data in the `PhotoPath` column, we do not have functioning hyperlinks.

```
...
    <title>  TIO-0503-Hyperlink-1.aspx </title>
</head>
```

```
<body>
        <h2>Chapter 05 TIO #0503 Hyperlink version 1</h2>
    <form id="form1" runat="server">
    <div>
        <asp:GridView ID="GridView1" runat="server" AutoGenerateColumns="False"
DataKeyNames="EmployeeID" DataSourceID="SqlDataSource1">
            <Columns>
                <asp:BoundField DataField="EmployeeID" HeaderText="EmployeeID"
InsertVisible="False"
                    ReadOnly="True" SortExpression="EmployeeID" />
                <asp:BoundField DataField="LastName" HeaderText="LastName"
SortExpression="LastName" />
            </Columns>
        </asp:GridView>
        <asp:SqlDataSource ID="SqlDataSource1" runat="server" ConnectionString="<%$
ConnectionStrings:MdfNorthwind %>"
            SelectCommand="SELECT [EmployeeID], [FirstName], [LastName] FROM
[Employees]"></asp:SqlDataSource>
    </div>
    </form>
</body>
</html>
```

2. Close the browser and view the page in Design view. Open the `GridView` Smart Tasks panel, and choose Edit Columns. Delete the `PhotoPath` field. Add a hyperlink field with its `DataNavigationUrlFields` set to the `PhotoPath` field. Set the Text property to "Click For Photo" and click OK to apply the column edits. Save the page as version 2, and take a look at it in the browser. The hyperlinks now work, but we don't have the photos in your computer, so the links will be broken. If you look at the URL request, you will see that your browser is attempting to connect to the URL held in the database.

```
<Columns>
    <asp:BoundField DataField="EmployeeID"
        HeaderText="EmployeeID"
        InsertVisible="False"
        ReadOnly="True"
        SortExpression="EmployeeID" />
    <asp:BoundField DataField="LastName"
        HeaderText="LastName"
        SortExpression="LastName" />
    <asp:HyperLinkField DataNavigateUrlFields="PhotoPath"
        Text="Click for Photo" />
</Columns>
```

3. Create a second page, and see how you can transfer data from the hyperlink. Create a page named `TIO-0503-HyperlinkTarget.aspx` as follows by typing the shaded lines.

```
... <title>TIO-0503-HyperlinkTarget.aspx</title>
</head>
<body>
  <form id="form1" runat="server">
    <h2>
      Details for Employee
      <%= Request.QueryString("ID") %> :
```

```
        <%= Request.QueryString("FirstName") %>
        <%= Request.QueryString("LastName") %>
      </h2>
      To learn in later chapter: Look up more employee details here
    </form>
  </body>
  </html>
```

4. In VWD Design view and using the Edit Columns pane, modify your page `TIO-0503-Hyperlinks-2.aspx` by adding a second `Hyperlink` column as follows, and save it as version 3. See Figure 5-1.

```
<asp:HyperLinkField
       HeaderText="Details Link"
       Text="View Details..."
       DataNavigateUrlFields="EmployeeID,FirstName,LastName"
       DataNavigateUrlFormatString=
              "TIO-0503-HyperlinkTarget.aspx?ID={0}&FirstName={1}&LastName={2}"
     />
```

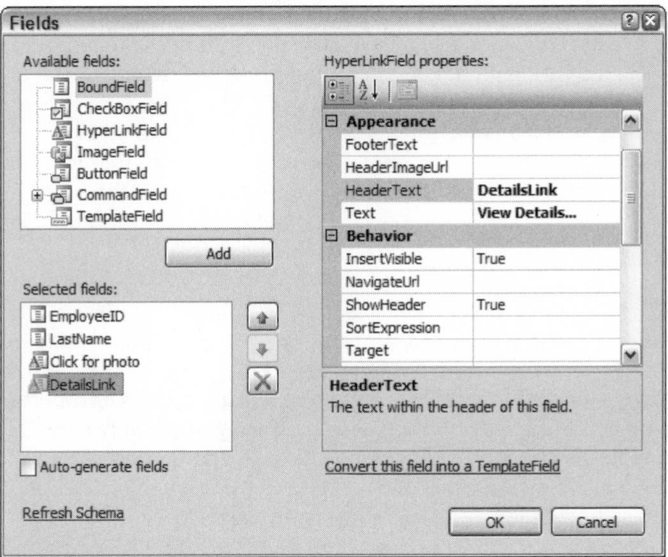

Figure 5-1

5. Save both files and view the `TIO-0503-Hyperlinks-3.aspx` in the browser. Notice that when you scroll over the new hyperlinks, the target reflects the data for the correct record. When a hyperlink is clicked, the appropriate information is sent to the target page.

How It Works

We began in Step 1 with a page that did not contain a hyperlink. Step 2 added a hyperlink field that rendered a hyperlink to a target page specified by the `PhotoPath` field. In this case, the field contained the complete target URL, so it was not necessary to use a format string. The text for each link was the same: "View Photo. . . ."

Steps 3 and 4 added another hyperlink field that rendered a link to a target page that accepts field values along the querystring. Step 3 created the target page for these hyperlinks. In Step 4, you specified a hyperlink field that passed three field values along the querystring, using the DataNavigateUrlFields and DataNavigateUrlFormatString properties. Note that the placeholders for the fields in the format string use an incremental number (`{0}`, `{1}`, `{2}`, and so on) to indicate the placement of each field in the URL.

Image Field

ASP.NET 2.0 includes an `ImageField` type, which is similar to the `HyperLinkField`, and can be used to render images in the grid. Instead of setting properties for the hyperlink's `Text` and `URL`, you set properties for the `AlternateText` and `URL` to an image file. The physical location of the image can be anywhere as long as it is URL addressable. For example, the URL might be to a physical image file, such as `Banner.jpg`, or to a dynamic Web page that returns an image based on field values passed to the URL, such as `GetImage.aspx?ImageID=1234`. Although the latter approach is outside the scope of this book, the former approach is demonstrated in the following example.

Like `HyperLinkField`, you can set the URL to the image as a static value using the `ImageUrl` property, but this would render the same image for all rows. A more useful approach is to specify the `DataImageUrlField` property to a field of the data source and use the `DataImageUrlFormatString` property to complete the URL with `http://` or other literal characters.

Alternatively, you may have a database field containing the name of an image file outside the database. In this case, you switch the mode to `ImageURL`. The trick is in the formatting. The image's filename is likely to be stored in your database image name field, such as one of the following values:

- JaneDoe
- JaneDoe.jpg
- `Images\JaneDoe.jpg`

To get that value in a form usable as a URL, you must make some modifications. That reformatting is done with the value in the `ImageUrlFormatString`. The syntax is of two parts. The value from the database is represented as `{0}`. Anything you need to add you type as a literal. So, in the case of the preceding first option, and where the image file is stored in the same folder as the ASPX page, you would use the following to add the file extension to the stored value:

```
ImageUrlFormatString = "{0}.jpg"
```

In the case of the second option, the image files are located in a sister folder named images; you would use the following:

```
ImageUrlFormatString = "../images/{0}"
```

In the case of the third option, you can just use the field value by itself, with no format string specified.

Command Field

Adding a CommandField to a GridView allows you to offer the user one of three behaviors: deleting, editing, or selecting. We'll focus on selecting later in the master-details section in Chapter 10. The general syntax for a select column follows:

```
<asp:GridView ID="GridView1" Runat="server"
         DataSourceID="AccessDataSource1">
         <Columns>
                <asp:CommandField ButtonType="Button"
                       ShowSelectButton="True">
                </asp:CommandField>
         </Columns>
</asp:GridView>
```

Alternatives for the ShowSelectButton include the following:

```
ShowEditButton ShowDeleteButton ShowCancelButton ShowInsertButton
```

You can also customize the exact text for each of the buttons that is rendered by the CommandField. Note that when CommandField is rendered in a control in Edit or Insert mode, it renders different buttons than in Read-Only mode. Also note that it is not sufficient to support updating, inserting, or deleting merely by adding a CommandField; there are other steps that need to be taken to fully configure a GridView for these scenarios, as we will explore in later chapters.

For now, we simply demonstrate that adding a CommandField to the GridView renders the appropriate button to perform a selection.

Try It Out Command Field Columns

Consider this exercise a preview of techniques discussed in detail later, namely, modifying data and using data from a selection in an event.

1. Create a new page named TIO-0504-CommandColumns-1.aspx. Add a data source control and a GridView to show the ProductID, ProductName, and Unit Price fields from the Products table in Northwind.
2. Select Edit Columns in the Smart Tasks panel of the GridView. In the Available Fields panel, expand CommandField to see the three options. Add a Select and then add an Edit. Save your work and take a look at it in your browser to see the command buttons. Note that with no coding they work at least partially; you can click Edit for a record and change its values. Note that if you click Update while the GridView is in Edit mode, it will not work yet. Also note that you can click Select and a selection occurs behind the scenes. But nothing will be visible in your browser. Later we will learn how to change the appearance of the row that is selected (check the index for SelectedRowStyle).

```
...     <title>TIO-0504-CommandColumns-1.aspx</title>
 </head>
<body>
    <form id="form1" runat="server">
      <asp:GridView ID="GridView1" Runat="server"
         DataSourceID="SqlDataSource1"
```

```
         AutoGenerateColumns="False"
         DataKeyNames="ProductName">
        <SelectedRowStyle BackColor="#cccccc" />
        <Columns>
          <asp:CommandField ShowEditButton="true" ShowSelectButton="true"/>
          <asp:BoundField HeaderText="Product ID" DataField="ProductID" />
          <asp:BoundField HeaderText="Product Name" DataField="ProductName" />
          <asp:BoundField HeaderText="Unit Price" DataField="UnitPrice" />
        </Columns>
      </asp:GridView>

      <asp:SqlDataSource ID="SqlDataSource1" runat="server"
      ConnectionString="<%$ ConnectionStrings:MdfNorthwind %>"
        SelectCommand="SELECT [ProductID], [ProductName], [UnitPrice] FROM
[Products]" />
    </form></body></html>
```

3. Close the browser and return to VWD. This time, go to Source view and add the following property to the `GridView` and then the following procedure:

```
<asp:GridView ID="GridView1" Runat="server"
   DataSourceID="SqlDataSource1"
   AutoGenerateColumns="False"
   OnSelectedIndexChanged="GridView1_SelectedIndexChanged"
   DataKeyNames="ProductName">
```

C#

```
<%@ Page Language="C#" %>
<script runat="server">
void GridView1_SelectedIndexChanged(object sender, EventArgs e)
{
    Response.Write("You selected: " + GridView1.SelectedValue + "<br/>");
}
</script>
<html>
...
```

VB

```
<%@ Page Language="VB" %>
<script runat="server">

Sub GridView1_SelectedIndexChanged(ByVal sender As Object, ByVal e As
System.EventArgs)
    Response.Write("You Selected: " & GridView1.SelectedValue)
End Sub
</script>
<html>
 ...
```

4. Save as version 2 and test in the browser.

How It Works

The real story here is how little you actually had to do to add tremendous functionality to the GridView. Simply adding a CommandField and setting one property modified our page so that it renders Edit and Select buttons. Note that when the GridView is in Edit mode, the CommandField renders appropriate buttons for that mode: Update and Cancel.

In the final step, we demonstrated the availability of values once a row is selected. The GridView triggers an event named SelectedIndexChanged whenever the user clicks on the Select button you enabled. Your single line of code then reads the selected value from the GridView and writes it to the page. Don't worry if you don't understand the relationships among all these properties right now. Future chapters will look at more sophisticated uses of the SelectedValue; for example, Chapter 10 explains how to use a selection in one control to limit the records in another control.

Button Field

ButtonFields provide a way for a user to invoke code the programmer writes. Compare that to a CommandField that can invoke one of several built-in operations (edit, select, delete). Confusion arises because a ButtonField can be set to invoke a built-in behavior just like a CommandField, but it is predominantly used to invoke user-defined code. Note that button columns have nothing to do with radio buttons (option buttons).

There can also be confusion because many solutions, like the last TIO, are hybrids. We used the built-in capability of the CommandField to perform a selection. Then we added some custom code (Sub GridView1_SelectedIndexChanged...) that was also invoked. Since the initial step was using the built-in code we used a CommandField instead of a ButtonField.

ButtonFields offer one of three appearances by the ButtonType property.

- **Link:** GridView will display its value in an appearance of a clickable string (typically blue with an underline) with your text as the link's text.
- **Button:** Will display a small button icon with your text on the button.
- **Image:** Will display an image that is clickable with your text as the accessible AlternateText.

The Text and CommandName properties can be a little confusing. Text is the string that will appear on the button, viewable by the user in the browser. Text has no role in the execution of code. CommandName carries to the code an identifier for which button was clicked. CommandName is not known to the user, only to the programmer. For example, a button to sell stocks might have a Text of "Sell This Stock," whereas the CommandName might be "Sale."

If you have worked with event handling in the past, you probably anticipate that each button column in a GridView executes its own procedure. For example, you would have buy and sell buttons that trigger buy and sell procedures. But this is not the way it works in a GridView. By default, all buttons and CommandFields in a GridView execute the same procedure, named MyGridView_RowCommand within the script tags. What if there is more then one ButtonField (like both buy and sell buttons)? The .RowCommand procedure has some incoming parameters, including CommandName. This parameter will hold the CommandName that you assigned in the Button property. By doing a simple IF THEN or SELECT CASE, you can determine which of the ButtonFields was clicked. This handler also receives a

CommandArgument, which is set to the index of the row that fired the command by default. So, by knowing the ButtonField (from CommandName) and row (from CommandArgument), you know the exact record and type of button pressed and can carry out the appropriate action in your RowCommand procedure. The intricacies of handling events are discussed in Chapter 16, but for now a simple Try It Out follows.

Try It Out Button Field Columns

In this exercise, you create the front end to enable a buy or sell click for each product of Northwind.

1. Create a page named TIO-0505-ButtonColumns-1.aspx. Add a GridView to display the ProductID and ProductName values from all the records of the Products table of Northwind. Test the page in your browser, and then close your browser.
2. Back in VWD, save the page as version 2 and, in Design view, open the common task panel, and then click Edit Columns. Add a ButtonField and set its CommandNameProperty to Buy and the Text property to Buy This Product. Repeat with a second button field that uses Sell and Sell This Product. The button does not do anything yet, but you can check your work in the browser.

```
<%@ Page Language="VB" %>
<html>
<head>
    <title>Displaying Data in a GridView - ButtonField</title>
</head>
<body>
    <form id="form1" runat="server">
      <asp:GridView
        ID="GridView1"
        Runat="server"
        DataSourceID="SqlDataSource1"
        AutoGenerateColumns="False">
        <Columns>
          <asp:BoundField HeaderText="Product ID" DataField="ProductID" />
          <asp:BoundField HeaderText="Product Name" DataField="ProductName" />
          <asp:ButtonField CommandName="Buy" Text="Buy" />
          <asp:ButtonField CommandName="Sell" Text="Sell" />
        </Columns>
      </asp:GridView>

      <asp:SqlDataSource ID="SqlDataSource1"
      ConnectionString="<%$ ConnectionStrings:MdfNorthwind %>"
      SelectCommand="select * from Products"
      Runat="server" />
    </form>
</body>
</html>
```

- ❑ Now you will create the custom code to run when the buttons are clicked. First, you must modify the GridView to handle the clicks.

3. Add two lines, as follows. If VWD has already added a DataKeyNames (most likely to ProductID), then remove it and instead use the settings to ProductName, as shown here:

```
<asp:GridView
  ID="GridView1"
  Runat="server"
  DataSourceID="SqlDataSource1"
  AutoGenerateColumns="False"
  OnRowCommand="GridView1_RowCommand"
  DataKeyNames="ProductName">
```

- ❑ Next, add the following procedure (in C# or VB) to your page.

C#

```
<%@ Page Language="C#" %>
<script runat="server">
void GridView1_RowCommand(Object sender,
System.Web.UI.WebControls.GridViewCommandEventArgs e) {
    Response.Write("Command Name: " + e.CommandName + "<br/>");
    int rowIndex = Int32.Parse(e.CommandArgument.ToString());
    if (e.CommandName == "Buy")
      Response.Write("You Bought: " + GridView1.DataKeys[rowIndex].Value);
  else if (e.CommandName == "Sell")
      Response.Write("You Sold: " + GridView1.DataKeys[rowIndex].Value);
  }
</script>
<html>
...
```

VB

```
<%@ Page Language="VB" %>
<script runat="server">
  Sub GridView1_RowCommand(ByVal sender As Object, ByVal e As
  System.Web.UI.WebControls.GridViewCommandEventArgs)
    Response.Write("Commmand Name: " & e.CommandName & "<br/>")
    Dim rowIndex As Integer = e.CommandArgument
    If e.CommandName = "Buy" Then
      Response.Write("You Bought: " & GridView1.DataKeys(rowIndex).Value)
    ElseIf e.CommandName = "Sell" Then
      Response.Write("You Sold: " & GridView1.DataKeys(rowIndex).Value)
    End If
  End Sub
</script>
<html>
...
```

4. Save the file as `TIO-0505-ButtonColumns-2.aspx` and test it in your browser.

How It Works

The `ButtonField` enables the `GridView` to raise events that you can handle with user code. You started by adding the `ButtonField` just as you would for any other column type. You then specified the `Text` and `CommandName` properties for the button.

Then you modified the GridView in two ways. First, you added an event to specify that when a RowCommand is clicked, it should call the GridView1-RowCommand event handler. Second, you established which column should be the data key. (Data keys are further discussed in the modifying chapters, but for now, understand that a data key is a set of values to uniquely identify each record, even when the record's identifying field is being changed).

```
        OnRowCommand="GridView1_RowCommand"
        DataKeyNames="ProductName">
```

Last, you wrote the code in the GridView_RowCommand procedure. You had to name the procedure to match your specification in the GridView for the OnRowCommand event. When the event is raised, it will pass a set of GridViewCommandEvent arguments that are put into a collection. One of those arguments is CommandName, the string you provided when you created the button. This will identify which button was pressed if there is more than one button column.

A second argument of interest is the CommandArgument, which will be the index of the clicked row within the record set. Because you designated ProductName to be the data key name, you can use that number to look up the ProductName by using the index from the event and the DataKeys collection of the GridView. The code is wrapped in an If-Then statement that formats your values into either a You bought or You sold string.

Note that the RowCommand event is also raised automatically when clicking a button rendered by a CommandField column, such as Update or Select. This is another reason why it is important to check the CommandName value before processing the event. In the case of built-in commands from CommandField, GridView automatically handles the command, so you don't need to write code to explicitly handle these types of events.

Template Field

ASP.NET 2.0 allows you to create columns with even more elaborate customization than the column types discussed in the preceding text. The sky is the limit when you use TemplateFields. A TemplateField gives you a blank space, almost like a form, upon which you can add controls such as a Label or Image. Once added to a template, a control can have its properties "data-bound" to fields from the data source of the GridView, and this control will be rendered for each row of the GridView with data-bound values appropriate for each row.

Templates in ASP.NET 2.0 contain user-defined controls and HTML elements to be rendered for a region of a control. Instead of using the control's built-in rendering, a template allows you to replace this rendering with your own. Data-bound controls such as GridView support templates for a variety of regions such as the grid header, footer, pager, and individual column cells. When a control is data-bound, controls inside its templates can be bound to a data field and their values will stay synchronized with the current record of the data-bound control. Templates give the designer support for multiple controls and flexible layout within a section of a data-bound control. Note that templates are not the same as styles that apply formatting but don't enable creation of multiple subcontrols. (Templates are discussed in more detail in Chapter 10.)

You can add a TemplateField to the GridView's Columns collection the same way you do other columns. The TemplateField provides you with a blank workspace. Close the Edit Columns dialog box, and then choose the Edit Templates task on the GridView control's Smart Tasks panel. Select the ItemTemplate for the TemplateField column that you added, and the GridView will render a blank workspace upon which you can drag and drop labels, images, or other controls, as well as type literal strings or HTML tags. (More options are covered in Chapter 10 on templates.) When finished, don't forget to end template editing. An exercise using TemplateFields follows.

Try It Out Template Field Columns

You will create a new products table with two new goals. First, you want more than one value in a cell (such as product ID and product name). Second, you want some literal text to be in every cell, for example, the words "in stock" next to the stock amount.

1. Start with a new page named TIO-0506-TemplateColumns-1.aspx. Add a GridView with a new data source control set to Northwind's Products table and show all of the fields. Then choose the GridView Edit Columns task and set AutoGenerateColumns to false. Add a TemplateField, the last option in the list of "Available fields." Set the HeaderText property to Product, and then add a second template column with the header Price. Click OK to close the Fields dialog box and give the page a test. Notice that you have columns but no values assigned to the columns. Your GridView source code will be similar to that shown here:

```
<asp:GridView ID="GridView1" Runat="server"
            DataSourceID="NorthwindProductsSqlDataSource"
            AutoGenerateColumns="False">
            <Columns>
                <asp:TemplateField HeaderText="Product" />
                <asp:TemplateField HeaderText="Price" />
            </Columns>
</asp:GridView>
```

2. Close your browser and go back to the Design view. Save the page as version 2. Select the GridView, open the Smart Tasks panel, and click on Edit Templates. Drop down the list of templates to display and select Column (0) - Product, Item Template. You are now in template editing mode. You can add, delete or edit controls and text in the template field of the GridView.

3. Drag a label from the Toolbox onto the template. Click on the Smart Tasks panel for the label and select Edit Data Bindings. On the left, from the list of bindable properties select Text. In the radio button choices, select Field binding and then drop down the Bound To list of fields (click on Refresh Schema if field binding is not available). Select ProductName. Click OK to close the binding dialog box, and then close the Smart Tasks panel. The label will still be selected, press the right arrow to move the selection off the label. Press Enter to add a return. Add another label and bind its text to ProductName. You now have two labels in the template, one above the other. Open the GridView's Smart Tasks panel (not a label's Smart Tasks panel), and click End Template Editing. Your GridView source code will now appear as follows. Save it as version 2, and run it in the browser. Observe that you have two values displayed in each template, as shown in Figure 5-2.

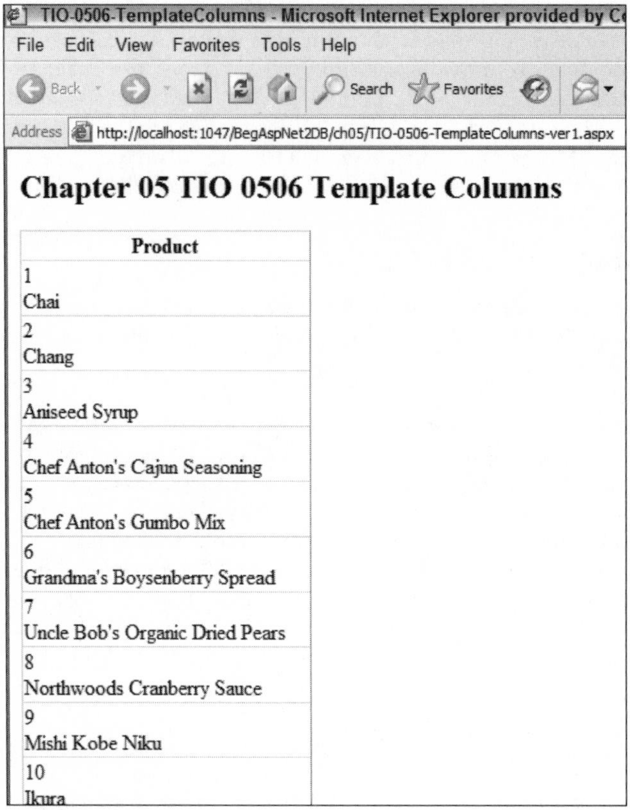

Figure 5-2

4. Close the browser and go back to VWD. Save the page as version 3. This time, we will add some hard-coded text and a label to hold a data value. Go to the `GridView`'s Smart Tasks panel, and select Edit Templates, then select the `Price Column [1]- Item Template`. This time just type into the template the text `on hand`. To the right of that, add a label and open the labels' Smart Tasks panel and select Edit DataBindings. From the left select Text property and bind it to the field named `UnitsInStock`. Click OK to close the DataBindings dialog box, and then don't forget to open the `GridView` Smart Tasks panel and end template editing. Your `GridView` source code will be similar to the following. Then save the code and view it in your browser, as shown in Figure 5-3.

```
... <title>TIO-0506-TemplateColumns-3</title></head>
<body>
<h2>Chapter 05 TIO 0506 Template Columns ver 3</h2>
    <form id="form1" runat="server">
    <div>
        <asp:GridView ID="GridView1" runat="server"
DataSourceID="SqlDataSource1" AutoGenerateColumns="False">
            <Columns>

                <asp:TemplateField HeaderText="Product">
```

```
                <ItemTemplate>
                    <asp:Label ID="Label1" runat="server"
                        Text='<%# Eval("ProductID") %>'></asp:Label><br />
                    <asp:Label ID="Label2" runat="server"
                        Text='<%# Eval("ProductName") %>'></asp:Label>
                </ItemTemplate>
            </asp:TemplateField>

            <asp:TemplateField HeaderText="Price">
                <ItemTemplate>
                    On hand:
                    <asp:Label ID="Label3" runat="server"
                        Text='<%# Eval ("UnitsInStock") %>'></asp:Label>
                </ItemTemplate>
            </asp:TemplateField>
        </Columns>
    </asp:GridView>
    <asp:SqlDataSource ID="SqlDataSource1" runat="server"
        ConnectionString="<%$ ConnectionStrings:MdfNorthwind %>"
        SelectCommand="SELECT * FROM [Products]">
    </asp:SqlDataSource>
</div>    </form> </body> </html>
```

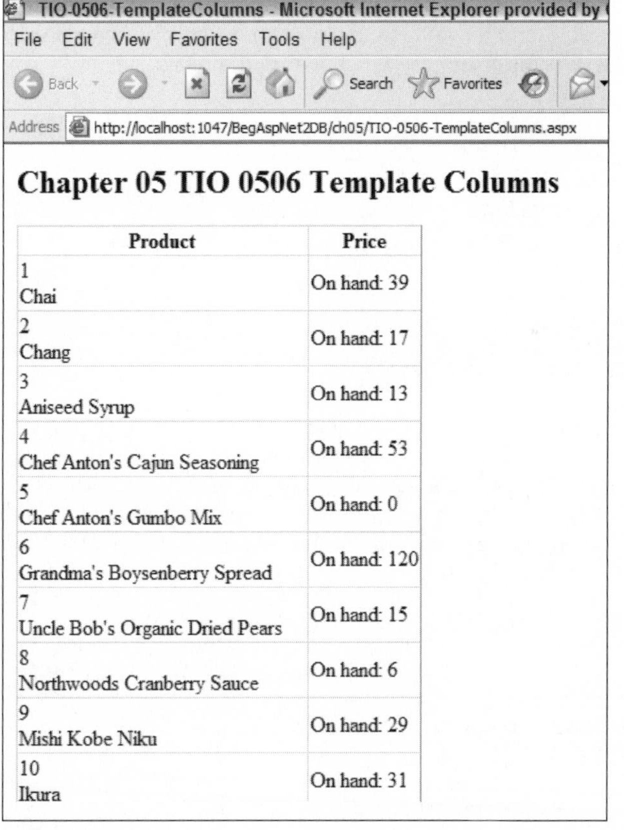

Figure 5-3

How It Works

Template columns offer tremendous versatility. You get a blank slate upon which you can create almost any arrangement of controls, all bound to the values for the current record. Template columns are added in the same way as other columns. After adding a template column, you use the `GridView`'s Smart Tasks panel to begin editing the templates. Drag and drop labels, and then select a field to which they bind. Remember to end template editing. More template techniques are discussed in Chapter 10.

Using the AutoGenerateColumns Property of the GridView

ASP.NET 2.0's `GridView` can display columns in two ways: `AutoGenerateColumns=true` or `false`. When it is set to true, the `GridView` or `DetailsView` displays all the columns that are sent from the data source control. When it is set to `false`, we are responsible for adding a `<Columns>` tag and then within there tags for each field. Also, there is actually a third possibility where you have the `AutoGenerateColumns` set to `true` but also roll a few of columns your own. Because you will frequently have to look at source code, it is important to have clear sense of each possibility, as we will discuss here.

- **AutoGenerateColumns = True and no predefined fields** will give you one column in the `GridView` for each field in the data source. If you have the right combination of fields in your data source control, you do not have to do any work in the `GridView`. This option is the easiest and least flexible, and it results in the most compact ASPX page. AutoGenerateColumns is, by default, true. So, this is the case as follows, with no tag:

```
  <asp:GridView
ID="GridView1"
runat="server"> ...
  </asp:GridView>
```

- It is also the case with an explicit tag, as follows:

```
  <asp:GridView
ID="GridView1"
runat="server"> ...
 AutoGenerateColumns="true" ... >
```

- **AutoGenerateColumns = True and also some predefined fields** will give you one column in the `GridView` for each field in the data source, plus it will display your predefined fields from the Columns collection. This option allows you to add a `CommandField`, such as Select or Edit, to the `GridView`, but keep the columns that are autogenerated from the data source. For example, the following autogenerates all of the columns but also adds another column that creates a column to perform selections:

```
<asp:GridView... AutoGenerateColumns="true" ... >
       <Columns>
              <asp:CommandField ShowSelectButton="True">
              </asp:CommandField>
       </Columns>
</asp:GridView>
```

- **AutoGenerateColumns = False (must have predefined fields)** will give you nothing beyond the fields that you define in the `Columns` collection. If you don't predefine fields, you get nothing. This option gives you the most control over exactly which columns will appear and in what order.

```
<asp:GridView... AutoGenerateColumns="False" ... >
       <columns>
              <asp:BoundField datafield="MySourceField1">
              </asp:BoundField>
              <asp:BoundField datafield="MySourceField2">
              </asp:BoundField>
              <asp:BoundField datafield="MySourceField3">
              </asp:BoundField>
       </columns>
</asp:GridView>
```

> **The defaults for `AutoGenerateColumns` are a little confusing. The default for the `GridView` control itself is `AutoGenerateColumns=True`. That is what you get if you typed, by hand, a `GridView` control into your page. But normally you will add a `GridView` in VWD by dragging a `GridView` control from the Toolbox. In that case, the default for how VWD builds a `GridView` is that it will set the `AutoGenerateColumns` property to `=false` and VWD builds the column list tags.**

In summary for `AutoGenerateColumns`, turn it on when you simply want to display all fields in the data source with no extra columns. Feel free to add a few additional columns if you want. But if you want a particular selection and arrangement of columns, take the time to set them up by adding explicit fields to the `GridView`'s `Column` collection using the Smart Tasks panels' Edit Columns feature.

Handling Null Field Values

The `GridView` offers an easy solution for handling null data. Users generally want to have more descriptive content for a cell than just emptiness. The `NullDisplayText` will render an alternate string when the value from the data source control is `NULL`. There is another case wherein the data source control does not return any rows at all — this is handled by the `EmptyDataText` property covered in the next chapter.

> **In Chapter 6, we will cover a similar topic — how to display a `GridView` for which no values come from the data source control, for example a search for data on an employee at Northwinds named Mr. Gates. If you want to jump ahead, check the index in this book for "EmptyDataRowStyle," "EmptyDataTemplate," or "EmptyDataText."**

Try It Out Handling Null Values

In this simple exercise, you will handle nulls from two fields of the `Suppliers` table.

1. Start with a new page named `TIO-0507-HandlingNullValues.aspx`. Drag a `GridView` from the toolbar to the page and set it up to display from Northwind's `Suppliers` table the fields

for `Company Name`, `Region`, and `Fax`. VWD will create the `GridView` control with three fields as simple bound columns (`AutoGenerateColumns=false`). Save the page (which should look similar to the following), and check it in your browser. Note that there are some missing data in the FAX and region columns, as in Figure 5-4.

```
<asp:GridView ID="GridView1" runat="server"
AutoGenerateColumns="False"
DataSourceID="SqlDataSource1">
    <Columns>
        <asp:BoundField DataField="CompanyName"
         HeaderText="CompanyName"
         SortExpression="CompanyName" />
        <asp:BoundField DataField="Fax"
         HeaderText="Fax"
         SortExpression="Fax" />
        <asp:BoundField DataField="Region"
         HeaderText="Region"
         SortExpression="Region" />
    </Columns>
</asp:GridView>
```

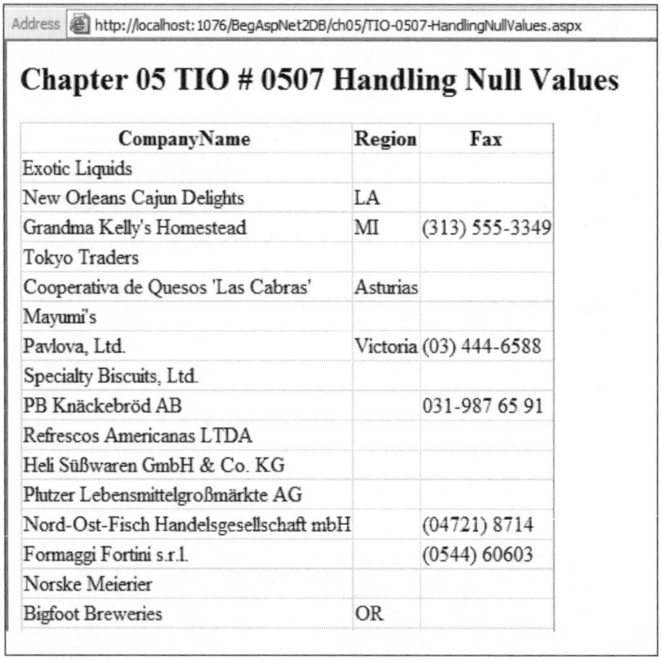

Address http://localhost:1076/BegAspNet2DB/ch05/TIO-0507-HandlingNullValues.aspx

Chapter 05 TIO # 0507 Handling Null Values

CompanyName	Region	Fax
Exotic Liquids		
New Orleans Cajun Delights	LA	
Grandma Kelly's Homestead	MI	(313) 555-3349
Tokyo Traders		
Cooperativa de Quesos 'Las Cabras'	Asturias	
Mayumi's		
Pavlova, Ltd.	Victoria	(03) 444-6588
Specialty Biscuits, Ltd.		
PB Knäckebröd AB		031-987 65 91
Refrescos Americanas LTDA		
Heli Süßwaren GmbH & Co. KG		
Plutzer Lebensmittelgroßmärkte AG		
Nord-Ost-Fisch Handelsgesellschaft mbH		(04721) 8714
Formaggi Fortini s.r.l.		(0544) 60603
Norske Meierier		
Bigfoot Breweries	OR	

Figure 5-4

2. Close your browser and return to the VWD Design view. Select the `GridView` and open its Smart Tasks panel. Select Edit Columns and, in the lower left, select the Region field. In the Property window, in the Behavior pane, find the `NullDisplayText` property, and enter `Region unknown`. For the `Fax` field's same property, enter `NullDisplayText = "Not on record"`. Click OK in the Fields dialog box, and then save your work and view the page in the browser.

Those two columns of the `GridView` will be modified in the source code as follows and will result in the table shown in Figure 5-5:

```
<asp:BoundField DataField="Fax"
 HeaderText="Fax"
 NullDisplayText="Not on Record"
 SortExpression="Fax" />

<asp:BoundField DataField="Region"
 HeaderText="Region"
 NullDisplayText="Region Unknown"
 SortExpression="Region" />
```

CompanyName	Fax	Region
Exotic Liquids	Not on Record	Region Unknown
New Orleans Cajun Delights	Not on Record	LA
Grandma Kelly's Homestead	(313) 555-3349	MI
Tokyo Traders	Not on Record	Region Unknown
Cooperativa de Quesos 'Las Cabras'	Not on Record	Asturias
Mayumi's	Not on Record	Region Unknown
Pavlova, Ltd.	(03) 444-6588	Victoria
Specialty Biscuits, Ltd.	Not on Record	Region Unknown
PB Knäckebröd AB	031-987 65 91	Region Unknown

Figure 5-5

How It Works

Handling nulls is very easy; merely set the `NullDisplayText` value to the string you want the user to see when a value is missing. Note that the string is set on a per-column basis, not for the entire `GridView`.

The DetailsView Control

The `DetailsView` displays fields from only one record at a time. It displays the fields of that one record as rows in a table. To see more records, the user can click on navigation tools, but he will see only one record at a time. Note in Figure 5-6 that we see only one record, and we have navigation tools across the bottom of the `DetailsView`.

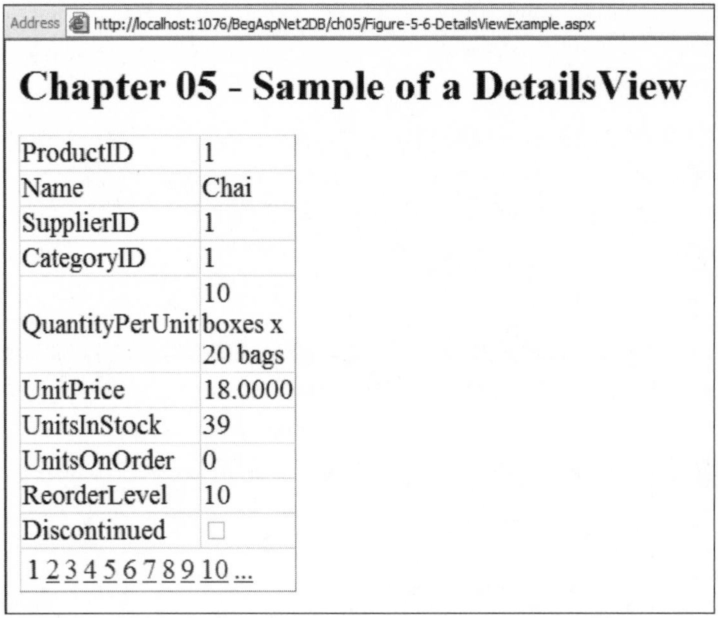

Address http://localhost:1076/BegAspNet2DB/ch05/Figure-5-6-DetailsViewExample.aspx

Chapter 05 - Sample of a DetailsView

ProductID	1
Name	Chai
SupplierID	1
CategoryID	1
QuantityPerUnit	10 boxes x 20 bags
UnitPrice	18.0000
UnitsInStock	39
UnitsOnOrder	0
ReorderLevel	10
Discontinued	☐
1 2 3 4 5 6 7 8 9 10 ...	

Figure 5-6

The `DetailsView` control was created as a sibling control to `GridView`. The two controls share almost exactly the same object model, and all of the preceding concepts apply equally to this control, including the types of fields (columns). Additionally, `DetailsView` supports inserting rows, which the `GridView` does not support (discussed in Chapter 9 on modifying data).

> **The `DetailsView` renders fields from a single record at a time. The `GridView` renders fields from many records at once.**

DetailsView Rendering Elements

The `DetailsView` rendering divides the control up into several regions, as listed below. Some of these are rendered only once per `DetailsView` control (`Header`, `Footer`). Others are rendered once for each field in the `DetailsView` (`DataField` and `Data Header`). The `Pager` can be rendered at the top, bottom, or both.

Header	Single row at the top of `DetailsView` that contains a header for the `DetailsView` as a whole (usually the name of the items represented by rows of the table). It can be specified by `HeaderText` or `HeaderTemplate` properties.
Data Fields	Each data row in the `DetailsView` corresponds to a single field from the data source. The values for the current record will be rendered and changed as the user clicks through the records.

Data Field Headers	The leftmost cell of each data field contains the header for the data field. This is the same value that is normally rendered as a column header in `GridView`.
Footer	Single row that contains footer information
Pager	Single row that holds page navigation tools such as First or Previous and can display at the top or bottom or both.
Empty Data Row	A single cell shown as an alternative to the `DetailsView` if there are no values for a given record.

Like the `GridView`, `DetailsView` offers an alternate one-cell rendering if there are no records available from the data source control. The layout and values for this case are held in the `EmptyDataTemplate`.

Connecting the DetailsView to Data

The `GridView` and `DetailsView` controls are derived from the same class but have different appearances and behaviors. The `DetailsView` is connected by its DataSourceID property to a data source control. The `DetailsView` retrieves data from the data source control and automatically generates a table of values for the first record.

```
<%@ Page Language="VB" %>
<html>
<head><title>Displaying Data in a DetailsView</title></head>
<body>
    <form id="form1" runat="server">

        <asp:DetailsView ID="DetailsView1" Runat="server"
          DataSourceID="SqlDataSource1" />

        <asp:SqlDataSource ID="SqlDataSource1" Runat="server"
        ConnectionString="<%$ ConnectionStrings:MdfNorthwind %>"
          SelectCommand="select * from Products"/>
      </form>
</body></html>
```

The VWD Designer facilitates the addition and modification of a `DetailsView` control. The first option is to go to the Smart Tasks panel of the `DetailsView` control and turn on paging. Another option is Edit Fields, which corresponds to the same dialog box that we used to customize the `GridView` columns. This dialog box allows you to add a `BoundField`, `HyperLinkField`, `CheckBoxField`, `CommandField`, `ButtonField`, or `TemplateField` to the `DetailsView`. Last, `DetailsView` also supports the Edit Templates task for manipulating its templated fields and other top-level template properties, a topic introduced in the preceding text and covered in more detail in Chapter 10.

> **Like `GridView`, `DetailsView` supports editing and deleting data items, but unlike `GridView`, it also supports inserting new records. This feature is discussed in the Chapters 5 to 10, which cover modifying data.**

You will note two small but important differences in the syntax of DetailsView from GridView:

- DetailsView uses the <Fields> tag, whereas GridView uses <Columns>.
- DetailsView also has an AutoGenerateFields property, whereas GridView has AutoGenerateColumns.

Both of these differences are logical, given that DetailsView does not actually render the fields as columns.

Try It Out DetailsView Control

In this exercise, you create a DetailsView that shows information about the Northwind products. We'll start with a basic sample and then add paging and templated fields.

1. Create a new page named TIO-0508-DetailsView.aspx. Add a SqlDataSource control connecting to all the fields of the Products table of Northwind using, as always, the MdfNorthwinds connection.
2. Drag and drop a DetailsView control from the Toolbox. On its Smart Tasks panel, set the data source to the data source control, the one you just created. Save and run the file to see the default layout. By default, you see every field in the table.
3. Close the browser and use VWD in Design view. Open the DetailsView Smart Tasks panel and enable paging. Then click Edit Fields to see a dialog box very similar to the one for GridView. Select the ProductName field from the list at the lower left, and in the properties list on the right, change its HeaderText property to just name.
4. Save and run the page, noting how paging was implemented with a single click and how the HeaderText property is rendered to the left of the value.

```
...  <title>TIO-0508-DetailsView.aspx</title>
</head>
<body>
  <form id="form1" runat="server">
      <asp:DetailsView ID="DetailsView1" Runat="server"
           DataSourceID="SqlDataSource1"
           DataKeyNames="ProductID"
           AllowPaging="True" AutoGenerateRows="false">
           <Fields>
                <asp:BoundField ReadOnly="True" HeaderText="ProductID"
InsertVisible="False" DataField="ProductID"
                     SortExpression="ProductID" />
                <asp:BoundField HeaderText="Name" DataField="ProductName"
SortExpression="ProductName" />
                <asp:BoundField HeaderText="SupplierID"
DataField="SupplierID" SortExpression="SupplierID" />
                <asp:BoundField HeaderText="CategoryID"
DataField="CategoryID" SortExpression="CategoryID" />
... (additional bound fields)
                <asp:CheckBoxField HeaderText="Discontinued"
SortExpression="Discontinued" DataField="Discontinued" />
           </Fields>
```

```
    </asp:DetailsView>

  <asp:SqlDataSource ID="SqlDataSource1" Runat="server"
    ConnectionString="<%$ ConnectionStrings:MdfNorthwind %>"
      SelectCommand="SELECT * FROM Products" />
</form></body></html>
```

How It Works

As you can see, the `DetailsView` control is very similar to the `GridView`. They have similar and similar persistence. But the `DetailsView` shows just one record at a time. Note that the label to the left of the value is actually called the `HeaderText` (we guess "LefterText" wouldn't have caught on). In the next few chapters, you will return to this control to see how it works in a master-details scenario and how it is used to add new records to a data source.

Common Mistakes

The following list describes some of the common mistakes developers make in trying to display data in tables:

- Attempting to render a `GridView` from a data source control that does not return data. If there is no data returned and the `EmptyDataText` or `EmptyDataTemplate` is not defined, the `GridView` will not render anything at all.
- Forgetting to set `AutoGenerateColumns=false` when only explicit columns are desired.
- Attempting to show values from two data sources in one `GridView` control. The `GridView` itself is not able to join data from multiple tables. That must be done either in the RDBMS or in the `SelectCommand` of the data source control.
- Attempting to set the properties of a `GridView` when it is not selected. If your properties options are ASP.NET, Body, and Misc, you have the page (background) selected, not the `GridView`. Click once on the middle of the `GridView` to select it, then you should have the property options for Accessibility, Appearance, and so on.
- Creating malformed tags. When typing and rearranging many attributes in the Source view of a `GridView`, it is easy to end up without a closing angle bracket on the `GridView` tag. The error message "The server tag is not well formed" stops on the line the tag starts, which misleads your eye as to the position of the problem — after the last attribute at the absence of the tag ending bracket (>).
- Attempting to display a field in a data-bound control when that field was not included in the `SelectCommand` of the data source control.
- Using the wrong name for a field in a data-bound control. This arises from an error in typing or an error recalling the name of the field. Whenever possible, use VWD's pick list or drag-and-drop.
- Committing a SQL mistake when using the AS clause in a SQL statement that also has a `WHERE` or `ORDER BY` clause. (See Appendix A for examples of using the `AS` clause.) Use the alias (new

name) in the WHERE if the AS clause is in the data store's query or view. Use the old name in the WHERE clause if the AS clause is in the data source control's SELECT statement.

- Attempting to place a GridView outside of a form tag. This can occur when you are dragging and dropping into source view or when you are moving controls around in Source view and accidentally move on outside the <form>.

Summary

Recall from earlier chapters that the basic architecture to display data on an ASP.NET 2.0 page utilizes two controls: a data source control and a data-bound control. Data source controls can connect to Access, SQL, or other sources. The data-bound controls work, for the most part, with any data source control. This interoperability reduces the learning curve and maintenance costs as databases and displays are modified over the life of a Web site.

With almost no coding, the GridView provides many of the functions that you had to create by hand in earlier versions of ASP.net. In most cases, the GridView can be created and modified through the VWD Design view tools, eliminating the need to work with tags. The GridView binds to a data source control and then displays the data in tabular form, that is, one or more columns and all of the rows sent from the data source.

The GridView's columns can be created automatically (one for each field) using AutoGenerateColumns=true or by specific definitions. Columns can be added, deleted, moved, and modified through the GridView's Smart Tasks panel⇨Edit Columns. If you use both, you will get one column for each field, plus any columns you defined by hand. Columns that display values from the database have the NullDisplayText property to display a string if the data source sends a NULL to the GridView for that record's field.

The basic type of column that shows a value is the BoundField. The value to display can be formatted into standard presentations for numbers or dates and can include leading or trailing text. These formatting features use the DataFormatString. The value from the database will be represented in the string by the {0} symbol.

A CheckBoxField binds to Boolean data and then automatically formats the results as a CheckBox icon. A HyperLinkField allows you to redirect the user to an appropriate target for the current that was clicked. First, you must set the HyperLink text that will appear in the HyperLink column and then the HyperLink's target. You will probably have to add strings using the DataNavigateFormatString to get a properly formed URL.

GridView offers ImageField columns that will display an image in the browser. The image comes from a value in the database referencing an external file (mode=ImageURL). You may need to modify the value's string to properly point to the image file, for example, by adding the path or extension.

CommandField columns and ButtonField columns both invoke code. The CommandField will run one of several standard operations provided by the GridView, including edit, select, and delete. A ButtonField will call event handlers wherein you write custom code.

The most flexible column is the `TemplateField`. This option provides a blank space into which you can place controls bound to values, HTML tags, or text. This flexibility allows you to completely customize the rendering for a `GridView` cell.

The `DetailsView` is a sibling control to the `GridView` in appearance, function, and internal design. Whereas the `GridView` displays a table of many records and a series of vertical columns, the `DetailsView` displays two columns, one showing the names of fields and the other showing values from just one record. It is easy to add page navigation, and the ability to modify its template fields offers great freedom in the layout.

This chapter explained how to build the structure of `GridView` and `DetailsView` controls. The next chapter looks at techniques to improve their overall appearance using styles.

Exercises

1. Describe the difference between `GridView` and a `DetailsView` controls.
2. Describe the difference between a `CommandField` and a `ButtonField`.
3. Describe the difference between a ButtonField's `Text` and `CommandName` properties.
4. What `GridView` Column type would be useful for a Boolean field?
5. How is a `GridView` `TemplateField` different from a `BoundField`?

Customizing the Appearance of Tables

All data is not of equal importance. A higher priority may come from the reader (who wants to highlight her record) or from the enterprise (that wants to focus on their discount price). The goal of this chapter is to take a few values out of an entire table and give them priority in the reader's eye. The design challenge is to focus the reader on the key values of interest among the deluge of data.

The `GridView` and `DetailsView` controls offer a wide variety of options for formatting the appearance and style of their major rendering elements (rows, columns, and cells). Whereas the last chapter focused on creating the structure of these controls from the fields in the data source, this chapter focuses on their overall appearance, covering six major areas:

- Customizing the appearance of an entire table
- Customizing styles within a table
- Using Cascading Style Sheets (CSS)
- Understanding the precedence of styles
- Using AutoFormat in Visual Web Developer Express
- Implementing themes and skins

Customizing the Appearance of an Entire Table

The properties, events, and methods of a `GridView` or `DetailsView` control can be roughly categorized into two groups: those that affect the appearance and those that affect the behavior. Each of these areas has several subcategories. Behavioral properties include the access key, ToolTips, autogeneration of columns, clickable elements, and scripted actions. Formatting features include colors, lines, styles, and the control of formatting by a Cascading Style Sheet (CSS). Furthermore, you can divide the formatting properties into those that affect the `GridView` as a whole and those that are specific to only some columns, rows, or cells. The appearance of a table can be modified quickly using the design features of Visual Web Developer (VWD). The resulting source code is also provided so that you can create the page using another editor.

As a quick review, recall that in the last chapter we used two techniques to make changes to a table's properties. Some properties were set through the Smart Tasks panel or its wizards. Others were changed by selecting the table and then making changes in the Properties window.

Setting the BackColor and a BackImageUrl

You can specify a background color for the entire grid. There are three ways to specify a color. The Visual Studio BackColor dialog box divides these options across three tabs:

- The Custom tab displays an RGB system with three hexadecimal values for Red, Green, and Blue in the format RRGGBB (see Figure 6-1). Each value ranges from 00 to FF. A good tool to experiment with the RGB hexadecimal color system is the VWD Custom Color tab in the dialog box for setting a `GridView`'s border color. The custom tab colors are a basic palette offering 48 values in a range of hues and intensities that will insert an RGB value into the tag. RGB colors are a logical selection for desktops, but they do not always translate well to the Web. The syntax follows for a shade of purple, where Red is a medium value (C0), Green is nothing (00), and Blue is also medium (C0).

```
<asp:gridview ... backcolor="#C000C0" ... >
```

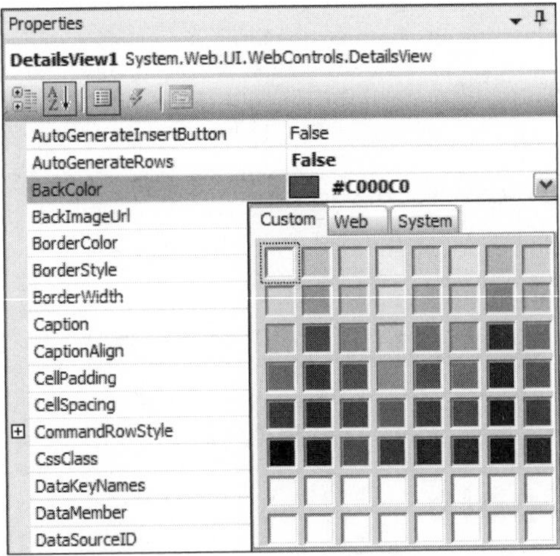

Figure 6-1

- The Web tab is the palette of approximately 150 specific colors that have been recognized and named by the World Wide Web (W3C) Consortium (see Figure 6-2). These colors should be available in every modern Web browser. VWD offers this palette in the Web tab, or typists can find the list in just about any HTML book.

```
<asp:gridview ... backcolor="DarkGray" ... >
```

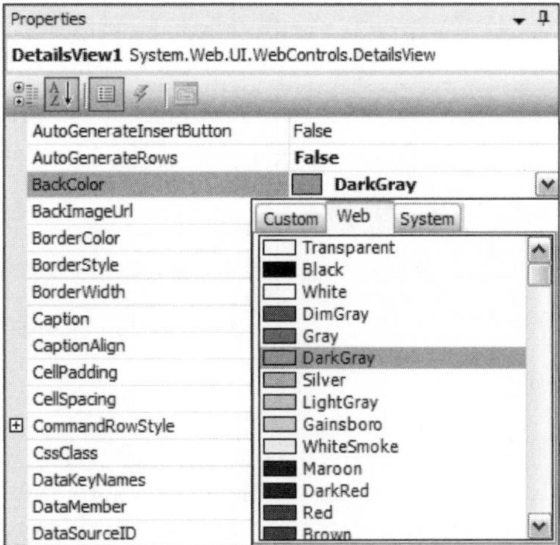

Figure 6-2

- The System tab will display a color that depends on the user's Windows settings (see Figure 6-3). Most Windows users right-click on the desktop and then select Properties➪Appearance➪Scheme and change from Windows Standard to something like Wheat or Spruce. That scheme then sets a color for each part of a window, including the Button Face, Border of an Active Window, Disabled Menu Options, and Menu Bar Background. As a result of selecting a Windows system color, your `GridView` background color will be set to match that Window part for each user. For example, you might set your `GridView` backcolor to MenuBar. If a visitor to your Web site is using the Spruce scheme (which has an Active Title color of green), her `GridView` backcolor will autoset to green. Other visitors will have other backgrounds, depending on their personal Windows settings. The net result is that your page looks well integrated with every user's Windows system.

```
<asp:gridview ... backcolor="MenuBar" ... >
```

An alternative to a backcolor is a background image. Browsers can handle GIF, JPG, BMP, and WMF file formats. However, be aware that some older browsers don't support formats such as PNG and BMP, so GIF and JPG are safest. Considering that your entire Web site may move to different folders or machines, it is best to use a path to the image file that is relative to the page that contains the `GridView`, instead of a fully qualified path that depends on the file system of your development machine. In VWD, simply navigate to and select the image; for typists, use the following syntax:

```
<asp:gridview ... backimageurl="~/MyImages/MyCompanyLogoInBlackAndWhite.gif" ... >
```

Carefully consider the user's experience when setting background images. Most images interfere with the legibility of the data in the grid. Because a background image will have a variety of color hues, it will be difficult to select any font color that will contrast well with all areas of the image.

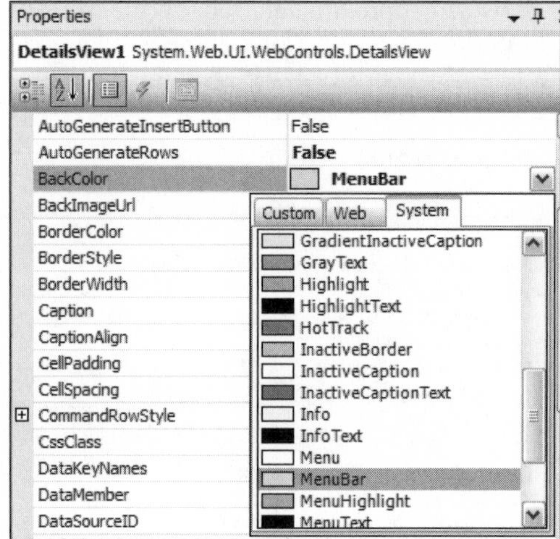

Figure 6-3

A second problem with background images is that they are not scaled or stretched to fit the `GridView`. A large image will have only its top-left corner visible in a small `GridView`. And a small image will be repeated in a large `GridView`, with parts of its right and bottom sides cut off. Considering that the dimension of a `GridView` will change with each request according to the amount of data and the size of the browser display, your chances of obtaining a consistent `GridView` background image are small.

We know of only two cases where a background image works well. First is a single color image with a very low contrast, such as a faint watermark of a company logo. Another is to have an artist design an "image," which is just a gradation of color from the very faintest to light as you go from left to right. You want to make this image a little larger than the largest the `GridView` can render. It will not be trouble-some to the eye when a "wash" like this cuts off.

Using a background image will override a backcolor setting.

Font and ForeColor

You can set the characteristics of the text displayed in the entire table. This operation is no different from modifying the font in standard HTML. Keep in mind that selecting the table control and setting font attributes makes changes to the entire table (information about changing to specific columns and rows will come in the next section of this chapter). You can change general characteristics of the font in the font property of the table control (note the plus sign [+] for expansion to the left of the property name in the property window).

```
<asp:gridview ... font-bold="True" font-underline="False" ... >
<asp:gridview ... font-name="Verdana" font-size="10pt" ... >
<asp:gridview ... forecolor="#10E4DD" ... > color defined by RGB hexadecimal code
<asp:gridview ... forecolor="PeachPuff" ... > one of the standard WWW colors
<asp:gridview ... forecolor="ActiveCaptionText" ... > color of user's Windows setup
```

Height and Width

The `GridView` control will automatically size itself to accommodate the values on the screen. However, you have the ability to override this default and specify a custom width and height. Select the table and use the VWD Properties window to specify the height and width. The result will be:

```
<asp:GridView ID="GridView1" Runat="server"
        ...
        Height="5cm"
        Width="200">
```

In this case, the available units are in for inches, cm for centimeters, and px for pixels (the default). Although absolute sizing options are available, you gain flexibility by leaving them out and letting the table size itself to the values. On the other hand, absolute values for a table slightly reduce the amount of time it takes the browser to generate the rendering. In the Design View pane, you can also drag the handles on the sides or corners of the `GridView` to resize it. VWD will automatically pop up a real-time notifier of the value as it is being revised.

> **Note that if the height and width values are set too low, they will be ignored by the browser. The exact numbers are dependent on the browser and monitor.**

CellSpacing and CellPadding

Cell spacing determines the distance between cells. Effectively, that becomes the width between the gridlines around each cell. *Cell padding* creates the space inside the cell, between the values and the cell walls. Increasing padding gives the values more space between each other. Units for both of these properties are always expressed in pixels. The default for CellPadding is `-1`, which indicates that no HTML value is rendered. The browser will then use its own default which is generally zero, meaning there will be no gap created between the gridlines of adjacent cells.

```
<asp:gridview ... cellpadding="2" cellspacing="5" ... >
```

Borders and GridLines

Border refers to the single rectangle around the entire `GridView` or `DetailsView` control. *Grid lines* refer to the internal lines that separate the cells. You can modify grid lines in two ways. The default settings for the entire table control are done as described here. Specific columns, rows or cells can then override the default, as described in the "Customizing Styles within a Table" section of this chapter.

You can change the grid lines for the entire table by setting the `GridLines` property to one of the following four values. The default is `Both`.

```
<asp:GridView...  gridlines="None"...
<asp:GridView...  gridlines="Horizontal"
<asp:GridView...  gridlines="Vertical"
<asp:GridView...  gridlines="Both"
```

The border color is set in the same manner as the table's background color, using either a standard color name recognized by the W3C, a color that the browser picks up from the user's Windows settings, or an RBG hexadecimal value.

The border width can be set in the Properties window when the table is selected. The options for units include `in`, `cm`, and `px`. The border style can be one of ten options, as follows. Always use the text name when setting properties; the parenthetical numbers shown below are only for reference in code.

```
<asp:GridView... borderstyle="NotSet" ...>
or
<asp:GridView... borderstyle=0 ...>

NotSet (0)      None (1)
Dotted (2)      Dashed (3)      Solid (4)           Double (5)
Groove (6)      Ridge (7)       Inset (8)           Outset (9)
```

Note that numbers six to nine inclusive will render the four borders in different configurations to create a three-dimensional effect. The value in parentheses is the integer setting held by the control and the value reported if you look at the contents of the property. The `Double` style must have a width of at least `3` to accommodate the dimensions of two lines; widths less than `3` will appear as a single line. Don't be surprised that when using a setting of `None`, depending on the `GridView.GridLines` value, there will still be some or all lines around the table because the outside edge of the outer cells will create a line around the entire table that appears the same as a table border. Note that when setting any of these values using the English name in code, you'll need to use the syntax that qualifies the value with the `BorderStyle` enumeration, as follows:

```
GridView1.BorderStyle = BorderStyle.Dashed
```

The preceding properties will change the appearance of the entire `GridView` or `DetailsView`. However, Themes and Style Sheets (to be discussed shortly) make it easier to change all of the grids in your site at once. You can also apply several formatting changes at once using the Auto Format feature of VWD. But before we move on, we'll try out what we've covered so far.

Try It Out Colors, Grid Lines, and Backgrounds

In this exercise, you will create two `GridViews`, separated by a horizontal line, `<hr/>`. Both will show the first and last names of the first three Northwind employees, but with different appearances. Of course, you can use more colorful options, but in this exercise you will use shades of black, white, and gray so that they are obvious in the black-and-white printing of the book.

1. Create a folder named `C:\Websites\BegAspNetDB\ch06` and, within it, a page named `TIO-0601-ColorAndBorder.aspx`. Add a single `SqlDataSource` control named `NorthWindEmployees` using your `MDFNorthwind` connection. Select the `LastName` and `FirstName` of the first five employees. To review limiting the number of records returned, in the SqlDataSource Control Wizard step for configuring the `Select` statement, click the WHERE button and set the column equal to `EmployeeID`, the operator to `<=`, the source to none, and the value to 5. Don't forget to click the Add button.
2. Create two `GridViews` with IDs set to White and Black, both linked to the `NorthWindEmployees` data source.

3. In VWD's Design view, select the White GridView and then turn your attention to the Properties window. Format it to have a wide (`4px`) `DarkGray` border that appears `Outset`. Set the font to be a typeface that is *sans serif* and about a quarter-inch tall (`Large`). There should be no internal lines dividing cells.

4. Format the `GridView` with `ID=Black` to have a black background with white letters in a block font with bold italics. Set the border to be `Double`, and display white lines between all cells. Your page will resemble the following, which you can view in your browser (see Figure 6-4):

```
<%@ Page Language="VB" %>
<!DOCTYPE html PUBLIC "-//W3C//DTD XHTML 1.0 Transitional//EN"
"http://www.w3.org/TR/xhtml1/DTD/xhtml1-transitional.dtd">
<script runat="server"> </script>
<html xmlns="http://www.w3.org/1999/xhtml" >
<head id="Head1" runat="server">
    <title>TIO-0601-ColorAndBorder</title>
</head>
<body>
<h2>Chapter 06 TIO #0601 Color and Border</h2>
    <form id="form1" runat="server">
    <div>
        <asp:SqlDataSource ID="SqlDataSource1" runat="server"
            ConnectionString="<%$ ConnectionStrings:MdfNorthwind %>"
            SelectCommand="SELECT [LastName], [FirstName]
                FROM [Employees]
                WHERE ([EmployeeID] <= @EmployeeID)">
            <SelectParameters>
                <asp:Parameter DefaultValue="5" Name="EmployeeID" Type="Int32" />
            </SelectParameters>
        </asp:SqlDataSource>
        <h3> White </h3>
        <asp:GridView ID="White" runat="server"
            AutoGenerateColumns="False"
            DataSourceID="SqlDataSource1"
            BorderColor="DarkGray"
            BorderStyle="Outset"
            BorderWidth="4px"
            Font-Names="Microsoft Sans Serif"
            Font-Size="Large"
            GridLines="None">
            <Columns>
                <asp:BoundField DataField="LastName"
                    HeaderText="LastName"
                    SortExpression="LastName" />
                <asp:BoundField DataField="FirstName"
                    HeaderText="FirstName"
                    SortExpression="FirstName" />
            </Columns>
        </asp:GridView>
        <hr />
<h3>Black</h3>
        <asp:GridView ID="Black" runat="server"
            AutoGenerateColumns="False"
            DataSourceID="SqlDataSource1"
```

```
                BackColor="Black"
                BorderColor="White"
                BorderStyle="Double"
                Font-Bold="True"
                Font-Italic="True"
                ForeColor="White">
                <Columns>
                    <asp:BoundField DataField="LastName"
                        HeaderText="LastName"
                        SortExpression="LastName" />
                    <asp:BoundField DataField="FirstName"
                        HeaderText="FirstName"
                        SortExpression="FirstName" />
                </Columns>
            </asp:GridView>
        </div>
        </form>
</body>
</html>
```

5. Save your work.

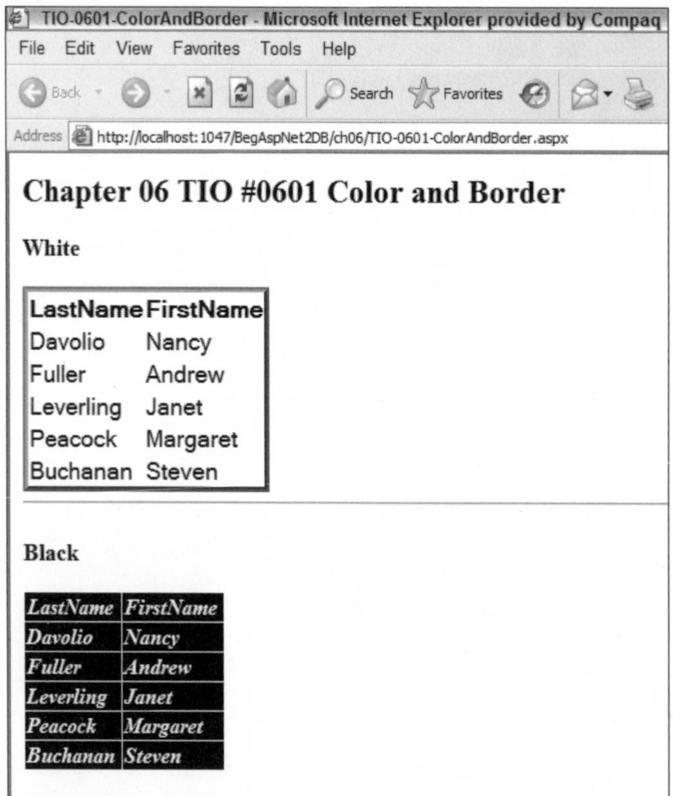

Figure 6-4

How It Works

These concepts are simple; you just have to know the exact name of each property and where to find it in the properties list. When you set the font using VWD, you do not get a sample in a dialog box (as in Microsoft Word). You will probably be most comfortable with one of the three color-naming methods, but keep in mind that pages you view from other programmers may use another method. Be prepared to work in all three methods.

The highlighted section of code above sets the `Select` statement to return only the first five employees (actually, it returns all the employees with `EmployeeID` numbers of five or less). The `WHERE` clause (first shaded line) limits the number of records returned to those that match the pattern of `EmployeeID` is equal to or less then the value in the parameter named `@EmployeeID`. That parameter is filled with a value of `5` by the `SelectParameters` tag highlighted in the bottom three shaded lines. We will discuss parameters in more depth in Chapters 11 and 12.

HorizontalAlign

An entire table can be located on the page at the left, center, or right as per the HorizontalAlign property. Keep in mind that, when this property is used in the `GridView` or `DetailsView` control, it applies to the location of the entire table, not the values within the cells. Alignment of values within cells is covered in the "Customizing Styles within a Table" section later in this chapter.

ShowHeader and ShowFooter

A `GridView`, by default, will show a header but not a footer. The header will contain the names of the fields in the data source, as column headers. If you want to show a footer, you must set the `ShowFooter` property to `True` and optionally specify a value to display in the footer style (covered shortly).

A `DetailsView` control has an optional header that goes at the top of the control. For `DetailsView`, *Field Headings* refers to the column of labels stacked along the left side, next to the values. In `DetailsView` there is no option to ShowFooter. But if a string is specified for the FooterText, then the footer appears as the bottom row of the `DetailsView` (but above the page navigation row, if that is turned on).

ToolTip

A ToolTip specific to a control appears whenever the mouse is held over the control. For example, in almost any Microsoft toolbar, if you hold the mouse over one icon, you will get a short text identifying the tool. These are easy to implement for a `GridView` or `DetailsView`, using the `ToolTip` property to create source code, as follows:

```
<asp:gridview ... tooltip="My tooltip for the entire table" .../>
```

You can have a very long ToolTip, although text over a few hundred characters has been found to be unstable (it sometimes flashes). However, you cannot include any formatting characters such as `vbTab` or `chr(10)` or a `Shift+Return`.

ToolTips are particularly useful to remind users that clicking on the column heading will perform a sort. In some applications, selecting a record will automatically start a process or lead to a new page — that can also be indicated in a ToolTip.

Try It Out — Headers, Footers, Alignment, and ToolTips

In this exercise, you will experiment with the three behaviors of the `GridView` previously listed.

1. Create a new page named `TIO-0602-HeadFootAlignTip.aspx`. View the Database Explorer, expand your connection to `MDFNorthwind`, and expand the Employees table. Select the employee's ID and both names, and then drag them to the page.
2. Add a ToolTip for the entire `GridView` with the text `Employee list is updated each midnight`.
3. Turn on the `ShowFooter` and turn off the `ShowHeader`. Save the page and look at it in your browser. Note that the footers are empty by default.
4. Close the browser and set the entire `GridView` to be on the right side of the page. Save your work and observe it in the browser.
5. Now go to the bottom of the page and add a `DetailsView` that gets its data from the same data source control. Open the Smart Tasks panel and enable paging (we explain details of paging in Chapter 7). Set its ToolTip to read `More employees visible by clicking navigation tools below`. Align the `DetailsView Right`. Scroll through the properties and note that a `DetailsView` does not have `ShowHeader` and `ShowFooter` properties

   The table controls of the page should be similar to the following:

```
...
<h2>Chapter 06 TIO #0602 </h2>
<h2>Headers, Footers, Alignment and ToolTips</h2>

    <form id="form1" runat="server">
    <div>
        <asp:GridView ID="GridView1"
                runat="server"
                AutoGenerateColumns="False"
                DataKeyNames="EmployeeID"
                DataSourceID="SqlDataSource1"
                EmptyDataText="There are no data records to display."
                HorizontalAlign="Right"
                ShowFooter="True"
                ShowHeader="False"
                ToolTip="Employee list is updated each midnight">
            <Columns> ... </Columns>
        </asp:GridView>

        <asp:DetailsView ID="DetailsView1" runat="server"
            DataSourceID="SqlDataSource1"
            HorizontalAlign="Right"
            ToolTip="More employees visible by clicking the navigation tools below"
            Height="50px"
            Width="125px">
        </asp:DetailsView>
```

How It Works

With this exercise, you see a ToolTip in action and then observe the default and modified behavior of `ShowHeader` and `ShowFooter`. Last, you modified the `HorizontalAlign` property of the tables. Keep in mind that the `HorizontalAlign` property moves the entire table, not the text within one cell. When we discuss column-level formatting, we will cover how to align data within a cell.

Customizing Styles within a Table

We've looked at a number of properties that affect the appearance of a table as a whole, from colors and borders to alignment and ToolTips. This section examines the set of style properties that can be applied to individual elements in the `GridView` and `DetailsView` renderings. A *style* in ASP.NET is a collection of properties that affect the look and feel of a portion of a control. A portion means, for example, the header row. The properties you can set in an ASP.NET style roughly correspond to the same style properties you might apply to an HTML tag directly (for example, colors, sizes, and borders). In fact, some of the table properties we've looked at so far are in fact style properties (inherited by the base ASP.NET `WebControl` class). However, this section looks at specific styles that apply to a portion of the table. In particular, there are styles that apply to rows in the table, and there are styles that apply to cells.

GridView and DetailsView Styles

The `GridView` and `DetailsView` control renderings are made up of a table with rows, and these row controls provide a set of properties you can set for applying style customizations to a row or group of rows in this rendering. The following style properties are supported:

- **RowStyle:** Applies to each row containing data from the data source.
- **AlternatingRowStyle:** Applies to every other row containing data from the data source. The properties set on this style override the same properties on `RowStyle`.
- **HeaderStyle:** Formats the top row.
- **FieldHeaderStyle:** Formats the cells in the header column on the left. (`DetailsView` only).
- **FooterStyle:** Formats the footer row.
- **PagerStyle:** Formats the pager row (more on that in Chapters 11 and 12) that contains tools for navigations, such as buttons for First, Last, Previous, and Next.
- **SelectedRowStyle:** Formats a row after it has been selected. This style is typically used when the `GridView` has a `CommandField` with the `ShowSelect` set to `true`.
- **EditRowStyle:** Formats a row that has been shifted into Edit mode, for example, when a user clicks an Edit button rendered by a `CommandField` with `ShowEditButton` set to `true`.
- **CommandRowStyle:** Formats a row with the command buttons to edit, delete or insert data (`DetailsView` only).
- **EmptyDataRowStyle:** Applies to the table rendered when no data is received from the data source control. The name of this style property is a bit misleading. This is not for a row representing a phantom record that does not have data. Rather, this is a single row that is substituted for the all the other rows in the entire table control (`GridView` or `DetailsView`) when the data source control delivers zero records.

Note that a feature must be turned on in order for its style to have an effect. For example, footers are turned off by default in `GridView`. In `DetailsView`, footers only appear if the footer text is not null Likewise, paging rows are not turned on by default. Also note that a border style, as discussed earlier in the book, is not the same kind of style. Border style refers to the thickness and pattern of the border line.

> **The term *Row Style* is used two ways. In a larger sense, as we discuss in the intro to this section, row styles means any style that applies to rows as opposed to the entire table or columns. In this meaning, row styles include all the style properties in the preceding list.**
>
> **In a more specific sense, row style means just the style applied to the row of a normal record. With this meaning, the term applies only to the first style property in the preceding list.**

With VWD, you can modify the format of a row style by using the properties of the control. You will see a long list of options for each row type. (You may have to click the plus sign to expand the options. If you are typing in another editor, styles for a type of row are held in `<style>` tags within the control tag. They can be located before or after the `<Columns>` tag but not within the `<Columns>` tags. For example, the following creates white characters on a black background for the header row:

```
<asp:GridView ID="GridView1" Runat="server">

    <HeaderStyle
            BackColor="black"
            ForeColor="white">
    </HeaderStyle>

    <Columns>
      <asp:BoundField DataField="MyField1"></asp:BoundField>
      <asp:BoundField DataField="MyField2"></asp:BoundField>
      <asp:BoundField DataField="MyField3"></asp:BoundField>
    </Columns>

</asp:GridView>
```

There is an alternative syntax supported for setting styles that does not require a separate `<style>` inner tag. Instead, you can type within the `GridView` tag the name of the style property, followed by a dash, followed by the property of the style you wish to set, as an attribute of the `GridView` tag itself.

```
<asp:GridView ID="GridView1" HeaderStyle-BackColor="black" HeaderStyle-
ForeColor="white" Runat="server">
```

Note that if the style property has subproperties, these can be nested using additional dashes between the property names. The most common example of this is the `Font` style property.

```
<asp:GridView ID="GridView1" HeaderStyle-Font-Bold="true" HeaderStyle-Font-
Name="Verdana" Runat="server">
```

Try It Out Formatting Row Styles

This exercise formats styles in several types of rows, including Header Style, Pager Style, and Row Style.

1. Create a new file named `TIO-0603-RowStyles`, and use it to simply display a `GridView` with the `ProductID`, `ProductName`, and `UnitPrice` of the first 10 items in the Products table. Save the file and check it in your browser to see that, by default, there is no formatting other than the default bold applied to the header row.
2. Create a `HeaderRowStyle` with a larger font, as follows. Select the `GridView`, then go to the Properties window. Expand the `Style` pane and then the `HeaderStyle` pane, and then expand the `Font` pane. Change the size to `Large`.
3. Set your basic rows to be italic using similar steps in the `RowStyle` pane. Note that you don't have to worry about selecting rows. Just select the `GridView` as a whole and find the appropriate property. This time, you change row style to `RowStyle Font-Italic`.
4. Differentiate every other row by setting a very faint gray background using `AlternatingRowStyle/Backcolor` set to something like `#E0E0E0`.
5. Turn on paging (GridView⇨Smart Tasks panel), and then set the `PagerStyle` to a sans-serif font such as `Arial Black`. Set the `GridView` to a PageSize of five. Save the file (the data-bound control is shown in code below) and take a look in the browser, which should be similar to the page shown in Figure 6-5.

```
<h2>Chapter 06 TIO #0603 Row Styles</h2>
...
<asp:GridView ID="GridView1"
        runat="server"
        AutoGenerateColumns="False"
        DataKeyNames="ProductID"
        DataSourceID="SqlDataSource1"
        EmptyDataText="There are no data records to display."
        AllowPaging="True"
        PageSize="5">
        <Columns>
            ...
        </Columns>
        <RowStyle Font-Italic="True" />
        <PagerStyle Font-Names="Arial Black" />
        <HeaderStyle Font-Size="Large" />
        <AlternatingRowStyle BackColor="#E0E0E0"/>
</asp:GridView>
```

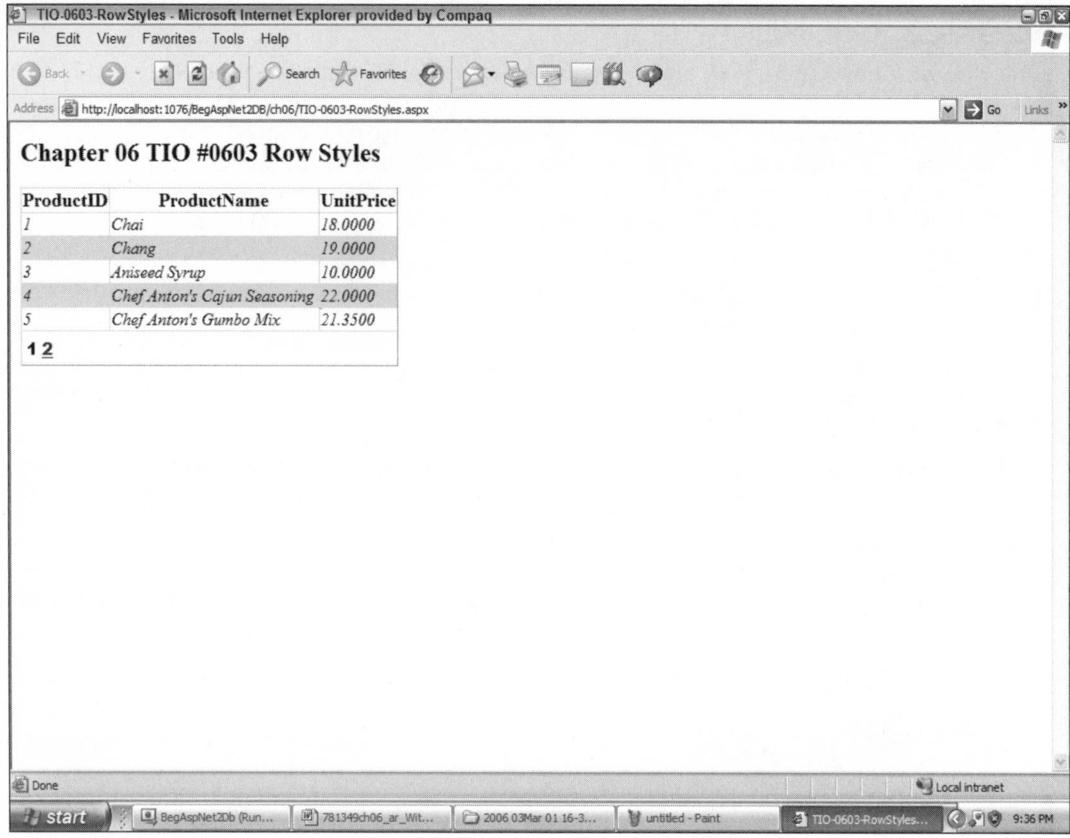

Figure 6-5

How It Works

Formatting rows is easy; however, there are a few syntax tricks. Note that VWD created `<XXXstyle>` tags within the `GridView` but outside the `<Column>` tags. When you set a row style, it applies to the appropriate row right across the `GridView`.

Empty Tables

The last chapter discussed how to use the `BoundField.NullDisplayText` to display a string when a single value is `NULL`. But what if the data source control returns no records at all? Perhaps the `SelectCommand` had a `WHERE` clause (for example, `DOB < 1/1/1800`) that is unfulfilled by any of the records. The result will be that your `GridView` or `DetailsView` does not render at all; you get blank space on the page. You can improve the appearance using the properties for `EmptyDataRow`, which will display to the page instead of the entire table.

> **The terminology here is confusing. *EmptyDataRow* implies that one row of a `GridView` is empty, but the term actually means that the set of data is empty of any rows at all. If there is one "empty" row, it will not show up in the `GridView`. An empty cell will show up as blank.**

`EmptyDataRowText` allows you to substitute a literal text where the table control would have been. Having a value for `EmptyRow` text actually does two things. First, it creates a table of one row and one cell. Second, it renders the text into the single cell of that little table. Once you have a value in `EmptyDataRowText`, you can set any of the dozen or so formatting properties of that little table row (background, width, and so on) by using the `EmptyDataRowStyle`.

Try It Out Empty Tables

In this exercise, you will build three versions of a page. The first will display the employee's data in a `DetailsView`. The second will seek to retrieve employees whose `ID = 999`, and there will be no result. In the third version, you will handle the lack of results by displaying an alternate message in the `EmptyDataRowStyle`.

1. Create a new file named `TIO-0604-EmptyTable-ver1.aspx`. Add a `DetailsView` control bound to the `DataSource` control that displays the ID and name fields from Employees in Northwind. Save and check the page in your browser to see that you see the values for the first employee. Close the browser.

2. Save the page as `TIO-0604-EmptyTable-ver2.aspx`. Change the `SelectCommand` so that it has a `WHERE` clause that will return no records, for example, `WHERE EmployeeID = 999`. You can do this manually in the source view or run through the data source control's wizard and click the WHERE button. The latter technique will result in code that has a select parameter. Save your work and note that the `DetailsView` control does not render at all. Close the browser.

```
<asp:SqlDataSource ID="SqlDataSource1" runat="server"
 ConnectionString="<%$ ConnectionStrings:MdfNorthwind %>"
 SelectCommand="SELECT [EmployeeID], [LastName], [FirstName] FROM [Employees] WHERE
EmployeeID = 999">
</asp:SqlDataSource>
```

3. Save the page as TIO-0604-EmptyTable-ver3.aspx. In Design view, select the DetailsView, go to the Properties window to find EmptyRowText, and set its value to No employees match your criteria. Then go to the EmptyDataRowStyle and assign a font of Arial Bold in size Large. Save your work and test it in your browser.

```
<asp:DetailsView ID="DetailsView1" runat="server"
 AutoGenerateRows="False"
 DataKeyNames="EmployeeID"
 DataSourceID="SqlDataSource1"
 EmptyDataText="No employees match your criteria">
 <Fields>
       ...
 </Fields>
 <EmptyDataRowStyle Font-Names="Arial Black" Font-Size="Large" />
</asp:DetailsView>
```

How It Works

This exercise starts by displaying a DetailsView without problems. When you change the SELECTCommand to return no records, the page does not give the user good feedback about the absence of the DetailsView control. There is no error, but the user is left wondering whether there might be an error. You recover by adding an EmptyDataText and formatting the resulting EmptyDataRowStyle.

Styles Specific to the DetailsView Control

Because of its different layout (fields stacked vertically rather than laid out horizontally) and capabilities (able to insert new records), the DetailsView has some special styles.

- **FieldHeaderStyle:** This region is the vertical list of field names to the left of the values. Functionally, it is the same as a header row in a GridView, but it is located to the left and rotated in a DetailsView. The header row in DetailsView doesn't contain column names, rather, just the value of HeaderText, if set on the DetailsView control.
- **CommandRowStyle:** When a CommandField, such as Edit, Delete, or Insert, is used in the DetailsView, it creates a new row for the command button(s). This row can be styled in the same way as other regions of the DetailsView.
- **InsertRowStyle:** Although the GridView and DetailsView are very similar, they have one major functional difference: DetailsView can add ("insert") new records. The functionality is enabled when a CommandField with ShowInsertButton="true" is added to the DetailsView. The DetailsView control then offers a special style for data rows when they are in insertion mode.

Try It Out DetailsView Styles

In this short exercise, you will modify the three styles mentioned in the preceding bulleted list.

1. Get a quick start by opening the TIO-0604-EmptyTableStyleVer1.aspx file you created earlier and save it as TIO-5-SpecialStylesForDetailsView.aspx. Change the title in the <head> and the <h2> text in the <body> using the text in the code list below.

```
...
<head id="Head1" runat="server">
 <title>TIO-0605-SpecialStylesForDetailsView</title>
</head>
<body>
 <h2>Chapter 06 TIO #0605 Special Styles For Details View</h2>
     <form id="form1" runat="server">
```

2. In VWD Design view, select the DetailsView control and open its Smart Tasks panel. Click on Edit Fields and add a field of type Command Field and the subtype "New, Insert, Cancel." Click OK to close the Edit Columns dialog box and the Smart Tasks panel. Observe that you now have a command row that holds the button "New."

3. Select the DetailsView control, and look in the Properties window to find the CommandRowStyle and set the Font and Italics to True.

4. Scroll down in the Properties window to the `InsertRowStyle` and set its background to light gray.
5. Last, with the `DetailsView` control still selected, look in the Properties window for the `FieldHeaderStyle` and change the font to `Arial Black`. Save the page and observe the results in your browser; the source code should look like the following listing:

```
...
<h2>Chapter 06 TIO #0605 Special Styles for Details View</h2>
...
<asp:DetailsView ID="DetailsView1" runat="server"
 AutoGenerateRows="False"
 DataKeyNames="EmployeeID"
 DataSourceID="SqlDataSource1">
 <Fields> ... </Fields>
<CommandRowStyle Font-Italic="True" />
<FieldHeaderStyle Font-Names="Arial Black" />
<InsertRowStyle BackColor="#E0E0E0" />
 </asp:DetailsView>
...
```

How It Works

For the `DetailsView` control, you have a few options beyond what we discussed for the `GridView`. You can use the `FieldHeaderStyle` to format the cells of the left column where the names of fields are listed. When the `DetailsView` contains a `CommandField`, the command buttons rendered by that field will be formatted according to the `CommandRowStyle`. Also, recall that the `DetailsView` offers the ability to add new records (called *inserting*), a function not available in the `GridView` (specifics are discussed starting in Chapter 12). The insertion function is available once there is a `CommandField` of the type `Insert`. When the Insert button (New) is clicked, the `DetailsView` control changes to Insert mode. The `CommandRow` now offers two different commands: `Insert` and `Cancel`. When in Insert mode, the body of the `DetailsView` changes to the format of `InsertRowStyle`.

Column Styles and Field Styles

Similar to rows, individual columns (in `GridView`) or fields (in `DetailsView`) can also have formatting. Each column or field style applies only to that column or field, as opposed to some row styles that can span multiple rows (like `RowStyle` and `AlternatingRowStyle`). Note that you must define your columns or fields to apply styles to their cells. You cannot use `AutoGenerateColumns` or `AutoGenerateFields`.

The style for a field or column is broken into four parts. In other words, you do not apply a style to an entire column. You apply four separate styles to the four parts of a field/column:

- Header
- Footer
- Item (cell displaying values)
- Controls in a cell

At first this may seem confusing—we covered header styles in the last section, so why again? Understand that you can format cells and groups in more then one way. You have two options for header cells, depending on where the HeaderStyle tag is located, as compared below.

Option one is to use the HeaderStyle *as a tag directly within the* GridView *tag* to format *all* the headers of all columns as follows. In this case, the header cells of all fields (one and two) will be red.

```
<asp:GridView ID="GridView1" Runat="server"
  ...
<HeaderStyle BackColor="Red" />
 <Columns>
        <asp:BoundField DataField="MyField1" />
        <asp:BoundField DataField="MyField2" />
 </Columns>
</asp:GridView>
```

Option two is to use *the* HeaderStyle *property of a given field* (such as an <asp:boundfield> tag), which means the header style only applies to the header of that *one* column. In the following code, the column one header is red and the column two header is orange.

```
<asp:GridView ID="GridView1" Runat="server"
  ...
 <Columns>
        <asp:BoundField1>
               ...
               <HeaderStyle BackColor="Red" />
        </asp:BoundField>
        <asp:BoundField>
               ...
               <HeaderStyle BackColor="Orange" />
        </asp:BoundField>
 </Columns>
</asp:GridView>
```

The following styles apply only to the cell(s) within one column or field. They can be seen in source code as a tag within a field tag. (To repeat, if you want to change the style of all the cells in one row of all the columns, use the GridView or DetailsView row styles.) Use the following four styles when you want cells of just one column to be different from the cells of the rest of the columns.

- **HeaderStyle:** Affects the header cell of the field or column. In a GridView, that is the cell holding the HeaderText.
- **FooterStyle:** Affects the footer cell of the field or column. In a GridView, this is an optional cell at the bottom of the column. In DetailsView, this has no effect.
- **ItemStyle:** Affects the actual data value cells in the middle of the column or field.
- **ControlStyle:** Affects the appearance of all WebControls in the data value cells of a field. For example, the button or hyperlink cells rendered by a ButtonField or HyperLinkField would have this style applied. In a BoundField column, this style also applies to the TextBox when the GridView row is put into Edit mode by the user clicking the Edit command button.

Note that the syntax is `RowStyle` (and `AlternateRowStyle`) for the `GridView`-level style. For the column-level equivalent, the syntax is `ItemStyle`. There is no `AlternateItemStyle` within a single column.

Try It Out Column Styles

In this exercise, you will set some overall formatting for a `GridView`. But you want one column to stand out, so giving its cells special formatting is necessary.

1. Create a new file named `TIO-0606-ColumnStyles.aspx`. Add a `GridView` to display the `EmployeeID` and first and last names from the Employees table of Northwind.
2. Select the `GridView` and set the row styles that will apply to all the columns of the table, as follows, using the Properties pane: `HeaderStyle = Large` font size and `RowStyle =` light gray background. Save and view in your browser (This is the same as `TIO-0606-ColumnStyles-1 in the downloads`). Observe that the `GridView` row styles apply to cells in all columns.
3. Close the browser and now, in Design view, select the `GridView`. Choose Edit Columns, select the `FirstName` column from the Selected fields list at the lower left, and go to the Properties section of the dialog box. Expand the `HeaderStyle` section and set the background to black, set the forecolor to white, and turn on italics within the `Font` section. Do the same for the ItemStyle. Click OK to close the Fields dialog box, save the code as version 2, and check it in the browser to see a page similar to Figure 6-6.

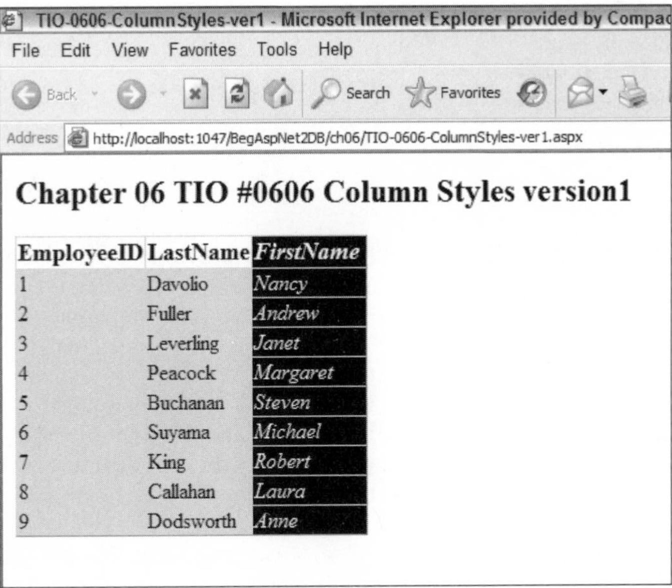

Figure 6-6

4. Examine the following source code to see the relationships between the controls. The upper shaded area sets header and item style within just the `BoundField` for `FirstName`. The lower shading sets the header and row styles for all the columns.

```
<h2>Chapter 06 TIO #0606 Column Styles version1</h2>
...
<asp:GridView ID="GridView1" runat="server"
 AutoGenerateColumns="False"
 DataKeyNames="EmployeeID"
 DataSourceID="SqlDataSource1" >
  <Columns>
    <asp:BoundField DataField="EmployeeID"
          HeaderText="EmployeeID"
          ReadOnly="True"
          SortExpression="EmployeeID" />
    <asp:BoundField DataField="LastName"
          HeaderText="LastName"
          SortExpression="LastName" />
    <asp:BoundField DataField="FirstName"
          HeaderText="FirstName"
          SortExpression="FirstName" >
         <ItemStyle
          BackColor="Black"
          Font-Italic="True"
          ForeColor="White" />
         <HeaderStyle
          BackColor="Black"
          Font-Italic="True"
          ForeColor="White" />
    </asp:BoundField>
 </Columns>
<RowStyle BackColor="#E0E0E0" />
<HeaderStyle Font-Size="Large" />
</asp:GridView>
```

How It Works

The key to understanding this exercise is to know what syntax applies to which section of the `GridView` and where to make the changes in the Designer. To apply formatting to the entire `GridView`, you select the `GridView` and use the editor's main Properties window. The result will be styles applied directly in the `GridView` tag.

To change just the cells of one column, select the `GridView` and then expand the Smart Tasks panel and click on Edit Columns. Then, select the column to change and then modify the style properties such as `ItemStyle`, `HeaderStyle`, and `FooterStyle` in the Properties window that is within the Edit Columns dialog box. The result will be styles created within one field tag.

Using Cascading Style Sheets

Cascading Style Sheets (CSS) are a system to create a single set of appearance definitions for an entire Web site and to do so with a minimum of coding and information transfer across the network. The sheet defines styles called Classes and then, for each style, provides a format consisting of the font, colors, indentation, and almost any other HTML formatting tag. Then, any control on the site with formatting (including table controls) can use a set of styles by setting a single `CssClass` property. When using CSS, three objectives are achieved:

- All pages will look the same because the style comes from one source.
- The description of the style must only be transmitted once across the connection because subsequent uses read from a copy of the style sheet cached on the browser machine.
- The developer has to make a change in only one place (the style sheet) to affect stylistic changes across every page of the site.

You can build a CSS definition quickly and accurately in Visual Studio by adding a new item to the root of your site of the type "Style Sheet" ending with the extension `.css`. By default, there will be a `body{}` definition, but you can add a new style by right-clicking after the braces and selecting Build New Style. The Build New Style dialog box accepts your input and then builds a class with a syntax similar to the following.

```
body{
}

.MyStyleGridView{
 color: white;
 font-family: Tahoma;
 background-color: black;
 text-align: right;
}
```

Then, in your ASPX page, you must add two items. First, in the `<head>` there must be a `<link>` to the CSS file, as follows. The example assumes that the CSS is in the root of your site. This establishes the style sheet for the entire page. To create the link in VWD, select the page and look in the Properties window. Double-check that the object selected in the top of the Properties window is the DOCUMENT; then set the `StyleSheet` to your CSS file. VWD will create the following code in the page.

```
<head runat="server">
 <link rel="Stylesheet" type="text/css" href="~/MyStyleSheet.css" />
</head>
```

Second, set a property for the `GridView` or `DetailsView` that determines which of the style classes in the CSS to apply to the table. Although you must have a leading period before your class name in the CSS file, you do not use the leading period in the `GridView` property. Again, do this in the VWD Property window by selecting the `GridView` object, scrolling down to the Appearance section and then the `CssClass` property. Type the name of the class, and press Enter to force VWD to create code as follows on the page:

```
<asp:gridview ... cssclass="MyStyleForGridView" ... >
```

When you create the CSS file, you have to translate the ASP.NET 2.0 control properties into the syntax allowed for style sheets.

> **The complete list of allowed style sheet format names can be found at** www.w3.org/TR/REC-CSS1 **or** http://msdn.microsoft.com/library/default.asp?url=/workshop/author/css/reference/attributes.asp.

The following table describes some of the conversions that trip up new designers.

Description	ASP Control Syntax	CSS Syntax
Text color	`Forecolor`	`Color: Green;` `Color: rgb(120,140,88);`
Background color	`Backcolor`	`background-color:blue;`
Italics	`Font-Italic="true"`	`Font-Style: italic;`
GridView border	`BorderColor`	`Table-border-color-light: Green;` `Table-border-color-dark: Red;`

Now that you've had an overview, use the following Try It Out for practice.

Try It Out Formatting by Cascading Style Sheet

In this exercise, you will create a style for a `GridView` and use it on three `GridViews` spread across two pages. Then you will change the style and see how it rolls out to all of the `GridViews`. Last, you will create a second style and apply it to some of the `GridViews`. Note that the downloads provide more than one CSS to reflect its state after various steps. On your machine, you will create just a single CSS and change it as instructed.

1. In the root of your site, create a style sheet named `StyleSheet.CSS` as follows. In VWD Solution Explorer, right-click on the root of your site and select Add new item. Double-check that you clicked on the root, not the `ch06` folder. Use the StyleSheet template and then proceed the same as you would for a new ASPX page. Within your new style sheet, we will make a simple change just to demonstrate the technique. Add a background color of gray for the entire document as follows. `E0` in hexadecimal is a medium value and when applied to all three colors results in gray. Save the style sheet.

```
body {
  background-color:#E0E0E0;
}
```

2. Now we will add a style sheet for `GridViews` using the VWD Style Builder tool (see Figure 6-7). At the bottom of the style sheet, type the new style name: .`GridViewOverall` followed by a pair of braces `{}`. Don't forget the beginning period. Place the insertion point between the braces, right-click, and select Build Style. By selecting categories from the left panel and then specific parameters from the right, create a `black` background with `white` letters in Arial with bold italics. Under the Edges category, set the border to be `double` line and use a weight of custom set to `5px`. Click OK to exit the StyleBuilder dialog box. VWD will create the source code.

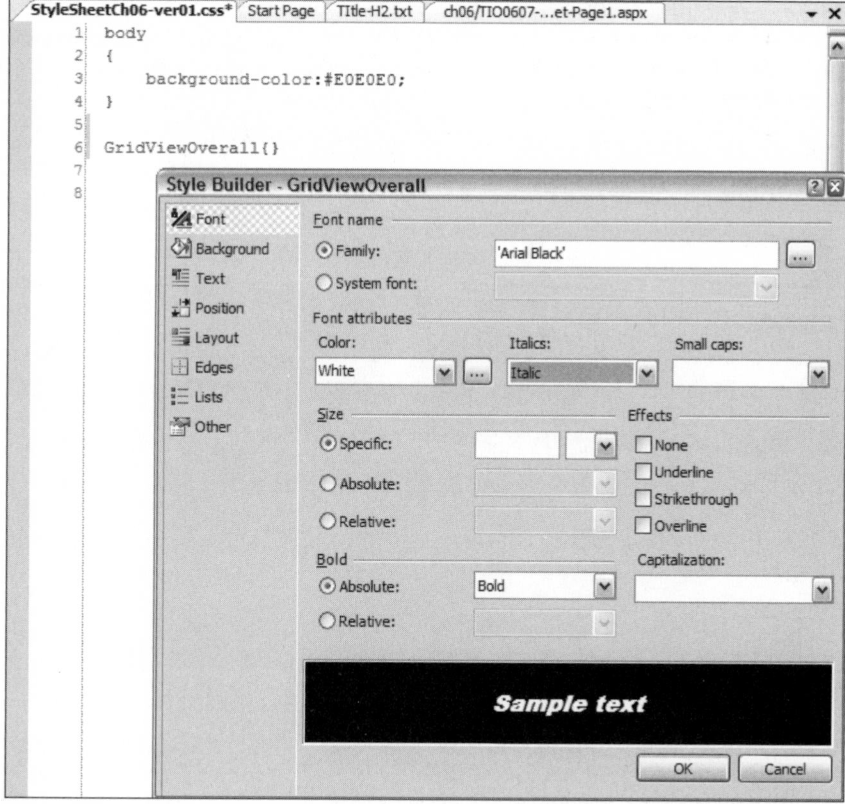

Figure 6-7

3. Save the style sheet. This will be the same as the sheet named `StyleSheet0601` in the downloads. Take a look at the code on the style sheet. The page should look similar to the following, although you may have picked a different font name and the attributes may be in a different order:

```
body {
     background-color:#E0E0E0;
}
.GridViewOverall
{
    border-right: 5px double;
    border-top: 5px double;
    font-weight: bold;
    border-left: 5px double;
    color: white;
    border-bottom: 5px double;
    font-style: italic;
    font-family: Arial;
    background-color: black;
}
```

4. In the ch06 folder, create a page named TIO-0607-GridViewFormatByStyleSheet-1.aspx. Add two GridViews that display data from Northwind; the first should show the last names from Employees, the second the names of categories from the Categories table. This will require separate data source controls.

5. Apply a StyleSheet to the entire document as follows. At the top of the properties window, drop down the object list and select the DOCUMENT, as shown in Figure 6-8. After selecting the document, go down the list of properties and set StyleSheet to StyleSheetCh06.CSS. Note that the page background is now gray, as per the body{} section of the CSS.

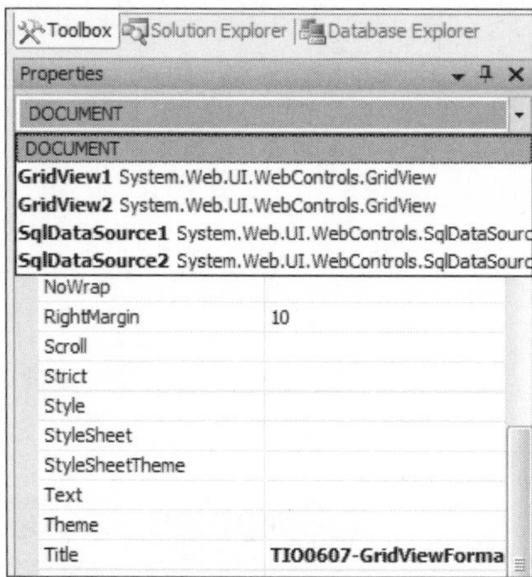

Figure 6-8

6. Apply an element of the style sheet to each GridView. Select the top GridView and set its CSSClass to your GridViewOverall from Step 1. You will have to type this — do not use the leading period. Press Enter to lock in the change. If you have saved your style sheet and not made any typos, your page in design view will now preview for you both the gray background for the entire sheet and the GridViewOverall style (black background) for the top GridView, as in Figure 6-9.

7. Give the second GridView the CssClass of GridViewOverall, as you did for the first GridView. In the ch06 folder, create a second page named \ch06\TIO-7-GridViewFormatByStyleSheet-2.aspx. You will use this to display in a GridView values from the CompanyName field from the Shippers table of Northwind. Again, format both the page and the GridView from the CSS.

8. Browse to the two pages and see how one style can be applied to GridViews on any page in the Web site.

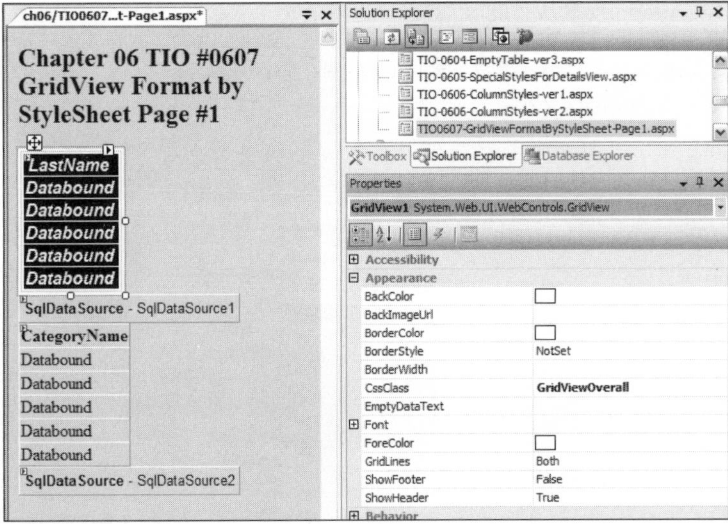

Figure 6-9

9. Change your style sheet by right-clicking on the `GridViewOverall` class and then selecting Build Style. Make changes so the class creates a wide gray border that appears `outset`, and make the font a typeface that is sans serif and about a quarter-inch tall. Save the style sheet with the same name (this will be the same as the sheet file named `StyleSheet0602` in the downloads). In your browser, refresh your two ASPX pages to see the changes rolled out to all three grids.

```
body {
     background-color:#E0E0E0;
}

.GridViewOverall
{
    border-right: gray 10px outset;
    border-top: gray 10px outset;
    font-weight: bold;
    border-left: gray 10px outset;
    color: white;
    border-bottom: gray 10px outset;
    font-style: italic;
    font-family: 'Microsoft Sans Serif';
    background-color: black;
    font-size: 0.25in;
}
```

10. In your style sheet, create a second style (class) called `GridViewBig`, which does only one thing—sets the font to `x-large`. Start by right-clicking anywhere on the style sheet, and from the menu, select Add Style Rule. Choose the Class Name option and type `GridViewBig`. Click the right arrow button to move `GridViewBig` onto the Style Rule Hierarchy list. Click OK to

close the Add Style Rule dialog box, and observe in the style sheet the new style class that you created. Right-click within the class braces and choose Build Style. Change the font size using the absolute option. Save the CSS (which will be the same as `StyleSheet3` in the downloads).

```
body {
}

.GridViewOverall{
border-width: 10px;
border-color: Gray;
border-style: Outset;
font-names: SanSerif;
font-size: larger;
}

.GridViewBig{
font-size: x-large;
}
```

11. On `TIO-0607-GridViewFormatByStyleSheet-Page1.ASPX` change the `Categories GridView` to utilize the `GridViewBig` style and view in your browser.

```
...
        <asp:GridView ID="NwCategoriesGridView" Runat="server"
            DataSourceID="NorthWindCategoriesSqlDataSource"
            CssClass="GridViewBig" />
...
```

12. Save your work.

How It Works

You start by creating your style sheet. With the VWD dialog for styles sheets, the `Body{}` style is automatically added by VWD. Right-clicking on the style sheet gives a menu option to Add Style Rule, which allows you to create a new style. Once you have created a style, you can then right-click within the braces of that style and select Build Style, which will actually create the various elements such as fonts and borders. If you are not using VWD, keep in mind that you create additional CSS class definitions with a period at the beginning of the name.

Don't forget the braces `{}` and use the syntax with a colon and semicolon. Do not use quotes around text values. The keywords for style sheets are different from what you use in attributes or properties. The CSS file is normally saved in the site's root.

Next, you created two pages with `GridViews`. You employed the style sheet with two commands. First, in the `<head>` you created a `<link>` to the name of the style sheet file. Note how easy it is to create the link's proper syntax by just clicking through the Properties pane in the designer. The second type of command is a property to set which style to use for each `GridView`.

When you make a change to the style sheet, the new format is automatically used by all `GridViews` employing that style. Furthermore, it is very easy to switch a `GridView` to a different style.

Understanding the Precedence of Styles

This and the preceding chapter have discussed many ways of formatting; in fact, there are six ways to set a format for a cell in a `GridView`. In the end, what is the order of precedence of these settings? There are two basic rules:

1. Smaller groups of cells have precedence over larger groups. For example, a setting for a column overrides a setting for the entire `GridView`.
2. Formatting properties in the control have precedence over the same setting made in a CSS style sheet.

You could view the hierarchy as follows, written out, with a style for an entire `GridView` in the CSS having the least precedence and a `Column/Field ItemStyle` property taking precedence over all others:

1. `Column/Field ItemStyle` property
2. `Column/Field ItemStyle CssClass`
3. `RowStyle` property
4. `RowStyle CssClass`
5. `GridView Style` property
6. `GridView CssClass`

Because a row can be in a variety of states (alternating, selected, editable) at different times, it is possible for a row to have more than one applicable `RowStyle` at a time. When there are multiple conflicting `RowStyles` defined, they are applied in the following order of precedence:

1. `EditRowStyle` or `InsertRowStyle`
2. `SelectedRowStyle`
3. `AlternatingRowStyle`
4. `RowStyle`

The overall effect is that styles (including CSS classes) are applied to the row in this order: `RowStyle`, `AlternatingRowStyle`, `SelectedRowStyle`, `Edit` or `InsertRowStyle`. Each style is overlaid on the style before it, accepting properties that are not in conflict and overwriting any properties set in both the existing style and the style being applied. Field styles are applied to the cell, not the row, so they are not merged at all. In this case, the browser takes care of precedence. CSS classes work similarly — ASP.NET 2.0 renders properties of both the inline styles and the CSS class, and the browser decides precedence.

Try It Out Precedence of Styles

In this exercise, you will set `GridView` cells to a background color in six different places and examine the results. You will use the colors in the following table.

Level	Background Color with Official W3C Name	RGB Code
GridView CSS	Light red ("mistyrose")	#ffe4e1
GridView Style Property	Red ("red")	#ff0000
RowStyle CSS	Light yellow ("lemonchiffon")	#fffacd
RowStyle Property	Yellow ("yellow")	#ffff00
Column ItemStyle CSS	Light green ("lightgreen")	#90ee90
Column ItemStyle Property	Green ("green")	#008000

Note that the CSS value is always lighter but is the same hue as the value set in the equivalent control-level attribute. Also note that the colors of lower frequency (red) are the least powerful in precedence, and the colors of highest frequency (green) are of the highest precedence. In general, the exercises of this book avoid color because they will not appear on the printed page, but in this case, color is a very useful tool for seeing the level of precedence.

1. Start by creating a CSS style sheet named `PrecedenceStyleSheet`.css in the root of your site. Under the `body` style, create three classes (styles) as follows. Right-click anywhere on the style sheet and select Add Style Rule. Select the Class Name option, type `GridView` and click the Add button. Click OK. Repeat for the other two styles listed below. Now go back to each and right-click inside their braces and select Build Style. The Background group includes the `BackColor`, and by clicking on the ellipses button and selecting Named Colors, you can get a style sheet like the following. (Note that all three colors are on the bottom row of the color grid.) Note how all of the colors in the style sheet are the light-colored tints. Save the style sheet.

```
body {
}
.GridView{background-color: mistyrose; }
.Row{background-color: lemonchiffon; }
.ColumnItem{background-color: lightgreen; }
```

The following code shows the same effect created with the RGB system:

```
body {
}
.GridView{background-color: #ffe4e1;}
.Row{background-color: #fffacd;}
.ColumnItem{background-color: #90ee90;}
```

2. In the folder named `ch06`, create a new file named `TIO-0608-Precedence-ver1.aspx`. Drag the `ProductName`, `UnitPrice`, and `CategoryID` columns from the Products table onto the page and complete the wizards. The page should now resemble the following. Note that there is no color in the `GridView`.
3. Close the browser and, in Design view, select the page (document). In the Properties window, set the `StyleSheet` property to `PrecedenceStyleSheet`. Now you can use the CSS styles in your controls.

4. Select the GridView and set its property CssClass="GridView". Save the page as TIO-0608-Precedence-ver2.aspx and take a look in the browser to observe the application of the pink BackColor.

5. Close the browser and, in VWD Design view, select the GridView and in the properties Window set its backcolor to Red (this is a local property, not from the CSS). Now save the page as TIO-0608-Precedence-ver3.aspx and take a look in the browser. Observe that a local setting (red) takes precedence over the StyleSheet setting (pink). Close the browser.

6. Let's move to the Row. Switch to VWD in Design view. Select the GridView, and in the Properties window, find RowStyle and expand to find CSSClass. Set it to Row, save it as TIO-0608-Precedence-ver4.aspx, and take a look in the browser (version 4 in the downloads). Observe that the data rows are now light yellow.

7. To see the precedence of local settings over CSS values for rows, select the GridView, and in the Properties Window change the RowStyle to a background of bright yellow. Save the page as TIO-0608-Precedence-ver5.aspx and take a look in the browser. Observe that a local setting for rows overrides the CSS setting.

8. Last, you will work with the ColumnItem styles. Close the browser, and in the Designer view, select the GridView. Open the Smart Tasks panel and select Edit Columns, and in the SelectedFields box select UnitPrice. In the Properties section of the dialog box, set ItemStyle/CssClass to ColumnItem. Save as TIO-0608-Precedence-ver6.aspx and take a look in the browser. The item cells of the UnitPrice column are now light green as set by the CSS.

9. As with the other settings, you can override the CSS setting with a specific attribute in the UnitPrice column's ItemStyle to set the background to green. Close the browser, and in the Designer view, select the GridView. Open the Smart Tasks panel and select Edit Columns, and in the SelectedFields box select UnitPrice. In the Properties section of the dialog box, set ItemStyle Background color to green. Save as TIO-0608-Precedence-ver6.aspx and take a look in the browser. The item cells of the UnitPrice column are now dark green from the column attribute rather then the light green of the CSS. Save as TIO-0608-Precedence-ver7.aspx. In the end, your page header and GridView control will be similar to the following.

```
...
<head id="Head1" runat="server">
    <title>TIO-0608-Precedence-ver7</title>
    <link href="../PrecedenceStyleSheet.css" rel="stylesheet" type="text/css" />
</head>
...
<asp:GridView ID="GridView1" runat="server"
AutoGenerateColumns="False"
CssClass="GridView"
DataSourceID="SqlDataSource1"
BackColor="Red">
 <Columns>
    <asp:BoundField DataField="ProductName"
    HeaderText="ProductName"
    SortExpression="ProductName" />
<asp:BoundField DataField="UnitPrice"
          HeaderText="UnitPrice"
          SortExpression="UnitPrice" >
```

```
                <ItemStyle CssClass="ColumnItem"
                BackColor="#00C000" />
        </asp:BoundField>
        <asp:BoundField DataField="CategoryID"
                HeaderText="CategoryID"
                SortExpression="CategoryID" />
    </Columns>
    <RowStyle CssClass="Row" BackColor="Yellow" />
    </asp:GridView>
```

How It Works

Although repetitious, this exercise reviews almost all of the formatting you have done to sections of the GridView and emphasizes the priority given to each style setting when rendering the GridView. You can set the entire GridView background by a CSS or local attribute. Then you do the same with rows and column cells (items). Note that local settings take precedence over CSS settings and that smaller units of cells take precedence over larger blocks of cells.

Styles provide a great flexibility to modify the appearance of a control. ASP.NET 2.0 also offers two techniques at larger scales, as we will see in the next section.

Implementing Themes and Skins

One of the principal advantages of CSS style sheets is that they allow the look and feel of your pages to be maintained centrally in a single file, so it is not necessary to update multiple pages in your site just to change a style setting you want to propagate to all pages. Although CSS is a great way to define styles in the W3C standard format that applies to the HTML elements rendered by the control, there are many control properties that affect the look of a control that cannot be represented in a CSS style sheet, for example, the GridView GridLines property. It would be nice if you could define this property in a single place to be used by all GridView controls in the site. Fortunately, ASP.NET 2.0 allows you to do this using a new feature called Themes.

A *theme* in ASP.NET 2.0 is a collection of skin files that are stored under an App_Themes subdirectory in the application root directory. A *skin file* is saved with the .skin extension and consists of a collection of control definitions with properties set on them. Each control definition will determine the properties to set for that control type across the entire site. For example, you could create a directory under the Web site root for a CustomBlue theme:

```
/ApplicationRoot
    /App_Themes
        /CustomBlue
            CustomBlue.skin
```

Inside the skin file, you can define a theme for a control by adding that control to the skin file and setting its properties. Note that the ID and DataSourceID properties on the control in a skin are intentionally left out, because they are not supported in a theme definition. The <Columns> collection is also left out, because each GridView in our site is likely to have a different set of fields. In fact, each control defines the set of properties that are themeable, which varies from control to control. Most often, the appearance properties of a control are themeable, whereas the behavioral properties are not. We set a few appearance and style properties on this control that we want to apply to all GridView controls in our site.

```
    <asp:GridView Font-Italic="true" ForeColor="LightBlue" BackColor="DarkBlue'
runat="server"/>
```

We then reference the theme from an ASPX page in our site that contains a `GridView` control with no style formatting specified on it (but bound to an appropriate data source). This is done using a Page directive at the top of the page. Note that there is no need to make any specific references in the `GridView` control of the ASPX page.

```
<%@Page Theme="CustomBlue" %>
...
<asp:GridView ID="GridView1" DataSourceID="SqlDataSource1" runat="server"/>
```

Although the `GridView` in the page has no style properties defined on it, when you run the page, the properties defined in the skin file are automatically applied. So, a theme is very much like a style sheet in that it can define a set of appearance/style definitions that can be maintained centrally but applied globally. In fact, a theme can contain a CSS style sheet as well, so you can apply a `CssClass` property as part of a skin. Note that if you place a CSS style sheet named `CustomBlue.css` in the `CustomBlue` directory, it will automatically be applied to pages that reference this theme, without having to define a `<link>` tag on each page.

A skin file can also define properties that apply to only some (but not all) `GridView` controls in your site. To do this, add a `SkinID` property to the control definition in the skin file:

```
    <asp:GridView SkinID="RedGrid" BackColor="Red" runat="server"/>
```

Any `GridView` control in your site with a matching `SkinID` property will have this skin applied instead of the default `GridView` skin that applies to all other `GridView` controls.

Themes can actually be applied to a page in one of two ways:

- **As a Theme:** When applied as a `Theme`, the properties on the control are applied first, followed by any properties defined in the skin for the control. This is the setting used in the preceding example. This mode is typically used to customize the look of a site that was previously developed without a theme. In this mode, the theme style settings (properties defined in the skin file) always win over style settings defined by control properties in the target page.
- **As a StyleSheetTheme:** When applied as a `StyleSheetTheme`, the properties defined in the skin files for the theme will be applied first, followed by the properties defined on the control in the target page. In this mode, the control properties always win over the theme. This mode is useful when you want to use a theme like a style sheet, that is, when you are developing an application to serve as a central place to define the styles for controls in the application.

In the preceding example, if you try to set the `ForeColor` to Yellow on the `GridView`, the `Theme ForeColor` will win and it will be `LightBlue` anyway. If you want the control properties in the page to be applied *after* the theme properties, set the Theme as a `StyleSheetTheme` instead:

```
<%@Page StyleSheetTheme="CustomBlue" %>
...
<asp:GridView ID="GridView1" DataSourceID="SqlDataSource1" ForeColor="Yellow"
runat="server"/>
```

We recommend that you use `StyleSheetTheme` to apply your themes when you develop applications. Another big advantage of using `StyleSheetTheme` is that the VWD designer shows a preview of what the control will look like with the theme applied. As you will see in the following section, the AutoFormat dialog box also allows you to easily preview and choose from the set of available skins in a `StyleSheetTheme` for a particular control.

Using Auto Format in VWD

Visual Studio (and VWD) offers a smart task option for automatically formatting a `GridView` and other controls using a set of predefined style settings. This is a great way to get a professionally designed table without having to define each and every style setting.

To invoke the AutoFormat dialog box, first switch to Design view using the tabs at the bottom left. Select your `GridView` or `DetailsView` and open the Smart Tasks panel. Click Auto Format and review the dozen or so Auto Format schemes. These designs include row colors, formatting of the header and footer, line settings, foreground and background colors, and other features. If you do not like the settings, note that there is a remove option at the top of the list. When you click OK, the Auto Format dialog box applies its settings as a single operation. There is no ongoing enforcement of those settings, so you can first apply an `AutoFormat` and then make changes to individual properties within the control tag.

The Auto Format dialog box will also show you the set of skins available in the applied `StyleSheetTheme`, if applicable. You can preview the look of each skin in the dialog, and when you choose to apply a skin, the dialog sets the `SkinID` on the control to apply the styles.

Solving Common Mistakes

The following list describes some common mistakes made while customizing the appearance of tables:

- Selecting the wrong object when applying a style using VWD Properties window. Drop down the list of objects and select the correct one.
- Including errors in syntax for the style names in the style sheet. For example, Body does not begin with a period. All other styles must begin with a period (except in the rare case of a self-reference). Do not use a period in the VWD Properties window or in the source code of the ASPX page.
- Using the wrong syntax or wrong keywords in a Cascading Style Sheet. The names of attributes in style sheets are different from those used in an AS.NET control properties. You can get the correct set of keywords from `www.W3.org` or from style sheets you can examine by searching your drive for `*.CSS`. In addition, VS and VWD IDEs will give you IntelliSense options for the correct keywords while editing a style sheet.
- Expecting a style setting to be applied but having that style overridden by a style of higher precedence.
- Improperly placing style tags within the `GridView` or `DetailsView` tag structure. It is best to rely on VWD to automatically generate these tags as you make customizations through the property grid.

- Omitting the handling of empty datasets and NULL values.
- Attempting to set the properties of a `GridView` when the `GridView` is not selected. If your properties options are ASP.NET, Body, and Misc, you have the page (background) selected, not the `GridView`. Click once on the middle of the `GridView` to select it, and then you should have the property options Accessibility, Appearance, and so on.
- Using malformed tags. It is easy, if typing and rearranging many attributes in Source view, to end up without a closing angle bracket on a control. The error message "The server tag is not well formed" stops on the line the tag starts, which misleads your eye from the position of the problem—after the last attribute at the absence of the tag ending bracket (>).
- Changing the right property in the wrong control. In a large page with many ASP.NET controls, it is easy to change a common tag or attribute in the wrong control and then wonder why your change is not taking effect.
- Attempting to use an incorrect Theme directory and file structure or attempting to use incorrect skin file contents (for example, setting properties in a skin that are not themeable, such as `ID` or `DataSourceID`).
- Trying to override a Skin property for a theme that is not applied as a `StyleSheetTheme`.

Summary

This chapter explained how to change the appearance of tabular data-bound controls, namely, the `GridView` and `DetailsView`. It discussed formatting at the levels of the entire table, rows, and cells within one column. Many formatting options in this chapter require the use of defined fields or columns, so `AutoGenerateColumns` must be turned off and your columns must be explicitly defined within `<Columns>` tags. The entire `GridView` is formatted by properties such as background color and font. These settings will be the defaults unless overridden by some finer degree of formatting.

You format entire rows using style properties of the `GridView` control. Each type of row can be specified, with `RowStyle` being the basic style applied to the records. `AlternateRowStyle` modifies the `RowStyle` for every other record. `Header` and `Footer` styles will be shown only if those rows are set to be visible in the `GridView`.

You can specify styles for cells within a single column using column or field `ItemStyles`. Note that you do not format an entire column. Rather, you set the formatting for one of the four kinds of cells within a column. This level of formatting is used when you want one column or a few columns to stand out from the default formatting of the table. These column-style settings will get the highest precedence if there is a conflict of values for a given setting.

The lowest priority goes to formatting applied to the `GridView` as a whole. For each level, a format can be set either in the tag as a specific attribute or by reference to a Cascading Style Sheet. The advantage of the CSS is that it can then be applied to (and easily maintained for) many `GridViews` in your site.

Also, you learned that the most effective way to handle formatting is with a CSS that is set up in a separate file. The ASPX page must have a `<LINK>` to the CSS file. Then, within a table control, row style, or column style, you set the `CssClass` to a style in the style sheet. A setting in a style sheet is overridden by a setting that is made directly in the control's property.

Another method for defining your site styles in a central location is using a `Theme/StyleSheetTheme`. A theme allows you to specify control properties and/or CSS style settings that should apply globally for all controls in your site. It is a powerful alternative to using CSS style sheets alone.

If no records are supplied by the data source, a single cell is created with the format of the `GridView`'s `EmptyDataRowStyle` and `EmptyDataText`. It is easy to add a ToolTip to the `GridView` so that users have an additional item of explanation for the control.

Finally, you learned that VWD offers a tool to automatically apply a set of formats with a single click. This is a one-time operation at design time, and each setting can then be modified as desired. It also allows you to set skin definitions found in the applied `StyleSheetTheme` for your page.

The last chapter explained how to create the structure of `GridViews` and `DetailViews`. This chapter explained how to modify their appearance. The next chapter looks at how to change their behavior in two major ways: breaking a large set of records into smaller pages and sorting the set of records.

Exercises

1. Compare and contrast the way that the term *Header* is used in the `GridView` and the way it is used in `DetailsView` controls.
2. State the precedence of formatting in different tags and files.
3. Describe the difference between the terms *borders* and *gridlines*.
4. Describe the three systems for defining a color in data-bound controls.
5. Describe the difference between cell spacing and cell padding.
6. Write the proper syntax for a dotted cell border.
7. Write the syntax for each of the two ways to set a property for a style.
8. In what situation will the `EmptyDataRowStyle` be applied to a data-bound control?
9. Why does the `DetailsView` control have an `InsertRow` style but the `GridView` lacks that style?

Sorting and Paging Data

The previous chapter presented strategies for bringing subsets of information (rows or columns) to the forefront of the viewer's attention. In this chapter, we further refine the concept by bringing individual values to a more prominent place in the realm of the user's attention. We explore two techniques offered by ASP.NET 2.0:

- We enable the sorting of data to bring specific values to the top of a list.
- We constrict the corpus of data down to smaller chunks by paging.

Sorting and paging in the `GridView` control represent the archetype of the advances in ASP.NET version 2.0. Microsoft saw features that everyone wants to utilize, but it takes considerable time and expertise to code in a set of functions. The ASP.NET team wrapped up the dozens of lines of code that were necessary in ASP.NET 1.0 and exposed them as simple Boolean (true/false) properties in ASP.NET 2.0. With a single click on a check box in the Designer, you can now add paging or sorting to a table.

This chapter discusses the basics of sorting and paging and then covers some embellishments that solve common real-world problems.

- Enabling sorting and basic sorting scenarios
- Creating more complex sorting expressions
- Enabling paging
- Setting the attributes of the pager
- Working with paging, sorting and selecting at the same time

Introduction

Paging is the ability to display only portions of the records at one time in a `GridView`—for example, just the first 10 products. A set of navigational controls then allows the viewer to switch to seeing other sets, or pages, of products. Paging gives the page designer the opportunity to reduce "information overload" for the user, albeit at some loss in comprehensiveness. Note that this "paging" is not concerned with switching between full ASPX pages in a Web site. That is a job for the site navigation features.

Sorting is the ability to change the order in which records are listed in a `GridView`. With sorting enabled, a user can find a given record more easily and make associations between similar records, such as all employees from one state. These techniques are very flexible in ASP.NET 2.0, so you will start with some basic scenarios and then study the enhancements and potential conflicts.

`DetailsView` and, as you will learn later, `FormView` present a special case because they show only one record at a time. Therefore, sorting is not applicable. You can change the order in which records are displayed by using an `ORDER BY` clause in the `SelectCommand` of a `SqlDataSource`. Paging, however, is implemented as the feature that allows the user to move from one record to another.

A common point of confusion arises between the sorting and paging we discuss here (within a `GridView`) and the Chapter 3 topics of the `ORDER BY` and `WHERE` clauses of SQL statement. An `ORDER BY` in the data source control SQL statement determines the order in which the records will be served up by the database and, thus, initially ordered in the data source control. That will be the default for the order of records served to the data-bound control. When a sort is further established by the data-bound control (for example, `GridView`), then that causes the data to be resorted just prior to the data's being served to the data-bound control.

When we use `WHERE` clause in a SQL statement, we are limiting the number of records that the database will return. When we use paging in the `GridView`, we are limiting only the number of rows that the data-bound control retrieves from and displays on the page at one time.

Sorting

Sorting in the `GridView` involves a special modification of the header row. When turned on, the header text for each column becomes a clickable text (looking like a hyperlink). When clicked, the `GridView` will sort all of its displayed rows so that they are ordered according to the values in the clicked column. The `GridView` will toggle between an ascending or a descending sort order each time the header text is clicked. The `GridView` first checks whether the column is currently sorted. If not, it sorts the records in increasing order based on the field values under the clicked header. If the data is already sorted on that field, the `GridView` reverses the sort order.

A SQL `SELECT` statement can establish an initial sort order for the data as it is sent from the database to the data source control. In the `ORDER BY` clause, list the field upon which to sort and then follow with `ASC` for ascending or `DESC` for descending. If there is no direction, then SQL will assume that `ASC` is the correct order.

Try It Out — Sorting Basics

This exercise gives the `Northwind` employees a way to look at all of the products in a sortable `GridView`—the `ProductID`, `ProductName`, and `UnitPrice` fields.

1. Create a new folder for Chapter 7 and a file named `TIO-0701-SortingBasics.aspx`. We want to add a `GridView` that uses `AutoGenerateColumns=True`. Because this is not the default for VWD, perform the following steps exactly.

2. From the Toolbox drag a `GridView` to the page. From the Smart Tasks panel, choose a data source of New and set it to a database type. Accept the default ID `SqlDataSource1`, and use the existing `MdfNorthwind` connection string. From the drop-down list, select the Alphabetical List of Products Query, and include the `ProductID`, `ProductName`, and `UnitPrice` fields. Then, finish the wizard. The nascent `GridView` will open its Smart Tasks panel.

3. Click on Edit Columns and turn on Auto-generate fields. Select each field in the `SelectedFields` list, and click the red X button to delete them. This removes the double-generation of fields (once from the specific list and once from autogenerate). Click OK to close the column editor.

4. In the `GridView`'s Smart Tasks panel, turn on Enable Sorting. Save the page (source code follows), and observe the results in your browser.

```
...
<body>
<h2>Chapter 07 TIO #0701 Sorting Basics</h2>
<form id="form1" runat="server">  <div>

<asp:GridView ID="GridView1" runat="server"
        DataKeyNames="ProductID"
        DataSourceID="SqlDataSource1"
        AllowSorting="True">
</asp:GridView>

 <asp:SqlDataSource ID="SqlDataSource1" runat="server"
        ConnectionString="<%$ ConnectionStrings:MdfNorthwind %>"
        SelectCommand="SELECT [ProductID], [ProductName], [UnitPrice]
               FROM [Alphabetical list of products]">
 </asp:SqlDataSource>
</div>   </form>         </body>         </html>
```

How It Works

Enabling sorting in VWD just means putting a check in the Enable Sorting check box in the `GridView` Smart Tasks panel. In the page tags, this corresponds to a Boolean `AllowSorting` property set to `true`, as shown in the highlighted line in the code listing above. When using `AutoGenerateColumns`, the defaults in `GridView` cover all other settings. Note that the defaults in the `SqlDataSource` control also support sorting.

Note also that in the browser, the first time you click on `ProductID`, there appears to be no change. Because the column was not previously sorted, `GridView` is sorting it into ascending order with no visible changes. Subsequent clicks result in toggles between ascending and descending order.

Requirements to Enable Sorting

As you saw in the preceding simple Try It Out, sorting works with a single click in the Designer with `AutoGenerateColumns` in `GridView` and the defaults in `SqlDataSource` controls. But in more complex scenarios, we have to ensure that the prerequisites for sorting are met.

First, consider the data source control. Different data sources support sorting under different conditions, and some data sources do not support sorting at all (for example, `XmlDataSource`). The `SqlDataSource` control supports sorting when its `DataSourceMode = DataSet`. Similarly, the `ObjectDataSource` control supports sorting when the `SelectMethod` returns a `DataSet`, `DataTable`, or `DataView`. The reason for this lies under the covers in the ADO.NET objects. The data source directly applies the `SortExpression` from the `GridView` to the `DataView.Sort` property, which can be accessed from any of the aforementioned types. When `SqlDataSource.DataSourceMode = DataReader`, sorting is not supported.

Second, look at the data-bound control, in this case a `GridView`, which requires four prerequisites for sorting to be allowed. These are set by the designer by default, but if you begin to customize columns, you will have to ensure that you meet the following requirements. Note that some of these requirements are set at the level of the `GridView` and some within each field that allows sorting. A fifth, optional property is generally also used.

- `GridView.ShowHeader`: Because the sort interface is rendered in the header, the `GridView` as a whole must have `ShowHeader` set to `true`, which is the default. If you change it to `false`, you eliminate the links that users click to sort.
- `GridView.AllowSorting`: This property, when set to `true`, makes the built-in sorting method available.
- `DataControlField.HeaderText`: This property is set on a field object (for example, `BoundField`) in the `GridView`'s `Columns` collection. Again, because sorting is exposed to the user through the header, you need some text rendered so that the user can click to invoke sorting.
- `DataControlField.SortExpression`: This property is set on a field object (for example, `BoundField`) in the `GridView`'s `Columns` collection. Sorting works only if you have designated which values to use in the sort for each column.
- `DataControl.Header` **Style (Optional):** This property is set on a field object (for example, `BoundField`) in the `GridView`'s `Columns` collection. Although the default is fine, most designers want to enhance the item that can be clicked to invoke sorting. This formatting can be set for all headers in the `GridView.HeaderStyle` or for only one column in `DataControlField.HeaderStyle`.

With the preceding settings, all columns will be sortable. But that does not always make sense. For example, it does not make sense to sort BLOB (binary large objects, such as pictures) or GUID (globally unique identifiers) data types. To turn off sorting for one column, open the `GridView`'s Edit Column dialog box, select the column, and set its `SortExpression` to an empty string (nothing).

Understanding How ASP.NET 2.0 Manages Sorting

A good start is to look at a graphic of how sorting works, as in Figure 7-1. In Step 1, a data-bound control makes a request for data to a data source control that has a sort expression. Then (Step 2) the data source control sends the select command to the database, including the `ORDER BY` clause. However, at this point there is no involvement of the `SortExpression`. The data source control gets the data from the database ordered according to the `ORDER BY` clause it sent (Step 3). Now, in Step 4, the data source control actually applies the sort expression to the data (that is, it performs a sort). The data is then sent to the data-bound control in Step 5. At this point, the `ViewState` setting of `SortAscending` is not changed and, thus, remains as the default of true.

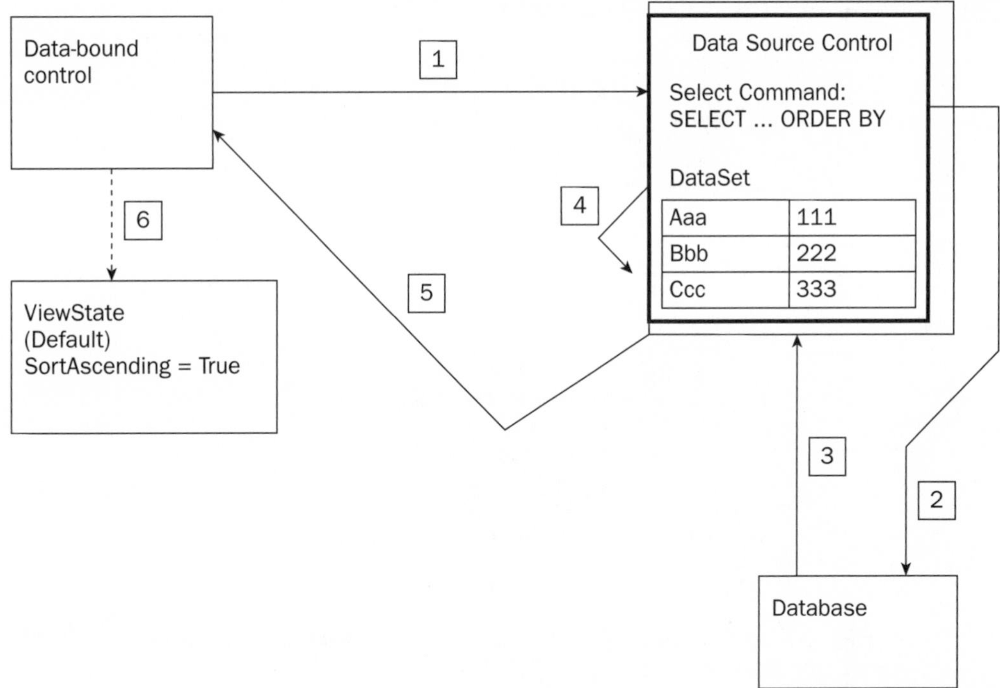

Figure 7-1

Also, ASP.NET 2.0 supports an advanced sorting technique supported by both `SqlDataSource` and `ObjectDataSource` that is not discussed in detail in this text. You can set the `SortParameterName` property to the name of a parameter in your `SelectCommand` (or `SelectMethod`) that corresponds to the `SortExpression`, and then in the implementation of your stored procedure or method, you can apply your own sorting (using `ORDER BY`) by parsing the expression that is passed in. This technique makes it possible to support sorting even in `DataReader` mode.

Try It Out Requirements for Sorting

This exercise returns to the Northwind Employees table but with a `GridView` that uses explicit columns rather than using `AutoGenerateColumns=true`. To review the sorting requirements previously mentioned, you will create one point of failure in each of three columns and observe the results.

1. Create a new file named `TIO-0702-SortRequirements-ver1.aspx`. Add a `GridView` that displays `BoundFields` for `EmployeeID` and both first and last names of employees from Northwind, using the existing connection to the MDF file. As you go through the wizard that creates the data source control, click the `ORDER BY` button to create a SQL statement clause that sorts by `EmployeeID`. Enable sorting with the check box in the `GridView`'s Smart Tasks panel. (If you did not follow these steps and have created the bound fields by hand, remember that you must set a `SortExpression` and a `HeaderText` by hand.)

2. Test the page. The source code for the `GridView` will be similar to the following:

```
... <h2>Chapter 07 TIO #0702 Sort Requirements ver 1 </h2>
    <form id="form1" runat="server"><div>
        <asp:GridView ID="GridView1" runat="server"
            AllowSorting="True"
            AutoGenerateColumns="False"
            DataKeyNames="EmployeeID"
            DataSourceID="SqlDataSource1">
            <Columns>
                <asp:BoundField DataField="EmployeeID"
                    HeaderText="EmployeeID"
                    InsertVisible="False"
                    ReadOnly="True"
                    SortExpression="EmployeeID" />
                <asp:BoundField DataField="LastName"
                    HeaderText="LastName"
                    SortExpression="LastName" />
                <asp:BoundField DataField="FirstName"
                    HeaderText="FirstName"
                    SortExpression="FirstName" />
            </Columns>
        </asp:GridView>
        <asp:SqlDataSource ID="SqlDataSource1" runat="server"
            ConnectionString="<%$ ConnectionStrings:MdfNorthwind %>"
            SelectCommand="
                SELECT [EmployeeID], [LastName], [FirstName]
                FROM [Employees]
                ORDER BY [EmployeeID]">
        </asp:SqlDataSource>
    </div></form></body></html>
```

3. Now let's see how this page fails when you leave out some of the sorting requirements. First, save the page as `TIO-0702-SortRequirements-ver2.aspx`. Now in VWD, using the `GridView` Edit Columns dialog box (accessible from the Smart Tasks panel), make the following modifications and test the page in the browser after each.

    a. `EmployeeID` column—Remove the sort expression.

    b. `LastName`—Set the sort expression column to `EmployeeID` (weird, but an interesting lesson)

    c. `FirstName` column—Remove the header text value so that it is empty.

4. Save the page (still as `TIO-0702-SortRequirements-ver2.aspx`). The page source code for the data controls should now be similar to the following:

```
... <h2>Chapter 07 TIO #0702 Sort Requirements ver 2 </h2>
<asp:GridView ID="GridView1" runat="server"
AllowSorting="True"
AutoGenerateColumns="False"
DataKeyNames="EmployeeID"
DataSourceID="SqlDataSource1">
<Columns>
<asp:BoundField DataField="EmployeeID"
```

```
HeaderText="EmployeeID"
InsertVisible="False"
ReadOnly="True" />
<asp:BoundField DataField="LastName"
HeaderText="LastName"
SortExpression="EmployeeID" />
<asp:BoundField DataField="FirstName"
SortExpression="FirstName" />
</Columns>
</asp:GridView>

<asp:SqlDataSource ID="SqlDataSource1" runat="server"
ConnectionString="<%$ ConnectionStrings:MdfNorthwind %>"
SelectCommand="SELECT [EmployeeID], [LastName], [FirstName]
FROM [Employees]
ORDER BY [EmployeeID]">
</asp:SqlDataSource>
```

How It Works

When setting up a `GridView` to be sortable, you must complete several tasks. First, double-check that your data source (including its modes) supports sorting. Then check that each column that should be sortable has a heading text and a sort expression. Double-check that the sort expression matches the field of the column. Last, enable sorting on the `GridView` Smart Tasks panel.

Sort Expressions

ASP.NET 2.0 `GridView` separates the properties for the data to display (`DataField`) and the data to use in the sorting (`SortExpression`). In most cases, these will be the same. But in this section you will look at some cases where you may want to break out of the mold. For example, you might want to sort on the first letter of the second word in a set of values.

First, your initial order of records should be set in the SQL clause of the data source `SelectCommand`. This is not a `GridView` sort expression issue, but it answers a common question. The SQL `ORDER BY` clause also offers the `DESC` option to reverse the sort order. For example, to display employee records starting with the most recently hired, use the following:

```
SelectCommand="
  SELECT EmployeeID, FirstName, LastName, HireDate
  FROM Employees
  ORDER BY HireDate DESC"
```

Sometimes you want to sort on a value that is not in any field, for example, the result of a string function such as `TRIM()`, `LEFT()`, or `MID()`. This cannot be done directly in the sort expression. However, you can add a column to your data source control `SelectCommand` (SQL `SELECT` statement) and use it as a sort expression rather than display the column in the `GridView`.

Tiebreaking in the sort requires some custom code. The way sort works is by keeping track of the current sort order in a variable named `SortDirection`. After each sort that is changed from true (the original, usually `ASC`) to false (the opposite, usually `DESC`). The problem comes if there is a tiebreaking field, say

Field2. Then we use the SQL syntax `Field1 ASC, Field2 ASC`. When ASP.NET 2.0 reverses the direction at the end of the expression, there is no change to the primary sort field. You can solve the problem by ignoring the built-in sort feature and substituting your sort expressions based on a sort order that you track in a variable held in ViewState. See the following Try It Out for the specifics.

> *More information on tiebreaking is available at* `http://msdn.microsoft.com/library/default.asp?url=/library/en-us/cpref/html/frlrfsystemdatadataviewclasssorttopic.asp`.

Try It Out Sort Expressions

This exercise presents the table of orders from Northwind with several sorting options. First, you build the default. Then, you limit the sort to just employees and use `CustomerID` for a tiebreaker. You will see some problems, however, and replace the default sorting behavior with custom code.

1. Create a page named `TIO-0703-SortExpression-ver1`, and add a `GridView` to show just the `OrderID`, `CustomerID`, and `EmployeeID` from the Orders table of Northwind. Using the `GridView`'s Smart Tasks panel, turn on sorting. Save and test the page.

For the rest of this exercise, you will work on the objective of being able to sort the table on `EmployeeID` with `CustomerID` as a tiebreaker. In other words, the top of the `GridView` will have all the orders taken by employee #1; and within that employee's orders, the records will be sorted by the customer ID. Regardless of whether the `EmployeeIDs` are ascending or descending, the `CustomerIDs` within one employee should always be ascending.

2. Save the page as `TIO-0703-SortExpression-ver2`. Start with two steps that can be performed in Source view (directly in the code) or in the Properties window after selecting the bound field in Source view. Or you can change the properties in the `GridView`'s Fields dialog box (use the `GridView` Smart Tasks panel /Edit columns).

First, eliminate sorting on the OrderID and CustomerID columns by deleting their sort expressions. Then change the sort expression for `EmployeeID` to `"EmployeeID,CustomerID"` (use quotation marks if you are typing directly into the source code; leave them out if you are using a dialog or properties window).

Your source code for the GridView control will end up as follows. Save version 2, open in the browser, and observe the problem as you perform several sorts and resorts.

```
... <h2>Chapter 07 TIO #0703 SortExpression</h2><h2>version 2</h2>
    <form id="form1" runat="server">
    <div>
        <asp:GridView ID="GridView1" runat="server" 0
            AllowSorting="True"
            AutoGenerateColumns="False"
            DataKeyNames="OrderID"
            DataSourceID="SqlDataSource1">
            <Columns>
                <asp:BoundField DataField="OrderID"
                    HeaderText="OrderID"
                    InsertVisible="False"
                    ReadOnly="True" />
                <asp:BoundField DataField="CustomerID"
                    HeaderText="CustomerID" />
                <asp:BoundField DataField="EmployeeID"
                    HeaderText="EmployeeID"
                    SortExpression="EmployeeID,CustomerID" />
```

```
            </Columns>
        </asp:GridView>
        <asp:SqlDataSource ID="SqlDataSource1" runat="server"
            ConnectionString="<%$ ConnectionStrings:MdfNorthwind %>"
            SelectCommand="
                SELECT [OrderID], [CustomerID], [EmployeeID]
                FROM [Orders]">
        </asp:SqlDataSource>
    </div></form></body></html>
```

3. Save the page as `TIO-0703-SortExpression-ver3`. Experiment with some alternate tiebreaking sort expressions for the `EmployeeID` field as follows. Test in your browser and consider the behavior of sorting in context of the sorting theory presented earlier in this chapter.

```
SortExpression="EmployeeID ASC,CustomerID ASC"

SortExpression="EmployeeID DESC,CustomerID ASC"
```

4. Save the page as `TIO-0703-SortExpression-ver4`. Before we solve the tiebreaker problem in the next step, we will create tools that allow us to look more closely at what is happening. Add two labels to the top of the page, switch to Source Code view and then add the following block of code. (We will cover the coding in detail in Chapter 10, but for now you can get VWD to do a lot of typing for you by using two drop-down lists at the top of the Source View panel.)

    - At the top left, select `GridView`, and at the top right, select Sorting, as shown in Figure 7-2. Then type the two lines of code from the listing below into the `Sub . . . End Sub` frame that VWD created. This script will run before the re-sort is performed by the `GridView` and will display the contents of two sort properties in the labels: sort order and sort expression. Note that for sort direction 0 represents ascending and 1 represents descending. Save your work and then experiment in the browser with the preceding alternate sort expressions. Although we now have some diagnostic tools, the problem is not yet solved.

```
<script runat="server">
Protected Sub GridView1_Sorting(ByVal sender As Object, ByVal e As
System.Web.UI.WebControls.GridViewSortEventArgs)
        Label1.Text = e.SortExpression
        Label2.Text = e.SortDirection
End Sub
</script>
```

5. Save the page as `TIO-0703-SortExpression-ver5`. Add the following code to solve the problem (discussed in depth in the "How It Works" section that follows).

```
<script runat="server">
Protected Sub GridView1_Sorting(ByVal sender As Object, ByVal e As
System.Web.UI.WebControls.GridViewSortEventArgs)
        Label1.Text = e.SortExpression
        Label2.Text = e.SortDirection

        If ViewState("SortAscending") Then
            e.SortExpression = "EmployeeID DESC,CustomerID ASC"
        Else
            e.SortExpression = "EmployeeID ASC,CustomerID ASC"
        End If
        ViewState("SortAscending") = Not ViewState("SortAscending")
End Sub
</script>
```

6. Save the code and then test it in the browser.

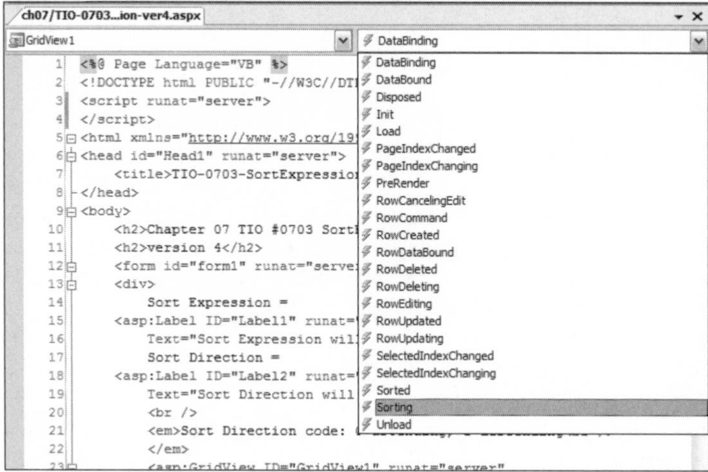

Figure 7-2

How It Works

In version 1, you just set up a page and turned on sorting. If you drag and drop from the Database Explorer, you will have additional lines such as insert and update commands and parameters. They do not affect the exercise.

Version 2 adds a tiebreaker `SortExpression="EmployeeID,CustomerID"`, but this creates problems. When the `GridView` sorts, it reads the order (ASC or DESC) from the end of the sort expression, deletes it, and replaces it with the opposite. So, in this case, it is reading the sort order from `CustomerID`. By default, the sort order is `ASC`, so `ASC` is clipped off and replaced with `DESC`. The next time, `... CustomerID DESC` is changed to `... Customer ASC`. Notice that the primary sort field, `EmployeeID`, is never touched.

In version 3, we did some experimenting to try to solve the problem with clever sort expressions. Unfortunately, none worked. We are always left with the problem that ASP.NET changes between `ASC` and `DESC` at the end of the string. Because the last field is the tiebreaker and not the primary sort order, we keep getting spurious results.

Version 4 shows you the sort properties. You get a glimpse of the behavior using a standard troubleshooting technique, displaying control properties on a development page. Coding is covered in detail at the end of the book, but for now, notice that the name of our code is `GridView_Sorting`, which means that the code will execute just after the user clicks to begin a sort but just before the `GridView` actually performs the sort. (Think of it as a set of custom presort instructions.) At this point, the code merely checks the current state of the sort expression and direction and displays those values. This `Sub` will use `e` to represent the `GridView`'s state and picks up two of the `GridView`'s properties to display in the labels.

Version 5 solves the problem in several steps. First, we create a variable in the `ViewState` named `SortAscending` that keeps track of the current sort order. This relieves the page of relying on the `GridView`'s SortDirection property, which checks only the last field. When the `ViewState("SortAscending")` is set to `true`, the first item on the page is loaded in the `Sub` named `Page_Load`. Subsequent sorts will cause the `ViewState("SortAscending")` to flip to the opposite value.

In the second part of Step five, you create an exact sort expression for each of the two cases:

- Employees `ASC` with tiebreaker of Customer `ASC`
- `EmployeeID DESC` with tiebreaker of Customer `ASC`

Then an `IF` structure decides which sort expression to use. Each time a sort occurs, there is an inversion of the value for a variable stored in the `ViewState` named `SortAscending`; it flip-flops between `true` and `false`. The first time the page loads, the `GridView` will be in the order of the primary key in the table (`OrderID`). At this point, the custom code has not been executed. The first sort click will run the Sub and check `ViewState("SortAscending")` to find that the variable does not exist, which evaluates to false, so the `e.SortExpression` is set to the one with `EmployeeID ASC`. At the end of the `Sub`, the value in `ViewState("SortAscending")` is flipped to its opposite.

This brings us to the end of the themes and variations in sorting. Next, we explore paging.

Paging

When paging is added to a `GridView` or `DetailsView`, the following happens:

- Only a portion of the total number of records is shown.
- The `GridView` creates a page navigation UI used to move between records.

`DetailsView` displays only one record of the total records at a time, as opposed to `GridView`, which displays a few records of the total at a time. Therefore, paging in `DetailsView` only formats and configures the pager navigation tool.

> ***Paging* is a feature used to control the display of sets of records within a `GridView`. Do not confuse paging with *page navigation,* which is a set of features used to help the user move between entire pages on the site.**

Enabling Paging

Paging can work only if the data source supports paging directly or returns a list that implements the `ICollection` interface. The `GridView` uses this interface to determine the total number of rows in the collection using the `Count` property and to display the correct subset of rows. When `DataSourceMode=DataSet`, paging will work because the `DataView` retrieved from the `DataSet` implements `ICollection`. `GridView` paging will not work if `DataSourceMode=DataReader`. For an

ObjectDataSource, your SelectMethod must return a DataSet or DataView or a list that implements ICollection in order for paging to work. For example, an ObjectDataSource will wrap a set of results in an ICollection.

> **The ICollection interface is a group of similar items grouped together so they can take advantage of features in the programming language. Those features include an enumerator (like a pointer that can move through the collection), the maximum size (capacity) of the collection, and count of the current number of items.**

To summarize:

1. ICollection is required for GridView to perform paging.
2. This "just works" for the DataSet and DataView, because GridView knows how to extract the ICollection from those objects.
3. GridView is requesting all rows from the data source and only rendering a subset.

> **To do custom paging where only the subset of rows is selected in the first place (a performance optimization), you can use ObjectDataSource.EnablePaging. However, because this technique is outside the scope of this book, it is not covered here.**

Once the data source control is configured, the data-bound control requires one setting: AllowPaging=true. This single setting sets up the entire paging function with defaults, a procedure that would have taken at least several hours of programmer time in the older versions of ASP.NET.

A simple ASPX page with a paging-enabled GridView yields an HTML page, as shown in Figure 7-3.

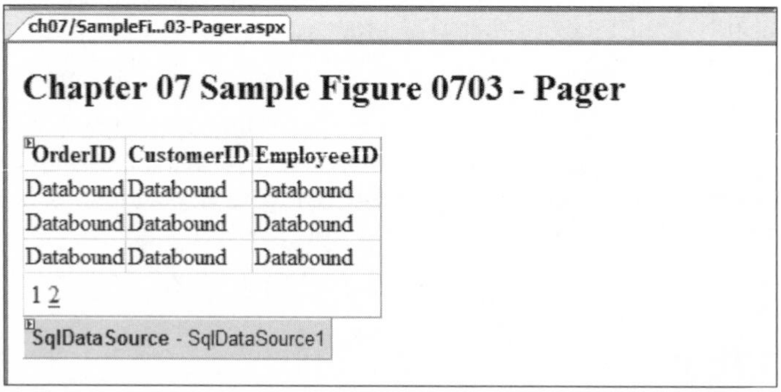

ch07/SampleFi...03-Pager.aspx

Chapter 07 Sample Figure 0703 - Pager

OrderID	CustomerID	EmployeeID
Databound	Databound	Databound
Databound	Databound	Databound
Databound	Databound	Databound
1 2		

SqlDataSource - SqlDataSource1

Figure 7-3

First, observe that of the several hundred orders, only three are shown at a time (PageSize=3). Note also the gridwide pager column at the bottom. The navigation tools include a link to jump to the first or last pages, modified here so the links show text of "Oldest" and "Most Recent." Users can also jump to a given page with the hyperlink numbers in the pager.

Try It Out Paging Basics

We will start with a simple paging scenario where we want to look at 10 Northwind orders at a time and want to be able to navigate among the groups of 10.

1. Create a new page named `TIO-0704-PagingBasics.aspx`. Drag onto the page the `OrderID`, `CustomerID`, `OrderDate`, and `Freight` fields from the Orders table of Northwind. On the `GridView`'s Smart Tasks panel, enable paging.

```
...
<h2>Chapter 07 TIO #0704 Paging Basics</h2>
<form id="form1" runat="server">
<div>
<asp:GridView ID="GridView1" runat="server"
AllowPaging="True"
 AutoGenerateColumns="False"
 DataKeyNames="OrderID" DataSourceID="SqlDataSource1">
 <Columns>
...
 </Columns>
</asp:GridView>
...
```

2. Save your work and then open the page in your browser and enjoy one-click paging.

How It Works

In earlier versions of ASP.NET, this task took hours to custom code. Today, it requires a single click of a check box in the Designer. Notice in the code above that a single `AllowPaging` property of the `GridView` turns on paging. This is almost criminally easy. However, keep in mind that we have relied on defaults in the data source control that enable paging. This is fine when using the `SqlDataSource`.

Customizing Paging and Pager Navigation Tools

Paging creates a new row in the `GridView`, called the *pager row*. This is different from sorting, which modifies the existing header row. You can format the pager row as a whole and format the clickable navigation links within the pager. The properties to control and format paging are located across three locations in the tags of the `GridView` control:

- Some are simple properties directly `GridView` control, such as `PageSize`. These control the basic pager settings.
- Some are subproperties on the `GridView` `PagerStyle` property, persisted as a `<PagerStyle>` subtag under the `<GridView>` tag. These control the appearance of the pager.
- Some are subproperties on the `GridView` `PagerSettings` property, located as a `<PagerSettings>` subtag under the `<GridView>` tag. These control the behavior of the pager.

A common set is broken out by location in the table below.

Location	Paging Properties
<GridView> tag	AllowPaging PageSize PageCount (read-only) PageIndex
<PagerStyle> tag	Font, color CSS class Alignment (Other formatting)
<PagerSettings> tag	Mode (which navigation links will be shown in the pager) ImageURLs and Text for pager links PageButtonCount Position

The AllowPaging property within the <GridView> tag was already mentioned. Another other option is to set the PageSize property to determine how many rows will be shown in the GridView. The final two GridView-level properties are PageCount and PageIndex. They are used by the internal page navigation process and rarely needed by the beginning programmer unless the programmer is using the PagerTemplate or is implementing paging themselves. The following code is a typical set of properties for the GridView-level options.

```
<asp:GridView ID="GridView1" Runat="server" ...
AllowPaging="True"
PageSize="5"
...>
```

Recall that the pager is the row that contains the page navigation tools, usually at the bottom of the GridView. The PagerStyle contains the same kinds of formatting that we discussed regarding other row styles. You can set the color, font, and alignment of the text in the pager cell. When working in Source view, recall that any row styles, including PagerStyle, must be wholly located between the <asp:GridView> and </asp:GridView> tags, as follows in a typical example.

```
<asp:GridView ...>
  <Columns>
        ...
  </Columns>
 <PagerSettings>
        ...
 </PagerSettings>
 <PagerStyle
        BackColor="LightGray"
        BorderStyle="Double"
        Font-Bold="True"
        HorizontalAlign="Center">
  </PagerStyle>
</asp:GridView>
```

PagerSettings contains the most interesting and individualized properties for paging. Mode defines what kinds of clickable links to display in the pager cell.

```
<PagerSettings
     Mode=NextPreviousFirstLast
</PagerSettings>
```

The most constrained mode option is Next Previous, which does not allow the user to jump out of the page sequence. An alternative is Numeric, which gives the user the ability to jump to any page. Both of these options can be combined with First and Last links.

PagerSettings also supports flexibility in how a clickable link is rendered. The properties that end in "text" (FirstPageText, LastPageText, and so on) accept a literal value such as "Click here for the most recent orders." The properties that end in ImageUrl (LastPageImageUrl, NextPageImageUrl, and so on) typically accept the name of an image file. If you specify both a text and an image, ASP.NET will use the ImageUrl.

```
<PagerSettings
    Mode=NextPreviousFirstLast
    FirstPageText="Jump to first page"
    NextPageImageUrl="PageDown.gif"
    PreviousPageImageUrl="PageUp.gif"
    LastPageText="Jump to last page">
</PagerSettings>
```

The final setting in <PagerSettings> is for the PageButtonCount, which determines, if the mode is set to Numeric, how many numbers are shown. If more pages are available than shown, an ellipsis appears. Be careful of two similarly named properties. GridView.PageSize determines the number of rows in the GridView, whereas GridView.PagerSettings.PageButtonCount determines how many hyperlinks to pages will appear in the pager row.

Simple design changes can improve the appearance of your GridViews with paging enabled. If your data values are of different widths, your resulting GridView will become wider or narrower as the user pages because the browser will render each column only wide enough to accommodate the longest values in that set of records. Setting your column widths as follows gives a consistent appearance.

Try It Out Pager Settings

The Products table has about 80 items, but only about 25 rows fit in the vertical height of a typical browser screen. Let's enable paging to show only seven rows at a time and present some GIF images to allow the user to click through the pages. We will use two images in this exercise, so start by importing them into your site.

1. You should already have an Images folder in your site (if not, create it now). Right-click on the Images folder, and select Add Existing Item. Browse to where you stored the download for this book and in the Images folder, select the two GIF images named PageUp and PageDown. Alternatively, search your hard drive for *.gif and pick two that look appropriate.
2. Create a page named TIO-0705-PagerSettings-ver1.aspx, and from the Data Explorer drag the ProductID, Name, and UnitPrice fields from the Products table of the

(local)\SqlExpress connection onto the page. In the Smart Tasks panel, enable paging and then close the Smart Tasks panel.

3. Select the GridView, and in the Properties window set the PageSize to seven records per page. In the pager settings, set the mode to display page links for next, previous, first, and last. Save your work and then have a look in your browser.

```
<asp:GridView ID="GridView1" Runat="server"
    DataSourceID="SqlDataSource1"
    DataKeyNames="ProductID"
    EmptyDataText="There are no data records to display."
    AutoGenerateColumns="False"
    AllowPaging="True"
    PageSize="7">
    <PagerSettings Mode="NextPreviousFirstLast"></PagerSettings>
    <Columns> ... </Columns>
</asp:GridView>
```

4. Save the page as TIO-0705-PagerSettings-ver2.aspx. Again, select the GridView in Design view, and in the Properties window section for PagerSettings, set the first- and last-page links to display text, as follows. You may want to include some spaces as shown. Save this version and examine in your browser, jumping to the first and last page to see all options of the pager text.

```
<PagerSettings
    Mode=NextPreviousFirstLast
    FirstPageText="Jump to first page    "
    LastPageText="    Jump to last page">
</PagerSettings>
```

5. Save the page as TIO-0705-PagerSettings-ver3.aspx. Improve the pager by giving it a gray background and using the icons to represent moving to the next and previous pages. These properties are available, when GridView is selected, in the Properties window PagerStyle. Save this version, and then inspect it in your browser.

```
<asp:GridView ID="GridView1" Runat="server"
DataSourceID="adsNW"
AutoGenerateColumns=false
AllowPaging="true"
PageSize=7>

        <PagerStyle
            Backcolor=#f0f0f0>
        </PagerStyle>

        <PagerSettings
            Mode=NextPreviousFirstLast
            FirstPageText="Jump to first page"
            NextPageImageUrl="~/Images/PageDown.gif"
            PreviousPageImageUrl="~/Images/PageUp.gif"
            LastPageText="Jump to last page">
        </PagerSettings>
...
</asp:GridView>
```

6. Save the page as TIO-0705-PagerSettings-ver5.aspx, and switch the mode to NumericFirstLast. Note that when you use Numeric there is no opportunity for setting text or images.

```
<PagerSettings
    Mode=NumericFirstLast
     FirstPageText="Jump to first page"
    NextPageImageUrl="PageDown.gif"
    PreviousPageImageUrl="PageUp.gif"
    LastPageText="Jump to last page">
</PagerSettings>
```

7. Save your work, and then view it in the browser.

How It Works

You turned on paging with a single property in the GridView control: AllowPaging. You then began to override defaults, starting with setting the page size (also in the GridView). In Step 5, you changed the PagerStyle in the same way that you changed the HeaderStyle in Chapter 6.

You can make modifications to the appearance of the pager links themselves. You observed both how to create your own text and how to use an image instead of the default >> and << symbols. Last, you observed how the Numeric option gives useful feedback but is not modifiable.

Note that there is another option for customizing the pager that is not discussed here, which is using the PagerTemplate property to fully customize the UI for paging. Templates are discussed in more detail in Chapter 10.

Having seen how to put basic paging into effect, we can now loop back to look more closely at what is happening behind the scenes.

Paging Theory and Alternatives

Paging is performed at the level of the data-bound control. The data source control retrieves all of the records from the database, as defined in the SELECT command, and puts them into a data set. The data-bound control gets all of the records from the data source control, displays the current set, and sends the rest for garbage collection. This model works well for one-click enablement, as you have observed in this chapter. However, records can be retrieved from the database and stored in the data sets that are never used.

An alternative is to have data source–level paging that would work with the database to retrieve only one set of records at a time, thus reducing the database read and reducing the size of the data set held in server memory. This option can be implemented using an ObjectDataSource control. Look to future releases (or third-party controls) for implementation with Microsoft SQL Server.

The Relationship among Sorting, Paging, and Selecting

A number of questions arise when sorting and paging are used together. Fortunately, they are resolved in a logical way by the internal `GridView` code. But it is important for you, as a designer, to understand what will happen when these features intersect:

- When you perform a sort, it is for all of the records in the `GridView`, not only those that are in the set of the current page.
- When you perform a sort, your page is automatically reset back to page 1 of the new sort order.
- If a row is selected and a new sort is performed, the selected style stays on the physical row. The style does not move with the record.

By design, selection corresponds to the UI, not the underlying data row. You can set `SelectedIndex = -1` in the sorting and paging events to unselect the row when one of these operations is performed. The more difficult task is retaining the selection on the specific data row after data is paged and sorted or rows are inserted/deleted/updated. To do this, you retain the `SelectedDataKey` for the user-selected row and then enumerate each visible row in the `GridView` looking for this key to programmatically set the selection after a sort, a page, or an insert event.

Try It Out — Using Paging, Sorting, and Selecting Together

In this exercise, you will create a `GridView` that has paging, sorting, and selecting all enabled. Then you will observe its behavior.

1. Create an ASPX file named `TIO-0706-PageAndSortAndSelect` that displays the `ID`, `Name`, and `UnitPrice` fields of the Products table ordered by `ProductID` ascending, which displays pages of five records at a time, sorts, and selects. Make the selected record appear with a light gray background.

```
...
<h2>Chapter 07 TIO #0706 Paging, Sorting and Selecting Together</h2>
<form id="form1" runat="server">
<div>
<asp:GridView ID="GridView1" runat="server"
AllowPaging="True"
AllowSorting="True"
AutoGenerateColumns="False"
DataKeyNames="ProductID"
DataSourceID="SqlDataSource1"
PageSize="5">
<Columns>
...
</Columns>
<SelectedRowStyle BackColor="LightGray" />
</asp:GridView>
<asp:SqlDataSource .../>
</div>    </form>          </body>          </html>
```

2. Save and then view the page in your browser. When first opened, the page will be sorted by `ProductID` because that is the sort order of the primary key back in the database's table. Observe that if you sort on `Price`, it sorts all of the records, not just the five shown in this page.
3. Keep the sort on price and go to page 6 to see items in the $15 range. Now re-sort on `ProductID`. Note that your page goes back to page 1.
4. Observe selection issues with sorting by selecting Item #5, the gumbo mix. Its background should pick up the `SelectedRowStyle` of gray. Now jump to page 10 and observe that the selection format remains on the bottom row, thus applied to a different product.

How It Works

This selection does not require intricate coding; you are looking at a basic page to understand how sorting and paging work together. When you perform a sort, the paging is reset back to the first page of the new sort order. Note that when you have a selection and then page or sort, the wrong record will probably display the selected format.

Common Mistakes

The following list describes some mistakes commonly made while attempting to page and sort data:

- Attempting to set the initial sort order in the `GridView`. It should be set in the data source control's `SELECT` command.
- Attempting to sort a column that does not have a sort expression.
- Attempting to sort a column that does not have header text.
- Attempting to enable sorting or paging when the data source does not support sorting, for example when `SqlDataSource.DataSourceMode=DataReader`. Only `DataSet` mode supports sorting and paging. Paging is also only supported on `ObjectDataSource` (discussed later in the book) when the `SelectMethod` returns a `DataSet`, `DataView`, `DataTable` or a collection that implements the `ICollection` interface.
- Confusing two similar-sounding properties. The `PageSize` determines the number of records shown in the table. The `PageButtonCount` determines how many hyperlinks will appear if the Page Mode includes Numeric navigators.
- Creating user confusion when a sort is performed after a selection. Solve the problem with the code presented at the end of the chapter.

Summary

This chapter covered two tools that are high on the priority list for many clients: the abilities to sort and page within a table. Although powerful, the `GridView` implements these features, and your task as a designer is very simple.

To sort, you must turn on sorting and show headers in the GridView object. Within each field tag, you need header text and a sort expression. Optionally, you can set the appearance for all the headers (using the header row style of the GridView) or you can set the appearance of just one header (using the column's header style property).

Paging starts in the data source control. Fortunately, the SqlDataSource control has all the prerequisites for sorting built in and turned on. The AccessDataSource supports sorting as well because it is derived from the SqlDataSource control. However, be careful when using other data sources that may require specific properties to enable sorting.

To add paging to a GridView, your minimum act is to set AllowPaging to true within the GridView. This simple set enables the paging behavior and creates a pager cell at the bottom of the GridView. You can apply a style to the pager using the PagerStyle like any other row style. You can use the pager mode to determine which items of page navigation are available, including numeric, next, previous, first, and last. These options can be presented to the user as text arrows (default), literal text, or images.

This chapter concludes the discussion of tabular data-bound controls (GridView and DetailsView). Next, we will look at a different group of data-bound controls: the list controls.

Exercises

The answers to these review questions can be found in Appendix B.

1. What is necessary to enable paging in a GridView control?
2. Which two event arguments are useful when creating custom sort expressions?
3. Describe the syntax of the SortExpression property.
4. Name the user interfaces that enable the user to navigate through pages in a GridView or DetailsView control.
5. Where in the Properties window do you set the kind of paging links shown (First/Last, Numeric, and so on)?
6. Describe how a user might be misled about which record is currently selected.

Displaying Data in Selection Lists

The last three chapters discussed tables in the forms of `GridView` and the `DetailsView`. This chapter studies selection lists. Whereas tables present data in a two-dimensional format (rows and columns), lists present data in a single dimension, such as a bulleted list, a list box, a drop-down list, a group of radio buttons, or a set of check boxes. These selection lists support selection and hyperlinks, making them a tool for user input. In the simplest case, you can provide the items in the selection list from literal statements in your code. But the more useful technique provides items from a data source.

This chapter covers the following four topics, in addition to the usual list of common mistakes:

- Concepts common to selection list controls
- Data-binding list controls
- Drop-down list control
- Handling selection in a list

> **Although the `DataList` control has *list* in its name, it is completely templated and so is discussed in Chapter 10 with other templated controls.**

You will find that the Try It Out exercises, which help you practice the concepts of data lists, do not complete the kinds of objectives needed for most sites. The next few chapters will build on these listing techniques to allow user interaction with lists to set properties of other controls. For example, a selection from a list of customers can change a `GridView` to show only orders from the selected customer.

Introduction to Selection Lists

GridView and DetailsView provide information in two dimensions. Lists present information in a single dimension. But beyond the presentation of data, lists are the most useful and common form of user input when there is a finite set of choices. Rather than allowing users to type in their region, for example, lists offer them a set of acceptable region names in a list. Site designs that offer only acceptable choices fail less frequently.

Transition from GridView to Other Formats

Before starting with lists, let's review the way data-bound controls are categorized:

- **Tabular controls:** present data in a two-dimensional table. GridView offers many rows and fields, whereas DetailsView is specialized to offer two columns (the left for labels and the right for data) describing a single record.
- **Selection list controls:** Present data in one dimension and include the BulletedList, ListBox, DropDownList, CheckBoxList, and RadioButtonList, as discussed in this chapter.
- **Hierarchical controls:** Display nested relationships like trees. The ones covered in this book are the TreeView, menu, and site navigation controls (see Chapter 14).

DataList is a crossover of these categories. It is a list in the sense of repeated display on page and is a list in name; however, the DataList is more like a table in that it presents values of records. It does not send the user an instruction that one of the choices (or records) should be clicked to continue, which is inherent in the other List controls. The syntax and behavior of the DataList is fundamentally different from the selection lists we cover in this chapter, and so the DataList is covered in Chapter 10 on templates.

In Chapter 10, we will also be discussing the concept of templates. As a preview, a template is a space within which you can add and arrange subcontrols, HTML tags, and text. Templating is an option that is available for most of the above controls. And, for some controls, your only option is to start with a template and build the interface.

Types of Selection List Controls

ASP.NET 2.0 (beta 2 version) provides five types of selection list controls, as follows:

- <asp:BulletedList>: Provides a list of items with an image or icon next to each. Items in a bulleted list can support hyperlinks, but a bulleted list does not prompt users to make a selection.
- <asp:ListBox>: Provides a selection list of items in a standard format, indicating to the user that a selection is expected. The ListBox also supports multiple selections, unlike the DropDownList.
- <asp:DropDownList>: Provides a format similar to the selection list box but uses less space when not in use.
- <asp:CheckBoxList>: Provides a selection list of items from which the user can pick any number of items from zero to all.
- <asp:RadioButtonList>: Provides a selection list of items in a group from which the user can select only one.

The bulleted list is a crossover between a selection list and a data-bound display of items. It behaves as and supports the same syntax as the other selection lists (`DropDown`, `Checkbox`, etc.). But it does not actually offer items to the user for selection. And, therefore, it does not communicate to the user a notion that action is required. The bulleted list can support a hyperlink on the items, but hyperlinks send a message of navigation options rather then a sense of request to select an item to continue. But because bulleted lists are closer to the family of selection lists than any other group of controls, we include them here.

Concepts Common to All Selection List Controls

Lists have a set of values that are presented in a consistent and repeating format. These data are called *items*, a term used extensively throughout the chapter. The source of items can be hard-coded into the page (static) or from a data source control (dynamic). When using a `SqlDataSource` control, the list of items can be filtered, renamed, or ordered using the appropriate SQL statement.

From the list, a user can select the items. The selection can be used later in the page life, or the selection can invoke an immediate hyperlink or induce a page refresh. You will work with all these possibilities in this chapter and the next. Note that the bullet list provides flexibility on this point. It can merely present information, or it can present items that are indicated to the user as selectable.

Selection list controls have a standard hierarchy of organization. Lists consist of a collection of list items, represented by `<asp:ListItem>` objects in ASP.NET. You can add `<asp:ListItem>` objects to the list control's Item collection property, as in the following example:

```
<asp:BulletedList runat="server" ID="List1">
<Items>
  <asp:ListItem Text="Item One"/>
  <asp:ListItem Text="Item Two"/>
  <asp:ListItem Text="Item Three"/>
</Items>
</asp:BulletedList>
```

To help you, Visual Web Developer and Visual Studio handle the creation of lists of items through a simple dialog box.

A list item has two important properties: `Text` and `Value`. The `Text` property represents the text to display in the rendering of the list item and is what the end user will see in the page rendering. The Value property is held in the background and will not be visible to the user. This dual-property design proves useful when you want to show the user a text such as "Canada Post" but want to use a value of the shipper's ID code, such as `111`, to process a selection in the list such as in a `WHERE` clause. The source code is organized as follows, with the `Text` and `Value` properties both explicitly stated within the item tag.

```
<asp:ListBox runat="server" ID="List1">
 <Items>
   <asp:ListItem Text="Canada Post" Value="111"/>
   <asp:ListItem Text="Royal Mail" Value="222"/>
   <asp:ListItem Text="US Postal Service" Value="333"/>
 </Items>
</asp:ListBox>
```

An alternative is to locate the text between opening and closing tags without the `Text` property identifier or the equals sign or quotation marks, as follows:

```
<asp:ListBox runat="server" ID="List1">
<Items>
   <asp:ListItem Value="111"/>Canada Post</asp:ListItem>
   <asp:ListItem Value="222"/>Royal Mail</asp:ListItem>
   <asp:ListItem Value="333"/>US Postal Service</asp:ListItem>
 </Items>
</asp:ListBox>
```

If you do some experimenting, it might appear that if you want to use a single value for each list item, to both display and serve as the underlying value, you may set either the `Text` or `Value` property and leave the other property unset. However, you may have problems accessing the undeclared value in code, so it is better to explicitly set both values. Also, note that the `Value` property of `ListItem` is useful only if the control allows user selection. Therefore, the value property makes little sense for the `asp:BulletedList`, which only renders the items (no selection).

The following exercise is a simple example that creates two lists of items that are hard-coded into the page.

Try It Out Populating Static List Items

1. Create a new folder named `C:\Websites\BegAspNet2DB\ch08`, and in it create a new page named `TIO-0801-StaticList.aspx`.
2. Drag a bulleted list from the Toolbox (Standard section) onto the page. In the Smart Tasks panel, click Edit Items and then click the Add button. In the ListItem Collection Editor dialog box, in the right panel, set the Text property to one of your favorite authors (see Figure 8-1). Add several more authors and click OK to close the dialog box. Save your work, and then take a look at the resulting source code. Observe the page in your browser.

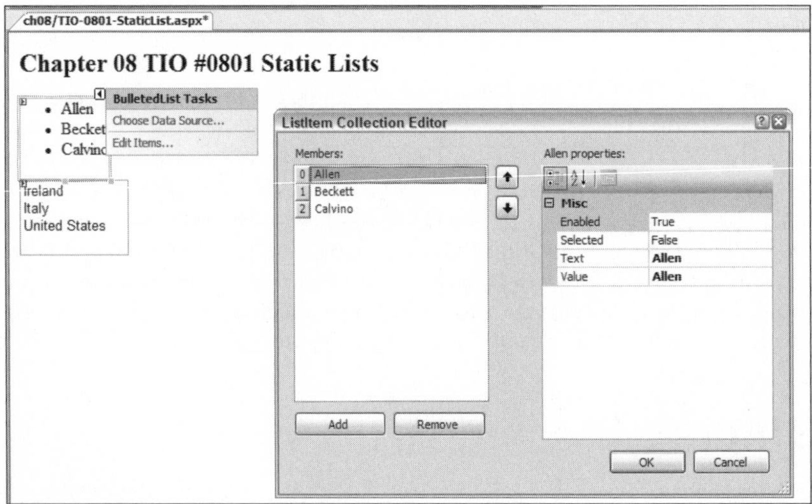

Figure 8-1

3. Drag a `ListBox` from the Toolbox (Standard section) onto the page. In the Smart Tasks panel, choose Edit Items. This time, add three countries. Enter the full country name in the Text field and the country code in the Value field. Click OK to close the `ListItem` Collection Editor, save your work, and then take a look at the resulting source code. Observe the page in your browser.

```
<%@ Page Language="VB" %>
<!DOCTYPE html PUBLIC "-//W3C//DTD XHTML 1.0 Transitional//EN"
"http://www.w3.org/TR/xhtml1/DTD/xhtml1-transitional.dtd">
<script runat="server"> </script>
<html xmlns="http://www.w3.org/1999/xhtml" >
<head id="Head1" runat="server">
    <title>TIO-0801-StaticList</title>
</head>
<body>
<h2>Chapter 08 TIO #0801 Static Lists </h2>
    <form id="form1" runat="server">
    <div>
        <asp:BulletedList ID="BulletedList1" runat="server">
            <asp:ListItem>Allen</asp:ListItem>
            <asp:ListItem>Beckett</asp:ListItem>
            <asp:ListItem>Calvino</asp:ListItem>
        </asp:BulletedList>
        <br />

        <asp:ListBox ID="ListBox1" runat="server">
            <asp:ListItem Value="IE">Ireland</asp:ListItem>
            <asp:ListItem Value="IT">Italy</asp:ListItem>
            <asp:ListItem Value="US">United States</asp:ListItem>
        </asp:ListBox></div>
    </form>
</body>
</html>
```

Now let's take a moment to see how this works.

How It Works

In this exercise, you had two simple objectives. The first objective was to practice using the VWD Designer interface, which allows you to easily add items to lists. The second objective was to observe the resulting code. Note the `<Items>` collection within the list tag and then the tags for each item in the collection. VWD creates code with the text between tags rather than setting the text string as a property within a tag. In the second step, we set two properties for each item. The text will be shown to the user, and the value will be available to us, as programmers, as an identifier of which item was selected.

We will be working with the contents of the value property for the next few dozen pages of this text.

Data-Binding List Controls

Setting list items statically (as in the preceding exercise) provides the best performance if items do not change (for example, a few types of membership categories). But if the list varies and the items are represented in your database, it behooves you to create the items collection dynamically. With ASP.NET 2.0, this is very easy. The list controls are data-bound controls that behave at design time and runtime almost the same as other data-bound controls. The list's DataSourceID property can be set to any data source control. You then have to set the Text and Value properties of the list control to fields that are available from the data returned by the data source control's Select method, for instance, in the SqlDataSource control's SelectCommand.

Recall from the introduction to list controls the contrast between Text and Value properties; Text is shown to the user, whereas Value is the datum available to other controls or processes after a selection is made. Text might be "Canada Post," but the Value represents that shipper's code of "101." When list controls are data-bound, you can specify separate fields to bind to the Text property and the Value property. Generally, you would bind the DataTextField to the more human-understandable field, such as ShipperName, and the DataValueField to the primary key such as the ShipperID field.

Many developers either forget to set the DataTextField or DataValueField or get them reversed. Using VWD's tools reduces errors. The Choose Data Source link opens a dialog box in which you can choose the data source and then reflects against the data source schema to allow (and remind) the user to choose field associations for DataTextField and DataValueField.

Note that when you use the VWD dialog box, you do not need to create an items collection; that will be done automatically by ASP.NET 2.0. However, you must be sure that the DataTextField is one of the fields returned by the data source control (for example, in the SelectCommand of a SqlDataSource control). Before going further, let's create a bulleted list that is dynamic.

Try It Out Data-Binding a BulletedList Control

In the last exercise, you created a bulleted list using items (favorite authors) that were hard-coded (static) in the page. This time, you will generate the list from the authors in the Pubs database.

1. If you did not create a connection string for Pubs in Chapter 3's second Try It Out, "Storing the Connection String in Web.Config", you should do so now. You can check for its presence by looking for the lines below (line breaks added below are artificial: the connection string will be on one line in web.config). If the MdfPubs connection string does not exist, then add it as a new connection string (of the type Microsoft SQL Server Database File – SqlClient) when you are working through the data source control wizard in Step 2.

```
...
  <appSettings/>
  <connectionStrings>
  <add name="MdfNorthwind"
connectionString=" Data Source=.\SQLEXPRESS;
AttachDbFilename=|DataDirectory|\Northwind.mdf;
Integrated Security=True;
Connect Timeout=30;
User Instance=True" />
  <add name="MdfPubs"
connectionString=" Data Source=.\SQLEXPRESS;
AttachDbFilename=|DataDirectory|\Pubs.mdf;
Integrated Security=True;
Connect Timeout=30;
User Instance=True" />
...
 </connectionStrings>
```

2. Create a new page named TIO-0802-BulletedList-Dynamic.aspx. Drag a bulleted list control onto the page and, in the Smart Tasks panel, select Choose Data Source. Select a new Data Source, and set it to a database named SqlDataSource1 that uses your MdfPubs connection. Retrieve just the authors' last names (au_lname) from the Pub's Authors table. Order by the author last name. After clicking Choose Data Source from the bulleted list Smart Tasks panel (see Figure 8-2), you will be cycled back to the original dialog box. Click Refresh Schema and, for the data field, select the only field, au_lname. You do not have to worry about the field for the value because the bulleted list is just a presentation tool, not a selection tool. Click OK, save the page, and view it in your browser.

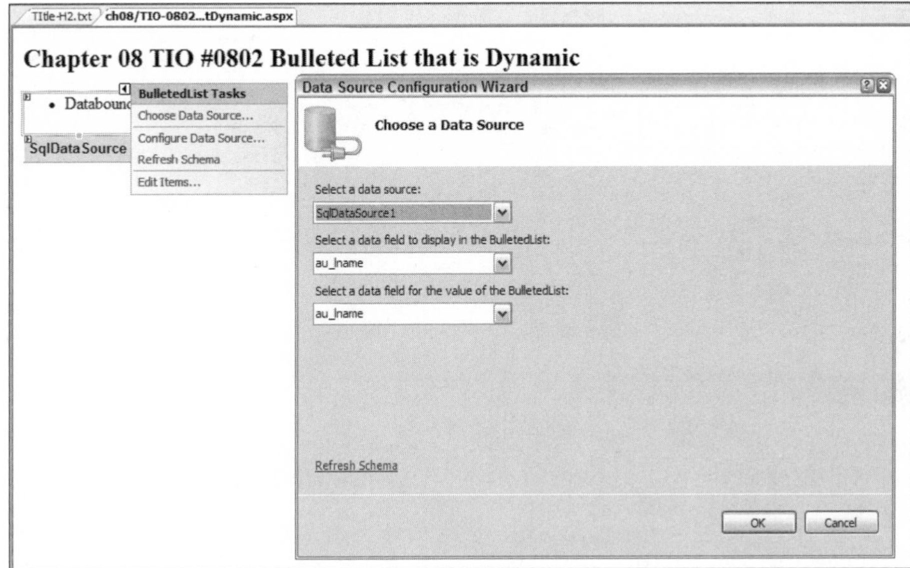

Figure 8-2

```
...
<h2>Chapter 08 TIO #0802 Bulleted List that is Dynamic</h2>
<form id="form1" runat="server">
    <div>
        <asp:BulletedList ID="BulletedList1"
                runat="server"
                DataSourceID="SqlDataSource1"
                DataTextField="au_lname"
                DataValueField="au_lname">
        </asp:BulletedList>
        <asp:SqlDataSource ID="SqlDataSource1" runat="server"
                ConnectionString="<%$ ConnectionStrings:MdfPubs %>"
                 SelectCommand="SELECT [au_lname] FROM [authors]
                        ORDER BY [au_lname]"></asp:SqlDataSource>
    </div>            </form>    </body>          </html>
```

3. Now we can change data and see our bulleted list automatically change. Let's say that we want to add a new author named Aardvark. Close your browser and switch to VWD. Open the Database Explorer, expand your pubs.mdf, and then expand the tables. Right-click on authors

and select Show Table Data. Scroll to the bottom of the table to find the row displaying an asterisk in the left column and all `NULL` values. Type the data for a new author named `Art Aardvark`. After you enter the first datum, the record is created and the asterisk in the left column will turn to a pencil to indicate that you are changing an existing record, as shown in Figure 8-3.

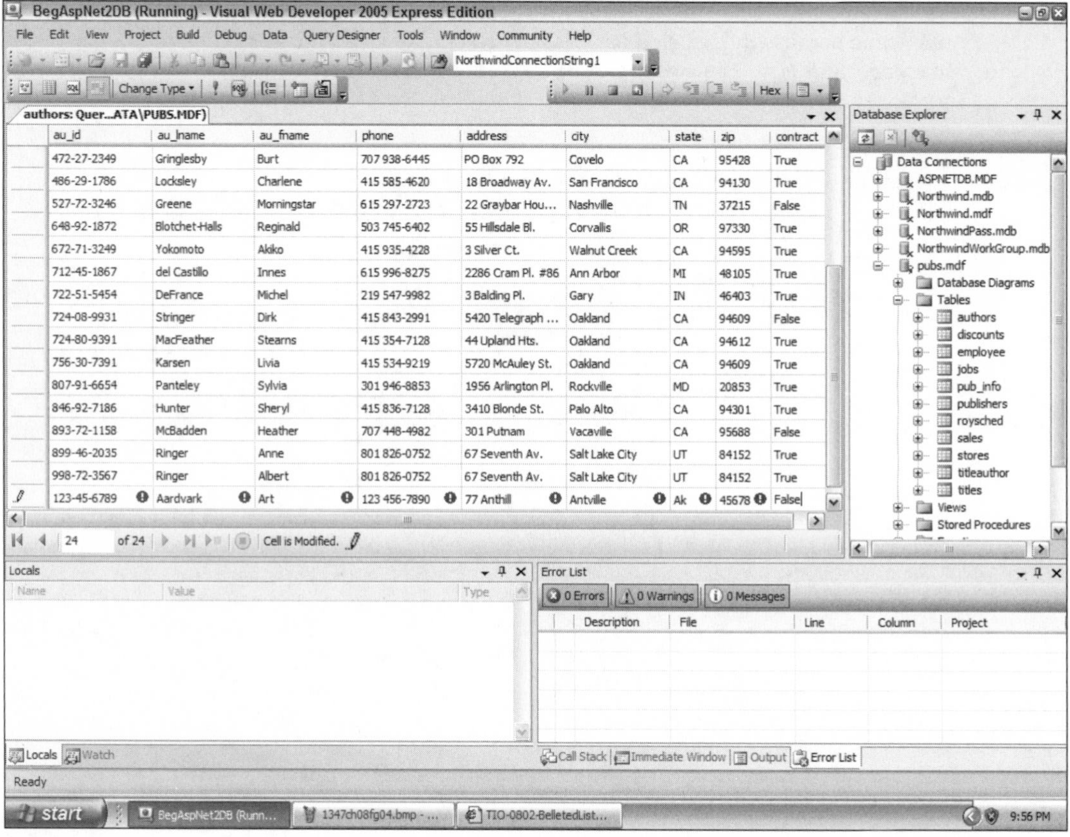

Figure 8-3

4. When you move off of the record using tabs or a mouse click, the record's new information is saved. At that point, the red warning icons disappear.

How It Works

The first exercise led you through adding all the items in a hard-coded list. If there were daily changes, you would have to go back and edit the ASPX page each time. In this exercise, we ascended one step on the ladder of enlightenment. You employed a list that displays information from a database, thus creating a dynamic list. The technique was simplicity itself. You just dragged and dropped. Now your bulleted list will automatically remain current with the database.

DropDownList Control

A bulleted list presents items, and those items can have hyperlinks. But a bulleted list does not signal to the user that a selection is expected. To invite the user to make a selection, you move to list boxes. Drop-down lists and list boxes are covered here at three levels: simple presentation, allowing selection with processing after a button is clicked, and allowing selection with automatic processing (`AutoPostBack`).

For simply presenting items, you can use the same technique as the bulleted lists. The only change is the name of the control. You still bind to a data source control and, in the list control, identify one field for the `Text` property (visible to users) and another as the `Value` property (values useful for processing in code).

```
<asp:DropDownList ID="DropDownList1" Runat="server"
  DataTextField="Field1"
  DataValueField="Field2"        DataSourceID="SqlDataSource1" />

<asp:SqlDataSource ID="SqlDataSource1" Runat="server"
  SelectCommand="SELECT Field1, Field2 FROM MyTable"
  ConnectionString=" ... "/>
```

Try It Out Data-Binding a DropDownList Control

In this example, you provide a list of authors in a drop-down list control.

1. Open the ASPX file `TIO-0802`, and save it as `TIO-0803-DropDownList`. Change the `<title>` and `<h2>` text to reflect the new file name and purpose.
2. In source view, change (typing by hand) the `<asp:BulletedList>` to `<asp:DropDownList>`. Change the closing tag as well.

```
...
<h2>Chapter 08 TIO #0803 Drop Down List </h2>
    <form id="form1" runat="server">
    <div>
        <asp:DropDownList ID="BulletedList1" runat="server"
                DataSourceID="SqlDataSource1"
                DataTextField="au_lname"
                DataValueField="au_lname">
        </asp:DropDownList>

        <asp:SqlDataSource ...
```

3. Save your work, and view it in your browser.

How It Works

Displaying a dynamic list of items in a drop-down list box is as easy as for the bulleted list. You merely create a data source control and then set the list's `DataSourceID` to the data source control's ID.

Other list controls are just as easy to create. In the following exercise, you review the drop-down list and then demonstrate the very similar syntax for list boxes, radio button lists, and check box lists.

Try It Out Data-Binding Other List Controls

In this page, you will create a single data source control and then display four lists from the one control.

1. Create a new page named `TIO-4-OtherListControls.aspx`. We'll be using the same `SqlDataSource` control for several data-bound controls, so let's create the data source control first. From the Toolbox, add a `SqlDataSource` control to read the authors' last names from the authors table of the Pubs database using the `MdfPubs` connection. Order the names by the author's last name.
2. From the VWD menu, select Layout⇨Insert table and add a table with one row and four columns. Select the row (using the Layout menu or the selection triangle to the left of the row), and in the Property window, set the vertical alignment to top. Drag the two right cells until they are `130px` wide.
3. Drag a `DropDownList` control onto the left (first) cell and set its `DataSourceID` to the `SqlDataSource` control. Set the Data Field to Display to `au_lname`.
4. Repeat for the next cells, adding `ListBox`, `CheckBoxList`, and `RadioButtonList` controls. In each case, set the `DataSourceID` to the `SqlDataSource1` as shown in Figure 8-4. Save and observe the file in your browser.

```
<table>
<tr>
<td style="width: 100px" valign="top">
        <asp:DropDownList ID="DropDownList1" runat="server"
        DataSourceID="SqlDataSource1"
        DataTextField="au_lname"
        DataValueField="au_lname">
        </asp:DropDownList></td>
<td style="width: 100px" valign="top">
        <asp:ListBox ID="ListBox1" runat="server"
        DataSourceID="SqlDataSource1"
        DataTextField="au_lname"
        DataValueField="au_lname"></asp:ListBox></td>
<td style="width: 130px" valign="top">
        <asp:CheckBoxList ID="CheckBoxList1" runat="server"
        DataSourceID="SqlDataSource1"
        DataTextField="au_lname"
        DataValueField="au_lname">
        </asp:CheckBoxList></td>
<td style="width: 130px" valign="top">
        <asp:RadioButtonList ID="RadioButtonList1" runat="server"
        DataSourceID="SqlDataSource1"
        DataTextField="au_lname"
        DataValueField="au_lname">
        </asp:RadioButtonList></td>
</tr>
</table>
```

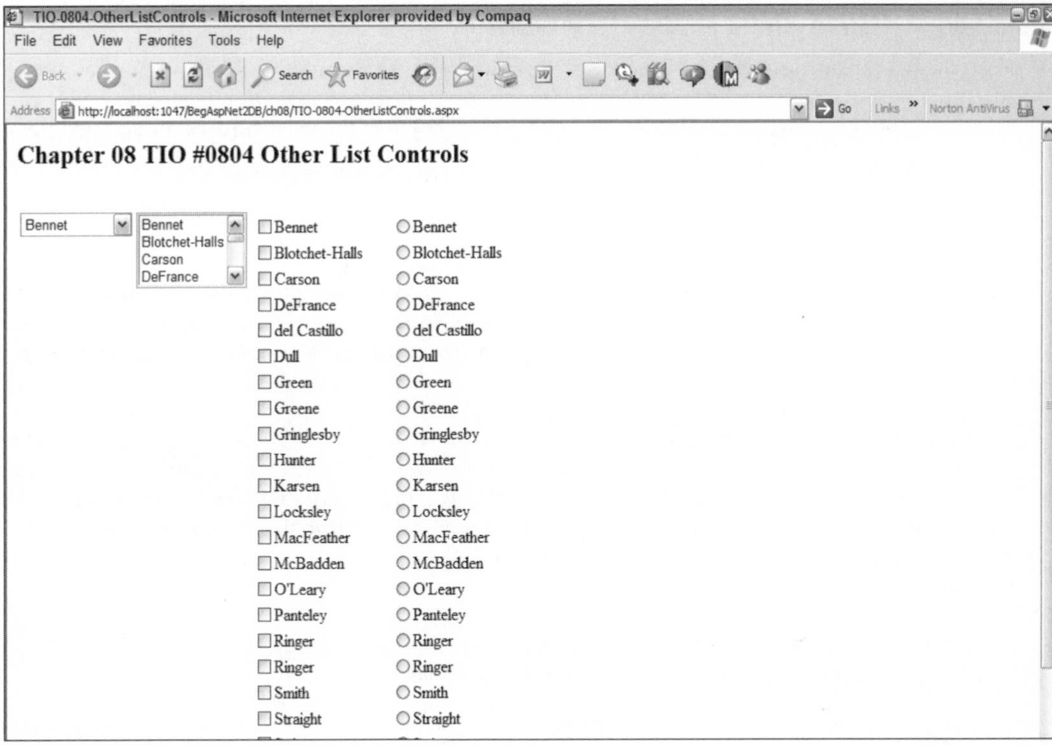

Figure 8-4

How It Works

VWD offers a consistent pattern to create list controls. You drag the control to the page and set its data source control. Then you specify a field to provide the text property. The resulting code generated by VWD is also very consistent—only the names of the controls change.

Selection in a List

It's time to move on to a more interactive level, where you permit the user to select one item in the list, and you react to that selection. Note that you can use the selected item at two points in time. If you enable `AutoPostBack`, the act of selecting causes the page to refresh, probably using the selected value to enact some sort of change to the page. If you do not use `AutoPostBack`, the page waits for the user to click on a button (typically Submit) before you use the selected item. For example, if a user is entering information as a new member, you may want to wait until selections are made from many lists before you process the page. In this case, `AutoPostBack` should be off so that a change by the user will not induce a page refresh. Both techniques are discussed below.

SelectedIndex and SelectedValue

When the user selects an item in a list control, three of the control's properties will receive values:

- `SelectedItemText`: Holds the string that was shown in the list control of the selected item.
- **SelectedValue:** Holds the datum in the `Value` property for the selected item.
- `SelectedItemIndex`: Holds the number (count starting with zero) of the item in the list that was selected.

The `SelectedIndex` property is useful if a list is generated from a hard-coded array, and you want to go back and look up data in the array (perhaps an additional dimension). However, if the list's item collection is being generated dynamically (for example, from a database), the index can vary from page to page and is, thus, less useful.

For example, if you load the selection list from a hard-coded list of states, you can be sure that Alabama is #0, Alaska #1 and Arizona #3. But if you are listing employees of Northwind arranged by last name, Buchanon will be #0 and Callahan #1 only as long as Callahan is not fired. When Callahan leaves, then Dodsworth will appear as #1 in the list. Most of the examples in this book will be using the `SelectedValue` in lookups back in the database because we expect the contents of the selection list to be dynamic.

If you work on more advanced scenarios of custom code, it is useful to know that `SelectedIndex` and `SelectedValue` may be set declaratively in code at runtime.

Try It Out Handling Selection with the Submit Button

In this exercise, you will present a drop-down list box of authors. The user can select one and then click a submit button. You report back on the page on which author was selected. For the benefit of the student programmer, also report the selection's value and index.

1. Create a new page named `TIO-5-DropDownList-Select.aspx`. Add a `SqlDataSource` control to the `MdfPubs` Authors table as you did earlier, but this time read two fields: author ID and author last name. Order by `au_lname` ascending.
2. Add a drop-down list with a connection to your data source control. Display the field `au-lname` (the wizard's way of setting the `DataTextField`). Set the data field for the value to `au_id` (the `DataValueField`).
3. Drag an `asp:` button control onto the page. With the button selected, in the Properties window set the `OnClientClick` property to `Button1_Click`.
4. Staying in VWD, go to the Source view and create the procedure in the `<script>`, as shown here for Visual Basic. VWD will create the frame of the procedure if in the top left drop-down box you select Button1, and at the top right drop-down you select Click (see Figure 8-5).

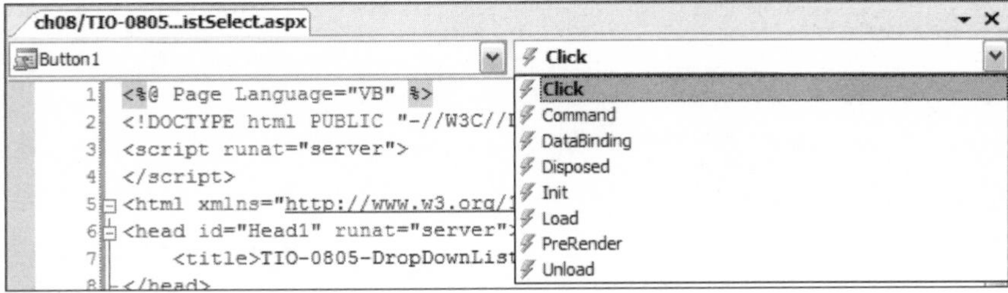

Figure 8-5

The following code demonstrates the source code if you use VB or C#.

C#

```
<%@ Page Language="C#" %>
...
<script runat="server">
    protected void Button1_Click(object sender, EventArgs e)
    {
        Response.Write("You Selected: " + DropDownList1.SelectedItem.Text );
        Response.Write("<br />(Value: " + DropDownList1.SelectedValue + ")");
        Response.Write("<br />(index: " + DropDownList1.SelectedIndex  + ")");
    }
</script>
```

VB

```
 <%@ Page Language="VB" %>
<!DOCTYPE html PUBLIC "-//W3C//DTD XHTML 1.0 Transitional//EN"
"http://www.w3.org/TR/xhtml1/DTD/xhtml1-transitional.dtd">
<script runat="server">
    Protected Sub Button1_Click(ByVal sender As Object, ByVal e As
System.EventArgs)
        Response.Write("You Selected: " & DropDownList1.SelectedItem.Text)
        Response.Write("<br />(value: " & DropDownList1.SelectedValue & ")")
        Response.Write("<br />(index: " & DropDownList1.SelectedIndex & ")")
    End Sub
</script>
<html xmlns="http://www.w3.org/1999/xhtml" >
<head id="Head1" runat="server">
    <title>TIO-0805-DropDownListSelect</title>
</head>
<body>
        <h2>Chapter 08 TIO #0805 Drop Down List Using Select </h2>
    <form id="form1" runat="server">
    <div>
        <asp:SqlDataSource ID="SqlDataSource1" runat="server"
            ConnectionString="<%$ ConnectionStrings:MdfPubs %>"
```

```
            SelectCommand="SELECT [au_id], [au_lname] FROM [authors] ORDER BY
[au_lname]">
          </asp:SqlDataSource>
        <asp:DropDownList ID="DropDownList1" runat="server"
            DataSourceID="SqlDataSource1"
            DataTextField="au_lname"
            DataValueField="au_id">
        </asp:DropDownList>
        <br />
        <asp:Button ID="Button1" runat="server"
            Text="Use My Selection"
            OnClick="Button1_Click" />
        </div>
        </form>
</body>
</html>
```

5. Save your work, and test it in your browser.

How It Works

This exercise differs from earlier exercises in several ways. First, you are going to handle selections and you want to use more than the string that was presented in the list — you want to display the `Value` and Index of the item the user selected. So, you specify a second property for the items and value, and you set it to the `au_ID`. As you will see in the next chapter, having that ID in hand makes it easy to create a `WHERE` clause that would look up only books from the selected author.

Second, you added a button to the page that, when clicked, triggered a procedure named `button1_click`. Third, you wrote the procedure (more details on handling events are presented in Chapter 16). The button-click event will send to the procedure `EventArgs` (arguments). These, in the case of a click on a list, reference back to properties of the control that was clicked: the list's selected item's text, value, and index number.

Automatic Postback

For some pages, you will want to react as soon as the user makes a selection in your list. Rather than having a button that requires a second user action, you can enable an automatic submit, that is, `AutoPostBack`. You can specify a procedure to perform when `AutoPostBack` is invoked. That procedure can utilize the selected item's text, value, and index. However, turning on `AutoPostBack` is not for every case, and the application developer needs to make a decision on which is the best choice. For example, if the `DropDownList` control is being used to alter the value of a record during editing, chances are good that you don't want the postback to happen until after the client has filled out all other input fields. In this case, a button submit (such as an Update button) makes more sense than `AutoPostBack`.

Try It Out — Handling Selection with Automatic Postback

This exercise builds on the previous exercise by adding a drop-down list that automatically posts back.

1. Open the `TIO-5-DropDownList-Select.aspx` file you created, and save it as `TIO-6-DropDOwnList-AutoPostback.aspx`.
2. Add a second `DropDownList` and configure its data source to `SqlDataSource1` (same as the first `DropDownList`). Set up its display the same way, with three exceptions. First, it will have a default name of `DropDownList2`. Second, in its Smart Tasks panel, turn on Enable Autopostback. Third, set its `SelectedIndexChanged` event handler to the procedure named `"DropDownList2_SelectedIndexChanged"`.
3. Add a second procedure named `"DropDownList2_SelectedIndexChanged"`, as shown in the following code. Save and observe in your browser.

The following lists demonstrate the source code if you use VB or C#.

C#

```
<%@ Page Language="C#" %>
...
<script runat="server">
...
    protected void DropDownList2_SelectedIndexChanged(object sender, EventArgs e)
    {
        Response.Write("You Selected From DropDownList #2: " +
                 DropDownList2.SelectedItem.Text);
        Response.Write("<br />(Value: " + DropDownList2.SelectedValue + ")");
        Response.Write("<br />(index: " + DropDownList2.SelectedIndex + ")");
    }
</script>
```

VB

```
<%@ Page Language="VB" %>
<!DOCTYPE html PUBLIC "-//W3C//DTD XHTML 1.0 Transitional//EN"
"http://www.w3.org/TR/xhtml1/DTD/xhtml1-transitional.dtd">
<script runat="server">
    Protected Sub Button1_Click(ByVal sender As Object, ByVal e As
System.EventArgs)
        Response.Write("You Selected: " & DropDownList1.SelectedItem.Text)
        Response.Write("<br />(value: " & DropDownList1.SelectedValue & ")")
        Response.Write("<br />(index: " & DropDownList1.SelectedIndex & ")")
    End Sub

    Protected Sub DropDownList2_SelectedIndexChanged(ByVal sender As Object, ByVal
e As System.EventArgs)
        Response.Write("You Selected From DropDownList #2: " &
DropDownList2.SelectedItem.Text)
        Response.Write("<br />(value: " & DropDownList2.SelectedValue & ")")
        Response.Write("<br />(index: " & DropDownList2.SelectedIndex & ")")
    End Sub
</script>
<html xmlns="http://www.w3.org/1999/xhtml" >
<head id="Head1" runat="server">
    <title>TIO-0806-DropDownListSelectWithAutoPostBack-VB</title>
</head>
<body>
        <h2>Chapter 08 TIO #0806 Drop Down List Using Select with AutoPostBack</h2>
```

```
        <form id="form1" runat="server">
        <div>
            <asp:SqlDataSource ID="SqlDataSource1" runat="server"
                ConnectionString="<%$ ConnectionStrings:MdfPubs %>"
                SelectCommand="SELECT [au_id], [au_lname] FROM [authors] ORDER BY
    [au_lname]">
            </asp:SqlDataSource>
        <asp:DropDownList ID="DropDownList1" runat="server"
            DataSourceID="SqlDataSource1"
            DataTextField="au_lname"
            DataValueField="au_id">
        </asp:DropDownList>
        <br />
        <asp:Button ID="Button1" runat="server"
            Text="Use My Selection"
            OnClick="Button1_Click" />
            <br />
        <asp:DropDownList ID="DropDownList2" runat="server"
            DataSourceID="SqlDataSource1"
            DataTextField="au_lname"
            DataValueField="au_id"
            AutoPostBack="true"
            OnSelectedIndexChanged="DropDownList2_SelectedIndexChanged">
        </asp:DropDownList></div>
        </form>
    </body>
    </html>
```

How It Works

When you added the second button, you introduced a new property. The `AutoPostBack=True` means that a selection in the list will also automatically perform the equivalent of a click on a submit button. Second, you set the `OnSelectedIndexChanged` event handler to point to a procedure to be run when that submission occurs.

```
        <asp:DropDownList ID="DropDownList2" Runat="server"
            DataValueField="au_id"
            DataTextField="au_lname"
            DataSourceID="SqlDataSource1"
            AutoPostBack="True"
            OnSelectedIndexChanged="DropDownList2_SelectedIndexChanged" />
```

The actual procedure is the same as in the previous example, except that you now write the data from the selected item of the second drop-down list.

`AutoPostBack` is useful but not always indicated. Only use it when you expect the change to the control to be the last action on the page prior to a refresh.

Common Mistakes

The following are mistakes commonly made while trying to display data in lists:

- Forgetting to set `DataTextField` or `DataValueField` (nothing renders in the list, or it renders the same thing for all items, such as `System.Data.DataRowView` when bound to a `DataSet`).
- Using `Text` when you want to use `Value`, and vice versa. These can be used interchangeably only when they point to the same field or value.
- Setting a list's `DataField` or `DataField` property to a field that is not included in the data source control's data, such as in the `SqlDataSource`'s `SelectCommand` statement.
- Expecting the `List.SelectedItem.Index` to be the same from page to page when the list is generated dynamically.
- Setting a list's `Text` or `Value` property to the original name of a field but the field's name has been changed with an alias in the `SqlDataSource`'s `SelectCommand` statement.
- Forgetting to set `AutoPostBack=true` when you want an automatic postback. If you do not have either `AutoPostBack` or a `Button` to initiate action, then nothing happens when you select from the list.

Summary

The last few chapters presented data in tables consisting of grids of rows and columns. When you have only one dimension of data, you can use one of the list controls, including the `BulletedList`, `DropDownList`, `ListBox`, `CheckBoxList`, or `RadioButtonList`. With the exception of the bulleted list, each of these presents choices to the user and implies that the user should make a selection. Ergo, they are referred to as selection lists.

They all work in very similar ways. A list contains a collection of items that will be displayed. Items have a `Text` property that is shown to the user. They also have a Value property that holds a datum that is hidden from the user but may be more useful when set for your code. Last, there is an Index property for each item.

The list of items can come from one of two sources. Option one loads the list from lines of code that contain literal strings and, thus, are static (that is, the same for all pages until the code is rewritten). Option two directs the page to load the list from the data of a data source control. Using this dynamic method, you get lists that are responsive to the current situation of the site and its business.

Lists go beyond just displaying data; they can also accept a user's click and react. At the time of reaction, three important bits of data will be available regarding the item that was selected: the aforementioned Text, Value, and Index properties. In this chapter, we reacted with a simple procedure that wrote the data to the page.

There are two options for when to react. First, a Submit button can be on the page. After performing multiple tasks on a page, the user can click the Submit button. Alternatively, you can have the page automatically and immediately perform a postback when the select is performed.

The exercises in this chapter were trivial; they did not solve real-world problems. But future chapters use the techniques of lists as building blocks for more complex solutions. For example, in the next chapter, you will react to a selection by re-rendering a `GridView` to show only the books of the selected author.

Exercises

The answers to these review questions can be found in Appendix B.

1. Describe the difference between a selection list's `DataValueField` and `DataTextField`.
2. How is a bulleted list different from a drop-down list or list box?
3. Which event is invoked when the user clicks on an item in a drop-down list?
4. When might it be ill advised to set `AutoPostBack` to `true` for a `DropDownList`?

Filtering and Master—Details Scenarios

The last few chapters discussed several data-bound controls, each with its own advantages. This chapter discusses how they can work together. We start with a basic technique to limit the number of records displayed in a data-bound table. Then we expand that technique to work with multiple controls, using the specialized strengths of each. For example, you will select one record from a `GridView` and display further details about that record in a `DetailsView` control. These concepts start our discussion of how to bring together multiple controls to create an efficient user interface.

This chapter tackles six major ideas:

- Filtering `GridView` records from a query string
- Filtering `GridView` records from user input in a `TextBox`
- The theory of selection and `ControlParameters`
- Filtering `GridView` Records Using a Selection List Control
- Showing a record in `DetailsView` based on a user selection in a `GridView`
- Cascading lists

Introducing Master–Details Scenarios

This chapter addresses how to give the user the capacity to change the scope of records or fields displayed in a data-bound control. It has two major objectives:

- **Showing only a subset of all the records in a control.** For example, you may want to see the orders for only one customer.
- **Showing more fields for just one of the records.** For example, after picking an employee from a GridView, you may want see additional details about that employee.

Both of these cases are solved in the same way: Use one data-bound control to change the *scope* (number of records or number of fields) of a second data-bound control.

> *The term* filtering *is often used in this chapter. Filtering in this chapter is the limiting of records to display by setting a* WHERE *clause in a data source control. This includes the case of displaying just one record when filtering determines which record. Note that this chapter does not discuss the* `FilterExpression/FilterParameters` *properties of SqlDataSource, which is typically used in special cases of caching and covered in Chapter 15.*

When using one data-bound control to filter another data-bound control, accurate wording must denote the two controls. The *master control* will be the one that accepts the user's input. The *details control* is the one that reacts with a filtered display. Note that the details (reacting) control does not have to be a `DetailsView control.`

Almost all controls can interact as master or details controls in a filtering scenario. For example, a `GridView` can be either the details control (another control determines which record `GridView` shows) or a master control (`GridView` determines which record is displayed in a details control). Also keep in mind that you may have two data source controls on a page, one to supply the master data-bound control and a second to supply the details data-bound control.

The basic theory for filtering involves three steps. In most cases in this chapter, that will mean the following:

1. You obtain a criterion from a master control.
2. You apply the criterion to the `WHERE` clause of the data source for the details control.
3. The details control will re-render display with a modified scope of records or fields. In most cases, this step will happen automatically.

The second step is the focus of much of our discussion. ASP.NET 2.0 passes the user's selection by first putting the value(s) into a parameter. The parameter is then read into the criteria of the `WHERE` clause.

Filtering GridView Records Using a Query String

We'll start with a focus on how the details control scope can be modified. This first example is so simple that it does not even use a master control; the criteria are provided in a query string. Recall that a *query string* is merely field names and values added to the end of a URL. For example, the following query string indicating a membership number could be sent to a site:

```
www.example.org?MemberNumber=123
```

The value `123` can be used in the page by asking the server for the query string value named `MemberNumber`. Query strings are intrinsic to all HTML pages; they are not special to ASP.NET.

The flow of information starts with the URL request for the page containing the query string. In this simple example, you will type the query string. Then, on your page, the data source control will pick up the value from the query string and put it into a parameter. The `WHERE` clause of the `SelectCommand` of the data source control will pick up the value from the parameter and use it as its criteria to scope (limit) records. The data-bound control will then show the scoped set of records and fields. Note that the `WHERE` clause gets a new query string value for every page request; thus, the page is dynamic, albeit in a crude way. The VWD IDE walks you through this setup, so you do not actually have to write code.

Try It Out — Filtering GridView Records Using a Query String

In this exercise, you want a page that accepts a request with a query string that indicates a state. The resulting `GridView` of authors will show writers from only the specified state. In this initial and simple exercise, we will plan on users submitting URLs with a query string containing a value for the state. Your page will scope the records to show just the requested state in a `GridView`. (Of course, your port number would vary from the sample 1111 shown here.)

```
http://localhost:1111/BegAspNet2Db/ch09/TIO-0901-QueryString.asp?state=IN
```

But first, there are two notes before we begin. First, the term *state* is also used to describe the condition of an ASPX page, but in this exercise we are using the word in its meaning as a geographic subsection of a nation. Second, this exercise uses the Pubs database instead of Northwind. Double-check that you installed the Pubs database in your SSE as described in Chapter 1 and that you have an `MdfPubs` connection string, the same as for `MdfNorthwind`.

1. Create a new folder named `C:\Websites\BegAspNet2Db\ch09` and a new page named `TIO-0901-QueryString.aspx`.
2. Add a `SqlDataSource` control to the page. Use the Smart Tasks panel and select Configure Data Source to connect to Pubs. Use the `MdfPubs` connection string. Select from the authors table the ID, names, city, and state. Click on `WHERE` and set `Column = state`, `Operator` to `equals`, and `Source` to `querystring`.

   Note that a Parameters Properties panel specific for query strings opens. Set `QueryString field = State` and a default of `CA`. Click Add, and note that the `WHERE` clause box now displays that the state will be set to the `Request.QueryString` value for `State`. Click OK, and continue the wizard.

   Test the query, accepting the default. Try the test again, this time noting that when the Parameter Values Editor dialog box pops up; you can try other values than the default; for example, there is an author from Michigan (MI).
3. Add a `GridView` to display records from the data source you just created. Your results should be similar to the following:

```
<%@ Page Language="VB" %>
<!DOCTYPE html PUBLIC "-//W3C//DTD XHTML 1.0 Transitional//EN"
"http://www.w3.org/TR/xhtml1/DTD/xhtml1-transitional.dtd">
<script runat="server">
</script>
<html xmlns="http://www.w3.org/1999/xhtml" >
<head id="Head1" runat="server"><title>TIO-0901-QueryString</title></head>
<body>
<h2>Chapter 09 TIO #0901 QueryString </h2>
    <form id="form1" runat="server">
    <div>

<asp:SqlDataSource ID="SqlDataSource1" runat="server"
```

```
            ConnectionString="<%$ ConnectionStrings:MdfPubs %>"
            SelectCommand="SELECT [au_id], [au_lname], [au_fname], [city], [state]
               FROM [authors] WHERE ([state] = @state)">

          <SelectParameters>
             <asp:QueryStringParameter
               DefaultValue="CA"
               Name="state"
               QueryStringField="state"
               Type="String" />
          </SelectParameters>
</asp:SqlDataSource>

        <asp:GridView ID="GridView1" runat="server"
AutoGenerateColumns="False"
DataKeyNames="au_id"
DataSourceID="SqlDataSource1">
            <Columns>
...
            </Columns>
        </asp:GridView>
    </div>      </form>         </body>         </html>
```

4. Test the page by first just opening it. Notice that the `GridView` is filtered by the WHERE clause applying the default query string value of CA.
5. Now go to the address line of your browser and type the URL with a query string such as the following:

```
http://localhost:1111/BegAspNet2Db/ch09/TIO-0901-QueryString.aspx?state=IN
```

6. Close your browser, and save the page.

How It Works

First, keep in mind that this is a preliminary example. Instead of using a master control, you are using a value typed into the query string:

```
SelectCommand="SELECT * FROM [authors] WHERE state = @state"
```

Within the data source control, note that the WHERE clause is not hard-coded. Rather, the value for state shall come from a parameter named state. The @ symbol indicates that the following term is a parameter in the data source control's parameter collection.

Now turn your attention to a new structure called the `SelectParameters` collection. This example uses a `QueryStringParameter`. Give the parameter the same name as that used in the `WHERE` clause, in this case, `state`. Two properties are set in the parameter. The first is that the value shall come from the query string field named `state`. If there is no `state` value, you will use a default of "`CA`".

```
<SelectParameters>
  <asp:QueryStringParameter Name="state"
      QueryStringField="state"
      DefaultValue="CA"  />
</SelectParameters>
```

The overall flow of information was as follows:

The user typed into the URL address bar a page name and value and then pressed Enter to request the page. At the server, that value was automatically put into the query string collection. Your page then read the value from the query string collection into your `SelectParameters` collection. When the data source control executed its `SelectCommand`, the `WHERE` clause read the value from the `SelectParameters` collection. Thus, the data source control created a set of records scoped down to just certain records. That smaller set of records was sent to the data-bound control for display.

Retyping an URL just to provide your site with a piece of data provides an interface reminiscent of the Neanderthals. Users want a way to interact with the page itself, not the browser's address line. In the remainder of the chapter, we will implement techniques that use the result of further evolution: the ASP.NET 2.0 controls.

Filtering GridView Records Using a TextBox

A value appended to a query string works fine if it is generated by another ASPX page. But query strings are awkward for direct input from a user. A better alternative is to give the user a `TextBox` and use that as the source for the parameter. This means that you are actually using one control to scope another, all on one page. As with the last exercise, it is easy to create the page by clicking through the VWD Designer.

The architecture of ASP.NET 2.0 provides programmers a very consistent syntax for parameters. Switching from a query string to a `TextBox` requires only changing your `SelectParameter` type from `QueryStringParameter` to `ControlParameter` and adding a property to specify the control.

Try It Out — Limiting GridView Records Using a TextBox

In this exercise, you want the user to be able to type a state into a textbox on the page rather than type the state value into the URL.

1. Create a new page named `TIO-0902-TextBox.aspx`. Start by adding a `TextBox` named `TextBox1` and a button control named `Button1`.
2. Add a `GridView` and use the Smart Tasks panel to Choose Data Source as New. Select the database option, accept the default name of `SqlDataSource1` and use the existing `MdfPubs` connection. Use the same data as the previous exercise (from the authors table, the ID, names, city, and state).

   As in the last exercise, click on `WHERE` and set `Column = state` and `Operator` to `equals`. But now you want the source set to a control. In the parameters properties, set the `ControlID = TextBox1` and a default of `CA`. Don't forget to click the Add button so your parameter actually gets added to the `WHERE` clause list at the bottom of the Add WHERE Clause dialog box.

   Finish the wizard (test if you want to) to get results similar to the following:

```
<%@ Page Language="VB" %>
<!DOCTYPE html PUBLIC "-//W3C//DTD XHTML 1.0 Transitional//EN"
"http://www.w3.org/TR/xhtml1/DTD/xhtml1-transitional.dtd">
<script runat="server">
</script>
```

```
<html xmlns="http://www.w3.org/1999/xhtml" >
<head id="Head1" runat="server"><title>TIO-0902-TextBox</title></head>
<body>
<h2>Chapter 0902 TIO #0902 Text Box Control of GridView Scope</h2>
    <form id="form1" runat="server">
    <div>
        <asp:TextBox ID="TextBox1" runat="server"></asp:TextBox><br />
        <asp:Button ID="Button1" runat="server"
            Text="Button"/>
        <br /><br />
        <asp:GridView ID="GridView1" runat="server"
                AutoGenerateColumns="False"
                DataKeyNames="au_id"
                DataSourceID="SqlDataSource1">
            <Columns>
                ...
            </Columns>
        </asp:GridView>

        <asp:SqlDataSource ID="SqlDataSource1" runat="server"
            ConnectionString="<%$ ConnectionStrings:MdfPubs %>"
            SelectCommand="SELECT [au_id], [au_lname], [au_fname], [city], [state]
                FROM [authors] WHERE ([state] = @state)">
            <SelectParameters>
                <asp:ControlParameter ControlID="TextBox1"
                    DefaultValue="CA"
                    Name="state"
                    PropertyName="Text"
                    Type="String" />
            </SelectParameters>
        </asp:SqlDataSource>
</div>   </form>          </body>          </html>
```

3. Test the page in your browser. By default, you will get the authors from California (`CA`). Try typing `IN` for Indiana or `KS` for Kansas into the textbox and clicking the button.

How It Works

Your improvement here allows the user to type a state into a textbox rather than into the browser's address tool. The primary change was in your `SelectParameters` collection. Instead of a `<asp:QueryStringParameter>`, you used a `<asp:ControlParameter>`. Without regard to the parameter type, the data source control just looks through the list of parameters until it finds one with a name to match its @ in the WHERE clause.

Note that the there is no explicit event created for the button (no `Button1_Click` in the `<script>` and no `OnClick=xxx` property in the `Button` control). The update happens automatically. The default behavior for a button click is a page load; that is, it causes a postback (i.e., a page reload). In this case, the user isn't trying to write custom code to execute when the button is clicked. Instead, the user is taking advantage of the smart declarative data controls and parameters, which is why no extra code needs to be written. When the page is posted back, the `ControlParameter` is evaluated (in this case, `TextBox.Text` is retrieved) and if the value is different than it was before, the `GridView` is rebound.

Using ASP.NET 2.0 data parameters like `ControlParameter` and `QueryStringParameter` helps improve the overall security of your site. An insecure approach to designing this page would be to concatenate the text into the `WHERE` clause. Such an approach would open your database to a SQL injection attack where a nefarious user could enter a string that aborts the encoded SQL statement and instead adds its own statement, such as `DELETE FROM Authors`. The code presented in the preceding Try It Out takes the text entry, and SQL encodes the string into a parameter that is more difficult to hack. As an additional measure towards security, it is also recommended that you perform validation on parameter inputs to ensure they conform to the values you expect. You can use the ASP.NET 2.0 validation controls or write your own code using the techniques of Chapter 16 on handling events.

The `ListBox` may overly limit the user, for example, when they have to enter one of very many choices, like the name of their city. But `TextBox`es lead to problems as well, as we will explore in the next section.

Using the SQL LIKE Operator

Like write-in political ballots, allowing users to write-in data is fraught with problems. A common problem is that a user types a value that is close, but not exactly correct. Our goal as programmers is to return not only records that match a criterion but also those records that are similar in some way. SQL Server (and most other databases) offers many tools to return a wider set of records. They are all part of the SQL language or the database features and not actually part of ASP.NET 2.0.

We detour from our ASP.NET 2.0 discussion to demonstrate one example in this section. The `LIKE` operator allows you to specify only part of the string to match. If you use the clause `...WHERE Name LIKE` "`Per%`" you will get records matching Person, Personn, Persone, and Persom. For more techniques, check a SQL text to understand the power of `BETWEEN`, `IN`, and nested SQL statements. Also, look at other wildcards in the SQL syntax.

Try It Out — Using the SQL LIKE Clause

This exercise allows the user to enter text in a textbox and then do a search for similar (not only exact) last name matches.

1. Create a new page named `TIO-0903-TextBoxWithLIKE.aspx`. Add a `TextBox` and button.
2. Add a `GridView`, and create a new data source set to show from `MdfPubs` the authors' ID, name, city, and state. When you go through the Configure Data Source Wizard, select `WHERE`, and set the column to `au_lname`. But for `Operator`, select `LIKE`. The source will be the control named `TextBox1`. Don't forget to click Add.
    - In the text screen, look at the SQL statement. The `WHERE` clause criteria have been given the `LIKE` keyword, and the percent symbols have been added, meaning "substitute any number of any characters here." Add a `GridView` and run the page; your source code should be similar to the following:

```
...
<head id="Head1" runat="server">
    <title>TIO-0903-TextBoxWithLIKE</title>
</head>
<body>
```

```
<h2>Chapter 09 TIO #0903 Text Box Input with the SQL LIKE Clause</h2>
    <form id="form1" runat="server">
    <div>
        <asp:TextBox ID="TextBox1" runat="server"></asp:TextBox><br />
        <asp:Button ID="Button1" runat="server" Text="Button" /><br />
        <asp:GridView ID="GridView1" runat="server"
         AutoGenerateColumns="False"
         DataKeyNames="au_id"
         DataSourceID="SqlDataSource1">
            <Columns>
                    ...
            </Columns>
        </asp:GridView>

        <asp:SqlDataSource ID="SqlDataSource1" runat="server" ConnectionString="<%$
ConnectionStrings:MdfPubs %>"
         SelectCommand="SELECT [au_id], [au_lname], [au_fname], [state], [city]
                FROM [authors]
                WHERE ([state] LIKE '%' + @state + '%')">
            <SelectParameters>
                <asp:ControlParameter ControlID="TextBox1"
                        Name="state"
                        DefaultValue="CA"
                        PropertyName="Text"
                        Type="String" />
            </SelectParameters>
        </asp:SqlDataSource>
</div>    </form> </body> </html>
```

3. Save and test the page first by entering **CA** in the textbox, and clicking the button.
4. Now enter just the single letter **C**, and note that you still get all of the California authors. Try entering just the letter **K**. Note that you get the authors from both AK and KS.

How It Works

When you pass a SELECT command such as

```
...WHERE au_lname LIKE "%smith%"
```

to SQL Server, SQL Server will match any values that have `smith` in them, including Smith, Goldsmith, and Smithers. The only trick is in making up the preceding string. You have to concatenate the percent symbols as a literal within quotes.

Note that you use the term `au_lname` twice in the `WHERE` clause. The first time refers to the field in the table. The second time, with the `@`, refers to the parameter value, which comes from the `TextBox`.

We will finish our discussion of `TextBox`es for input with a warning. Allowing users to type input opens you site to certain types of malicious hacking. Improve the security of your site by, whenever possible, limiting user input to selections from lists (as we discuss in the rest of this chapter). Second, always use the ASP.NET 2.0 parameters collection, as opposed to appending a user's input to a WHERE clause.

Having used parameters in our examples, we should pause and take a closer look at the theory behind them.

The Theory of Selection and ControlParameters

The overall pattern of the theory behind selection in ASP.NET 2.0 data-bound controls follows, where you have two data-bound controls, named `master` and `details`. In the last two exercises the `TextBox` was the master and the `GridView` was the details. The master control instructed the details control how to behave. The page reacts as follows:

1. The user makes a selection in a selectable master control.
2. The page automatically posts back and the `ControlParameters` look for that data in the `LoadComplete` event. That results in the selected value in any `ControlParameters` on a page that specifies the master control as their source.
3. One of those control parameters is in the data source control of the details control. The details' data source control uses the value of the control parameter as a criterion in a `WHERE` clause.
4. The details control shows the set of data limited by the details' data source control.

Tracing the process backward, you see that in the end you have the details control showing a limited set of records. That set is limited because the details' data source control used a `WHERE` clause. The criteria of the `WHERE` clause came from a control parameter in the details' data source control. The control `parameter` was filled at postback by a value in the master control. The postback occurred because one of two conditions invoked it: either the user clicked on a selectable master control with `AutoPostBack = True` or the user clicked on a button.

The following controls support selection and thus can be master controls. (Other controls, such as `Calendar`, support selection but are not covered in this text).The controls covered here include:

- `GridView` (with a `SelectCommand` column)
- `DetailsView` and `FormView` (current data item)
- `ListBox` and `DropDownList`
- `CheckBoxList` and `RadioButtonList`
- `TreeView` and `Menu`

As we have seen in the last two exercises, a `TextBox` *can be bound to a* ControlParameter, *so it can behave like a selection although, strictly speaking, it is not selectable.*

In the VWD Data Source Wizard, when you use the `WHERE` dialog box to configure the select command of a data source control, the only options are the data-bound controls listed above. Each selectable control has one or more properties with values useful for control parameters as well as properties of no use to control parameters (for example, backcolor, font). When a control parameter is created, it only needs to specify which control to get a value from. There is no need to specify the property because ASP.NET 2.0 recognizes a default property for each selectable control. The defaults are listed in the following table. Note that you always have the option to bind to a property other than the default by specifying it in the standard `Object.Property` syntax.

In the case of a `ListBox` and related controls, be aware that there are a text and a value property for each item in the box. The *text* for all items is shown to the user; the *value* is picked up by the control parameter for the one item that the user selected. For example, in Northwind you might show a list of employees' names in the `Text` property but store their employee ID in the values. The user would interact with the name, but under the covers, you would use the ID value as the selected value to put into the control parameter.

Data-Bound Control	Default Property for Binding to a Control Parameter
`TextBox, Label`	`Text`
`CheckBox, RadioButton`	`Checked`
`ListBox, DropDownList, CheckBoxList, RadioButtonList`	`SelectedValue`
`GridView, DetailsView, FormView`	`SelectedValue` (first field in the list of data key names)
`TreeView, Menu`	`SelectedValue`
`Calendar`	`SelectedDate`

The case of the `GridView` as a master control is more complex (several examples appear at the end of this chapter) because there may not be a single field in a `GridView` that uniquely identifies one record. So, when a `GridView` is created, you can specify a `DataKeyNames` property consisting of one or more field names. By default, VWD will set this to the table's primary key, which can consist of one or more fields (usually one). When a row is selected in a `GridView`, the automatic postback occurs, and control parameters that use the `GridView` will be filled with the value from the `GridView`'s `SelectedValue` property, which will be the value of the first field specified in `DataKeyNames`. In most cases, the data key name field will be the table's primary key, and the control parameter will end up holding the primary key value of the selected record. That is precisely what you want for criteria in the `WHERE` clause of the details' data source control. On rare occasions, you will need to fill a control parameter with a value from a property other than the default. In these cases, you can override the default by using the `PropertyName` property of the control parameter.

To summarize selection in data-bound controls, ASP.NET 2.0 takes care of coordinating all of the values behind the scenes when you use the VWD Designer. If you look at the resulting source code, you will see that the master control or button invokes a postback after the user makes a selection or clicks a button. The control parameter evaluates the value of the user's choice, then hands that value to the details' data source control. That value is used by the `WHERE` clause so that only a limited set of data is fed to the details data-bound control.

Scoping GridView Records Using a Selection List Control

Whenever you use a `TextBox`, you open the possibility of getting errant data from the user. The standard Windows interface for selecting from a finite number of choices is a list box. Switching from a query string or `TextBox` to a `ListBox` is easy because the ASP.NET 2.0 architecture uses a consistent parameters collection. There is no difference in theory between populating a drop-down list box and a simple list box. You can populate the list box

- From hard-coded values
- From a data source

- By using the SQL keyword `DISTINCT`

When using the `TextBox`, you had to include a button because the `TextBox` doesn't have a built-in sense of when the user is done typing, so you had to solicit user action (the button) to begin the filtering of the `GridView`. Alternatively, you can set the Enter key to be an invoker of postback in a `TextBox`. But a `ListBox` is more automatic. When `AutoPostBack` is set to `true`, a click registers the user's selection and that means the selection process is finished so the page can begin processing the selection. Therefore, you can build a page with data-bound selection lists as master controls with no need for buttons. The ASPX page takes care of triggering events and reacting appropriately.

Master Control by DropDownList with Hard-Coded Items

If the items in the `DropDownList` do not change frequently, you can add them to the `Item` collection in the page code. The VWD Designer walks you through the process and then builds the set of `ListItem` tags.

Try It Out Filtering GridView Records Using a DropDownList

In this exercise, you will offer the user a list of three states that you will hard code. Upon selection, the `GridView` will display only authors from the selected state.

1. In the `ch09` folder, create a page named `TIO-0904-DropDownList`, and drag a drop-down list from the toolbar onto it.
2. In the Smart Tasks panel, select Edit Items because you will hard code the list. Click Add and set text = CA and value = CA, as shown in Figure 9-1. Click Add again, repeat this for UT and IN, and then press OK to save your work.

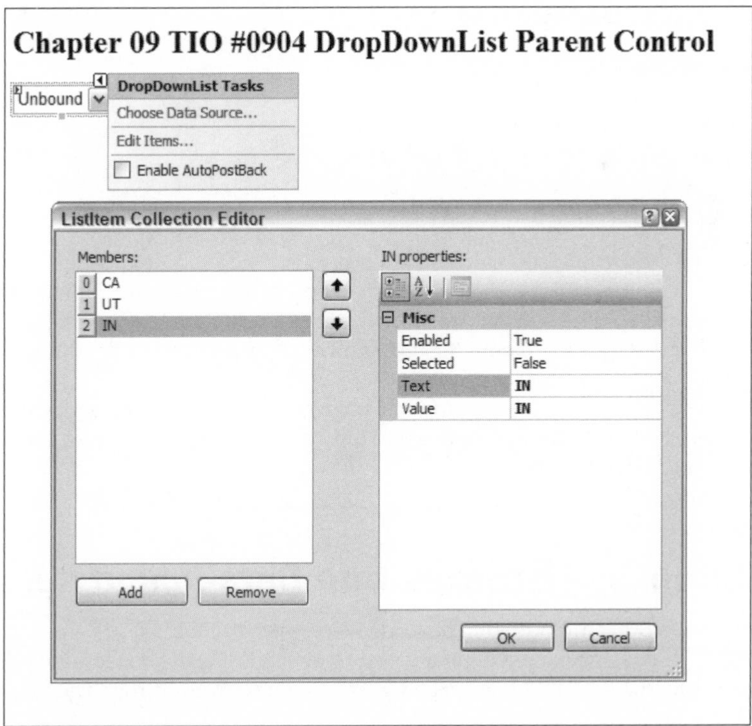

Figure 9-1

3. Keeping the list box selected, check its properties and be sure that Enable AutoPostBack is set to True.

4. Now, you will set up a `GridView` as a details control. Add a `GridView` to display author information as in the previous exercises, but this time in the source control wizard's `WHERE` clause, set your source to `Control = DropDownList1` and the `DefaultValue = CA`.

```
...
<h2>Chapter 09 TIO #0904 DropDownList Master Control </h2>
    <form id="form1" runat="server">
    <div>
        <asp:DropDownList ID="DropDownList1" runat="server" AutoPostBack="True">
            <asp:ListItem>CA</asp:ListItem>
            <asp:ListItem>UT</asp:ListItem>
            <asp:ListItem>IN</asp:ListItem>
        </asp:DropDownList><br />

        <asp:SqlDataSource ID="SqlDataSource1" runat="server"
            ConnectionString="<%$ ConnectionStrings:MdfPubs %>"
            SelectCommand="SELECT [au_id], [au_lname], [au_fname], [city], [state]
FROM [authors] WHERE ([state] = @state)">
            <SelectParameters>
                <asp:ControlParameter ControlID="DropDownList1"
                    DefaultValue="CA"
                    Name="state"
                    PropertyName="SelectedValue"
                    Type="String" />
            </SelectParameters>
        </asp:SqlDataSource>

    <asp:GridView ID="GridView1" runat="server"
      ...
    </asp:GridView>
</div></form></body></html>
```

5. Save your work, and test it in your browser.

How It Works

This exercise is like the previous in that we use a control for the source of a value in the parameter used in the `WHERE` clause of the data source control that supports the `GridView`. However, the control in this exercise is a `DropDownList`. You set up the `DropDownList` using the VWD Designer and double-checked that you added a string to both the text and value properties.

This example does not have a button because the page performs an automatic postback after a selection in the `DropDownList`. This behavior is automatic only if the master control (the `DropDownList`) has its `AutoPostBack` property set to `True`.

Master Control by ListBoxes with Data-Bound Items

Creating a `ListBox` with items added in the code works, but it would be a Sisyphean nightmare to maintain if the choices changed on a regular basis. Fortunately, the list box is a data-bound control (as discussed in Chapter 8). You build your page with two data source controls. The first supports the

GridView, as before, and takes its WHERE clause criteria from your list box. But now your list box also has a second data source control, which provides just the list of values held in the State field of the authors table. Note that SQL's keyword DISTINCT is used so that you do not get duplicates, such as CA listed eight times for the eight records of Californian authors. It would also be possible to load the list box from a new table named States, and in fact, this would be faster if there were hundreds of authors.

Try It Out — Filtering GridView Records Using a Bound DropDownList

In this exercise, you recreate your list of authors, but the master control DropDownList is dynamically created.

1. In the ch09 folder, create a page named TIO-0905-DropDownList-FromData.aspx. Now, drag a DropDownList to the page and set its source to a new data source that you name SqlDataSourceStates. Use the MdfPubs connection and set its SelectCommand to read just the state field of the author's table ordered by State, ascending. Check the check box in the SqlDataSource wizard that says "Return only unique rows." For the DropDownList set both the text and value to the state field. Check that the list has its AutoPostBack set to true.
2. Save and test the page with just the DropDownList.
3. Now you will add the details control. Add a GridView and create a new data source named SqlDataSourceAuthors that uses the MdfPubs connection to gather the authors' ID, names, city and states with its WHERE clause set so the state column equals the control named DropDownList1. You can leave the default value blank. Don't forget to click Add. The page should be similar to the following:

```
...
        <h2>Chapter 09 TIO #0905 DropDownList From Data</h2>
    <form id="form1" runat="server">
    <div>
        <asp:DropDownList ID="DropDownList1" runat="server"
            AutoPostBack="True"
            DataSourceID="SqlDataSourceStates"
            DataTextField="state"
            DataValueField="state">
        </asp:DropDownList>

        <asp:SqlDataSource ID="SqlDataSourceStates" runat="server"
            ConnectionString="<%$ ConnectionStrings:MdfPubs %>"
            SelectCommand="SELECT DISTINCT [state]
FROM [authors]
ORDER BY State ASC">
        </asp:SqlDataSource>
        <br />
        <asp:GridView ID="GridView1" runat="server"
            AutoGenerateColumns="False"
            DataKeyNames="au_id"
            DataSourceID="SqlDataSourceAuthors">
            <Columns>
...
            </Columns>
        </asp:GridView>
        <asp:SqlDataSource ID="SqlDataSourceAuthors" runat="server"
            ConnectionString="<%$ ConnectionStrings:MdfPubs %>"
            SelectCommand="SELECT [au_id], [au_lname], [au_fname], [city], [state]
```

```
    FROM [authors]
    WHERE ([state] = @state)">
                <SelectParameters>
                    <asp:ControlParameter ControlID="DropDownList1"
                        Name="state"
                        PropertyName="SelectedValue"
                        Type="String" />
                </SelectParameters>
            </asp:SqlDataSource>
        </div></form></body></html>
```

4. Save your work, and test it in a browser.

How It Works

In this exercise, you did not make changes to your GridView or its source control (SqlDataSource1). But you did add a new data source control for the DropDownList to read the list of state values from the authors table. The DISTINCT keyword in SQL filters out duplicate values in the list generated by SqlDataSourceStates. You also checked to be sure that the DropDownList as a master control had its AutoPostBack property set to True.

Note how the two data source controls operate completely independently. Also note that because the queries to retrieve the data for the GridView and DropDownList are different, we need to create two separate SqlDataSources. Although there may be data source controls in the future that can be configured for multiple queries simultaneously, the SqlDataSource control included in ASP.NET 2.0 supports only a single SelectCommand query at a time.

You may have observed some default behavior. A default for the state parameter for the GridView data source control does not appear when the page is rendered. Instead, you get the records that match the first item in the DropDownList. A DropDownList control always has an item selected, no matter what. Because of this, if you didn't explicitly specify which item was selected, the selected item will be the first item. In the end that's what the parameter sees, and that's why you get the authors from the first state.

Display Options for GridView in Master-Details Scenario

The last exercise limited the GridView records based on a user's selection in a DropDownList, but when the page first opened, the GridView displayed records from one state that was set as a default in the DropDownList. For example, the last exercise started with AR as the first state in the DropDownList and just the authors from Arkansas were visible in the GridView. A better interface would render a DropDownList without a selection and with no GridView visible until the user made a selection. Alternatively, the GridView would show all of the records until a selection in the DropDownList limited the scope. We will start with the display-none scenario in this section and then move to the display-all scenario. You will then try out both in TIO-0906.

The ASP.NET 2.0 team has built in the means to achieve the goal of initially hiding the GridView. In the SqlDataSource control, set CancelSelectOnNullParameter = True and remove a default from the master control. AS long as no parameter is coming from the Master, the SqlDataSource will not return data and no GridView will render.

Master Control by List Boxes with a Default Setting That Shows all Records in the GridView

In this section, we look at the opposite case from the last section. Instead of showing no `GridView` by default, we want to show all the records by default.

Try It Out Displaying a GridView with Default Scoping

In this exercise, you create a page that has a `DropDownList` that allows the user to select a state and then a `GridView` that displays only authors from the selected state (same as the last Try It Outs). However, you change the default for how the `GridView` is presented prior to user selection. You will create two pages, one that renders the page on first view with no records sent to the `GridView` and a second that starts with all of the records on display in the `GridView`.

1. In the `ch09` folder, open your page from the last exercise, `TIO-0905-DropDownList_From Data.aspx`, and save it as `TIO-0906-MasterChild-DefaultNone-1`. Change the title and `<H2>` text to reflect this new exercise.

2. Start by looking at it with the `DropDownList` control. If it is in the single-tag format (as follows), change it to the two-tag format:

   - Single-tag format:

```
<asp:DropDownList ID="DropDownList1"
     ...  />
```

   - Two-tag format:

```
<asp:DropDownList ID="DropDownList1"
     ... >
</asp:DropDownList>
```

3. Add an `Items` tag to the `DropDownList`, as follows (available as `TIO-0906-MasterChild-DefaultNone-1` in the downloads):

```
<asp:DropDownList ID="DropDownList1"
    AutoPostBack="True"
    Runat="server"
    DataSourceID="SqlDataSourceStates"
    DataTextField="state"
    DataValueField="state">
      <Items>
        <asp:ListItem Text="(Choose a state)" Value="" />
      </Items>
</asp:DropDownList>
```

4. Save and run the page. Don't panic; just notice that although you have added an item by hand, the `DropDownList` overwrites your item when it loads data from its data source control. Change that behavior by setting the `AppendDataBoundItems=True`. Save and test the page (`TIO-0906-MasterChild-DefaultNone-2` in the downloads).

```
<asp:DropDownList ID="DropDownList1"
    ...
```

```
        AppendDataBoundItems=true >
        ...
    </asp:DropDownList>
```

5. Ensure that in the SqlDataSource for the GridView, the SelectCommand will still be executed, even if there is a NULL in a control parameter (TIO-0906-MasterChild-DefaultNone-3 in the downloads).

```
    <asp:SqlDataSource ID="SqlDataSourceAuthors"
        ...
        CancelSelectOnNullParameter="false"
        ...
    </asp:SqlDataSource>
```

6. Last, you can change your WHERE clause so that it handles both the case of NULL and the case of a value from the DropDownList (TIO-0906-MasterChild-DefaultNone-4 in the downloads).

```
    <asp:SqlDataSource ID="SqlDataSourceAuthors"
        ...
      SelectCommand="SELECT * FROM [authors]
        WHERE state = IsNull(@state,state) " >
        ...
    </asp:SqlDataSource>
```

7. Save your page(s).

How It Works

In the preceding Try It Out, the page displayed, on first rendering, a default value in the DropDownList (CA) and a GridView that showed only authors from California. This exercise provides a more intuitive first rendering of the page that shows all of the GridView records until the user makes a selection from the DropDownList. The improvement required four changes.

First, after checking that the DropDownList was in two-tag form, an item added statically displayed a message to the user and held a value of an empty string. Because the behavior of a DropDownList is to use the first item in the list as a default, this will be the default when the page is first opened. Recall that an empty string will be converted to NULL when it is received into a ControlParameter used in a SqlDataSource control.

Second, to add the states to the DropDownList, a property was turned on that kept the static item and then appended the items received from the data binding.

Third, this page required overcoming a default behavior in the SqlDataSource control for the GridView. Normally, if a NULL value is present in a control parameter, the SqlDataSource control will just not execute its SelectCommand. That is fine in most cases because the NULL will cause no records to return, so there is no reason to execute the SelectCommand. But this employs a clever WHERE that handles NULLs, so the SelectCommand should execute even when a NULL is in the ControlParameters. This requires the following double negative. By setting CancelSelectOnNullParameter to false, the SelectCommand is executed.

```
    <asp:SqlDataSource ID="SqlDataSourceForGridView"
        v...
```

```
            CancelSelectOnNullParameter=false
            ...
        </asp:SqlDataSource>
```

Fourth, the WHERE clause of the GridView's data source control is modified to handle two cases. On first load, the ControlParameter will get a NULL. On subsequent loads, the ControlParameter will get the value of a state. To understand the solution, you must be comfortable with the two-argument behavior of ISNULL(argument1,argument2). If the first argument is not NULL, it is returned. If the first argument is NULL, the second argument is returned. As written in the code, the WHERE clause follows:

```
WHERE state=@state AND state = IsNull(@state,state) " >
```

When the page first renders, a NULL will be in the @state parameter. The left side of the AND clause will require records to have a state value of NULL, which should return no records. The right side of the AND clause will determine that @state is NULL and thus return state. To visualize the clause that SQL Server executes, substitute these results in the WHERE to get the following pseudocode, which will return no records.

```
WHERE state=NULL AND state = state" >
```

After the user selects a state in the DropDownList, a value will be in the @state parameter. The left side of the AND will require records to have a state equal to the value. The right side of the AND will determine that @state is not NULL and, thus, return the value in @state. As before, you can visualize the substitution of values into the WHERE to get the following pseudocode:

```
WHERE state=value AND state = value" >
```

The result is a redundant check to select only records where state=value. Good data servers eliminate that double request in their optimization schemas.

Another common master-details scenario is a GridView to show some fields of all records and then an option to select one record and see more fields in a DetailsView. The next section covers the specifics.

Displaying Details Using a GridView and DetailsView on the Same Page

The GridView optimizes the display of a few fields of many records. If you want to see many fields for just one record, you use the DetailsView control, as discussed earlier. Commonly, a designer wants to have one page with a GridView of all records, from which the user can select one record and open up a view of more details for that one record. This inverts earlier examples in this chapter because GridView is now the master instead of the details control. When the GridView is the master, you use a CommandField column with the ShowSelectButton set to true to render a button for selecting a row in the grid. When clicked by the user, the page will be refreshed with a DetailsView rendering more fields for the selected record. As when using a ListBox as a master control, all handling of events, and postback, can be automated by ASP.NET 2.0.

Before starting the next exercise, let us look at the persistence that explains what is required. These four blocks present the most basic properties (ignoring `ID` and `runat` properties). You will work with two data source controls and two data-bound controls. The first pair supports the displaying of a selectable `GridView` showing all authors. When a `SELECT` is performed, the other two controls come into play to show a `DetailsView` with additional fields for the selected row. So, start with the data source control for the `GridView`, as follows. Note that you are picking up only a few fields from the table including the pimary key (`FieldPK`).

```
<asp:SqlDataSource ID="MasterSource" ...
    SelectCommand="SELECT FieldPK, Field1, Field2 FROM MyTable />
```

Use that data source to support a `GridView` that must include a Select column. The `GridView` must also designate a `DataKeyName`, which is, essentially, a primary key to uniquely identify the records in the `GridView`. `DataKeyNames` are discussed in more detail in Chapters 11 and 12 on modifying data.

```
<asp:GridView ...
     DataSourceID="MasterSource"
     DataKeyName="FieldPK">
      <Columns>
         <asp:BoundField DataField="Field1" />
         <asp:BoundField DataField="Field2" />
         <asp:CommandField
                ShowSelectButton="True"
                SelectText="View Details..." />
      </Columns>
</asp:GridView>
```

The second data source control, shown in the following code, supports the `DetailsView`. When the user clicks on the preceding `GridView`'s Select button, the value from the data key name field for that record is passed into a select parameter named, in this case, `ForeignKey` in the following data source control. That value is then read into the `WHERE` clause and only the single matching record is requested from the database. The `@` symbol means that the following text is a parameter name.

```
<asp:SqlDataSource  ID="DetailsSource" ...
         SelectCommand="SELECT * FROM MyTable WHERE (ForiegnKey = @ForeignKey)">
      <SelectParameters>
        <asp:ControlParameter
         Name="ForeignKey"
         Type="String"
         ControlID="GridView1"/>
      </SelectParameters>
</asp:SqlDataSource>
```

Last, the details control (in this case, a `DetailsView control`) displays the limited set of records and fields that were retrieved by its data source control:

```
<asp:DetailsView ...
 DataSourceID="DetailsSource">
      <Fields>
         <asp:BoundFields .../>
      </Fields>
</asp:DetailsView>
```

Now, you can put the theory into practice in the following Try It Out.

Try It Out Displaying Details Using a GridView and DetailsView on the Same Page

In this exercise, you will create a `GridView` that displays just the author names and state fields, plus a Select button for each row. When the user clicks the Select button, all of the fields for the selected employee will be displayed. Even though you are not displaying the author ID, you will use it as the data key name, which becomes the `SelectedValue` for the `GridView` when a row is selected and the `WHERE` clause in the `DetailsView`'s data source control.

Note that the four controls (`GridViewAuthorNames`, `SqlDataSourceGV`, `DetailsView`, and `SqlDataSourceDetails`) can be in any order on the page. In this case, set the two data-bound controls side by side using an HTML table so that they can be rendered side by side.

1. In the `ch09` folder, create a new page, named `TIO-097-MasterDetails_SamePage.aspx`. To create an overall layout, switch to Design view. Create a table using Layout⇨Insert a table and select a size of one row, two columns. Set the border width of zero. While in the Insert Table dialog box, click on the Cell Properties button and change the Vertical align to `"= top"`. Click OK to close the Insert Table dialog box.

    - Widen the columns to about 350 px each. Drag a `GridView` into the left cell, choose Data Source as New, and name it `SqlDataSourceGV` that reads the `au_id` and the two name fields from the Authors table of `Pubs`. Do not use a `WHERE` clause, because you want to see all of the authors. Order the records by `au_lname`. Enable Selection in the `GridView` by clicking the check box in its Smart Tasks panel.

    - Last, while the GridView is selected, go to the VWD Properties window, find the DataKeyNames line. VWD should have added the au_id field. If that field is not listed, then click the ellipsis to open the Data Fields Collection Editor, as shown in Figure 9-2, and select `au_id`.

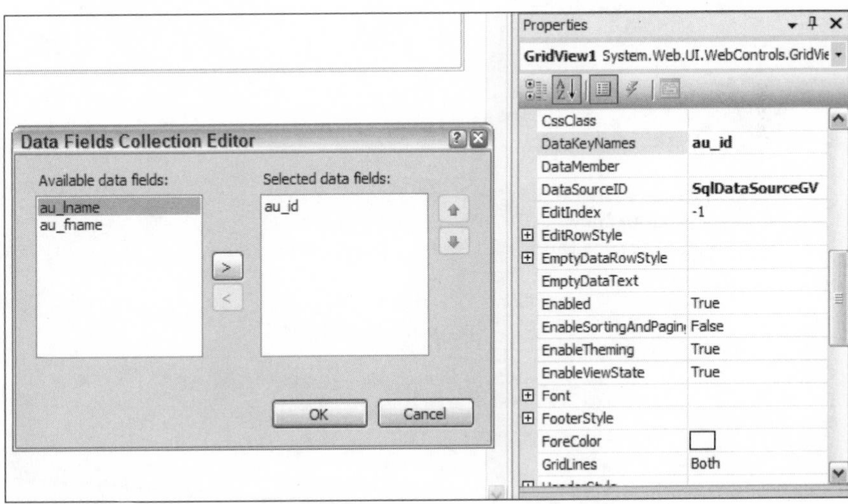

Figure 9-2

2. Save and test the page (the selection commands will not do anything yet). Close the browser.

3. In VWD Design view, drag into the right cell of the table a `DetailsView control` and configure its data source to a new data source control named `SqlDataSourceDetails`. Configure it to read all of the fields from the authors table, and then click the WHERE button. Set the column for `au_id` equal to a control; then set the `ControlID` to `GridView1`. Leave the default value blank, and click Add. Widen the details view to about `250 px` total.

```
...
<h2>Chapter 09 TIO #0907 Master and Details on the Same Page </h2>
    <form id="form1" runat="server">
    <div>
        <table border="0">
         <tr>
        <td style="width: 350px">
         <asp:GridView ID="GridView1" runat="server"
                DataSourceID="SqlDataSourceGV"
                DataKeyNames="au_id">
               <Columns>
                <asp:CommandField ShowSelectButton="True" />
               </Columns>
         </asp:GridView>

        <asp:SqlDataSource ID="SqlDataSourceGV" runat="server"
         ConnectionString="<%$ ConnectionStrings:MdfPubs %>"
         SelectCommand="SELECT [au_id], [au_lname], [au_fname]
                FROM [authors]
                ORDER BY [au_lname]">
         </asp:SqlDataSource>
       </td>
      <td style="width: 350px">
         <asp:DetailsView ID="DetailsView1" runat="server"
                AutoGenerateRows="False"
                DataKeyNames="au_id"
                DataSourceID="SqlDataSourceDetails"
                Height="50px" Width="250px">
                        <Fields>
                                ...
                        </Fields>
         </asp:DetailsView>

         <asp:SqlDataSource ID="SqlDataSourceDetails" runat="server"
         ConnectionString="<%$ ConnectionStrings:MdfPubs %>"
                SelectCommand="SELECT * FROM [authors] WHERE ([au_id] = @au_id)">
                <SelectParameters>
                        <asp:ControlParameter
                               ControlID="GridView1"
                               Name="au_id"
                               PropertyName="SelectedValue"
                               Type="String" />
                </SelectParameters>
       </asp:SqlDataSource>
 </td>
 </tr>
</table> </div>  </form> </body> </html>
```

4. Save the page, and test it in the browser.

How It Works

This page contains four controls: a GridView with its supporting data source control and a DetailsView with its supporting data source control. The GridView is the master because it accepts the user's click, and the DetailsView is the details. Let's analyze each of the four controls from the standpoint of its source code.

The SqlDataSourceGV presents nothing special other than a limited set of fields. Note that the au_id field is included even though you do not intend to display it because you need it as the primary key for the selection process.

The GridView displays the names fields plus the column created holding the Select buttons. Note in the source code that VWD has checked the table's primary key and used that field for the DataKeyNames property.

The SqlDataSourceDetails does the actual filtering so that the DetailsView control will display data for the single selected author. There are two sections of interest. First is the collection of SelectParameters, within which is one member of the type ControlParameter. The Designer, following your clicks in the dialog box, gave the parameter a name of au_id and set it to pick up the default property from the GridViewAuthorNames. Second, the SelectCommand is written to pick up your parameter named au_id for the criteria of the WHERE clause.

```
<asp:SqlDataSource ID="SqlDataSourceDetail"
  Runat="server"
     ConnectionString="<%$ ConnectionStrings: mdfPubs %>"
  SelectCommand="SELECT * FROM [authors] WHERE ([au_id] = @au_id)">
  <SelectParameters>
    <asp:ControlParameter
      Name="au_id"
      Type="String"
      ControlID="GridViewAuthorNames"/>
  </SelectParameters>
</asp:SqlDataSource>
```

Last, the DetailsView simply displays all of the fields from the one record returned by the SqlDataSourceDetails control.

What happens when the user clicks on the GridView? A postback is triggered that fills the au_id value of the selected record into the ControlParameter of the SqlDataSourceDetails control. That control then gets all the field values for that single matching record, and those field values are displayed in the DetailsView control.

Note that you do not have to show the DataKeyNames fields in the GridView. You can set the AutoGenerateColumns to false (it is true by default) and in the GridView, add the desired columns from the Smart Tasks panel's Edit Columns dialog box. The fact that the au_id is returned from the data source control is sufficient for it to be used as a data key.

Displaying Details Using a GridView and DetailsView on Different Pages

Frequently, you will find that a client wants details for a record shown on a separate page. This allows more fields to be shown and involves fewer layout constraints (and perhaps a new advertisement). The technique combines ideas from the "Displaying Details Using a GridView and DetailsView on the Same Page" Try It Out and the first Try It Out, "Filtering GridView Records Using a Query String."

There are two changes from the previous exercise, one on the master control page and one on the details control page. Recall that in the previous exercise (same page for `DetailsView`), you used a `CommandField` with a select button in the master control (`GridView`). But to display the details on a different page, you must use a `HyperLinkField` column instead. Within that hyperlink are two critical settings:

- `DataNavigateUrlField`: holds a field, in this case the primary key value of the selected field. You set it to the field holding the ID (primary key) for the records.
- `DataNavigateUrlFormatString`: You will use this to specify the details page's URL and to append the ID value from the preceding property.

The resulting code for the master control follows:

```
<asp:GridView ID="GridView1" Runat="server"
    DataSourceID="MyDataSource"
    DataKeyNames="MyPrimaryKeyField">
  <Columns>
     <asp:BoundField ... />
    <asp:HyperLinkField
            HeaderText="ViewDetails..."
            Text="View Details..."
            DataNavigateUrlFields="MyPrimaryKeyField"
            DataNavigateUrlFormatString="MyDetailsPage.aspx?ID={0}"/>
  </Columns>
</asp:GridView>
```

When the user clicks on a hyperlink button of the `GridView`, the record's primary key value is put into the variable `{0}`, and that is used as the query string on the end of the literal URL `MyDetailsPage.aspx?ID=` of the `DataNavigateUrlFormatString`.

On the details page, you now pick up the value from the query string, the same as in the first Try It Out of this chapter. The data source control is:

```
<asp:SqlDataSource ID="SqlDataSource1" Runat="server"
  ConnectionString="<%$ ConnectionStrings:MdfPubs %>"
  SelectCommand="
          SELECT * FROM MyTable
          WHERE (MyPrimaryKeyField = @ID)">
  <SelectParameters>
    <asp:QueryStringParameter Name="ID"
      DefaultValue="123"
      QueryStringField="ID"
      Type="String" />
  </SelectParameters>
</asp:SqlDataSource>
```

When the details page opens, it reads the query string and puts the values into the `QueryStringParameter`. When the data source control builds its `WHERE` clause, it will pull in the value of the record ID from the query string parameter.

Of course, the VWD Designer can generate all of this code automatically, as demonstrated in the following exercise.

Try It Out Displaying Details Using a GridView and DetailsView on Different Pages

This exercise is very similar in objective to the exercise it the previous Try It Out, but now you want the `DetailsView control` to appear on a second page, named `TIO-0908-Details.aspx`.

1. In the `ch09` folder, create a page named `TIO-0908-MasterDetails_DifferentPage.aspx`. Add a `GridView`, and set its source to a new data source to pick up the `au_id` and names fields from the Authors table of `Pubs`. Don't use a `WHERE` clause, because you want to see all of the authors' names; instead, add an `ORDER BY` ascending last name. In the `GridView`'s Smart Tasks panel, click Edit Columns, turn off Autogenerate Fields (if it is on) and (if not already there) add bound fields for the three author fields plus a hyperlink field. Staying in the Edit Columns dialog box, set four properties for the hyperlink field:

`HeaderText=`	`ViewDetails...`
`Text=`	`Click for more details`
`DataNavigateUrlFields=`	`au_id`
`DataNavigateUrlFormatString=`	`TIO-0908-Details.aspx?ID={0}`

2. The field should be similar to the following listing:

```
...
<h2>Chapter 09 TIO #0908 Master and Details on Different Pages </h2>
    <form id="form1" runat="server">
    <div>
        <asp:GridView ID="GridView1" runat="server"
                AutoGenerateColumns="False"
                DataKeyNames="au_id"
                DataSourceID="SqlDataSource1">
            <Columns>
                <asp:BoundField DataField="au_id"
                        HeaderText="au_id"
                        ReadOnly="True"
                        SortExpression="au_id" />
                <asp:BoundField DataField="au_lname"
                        HeaderText="au_lname"
                        SortExpression="au_lname" />
                <asp:BoundField DataField="au_fname"
                        HeaderText="au_fname"
                        SortExpression="au_fname" />
                <asp:HyperLinkField
                        DataNavigateUrlFields="au_id"
DataNavigateUrlFormatString="TIO-0908-Details.aspx?ID={0}"
                        HeaderText="View Details"
                      Text="Click for more details" />
```

```
            </Columns>
        </asp:GridView>
        <asp:SqlDataSource ID="SqlDataSource1" runat="server"
                ConnectionString="<%$ ConnectionStrings:MdfPubs %>"
                SelectCommand="SELECT [au_id], [au_lname], [au_fname]
                       FROM [authors] ORDER BY [au_lname]">
        </asp:SqlDataSource>
</div></form></body></html>
```

3. Save the file and test it (the hyperlinks are not enabled yet).

4. Now, create `TIO-0908-Details.aspx`, and add a `DetailsView control` that connects to a new data source that picks up all of the fields from the Authors table. Set its `WHERE` clause to make the column `au_id` equal to a query string field named `au_id`. Give it a default value of `213-46-8915`.

    - Back in the `DetailsView` Smart Tasks panel, the Autogenerate Fields option is fine here. After closing the Smart Tasks panel, expand the `DetailsView` to a total width of about `300 px`.

5. Finish the page by adding to the bottom a simple hyperlink back to `TIO-0908-MasterDetails_DifferentPage.aspx` and saving the page.

```
...
<h2>Chapter 09 TIO #0908 Details</h2>
    <form id="form1" runat="server">
    <div>
        <asp:DetailsView ID="DetailsView1" runat="server"
            AutoGenerateRows="False"
            DataKeyNames="au_id"
            DataSourceID="SqlDataSource1"
            Height="50px" Width="300px">
            <Fields>
                ...
            </Fields>
        </asp:DetailsView>
        <asp:SqlDataSource ID="SqlDataSource1" runat="server"
            ConnectionString="<%$ ConnectionStrings:MdfPubs %>"
            SelectCommand="SELECT * FROM [authors] WHERE ([au_id] = @au_id)">
            <SelectParameters>
                <asp:QueryStringParameter
                        DefaultValue="213-46-8915"
                        Name="au_id"
                        QueryStringField="ID"
                        Type="String" />
            </SelectParameters>
        </asp:SqlDataSource>
        <a href="../ch09/TIO-0908-MasterDetails-DifferentPage.aspx">
                Return to the list of all authors</a></div>
</form></body></html>
```

6. Open the first page (`TIO-0908-MasterDetails_DifferentPage.aspx`). Select an author, and more data about that person will be shown in the details page.

How It Works

When the user clicks a hyperlink in the master page `GridView`, the browser will navigate to the specified details page. Back on the server, ASP.NET 2.0 picks up the `au_id` from the selected row and copies the value into the details page's `QueryStringParameter`. When the details page data source control builds its `SelectCommand`, it will have an actual ID value for the field value. When that SQL statement executes, you get back only the one matching record. The values of that record are then displayed in the `DetailsView`. Note that is not a postback. A postback is only when the data is posted back to the page the data came from. This is simply a `GET` request (not a `POST`).

The same technique works if you want to display data from related tables. For example, page 1 may show a list of customers with selectability. Upon clicking, the user is directed to page 2, which shows all of the orders for the clicked customer. The only difference is in how you use the identification value received in the second page. For related records, you use it in a SQL statement that includes a JOIN. This is not an ASP.NET 2.0 topic, but it is worth an exercise so that you can see all of the code.

Try It Out Displaying Related Records Using a GridView and a GridView

This exercise uses the same `GridView` of authors as the master control, but on selecting an author, you jump to a page with all of the books by the selected author. Note that authors Marjorie Greene and Charlene Locksley have written more than one book.

1. Open your page from the last exercise (`TIO-0908-MasterDetails_DifferentPage.aspx`), and save as it `TIO-0909-MasterDetails-TwoGridVIews.aspx`. Change the target of the hyperlink to a new page by setting the `HyperlinkField.DataNavigationUrlFormatString` to the following:

```
<asp:HyperLinkField HeaderText="ViewDetails..."
    Text="View Details..."
    DataNavigateUrlFields="au_id"
    DataNavigateUrlFormatString="TIO-0909-Details.aspx?ID={0}" />
  </Columns>
</asp:GridView>
```

2. Open your details page from the last exercise (`TIO-098-Details.aspx`), and save as it `TIO-0909-Details.aspx`. Change the SQL statement for the data source control, title, and hyperlink, as follows:

```
<title>Ch09-TIO 09-View Book Details</title>...
<asp:SqlDataSource ID="SqlDataSource1" Runat="server"
        SelectCommand="
            SELECT authors.au_id, titles.title_id,
                titles.title, titles.type,
                titles.price, titles.notes
            FROM authors
                INNER JOIN titleauthor ON authors.au_id = titleauthor.au_id
                INNER JOIN titles ON titleauthor.title_id = titles.title_id
            WHERE (authors.au_id = @au_id)"
<a href="TIO-0909-MasterDetails_AllRelatedRecords.aspx">Back To Grid</a>
```

3. Delete the `DetailsView control` and replace with a `GridView` that uses the same `SqlDataSource1` and autogenerates fields. Last, change the hyperlink to go back to the `TIO-0909-MasterDetails-TwoGridVIews.aspx` page (instead of the page used in the previous exercise).

4. Save and test the details page on its own (all the books for the default author will be shown). Then test your work by opening the page with the master control.

How It Works 0909

The main change here is the SQL statement for the data source control of the details page. You select fields about titles (books) that come from tabular joins between `Authors` and `TitleAuthor` and then between `TitleAuthor` and `Titles`. This allows you to use the `au_id` value to select only those titles that match with a given author. More detail on the syntax of `JOINs` is available from a SQL text or the appendix at the back of this book.

Sometimes a single list will not be sufficient, as you will see in the next section.

Cascading DropDownLists

One of the most intuitive user interfaces is a cascade of lists. The user selects from the first list, for example, Countries, and then a second list is populated with appropriate choices, for example, Regions. The Regions choices would be only those regions within the selected country. The second list, when selected, can govern the population of a third list, such as Cities. In this architecture, the first list is a master. The second becomes both a details to the first and a master to the third. You need a data source control for each list. The details data source control will have a `ControlParameter` that points to the master data source control and uses the parameter value in its `WHERE` clause.

Try It Out Using Cascading DropDownLists

In this exercise, you will create a page that will help a clerk find all the products for a category that is selected from a `DropDownList`.

1. In the `ch09` folder, create a new page named `TIO-0910-CascadingDropDownLists.aspx`. Use Layout ⇨Insert Table to add a table of one row and three columns. Turn on the border, but set its width to zero.

2. In the left cell, add a `DropDownList` control that will show the categories of products from Northwind, and name it `DropDownListCategories`. Expand the Choose Data Source in the Smart Tag panel in VWD and choose `<New Data Source...>`. Get your data from a database, and name the control `SqlDataSourceCategories`. Use the `MdfNorthwind` connection to read the category ID and name from the Categories table of Northwind (order by CategoryName ascending). When configuring the `DropDownList`, set the field to display (`Text property`) to `CategoryName` and the value to `CategoryID`. On this `DropDownList` control's Smart Tasks panel, enable `AutoPostBack`.

```
...
<h2>Chapter 09 TIO #0910 Cascading DropDownLists</h2>
    <form id="form1" runat="server">
    <div>
```

```
        <table border="0">
            <tr>
                <td style="width: 100px">
                    <asp:DropDownList ID="DropDownListCategories" runat="server"
                        DataSourceID="SqlDataSourceCategories"
                        DataTextField="CategoryName"
                        DataValueField="CategoryID"
                        AutoPostBack="True">
                    </asp:DropDownList>
                    <asp:SqlDataSource ID="SqlDataSourceCategories" runat="server"
                        ConnectionString="<%$ ConnectionStrings:MdfNorthwind %>"
                        SelectCommand="SELECT [CategoryID], [CategoryName]
                               FROM [Categories]
                               ORDER BY [CategoryName]">
                    </asp:SqlDataSource>
                </td>
                <td style="width: 100px">
                </td>
                <td style="width: 100px">
                </td></tr>
</table></div></form></body></html>
```

3. Save and test the page.

4. Now add a second drop-down list, this one in the right table cell, and name it `DropDownListProducts`. Expand the Choose Data Source drop-down in the Smart Tag panel in VWD, and choose `<New Data Source...>`. Name it `SqlDataSourceProducts`. This time, read the product ID and product name from the Products table. Click the `WHERE` button, and set the `CategoryID` field equal to the `DropDownListCategories` control. Display the field named `ProductName`, and hold the value for `ProductID`. If you check the source code, you should have two new controls, as follows:

```
                <td style="width: 100px">
                    <asp:DropDownList ID="DropDownList1" runat="server"
                        DataSourceID="SqlDataSourceOrderItems"
                        DataTextField="Quantity"
                        DataValueField="ProductID">
                    </asp:DropDownList>
<asp:SqlDataSource ID="SqlDataSourceOrderItems" runat="server"
                        ConnectionString="<%$ ConnectionStrings:MdfNorthwind %>"
                        SelectCommand="SELECT [ProductID], [Discount], [Quantity]
                               FROM [Order Details]
                               WHERE ([ProductID] = @ProductID)">
                        <SelectParameters>
                            <asp:ControlParameter
                             ControlID="DropDownList1"
                             Name="ProductID"
                             PropertyName="SelectedValue"
                             Type="Int32" />
                        </SelectParameters>
                    </asp:SqlDataSource>
                </td>
```

5. Save and test the page.

How It Works

The first DropDownList, Categories, presents nothing new. The second list is supported by the SqlDataSourceControlProducts. That has a ControlParameter to read the selected value from the Categories DropDownList. The value selected is passed into the ControlParameter and then used as the criterion in the WHERE clause of the data source column for list 2.

Common Mistakes

Following are mistakes commonly made in filtering and working with master-details data:

- Forgetting to click Add after setting up a parameter in the WHERE clause dialog box of the data source control.
- Attempting to use the value property from a list box after only setting the text property for the list box's items. You need to set DataValueField in addition to DataTextField.
- Expecting a list box selection to automatically update a details control, but the AutoPostBack property of the list box is set to false. It must be true or else you must have a button to submit.
- Utilizing the wrong data source control for a data-bound control when the page contains multiple data sources. Use descriptive names for your data source controls to reduce errors.
- Improperly formatting a URL with a query string in a hyperlink column. Check the syntax in the examples of this chapter.
- Forgetting to set DataKeyNames on GridView when using it as a master control for selection or navigation to a separate page. The field set to DataKeyNames is used as a SelectedValue for the grid.
- Using a single data source for both the master and details controls. It will often be necessary to use separate data sources for each control because the data they display will be different.

Summary

This chapter demonstrated how one control can establish settings to change the scope of another control. You have implemented multiple scenarios of master-details controls without doing any VB or C# coding or even thinking about events. The chapter walked you through dialog boxes and wizards, and then the VWD Designer built all necessary code (with the exception of the complex SQL JOIN example). In particular, you used the Parameters dialog box, made visible by clicking the WHERE button, when configuring the data source control for the details data-bound control.

The basic theory is that the user will select an item on a master control. That will trigger a postback, and the value of the selected item will be placed into any ControlParameters on the page. You typically have such a parameter in the data source control for the details control. That data source control will then use the value in the parameter as the criterion for its WHERE clause. The resulting data (sometimes filtered to just one record) is displayed in the details data-bound control.

The first case demonstrated how to pass the value to the page in the query string. Although the technique is too crude for deployment, you saw how the details control picked up the parameter and used it to filter. Note that when a value comes from the query string, you must refer to it using a `QueryStringParameter`. The explanation then moved to the use of `TextBox` controls to refer to values in a `ControlParameter`. Although you can use the SQL keyword `LIKE` to overcome some problems, it is poor practice to rely on the user to type accurate input. When you use a list, you know that the user will not type invalid values.

Next, you explored how to use the `GridView` as a details by adding a parameter to its data source control and using that parameter as the criterion in a `WHERE` clause.

You also explored how to use the `GridView` as a master by adding a `CommandField` with a select button. When the user clicks on the select button of a record, a postback occurs. The selected record's ID (the value in the first field of the `DataKeyNames` property) is available from any control parameters on the page that specify the `GridView` as their source.

If you want the details to appear on a separate page, you use a hyperlink instead of a Select field in the `GridView`. The hyperlink uses the `DataNavigateUrlField` to hold the value from the ID column. You use the `DataNavigateUrlFormatString` to add the literal name of the details page. That details page then gets the ID value from the query string, deposits it in a `QueryStringParameter`, and uses the parameter as the criterion in the data source control's `WHERE` clause.

The chapter finished with cascading `DropDownList` controls. Each list gets its own data source control. The first list has no special modifications. The second data source control establishes a control parameter with the selected value of the first drop-down list. As per the pattern of this chapter, that parameter is used as the criterion in the WHERE clause of the second list's data source control.

The final topic to cover on displaying data involves templates, which are discussed in detail in the next chapter.

Exercises

The answers to these review questions can be found in Appendix B.

1. In a SqlDataSource control's `SelectCommand WHERE` clause, what is the difference between `Xxx` and `@Xxx`?
2. Write the syntax to include the value `567` in the `MemberID` field in a URL that calls a page named `MemberProfile.aspx` at the `MyYachtClub.org` site.
3. Continuing from Question 2, on the page `MemberProfile.aspx`, write the code for a SqlDataSource control to show information for only the member ID passed from the URL.
4. What is the default property for binding to a `ControlParameter` for a `DropDownList` and a `GridView`?
5. When populating a `DropDownList` from a SQL statement, how can you avoid multiple listings of the same value (for example, multiple `PAs` when four authors are from Pennsylvania)?

6. How can you display a combination of static and dynamic items in a `DropDownList`?
7. How does an ASP.NET 2.0 data source `ControlParameter` handle values that are an empty string?
8. How does a data source control react to a parameter containing a `NULL` value?
9. The `GridView` control was designed to display values for many records. What controls are designed to show values for only one record at a time?
10. Describe the difference between a HyperLinkField's `DataNavigateUrlField` and `DataNavigateUrlFormatString` properties.
11. How is the value from the `DataNavigateUrlField` put into the `DataNavigateUrlFormatString`?
12. How are the `DataNavigateUrlField` and `DataNavigateUrlFormatString` properties set when a `GridView` is calling for details of one record on another page?

Displaying Data in Templated Controls and Data Binding

Up until now we have studied data-bound controls that are rigid in their content and layout. For example, each cell of a `GridView` has held one value with no additional content, other than formatting. ASP.NET also offers the option of making that cell a workspace within which the designer can create a combination of values, static text and images, and layout. This workspace is called a *template*. Templates allow the designer to fulfill the exact needs of the client for each portion of an ASP.NET 2.0 control that can use templates.

As you will learn in this chapter, templates can be a part of a larger control, such as a templated column within a `GridView`. Templates can also be the entire representation of a control; for example, the `FormView` that is just one big empty template ready for your design.

This chapter covers the following topics:

- Introduction to templates
- General guidelines for using templated controls
- `GridView` template column
- `DataList` control
- `DataList` control internal layout
- Repeater control
- Templates in the `DetailsView` control
- `FormView` control
- Comparing and selecting the templated controls
- A few more advanced ideas on data binding

In addition, we offer a list of Common Mistakes, a Summary, and some Questions to check your knowledge, as we have done in other chapters.

Introduction to Templates

Chapters 8 through 10 discussed techniques to display data in tables. These controls offer quick results, but they have a prescribed layout for their format. For example, a `GridView BoundField` has one value per cell, and a list box presents its choices in a standard vertical format. Unfortunately, these are rigid in their rendering. To provide more flexibility, ASP.NET 2.0 also offers *templates*: spaces within which a designer can add one or more child data-bound controls, text, HTML, and images.

A *templated data-bound control* is bound to a data source, so controls inside the template can be bound to fields of the data source, and then each of the controls within a template will display the value for the current record. (There are a few cases where you can have templates that are not bound, such as a `LoginView` or `Panel`). When the current record changes by paging or from row to row, the values displayed in data-bound controls in the template change. The arrangement of the controls in the template is very flexible, as are options for laying out on the page the template holding the control.

As you can see in Figure 10-1, the `GridViews` we have created to date are like the one on the left. Each value is in one cell, and within that cell, there are no additional controls, images, HTML, or text. The `GridView` on the right side of the figure shows templates in which three values and an image (along with HTML for a little table) are presented within each cell, with one cell per record.

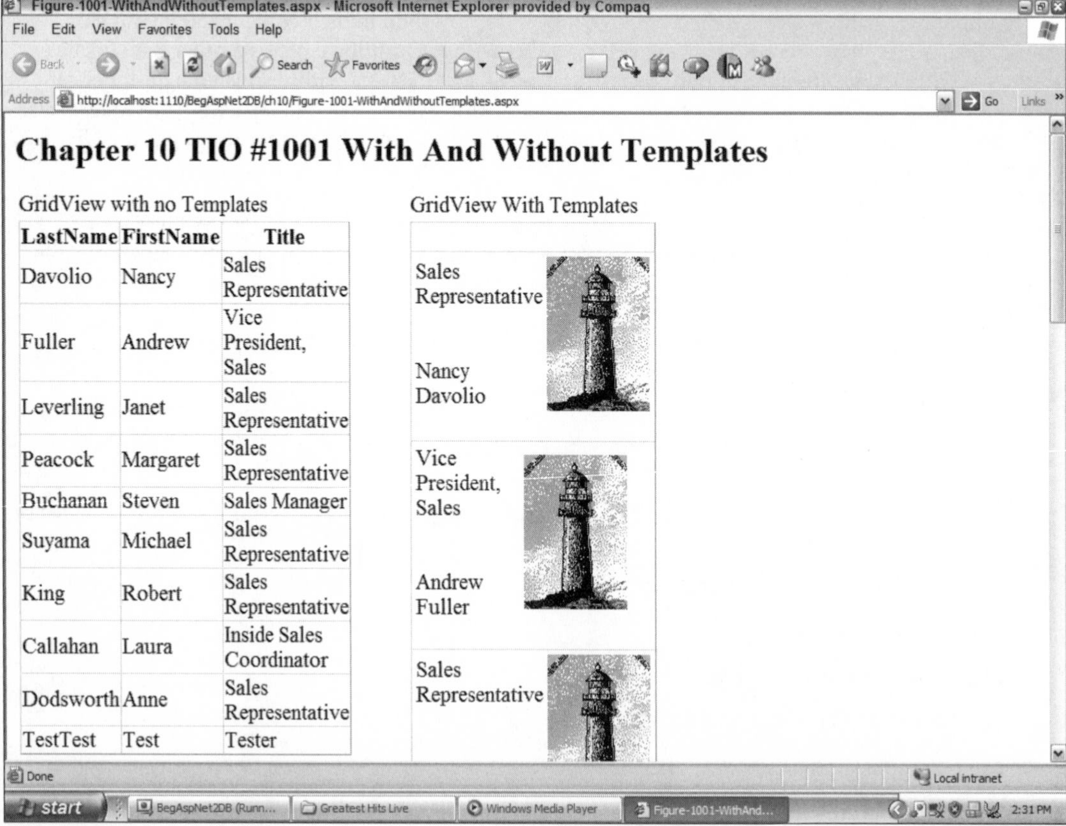

Figure 10-1

Two GridViews with bound columns displaying one value per cell (left) and with template columns that display multiple values and an image per cell (right).

> **The term *templates* arises in two places. When you create a new page, VWD offers you templates for Web Form, HTML Page, Style Sheet, and so on. These are not the topic of this chapter. In this chapter we discuss templates as spaces within parent controls that can hold child controls.**

To demonstrate how easy it is to use templates, we will start with an exercise. We will create a GridView of Northwind employees, as we've done previously, but this time we'll put the title, first name and last name into one template column instead of three separate columns.

Try It Out — Creating a Simple Template in GridView

In this first exercise, we will create a GridView with four columns that contain information about the Northwind employees. The first three will be the same as in prior chapters: Title, first name, and last name. However, the fourth will be a template that contains all three items of data in one column. Recall that in this book, connection strings are stored in the Web.config file per the second Try It Out in Chapter 3.

1. Create a new folder for this chapter: C:\Websites\BegAspNet2Db\ch10. Create a new page named TIO-1001-SimpleTemplate.aspx. Using the techniques of prior chapters, add a GridView with columns for the Northwind Employees' titles and names. The easiest way is to use the Database Explorer, open Northwinds.mdf, expand tables, expand Employees, and drag those three fields onto the page.
2. Your nascent GridView will open its Smart Tasks panel. Click Add New Column, select the type Template and give it the Header Text of Name combination. Save and test your page. When you are finished, close the browsers.
3. In Design view, select the GridView and open its Smart Tasks panel. Select Edit Templates. From the drop-down list, notice that you have a Column [3] named Name combination. Click on the menu choice for ItemTemplate. From the toolbar, drag a label into the ItemTemplate space in the GridView. In the Smart Tasks panel that VWD opens, click Edit DataBindings. Select the Text bindable property and bind it on the right to the field Title. Close the dialog box, and then close the Smart Tasks panel.
4. Repeat Step 3 for two more labels: first and last name. Finish by opening the Smart Tasks panel for the entire GridView and clicking on End Template Editing. Save and run the page. Notice that in your Template column you display three values in one cell.
5. Let's make two more improvements. Close your browser and return to VWD.
6. Open the GridView's Smart Tasks panel, and select Edit Templates again. From the drop-down list, select the Column[3] ItemTemplate and place your insertion bar between the title and first name labels. Press the Enter key so that the names are a line below the title. Drag an Image control to the template, and place it after the last name label. Do not edit the data binding. Instead, go to the Properties window and set the ImageUrl to the NorthWindLogo.bmp in your Image folder (or use any other image) to get code similar to the following.

```
...
<h2>Chapter 10 TIO #1001 Simple Template</h2>
    <form id="form1" runat="server">
    <div>
        <asp:GridView ID="GridView1" runat="server"
            AutoGenerateColumns="False"
            DataSourceID="SqlDataSource1"
            EmptyDataText="There are no data records to display.">
            <Columns>
                <asp:BoundField DataField="LastName"
                    HeaderText="LastName" SortExpression="LastName" />
                <asp:BoundField DataField="FirstName"
                    HeaderText="FirstName" SortExpression="FirstName" />
                <asp:BoundField DataField="Title"
                    HeaderText="Title" SortExpression="Title" />
                <asp:TemplateField HeaderText="NameCombination">
                    <ItemTemplate>
                        <asp:Label ID="Label1" runat="server"
                            Text='<%# Eval("Title") %>'></asp:Label>
                        <br />
                        <asp:Label ID="Label2" runat="server"
                            Text='<%# Eval("FirstName") %>'></asp:Label>
                        <asp:Label ID="Label3" runat="server"
                            Text='<%# Eval("LastName") %>'></asp:Label>
                        <asp:Image ID="Image1" runat="server"
                            ImageUrl="~/Images/NorthWindLogo.bmp" />
                    </ItemTemplate>
                </asp:TemplateField>
            </Columns>
        </asp:GridView>
        <asp:SqlDataSource ID="SqlDataSource1" runat="server"
            ConnectionString="<%$ ConnectionStrings:NorthwindConnectionString2 %>"
            ProviderName=
                "<%$ ConnectionStrings:NorthwindConnectionString2.ProviderName %>"
            SelectCommand="SELECT [LastName], [FirstName], [Title]
FROM [Employees]">
        </asp:SqlDataSource>
</div></form></body></html>
```

7. Save your work and test the page in the browser.

How It Works

This exercise walked you through the steps of adding a simple template to a `GridView` control. As you can see, the template column is similar to other columns in that it is created using the Add Column choice in the `GridView`'s Smart Tasks panel. You can then edit the template and add controls such as labels. As you observed, by using templates you created a workspace within which you could add one or more controls; these would all render within one cell of the `GridView` table. You also made a change in the layout by adding the line return by striking the Enter key. And last, we added a control that is not bound to data; the `Northwind` logo appears the same for every record.

Template Location and Scope

Templates are defined by tags within a parent (container) control. The pattern is similar to a `ListItem` within a `DropDownList` control. So in this chapter, we will frequently discuss both the larger container (parent) parent control and the internal control. We refer to this internal control as the child control, and it can be a label, textbox, check box, or another control.

Within their container control, templates can exist as part of the total rendering or as the entire rendering. These two categories include the following:

- `GridView` and the `DetailsView` controls have nontemplated columns or fields, headers, paging elements, and other nontemplated features as we discussed in prior chapters.
- `Repeater`, `DataList`, and `FormView` have their entire contents as templates.

Examples of these two cases can be observed in Figure 10-2, which is a rendering of the file named `Demo-1002-PartialAndTotalTemplates` (available in the downloads).

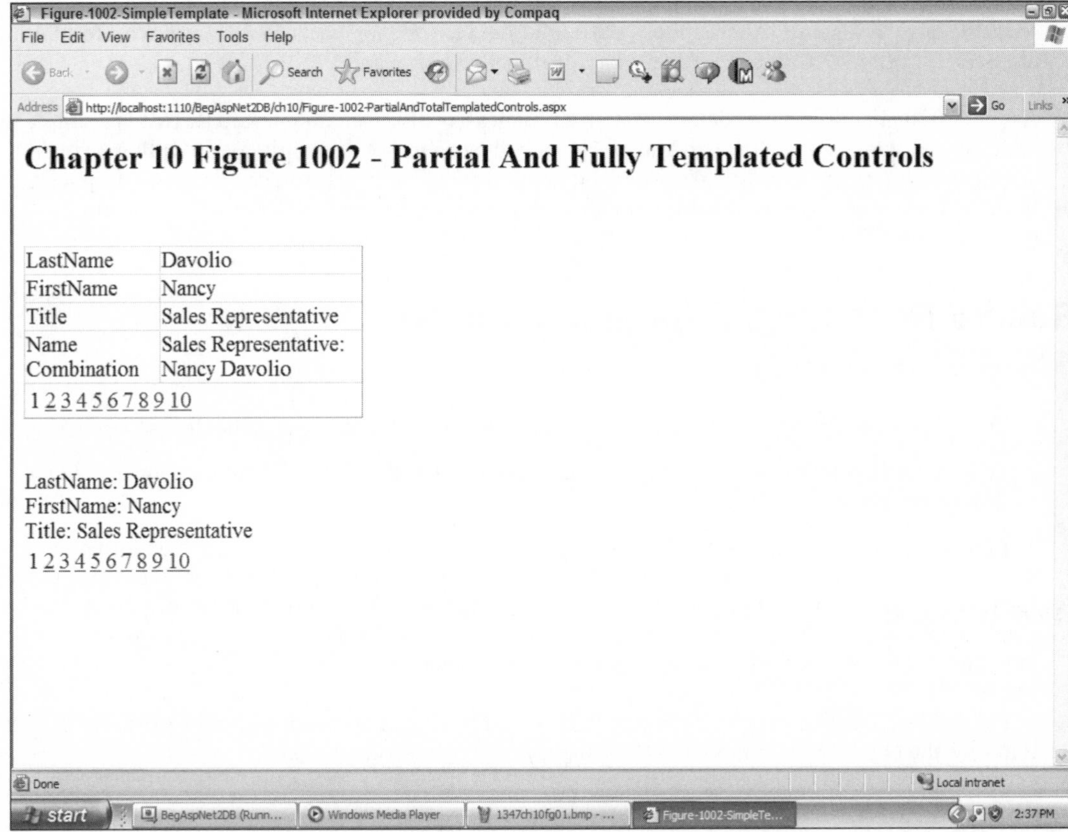

Figure 10-2

Having discussed the definitions and options, we can now turn to actually creating the contents of templates.

Template Contents

Templates can contain controls that render two types of information: bound and unbound. A *bound control* will show the value for the current record as read from the data source and, thus, is dynamic. An *unbound control* displays the same information in every record; that is, it is static. For example, an unbound label may display the text "Employee Profile:" at the top of a template. Then within the same template there could be a bound label that renders the string from the employee's profile field in the data source.

Furthermore, each *property* of a control in a template can be either bound or unbound. For example, a table of employees could have a template column that presents hyperlinks to employee's personal Web sites. For the hyperlink in the template, the property for `NavigateUrl` would be bound to the field in the data source that holds the URL of that employee's Web site. However, the hyperlink's `Text` property would be set to the unbound value of "Click here to see this employee's Web site" and, thus, be the same for each employee.

Do not confuse unbound information with formatting of bound information. For example, a list of fraternity members might have an unbound label with the text of `Brother` before the bound label that presents the member's name. Alternatively, the bound field to the member's name may have a formatting of `FormatString = " 'Brother' & {0}"` or something similar.

As previously mentioned and demonstrated, templates can also contain markup (HTML) or simple text. For example, it is often desirable to add an HTML table to a template simply for providing an overall layout structure to the template to contain data-bound server controls. You can drag and drop a table from the toolbar, or if you position the cursor within the template and click through the menu (Layout⇨Insert Table), you will get a handy dialog box to build the table.

Record Rendering: Repeat and Single

Templates can represent a set of multiple data records in one of two ways:

- Repeated iterations of the template on the page for each data item in the data source
- A single iteration of the template for the current data item, possibly with paging enabled to move between records

The `DataList`, `Repeater`, and `GridView` template column controls provide a repeated format, whereas the `DetailsView` and `FormView` provide a single record presentation (optionally with paging enabled to move between records). In Figure 10-3, you can see the repeated layout at the top of the page and the single record layout in the lower part of the page. You can download the file (named `Demo-1-TemplateLayout.aspx`), for this page from the downloadables for Chapter 10.

In Figure 10-4, note that in the top row the data-bound controls are showing all the records. In the bottom row, the `DetailsView` and `FormView` display only one record at a time.

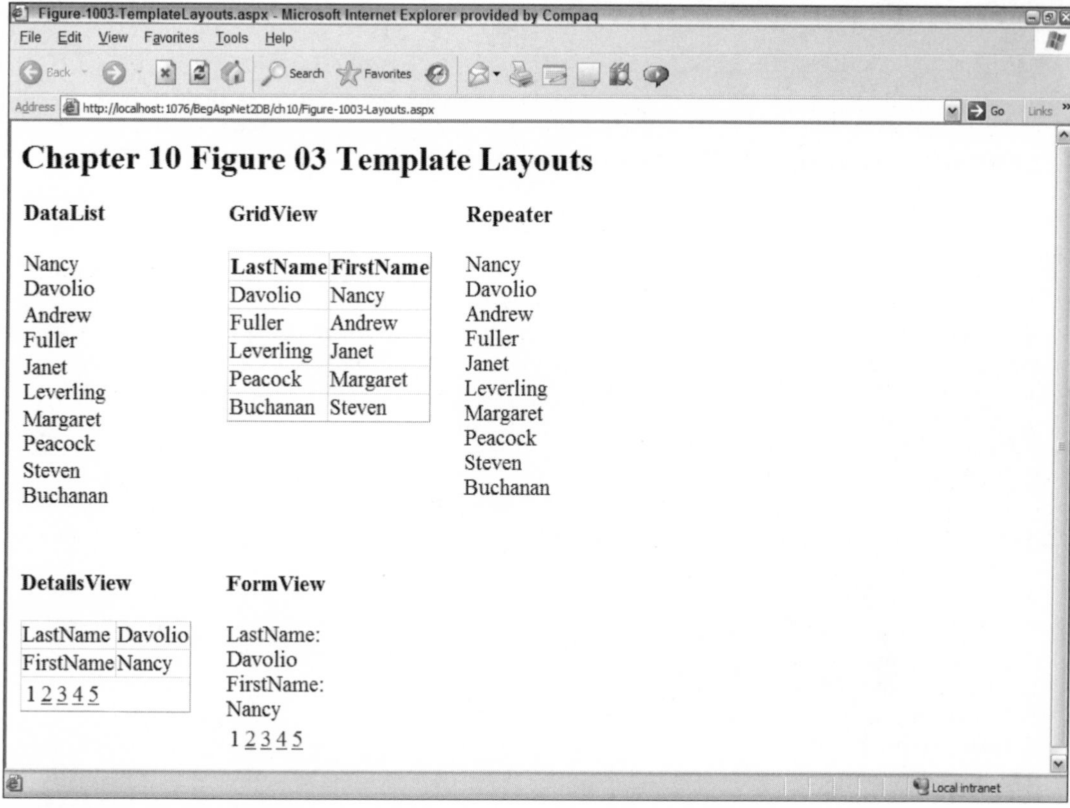

Figure 10-3

Subsections of Templates

Templated controls can have more than one templated area within them. For example, the `GridView` `TemplateField` represents the entire column. Within that template field, you actually have several regions that can be templated: the header, the footer, and the individual cells in the column. These have the logical names of `TemplateField.HeaderTemplate`, `TemplateField.FooterTemplate`, and `TemplateField.ItemTemplate`. Note that only the item template can contain data-bound controls; the header and footer templates are not data-bound and can only contain static controls and HTML markup. In order to see footers, you must set the `GridView.ShowFooter` property to true.

There is one Template column in this `GridView`, and it is divided into four subsection templates. The Header Template contains the text "Employee Name." The `ItemTemplate` has the values for names. The `AlternateItemTemplate` has the names in italics. The Footer Template has the text "Name."

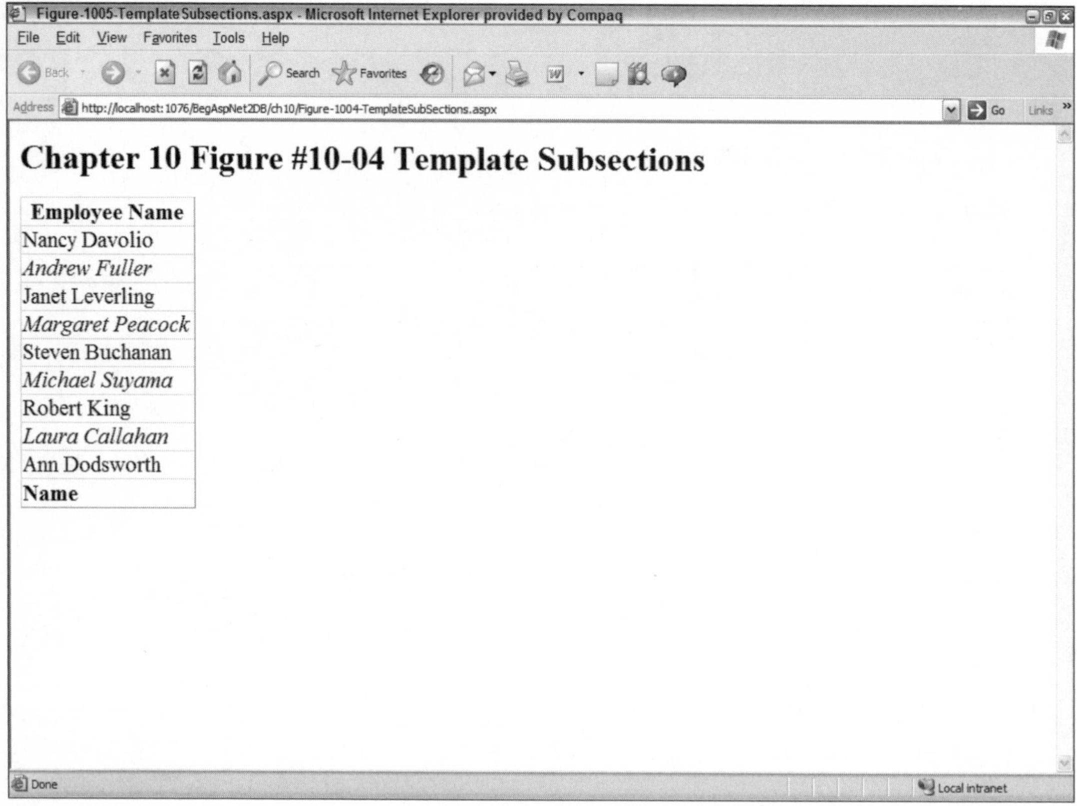

Figure 10-4

Now that you understand the sections of a template, we can look at the theory of how to bind data to child controls within templates.

Data Binding in Templates

Data-binding expressions are automatically created in the Designer when using VWD or Visual Studio (VS). It is worth understanding the source code for binding so that you can troubleshoot and maintain the page. Recall that you data-bind at two levels of controls. The entire *templated control* is bound to a data source control. Then the *controls within a template* that you add onto the template's workspace, such as labels and images, are bound to individual fields of the data source.

The binding of the entire templated data-bound control enables two features. First, it makes the fields of records from the data source control available to the controls within a template. Second, the templated data-bound control can set the current record and determine which record's values to display in the control within a template. This binding is done, as we have shown many times, by the `DataSourceID` property in the data-bound control as follows:

```
<asp:DataList ID="DataList1" Runat="server"
  DataSourceID="NorthwindShippersSqlDataSource"
```

```
    <ItemTemplate>
            <asp:Label />
            <asp:Image />
    </ItemTemplate>
</asp:DataList>
```

The properties of controls within a template are bound to fields of the data source. They must be bound to fields that are made available by the templated control's data source control. They can be bound as read-only or read-write (although write is not available for all templated controls). When you bind a control within a template to be read-only, you use the `Eval()` function. To add write capability, you substitute the `Bind()` function. In the VWD, you can direct the Designer to use `Bind()` (writability) by checking the Two Way Binding box when binding the control within a template.

```
<asp:DataList ID="DataList1" Runat="server"
        DataSourceID="MySqlDataSource">
                <ItemTemplate>
                        <asp:Label Text='<%# Eval("MyField") %>'  runat="server"/>
                </ItemTemplate>
</asp:DataList>
```

`Bind()` is available on both the new controls that were released with ASP.NET version 2.0: `GridView`, `DetailsView`, and `FormView` and the legacy data-bound controls (`DataList` and `Repeater`). (The writing of data from ASPX pages to a database is discussed in detail in Chapters 11 and 12.) The source code for a typical read-only bound control within a template follows.

Any server control can be added to a template, although some controls make more sense in certain templates than others. In the `ItemTemplate`, which is rendered for the read-only view of a data-bound control, you will most often place server controls that are simply for rendering the data, such as a `Label` control or `Image` control.

```
<ItemTemplate>
    <asp:Label Text='<%# Eval("CustomerName") %>'  runat="server"/>
    <asp:Image ImageUrl='<%# Eval("FileName", "~/Images/{0}") %>' runat="server"/>
</ItemTemplate>
```

In templates meant for editing, you will most likely place server controls that support input of data, such as a `TextBox` or `CheckBox` control.

```
<EditItemTemplate>
    <asp:TextBox Text='<%# Bind("CustomerName") %>'  runat="server"/>
    <asp:CheckBox ImageUrl='<%# Bind("IsActive") %>' runat="server"/>
</EditItemTemplate>
```

An editing template may also contain list controls, such as a `DropDownList`. As demonstrated in Chapter 8, the items in the list can be created statically or by binding the list to its own data source control.

```
<EditItemTemplate>
    <asp:DropDownList SelectedValue='<%# Bind("CustomerName") %>'
DataSourceID="CustomersDataSource" DataTextField="CustomerName"  runat="server"/>
</EditItemTemplate>
```

The terms `Bind` *and* `Eval` *have an etymology that indicates their difference.* `Eval` *simply evaluates a field and sets the property to that value.* `Bind` *actually creates the joining of the field on the page to the field in the database. One of us has suffered extensive studies in taxonomy and developed methods of memorization for academic survival. You may find this completely inane, but you can see that the shapes of the letters "E" for* `Eval` *and "B" for* `Bind`*, have a similar backbone. But the "B" shape more completely encircles the white spaces and, thus, you can remember that* `Bind()` *is the more complete function, that is, the one that supports both reading and writing.*

With the data-binding theory in mind, we can now look at the practice of creating templated regions of controls.

General Guidelines for Using Templated Controls

The technique to add templates depends on the template's parent control. However, you must have the parent control (for example the `GridView`) bound to a data source (except for those cases where you are using templates without data).

For controls that support both templated and nontemplated child controls (`GridView` and `DetailsView`), we can create a nontemplate column or field (for example a `GridView BoundField` column) in the same way we have in prior chapters. We can then use the Smart Tasks panel's Edit Columns, select the column, and click on the tool at the bottom right (it looks like a hyperlink) to convert the bound column to a template column. You can then edit the template as you desire, including adding text, images, additional bound controls, and HTML for layout.

The second technique is to create the template from scratch in the same way you would add a field to a `GridView` or `DetailsView`. Open the data-bound control's Smart Tasks panel, edit Columns, and add a new column of the Template type. Click OK to finish Edit Columns. Then, back on the Smart Tasks panel, you can select Edit Templates, select the template to change, and begin to fill it by dragging and dropping from the Toolbox.

The third option is for those controls that are only templated: `FormView`, `DataList`, and `Repeater`. When these controls are placed on a page, your only choice is to go into Edit Template mode and begin building in the workspace.

Note that there are three similar but different kinds of actions in the VWD's Smart Tasks panel for controls that can be templated:

- **Edit Columns:** Allows you to create a new column of the template type or convert a column to a template. It also permits making changes to a template column as a whole, but not within the template.
- **Add New Column:** Allows you to add a new column of the template type.
- **Edit Templates:** Switches to a mode where you can work within the template space, for example, adding new controls or changing the layout.

You cannot make changes to the *contents within* a templated field by using Edit Columns. This is because the Edit Columns feature was designed with a singular purpose in mind (one text property, one bound field property, etc.). Therefore, it is not suitable for the contents within a template where you can have many controls, with many text properties, bound field properties, and so on. To edit the multiple contents of a templated field you must use the Edit Templates choice on the Smart Tasks panel and then select the specific item in the template to modify. However, if you are making general changes to the templated field as a whole, for example the header text or backcolor, you can use the Edit Columns tool.

GridView Template Columns

We've already seen that you can add various fields to the GridView Columns collection. In prior chapters we have used hyperlink, command and button columns. The `TemplateField` is another field: one that allows you to define the contents of the column or field as a template region. The GridView's *template column* renders with multiple iterations down the grid, so it is like the other repeated templates in that all of the records are visible at once.

The template column offers layout flexibility not provided by other field objects, such as `BoundField`. You can use spaces and HTML line breaks (`<br>`) to arrange the internal controls in the template as well as tables for more complex layouts. When adding a table in VWD, go to Menu⇨Layout⇨Insert Table to take advantage of the design tool. The VWD allows easy conversion of a bound field to a templated field so that you can enhance a template without having to redrag and bind its first data-aware control.

Try It Out Converting a Column from Bound to Template in a GridView

In this exercise, you will create a page (named version 1) that displays a `GridView` with four bound columns from the Northwind Employees table. You will then (in version 2) convert one of those columns from a bound column to a template column and arrange three fields within that template column. This exercise is similar to the one in the preceding Try It Out, but you will convert a column from bound to template rather than add a new template column.

1. In the `ch10` folder, create a new page named `TIO-1002-ConvertBoundToTemplate-1.aspx`. In the Database Explorer, expand the `Northwind.mdf`, tables and employees. Select the IDs, names, and hire dates for employees of Northwind and drag the group to the page to create a `GridView`.

   Format the hire date to short date using {0:d} (use the `GridView`'s Smart Tasks panel then select Edit columns, select `HireDate` and modify the `DataFormatString` property). Also set the `HtmlEncode` for this column to false so the formatting will be employed. The code should be similar to the following:

```
...
<h2>Chapter 10 TIO #1002 </h2>
    <h2>Convert Bound Column To Template Column ver1</h2>
    <form id="form1" runat="server">
    <div>
        <asp:GridView ID="GridView1" runat="server"
            AutoGenerateColumns="False"
            DataKeyNames="EmployeeID"
            DataSourceID="SqlDataSource1"
            EmptyDataText="There are no data records to display.">
            <Columns>
                <asp:BoundField DataField="EmployeeID"
                    HeaderText="EmployeeID" ReadOnly="True"
```

```
                    SortExpression="EmployeeID" />
                <asp:BoundField DataField="LastName"
                    HeaderText="LastName" SortExpression="LastName" />
                <asp:BoundField DataField="FirstName"
                    HeaderText="FirstName" SortExpression="FirstName" />
                <asp:BoundField DataField="HireDate"
                    HeaderText="HireDate" SortExpression="HireDate"
                    DataFormatString="{0:D}"
                    HtmlEncode="False"/>
            </Columns>
        </asp:GridView>
        <asp:SqlDataSource ID="SqlDataSource1" runat="server"
            ConnectionString="<%$ ConnectionStrings:MdfNorthwind %>"
            ProviderName="<%$
                ConnectionStrings:MdfNorthwind.ProviderName %>"
            SelectCommand="SELECT [EmployeeID], [LastName], [FirstName], [HireDate]
                 FROM [Employees]"
        </asp:SqlDataSource>
    </div>
    </form>
</body>
</html>
```

2. Save the page and observe in your browser. When you are finished, close the browser.
3. Save the page as `TIO-1002-ConvertBoundToTemplate-2.aspx`. In the VWD Design view, select the `GridView` and open the Smart Tasks panel. Select the last name field, and click the red "X" button in the dialog box to delete it. Repeat for the last name field.
4. Click on the `EmployeeID` field. In the lower right of the Edit Columns dialog box, click on "Convert this field to a Template Field." Click OK to close the Edit Columns dialog box.
5. With the Smart Tasks panel still open, click on Edit Templates. From the drop-down list of available templates, you will now have `Column[0]` and its subtemplates. Select `Column[0].ItemTemplate` to begin editing that template.

   In the template (within the `GridView`), click just to the right of the `Label1`, and press Enter to go to a new line. From the Toolbox, drag and drop a label to the beginning of the second line and select Edit Data Bindings to bind the `Text` property to the `LastName` field (if the Field Binding list box is not populated, click the Refresh Schema button). Close the label's Smart Tasks panel and add a comma and space directly into the template. Now drag and drop another label and bind it to the first name. Open the entire `GridView`'s Smart Tasks panel and End Template Editing. You now have in your template the employee ID and names in a free-form layout within the cell with some static text (the space and comma).

   To be neat and accurate, change the heading text of your templated column by opening the `GridView` Smart Tasks panel, click Edit Columns, select EmployeeID and change its HeaderText property to just "Employee." The source code for the `GridView` will now be similar to the following:

```
... <h2>Chapter 10 TIO #1002 </h2>
...
        <asp:GridView ID="GridView1" runat="server"
            AutoGenerateColumns="False"
            DataKeyNames="EmployeeID"
            DataSourceID="SqlDataSource1"
```

```
            EmptyDataText="There are no data records to display.">
            <Columns>
                <asp:TemplateField HeaderText="Employee"
                        SortExpression="EmployeeID">
                    <EditItemTemplate>
                        <asp:Label ID="Label1" runat="server"
                               Text='<%# Eval("EmployeeID") %>'></asp:Label>
                    </EditItemTemplate>
                    <ItemTemplate>
                        <asp:Label ID="Label1" runat="server"
                               Text='<%# Bind("EmployeeID") %>'></asp:Label><br />
                        <asp:Label ID="Label2" runat="server"
                               Text='<%# Eval("LastName") %>'></asp:Label>,
                        <asp:Label ID="Label3" runat="server"
                               Text='<%# Eval("FirstName") %>'></asp:Label>
                    </ItemTemplate>
                </asp:TemplateField>
                <asp:BoundField DataField="HireDate"
                        HeaderText="HireDate"
                        SortExpression="HireDate"
                        DataFormatString="{0:D}"
                        HtmlEncode="False"/>
            </Columns>
        </asp:GridView>
...
```

6. Save your work and then observe the page in your browser.

How It Works

This exercise walked through the conversion of a `GridView` bound column to a template column, followed by modifications to that template column. In the following analysis, you will see how the VWD Designer produces slightly different code for the two kinds of labels.

First, in version 2 of the page, note that the template field now has a different control than the bound field.

```
        <asp:GridView ID="GridView1" Runat="server"
            DataSourceID="NorthwindEmployeesSqlDataSource"
            AutoGenerateColumns="False">
            <Columns>
                <asp:TemplateField>
```

Second, switch your attention to the following lines. Recall from the introductory section of this chapter that there are two bindings: `Eval()` is read-only, whereas `Bind()` is read/write, as shown in the following listing:

```
            <ItemTemplate>
                        <asp:Label ID="Label1" Runat="server"
                               Text='<%# Bind("EmployeeID") %>' />
        <br />
                        <asp:Label ID="Label2" Runat="server"
                               Text='<%# Eval("LastName") %>' />
        ,  
```

```
                    <asp:Label ID="Label3" Runat="server"
                           Text='<%# Eval("FirstName") %>' />
                </ItemTemplate>
            </asp:TemplateField>
```

Also observe in the following code how the VWD Designer added layout code and text for a return <br/>, comma, and space as per your keystrokes. You will see later in the chapter that even more complex layout (such as tables) can be added to a template.

```
          <ItemTemplate>
                    <asp:Label ID="Label1" Runat="server"
                           Text='<%# Bind("EmployeeID") %>' />
      <br />
                    <asp:Label ID="Label2" Runat="server"
                           Text='<%# Eval("LastName") %>' />
      ,  
                    <asp:Label ID="Label3" Runat="server"
                           Text='<%# Eval("FirstName") %>' />
                </ItemTemplate>
```

Now return your attention to the `GridView` as a whole. When there is an editable field, the `GridView` will have an additional tag for EditItemTemplate. The `EditItemTemplate` has a label for only ID because that was what the `BoundField` was bound to when you converted it to a template field. It's not a textbox because the ID field is a primary key field and, thus, normally is not editable.

```
<asp:GridView ... runat="server"
 <Columns>
        <asp:TemplateField>

               <EditItemTemplate>
               ...
               </EditItemTemplate>

                <ItemTemplate>
                       <asp:Label ... Text='<%# Bind("MyField") %> />
                </ItemTemplate>
        </asp:TemplateField>
 </Columns>
</asp:GridView>
```

Now that we have added a new column that is templated (in the first Try It Out) and converted a bound column to a template column (in the second Try It Out), we can turn our attention to templated subsections that are not data-bound to a database field, such as the `HeaderTemplate`, `FooterTemplate`, `EmptyDataTemplate`, and `PagerTemplate`. However, these controls are, under the covers, "bound" to properties of the `GridView` such as the `ItemIndex` and the `PageIndex`. They are amenable to holding multiple controls and mixes of controls, text, HTML and layout.

Try It Out Using Templates That Are Not Data-Bound

In this short exercise, we will modify the `GridView` of the second Try It Out so that it uses a header template.

1. Open TIO-1002-ConvertBoundToTemplate-2.aspx, and in the ch10 folder, save it as TIO-1003-TemplateDataNotBound.aspx. Change the title and H2 text. Note that the current headings were defaults created by VWD as the HeaderText property of the entire TemplateField, shown in the source code as the gray line in the following listing.

```
...
<Columns>
  <asp:TemplateField
     HeaderText="Employee"
     SortExpression="EmployeeID">
     <ItemTemplate>...
```

2. In VWD Design view, select the GridView, open its Smart Tasks panel and select Edit Templates. From the list choose the Column[0] HeaderTemplate. Type into the workspace the words Employee Information and then select them. Press Ctrl+B to make them bold and Ctrl+I to make them italic. Reopen the Smart Tasks panel and end template editing.
3. Save your work, and view it in the browser.

How It Works

By default, VWD will apply the name of a field to a HeadingText property of the entire template column. But ASP.NET offers the option to edit the Header subsection of the template column. We can add images, additional text and other controls; however, no controls within a HeaderTemplate can be bound. Even though the HeaderText property remains, it is superseded by the HeaderTemplate layout.

Templates are not only available for tabular controls such as a GridView or DetailsView. They can also be used in the DataList and FormView controls, as we will cover in the next few sections.

DataList Control

Like the GridView, the DataList control offers a technique to display all the records on the page at once, with each record getting a cell within an overall HTML table. DataList is the first example of a control you've encountered that actually requires you to define templates (at least, the ItemTemplate) in order for the control to render. Unlike GridView and DetailsView, DataList does not provide a built-in rendering for data records other than the outer table used to lay out the content defined in its templates.

The DataList can be formatted at two levels. At the larger level, the arrangement of the overall HTML table can be controlled, including the number of columns and horizontal or vertical ordering of records. Then, within each cell, you have a templated space to lay out the fields for one record. That layout can include small tables to arrange the internal controls within the DataList's templates within the overall table.

The arrangement of records is established by the DataList Page Layout Properties. Note that the formatting properties for the overall table are actually divided into two panels of the Properties window in the categorized view: Layout and Appearance. Within Layout, Direction determines whether the records will be ordered across the page (horizontal) or down the columns (vertical). RepeatColumns determines the number of columns. Note that if you change the RepeatLayout to flow (default is table), you will lose the overall HTML table that holds the records and the templates will instead be rendered inside span tags.

Within the Appearance panel of the `DataList`'s Properties window, you can set the borders. The properties that begin with "Border..." affect the single rectangle around the entire `DataList` (all columns and rows). The `two border` settings within the `ItemStyle` (and `Alternating ItemStyle`) determine the appearance of dividing lines between the records. As with any HTML table, you have properties for cell padding (space between the inside of the cell wall and the contents) and cell spacing (width of the space between cells).

Try It Out Experimenting with the Page Layout Properties of a DataList Control

In this exercise, you will lay out a `DataList` of employees and experiment with the overall appearance of the table.

1. In the `ch10` folder, create a new page named `TIO-1004-DataListPageArrangements-ver1.aspx`. Add a `DataList` to the page, and configure a new data source control that reads the IDs, names, and hire dates from the Northwind Employees table.
2. The `DataList` will automatically give you a default layout of fields in its `ItemTemplate`. View this by opening the Smart Tasks panel, and enter Edit Template mode for the `ItemTemplate`. If you want, add text or returns to change the layout of the group of fields.
3. End template editing and save the page, which should look similar to the following:

```
<%@ Page Language="VB" %>
<!DOCTYPE html PUBLIC "-//W3C//DTD XHTML 1.0 Transitional//EN"
"http://www.w3.org/TR/xhtml1/DTD/xhtml1-transitional.dtd">
<script runat="server">
</script>
<html xmlns="http://www.w3.org/1999/xhtml" >
<head id="Head1" runat="server">
    <title>TIO-1004-DataListPageArrangements.aspx</title>
</head>
<body>
        <h2>Chapter 10 TIO #1004 DataList Page Arrangements</h2>
    <form id="form1" runat="server">
    <div>
        <asp:DataList ID="DataList1" runat="server" DataKeyField="EmployeeID"
DataSourceID="SqlDataSource1">
            <ItemTemplate>
                EmployeeID:
                <asp:Label ID="EmployeeIDLabel" runat="server"
                        Text='<%# Eval("EmployeeID") %>'></asp:Label><br />
                LastName:
                <asp:Label ID="LastNameLabel" runat="server"
                        Text='<%# Eval("LastName") %>'></asp:Label><br />
                FirstName:
                <asp:Label ID="FirstNameLabel" runat="server"
                        Text='<%# Eval("FirstName") %>'></asp:Label><br />
                HireDate:
                <asp:Label ID="HireDateLabel" runat="server"
                        Text='<%# Eval("HireDate") %>'></asp:Label><br />
                <br />
            </ItemTemplate>
        </asp:DataList>
```

```
        <asp:SqlDataSource ID="SqlDataSource1" runat="server"
               ConnectionString="<%$ ConnectionStrings:MdfNorthwind %>"
                SelectCommand="SELECT [EmployeeID],
                       [LastName], [FirstName], [HireDate] FROM [Employees]">
        </asp:SqlDataSource>
</div></form></body></html>
```

4. View the page in your browser. By default, the `DataList` will show the records in a table one column wide, so they will run straight down the page.

5. Close the browser, and, in VWD Design view, save the page as `TIO-2-DataListPageArrangements-ver2.aspx. Select the DataList control and, on its Smart Tasks panel, click on the Property Builder. Select two columns and the direction of horizontal.`

6. `Save you source code, which should be similar to the following, and view the page in the browser. It should now display the records in two columns with the records (sorted by EmployeeID) from left to right horizontally.`

```
<asp:DataList ID="DataList1" Runat="server"
 DataSourceID="NorthwindEmployeesSqlDataSource"
 RepeatColumns="2"
 RepeatDirection="Horizontal">
        <ItemTemplate>
        ...
        </ItemTemplate>
</asp:DataList>
```

7. Close the browser. Save the file as `TIO-2-DataListPageArrangements-ver2.aspx`. Change the title and H2 text. Select the `DataList` control, and look at the Properties window. Change the RepeatDirection to vertical and the RepeatColumns to 4. Notice in the browser how the increasing employee numbers go vertically downward and then wrap up to the top of the next column.

```
  <asp:DataList    ...
      RepeatColumns="4">
      RepeatDirection="Vertical">
 </asp:DataList>
```

8. Finish by saving the file as `TIO-2-DataListPageArrangements-ver4.aspx`. Select the `DataList` and look at the Properties window. This time, click the Borders tab on the left side. Add both gridlines of a gray color and a width of 3 points. Set the cell spacing to 2.

```
<asp:DataList ID="DataList1" Runat="server"
     DataSourceID="NorthwindEmployeesSqlDataSource"
     RepeatColumns="3"
     CellSpacing="2"
     BorderColor="LightGray"
     BorderWidth="3pt"
     GridLines="Both">
</asp:DataList>
```

9. Save your work, and view it in the browser.

How It Works

In this exercise, you experimented with the overall layout of the `DataList`. You can see that the number of columns and the flow of information (`RepeatDirection`) are similar to those of any other HTML table. Note that the default `RepeatDirection` is vertical, as shown in the first sample code of Step 7.

Within a given template the `DataList` offers several options for layout of subcontrols.

DataList Control Internal Layout

Recall that the `DataList` can be formatted at two levels. The last section focused on the overall HTML table, where each cell holds one record of information. Now, we turn our attention to the templated space within each cell.

VWD offers an intuitive dialog box to add a table to a template. Select the templated control, and then edit the `ItemTemplate`. Click through the menu: Menu⇨Layout⇨Insert Table. You will see some predefined options at the top of the Insert Table dialog box under Templates. Below that are tools to design a custom table, including the appearance of borders. Click Cell properties to set defaults for all cells in the table. Even if you do not intend to display a border in the final version, you may want to turn on a border of width 1 to help in navigation while adding controls to the table. In the end, a typical table in a template might appear as follows:

```
<asp:DataList ID="DataList1" Runat="server"
    DataSourceID="NorthwindEmployeesSqlDataSource"
    RepeatColumns="3"
    GridLines="Both">
    <ItemTemplate>
            <table>
               <tr>
                   <td>
                       <asp:Label ID="Label1" Runat="server"
                           Text='<%# Eval("Field1") %>' />
                   </td>
                   <td>
                       <asp:Label ID="Label2" Runat="server"
                           Text='<%# Eval("Field2") %>' />
                   </td>
                </tr>
                <tr>
                   <td>
                       <asp:Label ID="Label3" Runat="server"
                           Text='<%# Eval("Field3") %>' />
                   </td>
                   <td>
                       <asp:Label ID="Label4" Runat="server"
                           Text='<%# Eval("Field4") %>' />
                   </td>
                </tr>
           </table>
    </ItemTemplate>
</asp:DataList>
```

We will try this technique in the next exercise.

Try It Out Using the Internal Layout Properties of a DataList Control

In this exercise, you will present the employees' information in a more pleasing layout within each record. You will start with a page from the last exercise, add a table, and relocate the fields into the table.

1. Start with your file `TIO-1004-DataListPageArrangements-ver4.aspx from the last exercise, and save it as TIO-1005-DataListWithInternalTable.aspx. Change the Title and H2 texts.`
2. `In the data source control, run through the Configure Wizard and add the field for Notes, as follows. Accept the warning that that the old layout will be lost.`

   `Layout: Please preserve shading in the following code. Thanks.`

```
<asp:SqlDataSource
 ...
SelectCommand="SELECT EmployeeID,FirstName,LastName,HireDate,Notes
    FROM Employees"/>
```

3. In the VWD Design view, select the `DataList`. Open its Smart Tasks panel and then click on Refresh Schema. Click on Edit Template mode. Click anywhere in the template; to create some working space at the top of the template, press Enter.
4. Click through Menu⇨Layout⇨Insert Table, and add a table of three columns and three rows. Click OK. Now select the three cells in the bottom row. Click Menu⇨Layout⇨Merge Cells.
5. From the Toolbox, add labels and set their data bindings so that the template's internal table will be displayed as follows. Note each cell's horizontal alignment, which is set by clicking in the cell and pressing Ctrl+L (left-aligned), Ctrl+R(right-aligned), or Ctrl+E (center-aligned).

	LastName, FirstName	HireDate (in short format)
Employee ID		
Notes		

6. Save the code (which should be similar to that below).

```
<%@ Page Language="VB" %>
<!DOCTYPE html PUBLIC "-//W3C//DTD XHTML 1.0 Transitional//EN"
"http://www.w3.org/TR/xhtml1/DTD/xhtml1-transitional.dtd">
<script runat="server">
</script>
<html xmlns="http://www.w3.org/1999/xhtml" >
<head id="Head1" runat="server">
    <title>TIO-1004-DataListPageArrangements-4.aspx</title>
</head>
<body>
        <h2>Chapter 10 TIO #1004 DataList Page Arrangements - version 4</h2>
```

```
    <form id="form1" runat="server">
    <div>
        <asp:DataList ID="DataList1" runat="server"
            DataSourceID="SqlDataSource1"
            RepeatColumns="4"
            CellSpacing="2"
            BorderColor="LightGray"
            BorderWidth="3pt"
            GridLines="Both">
            <ItemTemplate>
                <br />
                <table>
                    <tr valign=top>
                        <td style="width: 100px">
                        </td>
                        <td style="width: 100px">
                            <asp:Label ID="Label1" runat="server"
                                Text='<%# Eval("LastName") %>'></asp:Label>,
                            <asp:Label ID="Label2" runat="server"
                                Text='<%# Eval("FirstName") %>'></asp:Label></td>
                        <td style="width: 212px">
                            <asp:Label ID="Label3" runat="server"
                                Text='<%# Eval("HireDate") %>'></asp:Label></td>
                    </tr>
                    <tr>
                        <td style="width: 100px">
                            <asp:Label ID="Label4" runat="server"
                                Text='<%# Eval("EmployeeID") %>'></asp:Label></td>
                        <td style="width: 100px">
                        </td>
                        <td style="width: 212px">
                        </td>
                    </tr>
                    <tr>
                        <td colspan="3" style="height: 94px" valign=top>
                            <asp:Label ID="Label5" runat="server"
                                Text='<%# Eval("Notes") %>'></asp:Label></td>
                    </tr>
                </table>
            </ItemTemplate>
        </asp:DataList>
        <asp:SqlDataSource ID="SqlDataSource1" runat="server"
            ConnectionString="<%$ ConnectionStrings:MdfNorthwind %>"
            SelectCommand="
                SELECT [EmployeeID], [LastName], [FirstName], [HireDate], [Notes]
                FROM [Employees]">
        </asp:SqlDataSource>
</div></form></body></html>
```

7. View your work in the browser.

How It Works

Here, you see how you can achieve a spectrum of HTML table format options within each iteration of a template. Adding the table from the Layout menu gives you the dialog box for easy design. Within the table, you were able to merge cells and set horizontal alignment. In the final source code, you can also see the normal table elements such as <td>.

Having studied the DataList control we now turn to the Repeater control.

Repeater Control

The Repeater is similar to the DataList in that it iterates one template to the page for each record. The difference is that the Repeater does not wrap the iterations in an overall HTML table. Because there is no overall table, there are no properties for RepeatDirection, number of columns, or table elements such as border and cell padding.

The second difference between DataList and Repeater is that Repeater's templates can have parts of HTML tags in them, where DataList's (and every other templated control) cannot. So, you can put an open tag in one template and its close tag in another. This allows ultimate flexibility, but is also the reason that there is no design-time experience for Repeater.

Note that in templated controls, data and literal text must be within a template tag, most frequently <ItemTemplate>. It is easy to be in Source view and begin adding labels and images without first creating an ItemTemplate. The result is an error message that the Repeater does not have a property named "label." (See a demonstration of the failure in the download file Demo-3-RepeaterWithNoItemTemplate.aspx.)

```
<asp:Repeater ID="Repeater1" runat="server"
    DataSourceID="NorthwindEmployeesSqlDataSource">
    <ItemTemplate>
         Id #
        <asp:Label ID="Label1" runat="server" Text='<%# Eval("EmployeeID") %>' />
         =
        <asp:Label ID="Label2" runat="server" Text='<%# Eval("LastName") %>' />
        .<br />
    </ItemTemplate>
</asp:Repeater>
```

Because the Repeater does not automatically generate an overall table, the Designer has greater control over the rendering. The DataList provides less flexibility but much greater convenience. Of these two iterated (tiled) controls, DataList will cover most of your needs.

Again, in templated controls, data and literal text must be within a template tag, most frequently, the <ItemTemplate>. It is easy to be in Source view and begin adding labels and images without first creating an ItemTemplate. The result is an error message that the Repeater does not have a property named "label."

Templates in the DetailsView Control

The DataList, Repeater, and GridView templates all repeat their ItemTemplate for each record in the data source; that is, they show all of the records on the page at once. We now switch gears to look at templating aspects of the controls that render the ItemTemplate once for the currently displayed record: DetailsView and FormView. Although similar in appearance, they differ in the automatically generated structure of the ItemTemplate. DetailsView creates an internal table of all fields and their names, while FormView is a blank slate, within which you define the overall structure of controls in the template. That makes DetailsView faster to set up, but FormView is more flexible.

You've already encountered DetailsView to support a drill-down of data from a selection in a GridView. You will encounter it again in the next two chapters as the control to add a new record when working with a GridView. Like the GridView template column, the DetailsView Edit Fields dialog box allows you to switch a bound field to a templated field. The DetailsView Smart Tasks panel offers options to edit fields, just as GridView had an option to edit columns. You can also click to edit the template, select the ItemTemplate, and rearrange the fields to your heart's content.

FormView Control

The FormView is very similar to the DetailsView. They both show only one record at a time and support paging over records. They also both support reading, writing, and creating new records. The difference is that the DetailsView automatically creates an internal HTML table structure that holds the names and values of the fields. The FormView offers just a blank area (actually a single cell of a one-row table) in which to add controls. Unlike the DetailsView, which has a built-in rendering (using AutoGenerateFields, or explicit fields defined in the Fields collection), the FormView actually requires you to define its ItemTemplate in order to provide the rendering for the control. It is more similar to DataList and Repeater in this regard, as it is an entirely templated control. As with other controls, you can add an HTML table by hand to organize your controls.

Try It Out Working with DetailsView and FormView

Northwind occasionally needs to look at employees from the perspective of when they were hired. You want to create a page that displays information on one employee at a time in order from longest serving to most recently hired. Suppose that your client has asked for easily understood aids for navigating the list of employees.

1. In the ch10 folder, create a new page named TIO-1006-DetailsViewAndFormView-ver1.aspx. Add a SqlDataSource for the IDs, names, and hire dates of the employees of Northwind ordered by hire date (use ascending order).
2. Add a DetailsView and bind it to the data source. Click on the Allow Paging option in the Smart Tasks panel.

```
...
<h2>Chapter 10 TIO #1006 DetailsView And FormView </h2>
    <form id="form1" runat="server">
    <div>
        <asp:DetailsView ID="DetailsView1" runat="server"
            AllowPaging="True"
            AutoGenerateRows="False"
```

```
            DataKeyNames="EmployeeID"
            DataSourceID="SqlDataSource1"
            Height="50px" Width="125px">
            <Fields>
                <asp:BoundField DataField="EmployeeID"
                    HeaderText="EmployeeID"
                    InsertVisible="False"
                    ReadOnly="True"
                    SortExpression="EmployeeID" />
                <asp:BoundField DataField="LastName"
                    HeaderText="LastName"
                    SortExpression="LastName" />
                <asp:BoundField DataField="FirstName"
                    HeaderText="FirstName"
                    SortExpression="FirstName" />
                <asp:BoundField DataField="HireDate"
                    HeaderText="HireDate"
                    SortExpression="HireDate" />
            </Fields>
        </asp:DetailsView>

        <asp:SqlDataSource ID="SqlDataSource1" runat="server"
            ConnectionString="<%$ ConnectionStrings:MdfNorthwind %>"
            SelectCommand="
                SELECT [EmployeeID], [LastName], [FirstName], [HireDate]
                FROM [Employees] ORDER BY [HireDate]">
        </asp:SqlDataSource>
</div></form></body></html>
```

3. Save and run the page. In the browser, look at the source, and note that ASP.NET created an internal HTML table and populated it with the names and values of earlier fields.

4. Save a copy of the file as `TIO-1006-DetailsViewAndFormView-ver1.aspx`. Drag and drop a `FormView` onto the page. Bind the `FormView` to the data source control. In the Smart Tasks panel, set Enable Paging to `true`.

```
<asp:FormView ID="FormView1" Runat="server"
        AllowPaging="True"
        DataSourceID="SqlDataSource1">
            <ItemTemplate>
                <asp:Label ID="Label1" Runat="server"
                        Text='<%# Eval("LastName") %>' />
                 ... other fields ...
            </ItemTemplate>
        </asp:FormView>
```

5. Save your work, and view it in the browser.

How It Works

When you add a `DetailsView` control and bind to a data source control, VWD automatically gives you a default layout within the `ItemTemplate`. You can also turn on paging (page navigation) and specify custom text for the navigation hyperlinks. When you have more than one data-bound control, they can share the same data source. However, they will navigate through the records independently.

Comparison of the Templated Controls

To summarize, the ASP.NET 2.0 templated controls and their associated template properties include the following:

Templated Control	Template Properties	ItemTemplate Behavior
GridView	EmptyDataTemplate PagerTemplate TemplateField AlternatingItemTemplate EditItemTemplate FooterTemplate HeaderTemplate ItemTemplate	GridView repeats Template Field.ItemTemplate once per row for each record in the data source.
DetailsView	EmptyDataTemplate PagerTemplate HeaderTemplate FooterTemplate TemplateField Alternating-ItemTemplate EditItemTemplate FooterTemplate HeaderTemplate InsertItemTemplate ItemTemplate	DetailsView renders TemplateField.ItemTemplate for field's data cell the current record in the data source.
FormView	EmptyDataTemplate PagerTemplate HeaderTemplate FooterTemplate ItemTemplate EditItemTemplate InsertItemTemplate	FormView renders the ItemTemplate for the current record in the data source.
DataList	HeaderTemplate FooterTemplate AlternatingItemTemplate ItemTemplate EditItemTemplate SelectedItemTemplate SeparatorTemplate	DataList repeats the ItemTemplate once for each record in the data source.
Repeater	HeaderTemplate FooterTemplate AlternatingItemTemplate ItemTemplate SeparatorTemplate	Repeater repeats the ItemTemplate once for each record in the data source.

ASP.NET 2.0 supports five templated data-bound controls. The following information will help you decide which templated control to use. Historically speaking, the `DataList` and `Repeater` were available in ASP.NET version 1.*x*, whereas `GridView`, `DetailsView`, and `FormView` came out only with version 2.0.

First, we have already considered controls that render their templates once per data record (`DetailsView TemplateField` and `FormView`) versus those that repeat their templates (`GridView TemplateField`, `DataList`, and `Repeater`).

Now, think of the templated controls in a range from most rigid to most flexible:

[Most rigid] - `GridView TemplateField`

`DetailsView TemplateField`

`FormView`

`DataList`

`Repeater` **[Just a frame, thus, most flexible]**

Although there may be variations, here is a list of considerations to take into account when deciding which control best suits your scenario. Although we haven't discussed updating, deleting, and inserting data in detail (those topics are reserved for the next three chapters), we list below which controls support which operations to help you decide on the right control to use.

Choosing a control based on display, update, delete, and insert capability:

1. If you want to insert new records, your only choices are `DetailsView` and `FormView`.
2. If you want to update or delete data (but not necessarily insert new records), choose `GridView`, `DetailsView`, or `FormView`. Although `DataList` is capable of providing UI for editing, it does not take advantage of the data source's ability to do this automatically like `GridView`, and you'll need to write custom code to make it work. Refer to an ASP.NET v1 reference for more information (the topic is outside the scope of this book).
3. If you only want to display read-only values, you can use any of the templated controls we've discussed within this chapter.

   Choosing a control based on formatting and layout of the data records:
4. If you want to display multiple data records at the same time, choose between `GridView`, `DataList`, and `Repeater`:

   `GridView`: Displays each data record as a row in a table. Fields of the data record are displayed in the table cells (one field per cell, or using a template, as many fields per cells as you need). The contents of each cell are defined by the `TemplateField.ItemTemplate` property.

   `DataList`: Displays each data record as a cell in a table. The number of data records per row in the table is determined by the `DataList's RepeatColumns` property. The `ItemTemplate` property allows you to define the template rendering of each data record within the table cell.

   `Repeater`: Displays each data record as a user-defined item, defined by the `Repeater's ItemTemplate` property. There is no built-in table for layout, so the items simply flow from one to the next (within a `<span>` tag, so styles are applied).

5. If you want to display one record at a time, choose between `DetailsView` and `FormView`:

   `DetailsView`: Displays each data record as a table of two columns, where each row typically contains a single field (the left cell is the header and the right cell the value). Using TemplateField, you can define the contents of each value cell using the TemplateField.ItemTemplate property.

   FormView: Displays each data record as a single cell in a table with one row. The contents of the table cell are defined by the `FormView`'s ItemTemplate property.

To finish the comparison, study the following table.

	GridView	DataList	Repeater	DetailsView	Form View
From version 1.x?	No	Yes	Yes	No	No
Number of records shown at once	Multiple	Multiple	Multiple	Single	Single
Can update records?	Yes	No*	No	Yes	Yes
Can delete records?	Yes	No*	No	Yes	Yes
Can insert records?	No	No	No	Yes	Yes
Can select records?	Yes	No*	No	Yes**	Yes**
Supports paging?	Yes	No	No	Yes	Yes
Renders data record as...	Row in multicolumn table	Cell in multirow/ column table	Item in a <span> (no table)	Single table of two columns	Single cell in a one-row table
Templates are optional?	Yes	No	No	Yes	No
Supports header/footer	Yes	Yes	Yes	Yes	Yes

* Although the `DataList` provides the ability to render `Edit` and `Delete` UI (through custom command buttons in the ItemTemplate and EditItemTemplate), it does not automatically perform these operations through data source controls like `GridView`, `DetailsView`, and `FormView`. For more information about using `DataList` to update and delete data, consult a reference for ASP.NET version 1.*x*.

** Unlike `GridView`, selection in `FormView` and `DetailsView` is not performed through a Select command button, but rather through paging between data records. The `SelectedValue` property reflects the DataKey of the currently rendered data item.

A Few More Advanced Ideas on Data Binding

ASP.NET supports additional forms and embellishment of data binding. These are beyond the scope of this book, but we will summarize some of these options as food for your thought when solving more advanced scenarios:

- `Eval()` is shorthand for the `DataBinder.Eval` function (from ASP.NET version 1), that takes a separate container data item argument, for example, `DataBinder.Eval(Container .DataItem, "Field", "FormatString")`. The data item is what is commonly used to reflect against for properties, and could be anything. For `Eval()`, it just happens to always be `Container .DataItem`.
- `DataBinder.Eval` is valid outside a template of a data-bound control, whereas `Eval()` is not.
- Data binding happens automatically for data-bound controls, but in some cases scenarios it is necessary to force data binding to happen programmatically, just as was required for v1. In this case, the Page developer must call `DataBind()` from code. Where you call `DataBind()` in the page's lifecycle is dependent on the scenario.
- `DataBinding Expressions <%# ... %>` can contain more than just `Eval` and `Bind` statements. In fact, they can contain arbitrary code expressions. For example, if a public property on my page is named `MyControl.MyProperty`, it could be referred to as `<%# MyControl .MyProperty %>`.
- A data binding can use the results of a method like `<%# MyMethod() %>`, perhaps even passing arguments like `<%# MyMethod(Eval("MyField")) %>`.
- Data-binding expressions are valid outside of a templated control. In this case, the page's author just calls `DataBind()` on the entity being data-bound, for example, `Label1.DataBind()` or `Page.DataBind()`, which recursively databinds all controls on the `Page`.

Common Mistakes

The following list describes some of the mistakes commonly made when trying to display data in templates:

- Forgetting to end template editing mode and then not finding desired options on the Smart Tasks panel.
- Attempting to bind controls in a template when the outer templated control as a whole has not been bound to a data source.
- When creating a paged that includes the capability to write data, attempting to use `Eval` in an edit template, where `Bind` is required.
- Not seeing the fields available for binding to controls in a template. Click on Refresh Schema in the dialog box, and the drop-down list of fields will be repopulated.
- Building contents of a `Repeater` control in Source view without including a set of `<ItemTemplate>` tags.

Summary

This chapter presented data-bound controls that have templated regions that offer a canvas upon which you can place and arrange data-bound controls (such as labels, hyperlinks, and images), literal values (such as dashes or commas), and HTML tags (such as <br> or <table>). The data-bound controls will display values for the current record of the templated control. Keep in mind that data binding occurs at two levels. The templated control as a whole is bound to a data source control. Then, within the template, each control that displays values is bound to a field.

Templated controls display multiple records in one of two ways: either in a repeated fashion or singly. `DataList`, `Repeater`, and the template column of the `GridView` display values from all of the records at once in some type of repeated arrangement. `DetailsView` and `FormView` display just one record at a time, as if you were seeing the top record of a stack.

Templates are built by selecting the control, opening the Smart Tasks panel, and entering Edit Template mode. Controls can be dragged from the toolbar; then a Smart Tasks panel for that control is provided to expedite data binding. The Data Binding dialog box has a drop-down section to select a display format for the value. Don't forget to reopen the Smart Tasks panel and select End Template Editing to restore the normal options in the Smart Tasks panel.

HTML tables are used in two ways with templated controls. In some templated controls, all of the records will be rendered onto a cell within an *overall* HTML table. The second use of tables is *inside* a template to organize various fields when displaying one record. Be careful to keep the two uses of tables differentiated in your mind when selecting which templated control to use and when maintaining code in Source view.

In `DetailsView` and `FormView`, ASP.NET 2.0 offers tools to navigate through the stack (from record to record). These navigation controls are generally in a pager cell with a `PagerStyle`. They provide navigation by listing the record numbers or displaying Next/Previous or jumps to First and Last pages.

Selecting the control to use can be confusing. Keep these points in mind to differentiate data-bound controls by read and write capability.

- If you want to insert new records, your only choices are `DetailsView` and `FormView`.
- If you want to update or delete data (but not necessarily insert new records), choose between `GridView`, `DetailsView`, or `FormView`.
- If you only want to display read-only values, you can use any of the templated controls.
- Select a control based on layout as follows. If you want to display multiple data records at the same time, choose between `GridView`, `DataList`, and `Repeater`; to display one record at a time, select between `FormView` (an empty template space) and `DetailsView` (with a default internal table).

Now, you are about to move on to the fourth section of this book: how to use an ASPX page as a user interface to modify data stored in a database.

Exercises

The answers to these review questions can be found in Appendix B.

1. Describe the differences between a `BoundField` and a `TemplateField`.
2. Which controls can contain templates?

3. Which controls can and cannot create new records?
4. What is the fundamental difference between `DetailsView` and `FormView`?
5. Which two data-bound controls covered in this chapter are holdovers from earlier versions of ASP.NET?
6. Does ASP.NET 2.0 support HTML tables within a template? Explain.
7. Once a `BoundField` is added to a `GridView`, can it be converted to a `TemplateField`?
8. What is the main difference between the `DataList` and `Repeater` controls?

Updating and Deleting Data

The last few chapters discussed ways to read data from a source and display it on the page. But an old proverb notes that "only three things in life are certain: birth, death, and change" (although sarcastic quoters have added "taxes" as well). This chapter and the next cover these certainties as they apply to data. We start here with how to change values in existing records (updating) and how to remove a record (deleting). The next chapter explains how to create a new record.

As with almost every task in ASP.NET 2.0, the Visual Web Developer (VWD) makes the creation of a data-modifying page very easy. This chapter walks you through the drag-and-drop steps and then explains the source code. Beneath the surface lie theories that are trickier than those that have been discussed to date; this chapter explains those ideas. We finish with some special examples and the techniques to delete a record.

This chapter covers eight topics to enable you to change and delete data:

- Understanding the theory of modifying data
- Creating and using command fields
- Enabling a simple update
- Using `DataKeyNames` with `updates`
- Enabling updates in a `DetailsView`
- Using the parameters collections
- Handling `NULLs` in `updates`
- Deleting entire records

By the end of this chapter, you will be comfortable with changing existing data and removing entire records.

Since we will be changing data, you may want to get it back to its original form. You will also need to enter new values, and they must be within the constraints of the database. Therefore, heed the following notes.

> **Before beginning this chapter, make a copy of your `Northwind.mdf` and `Pubs.mdf` files to a safe folder. If you make mistakes in changing or deleting records, you can copy these files back into the `App_Data` folder of your site by right-clicking on `App_Data` and using Add Existing Item.**

In several exercises in this chapter, you will modify or delete data. If you want to return to the original values (recommended), here is the original information for the first author in the `Authors` table of `Pubs.mdf`.

```
ID = 172-32-1176        First name = Johnson        Last name = White        City =
Menlo Park
```

When changing values in the Pubs' Authors table, keep in mind the following rules:

- For ID, use the format *nnn-nn-nnnn*, where *n* is a number.
- Phone numbers should be of the form *nnn-nnnn*.
- For the state, use CA and for the zip code, use 12345.
- For the other fields, use any values, but do not leave any blank.

If you use an invalid value, you will get a failure notice, but no harm is done. And remember, you can always reimport the MDF file from your backup location.

Overview of Modifying

First, for readers who have not worked with SQL, you should be aware of three terms used for modifying data:

- **Update:** To change value(s) within a record that already exists
- **Delete:** To remove an entire record
- **Insert** or **Insert Into:** To create a new record (usually with a set of values, but it could be empty)

ASP.NET 2.0 adds two additional terms. Consider that when you first see data it is usually read from a database; you are seeing the existing values in a read-only mode. Then, to create or change values, you want to change your view mode to one that accepts user input. The display of values changes from labels to textboxes. To describe the process of changing the view from read-only to writable, ASP.NET 2.0 adds two additional terms:

- **New:** To change the viewing mode to accept data for an `insert` (create a new record)
- **Edit:** To change the viewing mode to accept data for an `update` (change the values within an existing record)

Although these are good descriptive terms to display to the site user, they can cause some confusion when the designer has to translate that into the proper SQL terminology. Sometimes there is confusion about the term *delete*. If you want to remove just one value from a record, but still keep the record, then use `Update` and replace the existing value with `NULL`. The term *delete* only applies to removing an entire record.

> **There is a technical difference between the operation of the SQL terms and the ASP.NET 2.0 terms. The SQL keywords cause an operation to be performed on the data. The ASP.NET 2.0 `New` and `Edit` terms are not true substitutes for `Insert` and `Update`. Instead, they are command button keywords used to cause data-bound controls to transition UI states (e.g., from Read-Only mode to Edit mode). In some cases, for example when you are in Edit mode and click Update, that change in UI state triggers the execution of the appropriate SQL statement.**

ASP.NET 2.0, particularly with VWD, makes it easy to create pages that allow a user to modify values in a database. The ease derives from the capabilities that are built into the data source and data-bound controls.

- **Data source controls have a built-in capability to modify data.** You've already read about some built-in capabilities, such as sending a `SELECT` command to the database. ASP.NET 2.0 data source controls also have three capabilities to modify data: update, insert, and delete.
- **Data source controls have properties to enable the capability to modify data.** The modification capabilities listed in the last point can be turned on or off.
- **Data-bound controls can automatically use capabilities that have been turned on in the data source control.** Smart data-bound controls "know" which capabilities are turned on for their data source control. However, this sensing is only for smart controls: `GridView`, `DetailsView`, and `FormView`.
- **Data-bound controls have properties that enable use of their source control capability.** The modification interface can be turned on or off by enabling smart data-bound controls to display options such as Edit or Delete.

To summarize, data source controls have the ability to modify data, and that ability can be turned on by setting properties of the control. Similarly, data-bound controls have the ability to send modification commands to their `DataSource` control, and that capability can be turned on by setting properties of the data-bound control. These concepts are covered here, in reverse order, starting with the basics of displaying commands and moving up through the preceding list.

Keep in mind that the techniques for this chapter are for the ASP.NET 2.0 smart data-bound controls (`GridView`, `DetailsView`, and `FormView`). Legacy controls from version 1.*x*, such as `DataGrid`, are supported in version 2.0, but they do not have the "smarts" to perform the techniques of this chapter. Also note that these techniques are not available for list controls such as the `DataList` or the `Repeater`. If you want to modify data using version 1.*x* controls, you must use the version 1.*x* techniques of instantiating and using ADO.NET objects directly.

Controls such as labels and textboxes are not inherently "smart" for participation in writing to data stores. However, when they are placed inside of a smart control's template, they become smarter and can participate in the data writing process.

Command Fields

Recall that for a smart control you can open the Smart Tasks panel and begin editing or adding a column or field. One of your choices is to add a column of the `CommandField` type. Your choices are fourfold, as described in the following list and shown in Figure 11-1:

- **Edit, Update, and Cancel:** For updating values in an existing record
- **Delete:** For removing an entire record
- **New, Insert, Cancel:** For adding an entire new record
- **Select:** Not directly part of modifying data; for choosing the active record

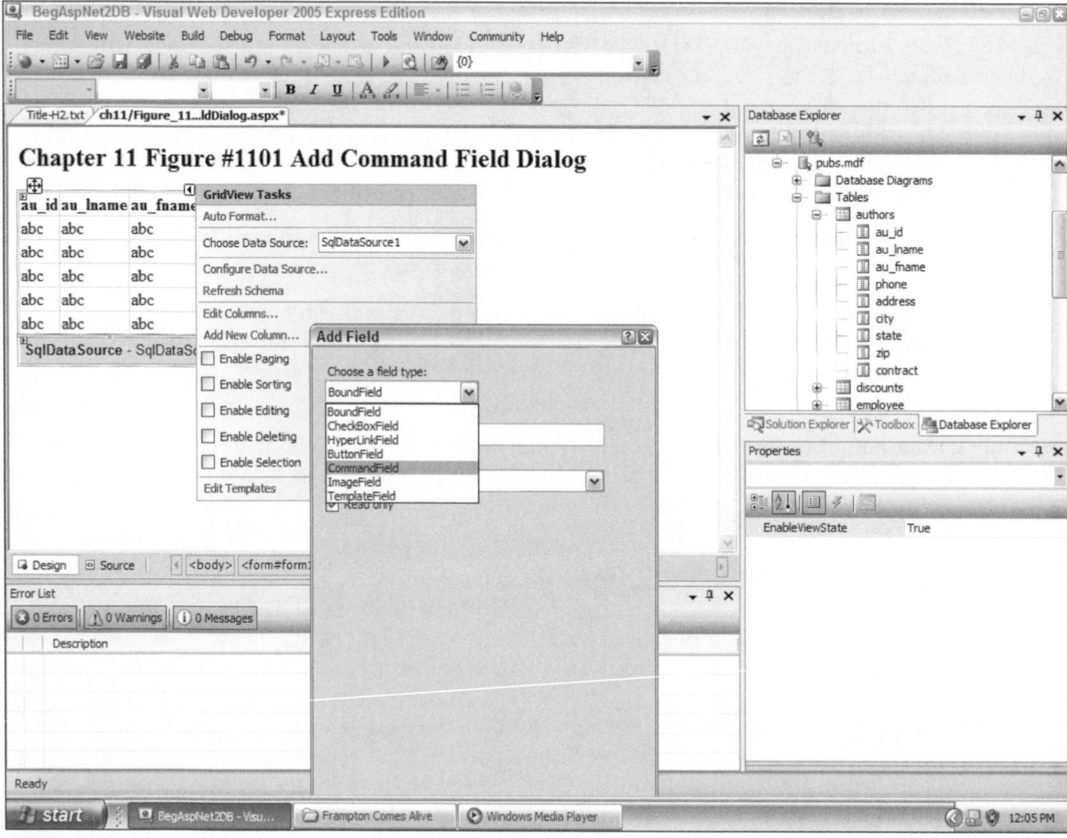

Figure 11-1

From a smart control's Smart Tasks panel, you can click on Add New Columns and select one of the type `CommandField`.

GridView does not have the New/Insert/Cancel command available because the control does not support the insertion of a new record. To insert a new record from a GridView, use a select CommandField in the GridView to switch to a DetailsView or FormView that does support an insert. See Figure 11-2.

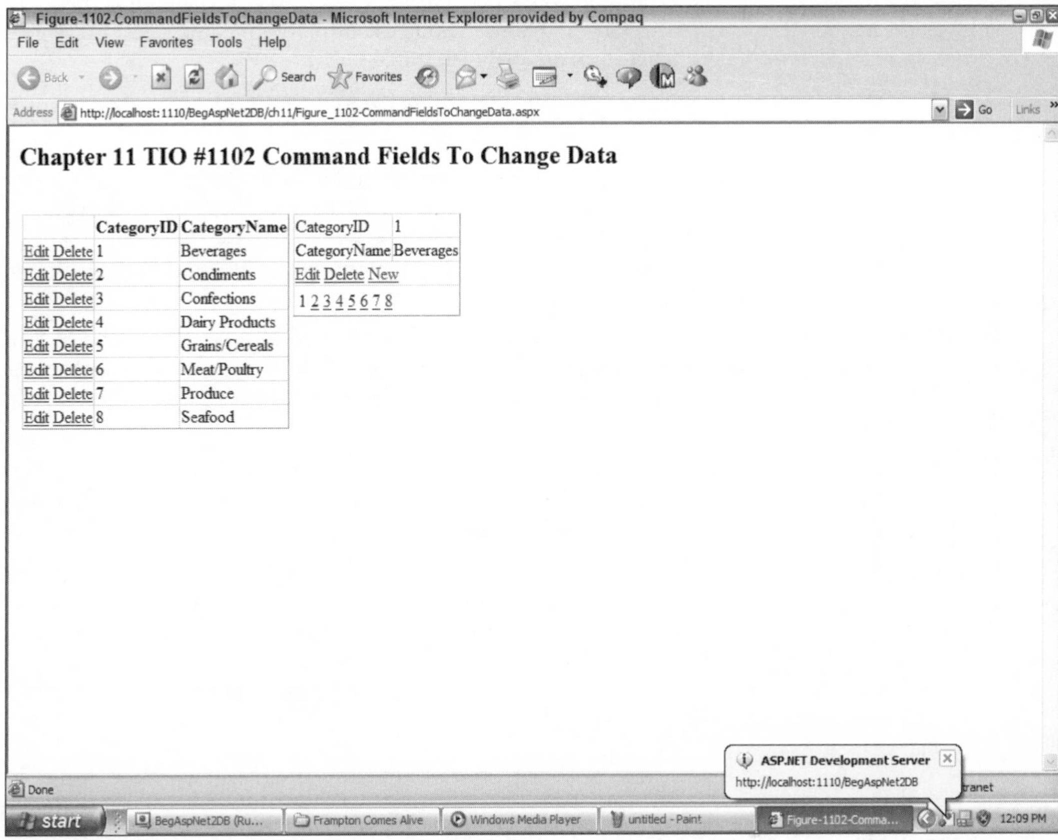

Figure 11-2

The GridView on the left sports two columns that enable the user to change or delete records. The DetailsView on the right does the same in its CommandField, and it allows the creation of new records.

You can give this a try in the first exercise for this chapter.

Try It Out Creating a Command Field

As a review, this first exercise will have you simply add CommandField to a GridView and to a DetailsView. But you will use two different techniques to create the controls so that you can see how VWD works. You will create the GridView in the most automated way — dragging fields from the Database Explorer. Then we will add the DetailsView by hand: first adding a data source control, then adding the data-bound control.

1. If you did not yet make a backup copy of the MDF files to another folder, do so now. Create a new folder named `ch11` and, within it, create a page named `TIO-1101-CommandFields.aspx`.
2. Add a `GridView` to the page as follows. Open the Database Explorer, open `Pubs.mdf`, and then expand the tables. Select the authors' ID, names, and city (use Ctrl+click) and drag them to the page. VWD will create a `GridView` and SqlDataSource control for you automatically. Using the `GridView`'s Smart Tasks panel, click on Enable Editing.
3. Save and test the page. Note that ASP.NET 2.0 has rendered the Edit column and added all appropriate code to make it work.
4. Now, you will add a DetailsView. Move your insertion bar to the bottom of the page and from the Toolbox add a `SqlDataSource` control that reads the same four fields from the Authors table of `Pubs.mdf`. Accept the default name of `SqlDataSource2`. Recall that in this book, connection strings are stored in the `Web.config` file per the second Try It Out in Chapter 3; use the one named `MdfPubs`.
5. Below the nascent data source control, add a `DetailsView` control and set its source control to `SqlDataSource2`. Open its Smart Tasks panel, and click on Edit Fields. In the Available fields list, scroll down to `CommandFields`, expand it, and select Edit, Update, Cancel. Click Add, and close the dialog.
6. Save your work, and test it. If you get an error that a control must be within a form tag, then close the browser and go back to VWD in source view. Select the entire offending tag, move it sot that it is within the `<form>` tags, and try again.
7. With the page open in the browser, try clicking on one of the Edit buttons in the `GridView` and changing a phone number. Complete the change by clicking Update. Now scroll down to the `DetailsView`. Click Edit to change some information, and click Update. This time the change fails. This is because you have not yet configured the data source for editing or inserting. You will learn that soon. Your code should look similar to the following listing:

```
...
<h2>Chapter 11 TIO #1101 Command Fields</h2>
    <form id="form1" runat="server">
    <div>
        <asp:GridView ID="GridView1" runat="server"
                AutoGenerateColumns="False"
                DataKeyNames="au_id"
                DataSourceID="SqlDataSource1"
                EmptyDataText="There are no data records to display.">
            <Columns>
                <asp:BoundField DataField="au_id" HeaderText="au_id"
                    ReadOnly="True" SortExpression="au_id" />
                <asp:BoundField DataField="au_lname" HeaderText="au_lname"
                    SortExpression="au_lname" />
                <asp:BoundField DataField="au_fname" HeaderText="au_fname"
                    SortExpression="au_fname" />
                <asp:BoundField DataField="city" HeaderText="city"
                    SortExpression="city" />
                <asp:CommandField ShowEditButton="True" />
            </Columns>
        </asp:GridView>

        <asp:SqlDataSource ID="SqlDataSource1" runat="server"
```

```
            ConnectionString="<%$ ConnectionStrings:MdfPubs %>"
            DeleteCommand="DELETE FROM [authors] WHERE [au_id] = @au_id"
            InsertCommand="
                INSERT INTO [authors] ([au_id], [au_lname], [au_fname], [city])
                VALUES (@au_id, @au_lname, @au_fname, @city)"
            ProviderName="<%$ ConnectionStrings:MdfPubs.ProviderName %>"
            SelectCommand="SELECT [au_id], [au_lname], [au_fname], [city]
                FROM [authors]"
            UpdateCommand="UPDATE [authors]
                SET [au_lname] = @au_lname, [au_fname] = @au_fname, [city] = @city
                WHERE [au_id] = @au_id">
            <InsertParameters>
                <asp:Parameter Name="au_id" Type="String" />
                <asp:Parameter Name="au_lname" Type="String" />
                <asp:Parameter Name="au_fname" Type="String" />
                <asp:Parameter Name="city" Type="String" />
            </InsertParameters>
            <UpdateParameters>
                <asp:Parameter Name="au_lname" Type="String" />
                <asp:Parameter Name="au_fname" Type="String" />
                <asp:Parameter Name="city" Type="String" />
                <asp:Parameter Name="au_id" Type="String" />
            </UpdateParameters>
            <DeleteParameters>
                <asp:Parameter Name="au_id" Type="String" />
            </DeleteParameters>
        </asp:SqlDataSource><br />

        <asp:SqlDataSource ID="SqlDataSource2" runat="server"
            ConnectionString="<%$ ConnectionStrings:MdfPubs %>"
            SelectCommand="SELECT [au_id], [au_lname], [au_fname], [city]
                FROM [authors]"></asp:SqlDataSource>

    <asp:DetailsView ID="DetailsView1" runat="server"
        AutoGenerateRows="False"
        DataKeyNames="au_id"
        DataSourceID="SqlDataSource2"
        Height="50px" Width="125px">
        <Fields>
            <asp:BoundField DataField="au_id" HeaderText="au_id"
                ReadOnly="True" SortExpression="au_id" />
            <asp:BoundField DataField="au_lname" HeaderText="au_lname"
                SortExpression="au_lname" />
            <asp:BoundField DataField="au_fname" HeaderText="au_fname"
                SortExpression="au_fname" />
            <asp:BoundField DataField="city" HeaderText="city"
                SortExpression="city" />
            <asp:CommandField ShowEditButton="True" />
        </Fields>
    </asp:DetailsView>
</div></form></body></html>
```

8. Save the page.

How It Works

In this exercise, you reviewed the design tools of VWD you can use to add a command to a `DetailsView`.

When you dragged fields from a database and let VWD do all the construction, you got a `GridView` control and data source control that had editing enabled. But when you created your own data source control and `DetailsView`, the capability to edit was not turned on, by default. Fear not; we will work on that next.

Simple Update

Recall the four concepts for data modification in ASP.NET 2.0:

- Many data source controls have a built-in capability to modify data.
- Data source controls have properties to enable the capability to modify data.
- Data-bound controls can automatically use capabilities that have been enabled in the data source control.
- Data-bound controls have properties that enable use of their source control capability.

You tested the last concept in the preceding exercise. The second-to-last concept happens automatically. Now, you want to enable the properties of the data source control so that you can modify data. The property to enable updating on the `SqlDataSource` control is the `UpdateCommand` (`UpdateQuery` in the property grid of Visual Web Developer), and its argument is the SQL statement to perform the update. This is very similar to the data source control's read capability that is enabled by having a SQL `SELECT` statement in the `SelectCommand` property. When creating a data source control, VWD offers the option (through the Advanced button) to generate this statement. The option will also generate statements to `INSERT` new records and `DELETE` entire records.

As a note for readers not familiar with SQL, the `UPDATE` statement has three clauses: an `UPDATE MyTable` clause, then a `SET` clause, which names the new values, and, finally, a `WHERE` clause that identifies which record to change. A typical statement follows.

```
UPDATE MyTable
SET
 Phone = 5551234,
 Name = 'My New Name'
WHERE Field_PrimaryKey = 'MyID'
```

Now, the trick is how to pass the new values entered by the user into this sort of syntax. Behind the scenes, ASP.NET uses parameters stored as a collection of values. The collection is automatically created and filled with the values the user types into the textboxes. The SQL `UPDATE` statement then reads those values from the parameters collection. You can see in the following statement how you refer to values in the parameter collection with an `@` preceding their field name.

```
UPDATE MyTable
SET
 Field1 = @Phone,
```

```
 Field2 = @Name
WHERE Field_PrimaryKey = @ID
```

Try It Out Enabling Data Source Update

In this exercise, you will modify the code you created in the preceding exercise so that SqlDataSource2 supports editing for the DetailsView control.

1. In the ch11 folder, open TIO-1101-CommandFields.aspx and save as TIO-1102-UpdasteSimple.aspx. Revise the <title> and <h2> content.
2. Open the Smart Tasks panel for SqlDataSource2. Click Configure Data Source, and then click Next to go to the dialog box to configure the Select statement. You will observe the field selections you made in the last exercise.
3. Click on Advanced, and then turn on the option for Generate INSERT, UPDATE and DELETE statements. You can leave optimistic concurrency off for now. Click OK, Next, and Finish to close the dialog boxes. When prompted, agree to refresh the fields for DetailsView.
4. Now select the DetailsView, and open its Smart Tasks panel to see that there are new options. Click Enable Editing. At this point, you hit a bug as the DetailsView fields disappear. Fear not; read on for a simple solution.
5. Open the Smart Tasks panel of the DetailsView, and set Choose Data Source = (none). Accept the offer to refresh DetailsView1, and clear all row fields. Open the Smart Tasks panel again, and set the Choose Data Source drop-down to SqlDataSource2. Enable Editing.
6. Save and test the page. The DetailsView can now perform edits.

How It Works

Recall that in the first exercise you added a GridView by dragging fields from the database. VWD gave you, by default, the full-service package with editing enabled. But when you built the DetailsView, you started by rolling your own data source control and adding the DetailsView by hand. In that scenario, VWD did not enable writing of data, by default.

In this exercise, you see how to use a VWD feature to activate the data source control the capability to edit. You merely check the choice in the dialog box and VWD builds the code. Note when you examine the code that VWD creates both SQL statements and sets of parameters for the UPDATE statement.

Last, you look at how the DataKeys work. In this exercise, you enabled updating in the data source control. Turning on that capability is simply a matter of adding an UpdateCommand. The SQL UPDATE statement, in its simplest form, specifies what value from the parameters collection to send to the database. The parameters collection is created automatically by the SqlDataSource control, using the values given to it by the GridView.

As you will see in the next few paragraphs, ASP.NET 2.0 uses *Dictionaries*. These are data structures that hold index/value pairs, where the index can be any object but is often a string. They are like an array, but you can use a string for look-up instead of an integer, and the members are not ordered. In this sense, they are like a paper dictionary: You find a word and you read out a value (definition) associated with the word you looked up.

Note that in order for the parameter values passed by the `GridView` to match up with the names of the parameters in the UPDATE statement, a naming convention is used. For parameters that correspond to values typed by the user into the `GridView` Edit `mode TextBoxes`, the parameter names in the UPDATE statement match the names of the fields in the `SELECT` command. The parameter name for the primary key matched in the `WHERE` clause is an exception to this rule. If you have turned on the Optimistic Concurrency option in the Data Source Wizard, then the parameter is given an `original` prefix. The reason is that the `GridView` passes fields defined in `DataKeyNames` as a separate "keys" dictionary to the data source control, and the `SqlDataSource` automatically renames these special values with the `original_` prefix. This leading text is defined by the `SqlDataSource OldValuesParameterFormatString` property, which is set to `original_{0}` by default. As you will see in the next Try It Out, this prefix is required in order to differentiate the original key value to match in the `WHERE` clause from the new value of the key field when you want to support updating the primary key.

DataKeyNames and Updates

`DataKeyNames` solves a specific set of problems that can occur behind the scenes when a page supports updates. In an update, you generally use a WHERE clause that equals the primary key in the table. In the preceding cases, you used the `au_id` field as the primary key. Frequently, the primary key is set by the database; for example, an exclusive serial number is created for each author. The database schema does not permit external values to be set for the field, in which case you make the key field read-only, as you saw in the previous example. But if the primary key is updateable, you face a potential problem. A user could change the primary key value in an update in a data-bound control. If you used the same parameter name for both the new value and the value to match in the `WHERE` clause, then when the `UpdateCommand` is executed, the `WHERE` would no longer match the original value of the primary key in the table. It would try to match the original value in the SQL statement's `WHERE` clause with the new value changed by the user in the `GridView`'s `TextBox` for the updatable primary key.

Data-bound and data source controls handle this problem by saving and differentiating both the new values and old (original) values for parameters. When the data-bound control (in this case, `GridView`) applies the update operation of its associated data source, it takes the original value of the primary key specified by `DataKeyNames` and stores it in a "keys" dictionary. It also creates and fills a "values" dictionary that contains the new values entered by the user in the `GridView` input `TextBoxes`. When the update operation of the data source is invoked, `GridView` passes both of these dictionaries to the data source. The data source then prepends each parameter name in the keys dictionary with a special prefix used to differentiate these original values from the new values. The prefix is defined by a property of the `SqlDataSource` called `OldValuesParameterFormatString`, set to `{0}` by default. However, if you turned on Optimistic Concurrency in the Data Source Wizard, it will be set to `original_{0}` by default. Like other format strings we've examined in this text, the `{0}` placeholder is replaced by the field name at runtime. For example, if the field name is `au_id`, the parameter name is formatted to become `original_au_id`. The `SqlDataSource` then applies the newly formatted parameters to the `UpdateCommand` before executing the statement. So now, even if the primary key has been changed, the update is still able to create a `WHERE` clause that can find the correct record to apply the update to in the table.

Sometimes, the primary key (and thus the `WHERE` clause) uses more than one field (a multikey primary key). If you are matching all of these fields in the `WHERE` clause, they should all be included in the `DataKeyNames` property as a comma-separated list, such as `primary_field1, primary_field2, primary_field3`.

Before you try using DataKeyNames, here are two advanced ideas to keep in mind:

- There is a complication when using Access as a database. The OLEDB provider for Access uses parameters by the *order* in which they were entered into the parameters collection, not as requested by parameter *name*. This makes the storing of parameters trickier because you have to be sure that the new value of a primary key is read from the parameters collection into the SET clause before the old value is read out in the WHERE clause. ASP.NET 2.0 arranges the parameter values so that new values are applied before key (original) values, so that parameters are applied in the order they most likely appear in the UPDATE statement.
- We haven't discussed optimistic concurrency yet, but essentially this means you are matching all the original values of the row, not just the primary key values. Data sources support this option by allowing you to include all original values as parameters of the WHERE clause, where each parameter is formatted using the original_ prefix, just as is done for keys. If you are using optimistic concurrency, you are attempting to ensure that no one else will be changing a value in the same record at the same time. You can check whether that was the case by getting an argument back from the database for the number of rows that were actually affected. Hopefully the value is 1; if it is 0 (zero), your update was not applied. You can find that value in the event arguments for the postevent handlers as the value of the AffectedRows property (see Chapter 16). You can check for AffectedRows =0 and responds with a failure notice to the user (or retries the update).

Keeping in mind these theoretical precepts of DataKeyNames, we can try an exercise.

Try It Out Utilizing DataKeyNames

In this exercise, you will create a new, simple page and observe how ASP.NET uses the DataKey property. Then you will add some code to show what is happening behind the scenes. We discuss writing code for data applications in Chapter 17, so the second part is optional.

1. In the Ch11 folder, create a page named TIO-1103-DataKeys-1.aspx. From the Database Explorer, drag the Pub Database's author ID and name fields to the page. Enable editing and paging. Set the GridView's PageSize property to 5.
2. Save your work, and test the editing feature in your browser.
3. Return to VWD, and switch to source view. Your page should appear as follows; take a closer look at the shaded lines:

```
...
<h2>Chapter 11 TIO #1103 Data Keys - 1</h2>
    <form id="form1" runat="server">
    <div>
        <asp:GridView ID="GridView1" runat="server"
            AutoGenerateColumns="False"
            DataKeyNames="au_id"
            DataSourceID="SqlDataSource1"
            EmptyDataText="There are no data records to display.">
            <Columns>
                <asp:CommandField ShowEditButton="True" />
                <asp:BoundField DataField="au_id" HeaderText="au_id"
                    ReadOnly="True" SortExpression="au_id" />
                <asp:BoundField DataField="au_lname" HeaderText="au_lname"
```

```
                    SortExpression="au_lname" />
                <asp:BoundField DataField="au_fname" HeaderText="au_fname"
                    SortExpression="au_fname" />
            </Columns>
        </asp:GridView>
        <asp:SqlDataSource ID="SqlDataSource1" runat="server"
            ConnectionString="<%$ ConnectionStrings:MdfPubs %>"
            ProviderName="<%$ ConnectionStrings:MdfPubs.ProviderName %>"
            DeleteCommand=...
            InsertCommand=...
            SelectCommand= ...
            UpdateCommand=
               "UPDATE [authors]
               SET [au_lname] = @au_lname, [au_fname] = @au_fname
                WHERE [au_id] = @au_id">
            <InsertParameters> ... </InsertParameters>
            <UpdateParameters>
                <asp:Parameter Name="au_lname" Type="String" />
                <asp:Parameter Name="au_fname" Type="String" />
                <asp:Parameter Name="au_id" Type="String" />
            </UpdateParameters>
            <DeleteParameters> ... </DeleteParameters>
        </asp:SqlDataSource>
</div></form></body></html>
```

4. Now, we will embellish the page by displaying the contents of the dictionaries that hold the original and new values. This requires some coding, so consider it optional at this point in the book.

5. Return to VWD and switch to source view. Save the document (and change the title and H2 tags) as version `TIO-1103-DataKeys-2VB`. We will work here in Visual Basic and show the C# code below.

6. In Source view, expand the drop-down list of objects at the top left of the code panel and click on `GridView1`. At the top right, drop down the events list and click on `RowUpdating`. VWD will build the framework for a `Protected Sub` procedure.

7. Enter the following lines of code; be very careful about the syntax. Follow that by typing the `Protected Sub` named `EnumerateDictionary`.

VB

```
<%@ Page Language="VB" %>
...
<script runat="server">
   Protected Sub GridView1_RowUpdating(ByVal sender As Object, ByVal e As
System.Web.UI.WebControls.GridViewUpdateEventArgs)
        Response.Write("<br/>Original Values read from the database and saved in
the dictionary:<br />")
        EnumerateDictionary(e.OldValues)

        Response.Write("<br/>New Values entered by user and saved in the
dictionary:<br />")
        EnumerateDictionary(e.NewValues)

        Response.Write("<br/>List of DataKeys:<br />")
        EnumerateDictionary(e.Keys)
```

```
    End Sub

    Protected Sub EnumerateDictionary(ByVal dictionary As
System.Collections.Specialized.IOrderedDictionary)
        Dim entry As DictionaryEntry
        For Each entry In dictionary
            Response.Write("<b/>" & Server.HtmlEncode(entry.Key) & "</b>=")
            Response.Write(Server.HtmlEncode(entry.Value))
            Response.Write(" type= " &
Server.HtmlEncode(entry.Value.GetType().Name) & "<br />")
        Next
    End Sub

</script>
...
<h2>Chapter 11 TIO #1103 Data Keys - version 2 VB</h2>
    <form id="form1" runat="server">
    <div>
        <asp:GridView ID="GridView1" runat="server"
    ...
            OnRowUpdating="GridView1_RowUpdating"
>
            <Columns>...
...
```

C#

```
<%@ Page Language="C#" %>
...
<script runat="server">

    void GridView1_RowUpdating(Object sender,
System.Web.UI.WebControls.GridViewUpdateEventArgs e)
    {
        Response.Write("<br/>Original values read from the database and stored in
the dictionary:<br />");
            EnumerateDictionary(e.OldValues);
        Response.Write("<br/>New values entered by the user and stored in the
dictionary:<br />");
            EnumerateDictionary(e.NewValues);
        Response.Write("<br/>List of DataKeys:<br />");
            EnumerateDictionary(e.Keys);
        }

    void EnumerateDictionary(System.Collections.Specialized.IOrderedDictionary
dictionary)
    {
        foreach (DictionaryEntry entry in dictionary)
        {
            Response.Write(" <b>" + Server.HtmlEncode(entry.Key.ToString()) +
"</b>=");
            Response.Write(Server.HtmlEncode(entry.Value.ToString()));
            Response.Write(" (" + Server.HtmlEncode(entry.Value.GetType().Name) +
")<br />");
        }
    }
```

```
</script>
...
<title>TIO-1103-DataKeys-2CS.aspx</title>
...
        <asp:GridView ID="GridView1" runat="server"
...
            OnRowUpdating="GridView1_RowUpdating">
            <Columns>...
```

8. Save your work. Run the page, and observe the additional information when performing an update.

How It Works

This exercise draws your attention to how the `DataKeys` are created and used. Recall that the dilemma arises from the SQL statement needing two different values for the primary key field in case the primary key field is updatable. ASP.NET 2.0 will use the *original* in the `WHERE` clause to find the correct record to change. The *new* value will be used in the `SET` clause to instruct the database of the new value to save.

The internal behavior of ASP.NET 2.0 data-bound controls differentiates and saves the old and new values, in this case for `au_id`. The multiple values are held in the `DataKeys` dictionary with an entry for each field listed in `DataKeyNames`. ASP.NET 2.0 then hands the appropriate values to ADO.NET in the `WHERE` and `SET` clauses.

The preceding statement will actually be filled with values from the parameters collection behind the scenes, as follows (assuming that you also changed Johnson's `au_id` to `999-88-7777`):

```
UpdateCommand="
    UPDATE [authors]
    SET
        [au_id] = 999-88-7777
    WHERE [au_id] = 172-32-1176"
```

We will discuss code and event handling in Chapter 17. For now, here is what happens in version 2 of your page. Start with the `GridView` control, as follows. When the `GridView` receives the `Update` command, it runs a procedure called `GridView1_RowUpdating` before it actually carries out the `Update`.

```
<asp:GridView ...  OnRowUpdating="GridView1_RowUpdating" ... >
```

Now, ASP.NET runs the code in the procedure called `GridView1_RowUpdating`. This code has three similar parts, each of which puts a heading onto the page and then a series of values. The line shaded below adds the first heading.

```
    void GridView1_RowUpdating(Object sender,
System.Web.UI.WebControls.GridViewUpdateEventArgs e)
    {
        Response.Write("<br/>Original values read from the database and stored in
the dictionary:<br />");
```

Then the line below runs another procedure (called `EnumerateDictionary`), and it sends one piece of information (an argument) about how to do the job: `OldValues`.

```
            EnumerateDictionary(e.OldValues);
```

So, ASP.NET 2.0 now runs the procedure called `EnumerateDictionary`. The first task is to take the argument `OldValues` and open that dictionary. Then the procedure goes through each item stored in the dictionary (`foreach` command) and writes three pieces of information to the page: the name of the dictionary entry, the value of the entry, and the data type of the entry.

```
    void EnumerateDictionary(System.Collections.Specialized.IOrderedDictionary
dictionary)
    {
        foreach (DictionaryEntry entry in dictionary)
        {
            Response.Write(" <b>" + Server.HtmlEncode(entry.Key) + "</b>=");
            Response.Write(Server.HtmlEncode(entry.Value));
            Response.Write(" (" + Server.HtmlEncode(entry.Value.GetType().Name) +
")<br />");
        }
    }
```

Once `EnumerateDictionary` is finished, program flow returns to the procedure named `GridView1_RowUpdating`, and it uses the following lines to repeat the above steps, but this time with the argument `NewValues`.

```
        Response.Write("<br/>New Values entered by user and saved in the
dictionary:<br />");
        EnumerateDictionary(e.NewValues);
```

Now we can look at an update using a `DetailsView` instead of a `GridView`.

Update in a DetailsView

The theory and practice remain the same when you switch from the `GridView` to the `DetailsView` or `FormView`. In the `DetailsView`, the command will be called a *field* instead of a *column*. The appearance of the control will be similar, with data values shown as labels in `ReadOnlyMode` and as textboxes in Edit mode, as shown in Figure 11-3.

The `DetailsView` control on the left of Figure 11-3 is in `ReadOnlyMode` where values are rendered in labels. If the user clicks on the Edit link, the `DetailsView` will appear as on the right, in Edit mode, where values are displayed in textboxes.

In many cases, you will have one or more fields that you do not want the user to be able to change. You can set these to be read-only using the property in the `BoundField`. However, this can only be set when your fields are explicitly stated; there is no way to make a field(s) read-only when using `AutoGenerateFields=true`. However, key fields are read only when `AutoGenerateColumns` is true. Sometimes people ask if they can use the `Direction` property of a `Parameter` object of the data source. The answer is no; that property only bears on how the data source passes parameters to the command.

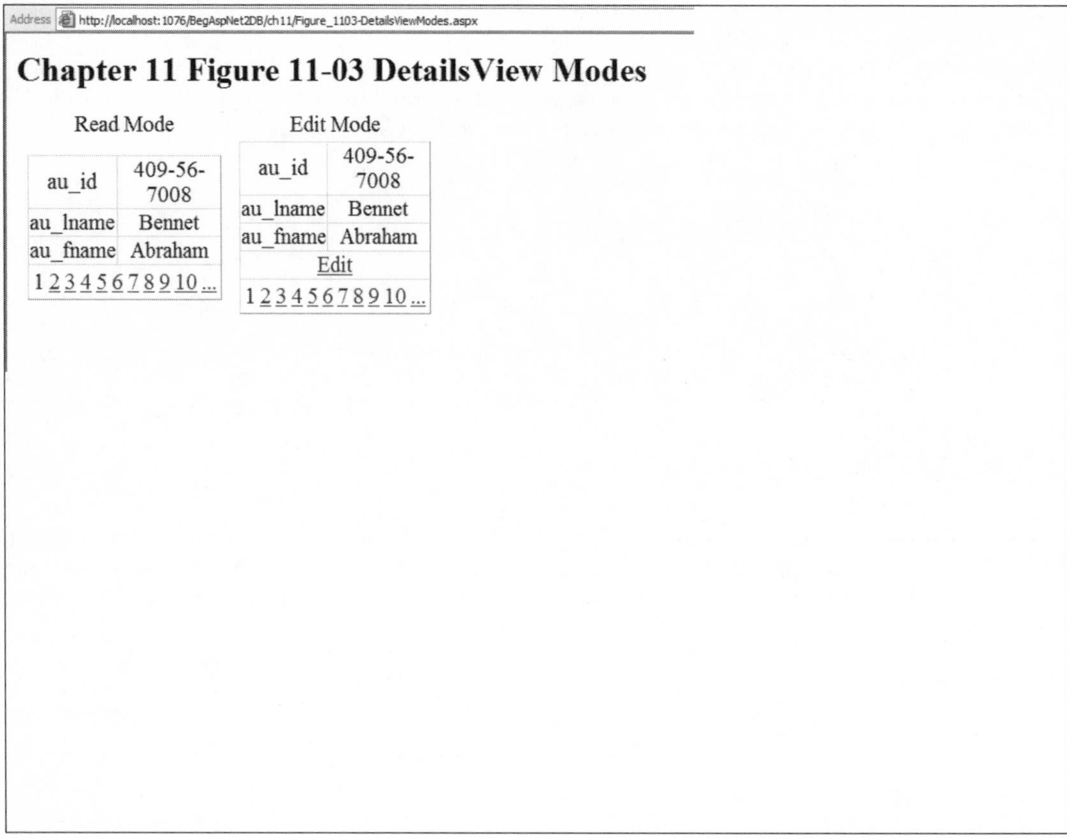

Figure 11-3

Try It Out Updating Using DetailsView

In this exercise, you will add editing (with ability to change the `ID` field) to a `DetailsView` control.

1. In the `Ch11` folder, create a new file named `TIO-1104-UpdateDetailsView.aspx`. Add a `DetailsView` control, and choose a new data source that provides from `Pubs.mdf` the author's ID and names. In the Configure Select Statement dialog box, click on Advanced and turn on Autogenerate INSERT....

2. Select the `DetailsView` control and open its Smart Tasks panel. Refresh the schema and then enable paging and editing. The page is partially shown here:

```
...
<h2>Chapter 11 TIO #1104 Update Details View</h2>
    <form id="form1" runat="server">
    <div><asp:DetailsView ID="DetailsView1" runat="server"
            DataSourceID="SqlDataSource1"
            Height="50px" Width="180px"
            AllowPaging="True" >
```

```
            <Fields>
                <asp:CommandField ShowEditButton="True" />
            </Fields>
        </asp:DetailsView>
        <asp:SqlDataSource ID="SqlDataSource1" runat="server"
            ConnectionString="<%$ ConnectionStrings:MdfPubs %>"
            DeleteCommand="DELETE FROM [authors] WHERE [au_id] = @au_id"
            InsertCommand="INSERT INTO [authors] ([au_id], [au_lname], [au_fname])
                VALUES (@au_id, @au_lname, @au_fname)"
            SelectCommand="SELECT [au_id], [au_lname], [au_fname]
                FROM [authors]"
            UpdateCommand="UPDATE [authors]
                SET [au_lname] = @au_lname, [au_fname] = @au_fname
                WHERE [au_id] = @au_id">
            <DeleteParameters>
                <asp:Parameter Name="au_id" Type="String" />
            </DeleteParameters>
            <UpdateParameters>
                <asp:Parameter Name="au_lname" Type="String" />
                <asp:Parameter Name="au_fname" Type="String" />
                <asp:Parameter Name="au_id" Type="String" />
            </UpdateParameters>
            <InsertParameters>
                <asp:Parameter Name="au_id" Type="String" />
                <asp:Parameter Name="au_lname" Type="String" />
                <asp:Parameter Name="au_fname" Type="String" />
            </InsertParameters>
        </asp:SqlDataSource>
    </div></form></body></html>
```

3. Save your work, and then view it in the browser. You should have no problems changing names, but notice that the ID numbers are read-only.

How It Works

Enabling the update capability in a data-bound control that displays one record at a time (`DetailsView` or `FormView`) is very similar to doing so for the controls that show many records (e.g., `GridView`). If you check the Autogenerate INSERT... option when configuring the data source control, VWD will automatically build the required tags. Then in the data-bound control, you only have to enable the Edit feature.

Take a look at the code listing in the preceding Try It Out. Observe three sections that make updating possible. Starting from the bottom (both logically and in the listing), the data source control has an `UpdateCommand` statement with a value that is a standard SQL `UPDATE` statement. The data source control also has a set of `Update` parameters that feed the user-entered values into the `UpdateCommand`. Moving on to the `DetailsView`, you can see that one of the fields is a `CommandField` set to show the Edit button.

Although we have used the parameters several times to date, it is now time for a closer look.

Parameters Collections

The parameters collections have been mentioned several times in this chapter. You may have been wondering why ASP.NET 2.0 creates an entire structure just to pass values from one control to another. This architecture allows you, the designer, more control over how those values are passed. Four major areas are available for manipulation, although the exact capabilities will depend on the provider.

- **Parameters can be typecast.** This means that although incoming data may appear to be of one type (perhaps the string `111`), they can be forced into another type (for example, the integer `111`). When you use VWD's parameter builder, this is done automatically.
- **Parameters can be set to be read-only or write-only.** The `Direction` property offers choices for `Input` (write-only), `Output` (read-only), or `InputOutput` (read and write). If you attempt to update a field whose parameter is set to `Output`, there will be no updating of that field.
- **Parameters can be given a default value.** This chapter focuses on updating, and the default value is generally left blank so that the old value stands. In the next chapter, you will appreciate a default value when you learn to insert new records
- **Parameters reduce exposure to SQL injection attacks**. Because of this, it is best practice to always pass user input through parameters rather than a build a raw concatenation into a SQL statement.

VWD automatically creates the hierarchy of parameter objects and their properties when you drag fields from the Data Explorer onto the page. A collection is created for each of the data source control's commands. If you drag a `DataSource` control to the page, you can walk through the Configure Wizard. After selecting the data connection, you have the opportunity to specify the columns. Click Advanced Options, and check Generate Insert, Update, and Delete Statements. When you finish this wizard, VWD will not only build the commands but also create collections of parameters to feed the appropriate values into the corresponding command.

If you are working in a non-VWD editor or need to make changes in Source view, you will work directly with the hierarchy. Note that not all collections must be present and that the parameters collections are nested within the data source control, not the data-bound control. Note also that the properties (typing, direction, and default) are described within each parameter.

```
<body><form id="form1" runat="server">
...
<asp:SqlDataSource ...
 SelectCommand="SELECT * FROM [authors]"
 DeleteCommand="DELETE ... "
 UpdateCommand="UPDATE ... "
 <SelectParameters>
          <asp:Parameter Type="String" Name="Field_ID" />
 </SelectParameters>
 <DeleteParameters>
          <asp:Parameter Type="String" Name="Field_ID" />
 </DeleteParameters>
 <UpdateParameters>
          <asp:Parameter Type="String" Name="Field_ID" />
          <asp:Parameter Name="Field1"
               Type="Int32"
               DefaultValue="999"
               Direction="Output"/>
```

```
            <asp:Parameter Name="Field2"
                 Type="DateTime"
                 DefaultValue="1/1/2005"
                 Direction="InputOutput"/>
    </UpdateParameters>
   </asp:SqlDataSource>
   </div></form>
   ...
```

We won't always have a value available when we change a record. The next section covers the handling of nulls.

Handle Nulls in Updates

When users enter Edit mode, they are expected to enter or revise a value for each editable field. What happens if they leave a field blank? Conversely, the database may have a `NULL` and the data-bound control shows an empty textbox for editing. You work with `NULLs` in several ways when modifying data.

A database may not have a value for a given field of a given record. You can display literal text as an alternative to empty space. This property is set for the `BoundField` as the `NullDisplayText`. When the user modifies data, if the `NullDisplayText` is left as is, ASP.NET will convert it back to a `NULL` value when the update is performed.

When the user updates a record but leaves a `TextBox` empty, you can substitute a default value. This property is set in the default value of the parameter object in the parameters collection. This property has no effect on reading, but if a user does not enter a value in a `TextBox` when updating, ASP.NET will automatically substitute the default value.

Confusion arises when a user enters an empty string into a textbox because an empty sting (in .NET 2.0 designated as `String.Empty`) is not the same as null to a database. You need to be able to tell the difference and use the intended value. Within each parameter object, there is a property to change empty strings to true `NULLs` for storage in the database.

When you consider the role of `BoundField.NullDisplayText` and `Parameter.DefaultValue`, you can envision some overlap and potential confusion. Keep in mind that the `NullDisplayText` determines how a null value will be displayed, whereas `DefaultValue` affects how data is saved. When you start with a `NULL` value that is displayed with a `NullDisplayText` alternate text and then save, you may wonder what is actually saved: a `NULL` or the display text? If the `BoundField` value is `NullDisplayText`, and `NullDisplayText` is not `String.Empty`, then the value passed back is `NULL`. If you have a `Default Value` set and perform an `Update`, the field will get the default value. A `BoundField` affects what the `GridView` passes to the data source. The properties of the parameter affect how the data source interprets that data.

Conversely, the `DefaultValue` does not affect the display in the data-bound control. If your parameter has a `DefaultValue` set, you will not see the default value in the field with a `NULL` when in Edit mode. You will see a blank (if there was a `NullDisplayText` in `ReadOnlyMode` that disappears in Edit mode). The `Default` value only comes into play when the `Update` is performed. So, your user can be surprised if she blanks out a value with the intention of creating a `NULL` and then updates. The `DefaultValue` will be stored, not the `NULL` that the user may be expecting. There is no intrinsic indication of this behavior to the user. So, it is incumbent on the page designer to make the business rule clear with a ToolTip or adjacent text.

Try It Out — Handling Nulls

In this exercise, you will modify a page to handle the absence of data.

1. In the ch11 folder, create a new page named TIO-1105-NullHandling-1.aspx.
2. Create a NULL in the database by deleting the city for the first author, Johnson White, as follows. In the VWD Database Explorer, expand the Pubs.mdf file and expand its tables. Right-click on the Authors table, and select Show Table Data. Click on the city value for Johnson White (Menlo Park), and delete the entire city name. Press Enter. Note that his city field is now empty. Close the Table Data window.
3. Back in VWD Design, view the TIO 1105-HandlingNulls-1.aspx page, and add a DetailsView control from the Toolbox that displays the ID, names, and cities of authors from the Pubs.mdf file. While setting up the data source statements, click on Advanced and uncheck the Generate Insert... check box.

   Once the DetailsView and its data source are created, open the DetailsView's Smart Tasks panel and click on Enable Editing. Click on Edit Fields and double-check that Auto-generate Fields is unchecked. In the Selected Fields list, select city, and in the BoundField properties box set NullDisplayText to No city available.
4. Save and view the page in the browser to see that the city is now unknown.
5. Using the VWD Database Explorer, reopen the table data display as in Step 2 and add a city for Johnson White (the original was Menlo Park).
6. Save your work, and then open the page in the browser to see the NullDisplayText replaced by a value.
7. Now, you will add a Default value and try updating the record with a NULL for city. Save the page as TIO 1105-HandlingNulls-2.aspx, and update the contents of the <title> and <h2> tags. Switch to source view, find the SqlDataSource control and within it find the gray line below. Be careful, because a similar line will be within the <InsertParameters tag>.

```
<asp:SqlDataSource ID="SqlDataSource1" runat="server"
...
          <UpdateParameters>
               <asp:Parameter Name="au_lname" Type="String" />
               <asp:Parameter Name="au_fname" Type="String" />
               <asp:Parameter Name="city" Type="String"  />
               <asp:Parameter Name="au_id" Type="String" />
           </UpdateParameters>
           <InsertParameters>
               <asp:Parameter Name="au_id" Type="String" />
               <asp:Parameter Name="au_lname" Type="String" />
               <asp:Parameter Name="au_fname" Type="String" />
               <asp:Parameter Name="city" Type="String" />
           </InsertParameters>
...
        </asp:SqlDataSource>
```

8. Locate your insertion bar anywhere within the <asp:Parameter Name="city"> tag and turn your attention to the Properties window. Within a second or two, the object drop-down list at the top of the Properties window will change to "city <asp:Parameter>". Find the

`DefaultValue` property and set it to "Venice" or another city of your choice. Press Enter. Your code should look like the following:

```
<asp:Parameter Name="city" Type="String" DefaultValue="Venice"  />
```

9. Save your work, and open the page in your browser.

10. Edit the Johnson White record. Note that the `NullDisplayText` disappears and a blank displays for the `NULL`. Leave the city blank and click Update. Observe that because the record was updated with a `NULL` for city, "Venice" was put in. The final code follows:

```
...
<h2>Chapter 11 TIO #1105 Null Handling ver 2</h2>
    <form id="form1" runat="server">
    <div>
        <asp:DetailsView ID="DetailsView1" runat="server"
            AutoGenerateRows="False"
            DataKeyNames="au_id"
            DataSourceID="SqlDataSource1"
            Height="50px" Width="125px">
            <Fields>
                <asp:BoundField DataField="au_id" HeaderText="au_id"
                    ReadOnly="True" SortExpression="au_id" />
                <asp:BoundField DataField="au_lname" HeaderText="au_lname"
                    SortExpression="au_lname" />
                <asp:BoundField DataField="au_fname" HeaderText="au_fname"
                    SortExpression="au_fname" />
                <asp:BoundField DataField="city" HeaderText="city"
                    NullDisplayText="No city available"
                    SortExpression="city" />
                <asp:CommandField ShowEditButton="True" />
            </Fields>
        </asp:DetailsView>
        <asp:SqlDataSource ID="SqlDataSource1" runat="server"
            ConnectionString="<%$ ConnectionStrings:MdfPubs %>"
            DeleteCommand= ...
            InsertCommand=...
            SelectCommand="SELECT [au_id], [au_lname], [au_fname], [city]
                FROM [authors]"
            UpdateCommand="UPDATE [authors]
                SET [au_lname] = @au_lname, [au_fname] = @au_fname, [city] = @city
                WHERE [au_id] = @au_id">
            <DeleteParameters> ... </DeleteParameters>
            <UpdateParameters>
                <asp:Parameter Name="au_lname" Type="String" />
                <asp:Parameter Name="au_fname" Type="String" />
                <asp:Parameter Name="city" Type="String" DefaultValue="Venice" />
                <asp:Parameter Name="au_id" Type="String" />
            </UpdateParameters>
            <InsertParameters> ... </InsertParameters>
        </asp:SqlDataSource>
</div></form></body></html>
```

11. Close the browser, and save your file.

How It Works

This exercise demonstrates two concepts. First, it shows that you can display an alternate text instead of a blank space when the database offers up a NULL value as established in the following:

```
<asp:DetailsView ID="DetailsView1" runat="server"
...
<Fields>
        <asp:BoundField DataField="city" HeaderText="city"
             NullDisplayText="No city available"
                SortExpression="city" />
```

The second step creates a default value for when an update occurs, but there is no value in the textbox while in Edit mode.

```
<asp:SqlDataSource ...>
 <UpdateParameters>
        <asp:Parameter Type="String" Name="city"
               DefaultValue="Venice" />
```

Note the difference in location in the source code of these two properties. `NullDisplayText` is located on the `BoundField` class, whereas `DefaultValue` is a property of the parameter in the data source control.

Having covered changing existing records, we will finish with deleting entire records.

Delete to Remove Entire Records

The capability to delete an entire record is similar in practice to the capability of updating a record. The main difference arises from a consideration of how the delete affects the rest of the database.

> **Recall from the introduction to this chapter that in SQL, *delete* means to remove an entire record. If you want to delete just one value from a record (but keep the remainder of the record), use Update (Edit) to change the one field to a `NULL`.**

To enable deletion using the data-bound control, you must first enable the deleting capacity of the data source and then the rendering of the data-bound control. You enable deletions in the data source control by specifying a `DeleteCommand`, which is a proper SQL `DELETE` statement. This command can be built by hand in source view or you can have VWD generate it automatically (along with the `INSERT` and `UPDATE` commands) using the Advanced button in the wizard for configuring a data source control. The command will have to identify which record to delete, so there will be a `WHERE` clause. The `WHERE` clause typically sets the record to be deleted based on its primary key (generally an `ID` field). If you set the `DataKeyNames` property of the data-bound control to the primary key, ASP.NET 2.0 automatically feeds the original value from the `DataKeys` dictionary when the parameter is requested in the `WHERE` clause. Switching attention to the data-bound control, the smart control merely needs a new `CommandField` with a delete button. Again, you can add it by hand or just use VWD's Smart Tasks panel to enable deleting.

But, as the German proverb goes, "To change and to change for the better are two different things." The biggest problem with a delete is the potential for conflicts in the database. For example, the Pubs database has an authors-titles table that determines the author for each book (title). If you delete an author, you are left with an orphaned book. To prevent these problems, a database will normally have constraints on deletions. This is called a foreign key restraint. If you attempt to delete a constrained record, the database will raise an error and pass it back to ASP.NET 2.0. At this point in your study, you will see the error in a form that is useful for programmers, not end users. Chapter 16 will discuss how to handle this error with grace.

Try It Out Deleting Entire Records

In this exercise, we create a `GridView` that can delete a sale of a book from the Sales table of Pubs. In the second part, we will set up a `DetailsView` that can delete an author record. But then we will find that because authors is a foreign key for other tables (like `TitleAuthor`), the deletion is not permitted by the database.

1. In the `ch11` folder, create a new page named `TIO-1106-DeleteRecord-1.aspx`. Drag and drop all the fields from the sales table of Pubs onto the page. After VWD builds the `GridView`, and its associated data source control, turn on Enable Deleting and Enable Paging in the Smart Tasks panel. While the `GridView` is selected go to the Properties window and set the page size to 5.
2. Save the page, and test it by opening in the browser and deleting one sale record. Don't go overboard; there is no way to get those records back.

> **If you went delete-happy and want to restore the database, you can copy the `.mdf` file from the download into your `App_Data` folder.**

3. Save the page as `TIO-1106-DeleteRecord-2.aspx`, and change the `<title>` and `<h2>` text. Below the `GridView`, add a `DetailsView` control by dragging it from the Toolbox. Configure for it a new data source control that reads the ID and names fields from the `Authors` table. In the Statement dialog box, click Advanced and check Generate INSERT, UPDATE and DELETE statements. Also, click the ORDER BY button and set the order to `au_id` ascending. In the `DetailsView` Smart Tasks panel, enable paging and deleting. Your code should look similar to the following:

```
<h2>Chapter 11 TIO #1106 Delete Record ver 2</h2>
<form id="form1" runat="server">
    <div>
        <asp:GridView ID="GridView1" runat="server"
            AutoGenerateColumns="False"
            DataKeyNames="stor_id,ord_num,title_id"
            DataSourceID="SqlDataSource1"
            EmptyDataText="There are no data records to display."
            AllowPaging="True" PageSize="5">
            <Columns>
                <asp:CommandField ShowDeleteButton="True" />
                <asp:BoundField DataField="stor_id" HeaderText="stor_id"
                    ReadOnly="True" SortExpression="stor_id" />
                ...
            </Columns>
```

```
        </asp:GridView>
        <asp:SqlDataSource ID="SqlDataSource1" runat="server"
            ConnectionString="<%$ ConnectionStrings:MdfPubs %>"
            ProviderName="<%$ ConnectionStrings:MdfPubs.ProviderName %>"
            DeleteCommand="DELETE FROM [sales]
                WHERE [stor_id] = @stor_id AND [ord_num] = @ord_num
                AND [title_id] = @title_id"
            InsertCommand= ...
            SelectCommand="SELECT [stor_id], [ord_num], [ord_date],
                [qty], [payterms], [title_id] FROM [sales]"
            UpdateCommand= ...
            <InsertParameters> ... </InsertParameters>
            <UpdateParameters> ... </UpdateParameters>
            <DeleteParameters>
                <asp:Parameter Name="stor_id" Type="String" />
                <asp:Parameter Name="ord_num" Type="String" />
                <asp:Parameter Name="title_id" Type="String" />
            </DeleteParameters>
        </asp:SqlDataSource><br />

        <asp:DetailsView ID="DetailsView1" runat="server"
            AllowPaging="True"
            AutoGenerateRows="False"
            DataKeyNames="au_id"
            DataSourceID="SqlDataSource2"
            Height="50px" Width="125px">
            <Fields>
                ...
            </Fields>
        </asp:DetailsView>
        <asp:SqlDataSource ID="SqlDataSource2" runat="server"
            ConnectionString="<%$ ConnectionStrings:MdfPubs %>"
            DeleteCommand="DELETE FROM [authors] WHERE [au_id] = @au_id"
            InsertCommand= ...
            SelectCommand="SELECT [au_id], [au_lname], [au_fname] FROM [authors]
                ORDER BY [au_id]"
            UpdateCommand= ...
            <DeleteParameters>
                <asp:Parameter Name="au_id" Type="String" />
            </DeleteParameters>
            <UpdateParameters> ... </UpdateParameters>
            <InsertParameters> ... </InsertParameters>
        </asp:SqlDataSource>
</div></form></body></html>
```

4. Save your work, and open it in the browser. Test the page as follows: Advance through the `DetailsView` until you get to about record 12, which should be a fellow named Blotchet-Halls, number 648-92-1872. Delete him and observe that the database refuses to execute the delete because this author has records in the `TitleAuthor` table that would be orphaned. Note that not all people listed in the authors table have written books and, thus, some do not have a title dependent on the existence of an authors record; if you delete an unpublished writer, the database will accept the deletion.

How It Works

When you do a drag and drop of fields from VWD's Database Explorer, VWD automatically performs several tasks. In the data source control, it generates all the statements and parameters needed for displaying, editing, deleting, and creating new records. However, those features are not automatically enabled in the data-bound `GridView`. We as programmers must enable them with check-offs in the `GridView` Smart Tasks panel.

When we build an interface by dragging a control from a Toolbox (as we did in version 2 with the `DetailsView`), VWD does a little less for us. When we walk through the configuration of the data source control, we must detour to the Advanced option and specifically say we want to build those SQL statements for changing data (but don't complain – you should have seen what you had to do in the days of classic ASP). And then we have to enable those features in the data-bound control. This system is well thought out. The designers of VWD did not want people who are slightly familiar with ASP to create pages that, by default, open up their data stores to modification. The ASP.NET 2.0 team follows a "secure by default" approach to these issues.

Common Mistakes

The following list describes mistakes commonly made by developers when attempting to update or delete data:

> **Whenever possible, use VWD tools (dialogs, wizards, IntelliSense, and the Properties window) to add properties or set options, since VWD will use the correct placement and syntax.**

- Forgetting to use the `DataKeyNames` property and then not being able to update changes to the database.
- Forgetting to use the `original_` prefix for parameter names in the `WHERE` clause.
- Having a different number of (or incorrect names for) parameters in the `UPDATE` or `DELETE` statements from parameters that are passed by the data-bound control. Make sure that you only have as many parameters as editable fields plus fields specified by `DataKeyNames`.
- Allowing the user to update fields that should be locked (direction is output only).
- Not handling the error of a delete or update that was not performed by the database (generally because of relational dependencies).
- Failing to typecast, causing an error when a wrong data type is rejected by the database.
- Accidentally changing the wrong set (`Select`, `Update`, `Insert`) of parameters when working in Source view.
- Placing the parameters collections in the data-bound control when coding without the VWD.
- Confusing the location of similar properties. `NullDisplayText` is in the `BoundField` object of the `Columns` or `Fields` collection. `DefaultText` is in the parameter object of one of the parameter collections.

Summary

This chapter explained two data modification techniques: updating values in an existing record and deleting an entire record.

Data source controls have the capability to modify data. They will automatically create and manage the appropriate ADO.NET objects to complete the modification. You enable these capabilities by adding an `UpdateCommand` or a `DeleteCommand` property. The argument for these commands is a suitable SQL statement.

The SQL statement generally needs to use values that were entered by the user. In the case of an update, these will be the new values; in the case of a delete, it will be the ID of the record to be deleted. Values are held in collections of parameters. There is one collection for each command object (`DeleteParameters`, `UpdateParameters`, and so on). In many cases, you can accept the default parameters collections made by ASP.NET 2.0, which will have a value for each field name. If you want to change the data type, set defaults, or limit the direction of information flow, you have to explicitly state the parameters and their properties.

Using the data-bound control requires you to go through the following steps. First, turn on the modification capability by adding a `CommandField` with appropriate buttons. This enables a whole set of behaviors including re-rendering the screen when the user switches into Edit mode. When the user clicks Delete or Update, the data-bound control will automatically write the user's input values into the parameters collection and instruct the data source control to perform the modification.

A special case arises when the primary key (usually an `ID` field) can be edited. The new value will inhibit the look-up of the record in the table containing the old values. The problem is solved by assigning the name of the primary key field(s) to the data-bound control's `DataKeyNames` property and using the `original_{0}` prefix for parameters in the `WHERE` clause.

The next chapter discusses the third modification option: creating new records with the INSERT command.

Exercises

The answers to these review questions can be found in Appendix B.

1. What is the difference between the SQL terms `UPDATE` and `INSERT`?
2. What is the difference between the commands `New` and `Edit`?
3. How do you configure a `GridView` to create a new record?
4. How does a command field know which command to execute?
5. What is the purpose of a `DataKey` property in a data-bound control?
6. What is the difference between a command field and a command column?
7. Values that a user types into a textbox will always be of the data type string. How can a typed value be changed to a number for a numeric field?
8. What property adds the capacity to delete records to a `DetailsView` control?

Inserting New Records

The last chapter discussed how to change values in existing records and how to delete an entire record. This chapter covers the third leg of modifying data — creating a new record. It starts with a section on theory and a comparison of the insert capabilities of ASP.NET 2.0 controls. It then examines enabling inserts in the data source controls and the data-bound controls in more detail. After that follows a quick example of inserts with templates and then a more careful study of specific controls on a template. The final section discusses issues specific to the `FormView`.

In this chapter, we cover 10 topics:

- Introducing the creation of new records, including enabling controls for insertions, displaying modes and how ASP.NET 2.0 handles insertions
- Understanding database considerations when using `Insert`
- Enabling `Insert` in a `DataSource` control
- Basic Insert using `DetailsView`
- Performing an insert using a `DetailsView` and `GridView`, both on one page and across two pages
- Using `TemplateFields` for inserting
- Employing `RadioButtonLists` and `DropDownLists` for user entry
- Entering data using `CheckBoxes`
- Inserting with `FormView`
- Comparing inserts using `DetailsView` and `FormView`

And, as always, we give you a list of common mistakes, a summary and some questions to check your understanding of the chapter. Several times in this chapter, you will add a new author to the Authors table in the Pubs database. Note the following constraints on data for an author:

- For ID, use *nnn-nn-nnnn*, where *n* is a number.
- Phone numbers should be of the form *nnn-nnnn*.

- For the state, use CA.
- For the zip code, use 12345.
- For the other fields, use any values, but do not leave any blank.
- If you add more than one record, you must use different ID numbers.

Theory of Creating New Records

Inserting, on a theoretical level, requires five operations. These are handled almost automatically in ASP.NET 2.0.

1. Provide a way to begin the insertion, typically a button.
2. Change to the insert interface, a display to accept values for the new record.
3. Provide a button to end the input and create the record (or cancel).
4. Send the command to the database.
5. Check for success and handle errors.

Although all of these operations were possible in version 1.*x*, many designers stumbled on the syntax and location of operations in the correct events. ASP.NET 2.0 handles all of those tricky parts and exposes a highly simplified (abstracted) interface for the designer to add insert capability.

ASP.NET 2.0 insertion uses a particular set of vocabulary to describe the operations in an insertion:

- **New:** This button performs the change from Display mode to Insert mode.
- **Insert:** This button actually executes the insertion using the values entered by the user and then returns to Display mode.
- **Cancel:** This button aborts the insertion and returns to Display mode.

> **Remember that Insert creates an entire new record in the table. To add or change a value in an existing record, use the `Update` command with an `UPDATE SQL` statement as discussed in Chapter 11.**

Support for Insert

Not all of the data-bound controls support ASP.NET 2.0 inserts. `DetailsView` and `FormView` do; `GridView` does not (you must shift to `DetailsView` or FormView to perform the insert). A user interface for `GridView` to insert rows would be clumsy. Would the rows be at the top or at the bottom? Should it be there all the time, or just sometimes? Where do you put the Insert button — you wouldn't want an empty `CommandField` column on every other row. In the end, the design team decided that using a dedicated control for inserting was a far better interface.

> **However, you can perform inserts on almost any control if you drop back to using the more cumbersome ASP.NET 1.x techniques.**

How do you choose between `DetailsView` and `FormView`? They both present one record at a time and both support inserting new records. `DetailsView` provides a very simple layout with a simple enablement of inserts, but you may not find the automatic layout to your liking. `FormView` requires you to build the insert capability into top-level templates for `Item` and `InsertItem` but gives you complete freedom in layout.

`DetailsView` does not, even after enabling inserts, offer top-level templates for `Item` and `InsertItem`. However, you can add a `TemplateField` to the `DetailsView`, and that `TemplateField` will have its own template for `Item` and `InsertItem` for a specific row in the `DetailsView` table.

What Happens under the Hood?

ASP.NET controls automatically carry out many tasks in reaction to user clicks. You can use Visual Web Developer (VWD) to design pages that insert new records, and you usually don't have to worry about the underlying operations. But it helps in troubleshooting to have some knowledge of what happens. The theory can be broken into three parts: the setup, the rendering modes, and the action after clicks.

Enabling the Data Source Control for Insert

As with updating and deleting, the `SqlDataSource` control can be enabled to perform inserts. The minimum requirement is an `InsertCommand` property. The argument will be a standard SQL `INSERT INTO` statement. Also in the `SqlDataSource` control, there is an `InsertParameters` collection that defines the parameters used in the `INSERT` statement. This collection will be used to transfer (and maybe modify) values from the data-bound control's input controls to the data source control's `InsertCommand`.

Display Modes

The `DetailsView` and `FormView` controls support three different rendering modes: ReadOnly, Edit, and Insert. We have already seen the ReadOnly and Edit modes in the previous chapters. Recall that `DetailsView` changes from ReadOnly to Edit mode when an Edit command button is clicked in the control. In Edit mode, the `DetailsView` renders input controls for modifying the data of the current record.

Similarly, `DetailsView` supports an Insert mode for rendering input UI to define a new record. `DetailsView` will change into this mode from ReadOnly mode when a button with `CommandName="New"` is clicked inside the control. There are three ways to include this button in the `DetailsView` rendering. You can:

- Set `AutoGenerateInsertButton="true"` on the `DetailsView`
- Set `ShowInsertButton="true"` on a `CommandField` object in the `DetailsView.Fields` collection
- Add a `Button` control with `CommandName="New"` to a `TemplateField` in the `Field` collection

In Insert mode, the display of values changes from labels to input controls (textboxes, lists, radio buttons, and so on) to allow the user to enter values for the new record. Once in Insert mode, the

`DetailsView` will submit the newly entered record in response to an `Insert` button command. Like Edit mode, Insert mode can be cancelled (without performing the record insert) by clicking a Cancel button. In both cases, the `DetailsView` reverts to ReadOnly mode (or to the mode set as `DetailsView.DefaultMode`, which is ReadOnly by default).

Action Performed by ASP.NET 2.0 on Insert

When the Insert button is pressed in Insert mode, the data-bound control collects the values entered by the user in the `DetailsView` input UI and creates a dictionary to pass to the data source `Insert` operation. When the data source receives these values, it packages them up and sends to ADO.NET to add to the `DBCommand Parameters`, using the data types specified in the `InsertParameters` collection. Going through the parameters greatly reduces the chance of a SQL injection attack. The data source then instructs ADO.NET to execute the command to insert the new record. The data source control automatically creates the appropriate ADO.NET objects and calls the methods on those objects to perform the insert into the database. The database surfaces any errors that occurred during command execution.

Database Considerations When Performing an Insert

Basic database rules require your attention when adding new records. Tables normally will have a *primary key*, which is a field or fields together that have values that are unique for each row. Primary key values can be entered by hand or autogenerated. If the value is autogenerated by the database, you must prevent the ASP.NET page from trying to add the value when it performs the insertion by omitting the field from Insert mode altogether. You can do this by setting `InsertVisible=false` on the corresponding field object or by removing that field name from the `InsertItemTemplate`. If you decide to make the primary key field editable and allow the user to enter a value by hand, the entered value cannot match a value that has already been taken by another record, because primary keys are unique for each row in the database. Therefore, you will have to check whether the user's entered value for the primary key was accepted or rejected by the database.

Some tables are designed so that a given field's value must match a value in the primary key of another table. For example, in an `Orders` table, the value in the `CustomerID` field must match a value in the `CustomerID` field of the `Customers` table. The best solution is to use an input control that accepts only valid values, such as a list or radio button. For example, Northwind has an Orders table with fields for the `CustomerID`. The best way to get the `CustomerID` from the user is to use a `DropDownList` list to offer legitimate options of `CustomerIDs` in the data-bound control's `InsertItemTemplate`. This technique will be discussed and practiced later in this chapter.

Enabling Insert in a Data Source Control

The first step for inserting is to enable the function in the data source control. To do this in a `SqlDataSource`, you add an `InsertCommand` and add items to the `InsertParameters` collection. There is no additional property to set such as `"EnableInsert=true"`; the existence of the `InsertCommand` and `InsertParameters` is all that is needed to enable inserting. When you walk through the wizard to create a data source control, VWD offers a step to configure the SQL `SelectCommand`. There is a button labeled Advanced that allows you to simply turn on the option for VWD to create commands for insertion. In the current version of VWD, the option is for three commands (Insert, Edit, and Delete) or none. Turning on the same option automatically instructs VWD to add appropriate items to the `InsertParameters` collection.

If you look at the source view, you will see the details. The `InsertCommand` is a standard SQL `INSERT INTO` statement. It lists values for each of the fields, and those values come from the `InsertParameters` collection (wholly held within the data source control). Each parameter can be set with its own tag with a type and name. A default value can also be specified. Note that the `InsertCommand` will read parameters from only the `InsertParameters` collection, even if there are parameters with the same name in other collections (such as `UpdateParameters`). In commands, values from SQL parameters are referred to with an `@` before their name, but in the parameters themselves there is no need for the @ symbol in the name.

Actually, you will not get a parameter for *every* field. SQL Server offers a field property called an `IDENTITY` for a primary key field. Every new record will receive a value of an incrementally larger integer, starting with a seed value. For example, if the identity seed is 0 and the increment is 1, then the values for the identity field of new records will automatically be 0, then 1, 2, 3, and so on. This is similar to Microsoft Access `AutoNumber` column type. You can see the designation by looking at the field's `IsIdentity` property in the VWD Database Explorer. If a field has the property of `IsIdentity=True`, then VWD will not create a parameter for said field or include it in the `INSERT INTO` list of values. If you create a page outside the VWD wizards that sends a value to a field for which `IsIdentity=True`, and the database will ignore the incoming value and substitute the next integer in the identity series.

Not all tables use the SQL Server Identity property to create the values for the primary key field. The database may use a system based on globally unique identifiers (GUIDs) or some internal logic to generate an `ID` value. In other cases, a look-up table of two fields may use the combination of both fields for its primary key, for example the `Pubs.AuthorTitle`. In these cases, the page designer must explicitly prevent the input of an `ID` value; VWD only obstructs input based on the `IsIdentity` property. And in other cases the primary key field must actually be entered by hand. These fields would not be identities (even though the values are unique). A good example is when a person's Social Security number is used for the primary key. We can't expect people to register in the order of their Social Security numbers (and without skips)! So, in this case, the primary key is entered from a textbox.

Try It Out — Setting Up a Data Source Control to Support Inserts

In this Try It Out exercise, you will create a page with a `SqlDataSource` control that allows the addition of new shipping companies to the `Northwind` database. We will then examine what VWD has constructed in the Source view. (We will add the data-bound control in the next section.)

1. Create a new folder for Chapter 12 in your project, and within that folder create a new page named `TIO-1201-EnableInsertionInDataSourceControl.aspx`. Drag a `SqlDataSource` control onto the page.

2. On the control's Smart Tasks panel, click Configure Data Source. Select the `MdfNorthwind` connection string and then the Shippers table. Select the three fields, and then click the Advanced button. Turn on Generate INSERT.... Click Next and then click Finish. Switch to Source view and examine your code, which should be similar to the below listing.

```
...
<h2>Chapter 10 TIO #12-01 Enable Insertion In DataSource Control</h2>
    <form id="form1" runat="server">
    <div>
        <asp:SqlDataSource ID="SqlDataSource1" runat="server"
            ConnectionString="<%$ ConnectionStrings:MdfNorthwind %>"
            DeleteCommand= ...
            SelectCommand= ...
```

```
        UpdateCommand= ...

        InsertCommand="
            INSERT INTO [Shippers] ([CompanyName], [Phone])
            VALUES (@CompanyName, @Phone)">

        <InsertParameters>
            <asp:Parameter Name="CompanyName" Type="String" />
            <asp:Parameter Name="Phone" Type="String" />
        </InsertParameters>

        ...
    </asp:SqlDataSource>
</div></form></body></html>
```

3. Save the page. There is no need to run in a browser.

How It Works

In this exercise, you instructed VWD to add the capability to insert new records. VWD responded by configuring two properties. First, it set the data source control's `InsertCommand` property to the value of a proper SQL `INSERT INTO` statement, as shown below. An insert command has three parts. The first states the `INSERT INTO [Shippers]` to indicate the kind of action and the table to modify. Second is a list of fields for which you intend to provide values. The last is the `VALUES`. If you leave out a value, it will get the default as set in the database. If there is no default in the database, then no value will be saved. Note that the values here are the field names preceded by an `@` sign, which means to use the value in the parameter with this name.

```
InsertCommand="
    INSERT INTO [Shippers] ([CompanyName], [Phone])
    VALUES (@CompanyName, @Phone)">
```

VWD configured a second property: the `InsertParameters` collection as shown below. There is a parameter for each field in the table (except the primary key that we will discuss below). Within the parameter, there is, at minimum, a name, and a data type. In some cases, there can also be a designation of size, default value, or other information.

```
<InsertParameters>
    <asp:Parameter Name="CompanyName" Type="String" />
    <asp:Parameter Name="Phone" Type="String" />
</InsertParameters>
```

Note that VWD did not create a parameter for `ShipperID`. ASP.NET 2.0 senses that this field is automatically assigned a value by the database. (Had `ShipperID` been the primary key but not with values auto-generated by the database, you would see it in the `Insert` command and a corresponding parameter in the `InsertParameters` collection.)

Basic Insert Using DetailsView

To review, enabling the creation of new records (inserts) requires enabling it in both the data source control and the data-bound control. We discuss enablement in the data source control in the last section, which is the addition of an `InsertCommand` and a list of parameters. We will now look at enablement for one of the data-bound controls.

`DetailsView` has a simple designer interface to enable inserting — a check box on the `DetailsView` Smart Tasks panel will do it for you. When turned on, the `DetailsView` will display a button in a `CommandField` named `New`. When clicked, the `DetailsView` will switch from ReadOnly mode to Insert mode and the labels will change to text boxes. The `CommandField` will now display buttons for Insert (meaning to actually create the record using the entered data) and Cancel (to abort the insertion).

In the source code, the enablement is simple. The data-bound control must include in its `<Fields>` list an `<asp:CommandField>`, where the `ShowInsertButton` property is set to `True`. Everything else is taken care of by the code written into the data-bound control by the good folks at Microsoft.

Try It Out — Simple Insert by DetailsView

In this exercise, you will create a page that uses the `DetailsView` control with insert capability to add a new author and then view some errors.

1. Open the `TIO-1201-EnableInsertionInDataSourceControl.aspx` page from the last exercise, and save it as `TIO-1202-EnableInsertionInDetailsView.aspx`. Change the title and H2 texts. Drag to the page a `DetailsView` control and set as its data source the `SqlDataSource1` you created in the last exercise. Select the `DetailsView` control, and enable paging and inserting.
2. View in your browser. Add a new shipper by clicking on New, filling in a name and phone number (no need to fill in the ID because that is an identity field) and then clicking on Insert. Observe your new record by paging to the end of the record stack in the `DetailsView`.
3. Save your page.
4. Try violating a table constraint by adding another shipper with no company name. Notice that the insert fails.
5. Remove the shipper with no company name, and save your work.

How It Works

Insert works when the data source control and the data-bound control are both enabled for inserting. The data source control was enabled by having the VWD generate an `InsertCommand` in the last exercise. At the same time, VWD automatically generated a set of `InsertParameters`. For our purposes, the command and parameters for Update and Delete can be excised from the page.

The `DetailsView` data-bound control was insert-enabled with a simple check box in the VWD Developer. That check added a `CommandField` that renders a button that will switch from New to Insert and Cancel. If your `DefaultMode` is not `Insert`, then you cannot access the commands at design time. But if you set the `DefaultMode` property to `Insert`, then you can work with the commands in VWD.

When the user opens the page, the `DetailsView` will be in ReadOnly mode. When you click on New, the rendering will change in two ways. First, the buttons change from New to Insert and Cancel. Second, the fields change from showing values in labels for the current record to showing empty textboxes. When the user clicks on Insert, the `DetailsView` control hands the values to the `SqlDataSource` control, which merges them with the values in the `InsertParameters` collection. The data-bound control then instructs the data source control to perform the insert. The data source control instantiates and uses ADO.NET objects as needed. They, in turn, instruct the database to perform the insertion. If there is a problem, an error message will bubble back up through ADO.NET and cause a page error.

DetailsView Insert Starting from GridView

As previously mentioned, you can't perform an insert using the `GridView` control. Instead, you must switch to a `DetailsView` or `FormView` control. Starting from a `GridView`, you have two layout options:

- ❑ Locate the `DetailsView/FormView` on the same page as `GridView`.
- ❑ Locate the `DetailsView/FormView` on a different page from the `GridView`.

Both of these scenarios are covered in this section.

GridView and DetailsView for Insert on Same Page

A layout of a `GridView` and `DetailsView` on the same page works well. Both can use the same data source control, provided the data source control is enabled to perform inserts (has an `InsertCommand` and a set of `InsertParameters`). The `DetailsView` has a `DefaultMode` property that can be set to insert. Its appearance with blank fields and a New button will signify to users its purpose.

GridView on One Page with DetailsView on a Different Page

An alternative is to add a button to a page that jumps to a new page for creating new records. The button can be in the `GridView`'s header or footer or located outside the `GridView`. The button is nothing more than a hyperlink to a page set up with a `DetailsView` for inserts. The `DetailsView` on the inserts page should have its `DefaultMode` set to `Insert`. Don't forget to add a button to go back to the `GridView` page. (Alternatively, you can create an automatic redirection in an event handler, as described in Chapter 16).

Try It Out — Insert by DetailsView, Starting from GridView

In this exercise, you will offer insertions into the Authors table in two ways. The first has a `GridView` and `DetailsView` on the same page. The second technique has a separate page for the insert function.

1. In the `ch12` folder, create a new page named `TIO-1203-Both.aspx`. This one page will sport three controls: one data source control with insert enabled, a `GridView` that is read-only, and a `DetailsView` that is for inserting.

2. From the Database Explorer, drag the Authors table onto the page. Enable paging and set the `PageSize` to `5`.

3. Switch to source view, and find the `SqlDataSource` that was created by VWD. Notice that when you create a `GridView` by dragging and dropping from the Database Explorer, VWD builds a data source control that enables inserts even though the data-bound `GridView` does not support inserts. (Is VWD reading your mind for the next step?)

4. Now, in Design view, add a `DetailsView` control to the bottom of the page. Notice that when the Smart Tasks panel first appears (prior to setting the data source control), there is no option to enable inserting. Set the data source to the existing SqlDataSource1, and enable paging and inserting. Last, with the `DetailsView` still selected, go to the Properties window and set `DefaultMode` (in the Behavior category) to `Insert`.

5. Save and test the page by adding a new author. (Keep in mind the constraints on the Authors table data listed at the beginning of the chapter.)

```
...  <h2>Chapter 12 TIO #1203 Both on One Page</h2>
    <form id="form1" runat="server"><div>

<asp:GridView ... />

<asp:SqlDataSource ID="SqlDataSource1" runat="server"
ConnectionString="<%$ ConnectionStrings:MdfPubs %>"
ProviderName="<%$ ConnectionStrings:MdfPubs.ProviderName %>"
InsertCommand="
         INSERT INTO [authors]
         ([au_id], [au_lname], [au_fname],
         [phone], [address], [city], [state], [zip], [contract])
       VALUES (@au_id, @au_lname, @au_fname,
         @phone, @address, @city, @state, @zip, @contract)"
SelectCommand=...
UpdateCommand= ...
DeleteCommand=...
<InsertParameters>
                <asp:Parameter Name="au_id" Type="String" />
                <asp:Parameter Name="au_lname" Type="String" />
                <asp:Parameter Name="au_fname" Type="String" />
                <asp:Parameter Name="phone" Type="String" />
                <asp:Parameter Name="address" Type="String" />
                <asp:Parameter Name="city" Type="String" />
                <asp:Parameter Name="state" Type="String" />
                <asp:Parameter Name="zip" Type="String" />
                <asp:Parameter Name="contract" Type="Boolean" />
</InsertParameters>
<UpdateParameters> ... </UpdateParameters>
<DeleteParameters> ... </DeleteParameters>
</asp:SqlDataSource>

<asp:DetailsView ID="DetailsView1" runat="server"
                AllowPaging="True"
                AutoGenerateRows="False"
                 DataKeyNames="au_id"
                DataSourceID="SqlDataSource1"
                DefaultMode="Insert"
                Height="50px" Width="125px">
```

```
            <Fields> ... </Fields>
</asp:DetailsView>
</div></form></body></html>
```

6. Now you will build a two-page solution, starting with the `GridView` page. Create a new page named `TIO-1203-GridView.aspx` and repeat Step 2. Now add a hyperlink from the toolbar to the page (outside the `GridView`) with the following properties: `Text = "Click here to add a new author,"` and leave the `NavigateUrl` empty for now.

7. Now, you will create the page that is the target of the last step's hyperlink. In the `ch12` folder, add a new item named `TIO-1203-DetailsOnly.aspx`. Drag the item onto it a `SqlDataSource` control and in the configuration wizard, get data from all fields of the Authors table and with the Advanced button, generate insert, delete, and update statements. On the `DetailsView` control, enable paging and set the default mode to `Insert`. Add to the page (outside the `DetailsView`) a hyperlink button to return to the `GridView` page with the properties of `ID="ReturnToGridView";Text = "Return to GridView page";NavigateUrl="TIO-1203-GridOnly.aspx"`.

8. Go back to the `GridView` page and select the hyperlink. Go to the Properties window, and set the `NavigateUrl` using the browse button.

```
... <h2>Chapter 12 TIO #1203 GridView Only </h2>
<asp:GridView ... </asp:GridView>
<asp:SqlDataSource ... </asp:SqlDataSource>

<asp:HyperLink ID="HyperNewAuthhor" runat="server"
NavigateUrl="~/ch12/TIO-1203-DetailsViewOnly.aspx">
Click to add a new author
</asp:HyperLink>

</div></form></body></html>
```

9. Save your work, and test it by starting in the GridView Only page and adding a new author.

```
TIO-1203-DetailsViewOnly:
... <h2>Chapter 12 TIO #1203 DetailsView Only </h2>
<asp:SqlDataSource ID="SqlDataSource1" runat="server"
ConnectionString="<%$ ConnectionStrings:MdfPubs %>"
SelectCommand= ...
DeleteCommand= ...
InsertCommand="INSERT INTO [authors]
        ([au_id], [au_lname], [au_fname], [phone], [address],
              [city], [state], [zip], [contract])
        VALUES (@au_id, @au_lname, @au_fname, @phone, @address,
              @city, @state, @zip, @contract)"
<DeleteParameters> ... </DeleteParameters>
<UpdateParameters> ... </UpdateParameters>
<InsertParameters>
        <asp:Parameter Name="au_id" Type="String" />
        <asp:Parameter Name="au_lname" Type="String" />
        <asp:Parameter Name="au_fname" Type="String" />
        <asp:Parameter Name="phone" Type="String" />
        <asp:Parameter Name="address" Type="String" />
        <asp:Parameter Name="city" Type="String" />
        <asp:Parameter Name="state" Type="String" />
        <asp:Parameter Name="zip" Type="String" />
```

```
        <asp:Parameter Name="contract" Type="Boolean" />
</InsertParameters>
</asp:SqlDataSource>

<asp:DetailsView ID="DetailsView1" runat="server"
AutoGenerateRows="False"
DataKeyNames="au_id"
DataSourceID="SqlDataSource1"
DefaultMode="Insert"
Height="50px" Width="125px">
<Fields> ... </Fields>
</asp:DetailsView>

<asp:HyperLink ID="ReturnToGridView" runat="server"
NavigateUrl="~/ch12/TIO-1203-GridViewOnly.aspx">
        Return to GridView
</asp:HyperLink>
</div> </form> </body> </html>
```

How It Works

GridView does not support inserting new records, so you use a DetailsView (FormView also works for inserts). The DetailsView enabled for inserting can be on the same page as the GridView or on an alternate page. If it is on the same page, the two data-bound controls can share a single data source control if the data source control is enabled for inserts (has an InsertCommand and has a set of InsertParameters). In your second set of pages, the GridView page contains a button that jumps to the DetailsView page. In both cases, the DetailsView should have its DefaultMode set to Insert so that it is ready for the user to begin entering values for the new record. When a new record is inserted, it automatically shows up in the related GridView control because they are bound to the same data source.

In the second part (two-page solution), you circled back to add the NavigateUrl property of the hyperlink on the GridView page. This route was chosen because at the time the hyperlink was first created the target (TIO-1203-DetailsViewOnly.aspx) did not exist. You could have typed what you anticipated the target's name would be, but it is always more accurate to pick the name from the lists offered with the browse button in the Properties window.

Insert Using TemplateFields

DetailsView renders in one of three modes, including ReadOnly, Insert, and Edit mode. By default, ReadOnly mode shows values in labels, and Insert mode displays a textbox for each BoundField. However, in many cases you want your Insert mode to offer a different input control or layout. Instead of a TextBox, you may want a ListBox, Calendar, or set of RadioButtons. You can change the input control type by adding a TemplateField in place of the BoundField and modifying the InsertItem Template of that field. A template, as discussed in Chapter 10, is a holder for other controls. The Details View will render different templates depending on its mode. By editing the InsertItemTemplate, you can change the type of input controls rendered to the user during Insert mode. In fact, if you want any option other than a textbox for input you *must* change to a TemplateField. There are two exceptions. A Boolean field will automatically give you a CheckBox field. An ImageField will give you a TextBox for changing the string that points to an image The bound fields are easy to use (automatically switching from label to textbox), but they are rigid.

As we saw in Chapter 10 on templates, it is easy to change from a `BoundField` to a `TemplateField`. Select the `DetailsView`, and on the Smart Tasks panel, click on Edit Columns. Select the `BoundField` from the list in the lower-left corner of the dialog box and then click on the hyperlink that says "Convert this field into a TemplateField" in the lower-right corner. Close the dialog box. Go to Edit Templates and select the `TemplateField` you just created, and within it you will see an `InsertItemTemplate`.

> `DetailsView` **does not have an** `InsertItemTemplate` **for bound fields.** `InsertItemTemplates` **are available only for template fields. So, you must remove the default bound field and replace it with a template field, within which you will find your** `InsertItemTemplate`**. (FormView offers an** `InsertItemTemplate`**, but that is because the FormView only offers templates, no top-level bound fields).**

There is no data binding available for header or footer templates. The `HeaderTemplate` and `FooterTemplate` for the entire control will not support data binding. Likewise, within a `TemplateField` there is a `HeaderTemplate`, and it will not support data binding. All controls in a template that are to be data-bound must be in one of the Item templates, including `ItemTemplate`, `AlternateItemTemplate`, `EditItemTemplate`, or `InsertItemTemplate`.

You can see the hierarchy of templates in Figure 12-1. There are two `TemplateFields` (`title_id` and `pub_id`). Within each one there are templates for the various modes, such as `ItemTemplate` and `InsertItemTemplate`.

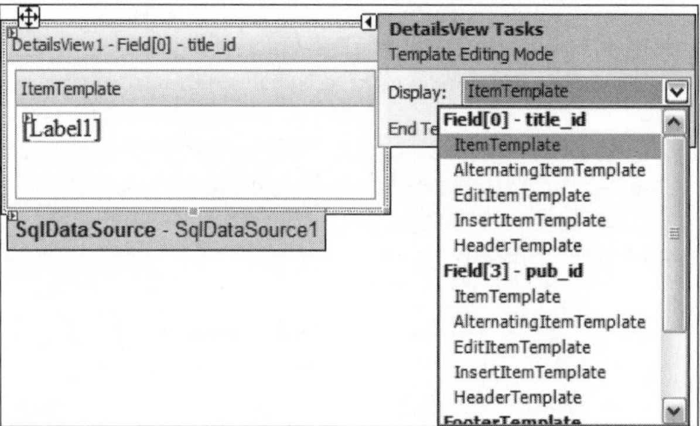

Figure 12-1

Using the Bind Syntax in InsertItemTemplate

Controls inside the `InsertItemTemplate` must be data-bound to a field of the `DetailsView` data source. In the chapter on templates, we mentioned the `Eval()` syntax to data-bind a field to be read-only. In this chapter, we use the `Bind()` syntax in order to create a two-way association to the field. This allows the `DetailsView` control to automatically extract the value from the data-bound control in order to pass to the data source `Insert` operation.

We did not need to specify data-bindings in the previous examples using `BoundFields`, because the `DetailsView` itself creates the `TextBox` input UI and, therefore, can automatically extract the values from these controls. In a template, the `DetailsView` doesn't necessarily know from which control property to extract the value unless you specify an explicit data-binding. In the next exercise, you will try this with a `Calendar` control.

Try It Out Insert Using Template Fields

In this exercise, you will create a `DetailsView` to add new employees. Instead of using a textbox for the hire date, you will use the ASP.NET 2.0 `Calendar` control. Along the way, you will find some points about how ASP.NET supports controls for data insertions.

1. In the `ch12` folder, create a new page named `TIO-1204-TemplateInserts.aspx`. Add a `DetailsView` control, and configure its data source to a new data source named `DataSource1` that lists ID, names, and HireDate fields from the Pubs Employees table.
2. Use Advanced Options to generate statements for `Insert`, `Update`, and `Delete`. In the `DetailsView`, enable paging and inserting. Click Edit Templates, and note that you have a very limited set of choices: `Footer`, `Header`, `EmptyData`, and `Pager`.
3. Save and test the page to see in Insert mode that all the fields are rendered as the default textboxes.
4. To change the `Hire Date` field to a `Calendar` control, close the browser and return to the page in VWD Design view. Select the `DetailsView` control, open the Smart Tasks panel, and select Edit Fields. In the lower-left panel, select `HireDate` and click Convert to Template; then close the Fields dialog box.
5. With the `DetailsView` control still selected, click Edit Templates. Now, you see the `HireDate` field template. Select the `InsertItemTemplate`, and delete the default `TextBox`.

   Drag and drop a `Calendar` control from the Toolbox onto the template. The Calendar's Smart Tasks panel will open; click on Edit DataBindings, select the `SelectedDate` property, and bind it to `HireDate`. Notice that the two-way data-binding checkbox is checked to indicate that the `Bind()` syntax will be used to create a two-way binding association.
6. Save your work, end template editing, close, and test the page.

```
...<h2>Chapter 12 TIO #1204 Template Inserts </h2>
    <form id="form1" runat="server">
    <div>
        <asp:DetailsView ID="DetailsView1" runat="server"
            AllowPaging="True"
            AutoGenerateRows="False"
            DataKeyNames="emp_id"
            DataSourceID="SqlDataSource1"
            Height="50px" Width="125px">
            <Fields>
                <asp:BoundField DataField="emp_id" HeaderText="emp_id"
                    ReadOnly="True" SortExpression="emp_id" />
                  ...
                <asp:TemplateField HeaderText="hire_date"
                    SortExpression="hire_date">

                    <ItemTemplate>
                        <asp:Label ID="Label1" runat="server"
```

```
                        Text='<%# Bind("hire_date") %>'>
                    </asp:Label>
                </ItemTemplate>

                <InsertItemTemplate>
                    <asp:Calendar ID="Calendar1" runat="server"
                        SelectedDate='<%# Bind("hire_date") %>'>
                    </asp:Calendar>
                </InsertItemTemplate>

                <EditItemTemplate> ... </EditItemTemplate>

            </asp:TemplateField>

            <asp:CommandField ShowInsertButton="True" />
        </Fields>
    </asp:DetailsView>

    <asp:SqlDataSource ID="SqlDataSource1" runat="server"
...
        InsertCommand="INSERT INTO [employee]
            ([emp_id], [fname], [minit], [lname], [hire_date])
            VALUES (@emp_id, @fname, @minit, @lname, @hire_date)"
...
        <InsertParameters>
            <asp:Parameter Name="emp_id" Type="String" />
            <asp:Parameter Name="fname" Type="String" />
            <asp:Parameter Name="minit" Type="String" />
            <asp:Parameter Name="lname" Type="String" />
            <asp:Parameter Name="hire_date" Type="DateTime" />
        </InsertParameters>
    </asp:SqlDataSource>
</div></form></body></html>
```

How It Works

When you created the page in Step 1, you took a peek at the templates. The `DetailsView`, holding only `BoundFields`, supports just four templates: `Footer`, `Header`, `EmptyData`, and `Pager`. With only `BoundFields` and no templates, there is no `ItemTemplate` or `InsertItemTemplate`. Although the `DetailsView` is very easy to use, it takes some work to modify its basic presentation.

To change from the default textboxes in Insert mode, you have to convert a `BoundField` to a `TemplateField`. Now, when you click Edit Templates, there are many more options because you can edit the `TemplateField's` mode templates. Note that instead of an `Item` and `InsertItem` template for the entire `DetailsView` you have an `Item` and `InsertItem` template for each `TemplateField`. Any `BoundFields` will get the default rendering of label and textbox.

When you add the Calendar, ASP.NET 2.0 will do all the work of rendering the calendar and accepting user input such as changing months and selecting a date. You have to set only one property: the calendar's `SelectedDate` property is bound to a field in your table.

Let's take a closer look at that `TemplateField` for `Hire Date`. When you create the `TemplateField`, VWD automatically creates four elements. First is the `TemplateField` within the data, along with its general `HeaderText` and `SortExpression`.

```
<asp:DetailsView ID="DetailsView1" runat="server" ...

<asp:TemplateField HeaderText="hire_date"
                    SortExpression="hire_date">
```

Within the TemplateField, VWD creates three templates that will be shown depending if the control is in ReadOnly, Edit or Insert mode:

```
<asp:TemplateField ...
<ItemTemplate> ...  </ItemTemplate>
<EditItemTemplate> ... </EditItemTemplate>
<InsertItemTemplate> ... </InsertItemTemplate>
  ...
</asp:TemplateField>
```

Our particular interest in this exercise was the InsertItemTemplate, within which you removed the default textbox and added a Calendar control.

```
<InsertItemTemplate>
<asp:Calendar ID="Calendar1" runat="server"
SelectedDate='<%# Bind("hire_date") %>'>
</asp:Calendar>
</InsertItemTemplate>
```

That covers the use of templates for inserting new records. But we can improve the user's data-entry experience by using some standard Windows tools: RadioButtons and DropDownLists as described in the next section.

Data Entry with RadioButtonLists and DropDownLists

RadioButtonLists provide the best input method when there is a short list of options and a rule that only one item can be selected at a time. DropDownLists and ListBoxes are better suited when there is a greater quantity of choices. These input controls can be populated either from the same data source control used by the DetailsView as a whole or from another data source. A SqlDataSource control can support only one SelectCommand statement, so if the RadioButtonList or DropDownList control is to have a Select that is to use values any different from the DetailsView, the input control must have its own data source control. It is also possible to statically populate the items of the list instead of binding to a data source, but this may not be maintainable if the items change frequently. For the sake of the examples, we will bind the lists to a data source.

If the list of values includes duplicates, you will probably not want the duplicates in your radio buttons or list box. The SQL keyword DISTINCT will eliminate the redundancy. However, a Select statement that uses DISTINCT will probably no longer be useful for the DetailsView as a whole. You will see this in the next exercise.

The overall technique is a modification of the general template discussion. There are five steps:

1. Create a data source to supply values to the input control.
2. In the `DetailsView` or `FormView`, convert the `BoundField` to a `TemplateField` using the Smart Tasks panel and Edit Fields.
3. Select Edit Templates and, in the `InsertItemTemplate`, delete the default textbox and replace it with a `RadioButtonList` or `DropDownList`.
4. Choose a data source from the input control's Smart Tasks panel and set the `DataTextField` and `DataValueField`. (Text will be shown to the user while the value will actually be stored in the database.)
5. From the input control's Smart Tasks panel, edit the data bindings to set the field in the `DetailsView` that will receive the selected value.

Although none of these steps is difficult, it is important to perform all of them in the order listed here to ensure success.

Try It Out Insert with a List Box and Radio Buttons

In this exercise, you will create a `DetailsView` to add a new sale. Because publishers sell to only a few stores, you will let the user select from a radio button list of stores. But when the user must select from more than 50 titles, a `DropDownList` is more appropriate. Because the three data-bound controls (`DetailsView` as a whole, `RadioButtonList`, and `DropDownList`) need fundamentally different sets of values, you will have to use three data source controls.

1. In the `ch12` folder, create a new page named `TIO-1205-InsertWithListBoxAndRadio.aspx`. Drag and drop a `DetailsView` control. Choose a new data source, name it `SalesSqlDataSource`, and configure it to display all fields of the Sales table of Pubs ordered by descending `Ord_Date` (most recent order will be on page 1). When creating the data source control, use the advance button to generate an `INSERT` statement. (These are the same techniques as used in previous Try It Outs in this chapter.) Finish by selecting the `DetailsView` and enabling paging and inserting. Select Edit Fields, and check that Auto-generate Fields is turned off.
2. Now, you will create the two data source controls needed for the subcontrols you will put in the `InsertItemTemplate`. Start with support for a radio button list that will list the stores. Drag to the bottom of the page a new `SqlDataSource`. Retrieve from the `Pubs Stores` table only the Store ID and name, ordered by Store name. After the wizard finishes, go to the new `SqlDataSource`'s Properties window and change the ID to `StoresSqlSource`.
3. Repeat Step 2 for another data source control that selects from the Titles table just the `Title_ID` and `Title`, ordered by title. Name it `TitlesSqlSource`.
4. Now, you need to change two of the `DetailsView` fields from simple `BoundFields` to `TemplateFields`, as follows. On the left of the Fields dialog box, select `Store_id` and click on the tool to "Convert this field into a TemplateField." Repeat for the `Title_id` field. Click OK to close field editing.
5. Edit the `Store_id` field as follows. In the `DetailsView` Smart Tasks panel, click Edit Templates and select the `Store_id InsertItemTemplate`. Delete `Store TextBox` and from the Toolbox, drag and drop a `RadioButtonList` control onto the template. Using its Smart Tasks panel, choose a data source of `StoresSqlDataSource` and set the display field to `Store_name` and the field for the value to `Store_id`. Going back to the radio button list's Smart Tasks panel, edit data bindings and set the `SelectedValue` property binding to the `Stor_id` field. Two-way data binding should be turned on. Click OK to end data binding.

6. Now change the input control for the Title field to a `DropDownList`, as follows. Open the Smart Tasks panel for the entire `DetailsView` control and, if you are not in template-editing mode, click Edit Templates. Select the `Title_ID` and `InsertItemTemplate`. Delete the textbox and drag a `DropDownList` from the Toolbox. Choose the `TitlesSqlSource` as its data source, and refresh the schema. Set the display field to `Title` and the data field to `Title_ID`. In the `DropDownList`'s Smart Tasks panel, edit data bindings and set the `SelectedValue` property to bind to the `Title_id` field. Two-way data binding should be turned on.

7. Save and run the page, as follows (large sections of code that were automatically generated for update and delete are replaced with ellipses). Try adding a new sale and note the ease of selecting a store and a title. For the text fields, use `111` for the order number, `1/1/01` for the date, `1` for the quantity, and `"Net 60"` for the terms.

```
... <h2>Chapter 12 TIO #1205 Insert with ListBox and Radio Buttons </h2>
<form id="form1" runat="server">
    <div>
        <asp:DetailsView ID="DetailsView1" runat="server"
        AllowPaging="True"
        AutoGenerateRows="False"
        DataKeyNames="stor_id,ord_num,title_id"
        DataSourceID="SalesSqlDataSource"
        Height="50px" Width="125px">
            <Fields>
                <asp:TemplateField HeaderText="stor_id" SortExpression="stor_id">
                    <ItemTemplate>
                        <asp:Label ID="Label1" runat="server"
                        Text='<%# Bind("stor_id") %>'></asp:Label>
                    </ItemTemplate>
                    <EditItemTemplate> ... </EditItemTemplate>
                    <InsertItemTemplate>
                        <asp:RadioButtonList ID="RadioButtonList1" runat="server"
                            DataSourceID="StoresSqlDataSource"
                            DataTextField="stor_name"
                            DataValueField="stor_id"
                            SelectedValue='<%# Bind("stor_id") %>'>
                        </asp:RadioButtonList>
                    </InsertItemTemplate>
                </asp:TemplateField>

                ... other bound fields ...
                <asp:TemplateField HeaderText="title_id"
                    SortExpression="title_id">
                    <EditItemTemplate>
                        <asp:Label ID="Label2" runat="server"
                            Text='<%# Eval("title_id") %>'></asp:Label>
                    </EditItemTemplate>
                    <InsertItemTemplate>
                        <asp:DropDownList ID="DropDownList1" runat="server"
                            DataSourceID="TitleDataSource"
                            DataTextField="title"
                            DataValueField="title_id"
                            SelectedValue='<%# Bind("title_id") %>'>
                        </asp:DropDownList>
                    </InsertItemTemplate>
                    <ItemTemplate>
                        <asp:Label ID="Label2" runat="server"
```

```
                    Text='<%# Bind("title_id") %>'></asp:Label>
                </ItemTemplate>
            </asp:TemplateField>
            <asp:CommandField ShowInsertButton="True" />
        </Fields>
    </asp:DetailsView>

    <asp:SqlDataSource ID="SalesSqlDataSource" runat="server"
        ConnectionString="<%$ ConnectionStrings:MdfPubs %>"
        SelectCommand="SELECT * FROM [sales] ORDER BY [ord_date] DESC"
        InsertCommand="INSERT INTO [sales]
            ([stor_id], [ord_num], [ord_date],
            [qty], [payterms], [title_id])
            VALUES (@stor_id, @ord_num, @ord_date, @qty, @payterms, @title_id)"
        DeleteCommand= ...
        UpdateCommand= ...
        <InsertParameters>
            <asp:Parameter Name="stor_id" Type="String" />
            <asp:Parameter Name="ord_num" Type="String" />
            <asp:Parameter Name="ord_date" Type="DateTime" />
            <asp:Parameter Name="qty" Type="Int16" />
            <asp:Parameter Name="payterms" Type="String" />
            <asp:Parameter Name="title_id" Type="String" />
        </InsertParameters>
    </asp:SqlDataSource>

    <asp:SqlDataSource ID="StoresSqlDataSource" runat="server"
        ConnectionString="<%$ ConnectionStrings:MdfPubs %>"
        SelectCommand="SELECT [stor_id], [stor_name]
            FROM [stores] ORDER BY [stor_name]">
    </asp:SqlDataSource>

<asp:SqlDataSource ID="TitleDataSource" runat="server"
    ConnectionString="<%$ ConnectionStrings:MdfPubs %>"
    SelectCommand="SELECT [title_id], [title] FROM [titles]
    ORDER BY [title]"></asp:SqlDataSource>
</div></form></body></html>
```

8. Save the page.

How It Works

This type of page can be built in two minutes with drag and drop in VWD but generates a lot of source code. You worked with data-bound controls at two levels: the `DetailsView` as a whole and at a lower level of your two data-bound input controls (`RadioButtonList` and `DropDownList`) within that `DetailsView`.

Your main data-bound control is the `DetailsView` that is bound to a data source enabled for inserts. The `DetailsView` can sense that enablement and, thus, you can turn on inserts for the user. The `DetailsView` self-generates an interface of labels in ReadOnly mode and textboxes in Insert mode. There is no overall template for the control's ReadOnly and Insert modes, but you can convert individual fields to `TemplateFields` that offer you editable templates for `ItemTemplate` (ReadOnly mode) and `InsertItemTemplate` (Insert mode).

Before you can add specialized data-bound controls within the DetailsView, you need data sources to supply them. Because the set of data to support the internal controls is different from the data source for the entire DetailsView, you must create separate data source controls. You created two, selecting values from the Stores table and the Titles table.

You then carried out several remaining tasks on your two input controls. Within the DataView, you converted the Store and Title BoundFields to TemplateFields so that you could modify their rendering. Second, within their InsertItemTemplates, you deleted the textboxes and replaced them with a RadioButtonList and a DropDownList. Then you opened the input control's Smart Tasks panel. You configured the data source and set a display to a field that would be useful to the human eye, namely store_name and title.

Data Entry with CheckBoxes

CheckBoxes are a special case in that they are set up automatically by DetailsView. They are automatically generated in the ItemTemplate and InsertItemTemplate for fields that the data source control detects as Boolean. So, there is no need to convert a CheckBox to a TemplateField.

However, if you choose to (or are using the FormView), you can add check boxes manually in two ways. In a DetailsView (not a FormView), without a template, you can add the field as a CheckBoxField in the Edit Fields dialog box, which puts in an <asp:CheckBoxField> control into the fields collection. Alternatively (and again, only in DetailsView, not FormView), you can create a TemplateField and insert a check box in the same way as previously described for radio buttons. Note that CheckBox is not a data-bound list control, so there is no need to specify a data source; simply two-way data-bind its Checked property to a field using Edit Databindings....

Inserting with FormView

FormView is similar to DetailsView in that they both display one record at a time and they both support inserting new records (provided, of course, that their underlying data source controls support Insert), but there is a significant difference in how they organize their templates. Recall that DetailsView offered the ability to add TemplateFields and then within those TemplateFields you had subtemplates for ItemTemplate, InsertItemTemplate and EditItemTemplate. FormView does not have templates for each field; rather it offers a top-level template for each of its modes. There is one ItemTemplate for all the fields that will be shown in ReadOnly mode. The same architecture holds for Edit and Insert mode, with the respective EditItemTemplate and InsertItemTemplate. You can customize these templates to define the UI that FormView should render for each mode, specifying your own custom layout of controls in the template.

The template organization varies between the two controls. When FormView is bound to a data source in VWD, it reflects against the schema (fields) of the data source in order to create default templates. VWD will also automatically create the EditItemTemplate and InsertItemTemplate to contain appropriate input controls that are two-way data-bound to the data source fields (even if the data source control does not have these behaviors enabled). You can modify these templates content to your liking. You can see the template options for FormView in Figure 12-2. For comparison, you might want to go back and review Figure 12-1 for DetailsView.

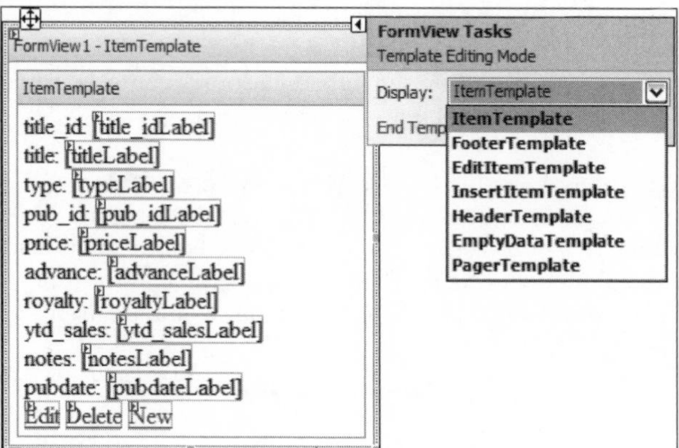

Figure 12-2

The layout generated by the control differs from `DetailsView` as well. `DetailsView` is created with more automatic layout features than `FormView`. You saw that `DetailsView` automatically creates a tablelike layout containing headers and values for each field of the data source.

The means to switch between modes differs between the two controls. Similar to the way `DetailsView` works, `FormView` will switch between its ReadOnly, Edit, and Insert modes in response to command button clicks. The same command names apply: `Edit` to transition into Edit mode, `New` to transition into Insert mode, and `Update/Cancel` or `Insert/Cancel` to transition back to `DefaultMode` (aborting the operation if Cancel is pressed). Unlike `DetailsView` however, `FormView` does not use a `CommandField` to generate these buttons. The buttons themselves are defined in the `ItemTemplate`, `EditItemTemplate`, or `InsertItemTemplate` with appropriate command names set for each mode. Fortunately, `FormView` will automatically create these buttons as part of the templates generated when it is bound to a data source. If you do not want to support a particular operation, you can delete the buttons that do not apply for your scenario.

Try It Out — FormView for Inserting New Records

In this exercise, you will create a `FormView` for inserting new records into the Titles table.

1. Create a new page named `TIO-1206-FormViewInserts-1.aspx`. Add a `FormView` that shows all of the fields from the Pubs database Titles table. Enable the data source control for inserts. Turn on paging in the `FormView`.

2. Select the `FormView` and, on the Smart Tasks panel, click on Edit Templates. Drop down the list of templates and examine the options. Note the different organization from what you used in `DetailsView`. Select the `InsertItemTemplate`, and rearrange the fields as shown in Figure 12-3.

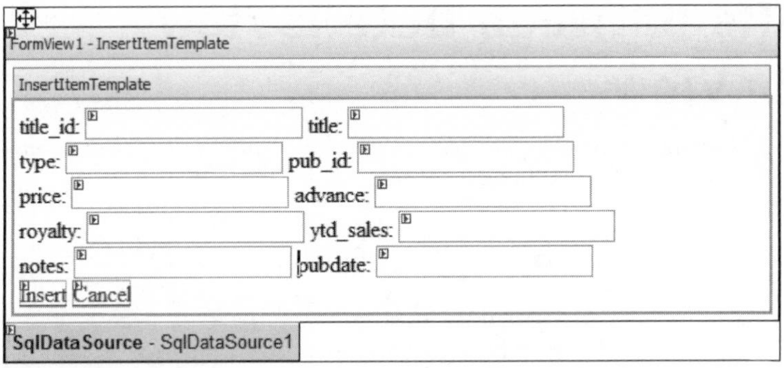

Figure 12-3

3. Save the page, and view it in the browser. Add a new title with a `Publisher ID = 9999`. The other fields can be values of your choice.

4. Let's improve that `PublisherID` field by making it a `DropDownList`. Close the browser, and go back to VWD Design view. Save the page as `TIO-1206-FormViewInserts-2.aspx,` and change the title and H2 text. Widen the `FormView` control to about 600 px. At the bottom of the page, add a second `SqlDataSource` named `PublisherSqlSource` to read (only) the `pub_name` and `pub_id` of the Publishers table.

   Now select the `FormView`, and edit the `InsertItemTemplate`. Delete the textbox for `pub_id`, and drag a `DropDownList`. Configure the data source to `PublisherSqlSource`, and set the `DataTextField` and `DataValueField` properties to `publisher name` and `publisher id`, respectively. Edit Data Bindings (a refresh may be necessary) so that `SelectedValue` is bound to `pub_id`. Two-way binding must be on.

   Save your work again, and view it in the browser to see an improved data-entry scheme.

How It Works

In this exercise, you created a `FormView` that could insert new titles. You started by enabling the inserting capability in the data source control. `FormView` supports whole-control templates (recall that `DetailsView` offers field-by-field templates).

You switched to the `InsertItemTemplate` and added two buttons and got the set of input controls. Of course, such a trick is not without problems. The field for `Title_ID` was set to read-only in `ItemTemplate`, and you needed to change it to read-write in `InsertItemTemplate`. You first changed the binding code from the `Eval()` function to the `Bind()` function. Then you changed the control type from `Label` to `TextBox`.

In the final step, you converted a textbox to a `DropDownList` in the same way that you did for `DetailsView`.

Trade-Offs between DetailsView and FormView

When enabling insertion on your pages, the DetailsView and FormView each have their place. To help you decide, here are the trade-offs.

	Advantages	Disadvantages
DetailsView	DetailsView provides some HTML layout for the field names and values. It is easy to add ButtonFields to execute code.	Very little customization of the layout of the fields.
FormView	Completely free to design ItemTemplate. Offers high-level templates such as one InsertItemTemplate for all fields.	Requires more work to build the template. Must do more work to create buttons.

Common Mistakes

If you are having problems with a page, we suggest you go through this list to check if you have made the kind of mistake that frequently shows up in the student labs.

- Looking for an insert technique in the GridView. You need to use DetailsView or FormView to add insert capability to the page.
- Changing values in a parameter of the wrong collection when using source view. When changing an InsertParameter, double-check that you are not in the list of UpdateParameters.
- Accidentally editing the ItemTemplate instead of the InsertItemTemplate. The former is to display in ReadOnly mode; the latter will appear in Insert mode.
- Attempting to insert a value for a field whose value is autogenerated by the database. In this case, you should remove this field from Insert mode by setting InsertVisible=false on the field or removing the input control for this field from the InsertItemTemplate.
- Attempting to insert a record with values that do not conform to the constraints of the underlying database.
- Looking for an ItemTemplate and InsertItemTemplate in DetailsView. They do not exist if the fields are all BoundFields. (Those fields are automatically changed from labels to textboxes). However, if you add a TemplateField to the DetailsView, you can work with an ItemTemplate and InsertItemTemplate for that field.

- Trying to find a function in the wrong Smart Tasks panel of a control. Because controls can be nested (for example, radio buttons within a `DetailsView`), it is easy to open the Smart Tasks panel for the wrong level of control.
- Trying to find a function on a Smart Tasks panel when the panel is in template editing mode. End template editing and then you will see the original list of options.
- Setting up a list box or radio button without following each of the five steps listed in this chapter.

Summary

This chapter walked you through increasingly more complex variations in inserting new records. Only the `DetailsView` and `FormView` support inserting (not the `GridView`). Using insert employs ASP.NET 2.0's ability to change the rendering of the `DetailsView` or `FormView` from ReadOnly to Insert mode. You started with a simple case of drag-and-drop and checked on enabling insertions in the data source control and data-bound control.

Next, you took a closer look at enabling insertions in the `SqlDataSource` control. There is no `EnableInsert=true` property; rather, the existence of an `InsertCommand` and an `InsertParameters` collection enables inserting. Both of these properties are set by the data source designer in the dialog box for Select Statement⇨Advanced Options. Don't be surprised if you look at the source code and see that the Designer also generates `Update` and `Delete` statements and corresponding parameters collections — in this version of VWD, you generate all three or none. You can delete the `Update` and `Delete` properties to condense code if you don't need them.

The data-bound control can sense the insert enablement in the data source control. By default, `DetailsView` will provide a label for each field in ReadOnly mode and a textbox for each in Insert mode. If you want to change that rendering, you can change a `BoundField` to be a `TemplateField` and then substitute a more robust input control such as radio buttons or a list box. That input control can be populated from a separate data source control, such as a list of states that come from a States table.

Using a templated input control in a `DetailsView` control is a five-step process. First, create a data source control to support the new input control. Second, change the field in the `DetailsView` from a `BoundField` to a `TemplateField`. Then edit the templates and replace the default textbox with your better input control. Next set the input control to read from your data source control of Step 1. And last, from the input control's Smart Tasks panel, data-bind display and value properties to fields in the input's data source control.

`FormView` is a less structured control. In contrast with `DetailsView`, it has `Item` and `InsertItem` templates for the control as a whole. By default, VWD populates the Read-Only template.

You have now completed the first three parts of the book: an introduction, how to read data, and how to modify data. In the last part, starting with the next chapter, you will work with special data sources and address performance issues.

Exercises

The answers to these review questions can be found in Appendix B.

1. In light of inserting new records, compare the major difference among `GridView`, `DetailsView`, and `FormView`.
2. Contrast the hierarchy of templates in the `DetailsView` and the `FormView`.
3. What is the easiest way to change a `DetailsView` with its default bound fields to bound fields within a template field?
4. Why might an ID field not show up in your `FormView InsertItemTemplate`?
5. What properties and subtags of a `SqlDataSource` control enable the behavior of inserting new records?

13 Validation

In the last two chapters, we created pages that allowed users to input values for storage in our database. We mentioned many times the importance of guarding against errant or malicious input. This chapter discusses validation controls, your first line of defense. Validation is not strictly a topic of the ASP.NET 2.0 data controls, because they can be used on forms that are not data-enabled. But because they are crucial to data operations, we will cover them in this chapter in seven sections:

- Overview of validation controls
- Common concepts of validation controls and their properties
- Types of validation controls including the `RequiredFieldValidator`, `CompareFieldValidator`, `RangeValidator`, `RegularExpressionValidator`, `CustomValidator`
- Validation in data scenarios
- Validation summary
- Validation groups (new to ASP.NET 2.0)
- Validation in code

We finish the chapter with our usual three aids: a list of common mistakes, a summary, and some self-test questions.

Overview of Validation Controls

The page designer is one of many guardians of the database. Web pages are a window into the data and, even more dangerously, a source of values in the database. With that capability comes the responsibility of using the best practices for data security. One of the first lines of defense is the careful validation of any data prior to presentation for writing to the database. Three kinds of problems arise from user input:

- Input that is not valid or uniform; for example, a user types "IND" for a state abbreviation that should be standardized as IN.
- The user mistypes input, such as AA for a state abbreviation.
- Input is malicious and attempts to compromise the security of the database.

ASP.NET 2.0 offers several tools to reduce these kinds of problems:

- Validation controls check that user input meets certain criteria. If the input does not meet the criteria, then the validation control triggers aborts on data-writing operations.
- Controls that prevent having the user type their input to eliminate frequent problems. Offering a list of states from which a user can select eliminates all of the problems of users typing a state into a textbox.
- The data source control `Insert`, `Delete`, and `Update` parameters provide a built-in defense against certain types of mistakes and malicious hacks.
- Although it is not part of ASP.NET, if you are designing the database, you can build in constraints that limit the kind of values that are accepted for writing.

When these four tools are used together, most problems can be eliminated. This chapter focuses on using validation to prevent errors.

What Are Validation Controls?

Validation controls check data entered into other controls and then issue a pass or fail. The kinds of checks range from simple, such as the mere existence of a value, up through very complex evaluations for patterns. Validation controls are like other ASP.NET 2.0 controls in that they are server-side code (with an exception discussed below) written by Microsoft. They are placed on the page, and their properties are set the same as manner as the data controls we have discussed in this book.

What Scenarios Do Validations Support?

Data can be obtained for an `Update` or `Insert` data source control in many ways.

- **Created automatically by the page:** For example, the page uses the system date as the creation date for a new record.
- **From another control:** For example, a list of states and provinces is offered, from which the user selects one.
- **From the server or request:** For example, the query string or session state.
- **By typing:** A textbox is offered, into which the user can type any group of characters.

The above list increases in risk of attack as you go down in the need for validation. In the topmost case, the page is providing the data and then validation is checking that the page is working correctly. In a selection list, the role of validation is to determine if a selection has been made. If there is a default value, then validation may not be necessary. Because of the reduced risk with the first two options, validation is not a high priority in most of those scenarios. But frequently we have to offer a textbox for input, especially when collecting raw user data such as a shipping address or email address. In these cases, validation should always be used.

To start the exercises in this chapter, we will set up a page with a simple validation.

Try It Out   Simple Form Scenario with RequiredFieldValidator Control

In this simple exercise, we will check that a textbox has data before the page is processed. Note that at this point we are not validating data controls, just that there is content in a simple textbox in a form.

1. Create a new folder for this chapter: `C:\Websites\BegAspNet2Db\ch13`. Create a new page named `TIO-1301-SimpleValidation.aspx`. Drag a textbox to the page, and name the textbox `NameTextBox`. Drag a button to the page, and in the Properties window, change the `Text` to `Submit` and confirm that the `UseSubmitBehavior` is set to true.
2. Save the page, and run it in the browser. Although the page does not actually do anything with your name, the Submit button sends the data to the server and calls the same page. Note that `Submit` works whether the `NameTextBox` has a name or not.

> **If you get an error about controls being within a form, check in VWD Source view that all of your ASP controls are inside the `<form>` tags.**

3. Close the browser and return to VWD. To the page, add a required `FieldValidator` control from the section of the Validation controls section of the toolbox. Set two properties in the Properties window: `ID` to `NameRequiredValidation` control and its `ControlToValidate` to `NameTextBox`. Now, find the `Text` property and change it to `"Please enter your name"`.
4. Save your work, which should match the following listing:

```
... <h2>Chapter 13 TIO #1301 Simple Validation</h2>
    <form id="form1" runat="server"> <div>
        <asp:TextBox ID="NameTextBox" runat="server"></asp:TextBox><br />
        <asp:RequiredFieldValidator ID="NameRequiredValidationcontrol1 "
runat="server"
            ControlToValidate="NameTextBox"
            Text="Please enter your name">
        </asp:RequiredFieldValidator control><br />
        <asp:Button ID="Button1" runat="server" Text="Submit" />
</div></form></body></html>
```

5. Test your work in your browser, noting that when you click the Submit button without having entered a name, you evoke a validation error.

How It Works

To start, the validation control sits on the page without rendering; we only see the Name textbox and the Submit button. When a page is submitted (the button clicked), the validation control applies its criteria to its `ControlToValidate`. For the `RequiredFieldValidator` control that we used, the only criterion is that the field contains a value (that is not `NULL` or `String.Empty`). If the `ControlToValidate` passes the test, then the submission proceeds. If the test fails, then the validation control becomes visible to display its `Text` property value. Later in this chapter, we will observe that the `Page.IsValid` property was set to `false` and the submission was incomplete.

Common Concepts of Validation Controls

Before exploring the details of each validation control, it is important to cover some common topics. In this section, we will:

- Study the properties that are common to all validation control controls
- Explore the general concepts of using validation controls
- Look at how validation controls work under the covers
- Examine how to use multiple validations together

Common Properties

ASP.NET 2.0 offers five validation controls, which differ primarily in the kind of check that they perform. Most members of this family offer the same set of properties, so we will cover these general properties prior to investigating the validation controls individually. These properties include:

- *ControlToValidate* identifies which of the controls on the page should be checked by this validation control. In the preceding simple exercise, the validation control was named `NameRequiredValidation` control and its property `ControlToValidate` was the `NameTextBox`.
- *Text* contains the string to be shown to the user if he or she enters data that violates the validation rule. If there is a value for `ErrorMessage` but no value in the Text property, then the `ErrorMessage` is automatically substituted for the Text property.
- *ErrorMessage* and *ValidationGroup* contain text to be shown in a summary of errors, as we cover later when we discuss `ValidationSummary`.

Two validation properties are similar in name: `Text` and `ErrorMessage`. Both are invoked when a control fails validation. `Text` is displayed in the position of the validation control. `ErrorMessage` is fed to the `ValidationSummary` control and displayed in the `ValidationSummary` control's location. If you are not using a `ValidationSummary`, then you should be putting your warning to the user in the `Text` property.

- The `Display` property determines how the page should handle the layout of the validation control when it is displaying its Text message. The three options include `None` that will not display the `Text` value. This option is employed when you want error messages to appear only in the `ValidationSummary` and not at the location of the validator control. `Static` will always reserve space for the validation control, even when its message is not being displayed. `Dynamic` will allocate space for the validation control text when it is shown, pushing the remainder of the page to the right and down.
- *SetFocusOnError* will change the focus of the page to the control that created the error, thus making it easier for the user to revise the input. If there is more than one validation control on the page and more than one reports a validation failure, then the first validation control on the page that with a failure will have its `ControlToValidate` receive the focus.

- ❑ *EnableClientScript* invokes a client-side check of the value. (This property is covered in more detail later in this chapter.)

There are, in addition, properties specific for the kind of test in each validation control. For the `RequiredFieldValidator` that we have used so far, the test is built in — a simple check that the value is not equal to `NULL` or `String.Empty`. In the next section, we will discuss the testing properties for comparing fields, value ranges, and regular expressions.

This chapter will also utilize one property of the button control. `MyButton.CausesValidation` allows you to turn off the validation programmatically. For example, if you create a custom Cancel button you would not want invalid data to abort the cancel operation. `CausesValidation` is set to true by default, so in most scenarios does not require modification.

Finally, we work in this chapter with one property of the page. The `Page.IsValid` property will be set to true only if all of the validation controls on the page report a pass for their `ControlsToValidate` (although there is a twist on that when we get to validation groups).

Try It Out Validation Properties

In this exercise, we will run through permutations of the properties discussed above. We will still be working with a simple form outside of a data-bound scenario.

1. In the `ch13` folder, create a new page named `TIO-1302-ValidationProperties-1.aspx`. Add a textbox to the page and accept the default name of `TextBox1`. Add a button. Position the insertion bar to the left of (before) the textbox and in the toolbox, double-click a `RequiredFieldValidator`. VWD will add the validator to the left of the textbox. In the validator's properties, set the text to `"This field is required"` and the `ControlToValidate` to `TextBox1`.
2. Save and test the page.
3. Before you close the page, observe that the textbox is in the middle of the page, with an empty space where the validator control is sitting. Close the browser.
4. Save the page as `TIO-1302-ValidationProperties-2.aspx` and adjust the title and H2 text. Change the validator's `Display` property to `Dynamic`.
5. Save and test the page. Note that the textbox starts to the left, and when a validation failure message appears, the page rearranges to shift the textbox right. Before you close the browser, note that if you do not enter data and click Submit, then the validation fails. If you immediately begin typing, the browser does not accept the input because the focus is not on the offending input control (the textbox).
6. In VWD, save the page as `TIO-1302-ValidationProperties-3.aspx`, and adjust the title and H2 text. Change the validation control property of `SetFocusOnError` to `true`.
7. Save and test the page by creating a validation failure and then immediately typing text into the box. Before closing the browser, observe that when you submit invalid data, the browser does not refresh from the server, as evidenced by a disabled Back button on your browser toolbar. This is showing that the browser is still showing the original page. A postback has not occurred. Close the browser.

8. In VWD save the page as `TIO-1302-ValidationProperties-4.aspx`, and adjust the title and H2 text. In the validator's properties, change the `EnableClientScript` to `false`.

9. Save and test in the browser. Notice that now when you submit invalid data, the browser's Back button appears, indicating that you are on a new page. The data went back to the server where it was deemed invalid. Close the browser.

10. In VWD, save the page as `TIO-1302-ValidationProperties-5.aspx`, and adjust the title and H2 text. Change `Button1`'s `CausesValidation` property to `false`.

11. Save you work and test it in the browser. Observe that validation is not being performed when the data is submitted.

How It Works

Most of these properties are self-explanatory, especially when you see them in action. Keep in mind that `Text` (not `ErrorMessage`) is the property that is displayed in the validator control when a validation fails. We have observed that prior to reacting to a validation failure the validation control can either take up space on the page (`Static`) or create space when needed to display a text message (`Dynamic`). In some scenarios, we may elect to turn off validation when a button is clicked, as we did by setting the `CausesValidation` property to `false`.

We will discuss more about the `EnableClientScript` in the next section, but this is how it worked here. In Step 8 the `EnableClientScript` started out set to `true` (the default). When it is true, the browser uses JScript to perform a validation locally. If the validation fails, then there is no communication back to the server. Because the page has not gone to the server, the browser will not show the option to go back. If the input is valid, then the page is sent to the server and another validation is performed (for security against spoofing). In this case, you see the Back button enabled because after the server has performed its validation it issues a new page.

> **Spoofing sends across the Internet information that pretends to be something else and, thus, hides its true identity. For example, a hacker could try to send to the server what looks like a postback but has actually been constructed without the client-side validation.**

Later in Step 8 we changed to `EnableClientScript=false`. In this case, every submit goes to the server and the Back button is always enabled. This scenario requires more communication with the server, but it works even when JScript is disabled or not supported on the client.

Implementation of Validation Controls

In keeping with the objectives of version 2.0 of ASP.NET, the entire validation scheme in ASP.NET 2.0 works with little customization by the page designer. If you add the validation controls and set their properties, then the validation will work without coding. Validation occurs in controls separate from the data-bound control. Not visible (like data source control) unless there is invalid data, validation controls can be placed anywhere on the page. If a validation fails, then the `Validator.Text` property's value will appear at the location of the validation control.

How Validation Works behind the Scenes

There are two scenarios for the sequence of events in validation:

- Validation is performed on the client *and* the server if the client supports JScript and the validation control's `EnableClientScript=true`.
- Validation is performed *only* on the server if either of the above two conditions are false.

Validation is always performed on the server, regardless of whether client validation was performed. This prevents *spoofing*, whereby a hacker fakes a valid postback to the server to try to bypass the client-side validation. The addition of the client-side option saves some time because a roundtrip is not made if there is a validation failure in the client validation.

Pages start with a setting that a page is not valid. If all of the validators report in with a `Valid=true`, then the page sums that up into setting `Page.IsValid=true`. The `GridView`, `DetailsView`, and `FormView` controls automatically check `Page.IsValid` before doing updates or inserts and will not instruct the `SqlDataSource` control to execute the SQL commands if the page is not valid.

Client-Side Validation

If validation is being performed on the client, then it occurs when the `ControlToValidate` loses focus. Note that this is generally before a Submit button is clicked. If the validation fails, then nothing is sent to the server, but the validators will still display their Text messages regarding the failure by using JavaScript.

Server-Side Validation

When received by server, another validation is performed. If the page passes validation, then the page goes on to perform its other tasks. If there are failures, then `Page.IsValid` is set to False. The page will then execute scripts, but these can be stopped if you, as the programmer, check the `Page.IsValid` state. Data controls on the page will not perform any writing tasks. Then the page is rebuilt with validation error messages and sent back in response.

Considerations for When to Use Server Side Versus Client–Side Validation

Always perform server-side validation (you can't turn it off anyhow for ASP.NET 2.0 validation controls). Client-side validation is an extra convenience if you know your clients use JavaScript. If some clients do not have JavaScript enabled, you can still turn on `EnableClientScript`, and it will be ignored for the limited browsers.

Multiple Validations

More than one validation control can target a single input control, for example that input is required and that input must be within a certain range. ASP.NET 2.0 will check all the validations and only report a pass for the input control if the input control meets all its validation controls.

In complicated cases, it may be best to use a regular expression validator with logical clauses that can perform multiple tests. For example, a North American postal code might meet the Canadian, Mexican, or U.S. patterns. Three different validation controls, one with each option, would fail because a value would never match all three. But you can create a pattern in a `RegularExpressionValidator` control with three clauses connected by `OR` symbols.

Types of Validation controls

Until now we have discussed validation on a theoretical level. ASP.NET 2.0 offers five kinds of validation controls, as described in the following table. We will go through the details of each, starting with a tabular overview.

Table of Types

Control Name	Applicable Situation
`RequiredFieldValidator`	To avoid empty values, for example when a user is entering a password for setting up a new account.
`RangeValidator`	To check if an entered value is within limits. For example, for a youth club the date of birth field should indicate an age that is less than 18.
`CompareValidator`	To check if two fields contain the same value. For example, when creating a password the user should enter it twice to ensure that the user has memorized it correctly.
`RegularExpressionValidator`	To check if the input matches a pattern about the nature of the characters, for example a letter versus a number, uppercase and lowercase, length and validity of a date.
`CustomValidator`	To check if the input conforms to rules that are written in code. This can include complex evaluations such verifying the pattern in an authorization number.

RequiredFieldValidator Control

As we have seen in earlier examples, the `RequiredFieldValidator` control checks that an input is not empty. As in most database work, one or more spaces would still be considered a value. Also, the fact that the data source control or database might add a default value is not considered by the `RequiredFieldValidator`.

When using a `DropDownList`, the first item in the list will be automatically selected until the user makes another selection. So, we get the counterintuitive behavior that a `RequiredFieldValidator` will pass even if the user does not make a selection. If you want to force a `DropDownList` selection, you can use the following code to add a new item to the top of the list, an item that does not have a value in it:

```
<asp:DropDownList ID="DropDownList1" runat="server"
DataSourceID="SqlDataSource1"
DataTextField="pub_name"
```

```
            DataValueField="pub_id"
            AppendDataBoundItems="true">
                <asp:ListItem  Value="" Text="Please select an option"/>
            </asp:DropDownList>
```

Consider the situation where NULL might be a legitimate value. If you expect the empty string to mean null, then you wouldn't use a required field validation control at all, since empty is actually a valid value (converted to NULL in the database). If you expect a specific value to mean null, such as "NA" or "NULL," then only use a required field validation control if empty string is considered an invalid value. You would convert the "NA" or "NULL" string to null on the server in code in the OnUpdating, OnInserting, or OnDeleting event of the data source or data-bound control.

CompareValidator Control

The CompareValidator control checks whether two items are the same, one of which is the ControlToValidate. The comparison can be made to one of three kinds of objects:

- The value in another control
- A hard-coded value, list of values or some kinds of ranges of values
- A data type

The CompareValidator control will has properties for ControlToCompare and Operator for the above scenarios. It also has a property for Type as listed below.

Comparing one input control to another input control is most obvious. This arises in many sites when you are asking for a crucial piece of information and you want to have the user enter it twice to ensure that the value is entered correctly (for example, an email address). Another common scenario occurs when the user is entering a password for the first time. Because the value in a password field is generally not shown (a camouflage character is substituted), the user can not visually check for accuracy. Entering the password a second time and using the CompareValidator control solves the problem. Note that the input textboxes for a new password will appear twice, but there is only one validation control. In this scenario, the ControlToCompare property is set to the second input control, and the Operator is generally set to equal.

CompareValidator controls can also be used against a set value. That can be a single value, such as a low-security scenario where the same password is used for all members to enter a page. The CompareValidator control would have no value in the ControlToCompare property but would have a value in the ValueToCompare property. The Operator property would be set to equals. CompareValidator control also offers the ability to make a quantitative comparison by setting the operator to Less Than, Greater Than or some similar options. These options bring the CompareValidator control close to the function of the RangeValidator control, but with much less flexibility. For example, CompareValidator could check that the value entered for a StartDate occurs before a value entered into EndDate.Last; the CompareValidator will check a data type for you. For instance, if you ask users to enter a date of birth, there are scores of formats. The Operator property can be set to DataTypeCheck and the Type set to DateTime.

> **If you accidentally include both ControlToCompare and ValueToCompare properties, then ControlToCompare is used.**

RangeValidator Control

The `RangeValidator` control ensures that an input value is within an upper and lower bound. The input value to validate can be a number, currency, date or (rarely) a string. In addition to the common properties discussed above, there are three testing properties to set: `MinimumValue`, `MaximumValue`, and `Type`, which means data type. The upper and lower bounds values are inclusive, so the comparison is like >= and <=. If they properties are set to 5 and 10, respectively, then an input of 5 and 10 are acceptable. If you will accept numbers with decimal values, then select the type `Double`.

One aspect of the `RangeValidator` control is counterintuitive. If no data exists in the input control, then the `RangeValidation` control will not validate the input and will not throw a validation failure. To ensure that there is a value entered and that the value is within a range, you must add a second validation control: a `RequiredFieldValidator`. This design supports scenarios where it is acceptable to leave a field blank. But if the user does enter something, it has to be valid.

The syntax for dates is flexible. First, set the `Type` to `Date`. Then the dates for `MaximumValue` and `MinimumValue` can be entered as YYYY/MM/DD, DD/MM/YY, or DD/MM/YYYY. You can leave off the leading zeros for days and months. Dates can be tricky to integrate across cultures. Most Web sites don't accept dates in a local format, because then you'd have to have logic to parse them in every language. It's much more common to require the dates, currency, and the like to be in the format of the culture of the server. The format for entry can be noted in text on the entry page. If you do attempt to globalize (a project with many other aspects than just date formats), there are three separate formats to consider.

- The syntax for dates in the `RangeValidator`'s properties is always the culture of the server, so the format shouldn't change no matter the culture in a culture page directive.
- The syntax that the `RangeValidator` will accept when users type in dates is culture-dependent and will be affected by the page directive's culture.
- The storage of dates in the database itself is always done in the format of the database server's culture.

Globalization of an application is not a trivial topic, because many things need to be considered, not just how to configure a `RangeValidator`. Prior to attempting globalization, you should study more advanced texts. The `RangeValidator` control will inspect a string and consider the range to be the alphabet in its Unicode order (Unicode has the same order as ASCII for the Western characters and also supports characters from other languages). So, if you want user input to be a code starting with a letter between A and F, then the entry will accept anything like A100 or Apple or F999. But if you enter a something starting with a lowercase letter, such as a100, validation will fail because "a" is listed after "A" and "F" in the Unicode sequence. If you need to regard upper- and lowercase letters as part of the same alphabet, then use the `RegularExpressionValidator` control.

You can limit entry to values that begin with a letter by making the `MinimumValue=A` and the `MaximumValue=z` (keeping in mind that the ASCII characters between the lower- and uppercase letters are also accepted, such as brackets, the backslash, and the caret). This works because the uppercase English alphabet comes before the lowercase English alphabet in Unicode. If you wanted to accept letters such as ñ, ü, or _, you would have to further expand the range within the ASCII order. Note that there is no option for using logical AND; that option becomes available with the `RegularExpressionValidator` control.

Last, we can set range maximum and minimum values programmatically, as we do other properties. For example, we might want the `MaximumValue` for a date of birth to be today and the `MinimumValue` to be calculated as 120 years prior to today. The following code will do the trick, but there are two places to be careful. First, be sure to set the data type in the `RangeValidator` and check that any values generated in code are acceptable within that type (especially dates). Second, the `MaximumValue` and `MinimumValue` properties of a `RangeValidator` require a value even before the `Page_Load` code executes. Ergo, you must have values in those properties, even if they are going to be changed in code.

```
<%@ Page Language="VB" %>
<!DOCTYPE html PUBLIC "-//W3C//DTD XHTML 1.0 Transitional//EN"
"http://www.w3.org/TR/xhtml1/DTD/xhtml1-transitional.dtd">
<script runat="server">
    Protected Sub Page_Load(ByVal sender As Object, ByVal e As System.EventArgs)
        RangeValidator1.MaximumValue = DateTime.Today
        DOBRangeValidator.MaximumValue = DateTime.Today.AddYears(-21)
        Response.Write(RangeValidator1.MinimumValue)
    End Sub
</script>
```

Actually, you would have to accommodate a maximum value of tomorrow. When it is January 1 in Hawaii, little bundles of joy have already entered this world on January 2 in Britain. Set `RangeValidator1.MaximumValue = DateTime.Today.AddYears(-21).`

Try It Out Compare and Range Validation Controls

This exercise will check numeric and date input for reasonable ranges. For the dates, we will fail dates that indicate that the user is less than 21 years old.

1. In the ch13 folder, create a page named `TIO-1303-CompareAndRangeValidation.aspx`. Add a textbox named `HeightTextBox` and a label asking the user to enter his or her height in centimeters. Add a `RangeValidator` of type double that limits acceptable values from 15 to 250 cm.
2. Save your work, and test it.
3. Drag a textbox to the page, name it `DOBTextBox`, and position a label next to it that renders `"Enter your date of birth."` Add a simple `RangeValidator` to ensure that the user enters between `1900 (MinimumValue)` and `2007` (`MaximumValue`).

```
...<h2>Chapter 13 TIO #1303 Compare And Range Validation version 1</h2>
    <form id="form1" runat="server"><div>
        <asp:Label ID="HeightLabel" runat="server"
            Text="Enter your height in cm" Width="250px"></asp:Label>
        <asp:TextBox ID="HeightTextBox" runat="server" Width="250px"></asp:TextBox>
        <asp:RangeValidator ID="HeightRangeValidator" runat="server"
            ControlToValidate="HeightTextBox"
            Text="Your entry for height is less than 15 or more than 250"
            MaximumValue="250"  MinimumValue="15"
            Type="Double"></asp:RangeValidator><br />

        <asp:Label ID="DOBLabel" runat="server"
            Text="Enter your Date of Birth"
            Width="250px"></asp:Label>
```

```
        <asp:TextBox ID="DOBTextBox" runat="server" Width="250px"></asp:TextBox>
        <asp:RangeValidator ID="DOBRangeValidator" runat="server"
            ControlToValidate="DOBTextBox"
            Text="Your DOB is too early or too recent"
            MaximumValue="12/31/2007" MinimumValue="1/1/1900"
            Type="Date"></asp:RangeValidator>
</div></form></body></html>
```

4. Save your work, and test it.
5. Now, improve the page by checking that the person is at least 21. Save the page as `TIO-1303-CompareAndRangeValidation-2`, and change the title and H2 texts. In source view, click the object list at the top left and then the Load event at the top right, as shown in Figure 13-1.
6. Type the following code into the nascent procedure, and change the text property to "You must be 21 to buy beer."

```
<script runat="server">

    Protected Sub Page_Load(ByVal sender As Object, ByVal e As System.EventArgs)
DOBRangeValidator.MaximumValue = DateTime.Today.AddYears(-21)
    End Sub
</script>
```

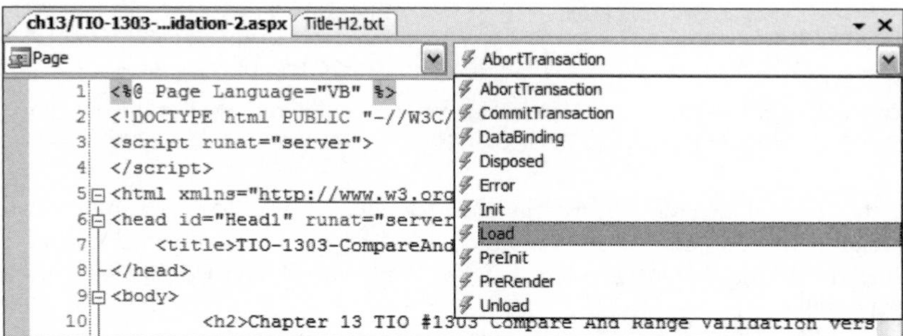

Figure 13-1

7. Save your work, and test it in your browser.
8. Add two textboxes named `EMailTextBox1` and `Email2TextBox` with a label that asks for entry of an email address. Add a `CompareValidator` to confirm that the two email addresses entered are the same. Add two `RequiredFieldValidators` to ensure that the user enters both email addresses.

```
<asp:Label ID="Email1Label" runat="server"
    Text="Enter your Email" Width="250px"></asp:Label>
<asp:TextBox ID="Email1TextBox" runat="server"
    Width="250px"></asp:TextBox>
<asp:CompareValidator ID="EmailCompareValidator" runat="server"
    ControlToCompare="Email1TextBox"
    ControlToValidate="Email2TextBox"
    Text="Your EMail address entries do not match">
```

```
</asp:CompareValidator><br />

<asp:Label ID="Email2Label" runat="server"
    Text="Re-enter your Email address" Width="250px"></asp:Label>
<asp:TextBox ID="Email2TextBox" runat="server"
    Width="250px"></asp:TextBox><br />
<asp:Button ID="Button1" runat="server" Text="Button" />
```

9. Save your work, and test it in your browser.

How It Works

For the height textbox, we merely have to think through the range of possibilities for humans. Fifteen centimeters should cover the smallest of premature babies, and two and a half meters will cover even basketball players. People may enter their height with a decimal, like 185.5 cm. This is accommodated with the type set to `Double`, which can support digits to the right of the decimal points (as opposed to `Integer`). And, as always with validators, we can't forget to test the `ControlToValidate` property. Fortunately, a missing value in this property raises an error at runtime.

A person's age is more complex, because it varies from day to day. In our page, we move to the more complex solution of actually calculating in code the `MaximumValue` acceptable for the birthdate. The code below runs before the page is validated. We refer to the validation property in code by its ID, the same as any other control. The function's parameters, in a generic definition, are `DateTime = DateTime.AddYears(NumberOfYears)`. The left side of the equals sign means any variable or instance of the type `DateTime`, in this case a value of today that we get from running the method `DateTime.Today`. (This is the same as the old VB code: `DateAdd`(*KindOfUnitsToAdd, Amount to Add(subtract), Date to which units are added*). Taken together, the line returns the date, which is 21 years before today.

```
DOBRangeValidator.MaximumValue = DateTime.Today.AddYears(-21)
```

The email address textboxes are compared for validation. Be sure to set the `ControlToValidate` as the input control that you expect the user to type in second. Otherwise, the validation will fire after the first receives data and at that point the second is still empty.

RegularExpressionValidator Control

A *regular expression* is description of a pattern of characters. For example, a Canadian postal code (examples include N1K 4R5 and B2R 7T8) is always six characters in the pattern of letter-number-letter-space-number-letter-number. Because this is always the case (the system is regular), we can write an expression that describes the pattern.

> **Regular expression can become very complex, to the extent that entire texts have been written on the topic (for example see *Beginning Regular Expressions* by Andrew Watt, ISBN: 0-7645-7489-2). Part of the problem is that we are using characters in the regular expression to describe characters in the value to test. Problems of recursion soon rear their ugly heads (see *Gödel, Escher, Bach: An Eternal Golden Braid* by Douglas Hofstadter, ISBN: 0465026567).**

A regular expression is made up of two kinds of characters:

- **Literal characters:** Describe specific characters that must be in specific locations. For example, there must always be a hyphen as the fourth character).
- **Metacharacters:** Describe allowable sets of characters (for example, in the second position there must be a number). The metacharacters also include options for how many characters are allowed and how the allowable criteria are to be applied.

The first rule is that if you expect your input to be one line (no line breaks), then begin the expression with a caret ^ and end it with a dollar sign $. Actually that means "the enclosed must match at the beginning and end of the string." In other words, do not allow matches on characters before or after these. If you will work with multiline input, you will need to study the topic beyond this short introduction. For a beginner, that is a good way to specify one line only.

The next fundamental rule of regular expressions is that a backslash \ is an escape character. That means the next character can be one of two things: a real metacharacter or an escaped literal character. For example, if you want parentheses or periods as literals, you have to prefix them with backslashes. So, if a value must be the digit 2 followed by another number, the expression would be: `^2\d$`. The leading 2 is a literal that means that the input must have the character "2" in the first position. Then the backslash indicates that the following character of the expression, the d, is a metacharacter. A metacharacter of "d" means any single digit (0 to 9). Similarly, a metacharacter of \w means a character that is part of a word (the letters). A simple regular expression to describe a Canadian Postal Code (a typical code is K2V 1A5) would be `^\d\w\d \w\d\w$`. Note the space character between the first and second set of three characters.

If a character in the value can be repeated, then that character's metacharacter in the expression should be followed by a pair of braces containing the exact number of repeats allowed, such as `^\d{5}$` for a five-digit USA postal code or `^\d{5}-\d{4}$` for a nine-digit USA code such as 12345-6789.

.NET regular expressions support the ability to accept a variable number of repeats of a metacharacter. Adding a comma in the repeater braces indicates that the number is a minimum value. A second number after the comma indicates a maximum. So, exactly five digits is `^\d{5}$`, five or more digits is `^\d{5,}$` , any number of digits is `^\d{0,}$`, and a number of digits that is at least three but no more than five is `^\d{3,5}$`.

You may also see a syntax for multiple characters that uses wildcards. A metacharacter followed by an asterisk * can be repeated zero or more times, which is the same as {0,}. A metacharacter followed by a plus sign + must be repeated one or more time (at least once), which is the same as {1,}. The question mark after a metacharacter means the character is repeated zero or once, which is the same as {0,1}. For example, an input that can only be digits and must be at least one digit and has no upper limit on length of digits could be described as `^\d+$`.

You can present a list of allowable characters in a position. The list just has to be enclosed in brackets [] and the items separated by commas. For example, you might have a password scheme (very weak) that requires a password of three letters and in which the middle letter must be a vowel. A regular expression for validation is `^\w[a,e,i,o,u,A,E.I,O,U]\w]$`. This permits "cat" and "CAT" and "dog" but not "adz".

Regular expressions support many special characters for tabs, line breaks, and so on. One of larger scope is the `\s`, which includes any kind of white space (spaces or tabs).

Regular expressions also permit the use of parentheses, as in algebra. This is particularly useful with the OR operator, for example in a pattern where a product code might be entered as `12-345` or as `12 345`.

```
^\d{2}(\-|\s)\d{3}$
```

To finish, the following table describes a few common regular expressions.

Purpose	Regular Expression	Note
Email address simple Joe@Does.org (However, the simple email address does not accommodate numbers in domain name, like an IP address. See following paragraph for a better alternative.)	`^\w+@[a-zA-Z_]+?\.[a-zA-Z]{2,3}$`	`\w+` Any number of letters `@` A literal `[a-zA-Z_]+?` Any number of letters `\.` A literal period (full stop) `[a-zA-Z]{2,3}` two or three letters
A 10-digit phone number (918) 123-4567 918 123-4567	`\(?\d{3}[) ]\s?\d{3}[- ]\d{4}`	`\(?` Matches none or one left parentheses `\d{3}` Matches exactly 3 numbers `[) ]` Checks for a right parenthesis or space `\s?` Checks for none or one spaces
Five- and nine-digit USA postal codes	`\b\d{5}-\d{4}\b|\b\d{5}\b`	`\d{5}-\d{4}` Matches the more modern zip plus four | The OR of an alternate pattern `\d{5}` Matches the older pattern of only five digits

The entry for Email address above would not accept an IP address composed of digits. We will cover that here, starting with the entire expression.

```
([\w-\.]+)@((\[[0-9]{1,3}\.[0-9]{1,3}\.[0-9]{1,3}\.)|(([\w-]+\.)+))([a-zA-Z]{2,4}|[0-9]{1,3})(\]?)
```

We can break this down into the following parts. First, we have any number of characters allowed for the personal part of the email address, followed by a literal `@` sign. This accommodates formats like `Joe@...` Or `Joe.Doe@...`. Note how the parentheses apply the plus sign to both the letters and a period.

```
([\w-\.]+)@
```

Next, we need to accept numeric IP addresses or domain names. So, we will set up an OR structure, indicated by the gray line below. The first line below is schematic, and the second is the actual expression.

```
(              ...option A...               )|( ...option b... )
((\[[0-9]{1,3}\.[0-9]{1,3}\.[0-9]{1,3}\.)|(([\w-]+\.)+))
```

In the above, option A matches an IP address with three sets of up to three numbers, each separated by a period symbol. A period on its own means "any single character." A backslash and followed by a period means a literal period.

```
((\[[0-9]{1,3}\.[0-9]{1,3}\.[0-9]{1,3}\.)
```

The option B is for a domain name represented by allowing any number of letters followed by a period.

```
[\w-]+\.
```

But addresses might have multiple parts to the domain, in the form of `Joe@NorthRegion.Sales.USA.MyCompany.com`. So, we take the above pattern and encase it in parentheses and allow that to be repeated as often as desired.

```
(([\w-]+\.)+))
```

The last bit is to the right of the final period. It can be either letters (like `.com` or `.org`) or numbers in an IP address. So, this is handled the same as the above with two options. The first option is 2 to 4 letters, whereas the second option is 1 to 3 numbers. Also included in the number option are the characters of parenthesis and backslash. The final question mark means there can be one or more of these two options.

```
( LetterOption| NumberOption  )
([a-zA-Z]{2,4}|[0-9]{1,3})(\]?)
```

As we mentioned above, entire books have been written on the art and science of regular expressions. But in this text we will limit ourselves to a few examples.

Try It Out RegularExpressionValidator Control

We will create a validation for a U.S. Social Security number. The numbers are always in the form of 123-45-6789, but we want to accept people entering them with spaces (123 45 6789) instead of hyphens or with no dividing characters at all (123456789).

1. In the `ch13` folder, create a page named `TIO-1304-RegularExpression-1.aspx` and add a label with a text of `"Please enter a social security number"`, a textbox, a button and a `RegularExpressionValidator` control. Set the `ControlToValidate` to `TextBox1` and the `Text` property to `"Invalid Social Security Number"`. Enter a basic `ValidationExpression` as follows:

```
^\d{3}-\d{2}-\d{4}$
```

2. Save the page, and test it in your browser.

3. Add the ability to accept no spaces by changing the validation expression to the following:

```
^(\d{3}-\d{2}-\d{4})|(\d{9})$
```

4. Save the page as `TIO-1304-RegularExpression-2.aspx`, and test it in your browser.
5. Finally, add the possibility of a number entered with spaces instead of hyphens, as follows:

```
^(\d{3}-\d{2}-\d{4})|(\d{9})|(\d{3} \d{2} \d{4})$
```

6. Save the page as `TIO-1304-RegularExpression-3.aspx`, and test it in your browser.

How It Works

Note that the entire `ValidationExpression` is between a ^ and $ to signify the entire line of input. When we use a backslash, it means that the following character will be a metacharacter, not a literal. In the first case, we use \d to mean any digit that is 0 to 9. A brace indicates how many times that character can be used, which in the left section is three times. We then follow this with a hyphen. Because the hyphen is not preceded by a backslash, it means that it is a literal hyphen.

When we add alternative formats, we enclose the entire format in parentheses and then divide it from the alternate format with a vertical line character, which means OR. Although the parentheses are not necessary in this particular case, they do make it easier for a human to read the code.

CustomValidator Control

This control raises an event called `ServerValidate` that you can use to perform the actual testing. The input value will be passed to the procedure as `ServerValidateEventArgs.Value`. You can set a Boolean with the results of your procedure in `ServerValidateEventArgs.IsValid`. If you set that property to `false`, the `CustomValidator` will behave like any other validator for which input has failed the test.

In the implementation of your event handler, you should reference the `ServerValidateEventArgs.Value` property instead referencing the control directly. This makes it possible to share the same event handler for multiple `CustomValidators` with potentially different `ControlToValidate` settings.

As an example, we will say that we issue authorization codes with a built-in pattern. A typical code is A65 or M77 or Z90, where the numbers represent the ASCII value of the preceding letter. We could perform a custom validation as follows. Note that the `CustomValidator` control has an event called `ServerValidate` that will invoke a procedure named `CustomValidator1_ServerValidate`. The procedure then has a single functional line that sets `ServerValidateEventArgs.IsValue` to true or `false` to return to the validator control. The test expression compares the ASCII value of the left character (the letter) against the right two numbers.

```
<script runat="server">
Protected Sub CustomValidator1_ServerValidate(ByVal source As Object, ByVal args As
System.Web.UI.WebControls.ServerValidateEventArgs)
        ' a few lines of diagnostic information for learning
                Response.Write("left" & Left(args.Value, 1) & "<br/>")
```

```
                Response.Write("ASCleft" & Asc(Left(args.Value, 1)) & "<br/>")
                Response.Write("right" & Right(args.Value, 2) & "<br/>")
        ' the actual test
        args.IsValid = (Asc(Left(args.Value, 1)) = Right(args.Value, 2))
End Sub
</script>

<h2>Chapter 13 Demo #1301 Custom Validation Control</h2>
    <form id="form1" runat="server">
    <div>
        Please enter your authorization code*<br />
        <asp:TextBox ID="TextBox1" runat="server"></asp:TextBox>
        <asp:Button ID="Button1" runat="server" Text="Button" /><br />
        <asp:CustomValidator ID="CustomValidator1" runat="server"
            ErrorMessage="Authorization code is not valid."
            ControlToValidate="TextBox1"
            OnServerValidate="CustomValidator1_ServerValidate">
            </asp:CustomValidator><br /><br />
        *(try A65 or M77 or Z90)
</div></form></body></html>
```

We will try implementing a custom validator in the next exercise.

Try It Out CustomValidator

This exercise will represent a part of a form to join a professional society. Most members have a `Professional` status. But members under age 25 can be `Students`, and those over 65 can be `Emeritus`. We will ask the user to input a date of birth and select a membership type. Then the page will check their membership type with a custom validator.

1. In the `ch13` folder, create a new page named `TIO-1305-CustomValidator.aspx`. Add a label with the text `"Please enter your date of birth"`. Add a textbox and then a `RequiredFieldValidator` and a `CompareValidator` that checks if the entry is a date (`ControlToValidate=TextBox1`, `Operator=DataTypeCheck`, `Type=Date`).
2. Add a `RadioButtonList` and in the Smart Task panel's edit items, add three items (Text/Value): Student/S, Professional/P, and Emeritus/E.
3. Add a button and a custom validator. In Source view, from the object list at the top left, select the `CustomValidator` and from the events list at the top right, select `ServerValidate`. Type the following lines into the procedure.

```
<script runat="server">
Protected Sub CustomValidator1_ServerValidate(ByVal source As Object, ByVal args As
System.Web.UI.WebControls.ServerValidateEventArgs)
        ' must be under age 25 to get a student membership
        If RadioButtonList1.SelectedValue = "S" And _
            CDate(DobTextBox.Text) < DateAdd("yyyy", -25, Today()) _
            Then args.IsValid = False
        ' must be over 65 to get an emeritus membership
        If RadioButtonList1.SelectedValue = "E" And _
            CDate(DobTextBox.Text) > DateAdd("yyyy", -65, Today()) _
            Then args.IsValid = False
End Sub
```

```
</script>

        <h2>Chapter 13 TIO #1305 Custom Validator </h2>
    <form id="form1" runat="server">
    <div>
        Membership Application<br /><br />
        Students members must be under age 25.<br />
        Emeritus members must be over age 65. <br /><br />
        <asp:Label ID="Label1" runat="server"
            Text="Please enter your date of birth as mm/dd/yy "></asp:Label>
        <asp:TextBox ID="DobTextBox" runat="server"></asp:TextBox>
        <asp:RequiredFieldValidator ID="RequiredFieldValidator1" runat="server"
            ControlToValidate="DobTextBox"
            Text="Please enter your date of birth">
            </asp:RequiredFieldValidator>
        <asp:CompareValidator ID="CompareValidator1" runat="server"
            Text="CompareValidator"
            ControlToValidate="DobTextBox"
            Operator="DataTypeCheck"
            Type="Date">
        </asp:CompareValidator><br />
        <asp:RadioButtonList ID="RadioButtonList1" runat="server">
            <asp:ListItem Value="S">Student</asp:ListItem>
            <asp:ListItem Value="P" Selected=true >Professional</asp:ListItem>
            <asp:ListItem Value="E">Emeritus</asp:ListItem>
        </asp:RadioButtonList><br />
        <asp:Button ID="Button1" runat="server" Text="Button" />
        <asp:CustomValidator ID="CustomValidator1" runat="server"
            Text="Your membership selection is not appropriate for your age"
    OnServerValidate="CustomValidator1_ServerValidate">
  </asp:CustomValidator>
</div></form></body></html>
```

4. Save the page and test in your browser.

How It Works

We added a custom validator that invoked when the server performed its validation (`ServerValidate` event). We do not need to use any values passed into our custom procedure; we can refer to the input controls directly. Because our testing will involve dates, we need to ensure that a date exists in the textbox and that the value entered is, in fact, a date.

Our object of interest is the procedure invoked by the `CustomValidator`. We have, below, a simple `If-Then` clause that sets `args.IsValid` to false if two conditions are both met. The first is that the selection in the radio button list is "S." The second is if the date of birth entered is older than 25 years before today. The `DateAdd` function has three arguments. The first is the kind of units to add or subtract, `YYYY` being years. The second is the number of units to add or subtract. The third argument is the date from which to start the addition; in this case, it is current date as returned by the `Today()` function.

```
' must be under age 25 to get a student membership
If RadioButtonList1.SelectedValue = "S" And _
    CDate(DobTextBox.Text) < DateAdd("yyyy", -25, Today()) _
    Then args.IsValid = False
```

We repeat to test that an applicant for emeritus status was born on a date less than (earlier than) 65 years before today:

```
        ' must be over 65 to get an emeritus membership
        If RadioButtonList1.SelectedValue = "E" And _
            CDate(DobTextBox.Text) > DateAdd("yyyy", -65, Today()) _
            Then args.IsValid = False
    End Sub
    </script>
```

So far in this chapter, we have looked at validation of user input in a general way. In the next section, we look at scenarios that are specific for working with databases.

Validation in Data Scenarios

Up until now, we have talked about validation in general, that is not bound to a data source. Now we shift our focus to using the validation controls specifically with the smart data controls of `GridView`, `DetailsView`, and `FormView`. Because validation is an issue of input data, we will be focusing on the update and insert modes.

The fundamental concept is that the validation control goes into the same template as the input control. This can occur at two levels. Recall that we discussed that in `GridView` and `DetailsView` we had field-level templates. Then within the field-level templates we had `EditItemTemplate` and `InsertItemTemplate` (among others). But `FormView` was different. `FormView` has the top-level `InsertItemTemplate` and `EditItemTemplate` (among others), and those hold the various input controls. We can summarize the rules as follows:

- If the smart data control supports field-level templates (`GridView` or `DetailsView`), then the validator goes into the field's `MyTemplateField.InsertItemTemplate` or `MyFieldTemplate.EditItemTemplate`
- If the smart data control does not have field-level templates (`FormView`), then the validators go directly into the control's `EditItemTemplate` or `InsertItemTemplate`.

In the first section of the chapter, we included on the page buttons that, by default, invoked validation in addition to the validation that occurred as focus left the input field. On smart data controls, the `Update` and `Insert` buttons of a `CommandField` also, by default, cause validation. However, the `ButtonField` (where you write custom code) is `CausesValidation=false` by default.

ASP.NET also has a clever timesaver built in. When an `InsertItemTemplate` is not specified, the `EditItemTemplate` will be used for both edit and insert modes. This allows you to skip the repetition of setting up two template contents (including validators) if they require exactly the same user interface.

Last, we may want to validate using a value that we reap dynamically from the data source. For example, column one might be `UnitsInStock`, and column two might be `QuantityToOrder` (the number of units the user wants to buy). Then our range validator for `QuantityToOrder` should have a

`MaximumValue` that is no more than the value shown in the `UnitsInStock`. We can write the source code as follows:

```
<asp:RangeValidator ... runat="server"
MaximumValue='<%# Eval("UnitsInStock") %>'
/>
```

To date, we have worked with individual validators. ASP.NET 2.0 also offers the option to wrap all validation reports in one control.

Validation Summary

Earlier we glossed over the property of `ErrorMessage`. Instead, we have focused on the `Text` message:

- *Text* value appears on the page at the location of the validator control if there are validation failures, usually when the input control loses focus.
- The `ErrorMessage` value appears in the `ValidationSummary` control if there are validation failures, generally when a Submit button that has `CausesValidation=true` is clicked.

The `ValidationSummary` control appears on the page in a postback action and displays a set of the error messages from all of validation controls where `IsValid=False`. These can be arranged as a list, paragraph, or bulleted list, as set in the `DisplayMode`. Furthermore, the display can also be in a message box, as set by `ShowMessageBox=true/false`. To repeat, the `ValidationSummary` control does not actually perform any validation itself; it has no `ControlToValidate` property.

However, you may want only the validation summary to display — instead of text messages at the location of the validation controls. You can achieve this hiding by setting the display of the validation controls to a value of `None`.

Validation Groups

Frequently, more than one set of inputs displays on a page. For example, there may be several kinds of searches that can be initiated from a page, each supporting its own input box. There is an expectation that the user will enter data in only one and press its button. It does not make sense to validate the controls that were not used. To overcome the problem, ASP.NET 2.0 offers the ability to group validators and then only perform validation on one group per submission.

All the input controls in one group should get the same `ValidationGroup` property. The button for that group gets the same group name. The button can be of any type that induces validation, including submit buttons, `ButtonField` or `CommandField` buttons such as `Insert` or `Update`. Then when that button is clicked, it fires a validation in all the validation controls of its group. The name of the property for the button is the same as for the validation controls in the group. There is no `Button.GroupToValidate` property.

> **If the `ValidationGroup` is not set on a validator or button, then it belongs to the `"default group" (ValidationGroup="")`.**

When you use the validation group feature in custom code, be aware that the `Page.IsValid` property will only be true or false for the validation controls in the group with the button that was clicked.

Try It Out Validation Summary and Groups

This exercise features a `GridView` and a `FormView` on one page, both displaying the same data of jobs from the Pubs table. The `GridView` is for reading and editing data, while the `FormView` is for new records. If an edit is performed, only the editing validations occur, and if a new record is inserted, only the insertion validations occur. In each case, a validation summary is displayed. We will add a new business rule that any new or changed levels must be from 25 to 250 inclusive.

1. In the `ch13` folder, create a new page named `TIO-1306-ValidationGroups.aspx`. Drag from the Data Explorer to the page the `Pubs.Jobs` table to make a `SqlDataSource` and `GridView`. Enable paging and editing in the `GridView`, and set `PageSize` to `5`. Drag a `FormView` to the page, use the same data source control, and set its `DefaultMode` to `Insert`.
2. To add validation to the `GridView`, first convert all of the fields, except `ID`, to `TemplateFields` (Open the `GridView` Smart Task panel, select Edit Columns, select a column, and click on Convert This Field into a `TemplateField`.)
3. Open the `GridView` template `job_desc.EditTemplate`, and add a `RequiredFieldValidator`. Set its `ControlToValidate` to `TextBox1` and its `Text` to `"This field is required"`. Set its `ValidationGroup` to `Edit-GV`. Repeat for the template columns of `min_lvl` with a `RangeValidator` of 25 to 200. Last, add a `RangeValidator` to the `max_lvl` template column with a range of 25 to 250. Don't forget to set the max and min column validators' `ValidationGroup=Edit-GV`.
4. Switch to the `FormView` and in its `InsertItemTemplate`, add the same validation controls as for the `GridView`. However, set their `ValidationGroups` to `Insert-FV`.
5. Add two `ValidationSummary` controls to the bottom of the page. One will have `ValidationGroup=Edit-GV` and the other, `Insert-FV`.
6. Save and test the page.

Validation in Code

Instead of using the built-in ASP.NET 2.0 validator controls, you can build validation in custom code. There are several methods and properties of the page that will be useful. `Page.Validate()` validates all validation controls in the default group. If you have assigned groups, then `Page.Validate("MyValidationGroup")` validates all validation controls in `MyValidationGroup`. If `Page.IsValid=True`, then all of the validation controls that have been validated up to this point have passed.

For data scenarios specifically, you may want to programmatically validate parameter collections in data source control events. `SqlDataSource` provides events, which call event handlers into which you can place code, including `Update`, `Insert`, and `Delete`. They will raise the events and call your event handlers prior to their built-in function. When performing your validation code, you can read the contents of the parameters in the procedure's event arguments.

Common Mistakes

The following list describes some common mistakes.

- When using the `RangeValidator` control, entering the lower bound in the `MaximumValue` property. Although this sounds like an improbable mistake, the `MaximumValue is listed` higher in the Properties window than the `MinimumValue` when the properties are alphabetized, so it is easy to glance at it and enter the range from low to high, going from top to bottom in the Properties window.
- Forgetting to set `RangeValidator.Type` for an entry that accepts numbers. The default type is String, which will accept numbers but as strings, not as numeric types.
- Expecting to accept decimal numbers when the `RangeValidator.Type` is set for integers. The `Type` named `Double` accepts decimal values.
- Assuming that all controls have been validated when using validation groups. Only the controls in the same group as the clicked button will be validated.

Summary

Validation is one of several tools a page designer can implement to protect the database. Other tools available in ASP.NET 2.0 include the membership logon scheme, forcing users to enter input without typing, and using parameters to process all user input. Validation controls check data entered into other controls and then issue a pass or fail. A failure will prevent data operations, such as a write, from proceeding.

Validation controls include a `ControlToValidate` property to identify which control on the page should be checked. The `Text` property displays a message in the space of the validation control when validation fails. An `ErrorMessage` is fed to the `ValidationSummary` control. You can set the control to hold a space for its validation failure text (`Display=Static`) or to make space only when the text is displayed (`Display=Dynamic`). There is also an option to automatically move the focus to the input that failed validation. ASP.NET also allows more than one validator to check a single control, for example both a `RequiredFieldValidator` and a `RangeValidator`.

Validation always occurs on the server. In addition, you can use `EnableClientScript` to perform a validation on JavaScript-enabled browsers. In the case of a validation failure, nothing is sent to the server.

The `RequiredFieldValidator` control checks that an input is not empty. The `CompareFieldValidator` control checks a comparison (equals, greater than, etc.) to: (1) a set value, (2) compare the value in another control or (3) compare a value to a certain data type (equals only). The `RangeValidator` control checks that an input value is between an upper and lower boundary. The input value to validate can be a number, currency, date, string, or any other .NET data type.

The `RegularExpressionValidator` control checks that a value matches a pattern. The pattern is described using a rich syntax. Patterns can be described for numbers, characters, and dates. When writing the expression, remember that a backslash means the following is a metacharacter and has some meaning other than its literal definition. Regular expressions support an OR symbol to build even more complex expressions.

The `CustomValidator` control invokes a procedure that you write to perform the actual testing. The input value will be passed to the procedure as `ServerValidateEventArgs.Value`. In the end, you assign `true` or `false` to an argument named `ServerValidateEventArgs.IsValid`.

When using validation with data-bound controls there are two basic rules. First, the validation must occur in `TemplateFields`, not in `BoundFields`. VWD makes it easy to convert a bound field column to a template field column. Second, the validator control must go in the same template as the input it is checking. Frequently, `InsertItemTemplate` will be the same as `EditItemTemplate`; in these cases, only create the `EditItemTemplate`. When an `InsertItemTemplate` is not specified, `EditItemTemplate` will be used for both edit and insert modes.

In addition to or in lieu of displaying a validator control's text, we can present to the user a summary of all the error messages from validators that failed to pass. Presented in a `ValidationSummary` control, the message can be arranged in several formats. Validation can also be performed in groups. This provides the option of having only the validators of one part of the page perform their checks. All of the validators with the same `ValidationGroup` value will be checked when a button is clicked with the same `ValidationGroup` value.

Last, as has always been the case, ASP.NET allows you to write your own validation routines in code. For instance, `SqlDataSource` offers events such as updating. You can create custom validation by handling those events and putting your code in your event handler before the new values are written to the database.

Exercises

The answers to these review questions can be found in Appendix B.

1. Compare and contrast the validator controls' `Text` and `ErrorMessage` properties.
2. How do you eliminate the blank space on the page that is created by a validator control when it is not showing its `Text` value?
3. Describe the differences between a `RangeValidator` and a `RegularExpressionValidator`.
4. The `CompareValidator` can be used to compare two input controls. What else can it compare?
5. How does a custom validator know if its custom code has passed or failed the validation?
6. Describe the location of validation controls for data to be edited in a `GridView` or `DetailsView`.
7. Describe the location of validation controls for a new record in `FormView`.
8. How do you add a validator to a `BoundField` in `GridView`?
9. How do you display only the `ValidationSummary` with no notices at the location of the validator control?

Business Objects As a Source of Data

Developers must realize that there is more to programming than simply adding controls and setting properties. Application architecture is a very important issue that is often overlooked. For reasons of clean separation and easier maintenance, you should create most Web applications using *N*-tier principles. In short, *N*-tier means dividing the programming functions across more then one layer. Traditionally, there is a data layer to hold and manage the data, a business layer that enforces the rules, and a presentation layer that interfaces with users. Because each layer has a defined interface with the others, they are modular. A layer can be replaced with an updated version. Also a layer could be used by more then one other layer. For example, a Web- and Windows-based front end could be created, both of which use the same business and data layers. When you work with an *N*-tier application, it is most likely that your middle-layer objects will return complex objects that you have to process in your ASP.NET presentation. Keeping this in mind, Microsoft has created a set of new data source controls that will allow you to seamlessly integrate the data returned from the middle-layer objects with the ASP.NET presentation layer.

This chapter explains the different variations of the *N*-tier application design principle and how they can provide flexible and easily maintainable application architectures. It also demonstrates how the new data source controls provided by ASP.NET 2.0 will aid you in creating true *N*-tier applications.

This chapter will cover nine concepts, as follows.

- Introducing the concepts of objects as a source of data, including the advantages of multiple-tier architecture
- Building an object that is an invariable array
- Building an array that uses the .NET generics
- Creating an object that is bound to a data source
- Using VWD to build objects with data
- Developing an object that returns a `DataSet` list

- Enabling objects to modify data
- Using `MasterDetails` with a data object
- Sorting in a data object

Introduction to the ObjectDataSource Control

When you are creating a distributed ASP.NET application, you will most likely split your application into multiple layers, such as presentation, business, and data access. This approach results in an extensible application that can be easily maintained and enhanced over a period of time. ASP.NET complements this type of application design by providing a new `ObjectDataSource` control that can be used to directly bind an object's methods to data-bound controls such as `GridView`, `DataList`, `DropDownList`, and so on. This approach provides for clean separation and encapsulation of code, eliminating the need to write data access code in the presentation layer. Now that you understand the theory behind the `ObjectDataSource` control, let's explore *N*-tier application design and the different layers that are part of a typical *N*-tier application.

Layers of an N-Tier Application

In a typical *N*-tier environment, the client implements the *presentation logic* (thin client). The business logic and data access logic are implemented on an application server(s), and the data resides on a database server(s). N-*tier architecture* is typically defined by the following three component layers:

- **Presentation Logic Layer:** A front-end component that is responsible for providing portable presentation logic
- **Business Logic Layer:** Allows users to share and control business logic by isolating it from the other layers of the application
- **Data Access Logic Layer:** Provides access to the database by executing a set of SQL statements or stored procedures

Presentation Logic Layer

The presentation logic layer consists of standard ASP.NET Web forms, ASP pages, documents, Windows forms, and so on. This is the layer that provides an end-user interface into your application. That is, it works with the results of the business logic layer to handle the transformation into something usable and readable by the end user.

Business Logic Layer

The business logic layer is basically where the brains of your application reside; it contains things like the business rules, data manipulation, and so on. For example, if you're creating a search engine and you want to rate or weight each matching item based on some custom criteria (say a quality rating and number of times a keyword was found in the result), place this logic at this layer. This layer does not know anything about HTML, nor does it output HTML. It does not care about ADO.NET or SQL, and it shouldn't have any code to access the database or the like. Those tasks are assigned to each corresponding layer above or below it.

Data Access Layer

The data access layer is where you will write some generic methods to interface with your data. For example, write a method for creating and opening a `SqlConnection` object, create a `SqlCommand` object for executing the stored procedure, and so on. It will also have some specific methods, such as `UpdateProduct`, so that when the `Product` object calls it with the appropriate data, it can persist it to the database. This data access logic layer contains no data business rules or data manipulation/transformation logic. It is merely a reusable interface to the database.

Advantages of N-Tier Architectures

Here are some of the advantages of *N*-tier architectures:

- Changes to the user interface or to the application logic are largely independent of one another, allowing the application to evolve easily to meet new requirements.
- Network bottlenecks are minimized because the application layer does not transmit extra data to the client, only what is needed to handle a task.
- When business logic changes are required, only the server has to be updated. In two-tier architectures, each client must be modified when logic changes.
- The client is insulated from database and network operations. The client can access data easily and quickly without having to know where data is or how many servers are on the system.
- The organization can have database independence because the data layer is written using standard SQL, which is platform-independent. The enterprise is not tied to vendor-specific stored procedures.
- The application layer can be written in standard third- or fourth-generation languages, such as Java, C, or COBOL, with which the organization's in-house programmers are experienced.
- It is also possible to add total dependence between layers by allowing multiple clients to consume the services of the same business logic layer. For example, both a Windows forms application and a Web application could use the same underlying business tier. This way you can provide a richer experience to folks on the local intranet, but still be able to provide an interface to the application for customers over the Web.

Simple Objects with Hard-Coded Data

To start this chapter, we will explore scenarios where we create an object but the object does not get its data from a database. Instead, the data will be hard-coded in the object. Even though the object is not reading from a database, we will still refer to it as a data object because that is our objective by the end of the chapter. We will also start by building our objects by hand because although VWD does a great job of building data objects, it adds many lines of code that we don't need in our simple cases. After you have some basic experience, we will move on to using the full power of VWD to build objects that use a database.

Creating a data object requires two steps, and then on your ASPX page you perform three steps to utilize the object.

1. Create a data object.
   - ❑ In the data object, create a `public` function.
   - ❑ In the `public` function, write code that returns data (for now, a simple string).
2. Create an ASPX page.
   - ❑ Add an `ObjectDataSource` control, and set its `TypeName` to the data object.
   - ❑ In the `ObjectDataSource` control, set the `SelectMethod` to the `public` function in the data object.
   - ❑ Add a data-bound control, and set its `DataSourceID` to the `ObjectDataSource` control.

Typically, a data object will have multiple `public` functions. For example, there might be one that returns all of the employees, while another accepts information to add a new employee. These will have a role on the ASPX page similar to the multiple commands in a `SqlDataSource` control (`SelectCommand`, `InsertCommand`, etc.). As you will see later, you can instruct the `ObjectDataSource` to use various functions in the data object for various tasks. In the data object, these blocks of code are referred to as *methods* (or, less conventionally, *public functions).* But from the outside (i.e., the perspective of the `ObjectDataSource` control), these are called *methods.*

In the end, your ASPX page will have a data-bound control such as a `TextBox` that is bound to an `ObjectDataSource` control. The `ObjectDataSource` control has as its source of data (its `TypeName`), the data object. This is similar to a `SqlDataSource` control having its `ConnectionString` set to an MDF file. Also in the `ObjectDataSource` control, we specify which of the data object's functions we want to use to get the data. Down in the data object, we create a `public` function that will return data.

In our first exercise, we will build the simplest possible data object, holding just two `public` functions. Neither of them will actually read a database; instead they just generate name(s) in code.

Try It Out Data Object with Hard-Coding

In this exercise, we will create a `DropDownList` that gets its items from an `ObjectDataSource`. We will create the data object first so that it returns a single string and then returns the names of four people. We will work with C# in these steps. In the downloads, there is a folder within `ch14` named `App_CodeInVb` with the samples in VB. Note that you can not have two files with the same name in the `App_Code` directory, even if their extensions are different. Specifically, having `MyObject.cs` and `MyObject.vb` will not work. In fact, if you have an `App_Code\MyObject.cs` you can't have `MyObject.vb` anywhere in the site, even in another folder.

1. Create a new folder named `C:\Websites\BegAspNet2Db\ch14` and a new page named `TIO-1401-...aspx`.
2. To your root add a folder named `ch14` and within there a page named `TIO-1401-ObjectHardCode-1`.
3. Right-click on your root directory and select Add New Item, and then click on the Class template. Name the object `MyDataObject` and select C#. Accept the suggestion to place the nascent class within the `App_Code` folder (which will be created)

4. Notes that for objects in C#, VWD automatically gives you a set of namespaces in the Using... commands. When using VB, they must be added by hand.

5. Add the following function inside the `public` class.

```
// following one declaration needed for all exercises in Chapter 14
using System;

public class MyDataObject
{
    //////////////////////////////////////////////////////
    // for TIO-1401
    public String[] GetLastNameOneOnly()
    {
        String[] lastNames = { "Millington" };
        return lastNames;
    }
}
```

6. To `TIO-1401-ObjectHardCode-1` add an `ObjectDataSource` and configure its data source. In the Configure Data Source dialog box, turn off the option to show only data components, and then drop down the list and select `MyDataObject object you created in Step 1.` Click Next and choose the one method that you made, named `GetLastNameOneOnly`, and then click Finish.

7. Add a `DropDownList` to the page and choose its data source to be the `ObjectDataSource` control. Set the `DropDownList` to `AutoPostBack`. Also add a short procedure within the Script tags to display the selection.

8. The ASPX page is shown in the code list below. There is no need to set a text or value, because only one string of data is returned. Save and test in your browser. Note that it takes a while (maybe 40 seconds) for ASP.NET to get the object set up for the first viewing. After that, of course, it will be very responsive.

```
... <h2>Chapter 14 TIO #1401 Object With Hard Coded Data <br />
      version 1 with a single name</h2>
    <form id="form1" runat="server">
    <div>
    <asp:ObjectDataSource ID="ObjectDataSource1" runat="server"
SelectMethod="GetLastNameOneOnly"
TypeName="MyDataObject">
   </asp:ObjectDataSource>
    <asp:DropDownList ID="DropDownList1" runat="server"
AutoPostBack="True"
DataSourceID="ObjectDataSource1"></asp:DropDownList>
    </div></form></body></html>
```

9. Save your work, and test it in your browser. Note that it takes a while (maybe 40 seconds) for ASP.NET to get the object set up for the first viewing. After that, of course, it will be very responsive.

How It Works

In this exercise, we created a simple object and used it as the source of data for a `DropDownList`. We created the new object named `MyDataObject`, and VWD automatically gave the `public` class framework typed for us:

```
public class MyDataObject
{ }
```

We added a directive at the top of the file to the namespace `System`.

Next, within the `MyDataObject` framework, we created a public function that returned some value. In this case, `String[]` indicates that the function will return an array of strings. We create a variable of the string array type named `lastNames` and then fill it with the single name.

```
public String[] GetLastNameOneOnly()
{
    String[] lastNames = { "Millington" };
    return lastNames;
}
```

Back in the ASPX page, the steps are simpler. We added the `ObjectDataSource` control, and in its configuration we set the `TypeName` to be the name of our new object. VWD then asked us to identify which method of the object would be used for the `Select`, and we specified the only method we made, `GetLastNameOneOnly`. When we added the `DropDownList`, we specified which data fields to use for text and value. You don't need to define those fields here because there's no property—it's the member itself, or the string, that you're binding to.

In the second half of the exercise (below), we created a second method, this one a bit more complex in that it returns several names in a string array. The `ObjectDataSource` returns each array item, one at a time, in exactly the same way that it would return rows from a database, one at a time.

```
public String[] GetLastNames()
{
    String[] lastNames = { "Millington", "Kauffman", "Washington", "Lincoln"};
    return lastNames;
}
```

Although this exercise introduces new techniques and terminology, it is too simple for practical uses. Now, we step up to creating an array in our object.

Binds to a Hard-Coded Array

We can use the commands of C# to create an array in our data object, and that array can be passed through the `ObjectDataSource` and to a data-bound control. The general technique to create an array in C# is to declare the array, then create items for the array, then put the items into the array. Last, we return the array from the function. As before, the `DropDownList` accepts the values as fed, item by item, from the `ObjectDataSource`. The data that comes from any data object must be an enumerable collection, as in the following for C#.

Because arrays will be so important in future exercises in this chapter, we will pause here to do an array with the simple hard-coded technique of the first Try It Out.

Try It Out Data Object with an Array

In this exercise, we will create a data object that delivers an array of names. We will display the data in a `GridView`.

1. Open your `MyObject.cs` in the `App_Code` folder. Scroll down to after the `GetLastNameOneOnly` method, and add a second method as shown in gray below.

```
public class MyDataObject
{
    public String[] GetLastNameOneOnly()
   { ... }

    ///////////////////////////////////////////////////////
    // for TIO-1402
    public String[] GetLastNames()
    {
        String[] lastNames = { "Millington", "Kauffman", "Washington", "Lincoln"};
        return lastNames;
    }
}
```

2. In VWD create a new ASPX page named `TIO-1402-Object-Array-1`. Add an `ObjectDataSource` control, and set its `TypeName` to `MyDataObject` and its `SelectMethod` to `GetPeople`. Add a `GridView` to the page, and set its data source to the `ObjectDataSource1`. You do not need to make any further changes to the `GridView`.

```
... <h2>Chapter 14 TIO #1402-1 Object Array using </h2>
    <form id="form1" runat="server">
    <div>
        <asp:GridView ID="GridView1" runat="server"
            DataSourceID="ObjectDataSource1">
        </asp:GridView>
        <asp:ObjectDataSource ID="ObjectDataSource1" runat="server"
            SelectMethod="GetPeople"
            TypeName="MyDataObject">
        </asp:ObjectDataSource>
  </div></form></body></html>
```

3. Save your work.

How It Works

The difference between this and the first Try It Out is that we added multiple names to the `lastNames` string to create an array.

```
        public String[] GetLastNames()
        {
            String[] lastNames = { "Millington", "Kauffman", "Washington", "Lincoln"};
            return lastNames;
        }
    }
```

The ASPX page is similar to the first exercise. We add an `ObjectDataSource` and set its `TypeName` to the name of the `class`. But this time we want to use our new data, so we set the `SelectMethod` to the name of that `public` function, `GetPeople`. We also display the values in a `GridView` instead of a `DropDownList`.

Having built two basic objects, we can now try incorporating .NET 2.0 Generics into our objects.

Objects That Use Generics

Generic collections are a new addition to .NET in the 2.0 version that allows you to make nontyped structures that then become type-safe when the page is compiled. Generics enable you to set up a data structure like a list, but without you having to make an initial commitment to a data type. But then when the generics are used, the .NET 2.0 compiler checks that the data types are consistent and, thus, safe.

They offer three advantages. First, in the past, if we had a collection we had to define the type of object that would be in the collection. Thus, we needed a different collection for each kind of contents. Generics offer a technique to make a general collection that can be used for various types of items. The collection is "generic" in the sense that it can hold any type of items. So, a generics `List<>` can be used to create a list of person, and then another copy (instantiation) of the same generic `List<>` can be instantiated to contain a different list of persons. The generic `List<>` collection itself is generic as to what type of contents it will receive.

Second, once a `GenericList` is instantiated, .NET 2.0 checks that the data types are consistent within the generics list. So, we do not have to commit to data types before we make the generics, but once we do instantiate we get the benefit of type checking.

Third, ASP.NET 2.0 comes with several generic built in. A generic collection such as a `List<>` will be of use to thousands of programmers, so Microsoft writes it and includes it in the .NET Framework 2.0. We can then take that and instantiate it to hold any kinds of items we want.

Using the generics `List<>` requires lines in three files:

- A file that defines the items that will be in the list
- A data object file that holds the Generics List<>
- An ASPX page

We will look at each line of code in a theoretical example and then build one in the exercise. They are shown schematically in Figure 14-1. The `MyItemType` file defines a class named `MyItemType`. Then in the data object file, we create a function named `GetMyItemsList`. That file uses `MyItemType` as the type of item in a generic `List<>` object and then fills some data into the `MyItemsType` of the generic `List<>`. Then in the ASPX page, we create an `ObjectDataSource` that refers to the data object and calls the `GetMyItemsList` to retrieve the data.

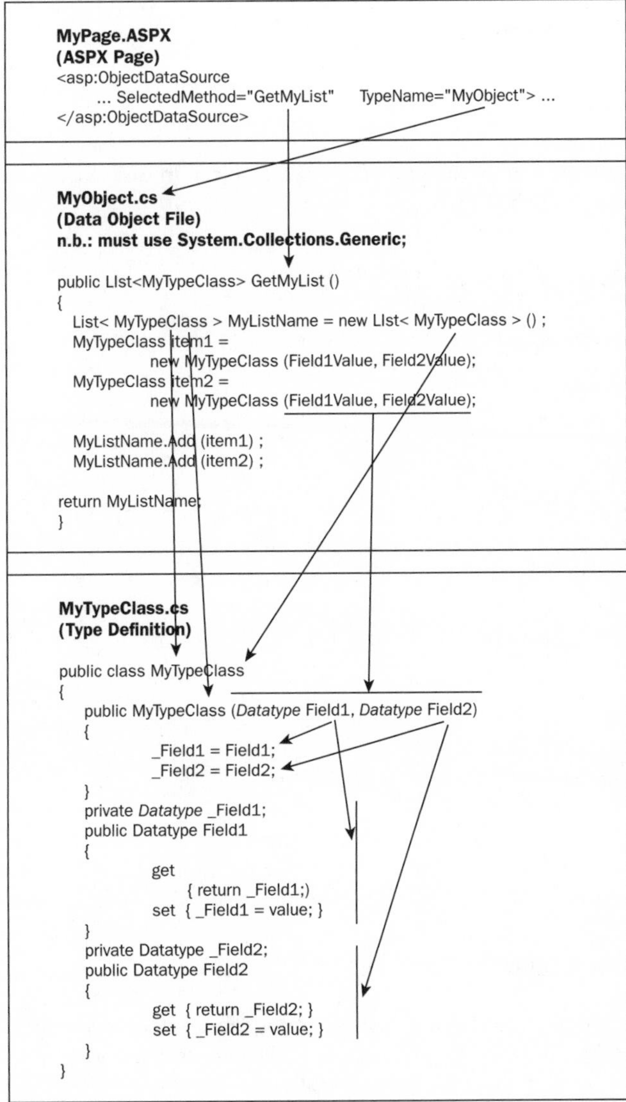

Figure 14-1

In the next few pages, we will walk through the whole process on a theoretical level; feel free to actually code the demonstrations or look at the files in your download. Check that you have downloaded `MyItemType.cs` and `MyDataObject.cs` into the `App_Code` folder; then run the ASPX page named `ch14\Demo-1401-GenericsList.aspx`. Then we will go through the process again, adding more detail to the steps in an exercise.

We start by creating a class that defines one item in the list and call it `MyItemType.cs`. VWD offers a template in the Add New Item choice of the root's quick menu. Within the class, we will add three items. The first is a declaration of namespaces as follows:

```
using System;
using System.Data;
```

The second item is a statement of the properties of the object. In this case, we will have an `id`, which is an integer, and a `Name`, which is a string.

```
public class MyItemType
{
  public MyItemType(int id, string Name)
  {
        _id = id;
        _Name = Name;
    }
```

The third item is code that will receive (set) and read out (get) a value for each of the two properties

```
    private int _id;
    public int ID
    {
        get { return _id; }
        set { _id = value; }
    }

    private string _Name;
    public string Name
    {
        get { return _Name; }
        set { _Name = value; }
    }
}
```

And that takes care of creating the class named `MyItemType`.

Next, we move to the data object, which does the same job that `MyDataObject` did in the last exercises. In the downloads, we include the following code at the end of `MyDataObject`. This file needs just two items. First is the declaration of namespaces, as follows:

```
// following is one item needed for all objects
using System;
// following are two items needed for generics
using System.Collections;
using System.Collections.Generic;
```

The second item is the public function that will be exposed as a method. We start by declaring that the function will return a generic `List<>`, and that list will be filled with objects of the `MyItem` (as described in `MyItemType.cs`). The name of the function will be `GetMyItemList()`. The gray line shows that we instantiate a new .NET 2.0 generic `List<>` item and name it `MyGenericsList`. Because we have told .NET that the list will contain `MyItemType` objects, we can start creating them on the next three lines with the names `MIT1` through `MIT3` and fill them with an integer and a name (remember that those are the properties of an `MyItemType` as we set up in `MyItemType.cs`). Then we have `MyGenericsList` and add those three items using an Add method, which we get for free because it is part of a .NET 2.0 generic `List<>`. Finally, we return to the caller (the ASPX page `ObjectDataSource` control) the `MyGenericsList`:

```
    ////////////////////////////////////////////////////////
    // Demo-1401
    public List<MyItemType> GetMyItemsList()
    {
        List<MyItemType> MyGenericsList = new List<MyItemType>();
        MyItemType MIT1 = new MyItemType(1,"Apple");
        MyItemType MIT2 = new MyItemType(2,"Banana");
        MyItemType MIT3 = new MyItemType(3,"Coconut");

        MyGenericsList.Add(MIT1);
        MyGenericsList.Add(MIT2);
        MyGenericsList.Add(MIT3);
        return MyGenericsList ;
    }
}
```

The third file of concern is the ASPX page. On that page, we add an `ObjectDataSource` control and set its `TypeName` to `MyDataObject`, and then within the control refer the `SelectMethod` to `GetMyItemsList`:

```
<asp:ObjectDataSource ID="ObjectDataSource1" runat="server"
    TypeName="MyDataObject"
    SelectMethod="GetMyItemsList">
</asp:ObjectDataSource>
```

In the above example, we create our own item type in `MyItemType.cs`. The .NET Framework 2.0 includes many built-in types that can be used as an item type in the examples above if your data has just one value. For example, if you were only holding the names of provinces, the `String` type would work fine; it would not be necessary to create a `Province` type.

To see this demo in action, check that you have downloaded `MyItemType.cs` and `MyDataObject` into the `App_Code` folder.

Try It Out — Object That Uses a Generic List

This exercise has the same objective as the last: to use a data object to create a list of names. But this time we will create the list in a generics `<List>` object. We will also add some more information about the people whose names are included.

1. Startby creating a new class that will define a "person" object. Right-click on the App_Code folder, and select Add New Item. Choose the class template, and name it Person.cs. We do not need all of the namespace directives; delete all but System.

2. Within the public Person class add a list of the properties that it will return when called. Follow that with the location that those values will come from inside the code. Note that a leading underline is a standard way to note that a variable is private to the class. In the gray lines below we are saying to return as the firstName the value that is filled in the class by firstName.

```
using System;
/// <summary>
/// This Class defines the type of a Person, including five properties of the
Person
/// </summary>

public class Person
{public Person(int id, String firstName, String lastName, String title, String
city)
  {
        _id = id;
        _firstName = firstName;
        _lastName = lastName;
        _title = title;
        _city = city;
    }
```

In Person.cs we now must add code that will internally handle the values for each of the five properties of a person. Add the following code shown in gray, and save your work.

```
public class Person
{public Person(... )
  {
        _id = id;
...
  }

    private int _id;
    public int ID
    {
        get { return _id; }
        set { _id = value; }
    }

    private String _lastName;
    public String LastName
    {
        get { return _lastName; }
        set { _lastName = value; }
    }

    private String _firstName;
    public String FirstName
    {
```

```
        get { return _firstName; }
        set { _firstName = value; }
    }

    private String _title;
    public String Title
    {
        get { return _title; }
        set { _title = value; }
    }

    private String _city;
    public String City
    {
        get { return _city; }
        set { _city = value; }
    }
```

1. Open your `MyDataObject`, and add two more namespace directives as follows, so you can use generics.

```
// following is one item needed for all exercises in Chapter 14
using System;
// following are two items needed for generics, starting with TIO-1402-2
using System.Collections;
using System.Collections.Generic;
```

2. Add another `public` function, as follows in gray. Save and close your `MyDataObject.cs` file.

```
public class MyDataObject
{
    public String[] GetLastNameOneOnly() ...
    public String[] GetLastNames() ...
    public Person[] GetPeople()...

/////////////////////////////////////////////////////
// for TIO-1403
    public List<Person> GetPeopleList()
    {
        // requires using System.Collections.Generic;
        List<Person> people = new List<Person>();

        Person p1 = new Person(74, "Brad", "Millington", "Program Mgr", "Redmond");
        Person p2 = new Person(58, "John", "Kauffman", "Author", "Ottawa");
        Person p3 = new Person(68, "-*", "Washington", "Developer", "Redmond");
        Person p4 = new Person(79, "Abraham", "Lincoln", "Developer", "Redmond");

        people.Add(p1);
        people.Add(p2);
        people.Add(p3);
        people.Add(p4);

        return people;
    }
```

1. Now create a new ASPX page named `TIO-1403-Object-GenericList`. Add an `ObjectDataSource` control, and set the `TypeName` to `MyDataObject` and the `SelectMethod` to `GetPeopleList`.

```
... <title>TIO-1403-Object-Array-2.aspx</title>
</head><body>
        <h2>Chapter 14 TIO #1403 Object Array<br/>
        with generic list</h2>
    <form id="form1" runat="server">    <div>
        <asp:GridView ID="GridView1" runat="server"
            AutoGenerateColumns="true"
            DataSourceID="ObjectDataSource1">
        </asp:GridView>
        <asp:ObjectDataSource ID="ObjectDataSource1" runat="server"
            TypeName="MyDataObject">
            SelectMethod="GetPeopleList"
        </asp:ObjectDataSource>
    </div></form></body></html>
```

How It Works

In this exercise, we worked in three files. In `Person.cs`, we created a type named `Person` in two steps. The first step, below, declares the constructor for `Person`.

```
public class Person
{public Person(int id, String firstName, String lastName, String title, String
city)
  {
        _id = id;
        _firstName = firstName;
        _lastName = lastName;
        _title = title;
        _city = city;
    }
```

Then we went through five blocks of code that took care of receiving and returning a value for a property of `Person`. The first (only) is listed below where `id` is the variable that holds the value inside the object while `ID` is the public presentation of the same value.

```
    private int _id;
    public int ID
    {
        get { return _id; }
        set { _id = value; }
    }
```

Next, we turned our attention to our `MyDataObject`. We started by adding directives to the two namespaces that enable us to use .NET 2.0 generics.

```
// following is one item needed for all exercises in Chapter 14
using System;
// following are two items needed for generics, starting with TIO-1402-2
using System.Collections;
```

```
using System.Collections.Generic;
public class MyDataObject
```

Then we added a new public function. We stated that it would return a generic of the `List` type named `Person`, as shown in the section below.

```
public class MyDataObject
{
    ... earlier publics  ...

///////////////////////////////////////////////////////
// for TIO-1403
    public List<Person> GetPeopleList()
    {
        List<Person> people = new List<Person>();

        Person p1 = new Person(74, "Brad", "Millington", "Program Mgr", "Redmond");
        Person p2 = new Person(58, "John", "Kauffman", "Author", "Ottawa");
        Person p3 = new Person(68, "George", "Washington", "Developer", "Redmond");
        Person p4 = new Person(79, "Abraham", "Lincoln", "Developer", "Redmond");

        people.Add(p1);
        people.Add(p2);
        people.Add(p3);
        people.Add(p4);

        return people;
    }
```

Last, we made a simple ASPX page that used an `ObjectDataSource` control to call the `GetPeopleList` method from the `MyDataObject`.

```
... <title>TIO-1403-Object-Array-2.aspx</title>
</head><body>
        <h2>Chapter 14 TIO #1403 Object Array<br/>
        with generic list</h2>
    <form id="form1" runat="server">    <div>
        <asp:GridView ID="GridView1" runat="server"
            AutoGenerateColumns="true"
            DataSourceID="ObjectDataSource1">
        </asp:GridView>
        <asp:ObjectDataSource ID="ObjectDataSource1" runat="server"
            TypeName="MyDataObject">
            SelectMethod="GetPeopleList"
        </asp:ObjectDataSource>
    </div></form></body></html>
```

A good wrap-up exercise for the reader is to go back to Figure 14-1 and review how the information flowed through the three files in the previous Try It Out.

We've bound controls for data display to hard-coded lists and to generics, now we can get to out real objective — an object that binds to a database.

Objects That Bind to a DataSource

Now we move to the real objective of the chapter: how to interface our data object with a database. This task requires that code using ADO.NET be written into the data object. In this section and its corresponding Try It Out, we will hand-code those commands. Next we will see how to direct VWD to type those lines of code for us. Don't dwell on the ADO.NET section if you are not familiar with the material.

Before we write a function that uses ADO.NET in the data object, we must add the following two namespaces:

```
using System.Data;
using System.Data.SqlClient;
```

We start by defining the name of our function and specifying that it will return a `DataSet` (the bold part of the command below).

```
public DataSet MyMethodToGetDataSet()
```

Inside the function, we create a variable named `connStr` and fill it with a connection string that is read from the `Web.config file`.

```
String connStr = ConfigurationManager.ConnectionStrings["MyConnectionString"]
.ConnectionString;
```

Then we test whether ASP.NET 2.0 actually put a string into the `connStr` variable. If it did, we will execute some code; if not we will return no data.

```
        if (connStr != null)
        { ... code to create the dataset ... }
        return null;
    }
```

Assuming that our connection string in the `Web.config` file is in good shape, we need something more useful for the true case of the above test. We start, in the shaded code below, by creating an ADO.NET `SqlConnection` object that has as its connection string the contents of our variable:

```
        if (connStr != null)
        {
            SqlConnection conn = new SqlConnection(connStr);
```

Then we create a variable named query and fill it with a SQL `SELECT` statement:

```
            String query = "SELECT MyField1, MyField2 FROM MyTable";
```

Next, we create an ADO.NET `DataAdapter` named `adapter` that uses the connection object and the query string.

```
            SqlDataAdapter adapter = new SqlDataAdapter(query, conn);
```

We create a `DataSet` named `ds` and then instruct `ouradapter` to `Fill` our data set with the result of the `SELECT` command. Last, the `public` function returns the data set back to whomever requested it.

```
            DataSet ds = new DataSet();
            adapter.Fill(ds);
            return ds;
        }
```

If you are familiar with the ADO.NET objects, you will see that this is very much like the standard data-reading operation we used in prior versions of ASP.NET. If you are not familiar with ADO.NET, don't worry. In a few pages, we will have VWD write the above code for us. But for now we will do one exercise by hand.

Try It Out Object-DatabaseSource

In this exercise, we add a `public` function to `MyDataObject` to gather employee data from `Northwinds` and then create an ASPX page to show the values in a `GridView`.

1. Reopen your `MyDataObject` from the `App_Code` folder, and add the following two new declarations:

```
// following is one item needed for all exercises in Chapter 14
using System;
// following are two items needed for generics, starting with TIO-1402
using System.Collections;
using System.Collections.Generic;
// following is one item needed for SQL connection to database, starting with TIO-
1404
using System.Data.SqlClient;
```

2. Add the code in gray below to create a dataset from `Northwind Employees`. This relies on your having the `MfdNorthwind` connection string in your `Web.config` file like the one we created in the earlier Try It Out exercise.

```
public class MyDataObject
{
    public String[] GetLastNameOneOnly() ...
    public String[] GetLastNames()...
    public Person[] GetPeople()...
    public List<Person> GetPeopleList()...
//////////////////////////////////////////////////////
// for TIO-1404
    public DataSet GetPeopleDataSet()
        // TIO-1403
        // requires using System.Data.SqlClient;
    {
```

```
        String connStr =
ConfigurationManager.ConnectionStrings["MdfNorthwind"].ConnectionString;
        if (connStr != null)
        {
            SqlConnection conn = new SqlConnection(connStr);
            String query = "select EmployeeID, LastName, FirstName, Title, City
from Employees";
            SqlDataAdapter adapter = new SqlDataAdapter(query, conn);
            DataSet ds = new DataSet();
            adapter.Fill(ds);
            return ds;
        }
        return null;
    }
}
```

3. Create a new page named `TIO-1404-Object-DataSet`. Add an `ObjectDataSource` control with `TypeName = MyDataObject` that uses the `SelectMethod` of the new `GetPeopleDataSet`. Add a `GridView` that uses the `ObjectDataSource1` and autogenerates its columns.

```
... <h2>Chapter 14 TIO #1404 Object Delivering a DataSet </h2>
    <form id="form1" runat="server"><div>
        <asp:GridView ID="GridView1" runat="server"
            DataSourceID="ObjectDataSource1">
        </asp:GridView>
        <asp:ObjectDataSource ID="ObjectDataSource1" runat="server"
            SelectMethod="GetPeopleDataSet"
            TypeName="MyDataObject">
        </asp:ObjectDataSource>
</div></form></body></html>
```

4. Save the page, and view it in your browser.

How It Works

In this exercise, we created yet another `public` function in our data object. But this time the code actually reads values from a database. The first step was to add namespaces so that we could instantiate ADO.NET data objects. This namespace requires the `System.Data` namespace, but that is added automatically by VWD when we create the class.

```
using System.Data.SqlClient;
```

Then we added the new `public` function, which will be referred to as a method when called by the `ObjectDataSource` control:

```
    public DataSet GetPeopleDataSet()
    {
```

Next we created and filled a variable with the connection string read from the `Web.config` file. We immediately tested that something was read into the variable:

```
        String connStr =
ConfigurationManager.ConnectionStrings["MdfNorthwind"].ConnectionString;
        if (connStr != null)
        {
```

For the true case, we created and filled SqlConnection, SqlDataAdapter and DataSet objects in the lines below:

```
SqlConnection conn = new SqlConnection(connStr);
String query =
"SELECT EmployeeID, LastName, FirstName, Title, City FROM Employees";
SqlDataAdapter adapter = new SqlDataAdapter(query, conn);
DataSet ds = new DataSet();
```

And last, we filled the data set and set it as the return object so that it would be sent up to the ObjectDataSource control:

```
adapter.Fill(ds);
            return ds;
        }
```

Once the function is created in the data object, the work on the ASPX page is trivial. We create an ObjectDataSource control and set its TypeName to MyDataObject and the SelectMethod to our new public function. The GridView gets the data from the ObjectDataSource the same as it would a SqlDataSource control.

In this section, we built an object by hand to bind to data. In the next section, we will use the VWD tools to achieve the same objective.

Using VWD to Build Objects with Data

Don't despair if you felt that working directly with ADO.NET objects seemed onerous. Many people feel that way. So, the development teams at Microsoft built into VWD the ability to construct the necessary code based on input from a wizard. You simply specify what database to use and how you want to use it; then VWD creates the DataSet and its associated files. The process is very similar to using the wizard that creates the properties for the SqlDataSource control. In the end, you have a data object that gives you all of the advantages discussed in the introduction to this chapter. In this section, we will walk through the wizard and then analyze the output. For the rest of the chapter, we will explore how to use the wizard to make more complex data objects.

Right-clicking on the App_Code folder gives an option to add a new item and within there a template for a DataSet. For this demonstration, we use the name Demo-1402 (available in the downloads). The design surface changes to a pinstripe and the TableAdapter Configuration Wizard starts. Select a connection, and click next. Then, as shown in Figure 14-2, you have the choice to build a SQL statement or to use stored procedures. Stored procedures are one or more lines of code that are, essentially, SQL statements. For this chapter, we will not use stored procedures.

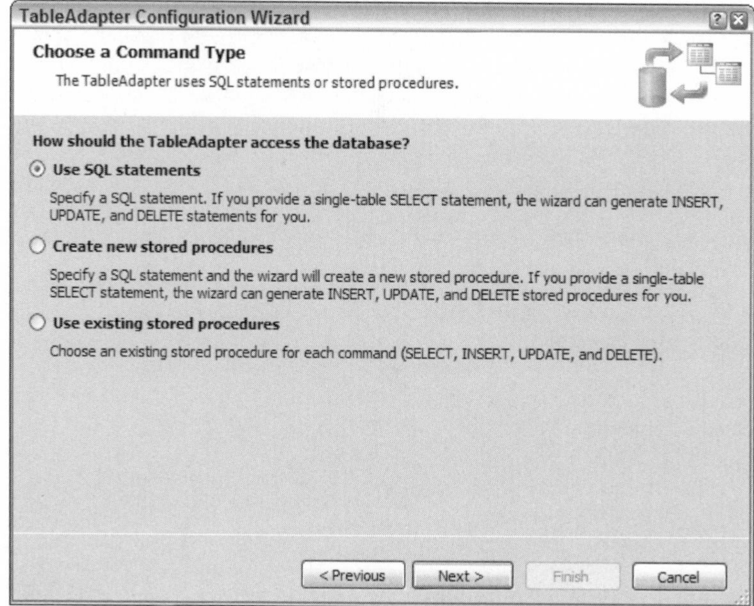

Figure 14-2

After clicking Next, you will have a pane to write your SQL statement.

The first step is to add the tables of interest as in Figure 14-3.

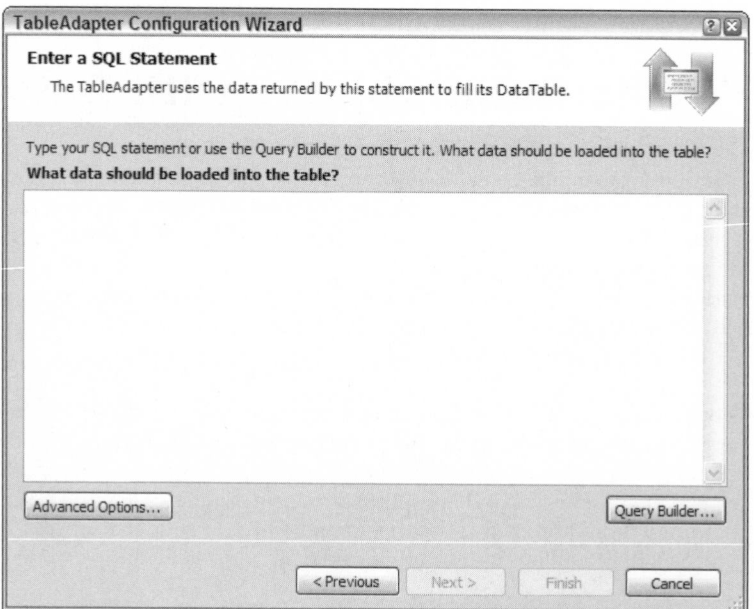

Figure 14-3

Click on the query builder for a visual interface. In the demonstration for these figures, we use the Employees table and select all the columns. VWD builds a SQL statement: `SELECT * FROM Employees`. Next, you see the TableAdapter Wizard, as shown below. The top option (Fill a Data Table) is more useful for Windows forms, so we generally turn it off for ASPX pages. The middle section returns a `DataTable`, so we leave it on and set the name to the method we want to use to get that table, typically something like `GetMyTable`. The bottom option, to create `Write` methods, should be on if you will be writing data. When you click Finish, the pinstriped designer will display a result similar to Figure 14-4.

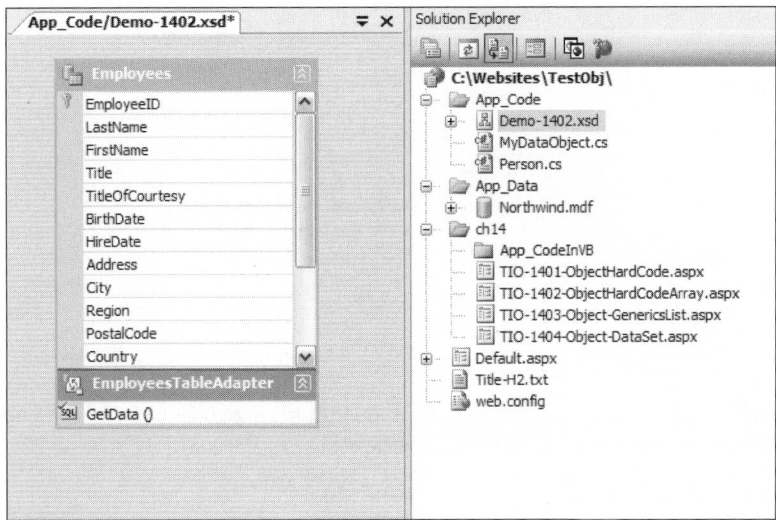

Figure 14-4

We can look at this `DataSet` in three ways:

- The representation in the designer
- The underlying code
- The way to use this `DataSet` in an `ObjectDataSource` control

What we see in the designer is a representation of an ADO.NET `DataSet`. At the top is the `DataTable`, which lists the output fields. These are the fields included in your SQL `SELECT` statement. Your data-bound control does not have to display all of these, but it cannot display any fields that are not in this list. At the bottom is the `TableAdapter`, which lists the one method VWD created, named `GetData`. It is only through the `TableAdapter` that you can access the data for reads or writes. We will learn how to add more methods later in the chapter. The names of the `DataTable` and `TableAdapter` can be changed by double-clicking on their current name in the title of the object. As a last note on the representation in the designer, if you look in the Solution Explorer at your `App_Data` folder, you will see your `DataSet` as an XSD file. Under that is an XSS file that sets the layout of the object in the representation. There is no need to use this XSS file directly, because you can drag and drop the object in the pane to rearrange it.

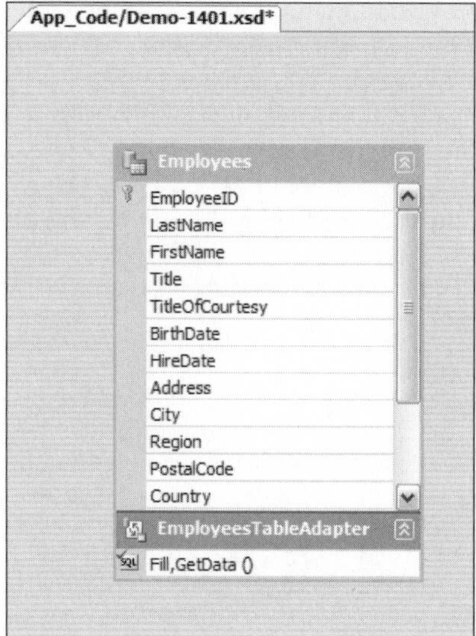

Figure 14-5

A second way to consider this object is to look at the underlying code, but you can only get halfway to that view when working in VWD. By right-clicking on the representation of the object, you get a View Code option. This leads to a page of tags that describe the goals of the object. There is no easy way to get all the way down to the ADO.NET commands. When the site is compiled, this set of tags is translated into actual `public` functions with their ADO.NET commands.

Last, we look at how to use this `DataTable`. When we add an `ObjectDataSource` control to the ASPX page, we now set its `TypeName` to the dataset's table adapter. Then we set the `SelectMethod` to the name of the method, as follows. Note in the syntax how `"TableAdapter"` is concatenated onto the end of the `DataTable` name.

```
<asp:ObjectDataSource ID="ObjectDataSource1" runat="server"
    TypeName="MyDataTableTableAdapter"
    SelectMethod="MyMethod"
</asp:ObjectDataSource>
```

Try It Out Using VWD to Build a Data Object

In this exercise, our goal is very similar to the last: create a data object to read the `Employees` from `Northwind` and to display those values in a `GridView`. However, this time we will use VWD to create a table adapter for us.

1. In VWD, right-click on the `App_Code` folder and select Add New Item. Choose the DataSet template, and name it `NorthWindDataSet`. VWD will automatically switch to the pinstripe designer, create a `DataTable1` and create a `DataTable1TableAdapter`.

2. When the wizard opens, select the `MdfNorthwinds` connection (set up in Try It Out of Chapter 3) and click Next. Choose to Use SQL Statements and click Next. Type into the text space `SELECT * FROM Employees`, and click Next. Deselect the Fill Data Table option, set the Return Data Table method name to `GetEmployees`, and keep selected the option to create methods for updates (we will not use these methods until a later exercise, however).

3. Take a look at what VWD has done for you by looking at the pinstriped page. At the top, we have the `Employees DataSet`. This is the list of fields that will be returned. Below we have a single `TableAdapter`, the one that reads the data. A great feature is that you can right-click on the method name and get a preview of the data that will be returned. Note that the data display window is initially empty; click the Preview button to fill it.

4. If you right-click anywhere on the `DataSet`, you can view the code. However, this is actually code that will build the ADO.NET commands when compiling; it is not the set of ADO.NET commands themselves. Close the `NorthWindDataSet` object.

5. We can use the `NorthWindDataSet` in an ASPX page directly; that is, without a new public function in `MyDataObject`. Create `TIO-1405-DataSetFromTableAdapterMadeByVwd`. Add an `ObjectDataSource` and configure it to use the `NorthwindDataSetTableAdaptors.EmployeesTableAdaptor`. Click Next, and select the `GetEmployees()` for your Select method. Then add a `GridView` as follows.

```
... <title>TIO-1405-DataSetFromTableAdapter.aspx</title>
</head><body>
    <h2>Chapter 14 TIO #1405 DataSet from a Table Adapter </h2>
    <form id="form1" runat="server">
    <div>
        <asp:GridView ID="GridView1" runat="server"
            AutoGenerateColumns="true"
            DataSourceID="ObjectDataSource1">
        </asp:GridView>
        <asp:ObjectDataSource ID="ObjectDataSource1" runat="server"
            TypeName="NorthwindDataSetTableAdapters.EmployeesTableAdapter"
            SelectMethod="GetEmployees">
        </asp:ObjectDataSource>
    </div></form></body></html>
```

6. Save your work and test it.

How It Works

In this exercise, we walk through the steps of VWD's wizard to create a data set. In the end, we have a representation in VWD with a top and bottom pane. The top is the `DataSet` that represents the largest set of fields that can be output. This is determined by the `SELECT` statement of the `DataSet`. In the bottom pane, we have a list of methods. So far we have just one method and that returns all of the fields from all of the records. As we work through the chapter, we will add more methods.

Next, we can improve our object so that it returns a `DataSet`.

Object That Returns a DataSet List

We used a generics <List> object in our third hard-coded Try It Out. Now, with our knowledge of how to connect to a DataSet, we can use the two techniques in one page.

Try It Out Object-DataSet from a Generic List

In this exercise, we use a data set to get the values and then use those values to populate a generic list of persons.

1. This exercise requires that you have the Person.cs file, which we created in the third Try It Out, in your App_Code folder. If it is not there, either copy it from the download or go through the steps of the third Try It Out. It also requires that you have the NorthWindDataSet.XSD file, which you created in the fifth Try It Out, in your App_Code folder.
2. Open your MyDataObject and double-check that you have the following namespaces; you will have to add the last one (in gray). They do not have to be in this order.

```
using System;
using System.Data;
using System.Data.SqlClient;
using System.Collections;
using System.Collections.Generic;
using NorthwindDataSetTableAdapters;
```

3. Add a new public function to MyDataObject named GetPeopleListFromDataSet. In the name, we state that we will be returning a generic List<> filled with items of the type Person that we defined in Person.cs. In the bottom line below, we actually create the generic List that will be populated with Person objects and we give it the name people.

```
public List<Person> GetPeopleListFromDataSet()
{
    List<Person> people = new List<Person>();
```

4. In the third Try It Out, we filled the list by typing three lines of names and then using the Add method three times. Now, we use the enlightened technique of reading data into the object. We start by instantiating a TableAdapter and telling the adapter to get a set of data as returned by the NorthWindDataSet's GetEmployees method.

```
    EmployeesTableAdapter adapter = new EmployeesTableAdapter();
    NorthwindDataSet.EmployeesDataTable table = adapter.GetEmployees();
```

5. Loop through each record, make that record a new Person item, and add it to the people object. We finish by returning that people object back to whomever called the MyDataObject.GetPeopleListFromDataSet():

```
    foreach (NorthwindDataSet.EmployeesRow row in table)
    {
        Person p = new Person(row.EmployeeID, row.FirstName, row.LastName,
row.Title, row.City);
        people.Add(p);
    }
    return people;
}
```

6. We can see the results by creating a page named `TIO-1406-DataSetWithGenerics.aspx` with an `ObjectDataSource` that uses `TypeName=MyDataObject SelectMethod=GetPeopleListFromDataSet`.

7. Save your work, and test it in your browser.

How It Works

In this exercise, we created a page that shows data that is not only read using a dataset and table adapter but also put into a .NET 2.0 generics `List<>` object. We used the `NorthwindDataSet` from the last Try It Out but did not have to make any modifications. The `GetEmployees()` method returns what we need. Note that this is an educational exercise (moving the data from a data set into a generic list). In this technique, we lose easy type and field name reflection.

In our `MyDataObject`, we had to add the `NorthwindDataSetTableAdapters` namespace. We made this object in the last Try It Out, and now it is fully qualified to help our code like the namespaces that come from Microsoft. We created a new `public` function that requested the values from `NorthwindDataSet.GetEmployees()` and put them into an object named `people` as follows:

```
public List<Person> GetPeopleListFromDataSet()
{
    List<Person> people = new List<Person>();
    EmployeesTableAdapter adapter = new EmployeesTableAdapter();
    NorthwindDataSet.EmployeesDataTable table = adapter.GetEmployees();
```

Then we use a `for-each` loop to loop through each of the rows in table and use their contents as values for another object named `p`, of the `Person` type. And for each we `add` the p to the `people` object.

```
    foreach (NorthwindDataSet.EmployeesRow row in table)
    {
        Person p = new Person(row.EmployeeID, row.FirstName, row.LastName,
row.Title, row.City);
        people.Add(p);
    }
    return people;
}
```

In our ASPX page, we only had one change from the last exercise: the `SelectMethod` of our `ObjectDataSource` now uses our new `GetPeopleListFromDataSet` method.

To date, we have only read data. `DataObject` can also write data, as you will see in the next section.

Objects That Modify Data

Continuing to move up in complexity, we can now study how to write through a `DataSet`. As before, we need three levels of code. The lowest is in the `DataSet.XSD` file, where we need the ADO.NET commands to perform an update. The intermediate level resides in the `DataObject.cs`, where we need an `update` function. At the highest level, we need to enable the writing behavior in the `ObjectDataSource` and the data-bound control.

Writing the ADO.NET commands to perform an Update is onerous for a beginner, so we can use the VWD tool. If you are creating a new DataSet, you can have VWD create these functions in the TableAdapter Wizard, as shown in Figure 14-3. If your DataSet already exists, you can right-click on its title bar, select Configure, and walk through the wizard to the point where you can ask VWD to create methods for Insert, Update, and Delete.

Either way, VWD will create a set of XML commands (viewable in the DataSet code) that will, at compile time, generate the necessary ADO.NET code to enable writing to the data. Once the method has been added to the DataSet, you can click on the method and use the properties window to change the name.

In the data object, we add another public function that requires some input values as listed in the parentheses. Then, in the two gray lines below, we create a new table adapter. In the lower shaded line, we use the table adapter to execute the UpdateMethod using our parameters and to return the results to the caller.

```
public int MyUpdateMethod(int MyFieldNumeric, String MyFieldText)
{
    MyTableAdapter adapter = new MyDataSetTableAdapter();
    return adapter.MyDataSetUpdateMethod(MyFieldNumeric, MyFieldText);
}
```

We have two tasks to perform in the ObjectDataSource. First, we need to specify that we want this particular data object function called when the user performs an Update, as indicated in the shaded line below.

```
<asp:ObjectDataSource ID="ObjectDataSource1" runat="server"
    TypeName="MyDataObject"
    SelectMethod="GetMyDataFromDataSet"
    UpdateMethod="UpdateMyData"
```

Second, in the ObjectDataSource, we need to provide the values for the update. This is done using a parameter collection, as you learned in the chapters on writing to SqlDataSources.

```
    <UpdateParameters>
        <asp:Parameter Name="MyFieldNumeric" Type="Int32" />
        <asp:Parameter Name="MyFieldText" Type="String" />
    </UpdateParameters>
</asp:ObjectDataSource>
```

And last, we make a change in our data-bound control to enable updating by providing a button for the user to initiate the action. For example, in a GridView we would use the following:

```
<asp:GridView ...
    DataKeyNames="ID">
    <Columns>
        <asp:CommandField ShowEditButton="True"></asp:CommandField>
    </Columns>
</asp:GridView>
```

In the next exercise, we build a page that uses a data object to write data.

Try It Out — Object That Updates Data

In this exercise, we create the ability to change the employee names.

1. Open your `NorthWindDataSet`, and check the Employees Data Tables list of TableAdapters for one named `UpdateEmployee(firstname...)`, as shown in Figure 14-6. If the `update` method does not exist, then right-click on the title of the `DataTable` and click on Configure. Click through the wizard until you get to the TableAdapter configuration (see Figure 14-2), and turn on the creation of the writing methods.

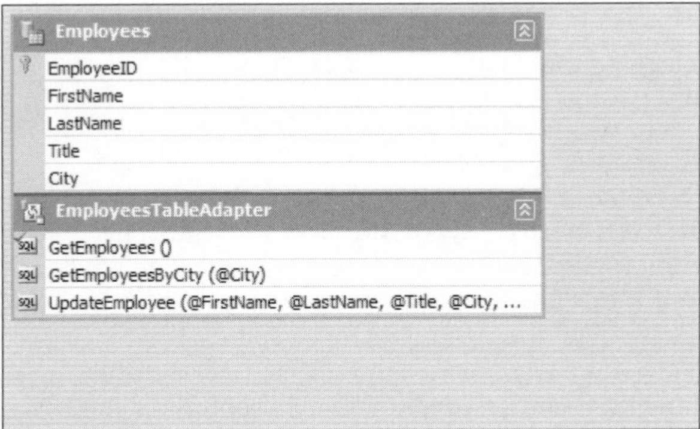

Figure 14-6

2. Open the `MyDataObject`, scroll down and create a new `public` function as follows and then save your work.

```
    ////////////////////////////////////////////////////////
    // TIO-1407 Update
    public int UpdatePerson(int id, String firstName, String lastName, String
title, String city)
    {
        EmployeesTableAdapter adapter = new EmployeesTableAdapter();
        return adapter.UpdateEmployee(firstName, lastName, title, city, id);
    }
```

3. Finish off the exercise by creating a new page named `TIO-1407-Object-Updating.aspx`. Add an `ObjectDataSource` as follows:

```
<asp:ObjectDataSource ID="ObjectDataSource1" runat="server"
        TypeName="MyDataObject"
SelectMethod="GetPeopleListFromDataSet"
UpdateMethod="UpdatePerson">
            <UpdateParameters>
                <asp:Parameter Name="id" Type="Int32" />
                <asp:Parameter Name="firstName" Type="String" />
                <asp:Parameter Name="lastName" Type="String" />
                <asp:Parameter Name="title" Type="String" />
                <asp:Parameter Name="city" Type="String" />
            </UpdateParameters>
        </asp:ObjectDataSource>
```

4. Continuing in the ASPX page, add a `GridView`, configure it to use `ObjectDataSource`, and enable editing. You can switch to autogenerate columns as we have done below, but be sure to not lose the `CommandField`.

```
<asp:GridView ID="GridView1" runat="server"
    DataSourceID="ObjectDataSource1"
    AutoGenerateColumns="true"
    DataKeyNames="ID">
    <Columns>
        <asp:CommandField ShowEditButton="True"></asp:CommandField>
    </Columns>
</asp:GridView>
```

5. Save your work, and run it in your browser.

How It Works

In this exercise, VWD did the toughest part. By enabling the creation of `write` methods in the `DataSet`'s Configuration Wizard, VWD created a set of XML tags in the XSD file that will generate the ADO.NET code at compile time and expose it as `UpdateEmployees`. We then wrote a new function in the `MyDataObject` that called that function and fed to it a set of values. In the ASPX page, we added an `ObjectDataSource` that put the values into a proper `UpdateParameters` collection. At the level of the `GridView` data-bound control, we added a `CommandField` brandishing an Edit button so that we could enable the behavior offered by the `ObjectDataSource` control.

Having learned to both read and write through a data object, you will now take a look at how to use a data object as part of a master-details scenario.

Master-Details with a Data Object

In the last exercise, we passed a set of parameters from our data-bound control to our data source control to our data object method to our `DataSet`. We can also pass parameters to be used in the `WHERE` clause of a SQL statement. This makes particular sense when we have a value from a master control (like a `DropDownList`) that we want to be the selector that limits the records of another control. We looked at this master-details scenario for the `SqlDataSource`, and now we can explore it when using a data object.

The master control is easy to set up. Create or use an existing `DataSet` and a function in your data object file that reads the desired data. Then, on the ASPX page, use an `ObjectDataSource` and a data-bound control. There is nothing in the master control that is any different from the one in the fifth Try It Out.

But the `DetailsView` control needs a number of modifications. First, in the `DataSet` we add a method that has a `WHERE` clause as follows:

```
SELECT MyFields FROM MyTable WHERE MyField = @MyValue
```

This syntax requires the caller of the method to pass a value that will go into `@MyValue`.

Up one level in the data object, we create a function as follows. We declare in the parentheses that we will be providing a value that will be referred to in the function as city. This is similar to an earlier harvest of values from a data set with one exception. In the shaded line below, we send the `MyValue` to the `TableAdapter`.

```
public List<MyItems> GetPeopleByCity(String city)
{
    List<MyItems> MyList = new List<MyItems>();
    MyTableAdapter adapter = new MyTableAdapter();
    MyDataSet.MyDataTable MyTable = adapter.MyFunctionWithWhereClause(MyValue);
    foreach (MyDataSet.MyRow row in table)
    {
        MyItem x = new MyItem(row.Field1, row.Field2);
        MyTable.Add(x);
    }
    return MyTable;
}
```

Last, we set up the ASPX page the same way we did in the master-details scenarios in Chapter 9. The master data-bound and data source controls are nothing special. The details data-bound controls are also no different; all the action is in the data source control for the details.

```
<asp:ObjectDataSource ID="MyObjectDataSource" runat="server"
TypeName="MyDataObject"
SelectMethod="MyGetMethodOfMyDataObject">
<SelectParameters>
<asp:ControlParameter
ControlID="MyMasterControl"
Name="MyValueName"
PropertyName="SelectedValue"
Type="String" />
</SelectParameters>
</asp:ObjectDataSource>
```

In the above code, when the `ObjectDataSource` calls the `MyGetMethodOfMyDataObject`, it will send along the `Select` parameter named `MyValueName`. That will be filled with the `SelectedValue` of the `MyMasterControl`.

Try It Out — Data Object with Master Details

In this exercise, we create a page that lists the cities of `Northwind` employees and then displays a `GridView` of just the employees selected from the `DropDownList`. For both the `DropDownList` and the `GridView`, we will provide the data using a data object and the generic `List<>`.

1. Start by creating a way to get a list of cities from our `DataSet`. Open your `NorthWindDataSet.XSD`. In the Database Explorer, expand the `MdfNorthWind` connection, expand the Tables, and then drag the `Employees` table to the pinstriped surface. Give it a minute to settle down, and then right-click on the `DataSet` (top) title bar and select Configure. Type the following SQL statement: `SELECT DISTINCT City FROM dbo.Employees`. Click Next, and disable Fill a Data Table and Create Methods to write. Click Next, and then click Finish.
2. Double-click on the new data set's name of `Employees`, and change it to `Cities`. Note that VWD will automatically create the `TableAdapter`. Now, change the name of the only method

by clicking on it and then in the Properties window, change the `name` from `GetData` to `GetCities`.

3. Create a method that will select a subset of the employees. In the `EmployeesTableAdapter`, right-click on the title bar and select Add Query. Use SQL statements and choose the `SELECT` which returns rows. Type or build the following statement. Do not select Fill a DataTable. Finish the wizard, and then in the Properties window, set the `GetMethodName` to `GetEmployeesByCity`:

```
SELECT EmployeeID, FirstName, LastName, Title, City
FROM Employees WHERE City = @City
```

4. Open `MyDataObject`, and go to the top to view the namespace declarations. Check that you have at least the following declarations shown in gray:

```
// following is one item needed for all exercises in Chapter 14
using System;
// following are two items needed for generics, starting with TIO-1402-2
using System.Collections;
using System.Collections.Generic;
// following are two items needed for SQL connection to database, starting with
TIO-1403
using System.Data;
using System.Data.SqlClient;
// following is one item for using the DataSet created by VWD, starting with TIO-
1406
using NorthwindDataSetTableAdapters;
```

5. Continuing in `MyDataObject.cs`, add a new public function as follows to simply read the values returned by the `GetCities` method. This will provide the data for our `DropDownList` of cities.

```
////////////////////////////////////////////////////////
// TIO-1408 Used for DropDownList
    public IEnumerable GetCities()
    {

        // requires using System.Collections;
        List<String> cities = new List<String>();
        CitiesTableAdapter adapter = new CitiesTableAdapter();
        NorthwindDataSet.CitiesDataTable table = adapter.GetCities();

        foreach (NorthwindDataSet.CitiesRow row in table)
        {
            cities.Add(row.City);
        }
        return cities;
    }
```

6. Continuing in `MyDataObject.cs`, add a new `public` function as follows, which will provide employee data for our `GridView`. Then close and save the `MyDataObject`.

```
public class MyDataObject
{
    public String[] GetLastNameOneOnly()
    ... the rest of our function so far ...
```

```
    public IEnumerable GetCities() ...

////////////////////////////////////////////////////////
// TIO-1408  Used for the GridView
    public List<Person> GetPeopleByCity(String city)
    {
        List<Person> people = new List<Person>();
        EmployeesTableAdapter adapter = new EmployeesTableAdapter();
        NorthwindDataSet.EmployeesDataTable table =
adapter.GetEmployeesByCity(city);
        foreach (NorthwindDataSet.EmployeesRow row in table)
        {
            Person p = new Person(row.EmployeeID, row.FirstName, row.LastName,
row.Title, row.City);
            people.Add(p);
        }
        return people;
    }
```

7. Create an ASPX page named `TIO-1408-ObjectWithParameters`. Start by dragging an `ObjectDataSource` to the page and setting its properties as follows. Then drag a `DropDownList` to the page, and set its data source to the nascent `ObjectDataSource` control.

```
... <h2>Chapter 14 TIO #1408 Object with Parameters <br />
        to support a Master-Details Scenario </h2>
    <form id="form1" runat="server"><div>

        <asp:DropDownList ID="DropDownList1" runat="server"
            AutoPostBack="True"
            DataSourceID="ObjectDataSource1">
        </asp:DropDownList>

        <asp:ObjectDataSource ID="ObjectDataSource1" runat="server"
            TypeName="MyDataObject"
            SelectMethod="GetCities">
        </asp:ObjectDataSource>
```

8. Add the `GridView` that will be based create an ASPX page named `TIO-1408-ObjectWithParameters`. Start by dragging an `ObjectDataSource` to the page and setting its properties as follows. Then drag a `GridView` to the page, and set its data source to the nascent `ObjectDataSource` control. Enable editing. You can set it to autogenerate columns, as we have below, or leave the `Columns` collection.

```
        <asp:GridView ID="GridView1" runat="server"
            AutoGenerateColumns="True"
            DataSourceID="ObjectDataSource2">
        </asp:GridView>
        <asp:ObjectDataSource ID="ObjectDataSource2" runat="server"
            SelectMethod="GetPeopleByCity"
            TypeName="MyDataObject">
            <SelectParameters>
                <asp:ControlParameter
                    ControlID="DropDownList1"
                    Name="city"
                    PropertyName="SelectedValue"
                    Type="String" />
```

```
            </SelectParameters>
        </asp:ObjectDataSource>
</div></form></body></html>
```

9. Save your work.

How It Works

This exercise brought together several concepts from the book. We used the master-child details techniques of Chapter 9 and data object techniques of this chapter. In this case, the best tool for the job is the generic `List<>`, which we use twice.

We started by adding a new `DataTable` named `Cities` to the `NorthWindDataSet`. This will return the list of all values of cities from the `City` field of the `Employees` table. Using the `DISTINCT` keyword weeds out any duplicates. We also added a new method to the `Employees DataTable`. But there is a crucial difference from earlier reads. This time, we specify a `WHERE` clause in the SQL statement. The value for the `WHERE` will come in with the call to the method as a parameter.

In our data object we added two functions. The first just passes the set of cities. The second gets a table of employee information but with a crucial difference from earlier reads. This time, we pass a parameter in with the call to the method. The parameter will contain the value of a city.

Now, we move up to the ASPX page. Here we use a master-details architecture the same way we did in Chapter 9. The key is the data source for the details control. We have a set of `SelectParameters` and within that a control parameter, because we get the value from a control (the master control, our `DropDownList`).

There are some changes in common data tasks when we use a data object. In the next section, we explore sorting.

Sorts in a Data Object

Sorting data from a `ObjectDataSource` control is not difficult. It primarily requires the addition of a `DataView` object in the data object.

First, in the data object, require an incoming parameter of `SortExpression` as follows:

```
public List<MyItem> GetMyDataSorted(String sortExpression)
{
```

Then, get the data into a table, as we did in the last few exercises:

```
    List<MyItem> MyList = new List<MyItem>();
    MyTableAdapter adapter = new MyTableAdapter();
    MyDataSet.MyDataTable MyTable = adapter.GetMyData();
```

But here we add an extra line. We take the information in the table and put it into a `DataView` object named `table`. A `DataView` object supports sorting, which we perform on the second line below:

```
        DataView view = new DataView(MyTable);
        view.Sort = sortExpression;
```

And now we do our adding of each item, but we loop through the `DataView` so that we are adding the items to the table in the sorted order.

```
        foreach (DataRowView row in view)
        {
            MyItem x = new MyItem((int)row["Field1"], (String)row["Field2"];
            MyTable.Add(p);
        }
        return MyList;
    }
```

Up in the ASPX file, we use an `ObjectDataSource` that states a `SortParameterName` whose value will be the `sortExpression` provided by the data-bound control. Because that parameter will ultimately be used in a SQL `SELECT` statement, we set up a `SelectParameters` collection. We only need one parameter, which we name `sortExpression`:

```
<asp:ObjectDataSource ID="ObjectDataSource1" runat="server"
TypeName="MyDataObject"
SelectMethod="GetMyDataSorted"
SortParameterName="sortExpression">
<SelectParameters>
<asp:Parameter Name="sortExpression" Type="String" />
</SelectParameters>
</asp:ObjectDataSource>
```

Last, still at the level of our ASPX page, we need a data-bound control that has sorting enabled:

```
<asp:GridView ID="GridView1" runat="server"
AllowSorting="True"
AutoGenerateColumns="True"
DataSourceID="ObjectDataSource1">
</asp:GridView>
```

We will try this sorting technique in the next exercise.

Try It Out — Sorting in a Data Object

In this exercise, we will enable sorting of the Northwind employee names. There is no need to change `DataSet.xsd`; we only have to change `MyObject.cs`.

1. Add the following new method to `MyObject.cs`.

```
/////////////////////////////////////////////////////////
// TIO-1409 Object With Sorting
    public List<Person> GetPeopleSorted(String sortExpression)
    {
        List<Person> people = new List<Person>();
        EmployeesTableAdapter adapter = new EmployeesTableAdapter();
        NorthwindDataSet.EmployeesDataTable table = adapter.GetEmployees();
```

```
        DataView view = new DataView(table);
        view.Sort = sortExpression;

        foreach (DataRowView row in view)
        {
            Person p = new Person((int)row["EmployeeID"], (String)row["FirstName"],
(String)row["LastName"], (String)row["Title"], (String)row["City"]);
            people.Add(p);
        }
        return people;
    }
```

2. Create a page named `TIO-1409-ObjectSorting.aspx` with an `ObjectDataSource` and a `GridView`, as follows.

```
... <h2>Chapter 14 TIO #1409 Object With Sorting </h2>
    <form id="form1" runat="server"><div>
        <asp:GridView ID="GridView1" runat="server"
            AllowSorting="True"
            AutoGenerateColumns="True"
            DataSourceID="ObjectDataSource1">
        </asp:GridView>
        <asp:ObjectDataSource ID="ObjectDataSource1" runat="server"
            TypeName="MyDataObject"
            SelectMethod="GetPeopleSorted"
            SortParameterName="sortExpression">
            <SelectParameters>
                <asp:Parameter Name="sortExpression" Type="String" />
            </SelectParameters>
        </asp:ObjectDataSource>
</div></form></body></html>
```

How It Works

We started in our data object with a new method. We will create a generics list of objects of the type `Person`. This is different from earlier generics objects because we added an incoming parameter that we named `sortExpression`.

```
    public List<Person> GetPeopleSorted(String sortExpression)
    {
```

The method then gets a batch of data from the `NorthwindDataSet` Table Adapter.

```
        List<Person> people = new List<Person>();
        EmployeesTableAdapter adapter = new EmployeesTableAdapter();
        NorthwindDataSet.EmployeesDataTable table = adapter.GetEmployees();
```

In order to sort, we now create a `DataView` and set its sort order to the value that came in on the parameter.

```
        DataView view = new DataView(table);
        view.Sort = sortExpression;
```

Last, we go through each record in the DataView (which was sorted) and create an item in the generics list.

```
        foreach (DataRowView row in view)
        {
            Person p = new Person((int)row["EmployeeID"], (String)row["FirstName"],
    (String)row["LastName"], (String)row["Title"], (String)row["City"]);
            people.Add(p);
        }
```

That generics list is then returned to the ObjectDataSource control, which then provides it to our GridView.

```
        return people;
```

Having covered a half-dozen new techniques in this chapter, we can pause and consider some common mistakes. If you are having problems, start your troubleshooting with this list.

Common Mistakes

- Inputting an incorrect username or password. Make sure that the connection string contains the correct username and password.
- Trying to use a component without creating it in the App_Code directory. Any time you are creating a reusable component, you should create it in the special App_Code directory. Only then will the component be compiled and available for use within the Web application. (Although there are some advanced options, such as compiling into the Bin directory or an install view the GAC. Neither of these is covered in this book.)
- Errors in table or column names. This mistake usually arises when typing; it is less problematic when using the designer wizards or drag-and-drop in Visual Studio and VWD.
- Using a type in a generics List<> but not defining the type. For example, we had to define the Person type before we could use it in a generic list of people.
- Attempting to sort data using a custom object that does not implement a sorting interface. Remember to set the SortParameterName on the ObjectDataSource to a parameter that accepts a sorting expression. (However, if the SelectMethod returns a DataSet, DataTable, or DataView, then ObjectDataSource can automatically apply sorting to the list by internally setting a DataView's SortExpression.)
- Attempting to bind an ObjectDataSource to a DataTable or DataRow type in a VS DataSet. Remember that it is the TableAdapter type that exposes the methods for binding.
- Attempting to bind an ObjectDataSource to a TableAdapter type without first saving the DataSet.xsd file in the designer. You must save the file in order for the TableAdapter type to be available to the ObjectDataSource.

Summary

In this chapter we discussed how to create a tier of objects in between the ASPX page (presentation layer) and the database (data access layer). By adding a *business logic layer* we achieve greater flexibility in development, additional options for security and improved efficiencies in serving the site. The middle tier can be modified without any changes in the ASPX page. It can be written to include additional security features. A middle tier could also be available to Windows forms for non-web applications within an enterprise and then changes to business rules only have to be made in one location. When changes are made to the location and nature of the database, only the business logic layer must be modified, not all of the presentation layers. Also, the business layer's programming language is independent of the presentation layer.

We started with a very simple object to demonstrate the needed files. We created a data object and added a public function with code that returned a simple string. Then in the ASPX page we added a `ObjectDataSource` control and set the TypeName to the data object and the `SelectMethod` to the public function in the data object. In the ASPX we set a data-bound control's data source to the `ObjectDataSource`, same as we would bind to any other data source control.

Next we built another function within our business object, but this time we created a string array so we could load several values. In the ASPX page the `ObjectDataSource` control handled them properly and feed the multiple values to the data-bound control on the page.

Generic collections (new with.NET 2.0) allow you to make nontyped structures that then become type-safe when the page is compiled. One generics `List<>` can hold persons items and another generics `List<>` a list of people. Both get the benefits of a collection like looping through contents or a count. Using the generics `List<>` required an additional file, one that defines the properties of the `MyItem` to be in the generics list. The data object must add a reference to using `System.Collections` and `System.Collections.Generic` and then the data object can create a generics list with `List<MyItem>`

Next we created an object that would bind to a database. However, our first example made the binding directly using ADO.NET objects. Although it worked, it was a cumbersome page of code. In fact, we did not go into the details of many of the ADO.NET objects.

To avoid creating the ADO.NET objects yourself, you can instruct VWD to build the objects. We simply specified what database to use and how to use it; then VWD created the `DataSet` and its associated files. We started by right-clicking on the App_Code folder and adding a new item from the template named `DataSet`. The TableAdapter Configuration Wizard started and walked us through the connection and building a SQL Select statement. The result was a dataset that had a representation (on the pinstriped background) that displayed the fields that would be returned and below them the table adaptors that allow access to those fields. We used the `DataTable` in an ASPX page by setting an `ObjectDataSource` control's TypeName to the dataset's table adapter concatenated onto the end of the `DataTable` name.

Next we combined our knowledge of the generics `<List>` with our ability to create a `DataSet` using VWD. Note that moving the data from a data set into a generic list lost field name reflection, so it was mainly an academic exercise.

Our next section covered modifying data by using three levels of code. Lowest was the `DataSet.XSD` file created by VWD that holds the ADO.NET objects that will perform the update. Intermediate was the `DataObject.cs`, where we added an update function. Highest was ASPX page holding the `ObjectDataSource` and the data-bound control.

A master-details scenario can be created because ASP.NET 2.0's `ObjectDataSource` permits passing of values from one control to another the same as the other ASP.NET 2.0 data source controls. Thus we can create Master-Detail scenarios as in earlier chapters. The master control is easy to set up, the same as for prior chapters. In the data object, we created a function with input arguments like `GetMyData(String MyValue)`. We could then refer to `MyValue` within the function. Last, the ASPX page is set the same way as master-details scenarios in Chapter 9 for the data source control for the details data-bound control; the `SelectMethod` will contain a `ControlParameter`. The values held in that parameter will be passed as the arguments to the function in the data object.

We studied how sorting in a data object requires the addition of a `DataView` object in the data object. We started with a function that creates a `Generics <List>`. Then we add an incoming argument to the function which contains the sort expression. Next we used a table adaptor with a view.sort property set to the sort expression. In the ASPX file's `ObjectDataSource` we added a `SortParameterName` of `sortExpression` and a parameter that holds the expression. Finally, in the data-bound control we set the `AllowSorting` to `true`.

Exercises

The answers to these review questions can be found in Appendix B.

1. Why are data objects important?
2. When you create a data object, it will contain blocks of code that execute tasks, such as returning data. What are these called by consumers of the data objects' services?
3. What is needed before we can use a generic list?
4. Where are data objects sorted on a Web site?
5. How can you add a new method to a `DataSet` in the VWD (pinstriped) designer?
6. What is needed to enable sorting in a data object?

XML and Other Hierarchical Data

Prior to this point in the book, you have worked with tabular data. In other words, the information could be organized in a series of rows, each of which had the same fields filled with data. This is the normal form of relational databases. But there are other ways to organize data, and one that now pervades IT is hierarchical data. ASP.NET has a series of controls that make it both easy and logical to utilize hierarchical data.

This chapter covers seven areas.

- ❑ Definition of hierarchical data, including the common types and the ASP.NET 2.0 hierarchical data controls
- ❑ The two main hierarchical controls: `XmlDataSource` and the `TreeView` control
- ❑ How to limit the scope of data returned from an XML file by using `XPath` with the `XmlDataSource`
- ❑ How to format the `TreeView`
- ❑ Handling events in the `TreeView` control
- ❑ How to use the `XmlDataSource` control with other data-bound controls, including `DropDownList`, `GridView`, and `DataList`
- ❑ How to work with the `SiteMapDataSource`, `SiteMapPath`, and the `Menu` control to provide navigation tools for the site

What Is Hierarchical Data?

In the first 14 chapters, our data sources were mostly organized into tables. But there are two common ways to store data:

- **Structured data (tabular):** This type of data is very rigid in that all records have the same fields. An example of structured data is a telephone book — every entry has a name, an address, and a telephone number. Relational databases are generally a better way to store highly structured data.
- **Semistructured data (hierarchical):** This type of data has some structure but is not rigidly structured. An example of semistructured data is a health record. For example, one patient might have a list of vaccinations, another might have height and weight, and another might have a list of surgical operations. Semistructured data is difficult to store in a relational database because it means you have either many different tables (which means many joins and slow retrieval time) or a single table with many null columns. Semistructured data is very easy to store as hierarchical data.

Hierarchical data is categorized by a structure of relationships where each item is a *child* to, or member of, an item above it. At the top of the hierarchy is a single item that has no parent. There is a specific vocabulary for hierarchical data. Each item is called a *node*. The topmost node is named the *root*. Nodes that have a node below them are *parents*, and all nodes except the root are *children*. As in families, a node can be both a parent and a child. Nodes with no children are called *leaf nodes*.

Types of Hierarchical Data

If you work in Windows, you are already familiar with one hierarchical data structure: the Windows file system of drives, folders, and files. When working with ASP.NET 2.0, you have three other sources (albeit one is a subset of another).

- **XML:** XML documents are *self-describing*, meaning that the metadata required to describe the data is actually contained in the XML document itself, providing a flexible way of handling XML data. Many Web sites exist to explain the rules for XML files, but the key points are that all information is in tags and the tags are within each other to organize a hierarchy branching down from a single, top-level tag.
- **SiteMap:** `SiteMap` is ASP.NET 2.0's XML format that provides a consistent way of describing the contents of a Web site, including all the pages contained in that Web site. Although it is possible in ASP.NET 2.0 to store a `SiteMap` as something other than XML using a custom provider, this book only covers the XML implementation of `SiteMap`.
- **Menu system:** (Subtype of XML) A menu system organized into an XML document as its input and displays the contents of the XML document in a hierarchical manner.

The next section details the support provided by ASP.NET for working with hierarchical data.

ASP.NET 2.0 Hierarchical Data Controls

The architecture of controls for hierarchical data is very similar to the design of controls for tabular data. ASP.NET offers both hierarchical data source controls and hierarchical data-bound controls:

- ASP.NET hierarchical data source controls
  - `XmlDataSource`
  - `SiteMapDataSource`

- ASP.NET hierarchical data-bound controls
  - `TreeView`
  - `Menu`
  - `SiteMapPath` (a highly specialized control only for displaying `SiteMap` data)

Because of the flexibility and common object model in the ASP.NET data story, in some situations you can use a data-bound control that normally used is for tabular data for hierarchical data. For example, an XML file holding the names of states can be used as the source for a list box. A `GridView` can display hierarchical data in a grid, but it tends to create very flat grids. The hierarchical data sources in ASP.NET implement a tabular interface that normal data-bound controls can bind against, so that in addition to using `TreeView` and `Menu` to bind to hierarchical data, you can also bind the tabular data-bound controls introduced in preceding chapters. As you will see later in this chapter, a new XML-based data-binding syntax also allows you to bind to hierarchical elements of a hierarchical data source in a templated data-bound control, such as `DataList`. Each of these applications of controls is discussed in the following sections.

XmlDataSource and the TreeView Control

The `XmlDataSource` and the `TreeView` data-bound controls are the workhorses of using XML data in ASP.NET 2.0. We will spend considerable time in this book discussing their intricacies. Both are optimized to support hierarchical data-bond controls For example, a `GridView` can be built from an `XmlDataSource`.

The `XmlDataSource` control is optimized for binding to XML data sources. Instead of a connection string property, the `XmlDataSource` needs a `DataFile` value that points to an XML file. There are also properties for transformations and `XPath` scoping, which we will cover later in this chapter, as well as for caching, which we discuss in Chapter 16. Compared to the `SqlDataSource` control, the properties are simple.

The `TreeView` control displays hierarchical information. Although it is not restricted to navigation, the `TreeView` control is found in VWD's Toolbox in the Navigation pane. Generally bound to a hierarchical data source control, the `TreeView` displays data in a clear parent-and-child arrangement. Its Smart Tasks panel offers the ability to edit nodes instead of edit columns. There is no templating within a `TreeView` like there is for smart data controls like `GridView`. `TreeView` does not offer options for inserting or updating (although these could be implemented in custom code).

Try It Out Creating a Simple XML Example

In this exercise, we will simply display the data from an XML file about books.

1. In VWD right-click on your `App_Data` folder and select Add Existing Item. From the book downloads, find `Bookstore.xml` and click Add. If you do not have the downloads, you can build the file as follows:

```
<Bookstore>
  <genre name="Fiction">
    <book ISBN="10-861003-324" Title="A Tale of Two Cities" Price="19.99">
```

```
        <chapter num="1" name="Introduction">Abstract... </chapter>
        <chapter num="2" name="Body">Abstract... </chapter>
        <chapter num="3" name="Conclusion">Abstract... </chapter>
      </book>
      <book ISBN="1-861001-57-5" Title="Pride And Prejudice" Price="24.95">
        <chapter num="1" name="Introduction">Abstract... </chapter>
        <chapter num="2" name="Body">Abstract... </chapter>
        <chapter num="3" name="Conclusion">Abstract... </chapter>
      </book>
      <book ISBN="1-861001-57-6" Title="The Old Man and the Sea" Price="27.95">
        <chapter num="1" name="Introduction">Abstract... </chapter>
        <chapter num="2" name="Body">Abstract... </chapter>
        <chapter num="3" name="Conclusion">Abstract... </chapter>
      </book>
    </genre>
    <genre name="NonFiction">
      <book ISBN="98-765142-654" Title="Italian-Thai Fusion cooking" Price="29.65">
        <chapter num="1" name="Pasta vs Noodles">Abstract... </chapter>
        <chapter num="2" name="Tomatoes and Mangos">Abstract... </chapter>
        <chapter num="3" name="Durian - the Miracle Fruit">Abstract... </chapter>
        <chapter num="4" name="Passion Fruit and Amore">Abstract... </chapter>
        <chapter num="5" name="Recipes">Abstract... </chapter>
      </book>
      <book ISBN="5-134685-85-5" Title="How to Live Forever (Thinly)" Price="128.95">
        <chapter num="1" name="Long, Long Term Investing">Abstract... </chapter>
        <chapter num="2" name="Picking Your Parents">Abstract... </chapter>
        <chapter num="3" name="Summary">Abstract... </chapter>
      </book>
      <book ISBN="6-6734-261548-8"
           Title="Air - A User's Guide to Breathing" Price="18.95">
        <chapter num="1" name="Inhale">Abstract... </chapter>
        <chapter num="2" name="Exhale">Abstract... </chapter>
        <chapter num="3" name="Repeat for Life">Abstract... </chapter>
      </book>
    </genre>
  </Bookstore>
```

2. Double-click the file to open it, and take a look at the pattern. We have an overall BookStore tag (the root), within which are two genres: fiction and nonfiction. Within the genre, we have book tags that hold an ISBN, title, and price. Within the book tags are chapter tags with a number, title, and abstract.

3. In your BegAspNet20Db site create a folder for ch15. Add a new ASP.NET 2.0 page named TIO-1501-SimpleXML-1.aspx. From the Solution Explorer, drag the entire Bookstore.xml file to the page. VWD will automatically create an XmlDataSource and a TreeView control.

4. Save your work, and view it in the browser. At this point, you will see the names of the tag levels, not the actual data.

5. Close the browser, and in VWD save the page as TIO-1501-SimpleXML-2.aspx. Select the TreeView and open its Smart Tasks panel. Click on Edit TreeNode Databindings. In the list of available bindings, select genre and click Add. In the properties, set TextField to name. Back in the list of available data bindings, select book and click Add. Set its TextField to Title.

```
..<h2>Chapter 15 TIO #1502 Simple XML  Example version 2</h2>
    <form id="form1" runat="server">
```

```
        <div>
            <asp:XmlDataSource ID="XmlDataSource1" runat="server"
             DataFile="../App_Data/Bookstore.xml">
            </asp:XmlDataSource>

            <asp:TreeView ID="TreeView1" runat="server"
    DataSourceID="XmlDataSource1">
             <DataBindings>
                    <asp:TreeNodeBinding DataMember="genre" TextField="name" />
                    <asp:TreeNodeBinding DataMember="book" TextField="Title" />
             </DataBindings>
            </asp:TreeView>
    </div></form></body></html>
```

6. Save your work, and view it in the browser.

How It Works

When we look over the XML, we see a mix of rigidity and flexibility. The format is absolutely rigid in that each opening tag must have a closing tag, there must be a single root tag, and the tags must maintain a strict consistency of hierarchy. But there is lots of flexibility in that tags such as `book` can contain various numbers and kinds of child tags. The book on `Italian-Thai Fusion cooking` has a different number of chapters from the other books. (This flexibility is inefficient in a single table of a relational database).

Note in the XML file that some data is within a tag (like the chapter number) and some data is located between the opening and closing tags (like the `Abstract`). The former is called a *name-value pair*, and the latter is called *inner text*. As you will see later, ASP.NET 2.0 handles them differently.

The `XmlDataSource` is very simple to implement, needing only the name of the file to read. There is no connection string, provider, or select command as required in the `SqlDataSource`.

The concept of data binding is interesting for `TreeView`. By default, as you saw in Step 3, the `TreeView` will do a default bind for each level to the name of the tag. Then you can actually data-bind each level to a specific datum within a tag. At the end of Step 4 (version 2 of the page), we have data-bound the names of genres and books, but the chapters are still in the default binding to the tag names.

DataBinding and Formatting the TreeView

As we saw above, the `TreeView`, by default, does a quasi-databind that results in the names of the nodes being displayed. In this sense, the word `name` means the first string after the opening of the node tag, for example the bold `<book isbn=...>` It is also possible that within the node there is a `Name` property, but that is not used in the default data binding. This section will explain how to move beyond that default.

To see the actual values, we have to set a `TextField` property for each node. Within the `TreeView` control, VWD will add a `DataBinding` collection that has a member for each level of node. The binding will contain two properties; the first is the `DataMember`, which contains the name of the level. By default, this is what is shown. The second property is the `TextField`, which identifies which property of the node to display. For example, in the `BookStore` XML file, we have a level, called `book`, that contains three attributes: ISBN, Title, and Price. If we wanted the title to be shown in the TreeView, we would use the following syntax. Note that for the levels other than <book>, we would get the default binding of the name word in the tag.

```
<asp:TreeView ID="TreeView1" runat="server"
    DataSourceID="XmlDataSource1">
    <DataBindings>
        <asp:TreeNodeBinding DataMember="book" TextField="Title" />
    </DataBindings>
</asp:TreeView>
```

Of course, VWD expedites all of this for you (not bad for free software). The TreeView Smart Tasks panel has a choice to edit TreeNode databindings. In that dialog you can select a node, add it to the bound nodes and then set its properties. The displayed value will be the property of TextField. If you expect to do some processing of user clicks, you can also set a ValueField . When you drop down the options for TextField, you will see two kinds of options. The ones that begin with a pound sign (#) are intrinsic to all tags. They include the #Name of the tag, which is the first string after the beginning of the tag; that is, the name of the level of the node. Another is the #InnerText between the start and end tags. Last is the #Value, which is not used for data controls. In addition, the options without the pound sign are the attributes that you may have added, such as the ISBN or Price.

> **If you really want to know about #Value..., it holds a datum that represents whether the node is a data element (#Value=NULL) or a nondata element like a comment. Because the ASP.NET XmlDataSource control already filters out nondata elements, there is no use for #Value in ASP.NET 2.0 scenarios.**

The TreeView offers options beyond displaying a value. The property for ImageUrl specifies a file to add a bullet or picture to each node. Setting a value for NavigateUrl makes the node into a hyperlink. Both of these properties can have values that are fields in the XML file or hard-coded to a single value for all nodes at one level.

Try It Out Using DataBinding When Formatting a TreeView

1. If the Bookstore.xml file is not already present in the App_Data folder, add it to the App_Data folder by right-clicking on the App_Data folder and selecting Add Existing Item from the context menu. In the Add Existing Item dialog box, select the Bookstore.xml file.
2. If you have not imported the images from the download, right-click on your site's image folder and select Add Existing item. Browse to your download and import all the images. You will need notepad.gif for this exercise.
3. In the Solution Explorer, select Ch15 and add a page named TO1502-TreeViewDataBinding.aspx from the template Web Form.
4. Take advantage of the VWD shortcut by dragging the file named Bookstore.xml from the App_Data folder to the page. VWD will automatically create an XmlDataSource control and a TreeView. Save your work, and view it in the browser to see the default data bindings.
5. Close the browser, and back in VWD, open the TreeView's Smart Tasks panel. Click on Edit TreeNode DataBindings. Select the book node in the Available DataBindings tree, and click the Add Command Button. Then, in the DataBinding Properties window, set the TextField to Title

and ImageUrl (not ImageUrlField) property to ~/Images/notepad.gif. Save the file. Your page should now appear as shown in Figure 15-1.

```
... <h2>Chapter 15 TIO #1502 TreeView DataBinding</h2>
    <form id="form1" runat="server">
    <div>
        <asp:XmlDataSource ID="XmlDataSource1" runat="server"
            DataFile="../App_Data/Bookstore.xml">
        </asp:XmlDataSource>
        <asp:TreeView ID="TreeView1" runat="server"
            DataSourceID="XmlDataSource1"
            Width="402px">
            <DataBindings>
                <asp:TreeNodeBinding DataMember="book"
                    ImageUrl="~/Images/notepad.gif" TextField="Title" />
                <asp:TreeNodeBinding DataMember="chapter"
                    TextField="name" />
            </DataBindings>
        </asp:TreeView>
</div></form></body></html>
```

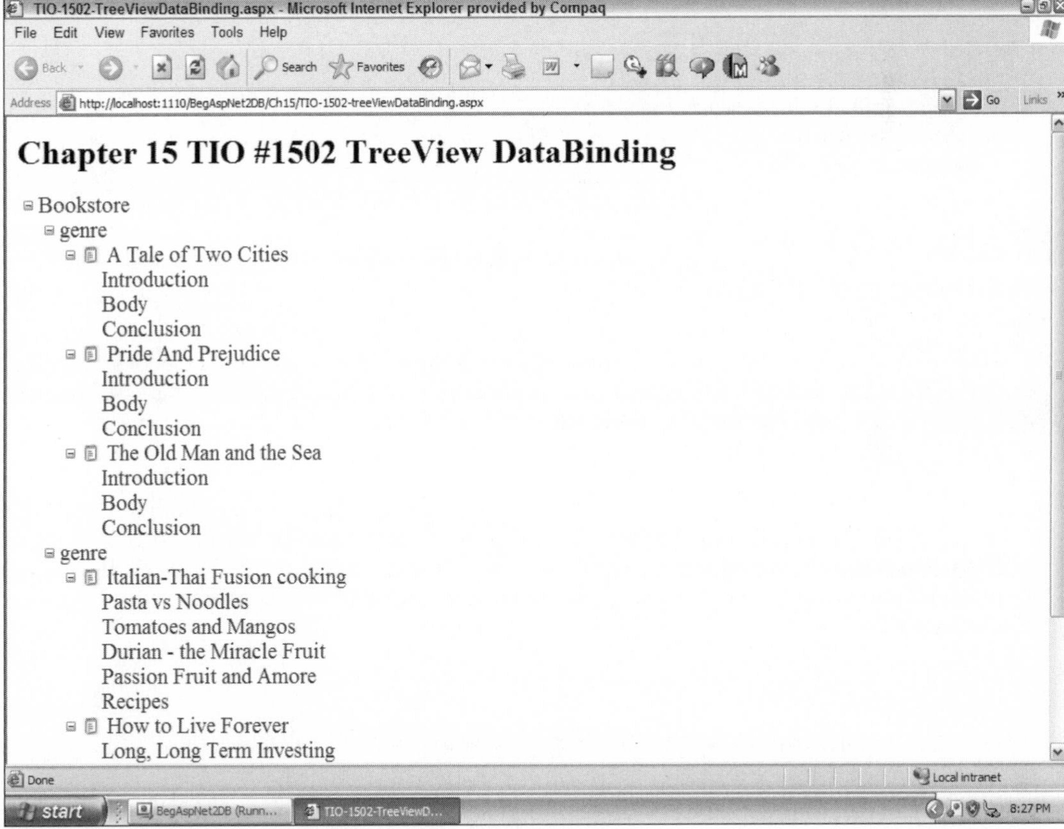

Figure 15-1

6. Close the browser and save the file.

How It Works

When you simply drag an XML file from the Database Explorer to the page, VWD sets up two controls on the page. The first, `XmlDataSource`, reads the `Bookstore.xml`. The second, the `TreeView`, takes that data and displays the information on the page.

VWD automatically bound the entire `TreeView` to the `XmlDataSource` control, as follows:

```
        <asp:TreeView ID="TreeView1" runat="server"
            DataSourceID="XmlDataSource1"
            Width="402px">
            <DataBindings>
...
            </DataBindings>
        </asp:TreeView>
```

Inside the `TreeView` control, VWD created a collection of `DataBindings` as follows. We can also see how VWD applied our specification to display `notepad.gif` next to each book node.

```
<DataBindings>
 <asp:TreeNodeBinding DataMember="book"
         TextField="Title"
         ImageUrl="~/Images/notepad.gif"/>
 <asp:TreeNodeBinding DataMember="chapter"
         TextField="name" />
</DataBindings>
```

XPath with XmlDataSource

`XPath` is a language to identify a set of nodes of an XML document. Its function is similar to that of a SQL `SELECT` statement. For example, an `XPath` definition can select only the nonfiction books from the `Bookstore.xml`. `XPath` statements can become complex; for example, only finding books that are priced over a set amount. We will apply `XPath` statements directly in our `XmlDataSource`. They can also be used in your further studies of XML when you use `XQuery`, `XSLT`, `XPointer`, and `XLink`. In addition, `XPath` provides basic functions for manipulating strings, numbers, and Booleans.

An `XPath` pattern is a slash-separated list of child element names that describes a path through the XML document. Only the nodes fitting that path will be returned. In all XML documents, there must be a root element, which is represented by the first forward slash (/) in `XPath`. In a standard XHTML document, the root element would be "html," so to match everything in an XHTML document, you would write the following:

```
/html
```

To match all the paragraphs in an XHTML document, you would write the following:

```
/html/body/p
```

/html/body/p would match all paragraphs within the body tag, but if there were paragraphs within a div tag or a td tag, these would be skipped. With XPath, you can specify all paragraph tags with two preceding slashes:

```
//p
```

This would match every paragraph tag in the XHTML document, no matter where it was. Or you could match only the paragraph tags that are inside a div tag, as follows:

```
//div/p
```

XPath can select multiple elements in a node with the symbol *. To match every element that is within a td tag (such as p, div, and so on), you would write the following:

```
//td/*
```

In an XML (not XHTML) file, you also start with a front slash to represent the root. Then you refer to lower-level nodes with additional slashes (the same as for Windows folders, but use front slashes). Within a node if you want to do limiting you use the following expression:

```
/.../.../MyNodeName[@MyAttribute='MyValue']/.../...
```

So, if we wanted to see only the books in the nonfiction genre, we would use:

```
/Bookstore/genre[@name='non-fiction']/book/chapter
```

To add a numeric range, use:

```
"/Bookstore/genre/book[@Price>25]"
```

The following Try It Out explores how to implement XPath expressions.

Try It Out Tightening the Scope of a TreeView from XPath

In this exercise, you will practice using XPath to filter data from an XML file.

1. Add a page to the ch15 folder named TIO-1503-XPath-1.aspx. Drag the Bookstore.xml file onto your page. Select the XmlDataSource control and in the Properties window, find its property for XPath. Enter the following.

```
Bookstore/genre[@name='Fiction']/book
```

2. Open the Smart Tasks panel of the TreeView control, and click Edit TreeNode databindings. From the available databindings, click on Bookstore, and then click Add. In the Properties window, set the TextField to #Name. Repeat the Add and bind as follows: genre to name, book to title, and chapter to name. Your page should now appear as follows:

```
<h2>Chapter 15 TIO #1503 XPath version 1</h2>
    <form id="form1" runat="server">
    <div>
        <asp:XmlDataSource ID="XmlDataSource1" runat="server"
```

```
            DataFile="~/App_Data/Bookstore.xml"
             XPath="/Bookstore/genre[@name='NonFiction']/*">
        </asp:XmlDataSource>

    <asp:TreeView ID="TreeView1" runat="server"
        DataSourceID="XmlDataSource1">
        <DataBindings>
            <asp:TreeNodeBinding DataMember="Bookstore" TextField="#Name" />
            <asp:TreeNodeBinding DataMember="genre" TextField="name" />
            <asp:TreeNodeBinding DataMember="book" TextField="Title" />
            <asp:TreeNodeBinding DataMember="chapter" TextField="#InnerText" />
        </DataBindings>
    </asp:TreeView>
</div></form></body></html>
```

1. Back in VWD, save your work as `TIO-1503-XPath-2.aspx`, and change the `XPath` expression to the following:

```
Bookstore/genre/book/chapter[@num='2']
```

2. Back in VWD, change the `XPath` expression to the following:

```
Bookstore/genre[@name='Fiction']/book
```

3. Save your page as `TIO-1503-XPath-3.aspx`, and test in your browser.

How It Works

The `XmlDataSource` applies the `XPath` expression to the contents of the XML file. When we set the `genre` equal to `NonFiction`, we limited the scope to only half the books. Note that when referring to an attribute of an XML node we use an `@` before its name. Also observe that `XPath` is case-sensitive, so the string case must match the nodes as named in the XML; using ". . . nonfiction" would not have worked.

Handling Events in a TreeView Control

Events in a `TreeView` are not significantly different from those used for `GridView` or other controls. We will go into the details in Chapter 17, but for now we can look at a basic example. The `TreeView` offers a dozen events, but the most useful are probably `SelectedNodeChanged`, `TreeNodeCollapsed`, and `TreeNodeExpanded`. We will write simple events for all three in the next exercise.

`TreeView` automatically raises an event at rendering, which you need to understand. If you select the `TreeView` object from the last exercise and look in the Properties window, you will see `ExpandDepth`. When the page is displayed, it will read this property and expand the `TreeView` to `FullyExpand` or expand a set number of levels, including zero.

Try playing with a settings from `Full` to `3` levels. This affects our procedures, because if this property is set above the zero level, then the `TreeView.OnTreeNodeExpanded` event is raised. Any code in the event handler is executed even before the user takes action on the page. If you want your handler to be executed only in response to a user-initiated expansion, then encase the code in the true section of an `If IsPostback Then...` clause.

Try It Out Handling Events in a TreeView Control

In this exercise, you will display, on your page, metadata about the elements contained in the XML document.

1. Add a page named `TIO-1504_TreeViewEvents.aspx` from the template Web form. Drag the `Bookstore.xml` file from the Database Explorer to the page. Open the `TreeView`'s Smart Tasks panel. Edit the `TreeNode` data bindings, as we did in earlier Try It Out exercises of this chapter so that `genre` nodes display `#name`, `book` nodes display `title`, and `chapter` nodes display `#InnerText`. Save your work, and test the page; close your browser.

2. Switch to source view. Drop down the object list and select the TreeView; then from the event list click on `SelectedNodeChanged`. Inside this event, add code to display the value of the selected node as follows. Alternatively, use the C# language listed at the end of the steps. Save your work, and test it in your browser.

```
Protected Sub TreeView1_SelectedNodeChanged(ByVal sender As Object,
                ByVal e As System.EventArgs)
 Response.Write("You selected " & TreeView1.SelectedNode.Text)
End Sub
```

3. Close the browser, and back in VWD source view, select the `TreeView1` object again and click on its event named `TreeNodeExpanded`. Add the following code:

```
Protected Sub TreeView1_TreeNodeExpanded(ByVal sender As Object, ByVal e As
System.Web.UI.WebControls.TreeNodeEventArgs)
If IsPostBack Then
         Response.Write("Click the - next to " & e.Node.Text & " to hide chapters")
End If
End Sub
```

4. Last, select the `TreeView1` object again, and click on its event named `TreeNodeCollapsed`. Add the following code:

```
Protected Sub TreeView1_TreeNodeCollapsed(ByVal sender As Object, ByVal e As
System.Web.UI.WebControls.TreeNodeEventArgs)
            Response.Write("Click the + next to " & e.Node.Text
                & " to see " & e.Node.ChildNodes.Count & " lower level items")
End Sub
```

C#

```
<%@ Page Language="C#" %> ...
<script runat="server">
    protected void TreeView1_SelectedNodeChanged(object sender, EventArgs e)
    {
        Response.Write("You Selected: " + TreeView1.SelectedNode.Text);
    }
    protected void TreeView1_TreeNodeExpanded(object sender, TreeNodeEventArgs e)
    {
        if (IsPostBack)
        { Response.Write("Click the - next to " + e.Node.Text
                + "to hide chapters"); }
    }
    protected void TreeView1_TreeNodeCollapsed(object sender, TreeNodeEventArgs e)
    {
```

```
            Response.Write("Click the + next to " + e.Node.Text
                + "to see " + e.Node.ChildNodes.Count + " lower level items");
        }
    </script>
```

5. Save and test in your browser.

How It Works

We cover events in Chapter 17, but for now the basic framework is in two parts. Within the data-bound control, VWD set attributes that specify which event handlers to execute for each handled event. Unless you have a strong reason, stick to the standard names.

```
<asp:TreeView ID="TreeView1" runat="server"
 DataSourceID="XmlDataSource1"
        OnSelectedNodeChanged="TreeView1_SelectedNodeChanged"
        OnTreeNodeExpanded="TreeView1_TreeNodeExpanded"
        OnTreeNodeCollapsed="TreeView1_TreeNodeCollapsed">
  <DataBindings>...</DataBindings>
</asp:TreeView>
```

Then we have to write those three procedures. In each case, we are merely writing some text to the page using the `Response.Write()` function. What to write goes within the parenthesis; literal strings go within quotes, and variables are naked. If you are putting together multiple items, you must use an ampersand (in VB.NET) or a plus sign between them.

For `OnSelectedNodeChanged` below, we read the contents of a property on the event `args` named `Node`, standing for the name of the node that was clicked. Within that variable, we want the string of the node's text.

```
Protected Sub TreeView1_SelectedNodeChanged(ByVal sender As Object, ByVal e As
System.EventArgs)
   Response.Write("You selected " & TreeView1.SelectedNode.Text)
End Sub
```

For the `TreeNodeCollapsed` event, we read a different value from the `Node` collection of the event `args`. This time we harvest the number of child nodes.

```
Protected Sub TreeView1_TreeNodeCollapsed(ByVal sender As Object, ByVal e As
System.Web.UI.WebControls.TreeNodeEventArgs)
        Response.Write("Click the + next to " & e.Node.Text &
        " to see " & e.Node.ChildNodes.Count & " lower level items")
End Sub
```

`TreeNodeExpanded` has a twist. When the page is first created, ASP.NET 2.0 automatically performs an expansion. This expansion is carried out to the extent of the `TreeView.ExpandDepth` property, by default fully expanded. Each of those node expansions raises the `TreeNodeExpanded` event, so we will end up with dozens of messages written to the beginning of the page before the user has done any clicking. To avoid the problem, we enclose the `Response.Write` within an `If-Then` statement that only does the write if this page is posted back, not a first rendering.

```
Protected Sub TreeView1_TreeNodeExpanded(ByVal sender As Object,
ByVal e As System.Web.UI.WebControls.TreeNodeEventArgs)
 If IsPostBack Then
         Response.Write("Click the - next to " & e.Node.Text & " to hide chapters")
 End If
End Sub
```

Hierarchical Data with Other Controls

You may need to display XML data in other controls apart from the `TreeView` control. For example, you may receive the latest postal code information from your government agency in an XML file, and you want that to be the source for a drop-down list of regions. This section explores how to use XML data with the `DropDownList`, `GridView`, and `DataList`. The data source remains the `XmlDataSource`; it is only the data-bound control that will change.

XmlDataSource and the DropDownList

By default a `DropDownList` with an `XmlDataSource` will display only the one level of nodes that are the first level below the root. In `Bookstore.xml`, that would be the two genre nodes. To display data from nodes lower in the tree, you must add an `XPath`. The data-binding options will be for attributes of the node that is last in the `XPath`. For example, to show the titles your `XPath` would be `/Bookstore/genre/*`, and your `DropDownList` to choose the data source would then offer the options for `ISBN`, `Title`, and `Price`.

XmlDataSource and GridView

As for `DropDownLists`, it is important to understand the mapping from the XML hierarchy to the `GridView` matrix. A `GridView` will display a row for each node in the lowest level specified in the `XPath`. That lowest level would commonly be an asterisk, meaning all the nodes at the level below the last listed level. An `XPath` of `/Bookstore/genre/book/*` will display a record for each chapter. The `GridView` then builds a column for each attribute in the opening tag of the first node of the record's level. Note that this can mean holes in the `GridView` for records for which a node has no attribute. You may also have an entire column created to support an attribute that exists in the first node of a level but no other nodes of that level.

You can also display a node's inner text (like *The Pennsylvania State University* below) as opposed to an attribute (like *Size* below):

```
<Institution Size ="35000">The Pennsylvania State University</Institution>
```

Use a `TemplateField` and an `XPath()` data-binding expression, like:

```
<%# XPath("text()") %>
```

Try It Out — Using XML As Source for a ListBox and a GridView

In this exercise, you will use the `XmlDataSource` as the source for a `GridView` and a `ListBox` control. We will experiment with how the data-bound control displays data from a tree hierarchy. Because the changes in each step are small and easy to follow, the download contains only the final version of the page.

1. Add a page named `TIO-1504-XmlListBoxAndGridView.aspx` from the template Web form. Add an `XmlDataSource` control that reads `the App_Data/BookStore.xml` file. Leave the `XPath` blank for now.

2. Add a `DropDownList`, open its Smart Tasks Panel, and choose as its data source `XmlDataSource1`. Your only options for text and value data will be `Name` because the default `XPath` is equivalent to `/Bookstores/*`, which points to the genre level, and the genre nodes have only one attribute. Save your work and test it; then close your browser.

3. Close the browser, and back in VWD open the Smart Tasks panel of the `XmlDataSource` control and add an `XPath` that points to the books that are `NonFiction`, as follows. Click the data source's refresh schema option. For the `DropDownList`, refresh the schema and click on Choose Data Source. Now you have the option to set the display to `Title` and the `Value` to `ISBN`.

```
<asp:XmlDataSource ID="XmlDataSource1" runat="server"
    DataFile="~/App_Data/Bookstore.xml"
    XPath="/Bookstore/genre[@name='NonFiction']/*">
</asp:XmlDataSource>
```

4. Save and test the page.

5. Add another `XmlDataSource` control that reads the same file and has no `XPath`. Add a `GridView`, and set its data source to the `XmlDataSource2` that you created in this step. Open the `GridView`'s Smart Tasks panel, and select Edit Columns. Remove the three columns, and turn on Auto-generate Fields. Run the page to see how the `GridView` displays data using the default `XPath` of `/Bookstore/*`.

6. Close the browser. Back in VWD, add an `XPath` of `/Bookstore/genre[@name='nonfiction']/book/*`. Save your work, and test it in your browser.

7. Close your browser. Back in VWD, open the `Bookstore.xml` file. In the node for `NonFiction/Italian-Thai Fusion cooking/chapter 1`, add a new attribute named `Difficulty`, as follows:

```
<genre name="NonFiction">Including Literary criticism
    <book ISBN="98-765142-654" Title="Italian-Thai Fusion cooking" Price="29.65">
      <chapter num="1" name="Pasta vs Noodles" difficulty="easy">
        Abstract...v
      </chapter> ...
```

8. Close the browser, and switch to VWD to edit `Bookstore.xml` again. Select `difficulty="easy"` from `chapter 1`, cut it, and then paste into `chapter 2`. So, now there is no `difficulty` attribute in the first chapter node read by the `GridView`. Save your work, and view it in the `GridView`. Observe that the attribute for `difficulty` is absent. See Figure 15-2.

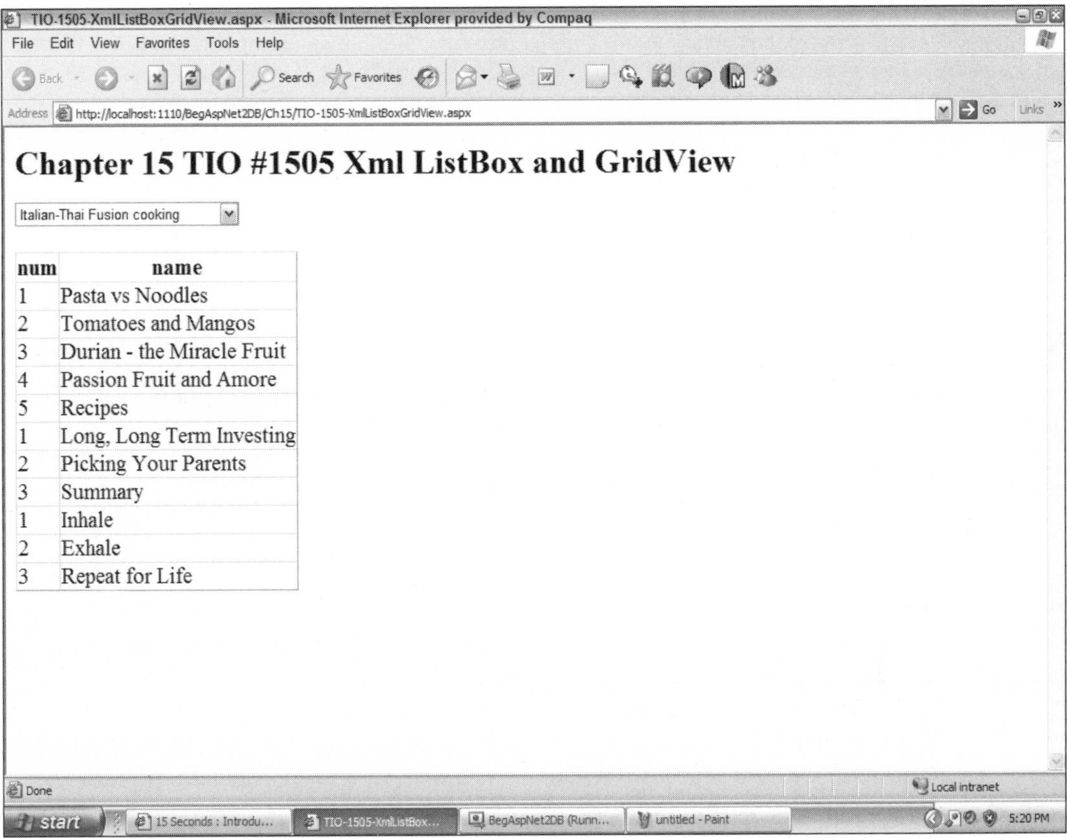

Figure 15-2

How It Works

The `DropDownList` and `GridView` bind to an `XmlDataSource` as they would to a `SqlDataSource`, by setting their `DataSourceID` properties. However, what they display from the XML file depends on the `XPath` that is used. In both cases, the data available for displaying will be the names and attributes for all the nodes in the lowest level specified in the path.

Note that in the `GridView` there is some forcing to get a tree hierarchy into a matrix. The `GridView` will create a column for each attribute in the first node of the lowest level of the `XPath`. If later nodes have additional attributes, then those values will not be represented.

XmlDataSource and DataList

The `DataList` control is used to display the data in an HTML table. (There is also the option for a flowing layout), with each cell holding all the data for one instance. With a `SqlDataSource` control an instance is a record, but with an `XmlDataSource` the instance is a node. As with other data-bound controls bound to the `XmlDataSource` control, they will display the items in the last level of the `XPath`.

Note that when we switch to using templates (as is necessary with the `DataList`), the binding syntax in our code changes. In prior exercises in this chapter, the data binding was completely implicit. As you will see in the next exercise, in a templated scenario we will see actual `Text='<%# Eval("MyField") %>'` statements.

Last, ASP.NET 2.0 supports using data as a look-up in the site file structure. For example, if we have a folder of images and the image names are the `employeeID` numbers, we can use the following code to display the appropriate image for each employee:

```
<img src='<%# Eval("EmployeeID", "../images/{0}.jpg") %>'>
```

Try It Out Using XML As Source for a DataList Control

In this exercise, you will use the `XmlDataSource` as the source for a `DataList` control.

1. Inthe `ch15` folder, create `TIO-1506-XmlDataList.aspx`, and add an `XmlDataSource` reading from the `BookStore.xml` file. Set an `XPath` to read the books, as follows.

```
/Bookstore/genre/*
```

2. Drag a `DataList` to the page, and set its data source to `XmlDataSource1`. Open the Smart Tasks panel, and click property builder. Select the Borders tab on the left, and set the `GridLines` to `Both`, the border color to `Black`, the style to `Double`, and the width to `4` points.
3. Switch to Source view, and have a look at the data-binding code within the `ItemTemplate` of the `DataList` control (as below). Back in Design view, open the `DataList`'s Smart Tasks panel, and click `EditTemplates`. Select the `ItemTemplate`, and rearrange the title to be at the top. Save your work, and view the result in the browser.
4. Close the browser to return to VWD. If you did not import all of the images from the download, then import the book cover JPGs as follows. Right-click on your images folder, click on Add Existing Items, and browse to your downloads. Select the six book covers and click Add to perform the import.
5. Save the page as `TIO-1506-XmlDataList-2.aspx`, and change the title and H2 text. Go back to edit template mode, and drag an HTML image control to the template. Bind its data as the shaded line in the following listing, which is also the final version of the page. Double-check your single and double quotation marks, then save your work and run it in the browser.

```
<%@ Page Language="VB" %>
<!DOCTYPE html PUBLIC "-//W3C//DTD XHTML 1.0 Transitional//EN"
"http://www.w3.org/TR/xhtml1/DTD/xhtml1-transitional.dtd">
<script runat="server">
</script>
<html xmlns="http://www.w3.org/1999/xhtml" >
<head id="Head1" runat="server">
    <title>TIO-1506-XmlDataList-2.aspx</title>
</head>
<body>
```

```
        <h2>Chapter 15 TIO #1506 Xml with a DataList version 2</h2>
    <form id="form1" runat="server">
    <div>
        <asp:XmlDataSource ID="XmlDataSource1" runat="server"
            DataFile="~/App_Data/Bookstore.xml"
            XPath="/Bookstore/genre/*"></asp:XmlDataSource>

    <asp:DataList ID="DataList1" runat="server"
        DataSourceID="XmlDataSource1"
        Width="490px"
        BorderStyle="Double" BorderWidth="4" BorderColor="Black">
        <ItemTemplate>
            Title: <asp:Label ID="TitleLabel" runat="server"
                Text='<%# Eval("Title") %>'></asp:Label><br />
            ISBN: <asp:Label ID="ISBNLabel" runat="server"
                Text='<%# Eval("ISBN") %>'></asp:Label><br />
            Price: <asp:Label ID="PriceLabel" runat="server"
                Text='<%# Eval("Price") %>'></asp:Label><br />
            Cover: <img src='<%# "../Images/" + Eval("ISBN") + ".jpg" %>' />
        </ItemTemplate>
    </asp:DataList>
</div></form></body></html>
```

How It Works

The DataList can display XML data without problems. As always with the DataList, our values will be in templates, and we can rearrange them. Note that when using a templated control, the XML data will be bound explicitly using the Eval() command. There is no option for writing, so there is no EditItemTemplate or use of the Bind() method.

When we added the image, we had to be cleverer because the image is not part of the XML file; rather it is a separate file. If the same image was used for all books, we would use the following code:

```
<img src="../Images/1-861001-57-6.jpg"/>
```

But some parts of the above code will change for each record, as shown in bold below.

```
<img src="../Images/1-861001-57-6.jpg"/>
```

So, we build up the entire file location with a mix of the outer parts (invariable) hard-coded and the inner part (varies by record) read from the XmlDataSource, as follows:

```
<img src='<%# "../Images/" + Eval("ISBN") + ".jpg" %>' />
```

XmlDataSource and DataList with Nesting

It is possible for you to nest multiple DataList controls in a Web form. Both the inner and outer DataLists will use the same XmlDataSource with an XPath pointing part of the way down the tree. Then, each data binding will state an XPath that continues further down the tree.

For example, we might want a DataList of genres and then within each genre an inner DataList to display the books. We would set an XPath on the XmlDataSource to /Bookstore because that is the lowest we can go that is common to both the outer and inner DataList. Then for each DataList, we add an XPath command that further defines what to display. The following exercise explores how to construct a page that utilizes an XmlDataSource control and nested data lists.

Try It Out Nesting with a DataList Data-Bind

In this exercise, you will use nested DataList controls to display information from the XmlDataSource.

1. Add a page named TIO-1507-XmlDataListNested.aspx. Add an XmlDataSource that reads from the Bookstore.xml file and uses an XPath of

```
Bookstore/genre/book
```

2. Add a DataList to the page, and set its data source to the XmlDataSource. VWD will automatically data-bind to display all the attributes of one book per cell in the table. Use the Smart Tasks panel's property builder to add both vertical and horizontal grid lines.
3. For the DataList switch to Edit Templates and select ItemTemplate. At the bottom of the template, add another DataList. Do not configure the data source; rather switch to source view to configure by hand. Add the DataList2 DataSource, and then within the DataList2.ItemTemplate add two data-bindings as follows:

```
<asp:DataList id="DataList2" runat="server"
 DataSource='<%# XPathSelect("chapter") %>'  >
 <ItemTemplate>
        Chapter <%# XPath("@num") %>: <%# XPath("@name") %>
 </ItemTemplate>
</asp:DataList>
```

4. Save your work and test it in your browser. Compare your work with Figure 15-3. The full file is available in the downloads.

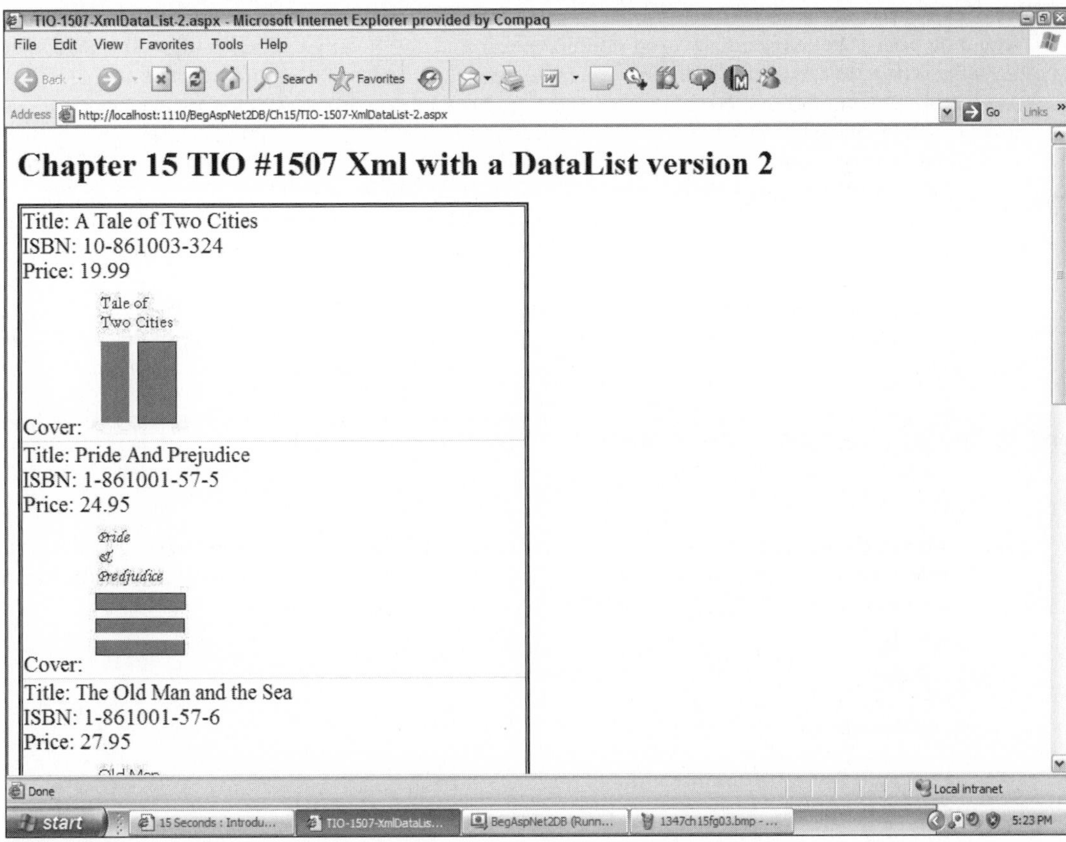

Figure 15-3

How It Works

Similarly to the previous example, you set the `DataSourceID` property of the `DataList` control to the `ID` of the `XmlDataSource` control, and then VWD automatically added labels for each field inside the `ItemTemplate` element. Then we added one more `DataList` control inside the `ItemTemplate` element. That `DataList` control uses a subset of the XML source as defined by its additional `XPath`.

SiteMapDataSource, SiteMapPath, and the Menu Control

ASP.NET 2.0 uses XML for an internal task of organizing pages on a site and assisting the user in navigation. The `web.sitemap` file is an XML file that is standardized for one kind of data: information about the pages and layout of a site. The `web.sitemap` specifies a list of nodes to describe the navigation structure of the site, which can be completely independent of the site folder layout or other structure. The file is generally located in the root of a site. VWD does not include a way to automatically build the file, but we can expect third parties to develop such a utility.

The `SiteMapDataSource` hierarchical data source control specialized for reading the `web.sitemap`. When a `SiteMapDataSource` is placed on the page, it will specifically look for a file with the name `web.sitemap`, read the contents of the `web.sitemap` file, and offer that information as an `XmlDataSource` would.

Having the site organize data in an XML file and a data source constitute two legs of a stool. The third leg is a data-bound control to display the data. ASP.NET 2.0 offers two options. The `SiteMapPath` offers a breadcrumb structure to indicate the path to the current page. Each level is hyperlinked so the user can work back towards the root. The `SiteMapPath` control does not require a data source. It gets its data directly from a `SiteMapProvider`, as configured in `web.config` (or the default provider, which is the one that reads from `web.sitemap` XML files). Another option two is the `Menu` that displays a `TreeView`-like arrangement of the pages in the site, again with hyperlinks enabled. Last, you can display the site layout in a `TreeView` control.

Try It Out Displaying the Navigation Structure of a Site

In this exercise, you will display information about an imaginary site that sells books.

1. Import the `web.sitemap` file from the downloads by right-clicking on the root of your site and selecting Add Existing Item. Navigate to your downloads, and select the `web.sitemap` file and click Add. If you do not have the downloads, you can create the following XML file:

```
<?xml version="1.0" encoding="utf-8" ?>
<siteMap>

  <siteMapNode title="Default" description="Home" url="default.aspx" >

    <siteMapNode title="Members"
      description="Members Home"
      url="members.aspx">
        <siteMapNode title="My Account"
          description="My Account"
          url="MyAccount.aspx" />
        <siteMapNode title="Products and Services"
          description="Products and Services"
          url="ProductsAndServices.aspx" />
    </siteMapNode>

    <siteMapNode title="Administration"
        description="Administration"
        url="~/admin/default.aspx">
        <siteMapNode title="Customer"
            description="Customer Admin"
            url="~/admin/customer/default.aspx" />
        <siteMapNode title="Add New Products and Services"
            description="Add Products and Services Admin"
            url="~/admin/productsAndServices/default.aspx" />
    </siteMapNode>

  </siteMapNode>
</siteMap>
```

2. In the `ch15` folder, create a new page named `TIO-1508-XmlSiteNavigation-1.aspx`. Add a `SiteMapDataSource`; there is no need to set any properties. Add a `Menu` control, and set its data source to the `SiteMapDataSource1`. Save the page, and run it in your browser.

3. Save the page as `TIO-1508-XmlSiteNavigation-2.aspx`. Select the `Menu` control, open its Smart Tasks panel, click on the AutoFormat feature, and choose a style (the download uses Professional). Take a look at the Menu control in Source view to observe the number of tags generated by the `AutoFormat`.

```
<%@ Page Language="VB" %>
<!DOCTYPE html PUBLIC "-//W3C//DTD XHTML 1.0 Transitional//EN"
"http://www.w3.org/TR/xhtml1/DTD/xhtml1-transitional.dtd">
<script runat="server">
</script>
<html xmlns="http://www.w3.org/1999/xhtml" >
<head id="Head1" runat="server">
    <title>TIO-1508-XmlSiteNavigation-2.aspx</title>
</head>
<body>
        <h2>Chapter 15 TIO #1508 Xml Site Navigation version 2</h2>
    <form id="form1" runat="server">
    <div>
        <asp:SiteMapDataSource ID="SiteMapDataSource1" runat="server" />
        <asp:Menu ID="Menu1" runat="server"
            BackColor="#F7F6F3"
            DataSourceID="SiteMapDataSource1"
            DynamicHorizontalOffset="2"
            Font-Names="Verdana" Font-Size="0.8em"
            ForeColor="#7C6F57" StaticSubMenuIndent="10px">
            <StaticMenuItemStyle HorizontalPadding="5px" VerticalPadding="2px" />
            <DynamicHoverStyle BackColor="#7C6F57" ForeColor="White" />
            <DynamicMenuStyle BackColor="#F7F6F3" />
            <StaticSelectedStyle BackColor="#5D7B9D" />
            <DynamicSelectedStyle BackColor="#5D7B9D" />
            <DynamicMenuItemStyle HorizontalPadding="5px" VerticalPadding="2px" />
            <StaticHoverStyle BackColor="#7C6F57" ForeColor="White" />
        </asp:Menu>
    </div>
    </form>
</body>
</html>
```

4. Save the page, and run it in your browser. Compare your work with Figure 15-4.

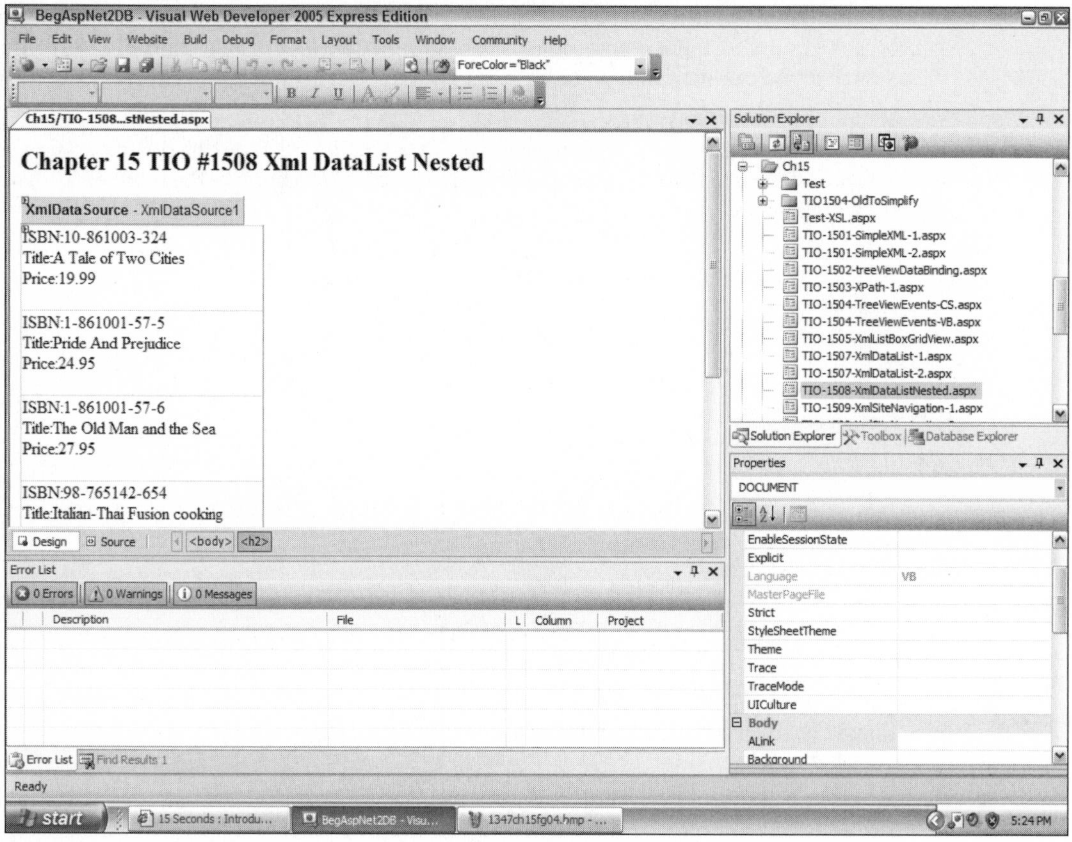

Figure 15-4

How It Works

The `SiteMapDataSource` control reads all the information from the `web.sitemap` file. Once the information is available in a `SiteMapDataSource` control, you can then consume it from a data-bound control. In this example, you used the `Menu` control.

Common Mistakes

The following mistakes are common when dealing with `XmlDataSource` controls:

- Using an incorrect name or path for the XML file. Recheck the exact name of the XML file and the path. To avoid errors in the pathnames, you can use the Browse button in the Configure Data Source Wizard to select the filenames.
- Using incorrect permissions to access the XML file. You need to make sure that the Web application has permissions to access the XML file.

- Trying to use a data-bound control when there is no data source control. A data-bound control must have a source of data, that is, a data source control, specified by its `DataSourceID` property (although there is the case when you might use a `Menu` or `TreeView` for static data in the form of declarative `TreeNodes` and `MenuItems`).
- Using an incorrect name or path for the XSL file. Recheck the exact name of the XSL file and the path. To avoid errors in the pathnames, you can use the Browse button in the Configure Data Source Wizard to select the filenames.
- Attempting to bind a hierarchical data-bound control, such as `TreeView` or `Menu`, to a nonhierarchical data source, such as `SqlDataSource` or `ObjectDataSource`. Hierarchical data-bound controls must be bound to hierarchical data sources.
- Attempting to bind a tabular data-bound control, such as `GridView` or `DropDownList`, to unstructured hierarchical data. Tabular data-bound controls expect data fields to be the same for every data item in the data source.
- Attempting to use `XPath` data-binding syntax with a data source other than the `XmlDataSource`.
- Attempting to create a `TreeView` that does not follow the hierarchical structure of the underlying data. If you need to change the shape of the data to match the expected tree, use an XSLT transform on an `XmlDataSource` before binding to `TreeView`.
- Attempting to bind to values of an XML hierarchy that are not exposed as attributes on the element node. Only XML attributes are bindable from `XmlDataSource`. To make nonattribute values bindable, use an XSLT transformation to reshape the data before binding to `TreeView`. This book does not cover XSLT; take a look at *XSLT 2.0 Programmer's Reference*, 3rd Edition, ISBN: 0-7645-6909-0.
- Specifying duplicate URL properties in a `web.sitemap` file. Each `siteMapNode` must contain a unique URL in order to be valid.
- Using incorrect case in an `XPath`. XML node names are case-specific.

Summary

This chapter discussed techniques of connecting an ASP.NET 2.0 Web page to XML-based data sources. ASP.NET 2.0 offers two options for reading XML data: `XmlDataSource` and `SiteMapDataSource` controls. Each requires the identification of the XML file to read, but for the latter the default is the `web.sitemap` in the root.

The scope of the data delivered from the XML file can be limited using an `XPath` statement. These statements can be large and complex (because they do a job similar to a SQL `SELECT` command) and are outside the range of this book. But at a simple level, we specify which levels of nodes to return and within a level we can constrain which nodes to include.

The display control optimized for hierarchical data is the `TreeView`. It can bind to the `XmlDataSource` and display data or images based on data. By default, it shows the names of the nodes. With data binding, which is easy to do through the dialog box, we can display any value within the node.

When the user selects, expands or collapses a `TreeView` node, the `TreeView` raises events. You can handle those events and put custom code in the event handlers. Keep in mind that expansion events occur when the `TreeView` is first displayed, assuming that the tree is set to be expanded when the page renders.

The `XmlDataSource` and an XML file can provide data for controls that, to date, we have used for relational data. Data-bound controls such as `GridView` will work with values form an `XmlDataSource` control, but you have to be careful of how the hierarchical organization of data maps to the tabular arrangement. In general, the second lowest level of the tree in your `XPath` will provide the records, and the lowest level will be the fields.

Exercises

The answers to these review questions can be found in Appendix B.

1. Does the `XPath` property reside in the `XmlDataSource` control or the `TreeView` control?
2. How do you set the number of levels that will be displayed in the `TreeView` when the page first is rendered?
3. By default, what does a row represent when a `GridView` displays data from an `XmlDataSource control`?
4. In `TreeView` data bindings, what is the difference between options that start with a pound sign (#) and those that do not?
5. Why is it generally necessary to put the `TreeView.TreeNodeExpanded` event within an `If IsPostBack Then...End If` statement?

Caching Data

In most cases, the most dramatic way to improve the performance of a database-driven Web application is through caching. Retrieving data from a database is one of the slowest operations that you can perform in a Web site. If, however, you can cache the data in memory, you can avoid accessing the database with every page request and dramatically increase your application's performance. This chapter discusses many of the new caching features in the ASP.NET 2.0 framework. You'll learn how caching support has been integrated into the new data source controls and how to configure and take advantage of SQL cache invalidation. Finally, you'll see how to enable partial-page caching using a new `Substitution` control that allows you to inject dynamic content into a cached page.

Caching and Its Benefits

When clients access an ASP.NET page, there are basically two ways to provide them with the information they need:

- The ASP.NET page can obtain information from outside the site, such as a database.
- The ASP.NET page can obtain information from within the application.

Retrieving information from a resource outside the application requires more processing steps and will, therefore, require more time and resources on the server than retrieving information that is within the application. If a set of information obtained from an outside source is to be used again, it can be brought into the application so it can be retrieved faster in subsequent requests. This technique, known as *caching*, can be used to temporarily store page output or application data either on the client or on the server, which can then be reused to satisfy subsequent requests, avoiding the overhead of recreating the same information.

When building enterprise-scale distributed applications, architects and developers are faced with many challenges. Caching mechanisms can be used to help you overcome some of these challenges:

- **Performance:** Caching techniques are commonly used to improve application performance by storing relevant data as close as possible to the data consumer, avoiding repetitive data creation, processing, and transportation. For example, storing data that does not change, such as a list of countries, in a cache can improve performance by minimizing data access operations and eliminating the need to re-create the same data for each request.
- **Scalability:** The same data, business functionality, and user interface fragments are often required by many users and processes in an application. If this information is processed for each request, valuable resources are wasted recreating the same output. Instead, you can store the results in a cache and reuse them for each request. This improves the scalability of your application because, as the user base increases, the demand for server resources for these tasks remains constant. For example, in a Web application, the Web server is required to render the user interface for each user request. You can cache the rendered page in the ASP.NET output cache to be used for future requests, freeing resources to be used for other purposes. Caching data can also help scale the resources of your database server. By storing frequently used data in a cache, fewer database requests are made, meaning that more users can be served.
- **Availability:** Occasionally, the services that provide information to your application may be unavailable. By storing that data in another place, your application may be able to survive system failures such as network latency, Web service problems, or hardware failures. For example, each time a user requests information from your data store, you can return the information and also cache the results, updating the cache on each request. If the data store then becomes unavailable, you can still service requests using the cached data until the data store comes back online.

When to Use Caching

It is important to remember that caching isn't something you can just add to your application at any point in the development cycle; the application should be designed with caching in mind. This ensures that the cache can be used during the development of the application to help tune its performance, scalability, and availability.

To successfully design an application that uses caching, you need to thoroughly understand the caching techniques ASP.NET provides, and you also need to be able to address questions such as the following:

- When and why should a custom cache be created?
- Which caching technique provides the best performance and scalability for a specific scenario and configuration?
- Which caching technology complies with the application's requirements for security, monitoring, and management?
- How can the cached data be kept up to date?

Before diving into caching technologies and techniques, it is important to have an understanding of state, because caching is merely a framework for state management.

Understanding State

Understanding the concept of state and its characteristics of lifetime and scope is important for making better decisions about whether to cache it. *State* refers to data, and the status or condition of that data, being used within a system at a certain point in time. The data may be permanently stored in a database, it may be held in memory for a short time while a user executes a certain function, or it may exist for some other defined length of time. It may be shared across a whole organization, it may be specific to an individual user, or it may be available to any grouping in between these extremes.

Understanding State Staleness

Cached state is a snapshot of the master state; therefore, its data is potentially stale (obsolete) as soon as it is retrieved by the consuming application. This is because the original data may have been changed by another process. A site designer must consider the rate that data becomes stale or the events that induce staleness and design the site to overcome problems created by stale data. *State staleness* is defined as the difference between the master state, from which the cached state was created, and the current version of the cached state. State can be defined in terms of the following:

- **Likelihood of changes:** Staleness will increase with time, because as time goes by, there is an increasing chance that other processes have updated the master data. However, the rate of change may be very slow.
- **Relevancy of changes:** It is possible that master state changes will not have an adverse affect on the usability of a process. For example, changing a Web page's style does not affect the business process operation itself. Depending on the use of the state within a system, staleness may or may not be an issue.

Caching is most useful when it takes a long time for data to become stale and, thus, the number of rereads increases. For example, a list of postal codes and their regions is likely to remain the same over many weeks or months, thus enabling thousands of reads from cache. In contrast, the total value of an investment portfolio of stocks is likely to change between every request during business hours. Interestingly, if the stocks are all traded in one time zone, that same value then becomes very amenable to caching during periods when the markets are closed.

Caching Options in ASP.NET 2.0

Storing frequently used data in memory is not a new concept for classic ASP developers. Classic ASP offers the `Session` and `Application` objects, which enable storing key/value pairs in memory. The `Session` object is used to store per-user data across multiple requests, and the `Application` object is used to store per-application data for use by requests from multiple users. ASP.NET introduces a new key/value pair object — the `Cache` object.

The scope of the ASP.NET cache object is the application domain. If a sever supports more than one site (as in a shared hosting scenario), the cached data of one site is not available to another site. The ASP.NET `Cache` object's life span is tied to the application, and the `Cache` object is recreated every time the application restarts, similar to the ASP Application object. The main difference between the `Cache` and `Application` objects is that the `Cache` object provides cache-specific features, such as dependencies and expiration policies.

ASP.NET provides five caching options that you can use in your applications:

- **Time-based Cache Expiration:** You can specify the amount of time you want to cache the data. This type of caching can be specified using the `OutputCache` directive at the page level or at the data source control level.
- **Caching with parameters:** You can cache the output of a parameterized SQL query. Depending on the parameters passed to the SQL query, you will have multiple versions of query results stored in the cache object.
- **Caching with filtering:** You can cache a larger amount of data and then apply filters to display different subsets on different pages.
- **Caching with data invalidation:** Cache invalidation enables you to automatically update data in the cache whenever Microsoft SQL Server observes that the data has changed in the database.
- **Partial page caching:** Page fragment permits caching for only parts of a page, using Web user controls or using a `Substitution` control.

A Note on Data for the Exercises

Our sample databases of Pubs and Northwind do not have a real-time, continuous business process built into them. There is no process running that accepts orders and restocks inventory, hires and fires employees, and registers new customers. Therefore, we do not have the kind of continuous change that is the test for managing staleness in cached data. Building an add-on to emulate these business processes would be a significant detour for this book. Instead, we will add to our datasets a piece of data that does change: the time on the server. We can include get that value with a SQL function as follows that will return the seconds part of the current time on the server as a value.

```
DatePart(second, GetDate())
```

We can place that value into a field named TimeStamp that we create in the SQL statement, as follows.

```
DatePart(second, GetDate()) As timestamp
```

Putting this into a full SQL statement and including all of the other fields from the Authors table, we get the following.

```
SELECT DatePart(second, GetDate()) As timestamp, * FROM [authors]
```

Each time we make the request we will get a new value for the seconds, but once the server reads the value into the set of data it is no longer linked to the server clock and will not change. We can expect that if we have no caching, the seconds value will change with every page refresh. If we have an unrefreshed cache, then it will never change with refreshes. When we use various types of smart caching, the value will change according to our intelligence rules.

Time-Based Cache Expiration

The data source controls enable the cache features. The first property to set, in all caching scenarios, is `EnableCaching = True`. Then for time-based cache expiration, you set the `CacheDuration` to a number of seconds:

```
<asp:SqlDataSource ... EnableCaching="true"  CacheDuration="300" />
```

ASP.NET 2.0 also offers an option of *sliding* for the cache expiration policy, as opposed to the default *absolute* policy. When absolute, the data is brought into the cache at the first call and a timer starts. Subsequent calls will hit the cache. When the timer gets to the `CacheDuration` number of seconds, the cache is emptied and the next call will go to the database and refill the cache. When using a sliding policy, the first call will still read from the database and store the information in the cache. But when a second call is made, it will reset the timer back to zero. As long as there are frequent calls to the cache, the `Cache` object is not refreshed. If there are no calls for the length of the `CacheDuration` value, then the `Cache` object is removed. The sliding option is useful when you are balancing the time it takes for a refresh versus the need to keep up with requests. If you place a higher premium on serving the requests fast than you do on insuring perfect data, then set the option to sliding. As long as the site is busy, the refresh will be put off. Then during slow times (less than one hit during the cache expiration time), the site will perform the refresh.

> **IIS constantly balances how it uses memory. Even though you have created a cache, that cache may be flushed prematurely if IIS needs to free memory for other tasks. More advanced texts on IIS performance can help you understand when you are in danger of losing the cache.**

The following Try It Out explores implementing a time-based cache technique.

Try It Out Time-Based Cache Expiration Policy

In this exercise, you will utilize the `Authors` table in the `Pubs` database and cache the results of the SQL query for five seconds.

1. Create a new folder for `ch16` and add a new Web Form page named `TIO1601_TimeCache.aspx`. Add a `SqlDataSource` that shows the first and last name fields from the `Authors` table of the `Pubs` database with no options to write.
2. Add a `GridView` with its data source control set to `SqlDataSource1`. Use only autogenerated fields as follows. In the `GridView`'s Smart Tasks panel, click on Edit Columns and remove all of the columns from the selected fields list. Turn on the Auto-generate Fields option.
3. Switch to Source view and find the `SqlDataSource`. Modify the `SelectCommand` so that an additional field is returned that will be filled with the seconds value of the server's clock, as follows. Then return to Design view, and click on the `GridView`'s Refresh Schema option.

```
... <h2>Chapter 16 TIO #1601 Time-Based Cache </h2>
    <form id="form1" runat="server"><div>
        <asp:GridView ID="GridView1" runat="server"
            DataSourceID="SqlDataSource1"
            AutoGenerateColumns="True">
```

```
    </asp:GridView>
    <asp:SqlDataSource ID="SqlDataSource1" runat="server"
        ConnectionString="<%$ ConnectionStrings:MdfPubs %>"
        SelectCommand="
            SELECT
                    DatePart(second,GetDate()) AS TimeStamp,
                    [au_lname], [au_fname]
            FROM [authors]">
    </asp:SqlDataSource>
</div></form></body></html>
```

4. Save and check your work in the browser. Try some refreshes.
5. Close the browser and open your page in VWD. Select the `SqlDataSource` and in the properties window set the `EnableCaching` to `True` and the `CacheDuration` to 10 seconds.

```
<asp:SqlDataSource ID="SqlDataSource1" runat="server"
            ConnectionString="<%$ ConnectionStrings:MdfPubs %>"
            SelectCommand="
                SELECT
                DatePart(second,GetDate()) AS TimeStamp,[au_lname],
[au_fname]
                FROM [authors]"
            EnableCaching="true" CacheDuration="10">
        </asp:SqlDataSource>
```

6. Save, open in the browser, and keep hitting Refresh. Notice that the page will keep reading from the cache until it expires after 10 seconds.

How It Works

While declaring the `SqlDataSource` control, you set the `EnableCaching` property to true, so the `SqlDataSource` will automatically save to memory the data it retrieves, rather then deleting the data. The `CacheDuration` property enables you to specify, in seconds, how long the data should be held before it is refreshed from the database. By default, the `SqlDataSource` will cache data using an absolute expiration policy, meaning that the data will be refreshed after the number of specified seconds set in the `CacheDuration` property.

Caching with Parameters

Caching works very well when the exact same data is requested by multiple pages, for example the list of postal regions in the country. At the other extreme, caching is close to useless if requests are for widely varying data, for example the postal regions of many different countries. In many cases, the best solution is a compromise somewhere in the middle. ASP.NET offers a solution between the extremes. The cache can use parameters (for example, a user choice from a `DropDownList`) to implement one of several cached sets of data, or not use the cache at all. With this tool, ASP.NET will create multiple caches for parameters. If a given parameter(s) is frequently requested, that cache will persist longer in memory and increase site performance.

> **Also read the next section on filtered caches for another solution.**

The technique is not difficult because the heavy lifting is down in the data source control. Of course, `EnableCaching` must be set to `True`. Other than that, parameter-based caching will be automatic if there is a parameter in the `SelectCommand`.

```
<asp:SqlDataSource ID="SqlDataSource1" Runat="server"
        ConnectionString="<%$ ConnectionStrings:LocalSqlPubs %>"
        EnableCaching="True"
        CacheDuration="10"

        SelectCommand="SELECT
         DatePart(second, GetDate()) As timestamp, *
         FROM [authors]" where state = @state" >

          <SelectParameters>
            <asp:ControlParameter Name="state"
                ControlID="DropDownList1"
                PropertyName="SelectedValue" />
          </SelectParameters>


</asp:SqlDataSource>
```

The subsurface behavior of the control is quite complicated to ensure that it will work correctly. ASP.NET 2.0 will create a cache entry for the first request. If the second request has a different set of parameters, then ASP.NET 2.0 will create a second cache entry. This will continue for each combination of parameters and connection strings. If there is a small set of parameters (like the list of postal regions of just a few countries), then these multiple caches are fine because the chances are good that they will be used for a subsequent hit. But if there are many permutations (many choices within each of several input controls), then the chances decrease of a subsequent page needing the exact same data as is sitting in a cache. If caches are not being hit then they were a waste of time and memory to set up.

The following Try It Out shows you how to pass parameters to the SQL query specified in the `SelectCommand` property of the `SqlDataSource` control.

Try It Out Cache with Parameters

In this exercise, you will utilize the `Authors` table in the `Pubs` database and cache the results of the parameterized SQL query for 10 seconds. As you refresh the page, you will see that the `GridView` records will be cached only for data requests that have already been made.

1. In the `ch16` folder, add a page named `TIO1602_CachingWithParameters.aspx`. Drag and drop a `DropDownList` control onto your page, edit the items to include `CA`, `IN`, and `UT` as values, and enable `AutoPostBack`.

```
<asp:DropDownList ID="DropDownList1" Runat="server"
 AutoPostBack="True">
  <asp:ListItem Value="CA" />
  <asp:ListItem Value="IN">IN</asp:ListItem>
  <asp:ListItem>UT</asp:ListItem>
</asp:DropDownList>
```

2. Add a `SqlDataSource` control to your page that connects with the `MdfPubs`, and specify a custom SQL statement of the code listing below. When prompted to define parameters, set the state parameter to a `ControlParameter` using `ControlID=DropDownList1` and a default value of `CA`.

```
SelectCommand="SELECT DatePart(second, GetDate()) As timestamp, *
    FROM [authors] where state = @state"
```

3. With the `SqlDataSource` selected, in the Properties window enable caching and set the cache duration for 60 seconds.

4. Add a `GridView` control to the page, and configure its data source to the `SqlDataSource`.

```
<h2>Chapter 16 TIO #1602 Caching With Parameters</h2>
<form id="form1" runat="server">
    <div>
        <asp:DropDownList ID="DropDownList1" runat="server" AutoPostBack="True">
            <asp:ListItem>CA</asp:ListItem>
            <asp:ListItem>IN</asp:ListItem>
            <asp:ListItem>UT</asp:ListItem>
        </asp:DropDownList><br />
        <asp:SqlDataSource ID="SqlDataSource1" runat="server"
                CacheDuration="60"
                ConnectionString="<%$ ConnectionStrings:MdfPubs %>"
                EnableCaching="True"
                SelectCommand="SELECT
                        DatePart(second, GetDate()) As timestamp, *
                        FROM [authors] where state = @state">
            <SelectParameters>
                <asp:ControlParameter ControlID="DropDownList1"
                        DefaultValue="CA" Name="state"
                        PropertyName="SelectedValue" />
            </SelectParameters>
        </asp:SqlDataSource>
        <asp:GridView ID="GridView1" runat="server"
                AutoGenerateColumns="False"
                DataKeyNames="au_id"
                DataSourceID="SqlDataSource1">
            <Columns>
                <asp:BoundField ...
            </Columns>
        </asp:GridView>
</div></form></body></html>
```

5. Save your work, and test it in your browser as follows (do all these tests within 20 seconds). Note the timestamp when viewing the CA data. Change the drop-down choice to IN.

6. Refresh the page several times quickly and note that the timestamp remains the same (it is reading from cache). Change back to CA and notice that it is still on the original timestamp, the cache for CA data has not yet expired. After 60 seconds all data will be refreshed.

How It Works

In this example, we have a `DropDownList` control that displays the list of states, and a `GridView` to display the list of authors based on the selected state in the `DropDownList` control.

For each possible request (three possibilities in this case: CA, IN, and UT), a new cache of data is created. This prevents data for one set of parameter values from being displayed for another set of parameter values. When the user returns to an already requested set of authors, the data is read from the cache.

Implementing Filtering Capability

One thing to note about this example is that each time a new item is selected for the `DropDownList`, a new copy of the cached data is created (the timestamp column updates). This is because the data source control stores a separate cache entry for each unique combination of parameter values applied to the data source control. While this is a perfectly valid use of the cache, it may sometimes result in more cache entries than are necessary. An alternative is to cache only one copy of the total data set and then use the parameters to filter from this large cache the desired subset.

The `FilterExpression` property of the `SqlDataSource` control sets an expression that is applied when the `SelectCommand` executes. The syntax used for the `FilterExpression` is the same syntax used for the `System.Data.DataSet.RowFilter` property. You can include parameters in the `FilterExpression;` using the syntax of `{0}` like you used in formatting string properties. At runtime, the data source substitutes parameter values obtained from its `FilterParameters` collection for these placeholders in the `FilterExpression`. If the type of the parameter value is a string or character type, enclose the parameter in single quotation marks, such as `"field = '{0}'"`. Quotation marks are not needed if the parameter is a numeric type.

Note that the `SqlDataSource` control only supports filtering data when in DataSet mode. This property delegates to the `FilterExpression` property of the `SqlDataSourceView` that is associated with the `SqlDataSource` control.

Try It Out Cache Filtering

In this exercise, we will cache the results of SQL query for five seconds. But we will use the `FilterExpression` property to pass in the appropriate value for a parameter in the `FilterParameters` collection.

1. Open your page from the last exercise named `TIO1602_CachingWithParameters.aspx`, save it as `TIO-1603-FilteringOnCache.aspx`, and revise the title and H2 text.
2. Switch to Source view, delete the collection of SelectParameters, and add a WHERE clause to the `SelectCommand` with the gray lines below:

```
<asp:SqlDataSource ID="SqlDataSource1" runat="server"
        CacheDuration="60"
        ConnectionString="<%$ ConnectionStrings:MdfPubs %>"
        EnableCaching="True"
        SelectCommand="SELECT
                DatePart(second, GetDate()) As timestamp, *
                FROM [authors]
                WHERE state = @state">
```

3. While the SqlDataSource is still selected, go to the Properties window and set the FilterExpression to:

```
state='{0}'
```

4. In Source view, change the following gray lines from SelectParameter to FilterParameter.

Here is the old:

```
            <SelectParameters>
                <asp:ControlParameter ControlID="DropDownList1"
                        DefaultValue="CA" Name="state"
                       PropertyName="SelectedValue" />
            </SelectParameters>
```

And here is the new:

```
            <FilterParameters>
                <asp:ControlParameter ControlID="DropDownList1"
                        DefaultValue="CA" Name="state"
                        PropertyName="SelectedValue" />
            </FilterParameters>
```

5. Save your page, which should look like the following, and test the page in your browser.

```
... <h2>Chapter 16 TIO #1603 Filter on a Cache </h2>
<form id="form1" runat="server">
    <div>
        <asp:DropDownList ID="DropDownList1" runat="server"
            AutoPostBack="True">
            <asp:ListItem>CA</asp:ListItem>
            <asp:ListItem>IN</asp:ListItem>
            <asp:ListItem>UT</asp:ListItem>
        </asp:DropDownList>

        <asp:SqlDataSource ID="SqlDataSource1" Runat="server"
            ConnectionString="<%$ ConnectionStrings:MdfPubs %>"
            SelectCommand="SELECT
                DatePart(second, GetDate()) As timestamp, *
                FROM [authors]"
            EnableCaching="True"
            CacheDuration="60"
            FilterExpression="state='{0}'">
          <FilterParameters>
             <asp:ControlParameter Name="state" ControlID="DropDownList1"
               PropertyName="SelectedValue" />
          </FilterParameters>
        </asp:SqlDataSource>

        <asp:GridView ID="GridView1" runat="server"
            AutoGenerateColumns="False"
            DataKeyNames="au_id"
            DataSourceID="SqlDataSource1">
            <Columns>
                <asp:BoundField ...
```

```
            </Columns>
        </asp:GridView>
    </div></form></body></html>
```

Try It Out Cache Filtering

This exercise demonstrates an alternative to the multiple cache entries generated by exercise TIO-1602. Note that the data request is for all the records, without a limiting WHERE clause, as follows.

```
SelectCommand="SELECT
        DatePart(second, GetDate()) As timestamp, *
        FROM [authors]"
```

We added a FilterExpression to the SqlDataSource that is applied any time the Select method is executed to retrieve data. In this example, the FilterExpression contains a placeholder for a filter parameter, which is '{0}' in this case. The FilterParameter collection we created by a quick and sneaky modification of the SelectParameter collection from the last Try It Out exercise. It holds one value named 'state' that was selected by the user in the DropDownList1 control.

SQL Server Cache Invalidation

In the above scenarios, we had to predict when we should refresh the cache. If you cache the contents of a database table in memory and the records in the underlying database table change before you refresh, your Web application will display inaccurate data. For certain types of data, you might not care if the data being displayed is slightly out of date, but for other types of data, such as stock prices and auction bids, displaying data that is even slightly stale is unacceptable. A better system would be to have communication with the database that would keep a cache valid until the underlying data changed. That would cover us for both very quickly changing data and for rarely changing data; this would also eliminate the need for the page author to predict the length of time a cache is valid. Microsoft has built this feature into its database product, SQL Server. Other database products, such as Oracle and DB2, can support this approach, but they require creation of custom code and communication channels.

The techniques for SQL Server cache invalidation depend on the version of SQL Server. If you are using a version prior to 2005, then you must use polling that requires more setup. Starting with SQL Server version 2005 (including the SSE we work with in this book), you can use notification, which is an easier setup.

For the polling technique (an early version of SQL Server), we take the following steps:

- Use aspnet_RegSql to enable SQL cache invalidation at the database and table levels.
- Add to the Web.config file the caching element, and specify the polling time and the connection string information.
- In the SqlDataSource control, specify the SqlCacheDependency attribute.

The setup on the command line (use the folder C:\Windows\Microsoft.NET\Framework\V2.0.40607) requires two tasks. First, use the line at the end of this paragraph. The -E option causes the aspnet_regsql tool to use integrated security, and the -d option selects the database by name. The -ed option enables the database for SQL cache invalidation. When you execute this command, a new database table named AspNet_SqlCacheTablesForChangeNotification is added to the database. This table contains a list of all of the database tables that are enabled for SQL Cache Invalidation. The command also adds a set of stored procedures to the database.

```
aspnet_regsql -E -d MyDatabase -ed
```

Second, on the command line, we run the command to select the particular tables in the database that you want to enable for SQL cache invalidation as follows. The -et option enables a database table for SQL cache invalidation. You can, of course, enable multiple tables by reexecuting this command for each database table.

```
aspnet_regsql -E -d MyDatabase -t MyTable -et
```

> **Instead of the** aspnet_regSql **command line tool, you can use methods of the** SqlCacheDependencyAdmin **class to configure Microsoft SQL Server. Its five primary methods include** DisableNotifications, DisableTableForNotifications, EnableNotifications, EnableTableForNotifications, **and** GetTables EnabledForNotifications.

Continuing for the polling technique, we add to the Web.config file a caching element.

```
<system.web>
   <caching>
      <sqlCacheDependency enabled="true" pollTime="1000">
        <databases>
          <add name="MyDatabase" connectionStringName="MyConnectionString"/>
        </databases>
      </sqlCacheDependency>
   </caching>
</system.web>
```

Last in the polling technique, we set up the SqlDataSource control on the ASPX page as follows:

```
<asp:SqlDataSource ID="SqlDataSource1" Runat="server"
ConnectionString="<%$ ConnectionStrings:MyConnectionString %>"
EnableCaching="True"
SelectCommand="SELECT ... "
...
```

Keep in mind that the above steps are for the older polling technique. If you are using SQL 2005 (or SSE), you will use the notification technique. This requires no action from the command line in the Web.config file. Rather, we start by adding a line in Global.ASAX that starts the method that handles the notification, as follows. As you type this line, be sure to use IntelliSense to avoid typos. Note that the DIM and following two lines should be on one line in your Global.ASAX, but are broken here to fit on the printed page.

```
<%@ Application Language="VB" %>
```

```
<script runat="server">
  Sub Application_Start(ByVal sender As Object, ByVal e As EventArgs)
    Dim MyConnString As String =
        ConfigurationManager.ConnectionStrings("MyConnectionStringInWebConfig")
        .ConnectionString
    System.Data.SqlClient.SqlDependency.Start(MyConnString)
End Sub
...
</script>
```

Next, for notification we set a property in our `SqlDataSource` control as follows.

```
<asp:SqlDataSource ID="SqlDataSource1" Runat="server"
ConnectionString="<%$ ConnectionStrings:MyConnectionString %>"
EnableCaching="true"
SqlCacheDependency="CommandNotification"
CacheDuration="Infinite"
... />
```

Last, two security rights must be granted: the right to create notifications and the right to send those notifications from SQL Server. These rights must be assigned to the process that is running ASP.NET. In our cases for this book, where we use the development Web server, we (the identity logged into Windows) are both the requestor and the administrator of SSE, so there is no problem. But at deployment, the ASPNET process must be added to the list of users that can create notification queries. Also, a right must be granted for the process to be allowed to send these notifications. To grant the two rights when using IIS, the database administrator will run commands similar to the following:

```
GRANT SUBSCRIBE QUERY NOTIFICATIONS TO username
GRANT SEND ON SERVICE::SqlQueryNotificationService TO username
```

That is all there is to the setup. However, when writing our SQL statements, we have to follow two new rules. First, we must refer to tables with the syntax that includes their owner's name, such as `dbo.MyTable`. Second, we cannot use the `*` wildcard for all fields. The fields must be individually listed.

Try It Out SQL Cache Invalidation

In this exercise, you will use a SQL Invalidation cache for the `Authors` table in the `Pubs` database. Because in this book we use SSE, a form of SQL Server 2005, we will use the notification technique.

1. Create a new page named `TIO-1604-SqlCacheInvalidation`. Open the Database Explorer and expand the Pubs tables. Select the author first and last name fields and drag them to the page. Switch to Source view and in the `GridView` change to `AutoGenerateColumns=True` and delete the columns collection. In the `SqlDataSource` control, modify the `SelectCommmand` to the following:

```
SelectCommand="
SELECT [au_lname], [au_fname], DatePart(second, GetDate()) AS TimeStamp
FROM [authors]">
```

2. Open your `Global.asax` file (or create one in the root if it does not exist), and add the following line of code to be run once when the application starts. Note that the DIM line and the following line should be on one line in your Global.asax. Here they are broken to fit on paper.

```
<%@ Application Language="VB" %>
<script runat="server">
    ... other subs...
    Sub Application_Start(ByVal sender As Object, ByVal e As EventArgs)
        ' Code that runs on application startup
        Dim MdfPubsConnString As String =
          ConfigurationManager.ConnectionStrings("MdfPubs").ConnectionString
        System.Data.SqlClient.SqlDependency.Start(MdfPubsConnString)
    End Sub
    ... other subs...
</script>
```

3. Turn on caching on the `SqlDataSource` by setting three properties on the control. You can do this in the Properties window or in Source view.

```
<asp:SqlDataSource ID="SqlDataSource1" runat="server"
...
EnableCaching=true
CacheDuration=Infinite
SqlCacheDependency="CommandNotification"
...>
</asp:SqlDataSource>
```

4. Save the page, and test it in your browser. Note how the seconds timestamp is not updated, even if you refresh forever.

5. Keep your browser open, but switch back to VWD. Open Database Explorer, navigate to the `MdfPubs` connection, `Tables`, and then the `Authors` table. Right-click on the `Authors` table, and select See data. Double-click on a name and change it.

6. Return to your browser and note the time, then refresh and note the change in time.

How It Works

First, we establish in `Global.asax` that when the application starts it will run a method named `Start`. That method actually starts the notification process for the stated connection string, in our case `MdfPubs`.

Next, on our ASPX page, we set three properties in the `SqlDataSource` control. The first turns on caching, the second sets the timed property of when to refresh to infinity, and the third establishes that the validity of the data in cache will depend on `SqlNotification`.

```
EnableCaching=true
CacheDuration=Infinite
SqlCacheDependency="CommandNotification"
```

In the `SqlDataSource`'s `SelectCommand`, we added a new field that will be created from the server's clock. Named `TimeStamp`, it will hold the same value for all records, the seconds part of the current date and time, as shown below. When we refetch, the value for seconds will stay the same because it is being read from the (static) cache instead of being regenerated by a request to the database.

```
SelectCommand="
SELECT [au_lname], [au_fname],
DatePart(second, GetDate()) AS TimeStamp
FROM [authors]">
```

Now, when we run the page we can refresh multiple times, but we get the same seconds value. If we make a change to the table, SQL Server sends a notification to ASP.NET that the cache is invalid and on the next refresh the request for data will go to SQL Server instead of reading from the cache.

Caching Partial Pages

Independently of our data source controls, entire ASP.NET pages can be cached. The following directive carries out the task. The duration value is in seconds, and the `VaryByParameter` allows the validity to be determined by a parameter (completely separate from any data issues).

```
<%@ Page Language="VB" %>
<%@ OutputCache Duration="6000" VaryByParam="none" %>
<!DOCTYPE html PUBLIC "-//W3C//DTD XHTML 1.0 Transitional//EN" ... >
```

Although we may want to cache an entire page to improve performance, we may know that certain sections of a page must be unique for each request. For example, the current value of a user's portfolio. Prior to ASP.NET 2.0, you could wrap the less variable sections in a Web forms user control and cache just that control.

ASP.NET 2.0 offers a new `asp:Substitution` control that isolates a section of the page and forces the section to not be cached. Therefore, the contents of a `Substitution` control are generated anew with every request. In our example of a page for financial services, the calendar of financial events could be cached for a day, but the visitor's portfolio value would be updated with every request.

The substitution control has a key property named `MethodName`. This key property specifies the method that will be invoked to provide the dynamic content. The method called by the `Substitution` control must be a `Shared` method. Furthermore, the method must take one parameter that represents the current `HttpContext`.

Try It Out Partial-Page Caching

In this exercise, you will utilize the `Substitution` control to implement partial-page caching. The entire page will be cached, so a timestamp on the page will remain the same after the first page build. But we will create a random number generator in a procedure, and the display of the random number will take place within a `Substitution` control so that it will be reread (generated) with every refresh.

1. In the `ch16` folder, add a page named `TIO1605-PartialPageCaching.aspx`, and change to Source view. To the top of the page, add the `OutputCache` directive as shown below:

```
<%@ Page Language="VB" %>
<%@ OutputCache Duration="6000" VaryByParam="none" %>
<!DOCTYPE html PUBLIC "-//W3C//DTD XHTML 1.0 Transitional//EN" ... >
```

2. Within the script tags, add a method named `GetRandomNumber` that looks like the following:

```
<script runat="server">
  Shared Function GetRandomNumber(ByVal context As HttpContext) As String
    Dim randomNumber As Integer
    randomNumber = New System.Random().Next(1, 10000)
    Return randomNumber.ToString()
  End Function
</script>
```

Alternatively, use the following script in C#:

```
<%@ Page Language="C#" %> ...
    <script runat="server">
      static String GetRandomNumber(HttpContext context)
      {
            int randomNumber;
            randomNumber = new System.Random().Next(1, 10000);
            return randomNumber.ToString();
      }
    </script>
```

3. From the Toolbox, add a `Substitution` control to your page. Select the control, and in the Properties window, set the `MethodName` property to `GetRandomNumber`. This allows you to execute the `GetRandomNumber` method every time the page is requested, even though the entire page is cached.
4. The page should appear as follows (VB version).
5. Save your work, and view it in the browser, hitting the Refresh button several times.

How It Works

At the top of the page, the `OutputCache` directive is used to cache the contents of the page in memory for 100 minutes. After that we wrote a short function (method) named `GetRandomNumber` that returned a random number between 1 and 10,000. Last, we added a `Substitution` control. You set its `MethodName` attribute of the `Substitution` control to our random number generator method.

When you run the page and begin hitting Refresh, you will find that the displayed current time always remains the same because you are actually reading the page from cache. It is not being regenerated (which would involve checking the server time). However, the portion of the page in the `Substitution` control is forced to be fresh with each request, and so it is requesting a new execution of the `GetRandomNumber` method every time.

Common Mistakes

The following is a list of common errors made while attempting to implement caching in ASP.NET 2.0:

- Using an incorrect connection string. Recheck the connection string specified in the `Web.config` file.
- Using an incorrect username. Make sure that the connection string contains the correct username and password.

- Trying to use a data-bound control when there is no data source control. A data-bound control must have a source of data, that is, a data source control, specified by its `DataSourceID` property.
- Trying to cache the output of a `SqlDataSource` control without setting the `EnableCaching` property. Before you can cache the output of a data source control such as `SqlDataSource` control, you need to set its `EnableCaching` property to `true`.
- Errors in table or column names. This mistake usually arises when typing; it is less problematic when using the designer wizards or drag-and-drop in Visual Studio and Visual Web Designer.
- Attempting to use SQL Cache Invalidation without first configuring the database and table using `aspnet_regsql.exe`.
- Typing an incorrect value for the `SqlCacheDependency` property of `SqlDataSource`. Note that this property is case-sensitive and must be typed exactly using the database and connection names specified when configuring them using `aspnet_regsql.exe`.
- Attempting to use SQL Cache Invalidation on an unsupported database server. SQL Cache Invalidation is only supported on Microsoft SQL Server version 7 or higher.

Summary

Caching may dramatically improve the performance of database-driven Web applications where multiple requests will be using the same or a subset of the same data. There are three main benefits to implementing caching in your applications:

- Reduction of the amount of data that is transferred between processes and computers
- Reduction of the amount of data processing that occurs within the system
- Reduction of the number of disk access operations that occur

ASP.NET 2.0 supports an `EnableCache` property on the `SqlDataSource` and `ObjectDataSource` controls with several options to determine the duration of the cached data. The most basic option is to set a fixed number of seconds during which the cache will be valid.

If similar but different requests are being made, ASP.NET will create several caches of data and select the correct one according to the parameters that are inserted into the request. The downside to this approach is that your page may have so many permutations of parameters that a duplicate request does not come in before the cache is invalid, so the memory spent on the cache is wasted.

An alternative is to cache a more inclusive set of data and then apply a filter to the request that will limit the records returned from the cache. This approach requires a set of `FilterParameters` and a `FilterExpression` that refers to the value in a parameter with the syntax `{0}`.

SQL Cache Invalidation enables you to automatically reload database data in the cache whenever the data is modified in the underlying database. This feature provides you with all the performance benefits of caching, without having to worry about stale data.

Finally, the new `asp:Substitution` control can be added to a page. Although the page as a whole might be cached, this control will force a fresh read to obtain its content.

Exercises

The answers to these review questions can be found in Appendix B.

1. List some advantages and disadvantages of caching.
2. Describe the difference between data invalidation in SQL Server 2005 and prior versions of SQL Server.
3. Discuss a disadvantage of caching parameterized SQL requests.
4. What is the role of the `<asp:Substitution>` control?

Handling Events for Data Controls

As much as we would like to have the fabulous ASP.NET 2.0 data controls do everything we need, that will not always be the case. As we have already seen in the last few chapters, writing code in event handlers is unavoidable as an application becomes complex. This chapter explains the basics of creating event handlers, and provides an explanation of page-level events and how to handle button clicks. Then you'll find sections on responding to events from lists and how to work with the events raised by data controls. Last is a look at the events raised when a page encounters an error.

We will cover seven topics related to events:

- Introduction to event handling, including the flow of execution when an event is triggered and the types of events
- General techniques for writing event handlers and how values are transferred to the event
- Location of event handlers
- Command and custom button events
- List selection events and page events
- Data control binding events
- General error events

Introduction to Event Handling

A major goal of the ASP.NET 2.0 design team was to greatly reduce the importance of this chapter. Whereas in the past we had to write large blocks of code to use data, in version 2.0 very little code is required to achieve the common scenarios. The ASP.NET team has cataloged the most common Web scenarios that required code and built those functions into the properties and methods of objects. You have seen this pattern in prior chapters for data source controls and data-bound controls. However, it is impossible for the ASP.NET team to cover every possibility. So the team has also included the capability to execute custom code that you write by using event handlers.

An event is an action like "Button1 has been clicked" or "The page has been loaded into memory." Events can have an *event handler*, which is a container for code to execute when the event occurs. Microsoft writes some code for event handlers; a page's designer also writes some. For example, Microsoft has written event handlers for its command buttons such as `Update` to gather values, put them in a parameters collection, append them to the data source control's `Update` statement, instantiate the appropriate ADO.NET objects, and execute the command. Similarly, designers can write their own custom code in an event handler.

Why would you need to go beyond the built-in event handlers? In most cases you won't, particularly for the predictable tasks of binding data to controls. But as pages and sites become more complex, it is necessary to create customized code beyond what Microsoft could have anticipated anyone using. After all, they can't predict everything for everybody. However, always first look carefully for a built-in way to achieve objectives; writing custom event handlers should be undertaken only if absolutely necessary.

Execution Control When an Event Is Triggered

When the user takes certain actions, an event is raised. For example, when the user clicks on a button, that button's `Button_Click` event is triggered. In addition, there are some cases where steps taken by ASP.NET 2.0 triggers events, such as `Page.Load` or `DataBinding`. Server-side controls such as `<asp:button...>` will have a property such as `OnClick`, which gets the event handler's name as a value to trigger when the button is clicked. The events raised by each control are listed in the control's property box after you click the event list (lightning bolt) icon. Designers can write code in the event handler that will be executed at the time that particular event is triggered.

Custom event handlers are written in two steps. First, in the server-side control, declare which handler to use for the event. This is usually a standard name, for example, `Button1_Click`. Then the code is written into an event handler within the `<script>` tags, using the name designated in Step 1.

Types of Events

When explaining events, it is useful to divide them into functional groups. There is no basis for this taxonomy in the ASP.NET 2.0 object model, but it helps when considering where to write code.

- **Events triggered by the page:** `Page.Load`, `Page.PreRender`, and so on.
- **Events triggered by command buttons (command fields):** `Insert`, `Update`, `Delete`, and `Select`. These buttons are available in data-bound controls.
- **Events from custom buttons:** Buttons that trigger custom code. These buttons can be inside or outside of data-bound controls.
- **Events triggered by server-side controls:** The selection event in a list select, for example.
- **Events that are triggered by data-binding:** `DataBound` and `RowDataBound`, for example.
- **Events raised by errors:** `Page.Error` and `Application.Error` events.

General Techniques for Writing Event Handlers

Event handlers are very similar to procedures that you may have studied in general books on ASP or a .NET-supported language. A procedure (or function) is called by another line of code. But an event handler is automatically invoked by an action that the user performs (such as a button click) or one in the life of the page (such as page load).

Event handlers, like all page methods, are located within script tags. Script tags (sometimes called *script blocks*) can be located anywhere on the page but are usually after the `<%@Page%>` tag and before the `<html>`. Note that in the `@Page` tag there is a language designation. ASP.NET 2.0 supports many languages, but only one language per page. Within a single set of script tags can be any number of individual event handlers. Procedures and functions are typically located within the same script tags, as well; however, they will be designated by a singular name, whereas event handlers are typically designated in the form `Object_Event`.

An event handler is just a method that is invoked automatically in response to an event. ASP.NET 2.0 supports multiple languages that can be used within an event handler. Each language has its own syntax for a method, including a syntax to begin and end an event handler. Visual Basic uses the `Sub` and `End Sub`, as follows:

```
Sub MyObject_Event (ByVal sender As Object, ByVal e As System.EventArgs)
    'Visual Basic Code goes here
End Sub
```

C# uses the keyword `void` along with braces. Note that the closing brace ends the handler; there is no need for an `END` statement because in C# the braces indicate the end.

```
void MyObject_Event(Object sender, EventArgs e)
{
    //C# Code goes here;
}
```

When you use VWD, the language framework is set up automatically for you in two steps. First, when you create the page, you select the language for scripts in the Add New Item dialog. Then, when you want to write code in a specific handler, you can select an object such as a button and in its Properties window, click on the lightning icon to see the list of available events. Double-clicking on one of the events will cause VWD to create an event handler stub (first and last lines) for the event. Alternatively, you can double-click on the control in Design view and you will be led to the default event (click for buttons; change in selected index for lists).

Try It Out — Trying a Simple Event Handler

In this exercise, we will display a `GridView` of `Northwind` employee names. We will pretend that there are employees constantly being hired. We will also add to the page a timestamp of when the data was read so that if a user walks away from the browser and returns they have guidance for their decision on whether to hit the refresh. We will then write a very basic event handler that advises users of about how many pages of data there are in the `GridView`.

1. Create a new folder named `C:\BegAspNet2Db\ch17` and within the nascent folder a file named `TIO-1701-SImpleEventHandler-VB.aspx`. In the dialog box, select either Visual Basic or C# language, but turn off the "Place code in separate file" option.
2. Add two labels to the top of the page. Name the first one `TimeLabel` and the other `PagesLabel`. Set their default text to empty strings.
3. Add a `GridView` supported by a new data source control that reads (no writing) the ID and names of the `Employees` of `Northwind`. Set the `GridView` to enable paging and have a page size of two records. Set the `PagerSettingsMode` to `NextPrevious`.
4. Switch to Source view, and from the object list at the top left, select the `Page`. From the events list at the top right, select `Load`. Add the following lines of code:

C#

```
protected void Page_Load(object sender, EventArgs e)
 {
     TimeLabel.Text = DateTime.Now.ToString();
 }
```

VB

```
<%@ Page Language="VB" %> ...
<script runat="server">
    Protected Sub Page_Load(ByVal sender As Object, ByVal e As System.EventArgs)
        TimeLabel.Text = Now()
    End Sub
</script>
```

5. Now we will add an event handler that will put a message into the `PagesLabel`. In Source view, select the `GridView` from the object list and then select its `PageIndexChanged` event. Add the following code:

C#

```
<%@ Page Language="C#" %>
...
<script runat="server">
  protected void Page_Load ...
  protected void GridView1_PageIndexChanged(object sender, EventArgs e)
   {
        GridView SendingGridView = ((GridView)sender);
        PagesLabel.Text = "You are on page #" + (SendingGridView.PageIndex + 1)
  + " of " + SendingGridView.PageCount;
   }
</script>
```

VB

```
<script runat="server">
Protected Sub Page_Load...

Protected Sub GridView1_PageIndexChanged(ByVal sender As Object, ByVal e As
System.EventArgs)
    PagesLabel.Text = "You are on page #" & _
        (Sender.PageIndex + 1) & " of " & Sender.PageCount
End Sub
</script>
```

6. Review the code (as shown below).

```
<%@ Page Language="VB" %>
...
<script runat="server">
    Protected Sub Page_Load(ByVal sender As Object, ByVal e As System.EventArgs)
        TimeLabel.Text = Now()
    End Sub
    Protected Sub GridView1_PageIndexChanged(ByVal sender As Object, ByVal e As
System.EventArgs)
        PagesLabel.Text = "You are on page #" & _
            (Sender.PageIndex + 1) & " of " & Sender.PageCount
    End Sub
</script>
...<h2>Chapter 17 TIO #1701 Simple Event Handler </h2>
    <form id="form1" runat="server">
    <div>
        <asp:Label ID="TimeLabel" runat="server" Text=""></asp:Label><br />
        <asp:Label ID="PagesLabel" runat="server" Text=""></asp:Label><br />
        <asp:GridView ID="GridView1" runat="server"
            AllowPaging="True"
            AutoGenerateColumns="False"
            DataKeyNames="EmployeeID"
            DataSourceID="SqlDataSource1"
            OnPageIndexChanged="GridView1_PageIndexChanged"
            PageSize="2" PagerSettings-Mode="NextPrevious">
            <Columns>
...
            </Columns>
        </asp:GridView>
        <asp:SqlDataSource ID="SqlDataSource1" runat="server"
            ConnectionString="<%$ ConnectionStrings:MdfNorthwind %>"
            SelectCommand="SELECT [EmployeeID], [LastName], [FirstName]
FROM [Employees]">
        </asp:SqlDataSource>
</div></form></body></html>
```

7. Save the page and run it in the browser, clicking on the `GridView` navigation links.

How It Works

This demonstration gives you an overview of several topics that are discussed in detail later in this chapter. First, event handlers can be created in source view by clicking on an object from the object list, (top left) and then one of its events from the list at top right. When an event handler is added, there are one or two changes to the page. First, if the event is of a control, then there is a reference from the control to the procedure. (If the event is associated with the `Page`, then no reference is needed).

```
<asp:GridView ...
OnPageIndexChanged="GridView1_PageIndexChanged"
```

Second, there is the actual handler within the `<script>` tags. In the handler, VWD gave us the opening and closing lines. The opening has two arguments that we will discuss shortly. For the `Page_Load` procedure, we merely set the `TimeLabel.Text` to the time we got from the server at the time that the page is loaded.

In the second case, we want an action after the user moves to another page, so we will place the code in the `GridView.PageIndexChanged` event. We displayed a property of the object that triggered the event. Within the handler we can reference the object that created the event by referring to `Sender`. We can also refer to controls on the page directly, as we do with `TimeLabel`, but as we will discuss later, keeping the reference as a generic `Sender` makes our code more flexible.

Frequently, we will need the event to use some data from the page, particularly from the control that raised the event. In the next section, we look at those parameters.

Transfer of Values When an Event Is Triggered

When an event is triggered, there is an automatic transfer of some information from controls (and the page in general) to the event handler. This data has been standardized into two parameters. The first is the object that triggered the event, and the second is a set of values called event arguments.

Object Sender

The `Object` sender argument seems odd at first thought. After all, if you are handling an event named `MyButton_Click`, there should be no ambiguity about what object initiated the event handler; it was `MyButton`. But you may use the same event handler for several buttons or several lists. For example, in a library catalog, you may have three lists for title, subject, and author. The user is to pick from any of the three. In each case, a similar action will occur — information for a book will be retrieved and displayed. For all three, the same event handler (perhaps named `LookUp`) will be set as the `OnClick` value. The `Object` sender argument allows you to determine which list the user clicked and create the appropriate SQL statement.

Accessing the properties of the sender is not as easy to use as it might seem. It does not contain a simple string with the name of the sender, nor does it contain a strongly typed reference to the control that fired the event. Rather it contains an object of the type of the sender, stored in an untyped `Object` variable. So, the object can be a button, a list, and so on. Extracting a value is different when using Visual Basic and C#. In VB, the value of a property can be referred to in the standard `Object.Property` syntax. For example, the `Object` will have an `ID` property holding the name it was given in the server-side control properties. To see the name of the object that initiated the event handler, you would use the following code:

```
Response.Write(Sender.ID)
```

Conversely, you can affect the sender with the following:

```
Sender.Text = "My string"
```

VB lets you get away with not typecasting the `Object`, but you do pay a performance penalty for late binding. It is always better coding practice, even in VB, to properly typecast variables before accessing their properties. You can typecast in visual basic as follows (third line then displays the button name in label1). This code is included in the download in `Demo-1701-TypeCast-VB.ASPX`.

```
Dim MyButton = CType(sender, Button)
Label1.Text = MyButton.ID
```

But C# is more exacting in how it handles types. You must first cast the object, then you can read from or write to the values of the sender's properties. The following code example achieves the same objectives as the preceding VB code:

```
Button SendingButton = ((Button)sender);
Label1.Text=SendingButton.ID;
```

EventArgs

The event arguments are a set of values sent from the control to the event handler. They are specific for each kind of event. You can see the event arguments that are returned by looking in the object browser (VWD Menu⇨View⇨ObjectBrowser). For example, click through System.Web⇨UI.Webcontrols⇨ GridViewSelectEventArgs and you will see the `NewSelectedIndex` argument. In some cases, you can also refer to the object and property directly without using the event arguments (for example, `MyGridView.SelectedItem`). You will practice using event arguments in the Try It Out that deals with selections.

Location of Event Handlers

Event handlers, like other procedures, can be located in several places. The two basic divisions are code-inline and code-behind (that is, code inside the ASPX page file or code inside a separate class file associated to the ASPX page). Same page is easier to read and easier to transfer to the host because there is one file only. Separate code makes it easier to separate the user interface definition (controls and HTML) from the programming code (event handlers and other functions). Therefore, the inline model is generally used for simpler sites, hobbyist sites, or projects with just one programmer. Generally speaking, enterprise-level sites with separate teams for the user interface (UI) and logic will favor a separate-page architecture.

An important traditional advantage of code separation was to precompile, and thus hide, the source code in the separate file. However, ASP.NET 2.0 can precompile entire sites with a command line utility named `aspnet_compiler`. In the balance, code on the page was easier because the designer or maintainer did not have to jump back and forth between pages. VWD also solves this problem by opening both the design and code-behind files and automatically jumping the view between them, as necessary.

So far, you have placed both server-side code and HTML object declarations on the same page. The code can be located almost anywhere on the page, as long as it is within `<script>` tags. The code can also be broken up into several script blocks, and ASP.NET 2.0 will find the event handler regardless of its location on the page. By default, VWD will locate all on-page code in one block near the top of the page.

Code can also be located on a separate page named `CodeFile`, in a technique called *code-behind*. The file is generally named with an `.aspx.vb` or `.aspx.cs` extension, indicating its language. (Note the syntax of two periods to create a double extension.) Start by declaring the partial class in the `CodeFile`, which could be named `MyCodeFile.aspx.vb`, as follows:

```
Imports Microsoft.VisualBasic
Partial Class MyPartialClass
     Inherits System.Web.UI.Page
     Protected Sub SeparatePageCodeButton_Click(ByVal sender As Object, ByVal e As
System.EventArgs)
         OutputLabel.Text = "From separate code page."
    End Sub
End Class
```

Then, in the ASPX page, you must indicate in the first tag which page holds the code, using the three directives in the following code. Assuming that the `CodeFile` page is named `MyCodeFile.aspx.vb`, you start your ASPX page as follows:

VB

```
<%@ Page Language="VB"
    AutoEventWireup="false"
    CodeFile="MyCodeFile.aspx.vb"
    Inherits="MyPartialClass"
    %>
```

Or, in C#, you would use the syntax that follows in the code-behind page, which could be named `MyCodeFile.aspx.cs`.

C#

```
public partial class MyPartialClass    : System.Web.UI.Page
{
    protected void SeparatePageCodeButton_Click(object sender, EventArgs e)
    {
        OutputLabel.Text = "From separate code page.";
    }
}
```

And in the ASPX page using C#, you would start with the following:

```
<%@ Page Language="C#"
 CodeFile="MyCodeFile.aspx.cs"
```

Of course, VWD writes this automatically for you when you designate code in a separate page in the Add New Item dialog box. `AutoEventWireUp` will connect the page functions events of the ASPX page (such as `Page_Load`) to their underlying ASP.NET equivalents (such as the `Page.Load` function). This eliminates the need to add specific reference to event handlers in the ASPX page. `CodeFile` designates the name of the file holding the code. By convention, that is the name of the ASPX file plus an extension indicating the language. The `Inherits` attribute indicates the partial class to use within the code file. Although it is possible to have one code file support several ASPX pages (each with its own partial class), most often each page has its own code file.

VWD provides several forms of assistance when creating an event handler. First, when VWD creates a new item in a folder, the dialog box has a check box option to locate code on a separate page. An alternative option is to place the code on the same page. Whichever option you choose, VWD will remember it for future new items. Second, if you select an event from the object and event lists at the top of the source view pane, VWD will generate boilerplate code for the event handler and add the `OnEvent` property to the control. You can also get the same behavior in Design view by double-clicking on a control. However, VWD will always create a handler for the default event. Alternatively, you can select a control, and in the Properties window, click on the lightning icon. This opens a list of events. Double-clicking on one will jump you to the appropriate handler in the source code.

There is a third, but fundamentally different, location for code. As discussed in Chapter 14, code can be placed in an object to be shared by all pages in the site, and the properties and methods of the object may be called from your pages.

Try It Out — Observing Event Code Locations

In this exercise, you will see code in four locations: three places on the same page as the presentation controls and then one page where the code is in a separate file.

1. Right-click on your `ch17` folder and select Add New Item. Use the WebForm template, name the file `TIO-1702-EventHandlerLocation` and check that `Code` is in a `Separate File`. Add a label named `OutputLabel` and three buttons named `TopCodeButton`, `MiddleCodeButton`, and `BottomCodeButton`. Set the buttons' `Text` property to be similar to their name.

2. In Design view, double-click on the `TopCodeButton`. VWD will take you to the script tags at the top of the file and create a `TopCodeButton_Click` event. Add the following code:

```
<%@ Page Language="VB" %>
<script runat="server">
    Sub TopCodeButton_Click(ByVal sender As Object, ByVal e As System.EventArgs)
        OutputLabel.Text = "From code located at top of page"
    End Sub
</script>
```

3. To demonstrate that you can place a script tag in the middle of the page, add the following:

```
... <body>
<asp:Button ID="MiddleCodeButton" Runat="server" ... />

<script runat="server">
    Sub MiddleCodeButton_Click(ByVal sender As Object, ByVal e As System.EventArgs)
        OutputLabel.Text = "From code in middle of page"
    End Sub
</script>

<asp:Button ID="BottomCodeButton" Runat="server" ...
```

4. Last on this page, create a script tag after the closing HTML tag and insert code for another event handler, as follows:

```
...</body>
</html>
<script runat="server">
    Sub BottomCodeButton_Click(ByVal sender As Object, ByVal e As System.EventArgs)
        OutputLabel.Text = "From code located at bottom of page"
    End Sub
</script>
```

Alternatively, if you prefer C#, your page should appear as follows:

```
<%@ Page Language="C#" %>
<script runat="server">
    void TopCodeButton_Click(object sender, EventArgs e)
        {
        OutputLabel.Text = "From code located at top of page";
        }
</script>
<html>
<head><title>Ch-17-TIO-02-CodeLocation-CS</title></head>
<body>
```

```
<h3>Chapter 17 TIO #02 Code Location - CS</h3>
    <p>Same Page -  C# version</p>
  <form id="form1" runat="server">
      <asp:Button ID="TopCodeButton" Runat="server" Text="Top Code Button"
OnClick="TopCodeButton_Click" />
      <br />
      <asp:Button ID="MiddleCodeButton" Runat="server" Text="Middle Code Button"
OnClick="MiddleCodeButton_Click" />
<script runat="server">
    void MiddleCodeButton_Click(object sender, EventArgs e)
        {
        OutputLabel.Text = "From code located in middle of page";
        }
</script>
      <br />
      <asp:Button ID="BottomCodeButton" Runat="server" Text="Bottom Code Button"
OnClick="BottomCodeButton_Click" /> <br />
      <br />
      <asp:Label ID="OutputLabel" Runat="server" Text="Default Text" Width="398px"
Height="39px"></asp:Label>
  </form>
</body>
</html>
<script runat="server">
    void BottomCodeButton_Click(object sender, EventArgs e)
        {
        OutputLabel.Text = "From code located at bottom of page";
        }
</script>
```

5. Save and run the page, noting that all three buttons work.

6. Now experiment with code on a separate page. Back in VWD's Solution Explorer, right-click on your `ch17` folder and click on Add New Item again. This time, turn on the option to `Place Code` in `Separate File`, and then create a file from the Web Form template named `TIO-2-EventCodeLocations-SeparatePage-VB.aspx`. Add a single label and button and give them appropriate names, as follows. Double-click on the button to begin coding, and note that you are jumped to a new file page that holds only code. Add the following highlighted line:

VB

```
Partial Class t3_aspx
    Sub SeparatePageCodeButton_Click(ByVal sender As Object, ByVal e As
System.EventArgs)
        OutputLabel.Text = "From separate code page."
    End Sub
End Class
```

If you prefer C#, select it in the New Item dialog box and double-click on the button to go to a C# code page. You will already see most of the following lines created by VWD. Add the single highlighted line.

C#

```
using System;
using System.Data;
using System.Configuration;
using System.Web;
using System.Web.Security;
using System.Web.UI;
using System.Web.UI.WebControls;
using System.Web.UI.WebControls.WebParts;
using System.Web.UI.HtmlControls;

public partial class TIO_2_EventCodeLocations_SeparatePage_CS_aspx
{
    protected void SeparatePageCodeButton_Click(object sender, EventArgs e)
    {
        OutputLabel.Text = "From separate code page.";
    }

}
```

7. Save and run the file in your browser, noting that code on a separate page works fine.

How It Works

The first example simply demonstrates that a `<script>` tag with event handlers can be located anywhere on a page and still work. By default, VWD will place all of the event handlers after the `<%@page>` tag but before the `<html>` tag. This convention allows you and other maintainers of the code to see all of the event handlers right up front.

In the second example, you instructed VWD, in the Add New Item dialog, to place code in a separate page. The code file was automatically created by VWD with a name extension of the language. You open and jump into that page by double-clicking on the control that will invoke the handler. Alternatively, you can select a control and open all of its events in the Properties window using the lightning icon. For both VB and C#, VWD generates several lines of code. You merely have to add the code specific to your goals using the proper syntax for the chosen language.

Our events to date have been raised by buttons outside of data controls. Now we start to look at responding to events raised by commands and buttons within a `GridView` or other data control.

Command and Custom Button Events

Buttons on an ASPX page raise events that are handled by page-level event handlers, as demonstrated above. However, when a button is placed inside a data-bound control such as `FormView` or `GridView`, it is actually the `FormView` or `GridView` control that handles the event on the button's behalf. This may be handled automatically or may raise an event on the `FormView` or `GridView` that you can handle yourself. In any case, you are not handling the button's click event, but an event of the outer data-bound control. The button only has a simple `CommandName` property (and optional `CommandArgument` property) that indicates to the outer data-bound control the action to perform. We call this *event bubbling* in ASP.NET because the command is "bubbled" up from the button to the outer control.

Consider the case where `GridView` has an edit button next to each row. You would not want to wire up a separate event handler for each of these buttons, because there may be many rows in the grid. Event bubbling allows you to handle a single `GridView OnRowEditing` event instead. You don't always need to handle the event, because the `GridView` will automatically perform some reasonable behavior in response to commands. Note that the commands that are handled automatically by the data-bound control can be different for each control. The `GridView` handles `Select`, `Edit`, `Update`, `Delete`, `Cancel`, `Page`, and `Sort`. You can also define your own command names and handle them yourself using the `GridView`'s `OnItemCommand` event.

Using Events Raised by Command Buttons or Command Fields

As discussed in the chapters on presenting and modifying data, command buttons can be divided into four general categories:

- **Selecting data:** Select
- **Modifying data:** Insert, New, Cancel, Update, Delete
- **Paging through sets of rows:** First, Last, Previous, Next, Number
- **Sorting Columns**

A `HyperLinkField` doesn't render a link button like `CommandField` does. It simply renders a direct hyperlink tag to the browser (no `postback` required).

The first concept to understand is that all of the code needed for these buttons to perform their tasks is prewritten by Microsoft into the control. After all, this is the great advance in the data story for ASP.NET version 2.0: displaying and modifying data is now codeless for most scenarios. However, the designer can augment those behaviors at two points: before they perform their built-in behavior and after.

Before a command button's behavior is executed, ASP.NET 2.0 triggers an "ing" event: `Inserting`, `Deleting`, `Selecting`, and so on. This is an appropriate time to execute validation, typecasting, or other customized qualifying steps prior to the behavior executing. After a command button's behavior is complete, there is an "ed" event: `Inserted`, `Deleted`, `Selected`, and so on. This event is appropriate for checking on the success of the operation. Like other command buttons, paging controls have `PageIndexChanging` and `PageIndexChanged` events.

Using Events Raised by Buttons with Custom Behavior

The buttons we described above raise built-in events. But we can also create a button that raises a custom event, that is, a block of code written by the page developer. For buttons with custom behavior, the designer must write all behavior, as expressed in the first few examples of this chapter where you put a button control on the page. The button was not in a data-bound control and, thus, could not be designated as a command button, such as `Select` or `Insert`. Instead, as the designer, you created all of the behavior in an event. One event is built into all buttons: click. Note that this is limited compared with Windows Forms or client-side code, where the page exposes events such as `MouseOver` and `Focus`. If these more ephemeral events were handled by server-side code, the number of page refreshes (and, thus, roundtrips) would become onerous.

Try It Out — Using Custom Events for Buttons

This exercise looks at a `GridView` of products that displays custom buttons that raise an event with a custom handler. We will use one event handler for both buttons so you can practice differentiating the sender.

1. In the `ch17` folder, create a new page named `TIO-3-EventsFromCommandButtons.aspx`, turning off the option to put code in a separate file.
2. Add a `GridView` that displays the products' ID and name from `Northwind`. Open the Smart Tasks panel of the `GridView` and select Add New Column. Set the field type to `ButtonField`, the `HeaderText` to `Buy`, the type to `Button`, and the text to `Buy`. You can leave the `CommandName` as Cancel (we will change it later). Add another `ButtonField` with the same properties, but this time set the `HeaderText` to `Sell` and `Text` to `Sell`.
3. Now switch to Source view and change the `GridView`'s `ButtonField`'s `CommandName` to `Buy` and `Sell`, respectively (as listed in the code below).
4. Now, we will create the event handler. Staying in Source view, drop down the list of objects at the top left and select `GridView1`. At the top right, drop the list of events and select `OnRowCommand`. VWD will create the framework for the event handler; then you can type the shaded lines of code below within the `<script>` tags:

```
<%@ Page Language="C#" %>
<!DOCTYPE html PUBLIC "-//W3C//DTD XHTML 1.0 Transitional//EN"
"http://www.w3.org/TR/xhtml1/DTD/xhtml1-transitional.dtd">
<script runat="server">
    Sub GridView1_RowCommand(ByVal sender As Object, ByVal e As
System.Web.UI.WebControls.GridViewCommandEventArgs)
        Response.Write("Commmand Name: " & e.CommandName & "<br/>")
        Dim rowIndex As Integer = e.CommandArgument
        If e.CommandName = "Buy" Then
            Response.Write("You Bought: " & GridView1.DataKeys(rowIndex).Value)
        ElseIf e.CommandName = "Sell" Then
            Response.Write("You Sold: " & GridView1.DataKeys(rowIndex).Value)
        End If
    End Sub
</script>
... <h2>Chapter 17 TIO #1703 Events From Command Buttons </h2>
    <form id="form1" runat="server">    <div>
      <asp:GridView ID="GridView1" runat="server"
        DataSourceID="SqlDataSource1"
        AutoGenerateColumns="False"
        DataKeyNames="ProductID"
        EmptyDataText="There are no data records to display."
        OnRowCommand="GridView1_RowCommand">
          <Columns>
              <asp:BoundField DataField="ProductID"
                HeaderText="ProductID" ReadOnly="True" SortExpression="ProductID"/>
              <asp:BoundField DataField="ProductName"
                HeaderText="ProductName" SortExpression="ProductName" />
              <asp:ButtonField CommandName="Buy" Text="Buy"
                HeaderText="Click to Buy"></asp:ButtonField>
              <asp:ButtonField CommandName="Sell" Text="Sell"
```

```
                HeaderText="Click to Sell"></asp:ButtonField>
         </Columns>
      </asp:GridView>
        <asp:SqlDataSource ID="SqlDataSource1" runat="server"
            ConnectionString="<%$ ConnectionStrings:MdfNorthwind %>"
            ProviderName="<%$ ConnectionStrings:MdfNorthwind.ProviderName %>"
            SelectCommand="SELECT [ProductID], [ProductName] FROM [Products]">
        </asp:SqlDataSource>
</div></form></body></html>
```

5. Save the document and view it in the browser.

How It Works

In this exercise, you used the RowCommand event to determine when the user has clicked the button in the GridView control. Within that event handler, you wrote custom code that will execute whenever the click event in any of the button controls in the GridView occurs. One of the arguments to the RowCommand event handler is of type GridViewCommandEventArgs. This object exposes two important properties: CommandName and CommandArgument. The CommandName property allows you to identify the button that was clicked inside the GridView control, and the CommandArgument property provides you with an index of the clicked row. In the code, you used the combination of these properties to write an appropriate message to the screen.

To retrieve the ProductName field value from the current row, you use the DataKeys collection of the GridView control. Note that as part of the GridView control declaration, the DataKeyNames attribute is set to the ProductName field. Also note that when VWD created the event it also added a line to the GridView that specified the event handler to call when a row is clicked in the GridView.

When we work with events raised by a selection list (e.g., a DropDownList), there are additional considerations, as we will discuss below.

List Selection Events and Page Events

Having covered generic event handling, you can begin to focus on events that are directly related to the topic of working with data on ASP.NET 2.0 pages. GridView exposes Selecting and Selected events. Selection list controls like DropDownList expose a SelectedIndexChanged event. They pass their own identity for the sender and a set of event arguments, including the index of the selected record. However, to identify the user's choice, it is easier just to refer to the GridView's or list control's SelectedIndex without using the EventArgs.

A series of events occurs when a page is prepared on the server to be sent to the browser: Page.Init, Page.Load, and finally Page.Unload (as well as many others). These events are automatic for every page; they do not depend on any user action. In earlier versions of ASP.NET, data had to be bound at critical times during the page events. However, in ASP.NET 2.0, binding is handled automatically, lessening the degree to which you must know the page events.

The most commonly used event is the Page.Load event. You can use this event to perform operations such as setting default values for the controls. In particular, you can use a property called

Page.`IsPostBack` to determine whether the page is being visited for the first time (`Page.IsPostBack = false`). For example, a page may have a label or `GridView` that should be visible only after the user has made an initial selection in the first rendering of the page. We have used `IsPostBack` in earlier chapters of the book, for example in TIO-1504 and will use it in the exercise below.

Try It Out Combining List Selection and Page Events Handling

This exercise demonstrates employment of a user selection in an event handler. The user will be able to select from a `DropDownList`, `TreeView`, or `GridView`.

1. In the `ch17` folder, create a new page named `TIO-1704-ListSelection.aspx` with the code on the same page. We will start by adding a label and three controls for data display. Then we will write the event handlers.

2. Drag and drop a `Label` control onto the page, and leave the `ID` of the control as `Label1`.

3. Drag and drop a list box, and bind it to a hand-entered list of three states (use `CA`, `UT`, and `IN`).

```
<asp:DropDownList ID="DropDownList1" Runat="server"
   AutoPostBack="True"
  <asp:ListItem>CA</asp:ListItem>
  <asp:ListItem>IN</asp:ListItem>
  <asp:ListItem>UT</asp:ListItem>
</asp:DropDownList>
```

4. Next add a `TreeView` and hard-code a few layers, as follows:

```
<asp:TreeView ID="TreeView1" Runat="server">
  <Nodes>
    <asp:TreeNode Value="Parent 1" Expanded="True" Text="Parent 1">
      <asp:TreeNode Value="Parent1.Leaf2" Text="Leaf 1" />
        <asp:TreeNode Value="Parent1.Leaf2" Text="Leaf 2" />
    </asp:TreeNode>
    <asp:TreeNode Value="Parent 2" Expanded="True" Text="Parent 2">
      <asp:TreeNode Value="Parent2.Leaf1" Text="Leaf 1" />
        <asp:TreeNode Value="Parent2.Leaf2" Text="Leaf 2" />
    </asp:TreeNode>
  </Nodes>
</asp:TreeView>
```

5. Add a `GridView` of the authors from the `Pubs` database, including just the ID number and last name. Enable selection for the `GridView`, and check that you have a `DataKeyNames` property set as shown below:

```
<asp:GridView ID="GridView1" Runat="server"
   DataSourceID="SqlDataSource1"
   DataKeyNames="au_id"
   AutoGenerateColumns="False">
  <Columns>
    <asp:CommandField ShowSelectButton="True" />
    <asp:BoundField ReadOnly="True" HeaderText="au_id"
          DataField="au_id" SortExpression="au_id" />
    <asp:BoundField HeaderText="au_lname"
          DataField="au_lname" SortExpression="au_lname" />
```

```
        </Columns>
      </asp:GridView>

        <asp:SqlDataSource ID="SqlDataSource1" runat="server"
            ConnectionString="<%$ ConnectionStrings:MdfPubs %>"
            SelectCommand="SELECT [au_id], [au_lname] FROM [authors]">
        </asp:SqlDataSource>
```

6. The first event handler will be for the page load event, with a report to the label. In Source view drop down the list of objects in the top-left corner and select `Page`. In the top right, drop down the list and select the `Load` event. Add the following code into the framework that VWD creates for you:

```
<%@ Page Language="VB" %>
<script runat="server">

    Sub Page_Load(ByVal sender As Object, ByVal e As System.EventArgs)
        If (Not Page.IsPostBack) Then
            Label1.Text = "This text was set in the Page_Load event"
        End If
    End Sub
```

7. The second event handler responds to a user selection in the `DropDownList`. Again selecting from the drop-down lists at the top left and right of the Source view, select the `DropDownList1` object's `SelectedIndexChanged` event. Add the code shaded below. Also note how VWD automatically added a property to the `DropDownList` that instructs it to use our new event handler. (Note: keep the `Label1.Text` command all on one line.)

```
Sub DropDownList1_SelectedIndexChanged(ByVal sender As Object,
ByVal e As System.EventArgs)

    Label1.Text = "You used the " & sender.ID + " to select " +
           DropDownList1.SelectedValue
End Sub

<asp:DropDownList ... OnSelectedIndexChanged="DropDownList1_SelectedIndexChanged"
...>
```

8. The second event handler responds to a user's clicking on a tree node. From the drop-down lists in Source view, select the `TreeView1 SelectedNodeChanged` event. Enter the code shown in gray below. Again, VWD added a property to the data-bound control that instructs it to use the new event handler. (Note: keep the `Label1.Text` command all on one line)

```
    Sub TreeView1_SelectedNodeChanged(ByVal sender As Object, ByVal e As
System.EventArgs)
            Label1.Text = "You used the " & sender.ID +" to select " +
 TreeView1.SelectedNode.Value
    End Sub

<asp:TreeView ... OnSelectedNodeChanged="TreeView1_SelectedNodeChanged" ... >
```

9. The last event is for the `GridView`. Again, VWD added a property to the data-bound control that instructed it to use our new event handler. (Note: keep the `Label1.Text` command all on one line.)

```
    Sub GridView1_SelectedIndexChanged(ByVal sender As Object, ByVal e As
System.EventArgs)
        Label1.Text = "You used the " & sender.ID + Label1.Text += " to select " +
 GridView1.SelectedValue    End Sub
</script>
<asp:GridView ... OnSelectedIndexChanged="GridView1_SelectedIndexChanged"> ...
```

Alternatively, you can create a page using C# with a script section as follows. (Note: keep the `Label1.Text` command all on one line.)

```
<%@ Page Language="C#" %>
<script runat="server">
void DropDownList1_SelectedIndexChanged(Object sender, EventArgs e)
        {
        if(Page.IsPostBack)
            {
            Label1.Text = "You used the " + ((DropDownList)sender).ID +
                " to select " + DropDownList1.SelectedValue;
            }
        }
void TreeView1_SelectedNodeChanged(Object sender, EventArgs e)
        {
        if(Page.IsPostBack)
            {
            Label1.Text = "You used the " + ((TreeView)sender).ID +
                " to select " + TreeView1.SelectedValue;
            }
        }
void GridView1_SelectedIndexChanged(Object sender, EventArgs e)
        {
        if(Page.IsPostBack)
            {
            Label1.Text = "You used the " + ((GridView)sender).ID +
                " to select " + GridView1.SelectedValue;
            }
        }
</script>
```

10. Save the file and admire your efforts in your browser.

How It Works

In this example, you wrote four procedures to demonstrate event handling. Controls used in this example include `DropDownList`, `TreeView`, and `GridView`. Apart from these controls, you also used the `Page.Load` event to set the default text for the `Label` control. The `Text` property of the `Label` control is set for the first time only when the page is requested from the client browser. That code never gets executed after the initial load, because of the `IsPostBack` property check. The `IsPostBack` property of the `Page` object returns `false` only when the page is requested for the first time. After that, it always returns `true`.

Similar to the `Page.Load` event, both the `GridView` and `DropDownList` controls expose the `SelectedIndexChanged` event that is raised whenever the selected index is changed in the page. You used those events to set the `Text` property of the label control to the appropriate value. There is also a `TreeView` control in the page for which the `SelectedNodeChanged` event handler is implemented. Inside this event handler, you set the value of the selected node in the `TreeView` control.

Data Control Binding Events

When you data-bind a `GridView` control with a data source, there are two important events that are raised before the `GridView` is rendered. They are as follows:

- **RowCreated:** Raised when each row in the `GridView` control is created. In this event handler, you can execute custom code, such as adding custom content to a row.
- **RowDataBound:** Raised when a data row is bound to data in the `GridView` control. You can use this event to modify the contents of a row when the row is bound to data.

Both of the preceding events pass a `GridViewRowEventArgs` object to their handlers. The `GridViewRowEventArgs` object can be used to access the properties of the row being bound. To access a specific cell in the row, use the `Cells` property of the `GridViewRow` object. You can get access to the current `GridViewRow` object by accessing the `Row` property of the `GridViewRowEventArgs` object. It is also possible to determine the type of the current row (header row, data row, footer row, and so on) by examining the `RowType` property of the `GridViewRow` object.

Try It Out Using Data-Binding Events for GridView

In this exercise, you will practice how to use the `RowDataBound` event to modify the value of a field in the data source before it is displayed in a `GridView` control. For the purposes of this example, the `Products` table in the `Northwind` database is used. When displaying the products information, wherever the category ID is to be displayed, you will replace that with the category name by using code in the `RowDataBound` event handler.

We will also use a different architecture wherein we create a generic procedure that is not part of a built-in event.

1. In the `ch17` folder, create a new page named `TIO-5-DataBindingEvents.aspx`. Add `GridView` that shows product ID, product name, and category ID fields from the `Northwind Products` table. Save and run the page, noting how the right column displays the number values of the Category IDs.
2. Switch to Source view and add an `OnRowDataBound` procedure, as shown below. Then, manually add a reference to this procedure in the `GridVew OnRowDataBound` event handler:

```
<%@ Page Language="VB" %>
<script>
  Public Sub OnRowDataBound(ByVal sender As Object, ByVal e As
GridViewRowEventArgs)
        If e.Row.RowType = DataControlRowType.DataRow Then
            e.Row.Cells.Item(2).BackColor = Drawing.Color.DarkGray
            Dim categoryName As String = _
```

```
                GetCategoryName(CType(e.Row.Cells.Item(2).Text, Integer))
            e.Row.Cells.Item(2).Text = categoryName
        End If
  End Sub
</script>
<asp:GridView ... OnRowDataBound="OnRowDataBound" ... >
```

3. Within the `<script>` tags, add a server-side function named `GetCategoryName`. As the name suggests, this method gets the name of the category based on the supplied category ID.

```
<%@ Page Language="VB" %>
<script runat="server">
    Public Sub OnRowBound...
    End Sub

    Function GetCategoryName(ByVal categoryID As Integer) As String
        Dim categoryName As String = ""
        Select Case categoryID
            Case 1
                categoryName = "Beverages"
            Case 2
                categoryName = "Condiments"
            Case 3
                categoryName = "Confections"
            Case 4
                categoryName = "Dairy Products"
            Case 5
                categoryName = "Grains/Cereals"
            Case 6
                categoryName = "Meat/Poultry"
            Case 7
                categoryName = "Produce"
            Case 8
                categoryName = "Seafood"
        End Select
        Return categoryName
    End Function
</script>
```

4. Save and run the page, noting how now the right column displays a descriptive word for the category ID, as provided by the `Select Case` statement.

How It Works

In this exercise, we created a `GridView` control that displayed information from the `Products` table in the `Northwind` database. Then we created procedures that replaced the category ID with the category name from a custom function. As ASP.NET 2.0 builds the page, it puts values from the `DataSource` control into rows. After completing each row, it raises off the `OnRowBound` event.

The `GridView` control identifies the procedure to perform for the `RowDataBound` event. Inside that procedure, you check to see whether the current row type is `DataRow`. If the row type is `DataRow`, you set the background color of the third cell (identified with the index of `2`) to dark gray. Then you retrieve the value of the category ID by using the Text property of the GridViewTableCell object. This category ID is sent as an argument to the GetCategoryName method. The GetCategoryName uses a select statement to return the proper category name based on the category ID. Once the category name is obtained, it is displayed in the third cell, replacing the category ID.

General Error Events

Errors will occur in your applications. Even though you try to trap most errors using Try-Catch blocks, you can't cover every possible exception. What happens when an unhandled error occurs? One option is to show the default error message produced by ASP.NET, which is not very intuitive for the normal user. Instead, you should strive to handle them gracefully. With this in mind, there are three things about the error that you should know:

1. When the error occurs
2. Where it occurs
3. The type of error

ASP.NET provides an excellent approach that allows you to identify and track the errors as they occur. There are three places in ASP.NET where you can define what happens when an error occurs:

- **On the page itself:** This is done by handling the Page.Error event. Handling errors at this level is very simple. All you need to do is invoke the Server.GetLastError method to get the error information. If you want to redirect to a specific page, simply call Response.Redirect from this event handler. From within this event handler, you can also call Server.ClearError to cancel the bubbling up of the error at any time so that the next level of error handler (which is the Application.Error event, in this case) is not invoked.
- **On the entire application:** This is done by handling the Application.Error event in the global.asax file. Logging the errors using the Application.Error event provides a centralized approach to handling errors. This event handler will be called only after the Page.Error event handler is called. Here also you can log the error message and redirect to another page.
- **In the customErrors section in the web.config file:** This is the last line of defense, and the configurations specified in the customErrors section will come into play only after the Page.Error and Application.Error event handlers are called and only if they don't do a Response.Redirect or a Server.ClearError.

When you handle errors in the Page.Error or Application.Error events, you can get more information about the error using the Server.GetLastError method. The GetLastError method simply returns a reference to a generic Exception object.

Try It Out Handling Error Events

The code in this exercise uses the previous example TIO-5-DataBindingEvents.aspx to demonstrate error handling. For the purposes of this demonstration, you intentionally generate an error by changing the table name in the SelectCommand attribute of the SqlDataSource control to an invalid value. For this error, you will employ different types of error handlers to catch the exception.

1. Make a copy of the `TIO-5-DataBindingEvents.aspx` page, and rename it `TIO-6-ErrorEvents-ver01.aspx`. Revise the title and H2 text.

2. In the `SqlDataSource` control, modify the `SelectCommand` attribute by changing the table name in the SQL `SELECT` clause from `Products` to `NonExistentTable`. After modification, the declaration of the `SqlDataSource` control looks as follows:

```
<asp:SqlDataSource ID="SqlDataSource1" Runat="server" SelectCommand="SELECT
    [ProductName], [CategoryID], [ProductID] FROM [NonExistentTable]"
    ConnectionString="<%$ ConnectionStrings:LocalSqlNorthwind %>">
</asp:SqlDataSource>
```

3. Save the page as `TIO-6-ErrorEvents-ver01.aspx`, and view it in the browser. You will get an error message that says `Invalid object name 'NonExistentTable'`. In the same screen, you will also see other error attributes such as `Description`, `Exception Details`, `Source Error`, and `Stack Trace`. This user-unfriendly error message appears because there is no event handler for handling errors.

4. Now add a handler for the `Page.Error` event to the server-side script block. The code for the `Page.Error` event is:

```
Public Sub Page_Error(ByVal sender As Object, ByVal e As EventArgs)
    Response.Write("Error Message is : " & Server.GetLastError().Message)
    Server.ClearError()
End Sub
```

5. Now save the page as `TIO-6-ErrorEvents-ver02.aspx` (revise the title and H2 text) and view it in the browser. You will notice that the page displays the message `Error Message is : Invalid object name 'NonExistentTable'`. This message is caused by the `Response.Write` statement in the `Page.Error` event. Because the error message is cleared by the call to the `Server.ClearError` method, the exception is not propagated up through the call stack.

6. Now, we will create a system to respond to any error in the application (Web site). On `TIO-6-ErrorEvents_ver02.aspx`, comment out the `Server.ClearError` line in the `Page.Error` event and save the code as `TIO-6-ErrorEvents-ver03.aspx`. Now, the page will rely on any application-level handling of error events.

7. Check whether your application root has a `global.asax` file (it would be in `C:\Websites\BegAspNet2Db`). If the file exists, add the code line listed following this step. If the file does not exist, add an item to the root of your site of the type `Global Application Class` and with the name `global.asax`. Double-check that it is in `C:\Websites\BegAspNet2Db`. In the new ASAX page, find the `Application.Error` event and modify it as follows to redirect to a page that you will build shortly.

```
Sub Application_Error(ByVal sender As Object, ByVal e As EventArgs)
    Response.Redirect("~/ErrorPage.aspx")
End Sub
```

8. Add a new page named `ErrorPage.aspx` to the root of the Web site, and modify the code in that page to look as follows:

```
<%@ Page Language="VB" %>
<!DOCTYPE html PUBLIC "-//W3C//DTD XHTML 1.0 Transitional//EN" "http://www.w3.org/
TR/xhtml1/DTD/xhtml1-transitional.dtd">
```

```
<script runat="server">
</script>
<html xmlns="http://www.w3.org/1999/xhtml" >
<head id="Head1" runat="server">
    <title>Application_Error_Page.aspx</title>
</head><body>
        <h2>Entire Application - Error Page</h2>
        <h2>Created in TIO-1706</h2>
    <form id="form1" runat="server">
    <div><br /><br />
        Error page for the entire application
</div></form></body></html>
```

9. Save the ErrorPage.aspx, and then view TIO-6-ErrorEvents-ver03.aspx in the browser. Because the Server.ClearError method is commented out in the Page.Error event, the control will be automatically transferred to the Application.Error event. In the Application.Error event, the control is transferred to the ErrorPage.aspx file by means of a Response.Redirect statement. This will ensure that any time an error occurs in the application, the users will be automatically redirected to the ErrorPage.aspx file.

10. When you are done with this exercise and have studied the "How It Works," go back to the global.asax page and comment out the Application.Error handler's call to Response.Redirect with a preceding single quotation mark, as follows. This will reenable the default ASPX yellow troubleshooting page, which is more useful during your studies. In the end, your Global.asax should be as follows:

```
Sub Application_Error(ByVal sender As Object, ByVal e As EventArgs)
    ' Code that runs when an unhandled error occurs
    ' Response.Redirect("~/ErrorPage.aspx")
End Sub
```

11. Save your work.

How It Works

In this exercise, you deliberately introduced an error by changing the table name in the SelectCommand attribute to an invalid value. That error was handled by providing the Page.Error event handler in the page script block. In the Page.Error event handler, a message describing the details of the error displayed, using the Response.Write statement. You also cleared the error by invoking the Server.ClearError method. This will ensure that the error is not propagated up through the call stack at the end of the Page.Error event.

Then you explored further by adding the Application.Error event handler to the global.asax file. The Application.Error event handler will be automatically invoked any time an error occurs anywhere in the application. Before you did that, you also uncommented the Server.ClearError method call in the Page.Error event handler. This is done to ensure that the error propagates up through the call stack to the Application.Error event. Then in the Application.Error event handler, the users are redirected to an error page by invoking the Response.Redirect statement.

Common Mistakes

The following list describes some mistakes commonly made when attempting to handle events for data controls:

- Failure to check `Page.IsPostBack` when you only want code to execute if the page is loaded for the first time.
- Attempting to directly handle the `Click` event of a command button inside a data-bound control. You should handle events of the outer data-bound control instead.
- Coding errors in the language for an event handler. Check the built-in help for your language to check proper syntax and conventions.
- Incorrect declaration of an event handler or using incorrect event arguments. Be sure to check the correct syntax of the event you want to handle.
- Attempting to refer to `EventArgs` properties that do not exist. Find the available event arguments in the object browser.
- Failing to typecast the sender argument of an event handler.
- Incorrect understanding of the error propagation mechanism through the call stack. `Page.Error` is raised first, then `Application.Error`, then custom error handlers defined in configuration.
- Failing to clear the current error (by calling the `Server.ClearError` method) while troubleshooting the error propagation mechanism.

Summary

This chapter explained how to write customized code to handle more advanced scenarios. However, recall that most common scenarios are handled automatically by ASP.NET version 2.0, including data-binding to controls and the concomitant instantiation of ADO.NET objects. When you must use custom code, you have two steps: create an event handler within a script block and specify that handler in the server-side ASP.NET control. Custom event handlers reside within script blocks that can be anywhere on the same page or in a separate file.

Event handlers have the same basic syntax as procedures because they are page procedures. They start, in VB or C#, with a `Sub` or `void` keyword, then contain statements, and end with `End Sub` or `}`. Following the name of the handler is an argument list with two parameters. First is the `sender`, which holds the object that invoked the event handler. In most cases, you know the `sender` independently of this argument and can refer to it directly (`Button1.MyProperty` as opposed to `Sender.MyProperty`). Second is an `EventArgs`, which holds various values depending on the type of control that fired the event. Again, you generally know the argument of interest and can refer to it directly as `MyControl.MyProperty` rather than `.MyProperty`.

Buttons on the page will be one of two types. Command buttons (which can be inside `CommandFields`) have a built-in behavior, such as `Update`, `Edit`, and `Select`. You can add code in event handlers, such as `Updating` and `Updated`, and so on. The "ing" event executes prior to the built-in behavior, and the "ed" event executes after the task is completed. Custom buttons have no built-in behavior and will only execute the code written by the designer in their event handler. `GridView` controls also provide various event handlers such as `RowCreated` and `RowDataBound` that you can use to customize or modify the data before it is rendered by the `GridView` control.

You can't debug a problem if you don't know that it exists. After you take your Web application live, you are no longer the only one who is using it (hopefully), so you need an effective plan to track errors when they occur while users are surfing your site. A great way to do this is to implement error handlers at different levels. One commonly used approach is to handle errors at the application level using the `Application.Error` event. This will allow you to consolidate the logging and notification parts of your exception handling in one convenient place.

Exercises

The answers to these review questions can be found in Appendix B.

1. Describe how to induce VWD to generate for you the first and last lines of an event procedure.
2. Contrast events that end in "-ing" with events that end in "-ed."
3. What is the data type of the object `Sender` in the arguments of an event handler?
4. List places where event handler code can be located.
5. Can you mix code languages on a single ASPX page?
6. Compare and contrast command buttons and custom buttons.
7. When a selection is made in a `GridView` or list control and you have written an event handler, how can you identify (from within the event handler) which item was selected?

18

Performance Checklist

Having covered a suite of topics of using data with ASP.NET 2.0 pages, we want to return to a fundamental topic: performance. No new topics are introduced here; rather, we view this as a place for you to turn during the design phase of your site to check that each page will give the best performance. A simple site will probably not tax the software or hardware that hosts it. By simple we mean, in very approximate terms, sites that meet all three of the following criteria:

- **Hit rate:** Fewer than 10 or so visitors per minute
- **Complexities of requests:** Requests to the database are simple `SELECT`s or writes. They do not involve multiple `JOIN`s, more complex aggregate fields, complex `WHERE` clauses or the use of `UNION`s.
- **Database size:** Database size does not exceed tens of tables, tens of columns, and thousands rows. Furthermore, the tables are more independent and, thus, less reliant on multiple joins to answer queries.

If your site exceeds any of the above, or could grow to exceed these parameters, it is well worth the time to implement measures that improve performance. The performance suggestions in this book, repeated and summarized in this chapter, are so simple to deploy that it is worth following them even for simple sites so as to avoid a rework later.

Improved performance goes beyond reducing the wait time for a browser to display a page. Pages that reduce the load on your database will reduce the frequency with which drives and other hardware must be replaced. If your data is held on a machine other than the IIS server, you will reduce the traffic over the connection between those machines. Code that operates more efficiently requires fewer resources from a host and may qualify for lower hosting costs. Pages with good performance can meet your needs longer during your growth and thus increase the time before a new design is required. During development on a nonserver (desktop or laptop), better-performing pages will leave more CPU/memory to do other things, like develop even more ASP.NET apps. Taken together, the benefits are worth the investment in using best practices for performance.

This is not an exhaustive list of performance topics. There are additional concepts that deal with server loading and issues of handling large numbers of visitors. But those techniques are supplements to what we list here.

Convert Pages from Earlier Versions to 2.0

Refer to Chapter 1.

ASP.NET 2.0 allows running of pages from earlier versions (ASP.NET 1.*x* and classic ASP). However, pre-.NET versions are interpreted instead of compiled. Classic ASP interprets programming instructions every time the page is requested, whereas ASP.NET 2.0 dynamically compiles pages on the server into native programming instructions that can be run much, much more quickly. Converting all pages to the 2.0 Framework will improve site performance.

Switch from Access to SQL Server

Refer to Chapter 3.

Access was designed for single-user or small-group environments. It was never designed to handle large numbers of command executions to support a Web server. The problem is made worse if the users can write data because the record-locking model is a bottleneck for loads of more than a few users.

Furthermore, you will have difficulty finding a host that is willing to run Access to support a Web site on their hosting machines. Microsoft offers tools to convert an Access MDB file to a SQL Server MDF file. Within Access, open your MDB file and look at Tools➪Upsize Wizard. The resulting MDF file can be copied into your `App_Data` folder.

Use the DataReader Instead of the DataSet

Refer to Chapter 3.

A `DataReader` rockets through the data and delivers a single nonwritable stream to the data source control and on to the data-bound control. A `DataSet` creates a more complex object holding the data and, thus, enables writing A `DataReader` can be 10 or 20% faster then a `DataSet`. As a general rule, you should turn on the `DataReader` option of a `SqlDataSource` when you are only populating a list or a read-only grid. But if your data-bound control will enable paging then you must use a `DataSet`. `DataSets` are used by various clients of .NET 2.0 (including Windows forms with VB or C#). In ASP.NET 2.0, the `DataSet` is not used for writing, only for paging, filtering, and caching.

However, there is a trade-off here. Chapter 16 talks about caching being the way to gain performance, but you have to put the `SqlDataSource` in `DataSet` mode to use caching. Therefore, you have to do some analysis and testing to determine if you are better off with an uncached `DataReader` or a cached `DataSet`. Likewise, `FilterExpression` and `FilterParameters` require a `DataSet`.

Use OLEDB Instead of ODBC

Refer to Chapter 4.

ODBC is one of the most universal of data access techniques. But ODBC involves more layers and, thus, lower performance. The OLEDB native .NET provider is much faster if your database exposes itself via OLEDB. If your data source does not have a .NET managed OLEDB provider from Microsoft, then check with the data source manufacturer or search for third-party solutions. Managed code OLEDB providers are constantly coming to market, and in some cases you can test and choose from competing products.

Of course, if you are data is stored in Microsoft SQL Server, your best option is to use the `SqlDataSource` control with the `SqlClient` provider and not worry about OLEDB versus ODBC.

Set List Items Statically

Refer to Chapter 8.

If items in a list change only rarely, then performance is enhanced by setting those items in hard code rather than initiating a read of the database. For example, the divisions of a company or the regions of a country are more efficiently changed as needed in the code rather then doing thousands of reads per day of the same data from a database.

On the other hand, if your data values are hard-coded in a static list, then you have greatly increased your maintenance costs. This is even truer if the same list is on several pages. Some designers argue aggressively that the performance hit of keeping data in a database is well worth the reduction in maintenance.

Cache Data

Refer to Chapter 16.

Enabling caching on the `SqlDataSource` or `ObjectDataSource` is so easy and so productive that it is, by far, the best return for your effort when increasing the performance of pages that use values from a database. Connecting to and reading from a database consumes more time than almost any other operation. The more of that information you can get kept in memory, the better your system performance. Of course, the trick is to get the right information in memory, that is, the information that you are most likely to need again later.

Cache Whole or Partial Pages

Refer to Chapter 16.

For many pages, there are regions that vary and regions that do not. For example, when finding a shipping cost, the general layout of the page, including the list of states, will remain the same while the label that displays the resulting shipping cost will vary. You can turn on page caching using the `OutputCache` directive at the top of the page. Then for sections that will vary (you do not want to page-cache them), you can place them within the new `asp:Substitution` control.

Use SQL Server Cache Invalidation

Refer to Chapter 16.

One of the tricks to caching is to keep data in memory as long as it is valid (that is, the same as the underlying values in the database) but to refresh the data in memory when it is out of sync with the underlying values. Many forms of caching rely on the designer making a calculation (or best guess) as to how long, in units of time, to keep the data in memory before performing a refresh. If your data is stored in Microsoft SQL Server 2005 or later, you have a better alternative. You can turn on the system that instructs SQL Server to send a message when the underlying data changes and to, thus, invoke a refresh. This provides the best of both worlds—data is kept in memory as long as possible, but it is not kept in memory for anytime after it is stale.

Typecast in Code

Refer to Chapter 17.

It is always better coding practice to properly typecast variables before accessing their properties. VB lets you get away with not typecasting an object, but that creates late binding for which you pay a performance penalty. C# is more exacting. You must first cast the object; then you can read from or write to the values of the object's properties.

Specifically List Columns Instead of using AutoGenerate Columns

Refer to Chapter 5.

When a `GridView` or `DetailsView` has `AutoGenerateColumns="True"`, then ASP.NET 2.0 must take an additional step. The `GridView` must reflect on the data item to get the columns and their types. Once that information is obtained, the `GridView` can begin laying out the columns and then the data. This additional step is not a big issue, but a `GridView` that specifically states the columns in a `<Columns>` collection will be a few percent faster.

Turn Off ViewState When Possible

Turn off `ViewState` on the page or control level if you don't need it. With ASP.NET 2.0's control state, a lot of scenarios don't need `ViewState` anymore.

Set Properties Declaratively

All control properties that are set in code will have their values maintained in the `ViewState`. However, if you set the properties declaratively in the control's tags, then you avoid increasing the size of the `ViewState`.

Use Best Practices in Code

Eliminate unnecessary code by follow best practices. For example, store values of properties in a variable rather than retrieving them multiple times. Use the minimum scope for variables.

Precompile Your Pages

The compilation of an ASP.NET page takes place on first request and takes significantly more time than the subsequent servings of the compiled page. Performing a compilation of the entire site before deployment will reduce the time to serve pages the first time.

Case Study: FAQ System

We will finish by bringing together most of the ideas from the book to build a system that helps users by offering answers to FAQs (frequently asked questions). Our objective is to have the system self-contained so that it can be copied directly into any ASP.NET 2.0 page. Introduction

We have three objectives in this chapter:

- ❑ Review many of the ideas presented in the book
- ❑ Leave you with a solution almost ready to cut and paste into your site
- ❑ Give you a feel for how fast it is to create a complete Web solution in ASP.NET 2.0

Take a look at the time and see how long it takes you to go through the exercises of this chapter.

The exercises are in sync with chapters, so Try It Out 1906 covers topics of Chapter 6, for example. The first exception is #1902 where we add a simple logon system instead of Chapter 2's connection to Access. The second exception is #1904, where we look at a more complex SQL statement rather than connect to MySQL or another database. The last exceptions are Exercises 19-18 and 19-19, which finish out the project without reference to the techniques of any one chapter.

Project Description

As any good project, we start with a specification. In this case, is the specification includes a list of Web pages and their capabilities. We will refer to them in the chapter as deliverable #1, deliverable #2, etc.

You will create the following Web pages:

1. Page that displays a list of keywords from which the user can select and then see the FAQs that have been tagged with that keyword.
2. Page that displays all FAQs for the user to peruse
3. Page that displays as the authors of FAQs

4. Admin page to create, edit, delete a FAQ
5. Admin page to create, edit, delete a new keyword
6. Admin page to create, edit, delete a new keyword association
7. A scoring system that allows users to make a rating for a FAQ and for the administrator to see the average scores for each FAQ

We also have some more general objectives:

- All pages should have the same look and feel.
- All information should be stored in a Microsoft SQL Server database (SSE version), except for small amounts of data kept in MDB and XML files for demonstration purposes.

Database Design

Knowing that we must deliver the above, we can design the database. Because database design is not a topic of this book, we have created and filled the database for you. Briefly, we use the following tables:

- **FAQs:** Holds an ID, the question and the answer.
- **Keywords:** Holds the approved set of keywords.
- **KeywordAssoc:** Association table where each record is one keyword matched to one FAQ. FAQs with more than one applicable keyword will have more than one record in this table.
- **Scores:** Holds records giving a score of usefulness from 1 to 5 inclusive for a FAQ, as submitted by users.

So that you get a little practice with using Access as a data source, we will assume that the FAQ authors come from a `FaqAuthors.MDB` file that is part of this book's download.

> **A note on the syntax of naming the ASPX pages. We add to the end of ASPX page name the number of the exercise. This allows you to see the page as it is at the end of each exercise. For the completed project, you would only use the pages with the highest version number.**

Development of Files

As we work through this chapter, we will, exercise by exercise, improve on a basic set of files. The following list helps you keep track of the file status after each exercise. The following files will be affected by the Try It Out exercises as listed.

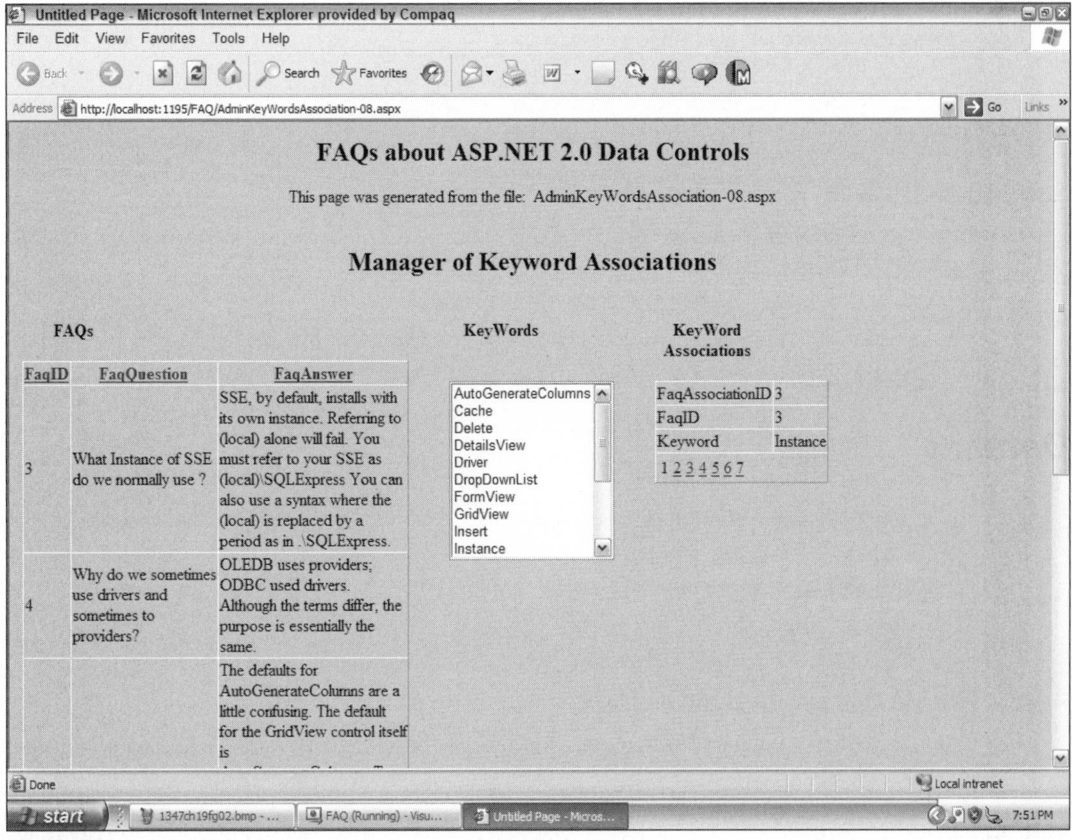

Figure 19-1

FaqsHome.aspx

Final objective: Create a home page with links to other pages.

- ❑ TIO #1918: Create a page that links to other pages.

FaqsDisplayAll.aspx

Final objective: A page that shows the first 50 characters of all of the FAQs in a `GridView` that contains paging and sorting capabilities. When the FAQ is selected, it will be shown in its entirety in a `DetailsView`. The user can give a FAQ a score of usefulness from 1 to 5, where five is most useful.

- ❑ TIO #1903: Create GridView with display of all FAQs. Store a connection string in `web.config`.
- ❑ TIO #1906: Improve appearance of table.
- ❑ TIO #1907: Add paging and sorting.

- ❑ TIO #1909: Change `GridView` to show only first 50 characters of answer and add a `DetailsView` to show entire `Answer`.
- ❑ TIO #1910: Modify `DetailsView` to use templates.
- ❑ TIO #1917: Add a scoring system.

FaqsSearch.aspx

Final Objective: `ListBox`(s) of keywords are shown. After selecting keyword(s) the user can get all of the FAQs with those keyword associations.

- ❑ TIO #1918: Create it.

AdminFaqsEditor.aspx

Final Objective: FAQs can be changed or deleted in a `GridView` of all FAQs. New FAQs can be created in a `DetailsView`. New information is validated prior to acceptance.

- ❑ TIO #1911: Create ASPX page. Add a `GridView`, enabling the editing and deleting of existing FAQs.
- ❑ TIO #1912: Add a `DetailsView` to create new FAQs.
- ❑ TIO #1913: Add validation of new FAQs and changes to FAQs.

AdminKeyWordAssociations.aspx

Final Objective: Allow Administrators to associate a keyword with a FAQ by selecting a FAQ from a `GridView` and a keyword from a `ListBox` and then clicking on a button.

- ❑ TIO #1905: Create `GridView` that displays FAQs and a `DetailsView` of the `Associations`.
- ❑ TIO #1907: Add paging and sorting to the `GridView` and paging to the `DetailsView`.
- ❑ TIO #1908: Add `ListBox` of keywords.
- ❑ TIO #1911: Enable `Edit` and `Delete` in the `GridView` and `DetailsView`.
- ❑ TIO #1912: Add ability to create a new association by hand.
- ❑ TIO #1917: Add ability to create an association by selecting and clicking.

AdminKeyWordEditor.aspx

Final Objective: Display a list of keywords in a `GridView` with paging, sorting, editing and deleting. Offer a `DetailsView` to add new keywords.

- ❑ TIO #1912: Create in entirety.

AdminScoreResults

Final Objective: Allow administrators to see, for each FAQ, the average "usability rating" score that has been entered by users, presented in a `GridView` that can be paged and sorted.

- ❑ TIO #1914: Create it (no further development).

MasterPage.master

Final Objective: Provide a common look and feel to the site, including navigation.

- ❑ TIO #1901: Create it.
- ❑ TIO #1915: Add navigation.

FaqAuthors.aspx

Final Objective: Administrators can see the list of FAQ authors.

- ❑ TIO #1902: Create the code to demonstrate reading from an MDB file (no further development).

FaqSqlTest.aspx

Final Objective: Enable Programmers to test various SQL statements against the FAQ database.

- ❑ TIO #1904: Create this to test more complex SQL statements (no further development).

FaqSearch.aspx

Final Objective: Allow users to search for FAQs that are associated with a given keyword.

- ❑ TIO #1918: Create it (no further development).

With this knowledge of the objectives, databases, and files, we can begin the creation of the site.

Try It Out 1901 Import the Database and Create the Default Page and Master Page

Our objective in the first exercise is to create the Web site, import the databases from the download, and create the master pages.

1. Open VWD, and using the menu, click File➪New Web Site. Use the ASP.NET template. Place it in `C:\Websites\FAQ`, and specify Visual Basic as the page's language.
2. We provide in the download a database to support this FAQ site. This database fulfills deliverable #9. Right-click on `App_Data` and Add Existing Item. Browse to your download, select the `FaqDatabase.mdf` in Chapter 19, and click OK. At the same time, import the `FaqEmployees.mdb` file.
3. In the Database explorer, expand the `FaqDatabase` and then Tables. Double-click on each table to see its structure, and then right-click on the table and select Show Table Data to view its values.
4. Now, we will create the master page for the site to fulfill deliverable #1. Right-click on the root of your site, and select Add New Item. Select the Master Page template, and accept the default name of `MasterPage.master`. Add the following gray lines of code:

```
<%@ Master Language="VB" %>
<%@ Import Namespace="System.IO" %>
<!DOCTYPE html PUBLIC "-//W3C//DTD XHTML 1.0 Transitional//EN"
"http://www.w3.org/TR/xhtml1/DTD/xhtml1-transitional.dtd">
```

```
<script runat="server">
</script>
<html xmlns="http://www.w3.org/1999/xhtml" >
<head runat="server">
</head>
<body bgcolor="#ccccff">
    <form id="form1" runat="server">
    <div style="text-align: center">
        <h2>FAQs about ASP.NET 2.0 Data Controls</h2>
        You are currently viewing a page from <%Response.Write(New FileInfo(Request
.FilePath).Name)%> <br />
        <asp:contentplaceholder id="ContentPlaceHolder1" runat="server">
        </asp:contentplaceholder>
        <br />
        Search for another FAQ   Administer Keywords  Administer
FAQs</div>
    </form>
</body>
</html>
```

Try It Out 1902 Displaying Data from an MDB File

To practice a connection to an MDB file, you add a small section to display the authors of the FAQs. This will satisfy deliverable #3. In the downloads, we provide a small database named `FaqAuthors.mdb`.

1. In VWD, right-click the `App_Data` folder and Add an Existing Item. Browse to `FaqAuthors.mdb` from your download folder named Chapter 19.
2. Create a new page named `FaqAuthors-1902` that uses the `MasterPage.master`. The "1902" designation is a reminder to you that this page is from TIO#02 of Chapter 19. In the Database Explorer, expand until you can see fields of the `FaqEmployees` table. Select the first and last names and drag them to the page. Save and run the page.

How It Works

Look at the source code to observe that VWD creates an `AccessDataSource`. That control uses a reference to an MDB file rather than a connection string as we use when connecting to SQL databases.

Try It Out 1903 Connecting to the SQL Database

In this exercise, you create deliverable #2, a simple `GridView` to display all FAQs. We pay particular attention to the connection string you will use throughout the rest of the chapter.

1. Create a page named `FaqsAll-1903.aspx` that uses the `MasterPage.master`. Open the Database Explorer and expand `FaqDatabase.mdf` and then Tables. Select the FAQs table and drag it onto the page. Save your work, and test it in your browser. If prompted, accept VWD's offer to modify `web.config` to enable debugging.
2. Close the browser and return to VWD. Open the page in Source view, and inspect the `SqlDataSource` control. Observe that the connection string refers to a string stored in the `web.config` file.

3. Open the `web.config` file, and observe the connection string that VWD created. Close `web.config`.

How It Works

At this point, we are performing the simplest technique to get data on a page—dragging a table from the Database Explorer to an ASPX page. Park your fingers and leave the typing to VWD. You get the default on everything—a `SqlDataSource` control and a `GridView`. VWD, in this scenario, will create a connection string for you and use it in the `SqlDataSource` control. In the last exercise of this chapter, we will review how to perform encryption.

Try It Out 1904 Using Other SQL Statements

Chapter 4 of this book focused on connecting to other sources of data. But in this case study you will use more complex SQL statements. This will also give you some practice in the kinds of statements you will need later in the chapter.

1. Open `FaqsAll-03` and save as `FaqsSqlTest-4`.
2. Change the SQL statement either by walking through the data source control's configure wizard or by typing into the Source view. Try to achieve the following outcomes (the answers are in the "How It Works," below.
3. Get the FAQs with the most recent FAQs at the top of the `GridView`, assuming that the ID values are chronological.
4. Get only the FAQ that has an ID number of seven.
5. Get only those FAQs whose questions start with "How"
6. Get all the FAQs with an ID of seven or greater.
7. Get only those FAQs where the question starts with "Why. . . ."
8. Get only those FAQs that contain the word `GridView` in `FaqAnswer`.
9. Return your page to a SQL statement with no `WHERE` clause and save it.

How It Works

The following SQL statements satisfy Steps 3 to 8 above.

```
SELECT [FaqID], [FaqQuestion], [FaqAnswer] FROM [FAQs] ORDER BY [FaqID] DESC
SELECT [FaqID], [FaqQuestion], [FaqAnswer] FROM [FAQs] WHERE [FaqID]=7
SELECT [FaqID], [FaqQuestion], [FaqAnswer]
FROM [FAQs] WHERE ([FaqID]<=7) AND ([FaqID]>=5)"
SELECT [FaqID], [FaqQuestion], [FaqAnswer]
FROM [FAQs] WHERE [FaqQuestion] LIKE 'Why%'
SELECT [FaqID], [FaqQuestion], [FaqAnswer]
FROM [FAQs] WHERE [FaqQuestion] LIKE '%GridView%'
```

Try It Out 1905 Creating Basic Tables

In this exercise, you will create two pages that administrators will eventually use to manage keywords and keyword associations (assignments of keywords to FAQs). At this point, you will not have all the features, but you will return to the pages later in the chapter. These pages will partially fulfill deliverables #5 and #6.

1. Create a page named `AdminKeywordsEditor-1905.aspx` that uses the master page. Add a table with one row and two columns.
2. From Database Explorer, drag the name of the keywords table into the left cell. In the resulting `GridView`'s Smart Tasks panel, enable paging (only). Into the right cell, drag a `DetailsView` from the Toolbox. Configure its data source to the existing `SqlDataSource` control. At this time, do not enable any features in the Smart Tasks panel. Save the page, and test it in your browser.
3. Create a page named `AdminKeywordsAssociation-1905.aspx` that uses the master page. Add a table with one row and two columns.
4. Into the left cell, drag from the Toolbox a `SqlDataSource` control. Configure it to use your `FaqDatabaseConnectionString1`, and use a custom SQL statement for the `SELECT`, as follows:

```
SELECT
FAQs.FaqQuestion, FAQs.FaqAnswer, FAQs.FaqID,
KeywordAssoc.Keyword
FROM KeywordAssoc
INNER JOIN FAQs ON KeywordAssoc.FaqID = FAQs.FaqID
ORDER BY KeywordAssoc.FaqID
```

5. Add to the left cell a `GridView` based on `SqlDataSource1`.
6. In the right column, add a `DetailsView` that uses a new `SqlDataSource` that reads all the fields from the Keywords table. Save your work, and test it in your browser.

How It Works

At this point, this page only reads the contents of the two tables. We will be jazzing it up later in the chapter. The `SELECT` statement for the `GridView` includes a `JOIN` that makes it possible to show the corresponding FAQs and keywords in one table.

Try It Out 1906 Changing the Appearance of Tables

Now, you can improve the appearance of the tables by changing the headers' texts to be more readable, making the `FaqID` values bold, changing the background of the answers and centering the `FaqID` column.

1. Open `FaqsAll-03` and save it as `FaqsAll-06`. In VWD Design view, select the `GridView`. Open its Smart Tasks panel and click on Edit Columns. Select the `FaqID` column, and sets its header text to just ID. Repeat this for each of the other columns, removing the "Faq" from the header text.

2. Staying in Edit Columns dialog box, change the style of the `FaqID` column's ItemStyle⇨Font to Bold. Change the background of the whole `FaqAnswer` column to Web color white. Set its border color to the same color as your master page background.

3. Staying in Edit Columns dialog box, select the `FaqID` column and set its `ItemStyle` and `HeaderStyle` to be horizontal aligned to center. Save the file, and observe your changes in the browser.

How It Works

Note in Step 2 that the column style colors are transparent to start with, so they appear to be the `MasterPage` background color. If you did not set the border color to contrast with white, the divisions between the rows of answers would be difficult to discern.

Try It Out 1907 Adding Paging and sorting

You will add paging and sorting options to the `FaqsAll` page.

1. Return to your `FaqsAll-06` page, and rename it as `FaqsAll-07`. Select the `GridView`, and open the Smart Tasks panel. Enable sorting and paging. Remove sorting from the `FaqAnswer` column by setting its sort expression to an empty string in the Edit Columns dialog box.

2. With the `GridView` still selected, go to the properties pane and set the page size to `5` records. Set the Pager Settings to `NumericFirstLast` mode. Save your work, and test it.

3. Back in VWD, open `AdminKeyWordAssociations-1905` and save it as `AdminKeyWordAssociations-1907`. Enable paging and sorting for the `GridView` and enable paging for the `DetailsView`.

How It Works

The only slight trick in this exercise is the method to disable sorting. Without a `SortExpression`, a column is not sortable.

Try It Out 1908 Creating a Selection List of Keywords

Now, you will improve the page that admins use to create associations between FAQs and keywords by adding a list of keywords. You still won't have the ability to add associations, but you are getting closer.

1. Open `AdminKeyWordsAssociation-1907`, and save it as `AdminKeyWordsAssociation -1908`.

2. In the top-right cell, position the cursor above the `DetailsView` showing the keyword associations. In the Toolbox, double-click on the `ListBox` icon. Open its Smart Tasks panel, click on Choose Data Source, and create a new `SqlDataSource` control that reads the values from the Keywords table.

3. Save your work.

How It Works

In this exercise, you added a `ListBox` and set its source to a `SqlDataSource` control that read values from the Keywords table.

Try It Out 1909 Using Master–Child Controls

In this exercise, you modify the FAQ `GridView` so that it only shows the first 50 characters of the answers and offers a `SELECT` command that the user can click to see the whole answer in a `DetailsView`. We will also add a feature to select for FAQs based on a user pick from keywords.

1. Open your `FaqsAll-1907` page, and save it as `FaqsAll-1909A`. We will start with a layout change. In the content pane, add a table with one rows and one column. Move the current controls (`GridView`, `DetailsView` and `SqlDataSource`) into the left cell. Modify the select command of `SqlDataSource1` control to create a smaller answer field named `FaqAnswerShort` that also concatenates on an ellipsis as shown in the second bar of gray code below. Then change the bound field for the answers from `FaqAnswer` to `FaqAnswerShort`, as shown in the first bar of gray code below.

```
...
    <asp:GridView ID="GridView1" runat="server"
        <Columns>
...
            <asp:BoundField DataField="FaqAnswerShort"
...

    <asp:SqlDataSource ID="SqlDataSource1" runat="server"
...
        SelectCommand="
SELECT [FaqID], [FaqQuestion],
LEFT([FaqAnswer],50)+'...' AS FaqAnswerShort
FROM [FAQs]"
...
```

2. Save and test the page. You should now be seeing only one line per record, without text wrapping (unless there are very long questions in the table).
3. On the `GridView`'s Smart Tasks panel enable Selecting.
4. Add to the page a `DetailsView` control, and configure its data source to a new `SqlDataSource` control that reads the FAQ table. Click the `WHERE` button in the wizard, and set the column to `FaqID`, Source to `Control`, `ControlID` to `GridView1` and be sure to click the Add button, then OK to finish out the wizard. Select the DetailsView, and stretch its right edge out to about 600 px. In the DetailView's Smart Tasks panel, select Edit Fields and make the `FaqAnswer ItemStyle` background equal to the white of the Web palette. Save your work, and test it in the browser.
5. Now we can add the second feature, a user pick of a keyword and the `GridView` contents change to display just FAQs with those keywords. Save your `FaqsAll-1909.aspx` page as `FaqsAll-1909B`. Into the right cell, drag a `ListBox` and enable `AutoPostBack`. Choose as its data source a new source of the type `Database`, and use your existing connection string. Keep the default name `SqlDataSource3`. Display the one field from Keywords in ascending order.

How It Works

In this exercise, the `GridView` is the master control, and the `DetailsView` is the child control. In the `DetailView`'s data source control, there is a `WHERE` clause that limits the record returned to the one that matches the `FaqID` in the parameters. The value in the parameter is automatically set to the `FaqID` of the row that the user clicked on in the `GridView`.

Try It Out 1910 Implementing Templates

Your `DetailsView` in `FaqsAll` looks rather boxy. We can switch those two fields to a single template field that will provide a nicer layout.

1. Open your `FaqsAll-1909` page, and save as `FaqsAll-1910`. Open the `DetailsView` Smart Tasks panel, select Edit Columns, and then remove the existing fields. Instead, add a single template field with the Header Text of `FAQ`, and close the Edit Columns dialog.
2. Back in the `DetailView`'s Smart Tasks panel, select Edit Templates and then select ItemTemplate. From the Toolbox, add a label and sets its Text property to Field Bind to `FaqQuestion` (not two-way). In the `Label1`'s Properties window, expand the Font property and turn on bold. Add another label and set its text to bind to `FaqAnswer`, again, not two-way. Set its Font to italic. Between them, drag from the Toolbox's HTML section a Horizontal Rule the template in edit mode should appear as in Figure 19-2.

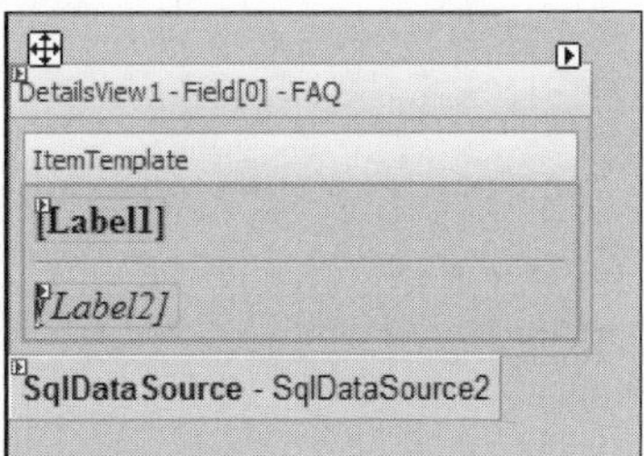

Figure 19-2

3. Save your work, and test it in your browser to see a page similar to the Figure 19-3.

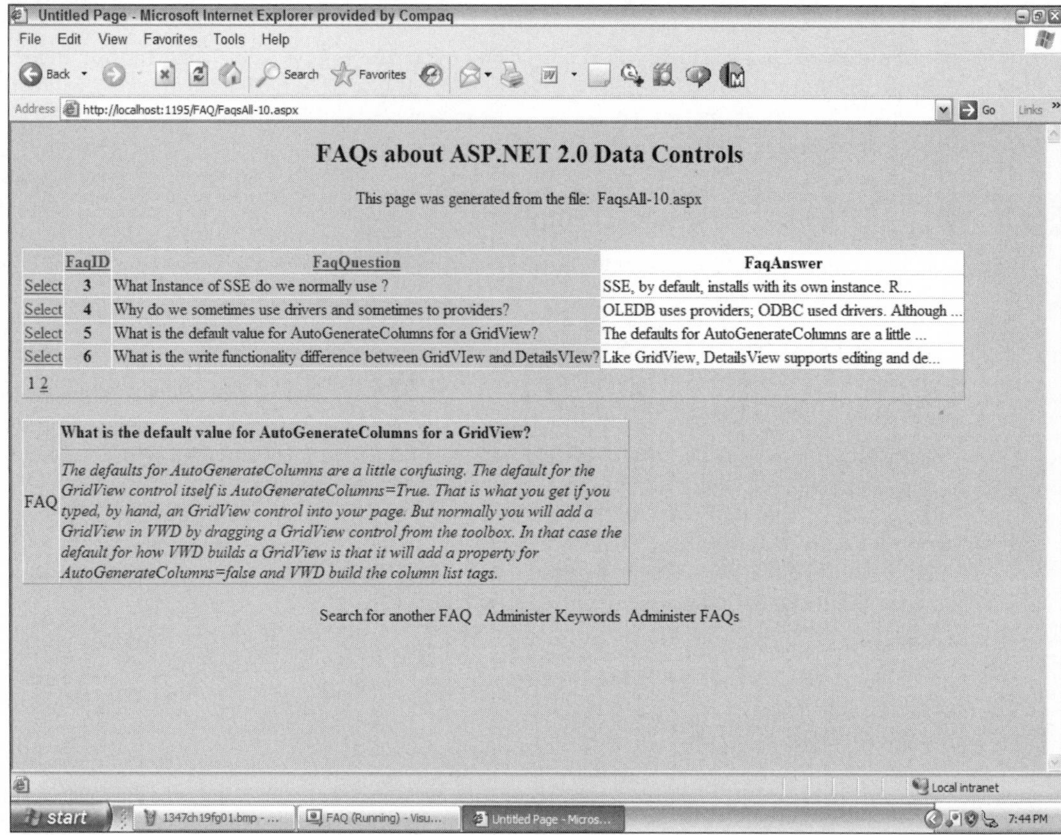

Figure 19-3

How It Works

In this exercise, you converted the `DetailsView` from displaying two fields in bound columns into a single `TemplateField`. The result is that you can do some rearranging for aesthetics and usability.

Try It Out 1911 Adding the Update and Delete of Records

To date you have been reading data. Now, you will create administrative pages to write modifications to FAQs and to edit the FAQ-keyword associations.

1. Create a new page named `AdminFaqsEditor-11A` that uses `MasterPage.master`. Drag to the page the FAQs table from the Database Explorer. On the GridView's Smart Tasks panel, go wild with the enablements by checking on Paging, Sorting, Deleting, and Editing (restrain yourself from enabling Selection).

2. Save and test the page. Try making some small changes to existing FAQs, and then try deleting one. If you want to get back all of the records, you can recopy the MDF from the downloads by right clicking on `App_Data` and selecting Add Existing Item.

3. We can improve the editing interface by making the labels larger so that the author can see more of the text. Save the file as `AdminFaqsEditor-11B`. Open the `GridView`'s Smart Tasks panel and select Edit Columns. Select the `FaqQuestion`, and click "Convert this field to a TemplateField." Repeat this for the `FaqAnswer` field, and click OK.

4. In the Smart Tasks panel, select Edit Templates. Drop down the "Display" list, and select `Column[2] - FaqQuestion's EditItemTemplate`. Select the label, and drag its bottom-right corner to be about 250 px wide and 200 px high (you can watch the size change in the Properties window). While the label is selected, go to the Properties pane and set the wrap to `true`. Repeat all these steps for the `FaqAnswer` but make it around 400 px wide. Save your work as `AdminFaqsEditor-11B`, and test it in your browser.

5. Open your file named `AdminKeyWordsAssociation-1908`, and save it as `AdminKeyWordsAssociation-1911`. Walk through the Configuration Wizard of `SqlDataSource2` (that supports the `DetailsView` of Associations), and select all fields from the `KeywordAssoc` table and turn on the advanced option to generate delete, update, and insert commands. Open the Smart Tasks panel for the DetailsView, and enable Deleting and Editing. Save your page, and test it in the browser by adding a new association.

For now, you will have to identify the FAQ by the `FaqID` number and type the keyword. But we will improve that later.

How It Works

How much simpler can it get? This exercise is an excellent display of how much power and efficiency Microsoft has built into the data controls of ASP.NET 2.0. First, we get editing and deleting by simply setting a check box to true.

In order to make the changes of Steps 3 and 4, we have to recall two facts from the text. First, to modify a mode (such as edit) of a `GridView`, we must work with templates. That capability is not in the default `BoundField` type of column. But that conversion is a single click. Second, we have to find the right template to edit. As you saw in the display list of Edit Templates, there are five templates per column, so you have to pick carefully.

Try It Out 1912 Inserting New Records

You will now improve the last exercise to enable the creation of new FAQs. You also create a page to do the same for keywords and for keyword associations.

1. Open `AdminFaqsEditor-11B`, and save it as `AdminFaqsEditor-12`. Drag to the bottom of the page a `DetailsView`, and set it to use the same data source control as the `GridView`. Drag the right side of the `DetailsView` out until it is about 700 px wide. While it is selected, go to the properties pane and set the `DefaultMode` to Insert. On its Smart Tasks panel, enable inserting and then click on Edit Fields. You don't want the `FaqID` field to appear in the DetailsView (that is autogenerated), so open the `DetailsView`'s Smart Tasks panel, go to edit fields, and click on Refresh Schema. Turn off Auogenerate Fields, and add just the `FaqQuestion` and `FaqAnswer` fields. Also add a command field of the type Insert, New, Cancel. Click OK and, if prompted, accept the regeneration of the `DetailsView` fields.

2. Now, you will set up the capability to edit, delete, and create keywords. Open `AdminKeywordsEditor-05`, and change to `AdminKeywordsEditor-12`. Open the `SqlDataSource1`'s Smart Tasks panel, and walk through the wizard. At the step to configure

the select statement, choose Specify Columns from a table or view. Select to use the Keywords table, select the one field of keywords, click the advanced button, and turn on Generate Insert... Statements. Also click on the Order By button, and set the order to Keyword Ascending. Click Next and Finish, accepting VWD's offer to refresh the `GridView` and `DetailsView`.

3. Now select the `GridView`, and enable sorting, paging, editing and deleting. Select the `DetailsView`, and enable inserting. Then in the properties pane set its `DefaultMode` to Insert. Save your work, and test it by adding a new keyword.
4. Last, you will give the administrators a tool to add new keyword associations. Open `AdminKeyWordsAssociation-1911`, and save it as `AdminKeyWordsAssociation-1912`. Select the `DetailsView` at the bottom right, and open its Smart Tasks panel. Enable inserting. In the properties pane, set its default mode to insert. Save your work, and test it.

At this point, the administrator must type in the FAQ ID number and keyword, but we will improve that shortly.

Try It Out 1913 Validating

You should not allow administrators to save a FAQ that does not have some text in both the `FaqQuestion` and `FaqAnswer`.

1. Open your `AdminsFaqsEditor-1912`, and save it as `AdminsFaqsEditor-1913`. For the `GridView`, select Edit Templates and select the template named `FaqQuestionEditItemTemplate`. From the Toolbox, drag to the template a `RequiredFieldValidator`, and in the Properties pane set its `ControlToValidate="Textbox1"`. Set its text to "The Question Field may not be empty" and set its Error message to "Please check that the Question field has a question." Repeat this for the `FaqAnswer` template column, setting its control to validate to `TextBox2` and using similar values for the text and error message. End template editing.
2. Below the `GridView`, place a `ValidationSummary` control. Save the page and test it by attempting to change a FAQ into an empty question or empty answer or both.

How It Works

To use validation controls on a `GridView` or `DetailsView`, the columns or fields must be templated. That was already done in a prior step of the chapter. The validation control must be placed in the same template as the control that it will validate. An optional summary can be placed on the page. If there is a validation failure, then the Text property value will appear at the location of the validation control, and the `ErrorMessage` property value will appear in the `Validation Summary` control.

Try It Out 1914 Using the Object Data Source

You want to know what users think of your FAQs. You will add a feedback option of radio buttons at the bottom of the FAQ page and then keep a record in a table named Scores. You will connect to the Scores table through a data object. You will start by making the administrator's page to view the results (a few records are in the table as downloaded). Then you will add to `the FaqAll.aspx` page the option for users to leave a rating.

1. Start by creating the `DataSet` object. Right-click on the root of your site, and select Add New Item of the type DataSet. Name it `Scores`, and accept the option to create it in a new `App_Code` folder. In the TableAdaptor Wizard, select the connection string `FaqDatabaseConnectionString1(web.config)`, which you have been using thus far in the chapter. Select the option to use `SqlStatements`, and click Next. When asked to enter a SQL Statement, click on the Query Builder. Add the Scores table, and select all of the columns. Click on Execute Query to test it. Click OK and then Next to accept the SQL statement that the Query Builder created. Accept all three options in the next page of the wizard: Fill a Data Table, Return a DataTable, and Create methods for updates. Accept the default names. VWD will finish the wizard and leave you with a `DataSet` named scores that includes a table adapter with `Fill` and `GetData` methods.

2. Create a page named `AdminScores-1914A`. Drag to the page a `GridView`, and configure its data source to a new data source. Select the `Object` type, and leave its name as `ObjectDataSource1`. Select the only business object, `ScoresTableAdaptor.ScoresTableAdaptor` and click Next. In the next page, under the Select Tab, choose the only method: `GetData()` and click Finish. On the `GridView`, enable paging and sorting. Save the page and run a test.

3. It would be more useful to see an average score. Start back in the `Scores DataSet`. Right-click on the title bar of Scores, and select Add, then Query. Select Use SQL Statements. Click the Next button, and select the Select type to return rows. Click on the Query Builder button, and perform the following steps:

    a. Add the Scores table and select just the `FaqID` and `Score`. In the pane of table, right-click and select Add Group By.

    b. In the query grid below, set the Score Group By to `Average`. Set the Score Alias to `ScoreAvg`. Click Execute SQL if you want to test it.

    c. In the table's pane, right-click and add the table named `Faqs`. Select the `FaqQuestion` and `FaqAnswer` fields. Set their aliases to `FaqQuestionShort` and `FaqAnswerShort`. Set the `SortType` to `Ascending` for `FaqID`.

    d. Modify the `SELECT` portion of the SQL expression in the gray lines that follow:

```
SELECT
 Scores.FAQID,
 AVG(Scores.Score) AS ScoreAvg,
 LEFT(FAQs.FaqQuestion.50) AS FaqQuestionShort,
 LEFT(FAQs.FaqAnswer,50) AS FaqAnswerShort
FROM         Scores INNER JOIN FAQs ON Scores.FAQID = FAQs.FaqID
GROUP BY Scores.FAQID, FAQs.FaqQuestion, FAQs.FaqAnswer
ORDER BY Scores.FAQID
```

    e. Click the Test button and click Finish. Select the resulting method (FillBy...) and in the properties pane, change its `FillMethodName` to `FillScoresAverage` and its `Get MethodName` to `GetScoresAverage`. Save your work, and close the `Scores.XSD` window.

4. Now we will show the averages to the Admins. Open `AdminScores-1914-A.aspx`, and save it as `AdminScores-1914-B.aspx`. To the top of the page, add a new `GridView`. Configure it for it a new data source of the object type that uses the `ScoresTableAdaptors.ScoresTableAdaptor`. In the Select tab, choose the method named `GetScoresAverage()` and click Finish. Save the page and test it in your browser.

In the Try It Out on events, we will build add a way for users to provide a score.

Try It Out 1915 Establishing Site Navigation Using an XML File

Because you will not create more pages, you can write up our site map and add a navigation tool to the master page.

1. Add an existing item to the root of your site, and browse to your downloads. In the Chapter 19 folder, find the `Web.Sitemap` and import (open) it. Open the file, and see that a site map that is valid is already set up — if you have followed the steps of this chapter.
2. Open `MasterPage.master` and from the Toolbox drag a `Menu` control to the bottom of the page. In the `Menu` control's Configure `DataSource`, select New and a data source of `SiteMap`. While the menu is still selected, go to the Properties window and set its `Disappear` property to `1000` and its orientation to horizontal.
3. Save your work.

How It Works

The hard part of a navigation system is creating the `Web.Sitemap`. As we mentioned in Chapter 15, do a Web search and see if third-party tools are available. For this study, we have created it for you.

Try It Out 1916 Caching

Prior to adding caching, you should consider the frequency of change of data. The FAQs and keywords will not change frequently, so you should cache them. The score will change frequently, so you will get less benefit from that cache. Because you are using SQL Server, you can go directly to the most efficient type of caching: `SqlNotification`.

1. Open your `FaqsAll-1910` file, and save it as `FaqsAll-1916`. Select `SqlDataSource1`, and set three properties:

```
EnableCaching=true
CacheDuration=Infinite
SqlCacheDependency="CommandNotification"
```

2. Repeat for the `SqlDataSource2`.
3. Save your work.

Try It Out 1917 Creating Events

In this exercise we will make two changes to the site. First, we will add a way for users to give a score to a FAQ. Second, we will enable a quicker way for administrators to create an association between a FAQ and a keyword.

1. Open the page named `FaqsAll-1910`, and save it as `FaqsAll-1917`. Add to the bottom of the page a radio button. Edit the Items List, and add an item with value set to `1` and the text to `1 - Least useful`. Repeat this for numbers `2` through `5`, with `5` being most useful. Set item `3` to selected, disable `AutoPostBack` for the list, and in the properties pane set the repeat direction to horizontal.

2. Add a `SqlDataSource` control that uses the `FaqDatabaseConnectionString1` and reads all of the columns from the `Scores` table.

3. Click Advanced and enable the generation of insert, update and delete statements. Click OK, Next, and Finish. In Source view, you can delete the tags for selecting, updating, and deleting. Add control parameters for inserting, as follows.

```
<asp:SqlDataSource ID="SqlDataSource3" runat="server"
 ConnectionString="<%$ ConnectionStrings:FaqDatabaseConnectionString1 %>"
  InsertCommand="
            INSERT INTO [Scores]
            ([FAQID], [Score])
            VALUES (@FAQID, @Score)">
 <InsertParameters>
        <asp:ControlParameter Name=FaqID
               ControlID=GridView1 Type=Int32 DefaultValue="7"  />
        <asp:ControlParameter Name=Score
               ControlID=RadioButtonList1 Type=Int32 DefaultValue="3" />
</InsertParameters>
</asp:SqlDataSource>
```

4. Add to the page a `Button` control, and set its text to `Submit Score`. Create an event handler for its `Click` event, and add the following line of code. Save the page, and test it by giving several scores to a FAQ. Open the `AdminScores` page to see the results.

```
<script runat="server">
Protected Sub Button1_Click(ByVal sender As Object, ByVal e As System.EventArgs)
        SqlDataSource3.Insert()
End Sub
</script>
```

5. Now, we will create a function the administrators can use to create a new keyword association. Open `KeyWordsAssociation-1912.aspx`, and save it as `KeyWordsAssociation-1917.aspx`. Select `SqlDataSource2` for the keywords association `DetailsView`, open its Smart Tasks panel, and configure its data source to specify all columns from the `KeywordAssoc` table. Select all fields, and in Advanced, enable generation of write statements. Finish the wizard and then modify the control in source code as follows to delete the unneeded commands and to change the insert parameters to be of the control type.

```
<asp:SqlDataSource ID="SqlDataSource2" runat="server"
 ConnectionString="<%$ ConnectionStrings:FaqDatabaseConnectionString1 %>"
```

```
    InsertCommand="
           INSERT INTO [KeywordAssoc]
           ([FaqID], [Keyword])
           VALUES (@FaqID, @Keyword)">
           <InsertParameters>
                  <asp:ControlParameter Name="Keyword"
                       ControlID="ListBox1"
                       Type="String" />
                  <asp:ControlParameter Name="FaqID"
                       ControlID="GridView2"
                       Type="int32" />
           </InsertParameters>
  </asp:SqlDataSource>
```

6. Save and test the page.

Try It Out 1918 Adding a Search Page

Now you will add a new page that does not introduce new concepts but will be very useful for your users: a way to search for all FAQs that are associated with a given keyword.

1. Using the master page, create a page named `FaqsSearch`.

```
<asp:SqlDataSource ID="SqlDataSource2"
  runat="server"
  ConnectionString="<%$ ConnectionStrings:FaqDatabaseConnectionString1 %>"
  SelectCommand="
    SELECT KeywordAssoc.Keyword, FAQs.FaqQuestion, FAQs.FaqAnswer
    FROM FAQs
    INNER JOIN KeywordAssoc ON FAQs.FaqID = KeywordAssoc.FaqID
    WHERE KeyWordAssoc.Keyword = @Keyword
    ORDER BY FAQs.FaqQuestion">
  <SelectParameters>
    <asp:ControlParameter Name="Keyword" ControlID="ListBox1" />
  </SelectParameters>
</asp:SqlDataSource>
```

Try It Out 1919 Wrapping Up and Deploying

We will finish with a few clean-up tasks and reminders for deployment.

1. Create a page named `Default.aspx`, using the master page. Add to the page two hyperlinks, one for the highest version of your `FaqsAll` page and one for the `FaqsSearch` page. Also, add a note that they can go to other pages using the tree below (which will show up from the `MasterPage`).

2. Staying with the default page, let's display one FAQ selected randomly from the collection. Add a `DetailsView` that uses a `SqlDataSource` control that reads all fields from the `FAQs` table. Resize the `DetailsView` to show all of the question and answer. Now, in Source view, modify the `SelectCommand` as follows. Save your work, and test it.

```
SelectCommand="
 SELECT TOP 1
       [FaqID],
       [FaqQuestion],
       [FaqAnswer]
from (
         select
              FAQID,
              FaqQuestion,
              FaqAnswer,
              RAND() as MyRandom
         from FAQs
         ORDER BY [MyRandom] ASC
    )">

SelectCommand="
SELECT TOP 1
[FaqID], [FaqQuestion], [FaqAnswer], RAND() as MyRandom
FROM [FAQs]
ORDER BY [MyRandom] ASC">
```

3. You may want to make a copy of the site for backup and then in the working version delete the early version of files. Change the names of the final versions by deleting the step names at the end of the files. Also, change their names in the listings of the `Web.sitemap`.
4. All of your data is stored in an MDF file, except for the list of FAQ authors in an MDB file. This MDB file is not used for any other purpose than to demonstrate the `AccessDataSource` control; you can delete this file and the page named `FaqAuthors-1902`.
5. When you deploy the site, encrypt the connection strings on the production server.
    a. Click on the Start menu, choose Run, type `cmd`, and then click OK. Change your directory to:

```
C:\WINDOWS\Microsoft.net\Framework\v2.0.50727
```

    b. Then type the following line, and press Enter:

```
aspnet_regiis -pef connectionStrings c:\Websites\FAQ
```

    c. Close the command line window and switch back to VWD to look at `web.config`. You will be prompted to refresh the page because the file was changed outside VWD. The result is a series of encryption tags and then a long `CipherValue` tag.
6. Save your work.

Finally, you may want to make some changes to the color schemes to fit in with your site.

How It Works

The only item of interest here is the SQL statement used to randomly select one FAQ to display.

Summary

Check your watch to get an idea of how long it took to create this site. Each of the topics in this section was covered in prior chapters. On each page, we followed the general pattern of adding data source controls and data-bound controls. Using the control's Smart Tasks panels, you were able to invoke wizards to walk you through most of the setup. In other cases, you turned to the Properties pane to change individual settings. And, in a few cases, you went down to the Source view of VWD to make changes by hand.

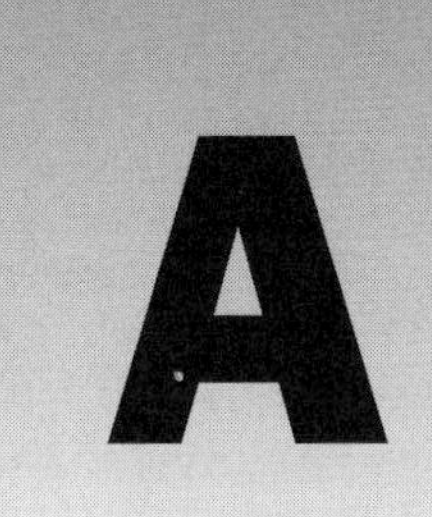

A Short and Practical Introduction to SQL Statements

Structured Query Language (SQL) is the most universal means to request data from a database. Almost every front end can send a SQL statement to a data source, and almost every kind of database can understand a SQL command. This book focuses on Microsoft ASP.NET 2.0 pages sending SQL statements from the data source controls. The same statements can be sent from Visual Basic, C++, Oracle front ends, Cold Fusion, Access, and WebSphere. Because SQL is the near-universal language for requesting a set of data, you can learn one syntax and be able to operate in dozens of environments.

SQL is primarily a declarative language, not a procedural language. Consider an example of getting a set of all the orders placed to you by your customer the Acme Company. In a procedural language, you would write several lines of code to move to the first record in the Orders table and open it. Then you would write more lines of code that would check to see if the customer for that order was Acme. If yes, you would copy the record into the results set. Then, another line of code would move you to the next record and restart the checking process. SQL statements work differently. You create one statement that describes what you want back and send that to the data source. How the database management system gets the result set is of no interest to us; that is completely internal and proprietary to that software vendor. After a few hundred milliseconds, you get back the result set. Because of this procedural model, you will generally send just a single SQL statement to the data source to achieve most objectives.

Having noted that SQL is declarative, it is possible to write multiple lines of SQL statements into a structure called a stored procedure (SPROC) that can include procedural commands such as looping and conditionals. SPROCs are used in more complex scenarios, where the declarative nature of the language is augmented with some simple procedural flow.

SQL is a standard for a language, not a software product. You can type a SQL statement any place that can hold text; there is no need for a development environment or editor. Having said that, there are tools to help you build SQL statements. Perhaps the most well known is the Query Builder in Access. Using this drag-and-drop interface, you can add fields, set criteria, and create alias names for fields. In this Access Query Builder interface, you can click through View⇨SQL, and you can see how Access has converted the GUI into the text of a SQL statement. If you are comfortable creating queries in the Access query builder, then this is a great way to learn the syntax. VWD will also build SQL statements for you. For example, when you drag and drop fields from the database explorer to the page, VWD writes SQL statements into several properties of the nascent data source control.

There is a consortium that sets the standards for SQL syntax, but many data source vendors have added various extensions to the language, and these are generally incompatible. Fortunately, these variations are minor, easy to learn, and not a factor for our basic discussion in this section. Microsoft uses a variation of the Data Manipulation Language (DML) called Transaction-SQL (T-SQL), which adds support for declared variables, transaction control, error handling, and row processing to the consortium's SQL functions. All of the statements in this presentation have been tested in Microsoft SQL Server Express (the lighter-weight version of SQL Server 2005).

The SQL consortium defines three broad areas of the language:

- The Data Definition Language (DDL) sets standards for SQL statements that create databases, tables, columns, and other elements of the schema.
- The Data Manipulation Language (DML) defines how to read and write to the data.
- The Data Control Language (DCL) outlines the statements for security schemes to determine who can perform what actions on the data.

This presentation concerns only the DML.

Try It Out SQL SELECT Statement Tester

This page allows you to test SQL `SELECT` statements against the Northwind database. Download the page from the book's Web site or type it as follows. On screen, the gray area gives you pretyped SQL `SELECT` statements to try. The green area is where you can drag and drop a statement and run it. The yellow area is for results. You can find the page in the downloads. The source code follows, along with some variations in the following paragraphs.

```
<%@ Page Language="VB" %>
<!DOCTYPE html PUBLIC "-//W3C//DTD XHTML 1.0 Transitional//EN"
"http://www.w3.org/TR/xhtml1/DTD/xhtml1-transitional.dtd">
<script runat="server">
    Sub Page_Load(ByVal sender As Object, ByVal e As System.EventArgs)
        SelectCommandInUse.Text = SqlDataSource1.SelectCommand
    End Sub

    Sub Button1_Click(ByVal sender As Object, ByVal e As System.EventArgs)
        SqlDataSource1.SelectCommand = SqlStatementNew.Text
        SelectCommandInUse.Text = SqlDataSource1.SelectCommand
        SqlStatementNew.Text = ""
    End Sub
```

```
</script>

<html xmlns="http://www.w3.org/1999/xhtml" >
<head runat="server">
    <title>Untitled Page</title>
</head>
<body>
<form id="form1" runat="server">
<div>
<h2>Appendix A - Short and Practical Introduction to SQL Statements </h2>
<table>
    <tr>
        <td style="width: 470px">
        <h3>From Beginning ASP.NET 2.0 and Databases<br />
            <em>by John Kauffman and Bradley Millington</em><br />
            ISBN ##781347</h3></td>
        <td style="width: 459px">
            <span style="color: #ff0033">
            This is a page for developer education and testing.
            In a deployed page never use in a SQL statement any text
            entered by users (danger of SQL injection attack).
            Instead allow the users to select from a list or radio buttons.<br />
            </span></td></tr>
</table>
<br />
<table bordercolor="black">
    <tr>
        <td bgcolor="#ccffff" valign="top" style="width:300px; height: 40px;">
            Enter a new SQL statement for the SelectCommand.<br />
            You can also  select, drag and drop statements
   from the gray region at right.</td>
        <td bgcolor="#ccffff" style="width: 542px; height: 40px;"
            align="center" valign="top">
            <asp:TextBox ID="SqlStatementNew" Runat="server"
                Width="384px" Height="200px"
                TextMode="MultiLine"
                Rows="5"></asp:TextBox><br />
            <br />
            <asp:Button ID="Button1" Runat="server"
                Text="Submit New statement"
                OnClick="Button1_Click" />
             <br /></td>
        <td style="width: 700px" valign="top"
            align="left" rowspan="4"
            bordercolor="black" bgcolor="silver">
            Try these SQL statements for the Northwind database:<br />
            <br />
            <span style="font-family: Courier New">
                SELECT FirstName,LastName FROM Employees<br /><br />
                SELECT EmployeeID FROM Employees<br /><br />
                SELECT EmployeeID,FirstName,LastName FROM Employees<br /><br />
                SELECT<br />  EmployeeID,   
                    FirstName,   LastName<br />
                        FROM Employees<br /><br />
                SELECT CategoryName,CategorySales
```

```
            FROM [Category Sales for 1997]<br /><br />
        SELECT * FROM Employees<br /><br />
        SELECT EmployeeID AS 'Associate Number',
                LastName FROM Employees<br /><br />
        SELECT OrderID, RIGHT(OrderId,3)
            AS 'ShortID' FROM Orders
        SELECT OrderID, YEAR(OrderDate) FROM Orders<br /><br />
        SELECT OrderID, OrderDate, CustomerID FROM Orders
            WHERE CustomerID = 'CHOPS'<br /><br />
        SELECT OrderID, OrderDate, CustomerID FROM Orders
            WHERE OrderID &gt;= 10500<br /><br />
        SELECT OrderID, OrderDate, CustomerID FROM Orders
            WHERE OrderDate='11/20/1997'<br /><br />
        SELECT OrderID, OrderDate, CustomerID FROM Orders
            WHERE OrderDate BETWEEN '1/15/1998'
            AND '1/31/1998'<br /><br />
        SELECT OrderID, OrderDate, CustomerID FROM Orders
            WHERE YEAR(OrderDate)&lt;1998<br /><br />
        SELECT OrderID, OrderDate, CustomerID AS 'Client'
            FROM Orders WHERE CustomerID = 'chops'<br /><br />
            ***Wrong Syntax:<br />
        SELECT OrderID, OrderDate, CustomerID AS 'Client'
            FROM Orders WHERE Client = 'chops'<br /><br />
        SELECT CustomerID, CompanyName FROM Customers
            WHERE CompanyName LIKE 'C%'<br /><br />
        SELECT CustomerID, OrderDate FROM Orders
            WHERE CustomerID='CHOPS' AND YEAR(OrderDate)=1997<br /><br />
        SELECT CustomerID, OrderDate FROM Orders
            WHERE CustomerID='CHOPS' OR YEAR(OrderDate)=1997<br /><br />
        SELECT OrderID, OrderDate FROM Orders
            WHERE NOT Year(OrderDate)= 1997<br /><br />
        SELECT OrderID, OrderDate, CustomerID
            FROM Orders ORDER BY CustomerID ASC<br /><br />
        SELECT OrderID, OrderDate, CustomerID
            FROM Orders ORDER BY OrderDate DESC<br /><br />
        SELECT OrderID, OrderDate, CustomerID
            FROM Orders ORDER BY CustomerID ASC, OrderDate DESC<br /><br />
        SELECT DISTINCT Country FROM Customers <br /><br />
        SELECT TOP 10 ProductID, UnitPrice FROM Products<br /><br />
        SELECT TOP 10 ProductID, UnitPrice
            FROM Products ORDER BY UnitPrice DESC
        </span></td></tr>
<tr>
    <td bgcolor="#ffffcc"
        valign="bottom"
        style="width:300px" height="100px" ><br />
        SelectCommand<br />
        in use below<br /></td>
    <td bgcolor="yellow"
        valign="bottom"
        height="100px" style="width: 542px">
        <asp:Label ID="SelectCommandInUse" Runat="server"
            Width="375px"></asp:Label></td></tr>
<tr>
    <td bgcolor="#ffffcc"
        valign="top" style="width: 300px"><br />
```

```
                Results:</td>
            <td bgcolor="#ffffcc" style="width: 542px" valign="top"><br />
                <asp:GridView ID="GridView1" Runat="server"
                    DataSourceID="SqlDataSource1">
                </asp:GridView></td></tr>
        <tr>
            <td valign="top" height="1000" style="width: 300px"></td>
            <td style="width: 542px" valign="top"></td>
           <td style="width: 700px" valign="top"
align="left" rowspan="1"></td></tr>
    </table>
    <asp:SqlDataSource ID="SqlDataSource1" Runat="server"
        ConnectionString= "<%$ connectionStrings:MdfNorthwind %>"
        SelectCommand = "SELECT OrderID,CustomerID,OrderDate FROM Orders">
    </asp:SqlDataSource>
</div></form></body></html>
```

If you have not set up a connection string in `web.config`, as in Chapter 3 Exercise 2, you can use this code for the `SqlDataSource`:

```
<asp:SqlDataSource ID="SqlDataSource1" runat="server"
         ConnectionString="Data Source=.\SQLEXPRESS;
         AttachDbFilename=|DataDirectory|\Northwind.mdf;
         Integrated Security=True;
         User Instance=True"
         ProviderName="System.Data.SqlClient"
         SelectCommand = "SELECT OrderID,CustomerID,OrderDate FROM Orders">
</asp:SqlDataSource>
```

Following is the script in C#:

```
<%@ Page Language="C#" %>
<!DOCTYPE html PUBLIC "-//W3C//DTD XHTML 1.1//EN"
"http://www.w3.org/TR/xhtml11/DTD/xhtml11.dtd">
<script runat="server">
    void Page_Load(Object sender, EventArgs e)
        {SelectCommandInUse.Text = SqlDataSource1.SelectCommand;
        }
    void Button1_Click(Object sender, EventArgs e)
        {SqlDataSource1.SelectCommand = SqlStatementNew.Text;
        SelectCommandInUse.Text = SqlDataSource1.SelectCommand;
        SqlStatementNew.Text = "";
        }
</script>
```

How It Works

On the first load, the `SqlDataSource` uses the `SELECT` statement that is hard-coded in the page. The user can see the SQL statement that was used in the yellow row and the results in the `GridView` in the beige area. At the top of the page is a textbox in which you can type SQL statements. You can also select a SQL statement from the gray area and drag that to the white SQL Statement box. In either case, when the Submit New Statement button is clicked, the statement in the textbox is set as the new `SelectCommand` of the `SqlDataSource`, and the page is refreshed.

Note that ASP.NET 2.0 uses separate commands for reading (`SELECT`) and writing or deleting (`INSERT`, `UPDATE`, and `DELETE`). This page sends only the typed SQL statement to the `SELECT` command, so data modifying commands such as `UPDATE` will not work.

Overall Syntax

The syntax of a SQL statement is designed to be parallel to a spoken English request for data. Common nouns and verbs are used to make a sentence-like statement in plain text. To start, here are some simple rules for typing the statement. Examples (partial code) follow each rule.

- ❑ Generally, SQL statement keywords are in all uppercase, whereas names of database objects (fields, tables) are in mixed case. Keywords in SQL aren't case-sensitive.

```
SELECT FirstName,LastName FROM Employees
```

- ❑ Spaces must surround keywords in the statement.

```
SELECT EmployeeID FROM Employees
```

- ❑ An optional semicolon signifies the end of a SQL statement.

```
SELECT EmployeeID,FirstName,LastName FROM Employees;
```

- ❑ Lists of items are separated by commas (spaces after commas are optional).

```
SELECT EmployeeID,FirstName,LastName FROM Employees
SELECT EmployeeID, FirstName, LastName FROM Employees
```

- ❑ Extra returns, tabs, and spaces (collectively called white space) are ignored. They can be used liberally to make the statement more readable to the human eye.

```
SELECT
  EmployeeID, FirstName, LastName
         FROM Employees
```

- ❑ If there is any ambiguity about names of fields that are in more than one table, use the table name followed by a period and the field name.

```
SELECT Employees.EmployeeID, Orders.EmployeeID
```

Most applications require the entire statement to be in double quotation marks because it will be a string that is handed off to the data source. For example, the `SelectCommand` used in ASP.NET 2.0 requires the statement to be in double quotation marks. However, when entering a SQL statement into the textbox of a property window, you do not need the double quotation marks because VWD will add them for you.

Objects in the database, such as field names, table names, views, and stored procedures (SPROCs), can be referred to directly by name. They should not be in quotes. The database will find the correct object from the schema. However, if the object name contains a space, there must be a designation that sets off the entire name. Depending on the provider, place the space-containing object name in square brackets, `[My Spacey Object Name]`, or in quotation marks, `'My Spacey Object Name'`.

When presenting values, such as a string to be matched or a new number to be added to a field, SQL has three rules. Note that these apply to values such as `Abraham`, not to object names such as a column `FirstName`.

- Literal strings are enclosed in single quotation marks, as are dates.

```
UPDATE FirstName VALUES('Abraham')
UPDATE DateBirth VALUES('01/01/2000')
```

- Numbers and Booleans do not need quotation marks.

```
UPDATE Price VALUES(2.34)
UPDATE Member VALUES(True)
```

- Values may be substituted from a parameters collection, in which case the syntax varies with the front end, provider, and database vendor. Some examples used in versions of ASP follow:

```
UPDATE Price VALUE(@PriceTextBox) WHERE ItemID=@DropDownListSelection)
INSERT INTO Authors (ID, Name, Address) VALUES (?, ?, ?)
```

For some providers, there is no naming of parameters; rather, they must appear in the correct order, and they are read into the argument from first to last.

Retrieving Columns of Data

The basic command to retrieve data is `SELECT`, followed by the columns desired and then the keyword `FROM` and the name of the table.

```
SELECT EmployeeID, FirstName, LastName FROM Employees
```

Records can be retrieved from Views, Queries, or SPROCs in the same manner:

```
SELECT CategoryName,CategorySales FROM [Category Sales for 1997]
```

If an object's name has a space in it, enclose the entire name in brackets, as follows. Note that this particular example does not work for the `Northwind` sample database, because these are not real field names.

```
SELECT [Order ID], [Order Date] FROM [Order Details]
```

If you want all of the columns, you can use the wildcard `*` instead of a list of columns.

```
SELECT * FROM Employees
```

You can create an alias, or renaming, of columns as follows. Then, in your front end, you must refer to the column by its alias.

```
SELECT EmployeeID AS 'Associate Number', LastName FROM Employees
```

Most databases support a set of functions that can be used to modify data in columns. Here is where you see large variability among vendors of databases because there is no mention of these functions in the SQL standards. Note that functions with the same name can have subtle differences between vendors. The following will return just the last three digits of the `EmployeeID` data from Microsoft products. The second example extracts the year data from the `OrderDate` field that contains time, day, month, and year.

```
SELECT OrderID, RIGHT(OrderId,3) AS 'ShortID' FROM Orders
SELECT OrderID, YEAR(OrderDate) FROM Orders
```

Limiting the Set of Records

Frequently, you won't want all of the possible records to be included in the answer set. A `WHERE` clause can be appended to the statement followed by an expression.

```
SELECT OrderID, OrderDate, CustomerID FROM Orders WHERE CustomerID =  'CHOPS'
SELECT OrderID, OrderDate, CustomerID FROM Orders WHERE OrderID >=  10500
SELECT OrderID, OrderDate, CustomerID FROM Orders WHERE OrderDate='11/20/1997'
```

SQL supports the `BETWEEN ... AND` keywords, as follows:

```
SELECT OrderID, OrderDate, CustomerID FROM Orders
  WHERE CustomerID BETWEEN '1/15/1998' AND '1/31/1998'
```

A function can be used in the `WHERE` clause:

```
SELECT OrderID, OrderDate, CustomerID FROM Orders WHERE YEAR(OrderDate)<1998
```

If a column is given an alias with `AS` and you use that column in a `WHERE` clause, you must refer to the column with its original name, not the alias.

```
SELECT OrderID, OrderDate, CustomerID AS 'Client' FROM Orders
  WHERE CustomerID = 'chops'

***Wrong Syntax (a common mistake):
SELECT OrderID, OrderDate, CustomerID AS 'Client' FROM Orders
  WHERE Client = 'chops'
```

SQL supports an option to match more than one target pattern in a string using `LIKE` and wildcard(s). The percent (`%`) wildcard represents any number of characters. The underscore (_) represents a single leading character. To see all of the customers whose names begin with the letter C, you use the following:

```
SELECT CustomerID, CustomerName FROM Customers WHERE CustomerName LIKE 'C%'
```

Multiple expressions can be included in the `WHERE` clause using the logical operators `AND`, `OR`, and `NOT`. The following example gives only orders placed by the customer coded `CHOPS` during 1997.

```
SELECT CustomerCode, OrderDate FROM Orders
  WHERE CustomerID='CHOPS' AND YEAR(OrderDate)=1997
```

The following example gives all of the orders from CHOPS in all years, as well as all the orders placed (by everyone) in 1997:

```
SELECT CustomerCode, OrderDate FROM Orders
  WHERE CustomerID='CHOPS' OR YEAR(OrderDate)=1997
```

The NOT keyword reverses the result of a logical expression. A list of orders but without the orders of 1997 follows:

```
SELECT OrderID, OrderDate FROM Orders WHERE NOT Year(OrderDate) = 1997
```

Ordering the Records

The set of records is ordered. By default, it will be ordered by the primary key of the table. You can override the order by appending an ORDER BY clause (after the WHERE clause, if used) followed by ASC for ascending (the default) and DESC for descending.

```
SELECT OrderID, OrderDate, CustomerID FROM Orders ORDER BY CustomerID ASC
SELECT OrderID, OrderDate, CustomerID FROM Orders ORDER BY OrderDate DESC
```

A tie in the order is broken by specifying a second order column. The following example lists orders starting with the lowest CustomerID. For the records with the same CustomerID, the presentation is from latest to earliest.

```
SELECT OrderID, OrderDate, CustomerID FROM Orders
  ORDER BY CustomerID ASC, OrderDate DESC
```

Distinct and Top

You can eliminate repeats in a results set by using the DISTINCT keyword, as follows. This technique is particularly useful when making a data set of choices for a list to present to the user, such as states or customers.

```
SELECT DISTINCT Country FROM Customers
```

Another option is to limit the number of results in a set according to a criterion by using the TOP keyword. For example, the most expensive items can be obtained by the following:

```
SELECT TOP 10 ProductID, UnitPrice FROM Products
```

Although an ORDER BY clause is not required, it is generally used as in the following example:

```
SELECT TOP 10 ProductID, UnitPrice FROM Products ORDER BY UnitPrice DESC
```

Changing Data

SQL supports three basic commands for changing data. INSERT INTO adds a new record and can optionally stock its fields with data. The first example creates a record and fills it with data that is hard-coded. The second uses ASP.NET-specific syntax to create a new record and fills it with data that comes from a parameter collection. Note that the values list must be in the same order as the columns list.

```
INSERT INTO Employees (FirstName, LastName) VALUES ('Abraham','Lincoln')
INSERT INTO Employees (FirstName, LastName) VALUES (@FirstName,@LastName)
```

UPDATE changes values in an existing record. Be careful to include a WHERE clause that identifies the one record to change, as in the first line in the following example. If you want to update a value in all records where it appears, you can use the second syntax. The third replaces a value with a NULL. The fourth example shows updating all records in the table.

```
UPDATE Employees SET Country = 'America' WHERE LastName = 'Davalio'
UPDATE Employees SET Country = 'America' WHERE Country = 'USA'
UPDATE Employees SET Country = NULL WHERE Country = 'America'
UPDATE Employees SET Country = 'United Nations'
```

Keep in mind when inserting or updating that some fields may automatically be given values from the database, such as an automatic numbering for the ID field. Trying to add or change a value for an ID field generally throws an error.

DELETE removes an entire record. The first case, rarely used, eliminates all records from a table. The second, more common, case eliminates only one record, assuming that the ID field is unique (a primary key). The third example eliminates a group of records. Use caution when experimenting with these statements; make a copy of your database for testing purposes to try these commands.

```
DELETE FROM Orders
DELETE FROM Orders WHERE OrderID = 10500
DELETE FROM Orders WHERE Year(OrderDate) = 1997
```

As with updating, constraints and built-in behavior may prevent you from carrying out a DELETE. If you are trying to delete a record that is a foreign key for another table, you will likely invoke an error. For example, deleting the customer CHOPS would leave all of their orders in limbo, no longer connected to a customer.

Joins

Last, we will cover a very basic example of returning a set of records that display values from more than one table via relationships. If you want a results set of all the orders and you want to show both the order date (from the Orders table) and the customer's telephone number (from the Customers table), you have a problem because they are in two different tables. The solution is to use a join, as in the following example:

```
SELECT Orders.OrderDate, Customers.Phone
  FROM Customers INNER JOIN Orders
       ON Customers.CustomerID = Orders.CustomerID
```

Joins have many permutations, which can become wickedly tricky. Read a SQL textbook to understand the `INNER JOIN` and `OUTER JOIN`.

SQL Injections

Beware of a major problem with using SQL statements. Strenuously avoid allowing input from a user to go into a SQL statement. Instead, require the user to make a selection from a populated control such as a list or set of radio buttons and then use the ASP.NET 2.0 parameter features to substitute the value into the SQL statement.

The problem derives from the fact that a second SQL statement can be added to a SQL statement and they will both be executed. So, if your page has a statement such as `Select * From Customers WHERE X`, you might (erroneously) set up your page to allow the user to type a string in a textbox and substitute that for *X* in the code. But a user could type something like `Acme;Delete FROM Orders`.The `Acme` would complete your intended SQL statement; however, the semicolon indicates that a new SQL statement will be coming, which means your database would get the statement `Delete FROM Orders`.

Exercise Answers

Chapter 1

Exercise 1 solution

Use two controls: a data source control to connect to the data and a data-bound control to display the data on the page.

Exercise 2 solution

SQL Server, Oracle, Access, XML files, any other OLEDB-enabled data source, and so on.

Exercise 3 solution

Grid (`GridView`), list of values for one record (`DetailsView`), tree (`TreeView`), and list boxes.

Exercise 4 solution

The framework is a set of standards for development of many types of software, including applications that run on the desktop without connection to the Internet. ASP.NET 2.0 is a technology to write Web-based applications. ASP.NET 2.0 subscribes to the standards of the .NET Framework as a whole and, thus, can communicate efficiently with other .NET-standardized software.

Exercise 5 solution

SQL Server is the full-scale database management software from Microsoft. MSDE and SSE are for local use by hobbyists or developers. Both MSDE and SSE have limited capabilities and are not designed to support public deployed Web sites. MSDE is based on SQL Server 2000, whereas SSE derives from the SQL Server version 2005 (which was codenamed Yukon).

Chapter 2

Exercise 1 solution

Access is an application that can store data, receive and display data, and support development of a user interface.

JET is the core of Access that stores and serves up data.

MDB is a file format for holding data and user interfaces such as forms and reports.

Exercise 2 solution

- `AccessDataSource` control
- A data-bound control such as the `GridView`

Exercise 3 solution

The second syntax is relative to the root of the Web site. When the Web site is deployed from your development to your production Web server, there is no need to change the reference. In the first code sample, a deployment to a host that uses a drive named D would require a change in your source code.

Exercise 4 solution

- Access cannot handle many simultaneous users.
- Access uses a slow procedure for preventing simultaneous changes.
- Access is less secure.
- Many hosts will not allow Access to be run on a Web server.
- The Access model for handling parameters makes coding more difficult.

Exercise 5 solution

Structured Query Language (SQL)

Exercise 6 solution

Purpose	Object Name
Connection with the MDB file	`AccessDataSource` control
Transfer arguments to the event handler	`SqlDataSourceStatusEventArgs`
Hold the exceptions raised by the connection	`System.Data.OleDb.OleDbException`

Chapter 3

Exercise 1 solution

SQL Server is designed for full-scale deployment. SSE is designed for development or for local and lightweight uses. MSDE is an older form of SSE: SSE is based on the Microsoft SQL Server 2005 version, whereas MSDE is based on SQL 2000.

Exercise 2 solution

```
Server = (local)\SQLExpress (or .\SQLExpress)
```

Exercise 3 solution

A connection string holds sensitive information, including the name of a server, name of a database, user ID, and password. By storing the connection string in the `web.config` file, that information is further hidden from the user. In addition, information in the `web.config` can be encrypted.

Exercise 4 solution

The `Selected` event of the data source control.

Exercise 5 solution

`e.Exception` identifies if there was a failure of any sort. Some types of data source control failures will be documented if the `e.Exception` equals a `System.Data.SqlClient.SqlException.`

Chapter 4

Exercise 1 solution

When connecting to an MDB without security, we use the `AccessDataSource`. If there is a password, we use the `SqlDataSource` so that we can pass the credentials.

Exercise 2 solution

One file name (`.MDB`) is the database and the other file (`.MDB`) is the workgroup file that contains the security information.

Exercise 3 solution

Catalog in general SQL terms translates to database in MySQL (and some other database systems.

Exercise 4 solution

The `System.Data.SqlClient` provider for Microsoft SQL Server is the default and, thus, does not have to be stated in the code.

Exercise 5 solution

Oracle: Microsoft includes a fully managed provider, named `System.Data.OracleClient`. This does not require a native provider.

`MySQL: SqlDataSource` with a nondefault provider of `System.Data.Odbc` and a native ODBC driver for MySQL. It is likely that in the near future a fully managed provider or an OLEDB native provider will be available and certified.

Exercise 6 solution

The smart data controls (data source controls and data-bound controls) automatically instantiate ADO.NET classes as needed and with the proper properties.

Exercise 7 solution

A MySQL driver. Currently, a driver is available for an ODBC connection. Expect one or more third-party OLEDB managed code providers to be available soon.

Exercise 8 solution

When used with an Access database password security scheme, the `Password` property means the password for the entire database. When used with an Access Workgroup security scheme, the `Password` property refers to the user's specific password.

Chapter 5

Exercise 1 solution

A `GridView` displays many records at once, whereas a `DetailsView` displays one record at a time. In a `GridView`, each horizontal row represents a record. In a `DetailsView`, each horizontal row represents one field of that one record.

A `DetailsView` can insert new records; a `GridView` cannot.

Exercise 2 solution

A `CommandField` executes one of several functions that were written by Microsoft into the control, including `Delete`, `Edit`, and `New`.

A `ButtonField` executes code that you, the programmer, write and put into an event handler.

Exercise 3 solution

The text is displayed to the user. The `CommandName` defines the name of the subroutine of code to execute when the button is clicked. As you will study in Chapter 17 on events, the value of the `CommandName` property gets sent to that method so that you know which command was invoked.

Exercise 4 solution

`CheckBoxField`

Exercise 5 solution

Within a `TemplateField`, you can add one or more controls, HTML tags, and text.

A `BoundField` can display only the value from its bound field.

Chapter 6

Exercise 1 solution

For both controls, the heading is a set of one cell per field that normally shows the name of the field. The difference is in the physical location of the heading. `GridView` has the heading as the first row, running horizontally across the top of the `GridView`.

The `DetailsView` has two similarly named styles. The `Header` and `HeaderStyle` apply to a top row in the `DetailsView` table (spanning both the field header column and value column). The `FieldHeaderStyle`, on the other hand, applies only to the field header column of `DetailsView`. The individual fields (in the `Fields` collection) of `DetailsView` have a `Header` property (and corresponding `HeaderStyle`) that apply only to the `DetailsView` header column cells.

Exercise 2 solution

The top-level `GridView` CSS setting is the least precedent and a `ColumnField` property takes precedence over all others:

```
GridView CssClass < GridView Style property < RowStyle CssClass < RowStyle property
< Column/Field ItemStyle CssClass < Column/Field ItemStyle property
```

When alternate display of rows is invoked (editing or selecting), the precedence becomes the following:

```
RowStyle < AlternatingRowStyle < SelectedRowStyle < EditRowStyle or InsertRowStyle
```

Exercise 3 solution

Borders refers to the single rectangle around the entire `GridView` or `DetailsView` control. *Gridlines* refers to the internal lines that separate the cells.

Exercise 4 solution

The three options include:

- RGB uses three hexadecimal values for red, green, and blue in the format RRGGBB. RGB colors are a logical selection for desktops but do not always translate well to the Web.
- WWW palette of about 150 colors that have been recognized and named by the W3C. They should be available in every modern Web browser.
- System will display a color that depends on the user's Windows settings with a scheme defining a color for each part of a window, as set by each Windows user.

Exercise 5 solution

Cell spacing is the distance between the borders of cells. It is spacing between cells. *Cell padding* is an empty space between the inner edge of a cell and its contents. It is a distance within cells.

Exercise 6 solution

```
The proper syntax is: GridView1.BorderStyle = BorderStyle.Dotted.
```

Exercise 7 solution

Option 1:

```
<asp:GridView ID="GridView1" Runat="server">
   <Columns>
   </Columns>
   <HeaderStyle
           Font-Bold="true">
   </HeaderStyle>
</asp:GridView>
```

Option 2:

```
<asp:GridView ID="GridView1"
   HeaderStyle-Font-Bold="true">
</ asp:GridView>
```

Exercise 8 solution

`EmptyDataRowStyle` will be applied when there is a set of no rows returned by the data source control. The single `EmptyDataRowStyle` will be used instead of all the other styles that would have been used if there had been row(s) returned.

Exercise 9 solution

Because the `GridView` is not a control for inserting new records. That task is available only in the `DetailsView` or `FormView`, as discussed in Chapter 12.

Chapter 7

Exercise 1 solution

A data source that supports paging and `GridView.AllowPaging=true`.

Exercise 2 solution

`e.SortExpression` and `e.SortDirection`.

Exercise 3 solution

Field name followed by `ASC` or `DESC`, then a comma. Repeat the pattern for a tie-breaking field. For example, to sort on last name with first name as a tie-breaker, you would use the following syntax:

```
LastName ASC,FirstName ASC
```

Exercise 4 solution

Numeric, First/Last, and Next/Previous.

Exercise 5 solution

Select the GridView. Look in Properties Windows⇨Paging⇨PagerSettings⇨Mode.

Exercise 6 solution

A selection is made, and then a sort is performed. The selected style will remain on the same line of the GridView, even though after the sort there is a new record on that line. Likewise, if a selection is made and then the user moves to a new page, the selected style will remain on the same line of the GridView, which will now be occupied by a new record.

Chapter 8

Exercise 1 solution

The value of the field specified by DataTextField is displayed to the user. The value of the field specified by DataValueField is hidden from the user but available to the programmer. Frequently, DataTextField is used to provide a field that is easy for the human mind to understand. In that case, the DataValueField holds a value, such as an ID number, that is useful for a database look-up.

Exercise 2 solution

A bulleted list does not imply to the user that a selection should be made.

Exercise 3 solution

OnSelectedIndexChanged

Exercise 4 solution

When your page gathers several items of information prior to responding, you would probably want to turn off AutoPostBack for each selection list. For example, a site that offers downloads for device drivers might want the user to click on two lists: the model of the device and the operating system. Then the user clicks a button to get the driver. If AutoPostBack was turned on for the selection list of devices, then the user would not have a chance to make a selection in the OS version selection list until the page reloaded, which would be cumbersome.

Chapter 9

Exercise 1 solution

Xxx refers to the name of the field in the database. @Xxx refers to a variable that holds a value filled by the <Parameters> tag. The value in the parameter could come from a query string (forwarded by the requesting page), a control on the page, or another source.

Exercise 2 solution

```
http://Example.Org/MemberProfile.aspx?MemberID=567
```

Exercise 3 solution

The code is as follows:

```
<asp:SqlDataSource ID="SqlDataSource1" Runat="server">
    ConnectionString=" ... "
    SelectCommand="SELECT * FROM [Members] WHERE MemberID = @MemberID"
  <SelectParameters>
    <asp:QueryStringParameter Name="MemberID"
        QueryStringField="MemberID" />
  </SelectParameters>
</asp:SqlDataSource>
```

Exercise 4 solution

`DropDownList.SelectedValue` (not `Text`).

`GridView.SelectedValue`, which is the value of the first field for the selected record in the list of the `DataKeyNames` property.

Question 5 solution

Use the `DISTINCT` keyword in the data source `SelectCommand`, as follows:

```
SELECT DISTINCT [state] FROM [authors]
```

Exercise 6 solution

In the `DropDownList` control, add the hard coded items within `<Items>` tags and set `AppendDataBoundItems = true`.

Exercise 7 solution

It converts them to a `NULL` as long as ConvertEmptyStringToNull is set to its default of `true`. (You can set `ConvertEmptyStringToNull` to `false`.

Exercise 8 solution

The data source control will not execute `SelectCommands` that contain a `NULL`. This behavior can be reversed with the data source control property `CancelSelectOnNullParameter=false`.

Exercise 9 solution

`DetailsView control` and `FormView` control.

Exercise 10 solution

`DataNavigateUrlField` holds the URL for that record's link (however, see the next two questions for a special case).

`DataNavigateUrlFormatString` allows the value of the `DataNavigateUrlField` to be formatted with characters such as a leading `http:` or a trailing query string.

Exercise 11 solution

In DataNavigateUrlFormatString, refer to the value of the DataNavigateUrlField with a {0}, as in the following:

```
DataNavigateUrlFields="MyIdField"
DataNavigateUrlFormatString=http://www.{0}.com
```

Exercise 12 solution

DataNavigateUrlField will hold an ID value for the selected record.

DataNavigateUrlFormatString holds the name of the target page (same for all records) with an appended "?ID={0}" to add the value from the DataNavigateUrlField.

Chapter 10

Exercise 1 solution

A BoundField shows the value in one field of the SELECT statement, with few layout options.

A TemplateField is a space into which the designer can add one or more controls with properties bound to data fields and arrange them as desired.

Exercise 2 solution

GridView and DetailsView.

Exercise 3 solution

DetailsView and FormView can create new records. GridView, DataList, and Repeater cannot create new records.

Exercise 4 solution

DetailsView provides some preformatting and default layout of all fields provided by the data source control.

FormView is a blank slate in which the designer builds a presentation by adding controls to its templates.

Exercise 5 solution

DataList and Repeater. Whenever possible in ASP.NET 2.0 pages, switch to using the version 2.0 controls: GridView, DetailsView, or FormView because they can update, delete, and insert data with data source controls codelessly.

Exercise 6 solution

Yes. VWD offers a useful interface to create HTML tables by using Menu: Layout⇨Insert Table.

Exercise 7 solution

Yes. In the Smart Task panel, click Edit Columns, select the bound column and click "Convert this field into a TemplateField."

Exercise 8 solution

The `DataList` control puts each record in a cell of an overall HTML table. This permits formatting, such as `RepeatDirection` and number of columns. The Repeater control does not use an overall HTML table. (However, both allow HTML tables inside each item template.) Furthermore, another big difference is that the Repeater control allows HTML snippets in its templates and, thus, there is no design-time support for Repeater.

Chapter 11

Exercise 1 solution

`UPDATE` changes values in an existing record. `INSERT INTO` creates a new record and, optionally, adds values to the nascent record.

Exercise 2 solution

`New` changes the `DetailsView` or `FormView` into insert mode with empty boxes for values. `Edit` changes it into edit mode with current values in boxes. Neither one actually executes any commands on the database. Assuming that the user then clicks on a command button for Insert or Update, respectively, `New` will create a new record, whereas `Edit` will change values in an existing record.

Exercise 3 solution

`GridView` does not support adding a new record. Instead, use a hyperlink to a `DetailsView` that can perform an INSERT INTO.

Exercise 4 solution

It will include one of the `Show` properties, such as `ShowEditButton` or `ShowDeleteButton`.

Exercise 5 solution

It stores the values of the primary key fields: (1) so you can retrieve them later (especially for use in a `WHERE` clause), and (2) as their native object types rather than as their string representations. It also tells the data-bound control which fields are the primary key fields so that it can present those appropriately to the data source control.

Exercise 6 solution

Command fields are in the DetailsView and command columns in a GridView.

Exercise 7 solution

In the `DataSource`'s Parameter for that field, set the type to one of the numeric types. ASP.NET 2.0 will then perform the conversion if it is possible.

Exercise 8 solution

In the DetailsView's data source control, add a DeleteCommand that is a proper SQL DELETE statement (almost always including a WHERE clause, so you only delete one record). Ensure that the DataKeyNames in the DetailsView includes the Primary key field that is used in the WHERE clause of the data source's DELETE command. Then, in the DetailsView, add a CommandField with its ShowDeleteButton=True.

Chapter 12

Exercise 1 solution

GridView cannot perform insertions. DetailsView and FormView can.

Exercise 2 solution

DetailsView offers TemplateFields. Within those fields there are templates for Item, EditItem, and InsertItem. These templates hold just one or a few fields and are displayed in their Edit mode. FormView offers only top-level templates for each mode, and all fields must be placed in the one template for that mode.

Exercise 3 solution

Select the DetailsView control, and open its Smart Tasks panel. Select Edit Columns, select the column to change and click "Convert this field into a TemplateField."

Exercise 4 solution

Fields that are flagged in the database as identity fields will not be offered in the InsertItem template for input because the values are provided by the database.

Exercise 5 solution

There must be a value for the InsertCommand. Except in certain cases (where parameters are set by code), there will an <InsertParameters> collection with parameter items.

Although not part of the data source control, the underlying database must allow inserts in terms of table rules and privileges.

Chapter 13

Exercise 1 solution

The Text message appears on the page in the location of the validator control. The ErrorMessage appears in a ValidationSummary. If there is a value for ErrorMessage but no value in the Text property, then the ErrorMessage appears.

Exercise 2 solution

Change the Validator.Display property to Dynamic.

Exercise 3 solution

A RangeValidator checks if the input value is between the minimum and maximum values, inclusive.

The RegularExpressionValidator checks that a value meets the pattern of the ValidationExpression property. Because the expression draws on a very large and rich syntax, pattern validation can be performed within a RegularExpressionValidator.

Exercise 4 solution

It can compare an input to a static value (or list of values). It can also perform a validity check for a data type.

Exercise 5 solution

The code must include setting a property on its event arguments named IsValid to True or False. That Boolean is passed back to the CustomValidator.

Exercise 6 solution

They must be in the same template as the ControlToValidate. In the case of a GridView that would be, for example, MyGridView.MyColumnTemplate.EditItemTemplate. In a DetailsView, it would be MyDetailsView.MyFieldTemplate.EditItemTemplate.

Exercise 7 solution

They must be in the same template as the ControlToValidate. However, in a FormView the Template hierarchy is flat. The controls would be in MyFormView.InsertItemTemplate.

Exercise 8 solution

First, convert the BoundField to a TemplateField, using the option in the GridView's Smart Tasks panel⇨Edit Columns.

Exercise 9 solution

Set the validator controls' display property to none.

Chapter 14

Exercise 1 solution

DataObjects allow an ASPX page to connect to an intermediate tier as opposed to directly to a database. Multiple tiers provide flexibility and efficiency in an enterprise.

Exercise 2 solution

Methods

Exercise 3 solution

An object type to go into the list. For example, we created the Persons type to go into a generics list of people.

Exercise 4 solution

`App_Code` folder

Exercise 5 solution

Right-click on the title of the `DataSet` or the title of the `TableAdaptor`.

Exercise 6 solution

- A `DataView` object
- An incoming parameter that will hold the `Sort Expression`
- A loop to add the items in the sorted order of the `DataView`

Chapter 15

Exercise 1 solution

XmlDataSource control.

Exercise 2 solution

`TreeView`'s `ExpandDepth` property can be set from 0 to `FullyExpanded`.

Exercise 3 solution

Each row represents one of the nodes from the first level below the root node.

Exercise 4 solution

Those with a pound sign are intrinsic, such as the name of the node and its inner text. The options with no pound sign are attributes that do not actually have a bearing on their use in an ASP.NET 2.0 page.

Exercise 5 solution

This event is raised when the `TreeView` is rendered, prior to the user's first viewing to expand the tree to the levels specified in `TreeView.ExpandDepth`. If the code in the procedure is designed to only be executed in response to a user click, then it must be used with an `If IsPostBack Then...End If` structure.

Chapter 16

Exercise 1 solution

Advantages:

- Caching greatly improves the speed with which a page is built if the page uses data that has recently been requested.
- Caching reduces the load on the database server.
- Caching reduces the amount of communication between IIS and the data servers.

Disadvantages:

- Cached data wastes server memory if it is not used.
- If caching is not set up correctly for the business situation, there is a risk of providing the user with erroneous data.

Exercise 2 solution

Prior to SQL Server version 2005 (which includes SSE) the ASP server was responsible for asking (polling) SQL Server if there had been a change to a table. To enable the feature you had to use `asp-net_RegSql` to enable SQL to give the results to the ASP Server. Then you had to specify the polling frequency and connection string information to the `Web.config` file. Then, and only then, you could enable `SqlCacheDependency` in the SqlDataSource control.

Starting with SQL Server version 2005 (and SSE), you can inform SQL Server that it should notify the server when a change has been made to at table. There is no more responsibility for the programmer to determine how often to poll. The newer technique is enabled by adding a line in `Global.ASAX` that starts the method that handles the notification. Then we set the SqlCacheDependency property to CommandNotification in our `SqlDataSource` control. Finally, two security rights must be granted to the process that is running ASP.NET: the right to create notifications and the right to send those notifications from SQL Server.

Exercise 3 solution

ASP.NET 2.0 will create a cache of data for each combination of parameters. If there are many permutations, then the cached data may rarely actually be hit by another exact same parameter set. In that case, the memory and time spent caching is for naught.

Exercise 4 solution

Content within the control is exempted form caching, so it is rebuilt with every request and never stale.

Chapter 17

Exercise 1 solution

Technique #1:

1. Switch to VWD Source view.
2. Drop down the list of object at the top left and select your control.
3. Drop down the list of events and select the one of interest.

Technique #2:

1. Switch to VWD Design view.
2. Select your control (or the page as a whole).
3. In the Properties window, click on the events list icon (lightening bolt).
4. Double-click on the event of interest.

Exercise 2 solution

Events ending in "-ing" are raised prior to the action occurring. Events that end in "-ed" are raised after the action is complete.

Exercise 3 solution

It is an untyped `Object` variable.

It can be cast into a control type as follows in VB:

```
Dim MyButtonObject = CType(sender, Button)
```

The `Sender` object can be cast into a control type as follows in C#:

```
Button MyButtonObject = ((Button)sender);
```

Exercise 4 solution

Anywhere on the page (top, middle, bottom)

A code-behind page

(Indirectly) in an object, which is called by the event handler

Exercise 5 solution

No, ASP.NET 2.0 permits only one language per page. But don't confuse that with the fact that ASP.NET 2.0 supports many languages (but only one per page). You can also use different languages on different pages within one site (as we have done in this book with VB and CS versions of pages in our one site.

Exercise 6 solution

Command buttons (command fields) raise standard events created by Microsoft such as `Insert`, `Update`, `Delete`, and `Select`. Custom buttons raise events that are handled by custom-written code.

Exercise 7 solution

Make reference to: `MyEventRaisingControl.SelectedValue`

Index

Index

SYMBOLS

A

H

I

J

K

L

M

N

O

P

Q

R

S

T

U

V

Professional ASP.NET 2.0

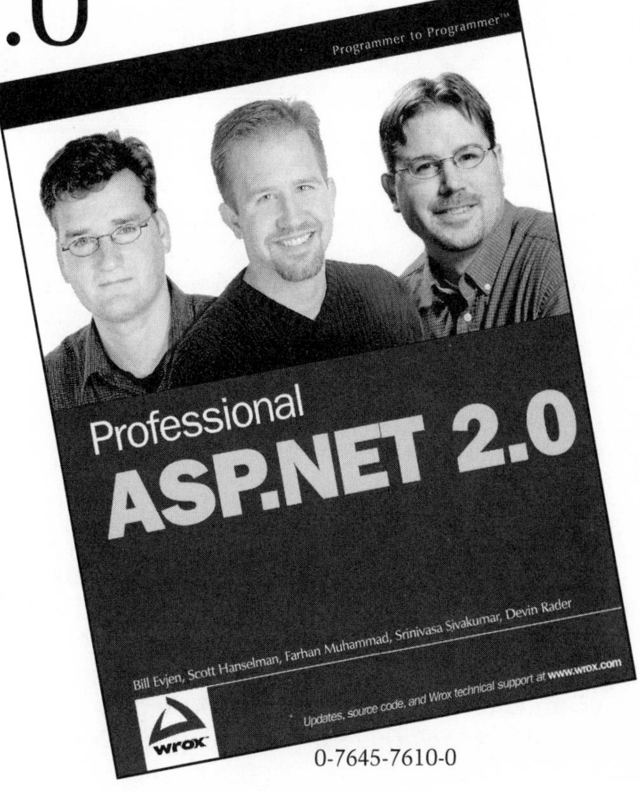

0-7645-7610-0

ASP.NET allows web sites to display unique pages for each visitor rather than show the same static HTML pages. The release of ASP.NET 2.0 is a revolutionary leap forward in the area of web application development. It brings with it a wealth of new and exciting built-in functions that reduce the amount of code you'll need to write for even the most common applications.

With more than 50 new server controls, the number of classes inside ASP.NET 2.0 has more than doubled, and, in many cases, the changes in this new version are dramatic. This book will alert you to every new feature and capability that ASP.NET 2.0 provides so that you'll be prepared to put these new technologies into action.

What you will learn from this book

- The idea of the server control and its pivotal role in ASP.NET development
- How to create templated ASP.NET pages using the new master page feature
- Techniques for debugging and handling errors
- The various frameworks that will enable you to extract, create, manipulate, and store XML
- Ways to package and deploy ASP.NET applications
- How to retrieve, update, and delete data quickly and logically

Who this book is for

This book is for experienced programmers and developers who are looking to make the transition to ASP.NET 2.0.

Check out Wrox.com for the latest ASP.NET 2.0 books.

An Imprint of WILEY
Now you know.

ley, the Wiley logo, and the Wrox logo are trademarks or registered trademarks of John Wiley & Sons, , and/or its affiliates.

Professional ASP.NET 2.0 XML

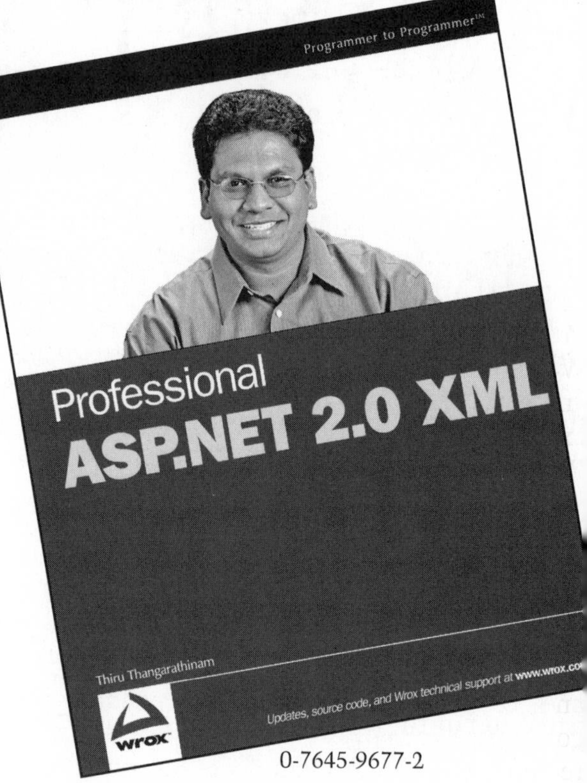

0-7645-9677-2

As the first book to cover the intersection between XML and ASP.NET 2.0, this resource explores the range of XML's various features and how they can be used in ASP.NET for developing Web applications. You'll find in-depth coverage of the key classes that implement XML in the .NET platform, and you'll gain a valuable understanding of Xpath® and XSL Transformations (XSLT), XML support in ADO.NET, and the use of XML for data display.

You'll also learn more about SQL Server™ 2005 XML features, XML serialization, and XML Web services. You'll see how XML can be used to increase application efficiency and reach. Two helpful real-life case studies used throughout the book demonstrate the many ways that XML documents can be created, transformed, and transmitted to other systems using ASP.NET.

What you will learn from this book
- How to read and write XML data
- Advanced Web service concepts such as SOAP headers and extensions
- Using XmlSerializer to serialize XML documents as XML data
- Techniques to build programs or scripts that create, read, and update settings in web.config and machine.config files
- How to create an XSD schema in Visual Studio® 2005
- Tips on working with typed and untyped data type columns
- How to get a head start with Microsoft's new "Atlas" Ajax technology for ASP.NET and XML

Who this book is for
This book is for intermediate to experienced programmers who are already familiar with XML and want to gain a clear understanding of ASP.NET development. Some basic knowledge of C# is necessary.

Check out Wrox.com for the latest ASP.NET 2.0 books.

Wiley, the Wiley logo, and the Wrox logo are trademarks or registered trademarks of John Wiley & Sons, Inc. and/or its affiliates. SQL Server is a trademark of Microsoft Corporation.

wrox
An Imprint of W
Now you know

Professional Web Parts and Custom Controls with ASP.NET 2.0

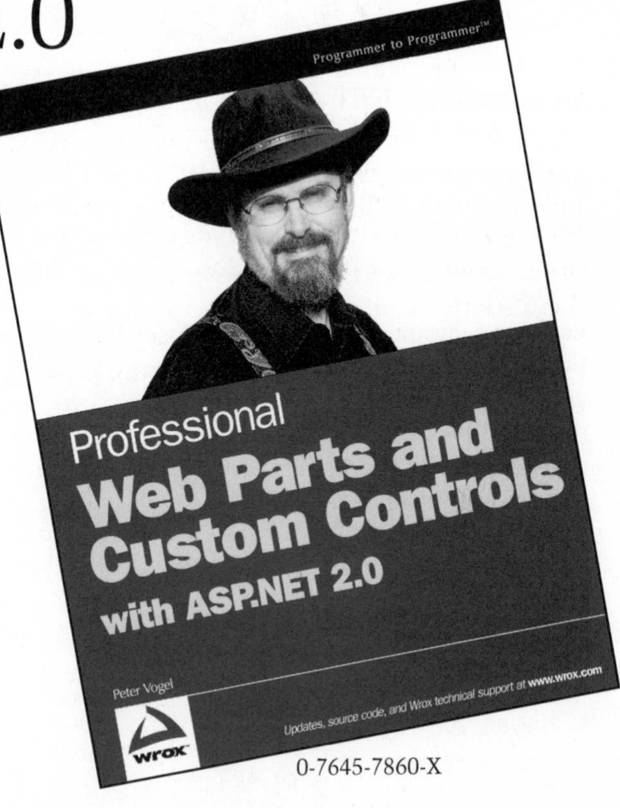

0-7645-7860-X

Custom controls, user controls, and Web Parts can make you more productive in many ways. You can create re-usable components for your WebForms, package a piece of your user interface and re-use it across several Web sites, and create exactly the ASP.NET controls you want. Web Parts, new with ASP.NET 2.0, allow you to create user interfaces with the user's involvement, making you more productive than ever before.

This book teaches you how to create controls using Visual Studio® 2005. Packed with business-related applications, it explains the costs and benefits of different ways to accomplish a goal, offers scenarios illustrating the use of each technique, and helps you make informed choices as you develop controls specifically geared to your business purposes.

What you will learn from this book

- The role of user controls, custom controls, and Web Parts in solving specific problems
- Methods for setting up your custom control project in Visual Studio 2005
- How to create a Web Part and extend the framework by adding functions
- New features in ASP.NET 2.0 that help you manage state in your controls
- How to add client-side code to custom controls, build your own validator control, and create a databinding control

Who this book is for

This book is for professional Web developers who already know how to create a WebForm and want to begin creating their own controls. Some experience with creating objects is helpful, but advanced skill as an object developer is not necessary.

Check out Wrox.com for the latest ASP.NET 2.0 books.

An Imprint of WILEY
Now you know.

ey, the Wiley logo, and the Wrox logo are trademarks or registered trademarks of John Wiley & Sons, Inc. and/or its affili-
s. Visual Studio is a registered trademark of Microsoft Corporation.

ASP.NET 2.0 Instant Results

If you're looking to quickly create dynamic Web pages with ASP.NET 2.0, your programming efforts just got a whole lot easier. Featuring a dozen ready-to-use projects on the book's CD-ROM that you can use immediately, this reference is a helpful guide that dives into working code so you can learn it rapidly.

Each project features step-by-step set-up instructions. The description of each project enables you to understand and then modify it so you can reuse it in different situations. By the end of the book, you'll be on the fast track to creating your own site from scratch.

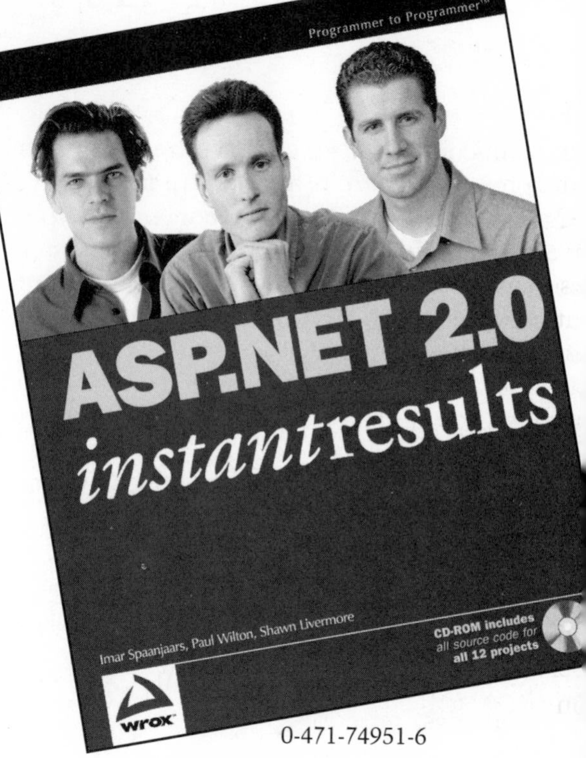

0-471-74951-6

CD-ROM includes the source code for all 12 projects

- •Online diary and organizer
- •File share
- •Chat server
- •Survey engine
- •CMS
- •Blog
- •Photo album
- •Customer support site
- •WebShop
- •Appointment booking system
- •Greeting cards
- •Bug base

Who this book is for

This book is for intermediate-level programmers with some .NET experience who need a quick-start reference book so they can use ASP.NET 2.0 at once.

Check out Wrox.com for the latest ASP.NET 2.0 books.

Wiley, the Wiley logo, and the Wrox logo are trademarks or registered trademarks of John Wiley & Sons, Inc. and/or its affiliates.

An Imprint of W
Now you know